Luxemburger Juristische Studien –
Luxembourg Legal Studies

edited by

Faculty of Law, Economics and Finance
University of Luxembourg

Volume 25

Stefan Braum (Ed.)

Experimental Law

The Rule of Law and the Regulation of the Corona Pandemic in Europe

Nomos

The Deutsche Nationalbibliothek lists this publication in the Deutsche Nationalbibliografie; detailed bibliographic data are available on the Internet at http://dnb.d-nb.de

ISBN 978-3-7560-0511-6 (Print)
978-3-7489-3834-7 (ePDF)

British Library Cataloguing-in-Publication Data
A catalogue record for this book is available from the British Library.

ISBN 978-3-7560-0511-6 (Print)
978-3-7489-3834-7 (ePDF)

Library of Congress Cataloging-in-Publication Data
Braum, Stefan
Experimental Law
The Rule of Law and the Regulation of the Corona Pandemic in Europe
Stefan Braum (Ed.)
476 pp.
Includes bibliographic references.

ISBN 978-3-7560-0511-6 (Print)
978-3-7489-3834-7 (ePDF)

Onlineversion
Nomos eLibrary

1st Edition 2023

Experimental Law

Rule of Law in the pandemic – Vertical and horizontal perspectives

Is it possible to combat a pandemic with the means of the liberal rule of law? And if so, how? What are the implications of combating the pandemic for basic principles of the rule of law and for the various system levels of the law? Are there such things as best practices in pandemic control? Finally, can models of legal regulation of a pandemic be derived from the geopolitical context?

These were the research questions at the beginning of the project *"Protection against infection through (European) regulatory law"*, funded by Luxembourg's Research Fund (Fonds national de la Recherche – FNR). In all these questions, the project was able to gain **both vertical and horizontal insights** into the legal handling of the pandemic that had not previously existed, without this process of gaining knowledge already having come to a comprehensive end. On the contrary, during the project it became apparent how dynamically and comprehensively European and international legislators reacted to the Corona crisis in constitutional, repressive and preventive terms. How lasting the influence on the legal system will be cannot yet be fully assessed.

From a vertical perspective, the following contributions contain – with a comparative legal intention – divergent national models of pandemic regulation. The following contributions refer to the states that were relatively severely affected by the pandemic and that have had – in part dramatic – experiences with the excessive demands and the failure of the respective national health system. On the one hand, legal-cultural differences in the prevention and repression of the pandemic become visible, but on the other hand, a hard core of legal control can be distilled from the comparative legal perspective. Conclusions and recommendations may be derived from this, which could be applied to the respective national legislation. As a normative consequence of these experiences, the question will arise to what extent the European legal framework must be strengthened, even harmonised. At the same time, a look at a regulatory model that is in part strongly divergent in terms of legal culture, such as in Singapore, may raise awareness of the geopolitical significance of pandemic regulation and thus also question the ability of the liberal constitutional state to effectively counter existential crises while at the same time protecting freedom.

Synthesis – Influences of Covid legislation in a nutshell

Synthesising both the vertical and horizontal research contributions, clear trends can be discerned as to how the regulation of the pandemic has influenced the legal system and its paradigms at the levels mentioned. There are **shifts and deformations due to emergency legislation**, a shift of **focus to executive law** can be observed, **a transformation of the principle of proportionality** and, last but not least, a **paradigm shift with regard to the digitalisation of preventive social control.**

Emergency legislation: At the beginning of the pandemic in February and March 2020, states such as Spain or France relied on constitutionally secured emergency articles. In spring 2020, the French legislature created a simple-law emergency rule in the "Code sanitaire" that was specifically geared to the pandemic situation. Other countries, such as Germany or the United Kingdom, were able to base their measures to contain the pandemic on simple legal emergency articles from the outset. They were provided for in the respective infection control or pandemic laws and which were supplemented in the course of the pandemic, in Germany, for example, by the concept of an "epidemic emergency of national significance". In the course of the pandemic, changes in the constitutional requirements for emergency legislation became apparent: despite virological polyphony, the continued maintenance of the Covid rules, which still date back to the state of emergency, was and is a problem that must be negotiated publicly, according to normative criteria. While at the beginning of the crisis both empirical ignorance and the risk of systemic failure led to a normatively justifiable narrowing to virologically advised and systemically explicable radical containment, in the course of the pandemic means-purpose relations increasingly came into view that require political – above all normative – justification. A **transformation of the principle of proportionality** can be observed, from an intervention barrier that must be based on empirically substantiated facts to a principle that justifies fundamental rights interventions based on risk models. **The law adapts like plasticine to the respective empirically recognisable pandemic situation.**

Executive law: In all countries involved, our studies show a shift in the focus of legislation to the executive, which decisively determines the content of covid laws even if they are – formally – passed by parliaments. This primarily affects the criminal justice system. Executive law is strongly accessory, i.e. its content follows from a complex technique of legal references to administrative law. Moreover, it has a tendency to criminalize minor misdemeanours in the context of crisis legislation. This creates problems for the legal principles of criminal legality as well as criminal liability.

Digitalisation and prevention: The project was able to draw inspiration from the **example of Singapore** in its research into instruments of pandemic regulation that have a preventive effect. Long before the introduction of digital certificates and effective covid apps, which are were just beginning to unfold effectively in Europe after the end of the so-called third Corona wave, the use of digitally supported prevention instruments was part of a strategy in Singapore from the very beginning. Singapore understood digitisation as part of a **strategy of trust in "good governance"** and at the same time an **empowerment of the population** itself to act. For Europe, however, this model is associated with the fear of the expansion of social control through digital technologies.

Experimental Law: beyond these core elements of pandemic regulation, a pattern of legislation is emerging that has the potential to have a lasting impact on the law even after the pandemic has ended: We see in "experimental law" the style of pandemic regulation law. What becomes visible is that this style counters the normative requirements of general legislation with a regulatory model that largely deviates from it. Little in it is permanent, much follows empirical knowledge and the technical or medical possibilities of pandemic control that are available at a particular time, in a particular place. Rules are not binding, their legal force only lasts for the moment. Nothing is universally valid, but follows selective medical imperatives. Experimental law is a right of resubmission, it refers to rules that always apply only until further notice. Just until medical expertise tries out new things and the law merely reproduces the empirically founded knowledge.

This may be a long-term problem in fighting crises under the rule of law. It is possible that a problem of legitimacy will arise for the democratic constitutional state in general, because its justification narratives will be transformed, namely from the idea of the citizen who makes self-determined use of his or her rights of freedom to a point of reference for (bio-) political optimisation.

These "findings" and "diagnoses" are reflected in the contributions to this volume and are confirmed in different ways.

Together they all have a moving target. They analyse, compare and criticise pandemic regulation in their respective moments. Therefore, the picture that emerges is in a sense the compilation of snapshots, drawn at a particular time in a particular place. That is part of the nature of things: nothing can be determined conclusively and with ultimate certainty. Nevertheless, common features crystallise, namely a new style of law: the experimental use of rules to manage systemic risks. In the system of law, only its recurring crisis mode seems to last. This would then also mean saying goodbye to normative bindingness, which should be constitutive for legislation that conforms to the rule of law. This volume is perhaps a kind of packaging supplement that points out the risks and side effects of this legal style for the democratic rule of law state.

Luxembourg, in August 2022 *Stefan Braum*

Table of Contents

Pandemic Regulation – Virus in the Rule of Law?

Stefan Braum

A. *Pandemic policy and the legal system*

I. *Juridical internal perspectives*

Is it possible to fight a pandemic with the means of the liberal constitutional state without damaging it permanently? An approach to this question can be attempted, on the one hand, by means of a normative perspective that looks for the legal basis for health prevention, for the resilience of the health system or for repressive measures to contain the pandemic, delineates fundamental rights from one another and weighs them against one another, establishes a normative balance between individual freedom and system interests and, last but not least, subjects any intervention in fundamental rights to the principle of proportionality. For the legal system, not least for the criminal justice system, the constraints of fighting the pandemic have an impact on three levels. One must distinguish between the macro-level of a constitutional and transnational legal framework, the application level of repression and the preventive control level. All levels capture the patterns of normative legitimation of pandemic policy, starting with constitutionally or transnationally available instruments of emergency legislation, continuing with their implementation through sanction, their procedures and legal control, and finally the preventive access to information and data for the purpose of health protection, which is enhanced by digitalisation. If the levels are put together, this may result in state models of pandemic control that, in European and international comparison, set different legal accents in the choice of legal basis, determine the scope of fundamental rights protection variously or interpret the principle of proportionality differently.

II. *The politics of pandemic regulation*

However, it became apparent during the crisis that lawyers tended to stand on the sidelines of the discussion about the legitimacy of the pandemic policy, even though constitutional lawyers in particular – rightly – urged that the political shaping and the determination of the democratic limits of the pandemic policy should not be left to virologists, epidemiologists, economists and health politicians alone. It corresponds to their role to demand respect for the legal principles that constitute the rule of law and democracy. "Constitution matters", indeed.[1] It may follow from this that the impact of the pandemic on the liberal rule of law cannot only be assessed normatively, not only with the technical means from the legal toolbox.

Rather, the problem of the extent to which – biologically speaking – the virus has also infected the rule of law can only be answered if one is aware of the socio-political context of the fight against the pandemic and sufficiently takes into account the interdependence of the legal system and pandemic policy. Political strategies in dealing with the pandemic make use of law and its forms and shape it. Already at the macro level of constitutional law, it becomes apparent that politics procures the constitutional legitimacy it needs to implement pandemic policy goals. Not normative legitimation, but "constitutional engineering"[2], i.e. the ongoing repair of the damage caused or threatened by the virus, appears as the actual juridical mode in dealing with the pandemic. Dangers to the rule of law, signs of its deformation and, at the same time, the possible guidelines for a legally constituted protection of the population against the dangers of the pandemic only become visible in the interplay of political techniques of pandemic policy and juridical reaction patterns.

1. *The pandemic – a challenge to the democratic sovereign's ability to act politically*

Interdependencies of law and politics are reflected in the idea of sovereignty. The political reactions to the pandemic, including their critical reflection and scientific processing, take up both the historical-political and the modern-normative discourse of sovereignty.

The core of sovereignty is the guarantee of political agency, the subject of which changes. In modernity, the people are the bearers of state power,

---

1 See Heinig/Kingreen/Lepsius/Möllers/Volkmann/Wissman, Juristenzeitung (JZ), 2020, p 861 et seq. versus Hase, Juristenzeitung (JZ) 2020, p. 697 et seq.

2 See Jörg Gerkrath, Constitutional Engineering of exception regimes within the European Union.

which is exercised in the legislative, executive and judicial branches. The idea of modernity creates the "res publica" – a form of law that allows the affairs of the state to be publicly regulated, complex systems to be managed, risks to be countered, the integrity of a society to be secured internally and externally, social justice to be ensured in the economy and society. While the idea of sovereignty was initially associated with the de facto coercive power of a ruler over a territory and a state people, in the political philosophy of the Enlightenment it gave way to a conception that limited political power – through its differentiation into three powers and through civil liberties to which all state action was bound if it wanted to claim legitimacy. Thus, traditional legitimation models of law are based on the idea of the social contract, whose normative fiction of an association of free citizens that takes place in mutual recognition is concretised in the model of the modern constitutional state. Political action and good governance are bound to the fulfilment of principles of the rule of law, which both limit and constitute political action. Legality takes the place of power. In the idea of the social contract, the law is at the same time linked to the overcoming of the ruleless state of nature. The law is a figure of thought and practice that subdues and restrains natural arbitrariness. Committing political actions to the form of the law is at the same time linked to the promise of somehow being able to exclude and control everything that is ambivalent and contingent.

"Nous sommes en guerre" – this declaration of war by French President Macron right at the beginning of the pandemic is not just political vocabulary to underline the seriousness of the situation. Against the background of political capacity to act as the core of sovereignty, this sentence must be taken seriously. On the one hand, because it makes clear that the principles of a legally legitimised sovereignty must give way in the face of the primal form of violence in order to enable the sovereign to defend its existence as such against an enemy.[3] On the other hand, because – also precisely in the face of such an existential threat – the political capacity of the sovereign to act is traced back to its historical origin – as a decision on life and death.[4] At stake, as Foucault puts it, is no longer the juridical existence of sovereignty, but the biological existence of a population.[5] For Foucault, a model of government characterised by “biopolitical” regulation joins the

3 M. Foucault, Recht über den Tod und Macht zum Leben, in: Folkers/Lemke (Eds), Biopolitik, p. 65 et seq. (p. 69).
4 M. Foucault, ibidem.
5 M. Foucault, ibidem (p. 67).

normative conception of sovereignty.[6] "Biopolitics" here refers to a technique of political power that partly complements, partly contrasts with other mechanisms of power such as sanctioning and disciplining, "surveillance and punishment".[7] The more we know about life, the stronger the political grip becomes to secure political capacity to act in the face of threats to vital interests and dangers to life itself. Since the second half of the 18th century, politics has been interested in birth and death rates, registering life spans, taking care of hygiene protection and combating epidemics. Biopolitical regulation has taken its place alongside the legal exercise of sovereignty.[8]

It is important to register this because it is not just abstract theory, but because it is about patterns that are relevant to the initial question. Felt powerlessness, shaken confidence in one's ability to act politically, exposed in a situation where a virus teaches us that everything can be ambivalent and contingent, call into question the political agency of states, of democratic constitutional states in particular. The challenge of politics to establish trust in liberal governance arises along the lines of normative decision-making – preferably by a democratic legislature – and knowledge-based regulation of life and its ever-changing dangers. This ***contrast – general legislation versus biopolitical regulation*** – is persistently reflected in the law of pandemic control, as we will see next.

2. *Pandemic regulation – a new style of law*

a) Modelling pandemic regulation versus general legislation

Along these lines, between the law and the political programme of protecting life and health, a specific style of regulation unfolds which on the one hand links to the law, and on the other hand makes this link as loose, as flexible, as close to the knowledge of risks and side effects of political protection strategies as possible. "Biopolitical regulation" – if one wants to stick to this formulation following Foucault – uses the form of law and its effects. It may thus be in line with liberal paradigms of "good gov-

---

6 M. Foucault, In Verteidigung der Gesellschaft, Vorlesung vom 17. März 1976, in: Folkers/Lemke, p. 88 et seq. (p. 92).

7 M. Foucault, ibidem, p. 94 and 95.

8 M. Foucault, ibidem, p. 96 and 96.

ernance".[9] However, patterns of political action, shaped by the necessity to stabilise or restore trust in the political capacity of state institutions, have an effect on law and its patterns of normative legitimation.[10] The dialectic between legality as the core of the liberal constitutional state and its appropriation by the technical regulation of the risks and dangers to life emanating from a pandemic also determines how compatible pandemic control is and can be with the requirements of liberal constitutional states. What has been emerging in Europe for more than two years is a style of law, as a law in crisis mode, which grasps, deforms, shakes, even destroys its basic rules or simply represents a new trace of political intervention as a new form of governance. Establishing such a trace, however, is not a neutral act of cognition, but above all a normative problem. All the subsequent contributions show this: for their respective national coordinate system, but also in a transversal, be it European or geopolitical perspective.

Containing the pandemic poses almost insoluble challenges to law in its methodology – hypotheses, subsumption, syllogism – and in its modes of decision-making – right or wrong, lawful or illegal, conforming to or deviating from the rules. Pandemic control as a political strategy does not primarily focus on the individual, neither with regard to his or her guilt or responsibility, nor, above all, as a natural bearer of fundamental rights. Rather, its point of reference seems to be the population as a whole, including the coincidences, ambivalences and contingency that constitute it. Its target is in constant flux, its empirical substance proves volatile, as the usual causality schemes of cause and effect no longer seem to apply. Consequently, pandemic policy has as its object the reduction, if possible the suppression, of the randomness necessarily associated with the free movement of liberal democracies. Curfews are elementary encroachments on fundamental rights – in the pandemic they are only a technique – used throughout Europe – to interrupt frequencies of movement in the population. Border closures and controls as well as entry restrictions interfere with fundamental freedoms guaranteed throughout Europe; in the pandemic they prevent movements across borders.[11]

Isolation and quarantine are, on the one hand, individual restrictions on freedom, but on the other hand and above all, measures to keep risks, dangers or simply ambivalences away from the population. In pandemic policies, technologies of power become visible that decouple from legal

---

9 M. Foucault, Die Geburt der Biopolitik, in: Folkers/Lemke, p. 115 et seq (p. 116).
10 M. Foucault, ibidem, p. 119.
11 J. Gerkrath, p. 45 et seq.

concepts, which instead seek a form they need for their implementation and enforcement. Pandemic policies access the population as a whole, their relationship to law appears just as functional as hygiene measures, the provision of masks or vaccines. Instead of normative decision-making between right and wrong, lawful or illegal, conforming to or deviating from the rules, pandemic policy is in permanent action mode: it is about quantification, measurement, statistical recording. All this with the aim of minimising hazard and – if you like – restoring the "homeostasis" of the natural cycle that has gone out of joint. In this way, scientific expertise penetrates legal codifications as a natural necessity.[12] This results in selective, temporary and at the same time *adaptable regulatory mechanisms*. These contrast sharply with and sometimes *replace general legislation.*

The tension between the *characteristics of pandemic regulation* and the *requirements of general legislation* takes hold of the system and application level of law and influences its functions, at the constitutional level, in its mechanisms of repression and prevention. Differences already emerge in the institutional anchoring of general legislation on the one hand and pandemic regulation on the other. While the former is based on normative, constitutionally anchored procedures and the state powers that support them, the latter seeks alternative forms of action and organisation that coordinate pandemic expertise and institutional action. This results in a picture of networking at the national and transnational levels. Ministries of health interact with affiliated or integrated institutions of disease surveillance and prevention, governments make use of the expert advice of ad-hoc "task forces", and at the European, even global level, this interweaving of crisis expertise and executive power is finally merged into an action of "good governance" guided by transnational experts.[13]

b) Pandemic regulation: security optimisation as a model

At the same time, the tension between modelling pandemic regulation and the legitimacy requirements of general legislation is no coincidence. Rather, it is an outflow and component of (post-)modern legal development itself, the core of which is not only repressive sanctioning, or even

---

12 Deleuze, Postskriptum über die Kontrollgesellschaften, in: Folkers/Lemke, p. 127 et seq.

13 See Heinig/Kingreen/Lepsius/Möllers/Volkmann/Wissman, Juristenzeitung (JZ), 2020, p. 861 et seq (p. 866).

preventive control, but is shaped by models of "post-preventive" control, i.e. control for its own sake.[14] Developments in the criminal justice system in recent history may serve as evidence of this. Criminal law – no longer even primarily – has a repressive or disciplinary effect; it not only claims to provide security, but also establishes mechanisms whose purpose is general control as such. Examples of this type of criminal law social control can be found in modern forms of legislative and executive security optimisation.[15] Throughout Europe, actors in the criminal justice system have powers of intervention independent of suspicion, risk profiles are scanned and screened, criminal liability can be based on suspicion of sympathy – in the context of anti-terror criminal law – and databases of law enforcement agencies, constitutional protection agencies or foreigners authorities are networked and designed to be inter-operable. Data collections are created on a stockpile basis – politics and the actors of internal security can make use of them or not, can condense and merge information or not, can intervene repressively or not – depending on what political expediency makes appear appropriate in view of changing security policy threat scenarios. The policy of pandemic regulation traces these vestiges of post-preventive social control, makes use of techniques of this control and perpetuates them.

What follows from the policy of pandemic regulation for the principles of the liberal rule of law can therefore also be seen in the consequences of the policy of security optimisation. The law, criminal law in particular, loses precision and binding force. Like post-preventive criminal law, the policy of pandemic regulation decouples itself from persons and their subjective rights. It is not the affected, the sick, the patients or the vulnerable who are of primary importance, but the statistically, mathematically or cybernetically recorded risk profiles of structures, spaces and organisms.[16] This depersonalisation is ritualised in the daily media communication of infection and death figures, of incidences, R-values, which – freed from any empathy – measure the effectiveness of pandemic regulation anew every day, and which form the seismograph for juridical intervention.

14 P.-A. Albrecht, Kriminologie – Eine Grundlegung zum Strafrecht, 4. Auflage, p. 65.

15 P.-A. Albrecht, ibidem, p. 75 et seq.

16 Paul Rabinow, Artifizialität und Aufklärung. Von der Soziobiologie zur Biosozialität, in: Folkers/Lemke, p. 385 et seq.

c) Experimental law

Complementary to the policy of security optimisation, the following applies to pandemic regulation: The law becomes a modelling mass that is adapted to its respective object. It deliberately refrains from a stable equilibrium, but reserves the option of dynamic regulation. Its leitmotif is the virological, epidemiological or simply sanitary seismograph of pandemic measurement. Thus, the law becomes part of an experimental set-up: in an experimental process of trial and error, measures are tested with regard to their respective effectiveness in containing the virus. If the test seems successful, the next question is which rule can be changed to keep the virus under control without having to intervene too deeply and for too long in fundamental rights. But it is precisely in the attenuation of the pandemic regulation that mistakes may arise that subsequently give rise to correction and tightening again.

This – experimental – style of law also runs counter to Giorgio Agamben's gloomy forecasts, which were discussed at the very beginning of the pandemic in March 2020. If one follows Agamben, the pandemic perpetuates the legal state of exception and makes it permanent.[17] The sovereign sees itself as a leviathan detached from the social contract, manifesting its political agency precisely through its decision on "bare life".[18] In truth, black-and-white or rule-exception thinking cannot properly capture the juridical response to the pandemic, and the deformation of the foundations of liberal democracies proves to be – possibly – much more sustainable in the end. Indeed, in the experimentation of pandemic regulation, normative frameworks and the policies of health protection become intertwined. Life, health, the resilience of social systems penetrate and take possession of law at all levels. The individual as a bearer of fundamental rights and as a citizen of the social contract experiences himself as in need of protection and vulnerable, be it as a health risk for others, be it as part of the structural problem – the threatening overload of the health system.

In Luxembourg, state institutions advertised voluntary participation in the "Large Scale Testing" campaign with the slogan "We are all part of the solution". This is only superficially an appeal to solidarity, but establishes a political collective of pandemic regulation, a model of "biosociality" as

---

17 G. Agamben, State of Exception, 2005, pp. 2, 40.

18 G. Agamben, Homo sacer. Die souveräne Macht und das nackte Leben, 2019, p. 37.

Rabinow puts it.[19] What normatively constitutes a society – freedom, fundamental rights, deliberative procedures of democratic decision-making – is overlaid and partially displaced by the common understanding of the biomedical preconditions of the liberal constitutional state. Therein may lie the beginning of a decisive change in the legitimacy of the rule of law itself. One no longer participates in fundamental rights as a – freely born – citizen, but only to the extent that they are to be exercised at all in one's own self-understanding and in that of others, mindful of a policy of health protection.

d) Risks and side effects

The politics of pandemic regulation has insidiously and tacitly captured the legitimacy and lived practice of liberal democracies and is in the process of permanently changing them. This is all the more true as the politics of pandemic regulation can hardly escape a geopolitical context. Nolens volens, the democracies of the West are in a systemic competition that also extends to the efficiency of pandemic control and containment. The development of national economies depends on this, as do geopolitical strategies to expand their own spheres of power beyond their own national borders. Finally yet importantly, it is about the legitimacy and acceptance of the political system itself. We have chosen Singapore as the point of reference for a legal comparison because the state and society embody the model of Asian values, which on the one hand differs from the discourse of fundamental rights, but on the other hand can serve as a regulatory model of "good governance" with exemplary character.[20] This may result in an intercultural dialogue on legitimacy through fundamental and human rights in the face of a severe crisis.

Is it possible to fight a pandemic with the means of the liberal rule of law is therefore not only a purely juridical question. It is not about traditional legal access patterns, but only the interdependence between the policy of pandemic regulation, its functional conditions and the code of the legal system that determines the price that the liberal rule of law pays for the consequences of the pandemic.

---

19 Paul Rabinow, cf. footnote 16.

20 See Li-ann Thio, Legal communitarianism and Pandemic Regulation in Singapore, p. 383 et seq.

The *challenge to the political agency of* democracies is reflected at the level of the constitution and in the diverse forms of the sanitary state of emergency. The *style of law*, which adapts like plasticine to the conditions of the pandemic, influences both repressive and preventive modes of law and its principles. After all, what is left of *freedom in crisis mode*? Can we do better than we have done to achieve both: effective crisis management and the preservation of rule of law principles?

The approaches to pandemic regulation and the presumably lasting consequences for the liberal rule of law are the subject of the following analyses from the Member States of the European Union and the United Kingdom most affected by the pandemic. If one wishes, the "general part" of pandemic regulation is reproduced above all on the following three levels, which are modelled in all the reference states of the present study:

- The state of emergency imposed in various legal systems in Europe leaves its mark on ordinary law (B);
- An executive right is created which reinforces an already existing imbalance between the three powers of the state (C);
- The concept of freedom, on which a constitutional criminal law is based à priori, continues to lose its contour and requires self-assurance and reconstruction (D). Only from this do conceivable alternatives for the protection of the physical integrity of the individual and the guarantee of those systemic conditions that make this protection possible in the first place emerge.

B. Emergencies – securing the democratic sovereign's ability to act politically

When the World Health Organisation declared a pandemic of global proportions in February 2020, the societies and democracies of the West, accustomed to stability and normality, were not prepared for it, neither medically, nor in the systems of services of general interest, especially in the health system, nor – and not least – in law. The imminent need to contain the spread of the virus and the resulting regulations on exit restrictions and contact bans, which, precisely because they are punishable and sanctioned, represent profound encroachments on fundamental and civil rights, were given different forms of legal legitimacy depending on the legal culture.

I. The state of emergency – basic norm of pandemic regulation

At the beginning of the pandemic in February and March 2020, countries such as Spain, France and Belgium relied on constitutionally protected emergency articles.[21] In France, the French president takes the necessary measures according to Article 16 of the French constitution, in Belgium, the parliament can authorise the government to use extraordinary powers of intervention, and in Spain, the government is legally allowed to impose the "estado de alarma" by decree according to Article 116 (2) of the Spanish constitution[22]. The French legislature also created a simple legal emergency rule in the "Code sanitaire" specifically for the pandemic situation in spring 2020. Other countries, such as Germany or Switzerland, were able to base their measures to contain the pandemic on simple legal emergency articles from the beginning, which were provided for in the respective infection control or pandemic laws and which were supplemented in the course of the pandemic, in Germany, for example, by the term "epidemic emergency of national significance".[23]

In a **traditional legal conceptual scheme** – such as that used by the Venice Commission – states of emergency can be distinguished into constitutionally integrated and non-constitutionally secured states of emergency. In the latter case, the executive acts on the basis of unwritten principles to deal with an exceptional crisis situation. The state then implements emergency measures without formally declaring a state of emergency.[24] As an integral part of European constitutions, the state of emergency is the constitutional response to crises and threats – mostly those to internal and external security.

Terminologies of states of emergency and the normative criteria that justify their imposition also differ according to the type of threat, depending on whether it is a threat from an external enemy, an internal danger to the democratic order itself or – in a geopolitical context – the duty to assist an ally – such as within NATO or to some extent also in the European Union. State of necessity", "martial law", "state of emergency", "state of siege", "state of defence", "state of alert" or "state of crisis" (Etat de Crise) can be found as normative descriptions of extraordinary crisis situations in the legal systems of the EU member states.[25]

21 See J.Gerkrath, p. 45 et seq.
22 See. A. Nieto, point B.
23 « Epidemische Lage von nationaler Tragweite », see Poscher/Kappler, p. 287 et seq.
24 See B. Baglayan, p. 65 et seq.
25 See J.Gerkrath, p. 45 et seq.

If one distils in detail the constitutional requirements that justify the imposition of a state of emergency from the legal systems of the EU member states, four normative aspects become visible:

- The material definition of the crisis;
- The power to decide on the emergency situation;
- The control of the emergency situation;
- The return of the state of emergency to ordinary law, i.e. the necessary temporal limitation of the state of emergency.[26]

From this legal, if one wishes constitutional positivist perspective, it seems possible to limit the state of emergency normatively – i.e. above all in its legal content and its temporal duration. Individual voices even advocate the legal conviction that the constitutionally enshrined state of emergency is a means of self-protection inherent in the constitution, in the sense of a kind of normative resilience of the democratic sovereign to the extraordinary challenges of a crisis, a health crisis in particular.[27] Including the idea of a state of emergency in the constitution may be interpreted as constitutional progress in some member states of the European Union.[28] However, it seems problematic whether the assumption that a state of emergency is legally controllable, in view of the **tension** just described **between the political laws of pandemic regulation and the legal system,** does not have to be supplemented by the **consequential effects resulting from this tension.** Afterwards, it seems questionable whether there is an "ideal" state of emergency, as it were, since it is constitutionally contained, which first displaces the actually liberal alternative – namely the ordinary state of law – in order to restore it afterwards – seamlessly and politically sovereign. A purely constitutional perspective would therefore have to address the question of how the practical application of the regulations of the state of exception is historically and politically mediated and what feedback this has on constitutional guarantees of freedom.

The **fragility of a normative limitation of states of emergency** arises – ex-negativo, as it were – from a higher human rights perspective. Ex-negativo because the case law of the European Court of Human Rights reveals the weaknesses of the derogation of the state of emergency according to

26 See J.Gerkrath, p. 45 et seq. with reference to Lemke, What does state of excpetion mean? A definitional and analytical approach, Zeitschrift für Politikwissenschaft (ZPol), 2018, p. 374.

27 See J.Gerkrath, p. 45 et seq. with reference to Catarina Santos Botelho on the state of emergency in Portugal.

28 See J. Gerkrath, p. 49 (Footnote 8).

Art. 15 ECHR.[29] It grants the signatory states of the ECHR a very wide margin of appreciation with regard to the criteria of a state of public emergency. In particular, with regard to the limitations of the state of emergency, such as its proportionality and duration, the scope of discretion is broad. In judicial review of the national emergency rules imposed in the context of the pandemic, the European Court of Human Rights would only intervene against the suspension of fundamental and human rights if they clearly go beyond what is really necessary to manage the crisis.[30]

Observers note a high degree of inconsistency at the level of application of Art. 15 ECHR during the pandemic. Only around thirty states notified the Convention bodies of their intention to derogate from their obligations under the ECHR. Only ten out of 47 signatory states have officially suspended human rights. An independent analysis of the extent to which human rights guaranteed in the transnational framework were affected by emergency measures did not even take place in most signatory states. Rather, a nationally narrowed automatism becomes visible. Limitations in national constitutional law – so the understanding goes – also contain a sufficient condition to be able to deviate from transnationally applicable human rights.[31] This is in line with the derogation doctrine, according to which, for the effective defence of life and health, fundamental and human rights may be suspended under Article 15. In contrast, the limitation approach reflecting the risks of the state of emergency hardly penetrates, although from the perspective of international law and human rights, states of emergency present themselves as serious challenges to the protection of human rights. Experience shows: States of emergency pave the way to systemic human rights violations and destabilise the balance of power by strengthening the executive at the expense of the legislature and judiciary.[32]

II. System resilience – Common denominator of emergency legislation

If one links this rule-exception problem and its normative consequences with the policy of pandemic regulation, a legal-political dynamic emerges that loosens the bonds of ordinary law and which is above all – in a legal-

---

29 See B. Baglayan, p. 65 et seq.
30 Ibidem.
31 See B. Baglayan, p. 65 et seq.
32 See B., p. 65 et seq.

historical perspective – the hallmark of long-term historical-political legal developments. Time and again, politically powerful criminal policy constructed regulations that established themselves as an alternative to a criminal law that protected freedom and was strictly oriented towards legality and guilt. Even in measures of correction and security, a concept emerged alongside the criminal law of guilt that focused not on the offence, but on the offender. A preventive criminal law of risk control and danger aversion shifts criminal law from repression to the control of risk structures, far in advance of the actual suspicion of a criminal offence. In the criminal law of the financial crisis, administrative and criminal sanctions become blurred, agencies of financial control mix with traditional actors of the criminal justice system. If this is taken as a basis, the tensions between the political laws of pandemic regulation and the legal system will ultimately contribute to its further deformation and – lasting – change, with the danger of its partial destruction.

If one unfolds the historical context of a policy of emergency, one arrives at the variable that stands before the bracket of the purely legal justification of constitutional or public health emergencies: Exceptional and emergency legislation, whether at the constitutional level or in ordinary law, are ***instruments for manifesting and stabilising systemic resilience***. Looking at the basic norms of pandemic regulation as European legislators have set, legitimised, expanded or limited them, they are part of executive and experimental reactivity to developments and unexpected swings of the crisis. Basic norms of Covid legislation are elements of a stress test: on the one hand, this concerns the relationship between central and regional or local governance.[33] The British example shows how normative systems adapt to the challenges of pandemic regulation, especially the shift from reactive to proactive strategies. Depending on the escalation threshold of the crisis, intervention competencies shift to the level of central government and, in parallel, expert bodies emerge to advise the intervening executive.[34] On the other hand, the multifunctionality of already existing legal emergency responses and their conversion to the constraints of the pandemic are proving their worth. In the United Kingdom, the emergency response to external threats was and is structured analogously to responses to health emergencies – always with the goal of system resilience as the starting point.[35]

33 See Poscher/Kappler, p. 287 et seq.
34 Cf. Mitsilegas/Wortmann, p. 187 et seq.
35 Cf. Mitsilegas/Wortmann, p. 187 et seq.

Both multifunctionality and historically evolving adaptation to the constraints of a crisis can be exemplified in the French legal system.[36] French law contains – for historical-political reasons – several traces of emergency powers, which were realised at different historical points for different political purposes. Already in the "State of siege", created in the course of the French Revolution by law of 10 July 1791, now Article 36 of the French Constitution, the executive was empowered to restrict public liberties, police power was transferred to the military.[37] Military courts were given jurisdiction over crimes and offences against public safety. The budget of victories was applied long before the 5th Republic at historical landmarks: the Revolution of 1848, the Franco-Prussian War of 1870, and at the beginning of each of the two world wars, 1914 and 1939.

In addition, Art. 16 of the French Constitution gives the President of the Republic extraordinary crisis powers in the event of a serious and immediate threat to the institutions of the Republic, the independence of the nation, the existence of its territory or for the fulfilment of its international obligations. These exceptional powers have only been used once so far: by President de Gaulle in the wake of the coup d'état by the generals in Algeria, between 23 April and 29 September 1961. Following assassinations by the National – Algerian – Liberation Front, a state of national emergency, introduced by the law of 3 April 1955, was imposed in the Algerian conflict of 1955. The imposition was repeated after the coup d'état in Algiers and the coup d'état of the generals for the period 1961 to 31 May 1963.[38] Finally, in more recent times, a state of national emergency was imposed in New Caledonia in 1984 and, last but not least, in response to the terrorist attacks in Paris in 2015. It is part of the experience of the historical modelling of the state of emergency that in view of the attacks on the Bataclan concert hall and the Stade de France on 13 November 2015, the state of emergency was extended three times and its regulations were – in large parts – transferred into ordinary law at its end.[39]

Traces of emergency powers can furthermore be found in ordinary law, namely in the law of 9 August 2004, which introduced a state of emergency in the case of serious threats to health ("menaces sanitaires graves").[40]

If one follows these traces, one concludes that states of emergency are only superficially the interplay of their respective preconditions in

36 Cf. Bachoué/Poelemans, p. 155 et seq.

37 Ibidem.

38 Ibidem

39 See Bachoué/Poelemans, p. 155 et seq.

40 Article L-3131-1 Code sanitaire.

positive law. Behind the normative façade are the political needs of the functioning of order and system.[41] The legislator responsible in each case defines the prerequisites needed to ensure the resilience of the system. In this context, the law provides the necessary adjustment services for regulating and overcoming crises that threaten the system. Against this background, it is coherent that the French legislature did not make use of the diverse and already differentiated instruments of its emergency powers, but created its own track to regulate the Corona crisis.[42]The emergency law 2020–290 of 23 March 2020 stands – especially in the first phase of the pandemic until the end of the first wave of infection – as a model for the style of law in the pandemic. At the beginning, there is the imposition of a hard lockdown with rigid contact restrictions and fundamental interference with individual freedom of movement, which – in a second phase – evolves into differentiated regulation guided by pandemic regulatory criteria such as the incidence rate, the reproductive factor, the positivity rate of corona tests and the burden on the health system, especially the occupancy of intensive care beds.[43]Starting from the differentiation of the pandemic measures, a next step then arises in the summer of 2020, namely the attempt to return to the norm. However, the French legislator does not end the pandemic emergency at any point, but rather declares it a transitional regime ("régime transitoire"), which on the one hand relaxes regulatory measures and offers the end of the emergency in perspective, but at the same time reserves the right to react to changes in the pandemic at any time.[44]What can be seen is that this track of the state of emergency must expand the already existing state of emergency regulations, because only in this way can the pandemic be adequately mapped repressively and preventively.

The rigid state of emergency, its withdrawal and differentiation on the one hand, the attempt to return to the norm and the yet permanent modelling of individual emergency measures on the other, are partial aspects of that experimental style of a law "in actio" that is always looking for answers to biopolitical imperatives.[45]

---

41 See S. Allegrezza, La réponse répressive des Etats face à la Covid ou le devoir à la santé du citoyen superlatif. Un aperçu de droit comparé, Revue pénale luxembourgeoise, p. 9 et seq (p. 10).

42 See Bachoué/Poelemans, p. 155 et seq.

43 Ibidem, p. 155 et seq.

44 Ibidem.

45 See for Italy Sicurella/Picicituo, p. 327 et seq.

Given these imperatives, the political unfolding of emergency legislation as an instrument of system resilience is accompanied by two further – interrelated – aspects: Time, on the one hand, and trust in the functioning of political, especially democratic, orders, on the other.[46] In the short time available, the only response to the spread of the virus – especially in the first wave – was acceleration. Emergency laws are an expression of this acceleration and at the same time its motor. They are the argument for a shift of political action to the executive, since – according to the assessment – strict adherence to parliamentary procedures could have resulted in disproportionately greater damage to the legal interests concerned.[47]In the face of empirical uncertainty about the spread of the virus and – at the same time – the associated loss of political capacity to act, politics was gripped by a desperate "something must be done" mentality. The fact that in some cases the democratic legitimacy of political action fell by the wayside was factored into the considerations that led to the imposition of emergency measures.[48]Part of these considerations was to stabilise trust in the functioning of the political order by means of accelerated legislation.[49] However, what seemed to provide the executive with legitimacy for the moment could prove counterproductive in the medium and long term, i.e. destabilising confidence in the functioning of democratic procedures themselves.[50]

III. Rule of the normative vs. the "plasticine" of law

In the microcosm of Luxembourg, one finds the type of emergency legislation that contains all the elements mentioned under I and II – the search for the basic norm of pandemic regulation, system resilience as a bracket, time and trust as legitimising formulas. As late as 16 March 2020, the Luxembourg government based the measures to contain the virus on a law dating back to 1885.[51] It was obvious that the 19th century

46 See Sicurella/Picicituo, p. 327 et seq.
47 Cf. for UK Mitsilegas/Wortmann, p. 187 et seq.
48 Cf. ibidem, p. 187 et seq.
49 See S. Allegrezza, La réponse répressive des Etats face à la Covid ou le devoir à la santé du citoyen superlatif. Un aperçu de droit comparé, Revue pénale luxembourgeoise, p. 9 et seq (p. 11).
50 Ibidem, p. 20.
51 Law of 25 March 1885, concerning measures against the introduction and spread of contagious diseases.

legal framework was normatively and practically unsuitable for regulating the pandemic. In the absence of legal alternatives, the only way out for the Luxembourg legislator could be the first-time application of Article 32 (4) of the Luxembourg Constitution and the subsequent Règlement Grand-Ducal of 18 March 2020. The answer to existing regulatory gaps in ordinary law was emergency – "Etat de Crise".[52]

In applying the state of emergency in March 2020, the legislator acted carefully: the fact that vital interests of the population were threatened was dramatically visible to everyone. The examination of proportionality, a normative limit of Art. 32 para. 4, is conscientious and made the lack of alternatives at the time of weighing individual liberties on the one hand and the right to physical integrity and health on the other hand very clear. The appropriateness of the measures could be based on medical expertise, and their rapid necessity follows compellingly from the threatening overload of the health system. The parliament remains as a control body of the executive. Finally, sanction rules secure the necessary measures to contain the virus. Article 6 of the Règlement Grand-Ducal of 18 March 2020 introduces administrative offences that threaten fines that are predictable for everyone. At the time, this was legally sophisticated crisis management, which was followed by an impressive switch to efficient crisis mode in politics, especially in the health system and the people who work in it.[53]

Despite all this, legal unease crept in as early as March 2020. In 2016, the legislator inserted Article 32(4) into the Constitution as a direct reaction to the attacks in Paris in November 2015. The legitimising context of the state of emergency is also closely linked to the policy of public security. The Luxembourg Council of State has always followed this introduction critically and with great legal restraint. It feared that the security paradigm would destroy fundamental rights and freedoms in the long term if the signal were given that ordinary (criminal) law was no longer capable of dealing with elementary violations of rights. Despite the limits that Art. 32 (4) places on the "Etat de Crise", the Council of State of Luxembourg – rightly – noted an inevitable shift in the balance of power of the state from parliament to the executive.

The European style of law that is unfolding with the pandemic regulation is fighting against its own unease, searching for boundaries and normative barriers that are losing clarity and force. The factual rule of

52 See S. Braum, Le droit pénal aux temps de Choléra, Revue pénale luxembourgeoise, 7/2021, p. 1 et seq. (p. 2).

53 S. Braum, ibidem.

the normative, which necessarily determines the claims of political action in the democratic constitutional state, must assert itself in the face of empirical uncertainty and crisis-like ambivalence.

To paraphrase Carl Schmitt's well-known dictum, not least the sovereign decides on the end of the state of emergency. In the European democracies, the democratic legislator, the people and the public that supports them have discussed when and under what conditions the encroachments on civil liberties must be relaxed and finally withdrawn. In essence, this is a matter of normative decision-making: neither economic calculation nor epidemiological expertise can claim normative precedence, even if both aspects must be weighty arguments in normative and ultimately legal decision-making. What counts is the domination of the normative, since otherwise fundamental and human rights – and the public sphere that makes them possible – are in danger of being structurally and sustainably damaged, indeed have already been damaged. What was emerging in Europe's legal systems was the struggle to prioritise conflicting rights. Again and again, the question was how these could be brought into a relationship of balance and practical concordance with each other.

States of emergency can only be legitimised if the principle of proportionality is respected. In a classical reading, the question is whether the imposition of a state of emergency is suitable and necessary to avert threats to the vital interests of society. Necessity presupposes that there are no milder means that are less detrimental to the fundamental rights of citizens. Adequacy must be maintained: The protection of vital social interests must not cause excessive damage to other legal interests, especially fundamental rights and civil liberties. Even at the beginning of the pandemic, it could be argued with a high degree of legal professionalism that there was no alternative to the use of emergency powers, that the resilience of the health system was at risk and, last but not least, that there was no milder means that could have made the imposition of curfews and contact bans superfluous.

Time as part of the legitimation of the state of emergency, however, becomes relevant not only in the initial justification of the state of emergency, but – not least – also in its outcome. Crises are indeterminate in time. Those who impose states of crisis must therefore know how and when they will leave them again. Crises are not fixed aggregate states, their normative preconditions are fluid: even after the formal end of emergency regulations in Europe, there are still interventions in civil liberties, which are sometimes tightened, sometimes relaxed, in order to flexibly adapt to the respective pandemic situation. Perspectives on the conflicting legal interests and the empirical assessment of the functioning of social systems change dynamically. Legislators try to follow this dynamic. ***Rules appear like plasticine*** that can be adapted to the risks of the pandemic situation that are known and apparent at the time.

In Europe, "task forces", virological and epidemiological expert committees, some of which were institutionalised by the governments, essentially determined the type and scope of measures to contain the virus, and thus also the severity of encroachments on fundamental rights and freedoms. The normative domination of political decisions was and is challenged by the ad-hoc changes in knowledge and demands of biopolitical expertise, whose understanding of rules tends to be selective and narrowed to short-term efficiency.[54] Rules can therefore be modelled, "kneaded", as it were, to suit the pandemic situation at hand. Lawyers, on the other hand, have insisted throughout Europe – often in vain but rightly so – on the autonomy of normative decision-making, especially in the face of ambivalence. Lawyers, not least in criminal law, are always confronted with the ambivalence of facts, with empirical uncertainty. At the same time, however, they are obliged to determine the truth. Truth is not a scientifically determinable object of knowledge, but a normative construction, a consequence of normative proof conducted in fair proceedings. What is true is what can be proven in accordance with just rules of criminal procedure. In criminal law, but also elsewhere, lawyers are therefore used to having to make legally binding decisions despite divergent, even contradictory expert opinions. It is not the expert who makes the judgement, but the judge, who places his expertise in the context of a free evaluation of evidence, at the end of which there is a reasonable conviction beyond all legal doubt, which decides on punishment or acquittal.

Normative, legal guidance for action is therefore politically required precisely when expert knowledge arrives at no, incomplete or very contradictory results. Despite the – medially intensified – virological polyphony, the continued maintenance of rules based on states of emergency was and is a problem that must be negotiated publicly, according to normative criteria.[55] While at the beginning of the crisis both empirical ignorance and

---

54 Empirical ambivalence remains the hallmark of pandemic regulation into autumn 2022, as evidenced by the crisis scenarios unfolded by the German government's Corona Expert Council alone in light of the expected autumn and winter wave of the Omicron variant. Cf. „Corona-ExpertInnenrat der Bundesregierung (11. Stellungnahme), 08.06.22, Pandemievorbereitung Herbst/Winter 2022/23", p. 4 et seq. Depending on the crisis scenario, the adaptation of the German Infection Protection Act (Infektionsschutzgesetz) may follow.

55 See Heinig et alii, JZ 2020, p. 861 et seq. (p. 866).

the risk of systemic failure led to a normatively justifiable narrowing to virologically advised and systemically explainable radical containment, the focus increasingly turned to means-purpose relations that require political – above all normative – justification.[56] The lack of knowledge about the appropriateness of a legal measure cannot in principle lead to an attempt to establish maximum biopolitical security, but rather requires mandatory compliance with the prohibition of excessive measures. However, its elements, namely necessity and appropriateness, are increasingly difficult to justify in legal terms.

Transformation of proportionality

The tensions between the traditional legal decision-making programmes (emergency as the basic norm of pandemic regulation), the requirements of system resilience and the modelling of rules adapting to biopolitical imperatives ("plasticine law") are also reflected in the pandemic-related application and interpretation of legal principles.

Thus, not surprisingly, the traces of necessity also include shifts in the understanding of proportionality. The triad of proportionality is necessarily dependent on empirical clarity. Proportionality as a principle binds law to empirical reason and obliges legislators to reflect on the practical consequences of their actions.[57] In view of the daily changing picture of the pandemic and the divergent scientific expertise of virologists, legal argumentation within the framework of proportionality loses the coordinates it actually needs for evidence-based assessments of the consequences of legislative action. An empirically based system of coordinates is replaced by a matrix of risks that are weighed against each other.[58] This weighing move along a red line, at the ends of which lie the subjective rights of the individual on the one hand and the collapse of the health system leading to the drama of triage decisions between life and death on the other. Between these extremes lie socio-cultural and socio-economic risks, for culture, religion, the economy and not least the rule of law itself, which must be publicly discussed and weighed up with the social actors.[59]

56 Ibidem

57 See A. Nieto's contribution to this volume, point D.

58 See Bachoué/Poelemans, p. 155 et seq.

59 See Poscher/Kappler, p. 287 et seq.

With the spread of vaccines, the premises of risk assessment are changing anew, one may even rediscover the evidence-based building blocks of the traditional coordinate system of proportionality. Obviously, the administration of a vaccine represents the milder means compared to other containment measures. In view of the fundamental availability of vaccines, the currently applicable encroachments on civil liberties appear to be justifiable only as long as the risk groups of the pandemic are not yet predominantly immunised. However, if the immunisation of society progresses continuously, the measures to contain the pandemic also lose their legitimacy. The principle of proportionality stands ready at the beginning of the pandemic as the principle limiting the state of emergency. Now also the hinge points the legal way out of the pandemic. What will remain is the temptation to replace the rational prognosis of the consequences of legislative action with a matrix of risk assessments that allows the legislator, not least the executive, a flexible, situation-related, even *experimental control of risks.*[60]

C. Executive law

Agamben's gloomy scenario of a quasi-totalitarian regime of biopolitical social control does not stand up to a differentiated legal consideration that emphasises the constitutional integration of the state of emergency. Its core element is the sovereignty of the parliamentary legislature, which decides on the reason for and extent of encroachments on fundamental rights. From an optimistic perspective, it may even be argued that in some states Covid legislation may well serve as a legislative model of how emergency powers of the executive can be shifted back to the parliamentary legislature. From a formal legal point of view, this may argue for a strengthening of parliament, especially in the face of a crisis of state and society that has rarely been seen before. In any case, the executive dominance that characterised the state of emergency seems – superficially – to be subject to legislative control.

The question is, however, whether this corresponds to the legal reality. Are there not system realities that overarch the legal framework of the constitution and deform its contents? Executive law is not just a formal attribution. It includes – not only – the law that is formally set by the executive. Executive law is a style of law cultivated throughout Europe

60 See A. Nieto, ibidem; Bachoué/Poelemans, ibidem.

in pandemic regulation: the executive thereby determines the content of legislation and is at the same time the determining force at the application level of the legal system, i.e. in the interpretation and execution of the law.

Knowledge is power

The tension between the normative domination of political action and its regulatory accompaniment by biopolitical expertise not only characterises emergency legislation as such, it also affects the form and content of pandemic regulation. Especially at the beginning of the pandemic, but also in its further course, the executive binds action competences and expert knowledge to itself. In ad-hoc groups or so-called "task forces", it acquires and generates data and information. Decisions derived from accumulated expert knowledge are directly incorporated into legislation, the justification and motives of which are only partially comprehensible to parliamentary legislators. The accumulation of expert knowledge at the level of the executive leaves formal control by the legislature in tact, but robs it of its substantive core. This is not only symbolic politics, but presents itself above all as a problem of the rule of law, since it thwarts the principle of democracy understood as a political culture in which normative conflicts of objectives and their resolution are publicly communicated and, above all, debated.[61] In the UK, 91 out of 102 laws and regulations in the first stages of Corona legislation were passed without appropriate parliamentary scrutiny.[62]Here, too, it is clear that the balance of state powers is shifting in favour of the executive.[63] Nolens volens, this shift threatens to be lasting and to shape the legal system even after the crisis.

Criminal law as a control of systemic risks

Executive law – in general – turns out to be a feature of modern criminal law that hopes to gain legitimacy through preventive control of systemic risks.[64] Five further characteristics mark executive law as a style-defining

---

61 See Sicurella/Picicituo, p. 327 et seq.

62 Mitsilegas/Wortman, p. 187 et seq.

63 See A. Nieto's contribution "Controls and Penalties in the time of Pandemic: The constitutional state on trial.

64 P.-A. Albrecht, Kriminologie, 4. Auflage, p. 222 (et seq.); See as well S. Allegrezza, La réponse répressive des Etats face à la Covid ou le devoir à la santé du citoyen

feature of pandemic regulation. It acts in an accessory, acceleratory, pedantic, escalatory and informalising manner:

Accessory: The content of a criminal law does not result directly from its legal characteristics. Rather, it is revealed by reference to further norms, ordinances or even decrees.[65] It is not only in the French criminal justice system that the question of the predictability of the application of the norm arises for the citizen as the addressee of the law. The principle of criminal legality finds itself fundamentally challenged.[66] Violations of residence and contact barring rules were criminalised by referring sanctioning provisions of the "Code sanitaire" to decrees, which in turn were characterised by indeterminate legal concepts.[67] The United Kingdom is a good example of how fundamental this accessoriness is and how serious the loss of legal predictability can be.[68]There, executive criminal law goes hand in hand with a – radicalised – administrative accessoriness that comprehensively criminalises those who violate Corona rules and guidelines and which at the same time abrades traditional principles of criminal attribution – such as "mens rea" and criminal responsibility.[69]The simplification of criminal attribution and penalisation results in a comprehensive overcriminalisation[70] – a model of criminal law that has already established itself as a crisis regulator in the past[71] and will find further imitation in the future in view of further foreseeable financial, health, climate and environmental crises.

Acceleratory: Time as a legitimising moment of accelerated pandemic regulation through emergency laws also perpetuates ordinary law. Acceleration is the imperative of a dynamic regulatory process. A connection between legislative dynamics, even legislative hectic, and the rapidly changing scientific knowledge becomes recognisable.[72] Legislation follows the fast rhythm of political action, which in turn is oriented to the pace set by scientific research and development[73]: Covid legislation is lawmaking at "warp speed". The consequence of a lack of legislative deliberation is

---

superlatif. Un aperçu de droit comparé, Revue pénale luxembourgeoise, p. 9 et seq (p. 13).

65 See Sicurella/Picicituo, p. 327 et seq.

66 Sicurella/Picicituo, ibidem.

67 Bachoué/Poelemans, p. 155 et seq.; Sicurella/Picicituo, p. 327 et seq.

68 Mitsilegas/Wortman, p. 187 et seq.

69 Ibidem, p. 187 et seq.; Sicurella/Picicituo, p. 327 et seq.

70 S. Allegrezza, p. 135 et seq.; Sicurella/Picicituo, p. 327 et seq.

71 S. Allegrezza, Ibidem, p. 135 et seq.

72 Mitsilegas/Wortman, p. 187 et seq.

73 Ibidem, p. 187 et seq. and p. 173.

over-criminalisation and the loss of legal guarantees – a model of criminal law crisis regulation that will tend to develop its significance beyond the days of the pandemic.

Pedantic: Social control and enforcement of the sanctions associated with the violation of the Corona rules are dense and intense. They do not stop at trivialities and the core of private lifestyles: the purchase of a lemonade in the supermarket is sanctioned because this alone is not a reason to break the curfews, as are lovers who meet secretly in remote places.[74] In France, 12.6 million police checks were carried out during the first month of the lockdown, resulting in 762,106 fines. Police custody was imposed 1733 times for repeated violations of the Corona rules.[75]In the United Kingdom, a ***shift in the classification and perception of wrong-doing*** can be described. Sanctioning violations of the Corona Rules is attributed to the tasks of the criminal justice system because this is the only way to ensure the safety of the population.[76]As a result, offences such as assault are also interpreted broadly and applied to coughing on people, especially police officers and members of health and care staff.[77] The broadness of criminal attribution and the loss of a concept of injustice that reserves punishment and sanction only for significant violations of rights or legal goods also leads to uncertainty among the actors of the criminal justice system itself.[78] Overcriminalisation by the executive has the overload and overactivity of the criminal justice system at its back.[79] Wave of criminalisation can only be reversed through effective judicial control.[80]

Escalatory: The density and severity of social control and the enforcement of punitive corona rules manifests itself – beyond the comprehensive criminalisation of actually minor violations of norms – also in an escalation of the level of sanctions, indeed the type of sanctions in the case of recurrence.[81] In France, the legislative will led to a true "regime d'exception", as for the first time ever in the French criminal justice system, more severe sanctions in the case of "contraventions" were provided for by law.[82]

---

74 See these examples in the A. Nieto's contribution, point C.
75 Poelemans/Bachoué, p. 155 et seq.
76 Mitsilegas/Wortman, p. 187 et seq.; A. Nieto, ibidem.
77 Ibidem, p. 187 et seq.; S. Allegrezza, p. 135 et seq.
78 See Mitsilegas/Wortman, p. 218 (footnote 102).
79 Mitsilegas/Wortman, p. 187 et seq.
80 Ibidem, p. 187 et seq.
81 See S. Allegrezza, p. 135 et seq.
82 Bachoué/Poelemans, p. 155 et seq.

Punishment and its communication, which underlines the system-relevant character of the violated norm, are intended to stabilise the system of pandemic regulation and assert it against norm deviation. This – positive general preventive effect – aims at the reassurance and internalisation of the norms created with the pandemic regulation. The criminal justice system becomes an instrument of biopolitical regulation.[83]

Informalising: Pedantic and escalatory executive law leads directly to another characteristic. The criminal justice system, overburdened in this way, develops its own mechanisms to limit the overload to a level that is feasible for the system. The extent and density of police control – as in the French criminal justice system – leads to an expansion of police or prosecutorial discretion, as does the term "reasonable excuse" in the British context. There, it is above all the police and public prosecutors who create standard examples that can lead either to freedom from sanctions or to an aggravation of sanctions. It is not only in British jurisprudence that this informalisation of criminal attribution is criticised and doubted, as it threatens to undermine the requirement of legal certainty of criminal measures.[84]

Loss of judicial control?

The question is whether and how this executive right can be limited by judicial control. We know from the processes of administrative rationalisation and informalisation of the criminal justice system that the access of the judiciary to executive law does not go far. This is almost in the nature of things. Those who undermine the legal determination of punishable acts or acts subject to sanctions by expanding police discretion, by using undefined legal terms, by speeding up legislation, by lowering thresholds of injustice, leave the judiciary little room for correction from the outset.

The density and intensity of judicial control in the EU member states referred to here varies. While Germany repealed and corrected a whole series of Corona measures[85], and in the United Kingdom or France the

---

83 Particularly clear again in the UK, see Mitsilegas/Wortman, p. 187 et seq. and p. 179.

84 See Mitsilegas/Wortman, p. 187 et seq.; Sicurella/Picicituo, p. 327 et seq.; see as well V. Covolo, Non-respect des mesures sanitaires et contamination à la COVID-19 : Quelle responsabilité pénale de droit commun?, Revue pénale luxembougeoise, 07/21, p. 16 et seq. (p. 19).

85 See Poscher/Kappler, p. 287 et seq.

existing over-criminalisation was partially curbed, it is all the more striking that in the Luxembourg context the judiciary hardly functions as a counterweight in the practical implementation of executive law.[86] The court rulings dealing with the legality and proportionality of individual measures – in contrast to the French or German context – can almost be counted on one hand. Regardless of their small number, their content proves that the executive application of Corona measures carries the risk of being disproportionate or inadequately justified.

For example, the manager of a pub was fined 8,000 euros because her guests illegally consumed drinks while standing.[87] However, she was not personally served with the fine notice. More seriously, and going beyond a mere formal error, in a second case the basis of evidence used for the conviction for a criminal offence proved to be completely insufficient. Rather, the conviction was based solely on the testimony of a witness who stated that the distance rules had not been observed in a pub.[88] The witness also supported his testimony with a video of what happened in the pub, which circulated on social media.[89] The administrative court declared the conviction null and void because the attribution of the offence on the spot ignored the formal requirements of the rule of law that are to be placed on the rationality of evidence, and it thus moved on the boundaries of arbitrary exercise of discretion. In view of this encroachment on civil rights, the importance of judicial control becomes apparent in order to set limits to the temptations of arbitrary attribution of administrative offences inherent in COVID-19 laws. This is especially true when the type and extent of the sanctions imposed are reviewed for their compatibility with the principle of proportionality, which in some cases led to milder fines than those originally imposed by the police.

Again, the formal shift of Covid legislation from the executive to parliaments is no guarantee of the integrity of democratic procedures. Rather, one sees emergency legislation perpetuating itself in an executive legal style of pandemic regulation. Unlike Agamben's oppressive perspective, there is no identity between the state of emergency and ordinary law, but its differentiation into several tracks of legal regulation. The executive style of law is reactive and accelerated, it is thus also fragmentary and accessory, that is, legal content only follows by reference to other norms. Not only

86 See Chaouche/Menétrey, Point B I.

87 Tribunal administratif, 7 octobre 2020, no 45051, 3ième chambre. See Fatima Chaouche and Séverine Menétrey in this volume, p. 87 et seq.

88 Tribunal administratif, 9 octobre 2020, no 45061, 1ière chambre.

89 Chaouche/Menétrey, p. 87 et seq.

does it elude the effective qualitative control of a parliamentary debate, but it would also require a condensed judicial control in order to avoid a drift into arbitrary exercise of discretion. From the beginning, there was a danger that the state of emergency, as the basic norm of pandemic regulation, would leave damage in the fabric of the democratic rule of law state. The executive right of pandemic legislation contributes causally to this damage.

D. *Rule of Law and Democracy – Saved, Endangered or Destroyed by Digitalisation?*

The pandemic limits our freedom – or what we understand by it. The normative answers we provide to the questions of pandemic regulation also say something about whether and to what extent freedom, as the essential and inalienable element of Western democracies, is deforming and thus coming under pressure from competing models of society and politics. Whether the virus in the constitutional state continues to spread through the digital aspects of pandemic regulation, perhaps becoming a part of juridical "long-covid damage", or whether new options of expansion, perhaps even the necessity of reconstructing traditional concepts of freedom arise, is an open question to be discussed. The ***intercultural divergences*** between a Southeast Asian gubernative communitarian model of regulation, as embodied by the Singaporean legal system, and the Western model of the democratic rule of law are suitable reference points against which the risks and side effects of digital pandemic regulation can be assessed. At the same time, they could offer options on how to reconstruct freedom in the face of seemingly unavoidable digitalised social control.

Is the Western model of the democratic constitutional state failing?

The state only legitimises itself insofar as it understands political action, especially the appropriate crisis response, as "res publica" and thus liberties are exercised reasonably and weighed against each other. Interventions in fundamental rights therefore require justification and are subject to limitations. Principles of legality and proportionality form the limits and conditions of sovereign action. Can it be that these basic convictions of liberal democracies are themselves reaching their limits in the face of the pandemic? The virus was rampant and out of control – a traumatic scenario of political sovereignty. Rising numbers of infections and victims in Europe and the USA even seemed to contrast with a – supposedly – controlled infection in China. At the beginning of the pandemic, China's geopolitical strategy of expanding the power of its authoritarian model of political rule internationally made use of the apparent difference in the effectiveness of state action. On the surface, it seemed as if liberal democracy is no longer up to the task of balancing the conflicts between divergent fundamental rights associated with the fight against the pandemic.

Southeast Asia as a geopolitical challenge and model

While China's geopolitical and power-political functionalisation of the pandemic may – immediately obvious – be delegitimised a priori by a universal concept of freedom and human rights, contrasts in pandemic control also become visible in other states of Southeast Asia that are worth closer examination.

The ***Singapore model*** documents on the one hand significant ***legal-cultural differences***, but on the other hand also clear ***quality differences in regulatory sustainability in*** combating the pandemic. Singapore, a country with a population of 6 million, was and is characterised by relatively low numbers of infections and victims.[90] Several reasons can be cited to explain this. While Western societies only internalise the Corona rules with difficulty, in the countries of Southeast Asia they prove to be a firmly implemented component of everyday coexistence. They are the result of a socio-culturally anchored ***legal culture of communitarianism.***[91] Limiting the individual through public interests is part of socio-political genetics. However, this also means that the principle of the rule of law is understood purely instrumentally as the implementation of effective government policy.[92]Normatively, this can hardly be a model worth emulating. Nevertheless, strategies can be derived from ***Southeast Asian experience to*** strengthen the resilience of the health system through specialisation in the fields of virology and epidemiology – instead of further deregulating it – and to empower individuals to take responsibility towards themselves and others.[93]

90 Li-ann Thio, p. 383 et seq.
91 Li-ann Thio, p. 383 et seq.
92 Ibidem.
93 Ibidem.

Digitalisation is crucial for naming intercultural divergences in pandemic regulation. This concerns, on the one hand, its extent, but also normative anchoring, criticism and acceptance in the respective political and social model. If one wishes, the system of digital pandemic regulation in Singapore is characterised by a – partly punitive – polycentric data control, which on the one hand enables contact tracking, on the other hand links freedom of movement to digital verification, and finally covers vulnerable population strata and residential areas.

For contact tracing, Singapore was one of the first countries in the world to develop an alert app (TraceTogether), which was also based on Bluetooth technology, like the contact tracing apps practised in the European Union.[94] Downloading and using the app is – in principle – voluntary, which about 40 percent of the population did. Unlike in Europe, users must share their contact details upon request by the Ministry of Health to enable necessary contact tracing. Refusal to do so carries the threat of prosecution under the Infection Disease Act.[95] The use of the warning app is also obligatory for population groups classified as vulnerable and the areas they inhabit. This applies above all to migrant workers.[96]

The alert app is complemented by freely portable tokens that also emit Bluetooth signals and can interact with other tokens or app users. In the event of an infection occurring, the token must be handed over to the health authorities to enable contact tracing.[97]

The polycentric data control is complemented by an access app that requires an unlocked Q&R code to enter public buildings. User data is registered by shop owners and stored on government servers for a period of 25 days, accessible to health authorities. Last but not least, surveillance devices such as remote-controlled drones and "robotic dogs" can be found in public spaces, which draw attention to violations of distance and hygiene rules, register them if necessary and report them to the police.

Viewed in a European context, these measures are likely to be largely incompatible with fundamental rights, especially the right to the protection of personal data.[98] Above all, massive public criticism and the – justified – fear of a data- and information-hungry surveillance state probably unfolded. In an open intercultural perspective, however, it must be noted that the legitimising strand of digital pandemic regulation in Singapore and other

94 Li-ann Thio, p. 383 et seq.
95 Li-ann Thio, p. 383 et seq.
96 Li-ann Thio, p. 383 et seq.
97 Li-ann Thio, p. 383 et seq.
98 See for Germany Poscher/Kappler, p. 287 et seq.

Asian societies (China is excluded here) is not characterised by preventive considerations of internal security. Rather, it is directly related to a model of society that, on the one hand, obliges the government to protect the health of all on the basis of the – moral – imperative of societal solidarity, and in return, political actors can demand trust in the practice of "good governance" as well as cooperation and tolerance for encroachments on civil liberties. Technological possibilities are part of a communitarian understanding of "good governance".[99]

Trust in "good governance" is also a constitutive element of constitutional democracy in the European context. Democratic procedures presuppose trust in the transparency and normative integrity of democratic institutions on the one hand and generate it on the other. The European problem lies in the close connection between digital technologies and their security policy purposes. Facial recognition with the help of artificial intelligence can serve health protection, but also universal, even totalitarian surveillance of public space. Contact tracking and tracing data can be part of pandemic control from a virological perspective. However, they have been and still are at the same time the instruments of a security law aimed at bringing forward police and criminal law interventions. Repeatedly, national and European courts – in the case of data retention or police hacking – have been able to point out the limits of security policy data processing – an arduous path to the defence of civil liberty in the face of the force of digitalisation. Digital pandemic regulation is thus located at this interface between security policy strategies, which carry the core of disproportionate access to personal data, and a policy of a proactive health policy approach, which is definitely also in the interest of self-empowerment.[100] It would therefore be important to understand digital pandemic regulation as an essential element of a public, deliberative health policy.[101] Political approaches to pandemic regulation must be disclosed and discussed in detail in public and transparent procedures.[102] This need for public debate, however, contrasts sharply with the acceleration imperatives of executive law and the threatened loss of normative subject-matter authority in the face of a technocratic understanding of law as "plasticine". The false di-

---

99 Li-ann Thio, p. 383 et seq. "Trust" in good governance is then also the starting point for criticism of inadequate data protection, which also forces a government committed to communitarianism to take public responsibility for undesirable developments.

100 See Poscher/Kappler, p. 287 et seq.; Sicurella/Picicituo, p. 327 et seq.

101 Poscher/Kappler, ibidem; Sicurella/Picicituo, p. 327 et seq.

102 Poscher/Kappler, ibidem.

chotomy of data protection or health prevention, or even blind faith in the benefits of digital technologies, would thus have to be countered by a carefully balanced multipolar weighing of technological options, their risks, data protection policies and, not least, consumer protection rights.[103]The intercultural difference would then be above all the source of trust in state institutions: a communitarian model on the one hand, legitimation through deliberative procedures on the other. The latter, however, would at the same time mean brushing the – executive and experimental – policy of pandemic regulation against the grain.

103 For the British context, see Mitsilegas/Wortman, p. 187 et seq.; see for the Spanish context A. Nieto, point D.

Part 1:
Transversal Perspectives

Constitutional Engineering of State of Exception Regimes within the European Union

Jörg Gerkrath

A. *Introduction*

In a number of European state's so-called "*state of emergency*" or '*state of exception*' or '*state of crisis*' rules (hereafter generally referred to as 'State of Exception (SoE)') have been relied on in order to develop quick executive responses to the COVID-19 pandemic.

The State of exception can be defined as an extraordinary mode of governance provided for by the laws of the country and **subject** to such laws for their declaration and implementation. Declarations of a state of exception precede or accompany executive interventions, which could not be justified in terms of the constitution or previously established laws.[1] Or, as Matthias Lemke has put it: 'In a legal sense, the term SoE refers to a multitude of different crisis reaction mechanisms that exist in the context of differentiated statehood. These mechanisms have in common that they all enhance the government's power of action and decision-making, if the relevant condition to call out a SoE are met. The declared aim of these instruments is to return as quickly as possible to the pre-crisis situation'.[2]

These definitions draw attention to the fact that recourse to a state of emergency regime corresponds to a certain respect for legalism, or at least the desire to demonstrate such respect and to organize the return to the normal state of legality in due time. Recent experiences of SoE declarations in Europe raise, however, the longstanding question whether emergency situations are at all amenable to constitutional or legal regulations that are meaningful and observe the principles of democracy, the protection of human rights and the rule of law.

In fact, political societies have always been confronted with this question: can the law, as an instrument of stability and social normality,

---

1 See International Commission of Jurists, *States of emergency: their impact on human rights*, Geneva 1983, 466 p, at p. 413.

2 Cf. Lemke Matthias, *What does state of exception mean? A definitional and analytical approach*, Zeitschrift für Politikwissenschaft (ZPol), 2018, pp. 373–383, at p. 374.

'grasp' the situation of exception and in which way? Thus, in case of imminent internal or external danger, the Roman Republic provided for recourse to the exception **through** the establishment of an extraordinary magistracy: the dictatorship.[3]

A first superficial comparison of the European constitutions in place reveals the existence of different models of SoE rules and regimes. The variety of names given to such regimes is in itself significant. Referring either to an emergency, a crisis, a siege, an armed attack, a state of necessity or an exceptional situation, they commonly address extraordinary and unpredictable situations which require measures that are themselves exceptional but necessary in order to react to a major threat and possibly derogatory to the constitutional standards applying in normal times.

David Dyzenhaus has rightly pointed out that with regard to SoE rules, at least three choices have to be made within each constitutional order.[4] The first is between entrenching such a regime in the written constitution and leaving it to be decided only when an emergency occurs. The second is between the 'executive model' and the 'legislative model' and the third is about the extent to which the judiciary will supervise the implementation of the SoE regime.

According to Catarina Santos Botelho such states of exception, 'are constitutional self-protective mechanisms aimed at restoring constitutional normality'.[5] Are these mechanisms, when enshrined within the Constitution itself, thus able to adjourn the normal constitutional legality? Or in other words, do they operate some kind of adjournment of constitutional rights and guarantees? This seems to be difficult to conceive if the Constitution explicitly prohibits the suspension of any constitutional provision as does for instance the Constitution of the Grand-Duchy of Luxembourg in article 113.

In the following, we will follow a large definition of 'constitutional regimes', 'constitutional frameworks' and 'constitutional law'. In this large understanding, we will encompass national and supranational rules of constitutional nature or relevance, as well as national and supranational

---

3 Cp. Stephane Pierré-Caps, *Constitutionnaliser l'état d'urgence?*, Civitas Europa 2016, p. 141 ff, at p. 143.

4 David Dyzenhaus, *States of emergency* in Michel Rosenfeld, András Sajó (eds.), The Oxford Handbook of Comparative Constitutional Law, OUP 2012, pp. 442–462.

5 Catarina Santos Botelho, *COVID-19 and stress on fundamental rights in Portugal: An intermezzo between the state of exception and constitutional normality*, Revista Catalana de Dret Públic, (special issue) 2020, 183–194. https://doi. org/10.2436/rcd p.i0.2020.3553.

legal norms that have a constitutional law significance without belonging always to the Constitution in the formal sense.

In the current European constitutional framework, often described as a multilayer constitutional system or multilevel constitutionalism, national and European rules coexist and have both to be taken into account in order to fully understand the law applying in each country.[6] This is particularly true for the 27 member states of the European Union (EU) that are bound by the law of the EU as well as by the European Convention of Human Rights (ECHR). As we will see in the following, both layers of constitutional law, the national and the European, are highly relevant when it comes to situations requiring the declaration of a SoE or the recourse to less radical extraordinary measures in order to react to an extraordinary situation as the one created by the COVID-19 pandemic.

Qualified by the German federal constitutional court (BVerfG) as a '*Verfassungsverbund*', which may be translated as a composite constitutional system or a 'constitutional compound', this complex of intertwined constitutional rules contains quite a number of provisions that apply to situations wherein exceptional measures are required. To give a clear presentation of this composite legal system we will recall the different existing rules and mechanisms in evoking separately the variety of national frameworks and the relevant supranational rules.

In order to assess the choices made within this composite European constitutional system and to identify some lessons for future constitutional engineering of the SoE, we will thus summarize the variety of solutions established on the national level (B.), present the existing framework at the supranational level (C.) and discuss the critical elements of constitutional engineering in the field (D.)

B. National frameworks of the State of exception

As William Feldman stated in 2005, 'Any democratic government faced with a war, an invasion, a domestic insurrection, or other types of emergency must determine how it will respond. How much power will the executive be given? What will be the role of the other branches of government? How long will the response last? How will the government administer justice during such a period? What, if any, fundamental rights will

6 For the original concept see Ingolf Pernice, *Multilevel constitutionalism and the treaty of Amsterdam: European constitution-making revisited?*, CML Rev. 1999, p. 703.

be sacrificed in order to protect the nation? The way in which a nation responds to such questions will undoubtedly determine how successful it will be in responding to the crisis with which it is faced.'[7]

The comparison of national responses to the challenge of drafting efficient SoE regimes reveals a wide variety of constitutional provisions. The different clauses have indeed been written in different contexts and with different objectives allowing the national authorities to respond to a broad range of extraordinary situations including situations of emergency, natural calamities, military aggression, occupation and others.

The scope of this limited contribution does not allow to realize a fully-fledged comparative study of the SoE regimes in all 27 EU member states. The ambition is much more modest. By discussing the genesis, the wording and the applications of the most exemplary existing regimes, based on single or multiple clauses, we will try to identify examples of good practice and models of efficient mechanisms that comply with the fundamental European principles of the rule of law, democracy and the protection of human rights.

While some member states' constitutions include indeed mechanisms allowing for recourse to a SoE or the entrustment of special powers to specific institutions, other legal orders do not, either for historic reasons or owing to institutional tradition. It seems however reasonable to infer that the inclusion of a well-designed SoE clause within the Constitution presents a number of advantages. It adds to legal certainty and legal security, it withdraws the matter from the fluctuating will of changing parliamentary majorities and allows to define clear boundaries to the executive power in this field. In the third part, we will raise a number of questions which should be addressed by lawmakers willing to introduce or to revise the SoE clause in their constitution.

The purpose of the analysis in this first part is to assess the formal differences between the national legal frameworks on SoEs. In this context, questions to be raised concern namely the legal basis of the SoE regime, which can be found in the Constitution, in ordinary legislation, in case law or in unwritten general principles of law as e.g. the principle of necessity. Furthermore, some legal orders have a unique SoE regime while others have enshrined a plurality of regimes. Finally, a classification of

---

7 William Feldman, *Theories of emergency powers: A comparative analysis of American Martial Law and the French State of Siege*, Cornell International Law Journal, vol. 38, no. 3, 2005, p. 1022.

different SoE regimes seems to be conceivable showing that the different names of the thing are not always the most relevant indication.[8]

I. The names of the thing

The various SoE regimes are mainly designed under the names of 'State of exception' (*Ausnahmezustand*), 'State of necessity' (*Status Necessitatis*), 'Martial Law' (*Kriegsrecht*), 'State of emergency' (*état d'urgence*), 'State of siege' (*Belagerungszustand*), 'Case of tension' (*Spannungsfall*), 'Case or State of defence' (*Verteidigungsfall, -zustand*), 'State of alert' (*estado de alarma*) or 'State of crisis' (*état de crise*).

Historically, a declaration of a 'state of siege' was the first manifestation of this phenomenon. It meant that all governmental power would be transferred to a military commander in an area under attack. Its application was a matter of custom and it remained in effect as long as a threat persisted. It was not until after the French Revolution when the state of siege was first articulated in statutory form. The French law of July 10, 1791, which established the rules governing the implementation and continuation of a state of siege, marked the beginning of its modern statutory basis. It has been constitutionalized since then and figures now in article 36 of the French Constitution where it coexists with article 16, establishing a SoE regime that doesn't bear its name. In addition, a so-called regime of 'state of emergency', was provided for in France by ordinary legislation in 1955.

In the Federal Republic of Germany, the constitution drafters of 1949 were reluctant to introduce a SoE regime because of the bad experiences made during the Weimar Republic when the emergency powers were invoked extremely often contributing to the unstable nature of the Republic.[9] When it came into force, the Basic Law (Grundgesetz, GG) did

---

8 In the following the author relies mainly on the comparative studies realized by the Conseil d'État of Luxembourg: Conseil d'État, *Avis du 15 juillet 2016 sur la proposition de revision de l'article 32 (4) de la Constitution*, doc. parl. No. 6938 (4); and on behalf of the European Parliament Research service: Diaz Crego Maria, Kotanidis Silvia, *States of emergency in response to the coronavirus crisis: Normative response and parliamentary oversight in EU Member States during the first wave of the pandemic*, EPRS 04-12-2020, 60 p.

9 C. Jakab András, German constitutional law and doctrine on State of Emergency – Paradigms and dilemmas of a traditional (continental) discourse, German Law Journal 2005, p. 453.

not contain any provisions for the case of emergency. This has, however, changed since then. The introduction of the so-called 'emergency constitution' was made by the 17th Amendment Act to the Basic Law in 1968. The two central provisions of the 'emergency constitution' concern the 'case of tension' (*Spannungsfall*, article 80a GG) and the 'case of defence' (*Verteidigungsfall*, articles 115 a – 115 l GG), the parliamentary determination of which is the prerequisite for the applicability of a number of other provisions of the 'emergency constitution' as well as the federal emergency laws. In addition, article 91 GG provides a regime for the so-called 'domestic emergency' (*innerer Notstand*). This clause allows a Land to request police forces of other Länder as well as forces and facilities of other administrations and of the Federal Border Police in order to 'avert an imminent danger to the existence or the free basic democratic order of the Federation or a federate state (Land)'. So, it is not accurate to pretend that Germany does not know a constitutional SoE regime, as it is sometimes written in literature.

These examples torn from the French and German constitutions show clearly that the generic term of 'State of exception' may refer to very different constitutional regimes. The Grand-Duchy of Luxembourg still opted for a different solution and introduced a clause on the 'State of crisis' (état de crise). The recently amended article 32 (4) of the Constitution provides notably that 'in the event of an international crisis, a real threat to the vital interests of all or part of the population or an imminent danger resulting from serious breaches of public security, the Grand Duke, having ascertained the urgency resulting from the impossibility of the Chamber of Deputies to legislate within the appropriate time limits, may take regulatory measures in all matters'.

Not a single EU member state has provided for something like a "State of health emergency" on the constitutional level. In Spain, however, the Organic Law 4/1981 of 1 June 1981 on states of alert, exception and siege, as foreseen by article 116 of the Constitution, provides, inter alia, for the declaration of a state of alert in the event of health crises, such as epidemics and serious cases of pollution (Article 4 b).

France also inaugurated some kind of "State of health emergency" legal regime in 2020. Article L 3131–12 of the Code of Public Health thus permits the declaration of a public health emergency. It differs from the 'ordinary' state of emergency provided for by Act No. 55–385 of 3 April 1955 (serious breaches of public order and public calamity) mainly in that the declaration of a state of public health emergency concerns only the case of 'a public health disaster which, by its nature and gravity, endangers the health of the population'. In both cases, infringements of civil liberties are possible.

II. The Legal Basis of a SoE Regime

The vast majority of EU member states' legal orders define one or several SoE regimes on the level of their Constitution. Only three out of the twenty-seven Member States do not provide for any sort of SoE clause at all (Austria, Belgium and Denmark). The latter provide, however, for alternative ways to react, allowing exceptional transfer of legislative powers to the monarch i.e. the executive (Belgium and Denmark), or to the Federal President (Austria).

Furthermore, seventeen Member States foresee a comprehensive constitutional emergency clause suitable to respond to a pandemic. Based on experiences of the first wave of the COVID-19 pandemic, a very thorough research study of the European Parliament identified four main normative responses, as there are: constitutional states of emergency, statutory regimes, the use of special legislative powers by the executive and, finally, the exclusive recourse to ordinary legislation.[10]

It is difficult to assess if one or the other of these different types of normative frameworks is better adapted to deal with an emergency situation like the one created by the COVID-19 pandemic. From a point of view of legal certainty, of predictability and the protection of constitutional values, as well as human rights and freedoms, it seems, however, preferable to opt for a single and comprehensive constitutional clause that is applicable to any case of emergency or state of exception.

III. Archetypes of SoEs

Matthias Lemke divides SoE regimes into three types: first, an 'extralegal', second a 'legally integrated and executive oriented' and, third, a 'legally integrated and non-executive orientated' arrangement. According to him a SoE is 'extralegal if its proclamation suspends the constitution for the

---

10 See Diaz Crego Maria, Kotanidis Silvia, States of emergency in response to the coronavirus crisis: Normative response and parliamentary oversight in EU Member States during the first wave of the pandemic, op. cit.

duration of the SoE'. It is 'legally integrated if the constitution is only partially suspended during the application of the SoE'.[11]

The different types of constitutional provisions on SoEs tend to respond to the various risks that can potentially threaten the existence of a state, its constitutional order or its population. From a systematic perspective, the most frequent constitutional threats that have been observed as a source of a state of emergency in the EU can be grouped into three main categories: i) external threat in the form of war (also often referred to as state of siege); ii) internal threat consisting of situations that endanger the democratic endurance of the state function, insurrection or internal state of tension; and iii) external natural events, such as natural disasters, catastrophes.

Some constitutions have established a graduated response to emergencies. In this case the choice of one of the available SoE regimes will have to be made according to the principle of proportionality and after a thorough analysis of the nature and the gravity of the internal or external threat. According to the adage 'who can do more, can do less', it does not seem indispensable to have different levels of SoE foreseen by the constitution.

IV. Unicity or Plurality of SoEs

Some member states' constitutions entail several regimes SoE which can be chosen according to the nature and/or the gravity or the nature of the threat. Thus, the French Constitution refers in article 16 to a sort of SoE defined by the existence of 'a serious and immediate threat to the institutions of the Republic, the independence of the Nation, the integrity of its territory or the fulfilment of its international commitments'. It furthermore adds the criterion of an interruption of the regular functioning of the constitutional organs. It also provides, in Article 36, for the proclamation of a 'state of siege', without providing the slightest clarification. A constitutional amendment initiated at the end of 2015 and abandoned in March 2016, aimed to add an article 36–1 containing a reference to the 'state of emergency' currently foreseen by ordinary legislation. The Spanish Constitution enshrines in Article 116 the concepts of 'state of alert' (estado de alarma), 'state of exception' (estado de excepción) and 'state of siege' (estado de sitio), which correspond to different scenarios of emergencies. A

11 Lemke Matthias, *What does state of exception mean? A definitional and analytical approach*, Zeitschrift für Politikwissenschaft (ZPol), 2018, p. 374.

similar, though more differentiated solution, is to be found in the German Grundgesetz, already mentioned.

Other member states, as Luxembourg, have drafted single SoE clauses that are meant to apply to any type of crisis. From the point of view of constitutional engineering, this choice presents the advantage of simplicity and transparency in the eyes of the citizens. It also circumvents any risk of political dispute about the best suited clause to apply in a given emergency situation.

Although this short study does not allow to identify the existence of a European standard of SoE clauses, the next developments will show that the influence of supranational European law provides for some common rules and constraints in this field.

C.Supranational legal rules

On the European supranational level, the main relevant rules that may interfere with national decisions, having recourse to constitutional clauses on SoE, are to be found within the European Convention on Human Rights (ECHR) (1.) and the EU legal order (2.) Both provide at least for a monitoring of the national decisions.

I. The European Convention on Human Rights

As many other universal and regional international human rights treaties, the ECHR provides for a mechanism allowing its contracting parties to derogate from the normal standard of protection of the conventional rights or to suspend their application. This clause for 'derogation in time of emergency' figures in article 15 ECHR. It applies 'in time of war or other public emergency threatening the life of the nation' and empowers the states to take measures derogating from their conventional obligations. Only measures 'strictly required by the exigencies of the situation' are, however, allowed and they must be consistent with the contracting state's other duties under international law. Derogations from Article 2, except in respect of deaths resulting from lawful acts of war, or from articles 3, 4 (paragraph 1) and 7 are excluded. Derogatory measures taken and the reasons, therefore, as well as the decision to end them returning to the full respect of the Convention are to be notified to the Secretary General of the Council of Europe.

During the COVID-19 pandemic, only ten out of forty-seven Council of Europe (CoE) members made notifications under article 15 ECHR.[12] Among those ten, there were only three EU member states: Latvia, Estonia and Romania. Estonia ended its emergency situation and withdrew its notification under article 15 ECHR from March 2020 on May 18, 2020. The notification of derogation issued by Romania in March 2020 was withdrawn on May 15, 2020. Latvia has made several derogation notifications in place starting from March 16, 2020. The latest notification, from October 25, 2021, was withdrawn on November 18, 2021.

The regime set up by article 15 ECHR fully corresponds to what David Dyzenhaus called the 'the derogation model'.[13] This model intends to integrate the imperative of efficiency of the executive response to the emergency situation. It does, however, also provide, in a second time, for the imperative of legality to be respected. This is reached through the judicial review of the European Court of Human Rights (ECtHR) or other international bodies. A more or less intensive international control on the implementation of the contracting states' right to derogate isn't indeed irreconcilable with the specific requirements of an emergency situation.[14]

The judicial review by the ECtHR follows three patterns: it excludes any control of the appropriateness of the state's decision to exercise the right to derogate, it comprises, however, a strict monitoring of the respect of the formal and material conditions of the derogation declaration or notification. This entails a judicial control of the adequacy of the derogatory measures in the light of the declaration of an emergency, as well as their necessity and proportionality.[15]

---

12 See the list on the CoE website, https://www.coe.int/en/web/conventions/derogations-covid-19, accessed on 1.12.2021.

13 Cf. David Dyzenhaus, *States of emergency*, in Michel Rosenfeld/Andras Sajo (eds.), The Oxford Handbook on Comparative Constitutional Law, Oxford 2012, at p. 451. See also Tom R. Hickman, Between human rights and the rule of aw: Indefinite detention and the derogation model of constitutionalism, Modern Law Review, 2005, pp. 655–668

14 See in this sense Ludovic Hennebel, Hélène Tigroudja, *Traité de droit international des Droits de l'Homme*, Paris, Pedone 2016, at p. 719 ff.

15 Cp. notably ECtHR, Ireland v. United Kingdom, 18 January 1978, application no. 5310/71, § 163 and ECtHR, Öcalan v. Turkey, 12 May 2005, application no. 46221/99, § 179.

II. Declaration of SoE and the EU Legal Order

The EU legal order does not contain any general rule considering explicitly the declaration of SoEs by its member states. There are, however, a number of provisions and principles that have to be respected by the member states in such an event or may apply in order to organize a joint reaction. The main relevant principles and rules that may come into play during a SoE in one or several member states result from what is known under EU law as the 'mutual defence clause', the 'solidarity clause', the 'duty of sincere cooperation' and the 'public order, public security and public health exception'.

The Treaty of Lisbon, which is in effect since December 1, 2009, strengthened the unity of the EU members in dealing with external threats by introducing a mutual defence clause in article 42(7) TEU. This clause postulates that if a member state is the victim of armed aggression on its territory, the other EU countries have an obligation to aid and assist it by all the means in their power, in accordance with article 51 of the United Nations Charter. This obligation of mutual defence is binding on all member states. However, it does not affect their possible neutrality and is consistent with their commitments as NATO members.

The solidarity clause, codified in article 222 TFEU, also by the Lisbon Treaty, provides that EU members are obliged to act jointly when one of them is the victim of a terrorist attack or a natural or man-made disaster. The clause was conceived in the following of the terrorist attacks in Madrid in March 2004. In 2014, the EU adopted a decision to lay down the rules and procedures for the operation of the solidarity clause. It ensures that all the parties concerned at the national and at EU level work together to respond quickly, effectively and consistently in the event of terrorist attacks or natural or man-made disasters.[16]

The duty of sincere or loyal cooperation, laid down in article 4(3) TEU, embraces a mutual legal obligation for the EU institutions and the Member States, 'to assist each other in carrying out the tasks which flow from the Treaties'. This general obligation is part of what is considered under EU law as the specific status of the member states, sometimes referred to as a status of 'integrated states'.[17] It applies generally and certainly

16 2014/415/EU, Council Decision of 24 June 2014 on the arrangements for the implementation by the Union of the solidarity clause, EUOJ L 192, 1.7.2014, p. 53.

17 See Jörg Gerkrath, *The Figure of Constitutional Law of the 'Integrated State': The Case of the Grand Duchy of Luxembourg*, EuConst 2014, p. 109.

also during an emergency or exceptional situation affecting one or several member states. It would at least require member states willing to adopt derogatory measures to consult with the EU institutions and the other member states before put in place measures, such as for instance unilateral border controls

The so-called 'public order (or public policy), public security and public health' exception is enshrined within the EU founding treaties, mainly in the field of free movement by article 52 TFEU, as well as in secondary law.[18] It does not, however, give a *'carte blanche'* to the member states. Rather to the contrary. Member states are closely controlled in the use they make of their public policy. ECJ case law and secondary law have indeed, not only defined the content of what might constitute a member state's public order concern, but also its concrete process of application.[19]

Regarding for instance the operation of border controls within the 'Schengen Area', defined as an area without internal borders controls, the EU Borders Code, also known as 'Schengen Borders Code', a regulation from 2016, imposes strict conditions on member states desiring to reintroduce such controls at the internal borders of the EU.

The ECJ has had occasion to state that 'article 25 of the Schengen Borders Code allows, exceptionally and under certain conditions, a Member State to reintroduce temporarily border control at all or specific parts of its internal borders where there is a serious threat to public policy or internal security in that Member State'.[20] It can be assumed that the notion of public order can include that of public health. Other texts of Union law thus refer typically to the triptych of public order, public safety and public health.[21]

According to settled case law, recourse to the concept of public policy presupposes, however, in any event the existence of 'a real, present and sufficiently serious threat to affect one of the fundamental interests of society' (recital 27 of the Borders Code). Articles 27 to 31 of Directive 2004/38

---

18 Notably in articles 27 -33 of Directive 2004/38/EC of the European Parliament and of the Council of 29 April 2004 on the right of citizens of the Union and their family members to move and reside freely within the territory of the Member States, EUOJ, L 158, 30.04.2004, p. 77.

19 Cf. amongst many contributions Catherine Kessedjian, *Public Order in European Law*, Erasmus Law Review, 2007, pp. 25–36.

20 ECJ,19 March 2019, Préfet des Pyrénées-Orientales v Abdelaziz Arib, C-444/17, ECLI:EU:C:2019:220, point 49.

21 Regulation (EU) 2016/399 of the European Parliament and of the Council of 9 March 2016 on a Union Code on the rules governing the movement of persons across borders (Schengen Borders Code), OJEU, L 77, 23.3.2016, pp. 1–52

on the free movement of citizens of the European Union codifies the material conditions that Member States have to respect when they want to take restrictive measures that affect the free movement of EU citizens, while being justified by threats to public policy, public security or public health.

D. Critical components of SoE regimes in Europe

Within the third part of this contribution, we will focus on the main elements of SoE regimes. Crucial aspects of the exercise of public powers under those regimes include not only the extent of the measures adopted, but also their legitimacy, raising the question of their initiation, their duration and the degree of parliamentary oversight and judicial review. Comparative studies conducted on the recourse to SoE regimes during the first wave of the COVID-19 pandemic show a broad variety of rules and practices.[22]

I. Initiation

Regarding the initiation of a SoE mechanism many questions have to be solved. According to the political system in place, the Constitution will usually recognize this power to the executive branch, the head of state or the head of government. Some constitutions require the executive to hold a prior consultation with the constitutional court (France) or to obtain a favourable vote in Parliament (Germany). Such requirements are to be welcomed as they tend to limit the risk of a purely executive driven response.

In many cases there will be no difficulty to determine the existence of a serious threat to the national or the constitutional order. In others, like the current threat generated by the COVID-19 pandemic, scientific expertise might be necessary in order to evaluate the seriousness of the threat and the necessity to react by the declaration of a SoE. This raises

22 Cf. the rich study of Maria Diaz Crego and Silvia Kotanidis, *States of emergency in response to the coronavirus crisis: Normative response and parliamentary oversight in EU Member States during the first wave of the pandemic*, (EPRS) European Parliamentary Research Service, 04.12. 2020, 60 p; see also Conseil d'Etat (Luxembourg), opinion of 15.7. 2016, doc. parl. n° 6938(4), pp. 3–7; and

the question who really declares the SoE and based on which evidence. Is it up to the scientific community or do we need to defend the classical political primacy in this field? The link between science and law becomes particularly evident.

In fact, there are strong similarities in this field to matters addressed by environmental and climate change law. It seems for instance highly relevant to apply the precautionary principle when making the proportionality test of measures taken during a SoE meant to tackle a pandemic. In both situations there is a strong connection to scientific expertise and a vital need of the political institutions to receive impartial scientific advice. The question how to organize the availability of such advice for the decision makers is, of course, central. It should not be over-institutionalized, and it should be made sure that all independent sources of scientific expertise are available to the constitutional organs.

Many events or circumstances may lead to the declaration of the SoE. It is difficult in terms of constitutional engineering to foresee all of them. The threats can have different origins, external or internal, political or military, natural or man-made. The SoE clause should tend to define these circumstances in a comprehensive manner without being too vague. Bearing in mind that only 17 EU member states know SoE clauses that are suitable to apply to a pandemic, there is certainly a gap to be filled.

The SoE clause should also take into account that the seriousness of a threat also depends on the potential victims of the threat. The subjects that deserve to be protected by the exceptional measures to be taken should indeed be identified. The liberal and democratic constitutional order, the nation, the population, the democratically legitimized institutions are certainly possible subjects to be mentioned in order to define the seriousness of an emergency situation. A menace for an individual head of the state or for a specific political party in power is however certainly not sufficient to declare the SoE.

We should also bear in mind that achievements realized on the European level should not be torn aside to easily. During situations that give rise to the declaration of SoEs national *Sonderwege* may lead to reinforce nationalistic tendencies that we thought we had overcome within the European Union. The unilateral re-instauration of border controls at the internal borders of the Union should thus be strictly monitored by the EU Commission and the conditions that are laid down in the Schengen Borders Code need to be respected, even in times of a pandemic.

As the conditions to be respected when switching from the ordinary 'state of constitution' to the 'state of emergency' are manifold, it is particularly important to decide who monitors whether these conditions are fulfilled. Safeguards against any kind of abuse are crucial in order to avoid that the state of exception becomes the normal situation. Such safeguards can result from different mechanisms as we will see in the following sections.

II. Cooperation of powers and parliamentary oversight

Regardless of the importance of the principle of separation of powers within the constitutional regimes of all EU member states, during an emergency or exceptional situation, it is vital to organize a fruitful cooperation between the three branches of sovereign powers.

The common feature of SoE regimes is to grant extraordinary powers to the (central) executive in order to allow a rapid and efficient reaction. Mainly this includes the transfer of legislative powers to the executive. The executive organs have indeed traditionally been considered better suited to deal with crises than legislatures, due to their hierarchical structure, their ability to respond more speedily and flexibly to immediate challenges and their better access to expertise.

This pattern is certainly core to any SoE regime. It should, however, not exclude the two other branches of government from exercising their constitutional role during the implementation of the extraordinary measures. A SoE regime that is consistent with the common European values of democracy, the rule of law and the protection of human rights that are enshrined within the status of the Council of Europe, as well as in the Treaty on the European union, must uphold these values as far as possible also in times of emergency.

More precisely, this leads to the requirement of a close cooperation of the three branches of powers and to the need to organize an efficient way to allow parliamentary oversight on the different stages of an implementation of a SoE. This oversight should be arranged from the declaration itself until the termination of the SoE.

The experience made within the Grand-Duchy of Luxembourg is, again, inspiring in this regard. When, in June 2020, the SoE ended after 3 months and Parliament regained its full rights, the statement of its President Fernand Etgen was clear: 'This delegation of powers was not a blank cheque for the government,' he explained during the last public session in 2020. 'I am proud to note that the Chamber has worked closely with the government and the Council of State in an exemplary and supportive manner, while at the same time remaining critical'. 'The Chamber has fully carried out its legislative and oversight duties', he added. Eighteen meetings at the highest level of elected representatives with members of the government were organised to provide weekly updates on the management and development of the pandemic in Luxembourg. The chamber held altogether 21 public sessions and 189 meetings in parliamentary committees and, unlike many parliaments abroad, the Chamber remained thus fully operational throughout the state of emergency. The deputies have voted about 60 bills in the three months of the 'state of crisis', including the 'covid statutes' which provide the rules of conduct to continue the fight against the virus. Twenty-one public sessions have been organised.

III. Duration

The declaration of a SoE must be limited in time. The shorter the better. Prolongations must, of course, be envisaged but should be limited in number and in duration in order to prevent the occurrence of the famous 'permanent situation of emergency' discussed by Giorgio Agamben. Article 32 (4) of the Constitution of Luxembourg seems to be a good example. It allows declaring the 'State of crisis' for an initial duration of ten days. Any prolongation going beyond these ten days needs to be approved by parliament (*Chambre des deputes*) voting with a two-thirds majority and cannot go beyond three months in any case.

As the genuine aspiration of any SoE or state of emergency law should be to secure the route back to the 'normal' constitutional state, a precise rule about the termination of the SoE undeniably has to be included in a SoE constitutional clause.

IV. The scope of the derogatory measures and their effects of fundamental rights and freedoms

A declaration of a SoE will usually be followed by the adoption of executive measures that may derogate from ordinary legislation during a certain lapse of time. Under the European constitutional model, it is not conceivable anymore that the SoE simply leads to the suspension of ordinary legality or even to the suspension of constitutional norms.

According to the derogation model, the SoE constitutes rather a limited derogation from the ordinary legality including the limited possibility to derogate from constitutional or conventional human rights.

As article 15 of the ECHR, article 4 of the International Covenant on Civil and Political Rights recognizes hence also the right of governments 'in time of public emergency which threatens the life of the nation' to derogate, with certain exceptions, from their obligations under the Covenant, 'to the extent strictly required by the exigencies of the situation'.

This is also consistent with the positive obligation of the state to protect the right to live and the right for corporal integrity against health risks of the individuals. During a SoE, which derives from a pandemic or another threat to life or the public health, the need to ensure a protection of the most vulnerable (elder persons, children, prisoners, refugees, detained or hospitalized persons, …) weighs heavily in the proportionality test to be made. Thus other fundamental rights may be limited as far as this is adequate and necessary.

Also, the enjoyment of fundamental rights and freedoms engenders human duties, even though the latter are rarely explicitly named. It is, however, reasonable to conceive a human duty to contribute to the public measures taken against the spreading of the Corona Virus in order to protect the life of others. Such a duty stems logically from the adage that 'one's personal freedom ends where the personal freedom of another begins'. This might then be understood as a supplementary justification for the need of (proportionate) restrictions to some fundamental rights as personal data protection, free movement, free speech and freedom of assembly. Their proportionality has to be assessed in the light of the precautionary principle and may thus be easier accepted than usually.

When it comes, however, to very intrusive executive measures that limit the personal freedom in an extreme manner as for instance measures imposing vaccination, a curfew, compulsory quarantine or forced hospitalization, the proportionality test should be very rigorous. This leads us naturally to the role of a judicial review during the application of a SoE regime.

V. Judicial Review

At first sight judicial review seems to be somewhat contradictory to the very nature of a SoE regime. The latter is designed to allow a prompt response to an imminent threat and the functioning of justice requires time. So, one might consider that the judicial control will normally take place only at a later stage and will be limited in order to respect the wide margin of appreciation that the SoE regime usually recognizes to the executive.

A first fascinating option is to provide for an action against the very decision of the executive to declare the SoE. Why shouldn't there be an action open for instance to the minority in parliament or to a certain number of representatives to refer the question to the constitutional court through some kind of urgency procedure. It would be up to this court to decide at least at first sight if the conditions for the declaration of a SoE have been met.

During a SoE regime the legality and the constitutionality of the executive measures should also be subject to ordinary judicial review. There should be no place for 'judicial self-restraint' in this field neither from the ordinary judges nor from the constitutional judges.[23] At the contrary the Constitution should underling the full applicability of constitutional rules on effective judicial protection in times of SoE.

The intensity of judicial review will naturally be limited. A certain margin of appreciation has to be recognized to the legislator and the executive. But an intensive judicial control can always be realized *a posteriori*, also on the supranational level. It would be crucial in order to deliver an authoritative interpretation of the SoE clause and the different conditions laid down therein.

E. Conclusion

The question of how to draft an excellent SoE regime is not easy to answer. Many aspects have to be taken into account. The main guidelines which should be followed by drafters of constitutional SoE regimes are still very clear. The objective must be to allow an efficient and rapid government action in order to respond to an unpredictable situation of emergency or crisis. This implies in practice a stronger role of the executive than in ordinary times. At the same time the rules that allow this executive response must also safeguard the main values of European constitutionalism: the rule of law, the protection of the fundamental rights of the individual as well as the separation – or better cooperation – of powers and democracy. The task is not an easy one. The experiences made during the COVID pandemic might, however, help to draft such SoE regime clauses that will

23 Cp. Stephane cp. Pierré-Caps, op. cit., p. 147.

allow us to tackle the threats resulting *inter alia* from climate change in the coming years.

Covid Stress Test for the Rule of Law: States of Emergency under International Human Rights Law

Basak Baglayan

A. *Introduction: Human Right Price-tag of COVID-19*

On 30 January 2020, within a few weeks after the emergence of the first known case of coronavirus (COVID-19), the World Health Organization (WHO) designated the disease as a pandemic.[1] Since then the disease has spread to almost all corners of the world[2] creating extraordinary challenges, not only for the preservation of human health and life but also challenges for the domestic legal orders. In order to combat the public health emergency states introduced various measures, including social distancing, travel bans, closure of non-essential businesses and public spaces, "lockdowns" and quarantines.

These restrictions have profound impact on certain core human rights as prescribed by international human rights instruments, including the rights to liberty and security, respect for private and family life, freedom of assembly and of association, freedom of religion, and freedom of movement.[3]

While the measures introduced by the states were more or less similar, the legal framework regulating those measures differed significantly, even within the EU, where the member states share similar constitutional

---

1 WHO, WHO characterizes COVID-19 as a pandemic, 11 March 2020, www.who.int/emergencies/diseases/novel-coronavirus-2019/events-as-theyhappen

2 The Guardian, 'Covid cases recorded in Antarctica for first time' (22 December 2020).

3 The implications of COVID-19 on human rights are well documented. See, for example, EU Fundamental Rights Agency, *Coronavirus Pandemic in the EU – Fundamental Rights Implications: Focus on Social Rights,* (November 2020), available at: https://fra.europa.eu/sites/default/files/fra_uploads/fra-2020-coronavirus-pandemic-eu-bulletin-november_en.pdf; The European Commission for Democracy through Law (Venice Commission), *Respect for Democracy, Human Rights and the Rule of Law During States of Emergency – Reflections* (Venice Commission, May 2020) (26 May 2020), paras 46–58; HRW, *Human Rights Dimensions of COVID-19 Response* (19 March 2020), available at; https://www.hrw.org/news/2020/03/19/human-rights-dimensions-covid-19-response.

traditions (for a comparative assessment of different Constitutional measures, see, ProLaw contribution Jörg Gerkrath).[4] Some States invoked constitutional provisions containing rules allowing for state of emergencies (SoE)[5] (without necessarily following the procedures established in human rights conventions including formal declaration/notification to the treaty bodies). Others addressed emergencies by opting for urgent legislative measures that would allow for a modification of the ordinary balance of powers without officially proclaiming SoE (i.e. *de facto* states of emergencies).

Whether formal (*de jure*) or *de facto*,[6] the SoEs are "critically important from human rights perspective considering that the suspension of legal order or important aspects thereof [...] during emergencies often paves the way for systematic human rights violations".[7] As put vividly by an international law scholar, "the response of a state to a public emergency is an acid test of its commitment to the effective implementation of human rights".[8] Frequently **cited effects** of SoEs include "changes in the allocation of powers within the government, more frequent invasion of absolute rights and

4 Note that in the field of public health, the EU has only a "competence to carry out actions to support, coordinate or supplement the actions of the Member States", which excludes the adoption of laws. Article 6, consolidated version of the Treaty on the Functioning of the European Union (TFEU).

5 Different concepts are used to refer to 'state of emergency', including "states of exception", "states of siege" and "public emergency". The primary treaty provisions addressed in this note, the ICCPR and the ECHR, use the term "public emergency" whereas "l'état de crise" is used in Luxembourg. While these terms are used interchangeably in the present contribution the preference is given to the notion of "state of emergency" in line with the Prolaw Project description.

6 The Venice Commission: "Two types of emergency powers exist: constitutional and extra-constitutional. In the first case emergency powers are based on the (written) constitution or on an organic or ordinary law enacted with accordance with the constitution; the state officially proclaims a state of emergency (in one of the forms foreseen by national law) and, usually, enacts emergency measures. In the latter case, executive authorities act – and are considered to be entitled to act – in an emergency on the basis of unwritten (constitutional) principles in order to overcome the emergency; the state enacts emergency measures without officially proclaiming a state of emergency", at Venice Commission, 'Opinions and Reports on State of Emergency' (16 April 2020), CDL-PI(2020)003, (Venice Commission, 'Opinions and Reports on State of Emergency' (16 April 2020), CDL-PI(2020)003,) 6.

7 Evan J. Criddle, Human rights, emergencies and rule of law, in *Human Rights Quarterly* (April 2010) (Criddle 2010) 4.

8 Dominic McGoldrick, The interface between public emergency powers and international law, International Journal of Constitutional Law 2, (2004), 380–429, 388.

greater restrictions upon other fundamental rights".[9] Moreover, SoEs pose significant challenges to states' commitments to rule of law by enhancing executive powers at the expense of legislative and judicial institutions.[10]

International law in general,[11] and international human rights law in particular,[12] provide legal frameworks for States to observe during states of emergencies expressed in derogation and limitation clauses. In general, "the idea of limitations is based on the recognition that most human rights are not absolute but rather reflect a balance between individual and community interests", whereas "a derogation of a right or an aspect of a right is its complete or partial elimination as an international obligation".[13]

Against this backdrop, part II of this contribution introduces the SoE regime in the European Convention of Human Rights and Fundamen-

9 J. M. Fitzpatrick, Human Rights in Crisis the International System for Protecting Rights During States of Emergency, (University of Pennsylvania Press, 1994), at 29.

10 Criddle 2010, *op. cit.*, 5. See, also, Venice Commission, SoE, warning states that: "a state of emergency does not involve the temporary suspension of the rule of law and does not allow those in power to act so that the law is violated, as they are bound by these principles *permanently*" (emphasis added). See also; J. Reynolds, *Empire, Emergency and International Law* (2017 CUP) stating: "the state of emergency is typically characterized by the deference or subordination of the legislative and judicial branches to an executive vested with increased powers", 191.

11 Leading international law treaties that stipulate standards to be followed during SOEs include; common Article 3 of the Geneva Conventions of 1949 (Convention for the Amelioration of the Condition of the Wounded and Sick in Armed Forces in the Field, Aug. 12, 1949, 6 U.S. I. 3114, T.I.A S. No. 3362, 75 U.N.T.S. 31; Convention for the Amelioration of the Condition of the Wounded Sick and Ship- wrecked Members of Armed Forces at Sea, Aug. 12, 1949, 6 U.S.T. 3217, 1.1.A S. No. 3363, 75 U.N.T.S. 85; Geneva Convention Relative to the Treatment of Prisoners of War, Aug. 12, 1949, 6 U.S.T. 3316, T.I.A S. No. 3364, 75 U.N.T.S. 135; Convention Relative lo the Protection of Civilian Persons in Time of War, Aug. 12, 1949, 6 U.S.T. 3516. T.I.AS. No. 3365, 75 U.N.T.S. 287).

12 See, for example; Convention for the Protection of Human Rights and Fundamental Freedoms, Art. 15.1, Nov. 4, 1950, 213 U.N.T.S. 221 [ECHR]; International Covenant on Civil and Political Rights, Art. 41, Dec. 16, 1966, 999 U.N.T.S. 171 [ICCPR]; European Social Charter, (1965) 529 UNTS 89, Art. 30(1); Revised European Social Charter 1999, ETS 163, 529 UNTS 89, art. F(1); League of Arab States, Revised Arab Charter on Human Rights Art. 4.1 (May 22, 2004), 12 INT'L HUM. RTS. REP. 893 (2005) [Arab Charter]; American Convention on Human Rights Art. 27.1, Nov. 22, 1969, O.A.S.T.S. No. 36, 1144 U.N.T.S. 123 [ACHR].

13 McGoldrick, *op. cit*,, 383.

tal Freedoms (ECHR),[14] with comparative references to the International Covenant on Civil and Political Rights (ICCPR).[15] The part discusses the extent to which derogating from human rights treaty obligations in the face of a public health crisis is necessary, considering less strict measures (in the form of limitations) exist. The following two parts describe the derogation and limitation clauses in the ECHR with references to the almost identical provisions in the ICCPR.[16] The parts explain both the substantive and procedural requirements of a legitimate derogation and limitation. Next, the contribution provides information on the current derogations from the ECHR in response to the pandemic and discusses the arguments in favour and against derogating from human rights treaty obligations. The final part concludes by arguing that derogating from human rights obligations at the time of public health emergencies, including the current COVID-19 pandemic, is neither necessary nor desirable considering that the existing limitation clauses in international law gives states sufficient freedom to deal with challenging circumstances in a legitimate way.

B. *Article 15 Derogations: Justification through the Emergency Concept*

Derogations are temporary suspensions of certain human rights guarantees during a state of emergency.[17] The European Commission for Democracy through Law (Venice Commission) defines a state of emergency as "a – temporary – situation in which exceptional powers are granted to the executive and exceptional rules apply in response to and with a view to overcoming an extraordinary situation posing a fundamental threat to a

---

14 European Convention for the Protection of Human Rights and Fundamental Freedoms, *signed* Nov. 4, 1950, *entered into force* Sept. 3, (ECHR) (1953), 213 U.N.T.S. 222.

15 International Covenant on Civil and Political Rights (ICCPR) (1966), 999 UNTS 171, Art. 4.

16 The derogations regime in the ECHR and ICCPR essentially "are equivalent in criteria, theory, and purpose"; see, Joan F Hartman, 'Derogation from human rights treaties in public emergencies – A critique of implementation by the European Commission and Court of Human Rights and the Human Rights Committee of the United Nations' (1981) 22 Harv Int'l L J 1, 3.

17 Venice Commission, *Respect for Democracy, Human Rights and the Rule of Law During States of Emergency – Reflections* (Venice Commission May 2020) (26 May 2020), para 41.

country".[18] Under international law, "not every disturbance or catastrophe qualifies as a public emergency".[19]

Aspects of what qualifies as public emergency is enumerated in derogation clauses. A derogation of a right is "its complete or partial elimination as an international obligation".[20] Some, but certainly not all,[21] international and regional human rights instruments contain derogation clauses. These include the International Covenant on Civil and Political Rights,[22] the American Convention on Human Rights,[23] the Arab Charter of Human Rights[24] and the European Convention on Human Rights and Fundamental Freedoms.[25]

Article 15 of the ECHR affords State parties the possibility of derogating from the Convention in exceptional circumstances.[26] It consists of three parts. The first paragraph sets out the substantive conditions according to which States can invoke a derogation clause and limits the measures they may take in the course of any derogation.[27] The second part lists those rights that are non-derogable even in state of emergencies and the third part lays out the notification requirements.

---

18 Ibid.

19 UN Human Rights Committee (HRC), CCPR General Comment No. 29: Article 4: Derogations during a State of Emergency, UN Doc. CCPR/C/21/Rev.1/Add.11 (Aug. 31, 2001) (GC29), para. 3.

20 McGoldrick, *op. cit.*, 383.

21 For example, the African Charter on Human and Peoples' Rights (ACHPR) does not contain a derogation clause and relies on general limitation clauses. African Charter on Human and Peoples' Rights, June 27, 1981, 21 ILM 58. Various human rights instruments within the UN system also do not incorporate derogation clauses, including; International Covenant on Economic, Social, and Cultural Rights, International Convention on the Elimination of All Forms of Racial Discrimination, Convention on the Elimination of All Forms of Discrimination Against Women, Convention Against Torture and Other Cruel, Inhuman or Degrading Treatment or Punishment, and Convention on the Rights of Persons with Disabilities.

22 ICCPR, *op.* cit., *Art. 4.*

23 American Convention on Human Rights (1969), 1144 UNTS 123, Art. 27(1).

24 Revised Arab Charter on Human Rights, reprinted in 12 International Human Rights Report 893 (2005), Art. 4.

25 ECHR, *op. Cit.*, Art 15.

26 For a detailed commentary on Article 15, see, William Schabas, *The European Convention on Human Rights: A Commentary* (OUP 2015).

27 See, CoE, *Guide on Article 15 of the Convention – Derogation in time of emergency* (31 August 2020) ("Guide on Article 15"), available at: https://www.echr.coe.int/Documents/Guide_Art_15_ENG.pdf.

I. Article 15 – Substantive Criteria

Article 15 paragraph 1 of the ECHR reads:

> In time of war or other public emergency threatening the life of the nation any High Contracting Party may take measures derogating from its obligations under this Convention to the extent strictly required by the exigencies of the situation, provided that such measures are not inconsistent with its other obligations under international law.

The clause in the ICCPR is slightly different, in that it refers to "time of public emergency which threatens the life of the nation..." without reference to "war".[28] This is the only difference between the two derogation clauses. However, the omission of this word from the ICCPR has "no real significance" upon the controlling operative language of the text which is *public emergency threatening the life of the nation*.[29]

The circumstances that justify derogation, i.e. what constitutes "public emergency threatening the life of the nation" was considered by the former European Commission of Human Rights (Commission)[30] and subsequently interpreted by the European Court of Human Rights (ECtHR or the Court) in *Lawless v. Ireland* case.[31] According to the Court "the natural

---

28 ICCPR, Art. 4(1). The derogation provision of the American Convention on Human Rights ("ACHR"), on the other hand, reads: "[times] of war, public danger, or other emergencies that [threaten] the independence or security of a [state]" (Art 27).

29 Oren Gross, Once more unto the breach: The systemic failure of applying the European Convention on Human Rights to entrenched emergencies' (1998) 23 *Yale J Int'l L* 437, 452.

30 Before entry into force of Protocol 11 on 1 November 1998, the Commission, together with the Court and the Committee of Ministers of the Council of Europe were overseeing the compliance by state parties with the Convention. The Commission would receive individual complaints, decide on their admissibility, investigate the facts and sought a friendly settlement. If no settlement could be reached, the Commission would bring the case before the Court or submit a report to the Committee of Ministers. Then, the final decision would be made either by the Committee or the Court. The Commission was abolished with the entry into force of Protocol 11 which replaced the old Court with a permanent Court with jurisdiction over all individual complaints. See, Basak Baglayan and Johannes H. Fahner, One can always do better' (2017) 17 *HRLR* 2, 3 (internal citations omitted).

31 ECtHR, *Lawless v. Ireland*, Application No. 332/57 (1 July 1961). The first time that the Commission dealt with the derogation clause of the Convention was the *Cyprus* cases (Greece v. United Kingdom *(Cyprus I)*, App. No. 176/56, 1958–1959). See also, Scott P Sheeran, 'Reconceptualizing States of Emergency under

and customary meaning" of public emergency refers to "an exceptional situation of crisis or emergency which affects the whole population and constitutes a threat to the organised life of the community of which the State is composed".[32] A more "comprehensive definition of public emergency"[33] in European Convention jurisprudence was provided in the subsequent *Greek Case*.[34] After reiterating the definition provided in the *Lawless Case*, the Commission listed four characteristics of a "public emergency" under Article 15: "(1) it must be actual or imminent; (2) its effects must involve the whole nation;[35] (3) The continuance of the organized life of the community must be threatened; (4) the crisis or danger must be exceptional, in that the normal measures or restrictions, permitted by the Convention for the maintenance of public safety, health and order, are plainly inadequate".[36]

The above definition of "public emergency" makes clear that the state of emergency has to be of an "exceptional" nature, which also separates and contrasts it with the state of "normalcy".[37] As such, the aim of any emergency regime is to "secure the route back to 'normal'" state of affairs.[38] The Human Rights Committee, in the context of ICCPR's derogation clause (Art 4), has come to a similar conclusion declaring that "the restoration

International Human Rights Law: Theory, legal doctrine, and politics' (2013) 34 *Mich J Int'l L* 491, 530.

32 *Lawless v. Ireland*, para. 28. In the later *Greek Case* concerning the interpretation of Article 15, the Commission has drawn attention to a distinction between the English and French versions of the *Lawless* judgment, the latter being the official text. The French text of the judgment, in its relevant part, reads; "une situation de crise ou de danger exceptionnel et imminent", adding the notion of "imminent emergency" which according to the former Commission "must be given weight" due to the authenticity of the French text, see; Eur. Comm'n on H. R., *The Greek Case*, *infra*, para 112, p 69.

33 Scott P Sheeran, *op. cit.*, 529.

34 ECtHR, *The Greek Case*, Application Nos. 3321/67, 3322/67, 3323/67, 3344/67 (1969).

35 This characteristic was later modified by the Commission and the Court in *Ireland v. United Kingdom* in which the "emergency was limited to Northern Ireland and therefore did not need to affect the entire nation", see; Sheeran, *op. cit.*, 533.

36 *The Greek Case, ibid.*, para 113, p 70.

37 A study on state of emergencies conducted by the International Commission of Jurists have analogized the exceptional nature of state of emergency in international law as "the counterpart of self-defence in penal law", International Commission of Jurists, *States of Emergency: Their impact on Human Rights* (1983), cited in Sheeran, *op. cit.*, 499.

38 See, Jörg Gerkrath, *Constitutional engineering of State of exception regimes within the European Union*, p. 45 et seq. (contribution ProLaw).

of a state of normalcy where full respect for the Covenant can again be secured must be the predominant objective of a State party derogating from the Covenant".[39]

First paragraph of Article 15, like the ICCPR Article 4(1), lay down the "principle of strict proportionality".[40] Both provisions enumerate the limitation criteria for measures derogating from the Convention: measures can be taken only to the "*extent strictly required by the exigencies of the situation*". The provisions refer to "the severity of measures, the geographical area they cover and the period for which they stay in place".[41] The latter, duration of derogation measures, is particularly relevant in the current context considering the ongoing nature of the pandemic. Neither the ECHR nor the ICCPR expressly requires that public emergencies be 'temporary'.[42] However, the Human Rights Committee (HRC) in General Comment 29, has stressed that "measures derogating from the provisions of the Covenant must be of an exceptional and temporary nature".[43] In the context of COVID-19 derogations, the HRC reiterated its position that the exceptional emergency powers must be on a "temporary basis"[44]

While the ECtHR acknowledged the HRC's position in General Comment 29, in *A and Others v. United Kingdom*,[45] it "explicitly disagreed with the HRC that an emergency, and consequently the derogation measures, can only be 'temporary'".[46] The Court, citing its own cases on UK's counter terrorism campaign in Northern Ireland, confirmed that "the Court's case-law has never, to date, explicitly incorporated the requirement that the emergency be temporary, although the question of the proportionality of the response may be linked to the duration of the emergency".[47]

---

39 Human Rights Committee, General Comment 29, States of Emergency (article 4), U.N. Doc. CCPR/C/21/Rev.1/Add.11 (2001).

40 OHCHR/IBA Manual, 852; General Comment 29, *op. cit.*, para. 4; Hartman, *op. cit.*, 17.

41 General Comment 29, ibid.

42 Criddle 2014, 204.

43 General Comment 29, *op. cit.*, para 2.

44 HRC, Statement on derogations from the Covenant in connection with the COVID-19 pandemic (24 April 2020), CCPR/C/128/2, para. 2.

45 *A & Others v. United Kingdom*, ECtHR, Application No. 3455/05, 19 February 2009, cited in Criddle 2014, *op. cit.*, 204.

46 Marko Milanovic, "European Court decides *A and others v. United Kingdom*" (19 February 2009) *EJIL:Talk*, available at: https://www.ejiltalk.org/european-court-decides-a-and-others-v-united-kingdom/.

47 *A & Others v. United Kingdom*, para 178.

The jurisprudence of the ECtHR leaves wide discretion to the states when interpreting whether there is a "public emergency threatening the life of the nation, as well as in deciding on "the nature and scope of derogations necessary to avert it".[48] It is likely that the Court will apply "a wide degree of deference to states" when scrutinizing the COVID-19 measures considering "the relatively unprecedented nature of COVID-19", as well as "at times, conflicting medical evidence guiding government responses and different impacts and rates of infections across different countries".[49] However, the derogating states "do not enjoy an unlimited power of appreciation. It is for the Court to rule on whether *inter alia* the States have gone beyond the 'extent strictly required by the exigencies' of the crisis".[50]

Another substantive aspect of the derogation regime in Article 15 of the Convention is that the emergency measures must not be "inconsistent with" a State's "other obligations under international law" (Article 15(1)). Those "other obligations under international law" can comprise legal obligations derived from international humanitarian law, other international human rights conventions, and norms of customary international law.[51] In the *Lawless Case*, the Court has stated that it will examine the consistency of derogatory measures with a Contracting State's "other obligations under international law" *proprio motu*.[52] However, according to the jurisprudence of the Court, as analyzed in detail in the OHCHR/IBA Manual, "unless the applicant has provided clear and well-founded submissions regarding the respondent State's alleged failure to act in conformity with its 'other obligations under international law', the Court will not entertain the complaint".[53]

As a final remark on the substantive aspect of the derogations, the ICCPR contains a non-discrimination clause which is absent in the ECHR. The ICCPR in relevant part reads that the measures may not "involve discrimination solely on the ground of race, color, sex, language, religion, or

---

48 OHCHR/IBA Manual, 855, citing the following ECtHR cases; *Ireland v. the United Kingdom*, (18 January 1978), para. 207; *Brannigan and McBride v. the United Kingdom*, (26 May 1993), para. 43; *Aksoy v. Turkey*, (18 December 1996), para. 68.

49 Sean Molloy, COVID-19 and derogations before the European Court of Human Rights (10 April 2020) *Vervassungsblog*, available at: https://verfassungsblog.de/covid-19-and-derogations-before-the-european-court-of-human-rights/.

50 *Brannigan and McBride v. the United Kingdom*, (26 May 1993), para 43, cited in OHCHR/IBA Manual, 855.

51 Gross, *op. cit.*, 451.

52 *Lawless Case*, paras 40–41, cited in OHCHR/IBA Manual, 878.

53 OHCHR/IBA Manual, ibid.

social origin" (Art. 4(1)). While no such provision exists in Article 15 of the ECHR, the commentators have argued that the "principle of proportionality also covers the issue of discrimination".[54]

II. Article 15 – Non-derogable Rights

Second part of Article 15 lists those human rights that no derogation is permitted even at times of emergency:

> No derogation from Article 2 (the right to life), except in respect of deaths resulting from lawful acts of war, or from Articles 3 (the prohibition of torture and other forms of ill-treatment), 4 (paragraph 1) (the prohibition of slavery or servitude) and 7 (no punishment without law) shall be made under this provision.

In addition to the above, additional protocols of the Convention also contain prohibition of derogation from certain human rights contained in them. These include; the abolition of the death penalty in time of peace and limiting the death penalty in time of war (Protocol 6, Art. 3), *ne bis in idem* (Protocol 7, Art. 4(3)), the complete abolition of the death penalty (Protocol 13, Art. 2).

In comparison to the ECHR, the ICCPR has broader scope of rights that no derogation is permitted, including; right to life (Art 6), prohibition of torture or cruel, inhuman or degrading punishment, or of medical or scientific experimentation without consent (Art 7), prohibition of slavery, slave-trade and servitude (Art 8, paras 1 and 2), prohibition of imprisonment because of inability to fulfil a contractual obligation (Art 11), the principle of legality in the field of criminal law (Art 15), (the recognition of everyone as a person before the law (Art 16), and freedom of thought, conscience and religion (Art 18).

III. Article 15 – Notification Requirements

Finally, the third paragraph of Article 15 defines the procedural requirements that need to be followed when a State derogates from the Convention. Article 15(3) of the European Convention stipulates that:

---

54 Ibid.

> Any High Contracting Party availing itself of this right of derogation shall keep the Secretary General of the Council of Europe fully informed of the measures which it has taken and the reasons therefore. It shall also inform the Secretary General of the Council of Europe when such measures have ceased to operate and the provisions of the Convention are again being fully executed.

Informing the Secretary General primarily serves two purposes: It makes the derogation public and informs, through the Secretary General, the other State parties of the derogation which serves the collective enforcement regime of the Convention.[55] According to the case law, absent of such public notice of derogation, Article 15 does not apply to the measures taken by the respondent State.[56] The term "fully inform" indicates that the State is required to provide comprehensive information regarding the derogatory measures, although there is **no express** requirement to indicate the provisions of the Convention from which the state is derogating.[57]

According to the Court's jurisprudence the notification has to be submitted "without delay",[58] which differs from the ICCPR's procedural requirements for derogations.[59] Under the ICCPR, States derogating from the Convention are required to "*immediately* inform the other States Parties".[60] While "failure to comply with the procedural obligations will not necessarily deprive states of their option to derogation, […] non-compliance may be taken as *prima facie* evidence of bad faith".[61] The ICCPR further requires "proclamation of a public emergency" which aims "to ensure that derogating states also complied with domestic legal requirements for states of emergency".[62]

---

55 Guide on Article 15, 12.

56 See, *Lawless v.* Ireland, *op. cit.*, para 80; ECtHR, *Cyprus v. Turkey, op. cit.*, 66–68.

57 OHCHR/IBA Manual, 883

58 *Lawless v. Ireland*, para. 47, cited in Wallace, *op. cit.*, 783.

59 See, Stuart Wallace, Derogations from the European Convention on Human Rights: The case for reform (2020), 20 *HRLR* 769–796, 782.

60 General Comment 29, para. 17 (emphasis added).

61 Gemmo Bautista Fernandez, Within the margin of error: Derogations, limitations, and the advancement of human rights' (2019) 92 *Phil. L.J.*, 5–6 (citations omitted).

62 Fitzpatrick, *op. cit.*, 59.

C. *Justification under Limitation Clauses*

States that have not officially derogated from their international human rights treaty obligations to address the current pandemic nonetheless can legally limit certain rights under limitation clauses. Limitations constitute "restrictions imposed on non-absolute human rights"[63] and "allow states to balance individual rights and public interests within pre-defined permissible restrictions".[64] They are "clearly distinct" from derogations, in that they are allowed "even in normal times".[65] "While derogations lead to rights being disregarded completely, limitations imply that the 'core of the right' should remain intact and may not be affected by a possible limitation".[66] According to Fionnuala Ní Aoláin, Special Rapporteur on the promotion and protection of human rights and fundamental freedoms, while countering terrorism "limitations are prudent measures designed to protect public goods and the rights of others without undermining essential human rights that provide the foundation for a dignity-based society".[67] Limitation clauses are also referred to as "accommodation clauses" to emphasize that "their main goal is, indeed, accommodating individual rights and liberties, on the one hand, and the interests and the needs of the community, on the other hand".[68]

Unlike derogation clauses, limitations or restrictions on the exercise of certain human rights "appear in most human rights instruments",[69] including ECHR,[70] ACHR,[71] and ACHPR,[72] ICCPR,[73] ICESCR,[74] and

63 Venice Commission (May 2020), para. 40.

64 Fernandez, *op. cit.*, 9 (citations omitted).

65 General Comment 29, para. 4.

66 Brigit Toebes, Human rights and public health: Towards a balanced relationship" (2015) 19 *Int. J. Hrs.* 4, 448–504, 497.

67 Fionnuala Ní Aoláin, *Report on the promotion and protection of human rights and fundamental freedoms while countering terrorism on the human rights challenge of States of Emergency in the context of countering terrorism*, A/HRC/37/52 (2018), para 8.

68 Gross, *op. cit.*, fn 41.

69 Ibid, 9.

70 See, ECHR, Articles 8–111.

71 See, ACHR, Articles 2, 13, 15, 16, 22.

72 See, ACHPR, Articles 8, 9, 11, 12, 13, 14, 27(2).

73 See, ICCPR, Articles 12, 18, 19, 21, 22.

74 See, ICESCR, Articles 4, 5.

UDHR.[75] The protection of "public health"[76] is explicitly contained in the limitation clauses of the ECHR (Articles 8–11 and Article 2 of Protocol 4) and the ICCPR (Articles 12(3) (freedom of movement), 18(3) (freedom of religion and belief), 19(2) (freedom of expression), 21 (peaceful assembly) and 22 (2) (freedom of association).

The Siracusa Principles on the Limitation and Derogation Provisions in the International Covenant on Civil and Political Rights (Siracusa Principles),[77] drafted by a group of international law experts in 1984, also lists "public health" as a legitimate ground for limiting certain rights. The relevant paragraph of the Siracusa Principles reads:

> "Public health may be invoked as a ground for limiting certain rights in order to allow a state to take measures dealing with a serious threat to the health of the population or individual members of the population. These measures must be specifically aimed at preventing disease or injury or providing care for the sick and injured."[78]

Like derogations, limitations are also subject to the proportionality analysis by the ECtHR in order to assess "if the state interference was necessary in a democratic society".[79] The proportionality analysis includes "a triple test of *legality* (are prescribed by law), *legitimacy* (pursue a legitimate aim) and *necessity* (are needed to reach the aim and proportionate to it)",[80]

75 Universal Declaration of Human Rights, Adopted and proclaimed by General Assembly resolution 217 A (III) of 10 December 1948, Article 29(2).

76 "Public health" is defined as; "the prevailingly healthful or sanitary condition of the general body of people or the community in mass, and the absence of any general or widespread disease or cause or mortality. The wholesome sanitary condition of the community at large", *Black's Law Dictionary*, 5th ed., p. 649, cited in Erica-Irene A. Daes,The individual's duties
to the community and the limitations on human rights and freedoms under Article 29 of the Universal Declaration
of Human Rights: A contribution to the freedom of the individual under law" (1983), E/CN.4/Sub.2/432/Rev.2, para. 294. International Covenant of Economic, Social and Cultural Rights (Art 12(2)c and European Social Charter (Revised Art 11(3)) requires States parties to protect public from epidemic diseases.

77 International Commission of Jurists, Siracusa, Principles on the Limitation and Derogation Provisions in the International Covenant on Civil and Political Rights (1985), available at: https://www.icj.org/wp-content/uploads/1984/07/Siracusa-principles-ICCPR-legal-submission-1985-eng.pdf

78 Ibid., para. 25.

79 Kanstantsin Dzehtsiarou, "Article 15 derogations: are they really necessary during the COVID-19 pandemic?" (2020) 4 *E.H.R.L.R* 359, 368.

80 Venice Commission, May 2020, *op. cit.*, para. 40.

once the Court decides that there is an interference with the Convention rights.[81]

The first step will be the *legality* test formulated in the ECHR as "prescribed by law".[82] The "law" in this context has a broad scope and may include common law, as well as legislation.[83] It must, however, be "formulated with sufficient precision to enable the citizen to regulate his conduct".[84] The law also "must be adequately accessible: the citizen must be able to have an indication that is adequate in the circumstances of the legal rules applicable to a given case".[85]

The second test concerns the *legitimacy* which is "the least contentious aspect of any case involving the application of a limitations clause".[86] The Court has been rather deferential to the State party in its assessment of a legitimate aim and has found a violation "only when no logical aim can be connected to the measure at issue".[87] In the context of the current pandemic, Kanstantsin Dzehtsiarou
has argued that "it will be relatively easy for the Contracting Parties to argue that they were in pursuit of a legitimate aim" considering that "protection of public health is recognised as one of the legitimate aims for the interference with the qualified rights enshrined in the Convention".[88]

Finally, the Court will assess the *necessity* of the interference, i.e. the extent to which the measure was needed to reach the aim and proportionate to it. Limitation clauses in the ECHR states that interferences with or restrictions on the rights and freedoms they contain must be "necessary

81 Dzehtsiarou, *op. cit.*, 368.

82 Oscar Garibaldi defines "the principle of legality" in following terms: "the principle of legality is the requirement that an individual command (such as a court judgment or an administrative act) be so related to a higher law in the same system that the former would not be considered valid as to both origin and content were it not for the existence of the latter", Oscar M Garibaldi, 'General Limitations on Human Rights: The Principle of Legality' (1976) 17 *Harv Int'l L J* 503, 506.

83 Berend Hovius, The limitation clauses of the European Convention on Human Rights: A guide for the application of section 1 of the Charter' (1985) 17 *Ottawa L Rev* 213, 226, citing Committee of Ministers, Resolution DH (81) 2, 3 E.H.R.R. 615 (1981), noting the United Kingdom response to *Sunday Times v. United Kingdom*, 2 E.H.R.R. 245 (Eur. Ct. of Human Rights 1979).

84 *Sunday Times v UK.* (1979), cited ibid.

85 *Sunday Times v UK.* (1979), cited ibid.

86 Hovius, *op. cit.*, 239.

87 Kanstantsin, *op. cit.* 369.

88 Ibid.

in a democratic society".[89] The word "necessary" according to the Court "implies the existence of a pressing social need".[90] A measure "can be considered necessary in a democratic society only if it is 'proportionate to the legitimate aim pursued'".[91]

Observers have often raised the question whether the derogation of the particular guaranteed right is the only way to cope with the emergency considering that there are less drastic alternatives such as limitations.[92] This question became even more prevalent in the current context of the pandemic considering that states adopted divergent approaches to the similar challenges posed by the pandemic.

D. *Article 15 Derogations in the Context of COVID-19*

Observers have noted a "striking lack of consistency" in state practice when it comes to derogations from human rights treaties in response to COVID-19.[93] Despite being exposed to a health emergency globally and having taken more or less similar measures, legally states have responded to the pandemic very differently. In comparison to many countries that have adopted emergency measures,[94] only around thirty have notified relevant treaty bodies of their intention to derogate from their human rights treaty obligations. Ten out of forty-seven Council of Europe states derogated from the ECHR in the context of the pandemic.[95]

After analysing all COVID-19 related derogations from ECHR, ICCPR and ACHR up to 5 May 2020, Niall Coghlan concluded that "regional derogations frequently appeared to be conceived of as ancillary to constitu-

---

89 Hovius, *op. cit.*, 241.

90 Ibid, citing *Sunday Times v. U.K.* (1979).

91 Ibid., 248.

92 Christoph Schreuer, Derogation of human rights in situations of public emergency: The experience of the European Convention on Human Rights' (1982) 9 *Yale J World Pub Ord* 113, 126.

93 N. Coghlan, Dissecting COVID-19 derogations" (5 May 2020) *Verfassungsblog*, https://verfassungsblog.de/dissecting-covid-19-derogations/.

94 COVID-19 Civic Freedom Tracker, available at: https://www.icnl.org/covid19tracker.

95 These include: Albania, Armenia, Estonia, Georgia, Latvia, Moldova, North Macedonia, Romania, San Marino and Serbia. For list of all derogation notices, see Council of Europe, Notifications Under Article 15 of the Convention in the Context of the COVID-19 Pandemic, available at; https://www.coe.int/en/web/conventions/full-list/-/ conventions/webContent/62111354.

tional derogation".[96] According to him "several states seemed primarily to analyse their state of emergency and consequent restrictions under constitutional law, and assumed that such restrictions entailed derogation from international human rights law".[97] One interpretation of this behavior suggests that certain states view derogation as "a natural result of a state of emergency".[98] However, as underlined by Coghlan, this practice also suggests "a failure to conduct a separate human rights analysis to determine whether the restriction of constitutional rights in fact requires derogation from international human rights law" which is rather "problematic".[99]

While derogation notifications mostly focus on freedom of movement, assembly, and association; in reality the scope of human rights that have been restricted by governments is much broader, including, rights to liberty, to respect for private and family life, to a fair trial, to the protection of property, to freedom of expression, and to education.[100] The divergent reactions to the same phenomena generated fertile discussions regarding the relevance of derogations in the face of a public health emergency and revived some old debates. The question at the heart of the discussions is whether existing limitation clauses provide enough leeway for governments in dealing with human rights issues related to the pandemic, or whether they should have a recourse to derogations. Three distinct positions can be observed.

According to one prevalent view, derogation clauses are entirely compatible with the notion of protecting human rights. Not only do they not contradict human rights protection, but they do "contribute to their effective protection".[101] This view sees certain positive effects in notifying international institutions about measures that derogate from human rights treaty obligations. Notification requirement of derogation pushes the State

---

96 N. Coghlan, Dissecting COVID-19 derogations (5 May 2020) *Verfassungsblog*, https://verfassungsblog.de/dissecting-covid-19-derogations/.

97 Ibid.

98 Ibid.

99 Ibid.

100 Laurence R. Helfer, Rethinking derogations from Human Rights treaties' (2021) *ASIL Editorial Comment*, 24. For a detailed empirical analysis see: Niall Coghlan, 'Dissecting COVID-19 d erogations' (May 5, 2020) *Verfassungsblog*, available at: https://verfassungsblog. de/dissecting-covid-19-derogations.

101 Gerald L. Neuman, *Constrained Derogation in Positive Human Rights Regime*, in Evan J. Criddle, *Human Rights in Emergencies* (CUP, 2016), pp. 15–31, cited in Audrey Lebret, 'COVID-19 pandemic and derogation to human rights' (4 May 2020), Advanced access publication,*Journal of Law and the Biosciences*, 1–15.

to clearly articulate emergency measures[102] and subjects it to international scrutiny under the terms of necessity and proportionality. While this argument may be true in theory however, the state practice has shown that notification of derogations is often vague and lacks precision in regard to the rights that are being derogated from.[103]

In recent discussions, Alan Greene has argued in favour of derogations in the context of the COVID-19 pandemic. According to him, the key risk of emergency powers in the current context is "the recalibration of rights protections downwards but without the quarantining effect of a state of emergency".[104] For him, failure to declare a state of emergency results in "a de facto state of emergency that enables the same powers but lacking the transparency, additional oversight, and supervision that should accompany a de jure state of emergency" and runs the risk of normalizing exceptional powers.[105] Therefore a *de jure* emergency under Article 15 provides a framework of legality and commitment to return to normalcy according to Greene.

Those who argue against derogations draw attention to various risks entailed in state of emergencies, be it *de facto* or *de jure*. Evan J. Criddle opines that "by authorising states to derogate from certain human rights commitments during public emergencies, [derogation clauses] effectively allow states to design their own temporary, *ad hoc* human rights regimes".[106] Often reiterated risk associated with derogations is the unclear temporal boundaries of state of emergencies. According to Oren Gross, "a substantial number of states of emergency in the modern world do not follow the 'normalcy-rule, emergency-exception' paradigm. Rather than provisional and temporary emergencies, the world increasingly faces *de facto*, permanent, institutionalized, or entrenched emergencies".[107] This

102 According to Niall Coghlan, a notable feature of the COVID-19 derogations is that, the derogating states "provide little to no explanation as to why derogation, rather than restriction, is necessary" in particular considering that majority of the rights in question are qualified rights, Coghlan; *op. cit.*

103 Fernandez, *op. cit.*, 24.

104 Alan Greene, 'Derogating from the European Convention on Human Rights in response to the coronavirus pandemic: if not now, when?' (2020) 3 *E.H.R.L.R* 262–276, 266.

105 Ibid.

106 Evan J. Criddle, "Protecting human rights during emergencies: Delegation, derogation, and deference", in M. Ambrus and R.A. Wessel (eds.), *Netherlands Yearbook of International Law 2014*, Netherlands Yearbook of International Law 45, 198–99 (Criddle 2014).

107 Gross, *op. cit.*, 455.

observation was confirmed in a recent empirical study that analyzed all Article 15 derogations to date and concluded that derogations are "being misused by States to derogate for protracted periods of time for entrenched emergencies and that emergency measures are remaining in place after declared emergencies have ended".[108]

Others point out that certain human rights are absolute, like the right to life, prohibition of torture, prohibition of slavery and retrospective implementation of criminal punishment, from which no derogation is permitted even in times of emergency, but many other rights and freedoms are qualified and states can limit the exercise of these rights on public health grounds under certain strict conditions. Then the question arises as to the "added value" of having recourse to emergency powers. This question becomes even more pertinent when one considers that derogation or even limitation clauses were "deliberately omitted" from the subsequent human rights treaties: "the drafters of these [...] treaties rejected the notion of derogation [...]. For these particular treaties, States' compliance with substantive obligations remains paramount, even in situations of emergency".[109]

Kanstantsin Dzehtsiarou argued that derogations are not useful in the case of pandemic since "regular mechanisms of interpretation of the Convention allow the state to fight the pandemic effectively".[110] Comparing derogations to limitations in the ECtHR jurisprudence, Dzehtsiarou states that the states are likely to be given broad margin of appreciation anyway whether they opt for derogation or not. Dzehtsiarou argues that lack of European consensus on the scope and precise nature of the pandemic measures will justify the deference to domestic authorities and will not significantly adjust the Court's standards of review.[111] The Court will consider the circumstances of the pandemic and as soon as these circumstances are over they will stop influencing the proportionality analysis.[112] Dzehtsiarou

108 See, Stuart Wallace, 'Derogations from the European Convention on Human Rights: The case for reform' (2020) 20 *H.R.L.R. 769–796*. The author has analysed all the derogations from the Convention, including the ten pandemic related derogations (in total 55). See also, Federica Paddeu and Michael Waibel, 'The final act: Exploring the end of pandemics' (July 2020) *University of Cambridge Faculty of Law Legal Studies Research Paper Series*, paper no. 27/2020, stating "In practice, states often maintain derogations for extended periods".

109 Diane A. Desierto, *Necessity and National Emergency Clauses: Sovereignty in Modern Treaty Interpretation Account* (Brill 2012), 252.

110 Dzehtsiarou, *op. cit.* 372.

111 Ibid., 364.

112 Ibid.

argues *against* Article 15 derogations, comparing the insignificant added benefit of formal derogations in terms of proportionality analysis to "symbolic and political costs" inherent in such derogations.

A similar concern was raised compellingly by Joan F. Hartman 40 years ago:

> It is a truism that fundamental rights take on their greatest importance precisely at times of social or political tension when temptations to abuse are greatest. For an authoritarian government unrest supplies a welcome camouflage and justification for drastic sanctions aimed at the indefinite abrogation of personal rights and freedoms. Especially vulnerable in such situations are political, religious, and racial minorities against whom a hostile majority may opportunistically take repressive measures under color of dealing vigorously with a national crisis. [...] Unfortunately, the derogation clauses seem to imply that respect for human rights is a 'luxury' that must be dispensed with in times of unusual stress or crisis".[113]

A third approach sees derogations and limitations "closely linked" and as forming a "legal continuum", the latter being referred to as an "extraordinary limitation" on the exercise of enjoyment of human rights.[114] The "continuum" argument suggests that, despite the fact that derogations can impose extraordinary limitation on rights, "such limitations must not annihilate the substance of the rights inherent in the human person" and that "at all times be a continuum in respect of the legally protected substance of a right".[115] Furthermore, the "continuum" implicitly suggests that invoking derogations should be seen only as a last resort.

Professor Martin Scheinin, former UN Special Rapporteur on Human Rights and Counter-terrorism and one of the drafters of HRC's General Comment 29, is among the experts supporting this view. Scheinin argues that: "In light of the risk of abuse, it appears as the safe course of action is to insist on the *principle of normalcy*, i.e. to handle the crisis through normally applicable powers and procedures and insist on full compliance with human rights, even if introducing new necessary and proportionate restrictions upon human rights on the basis of a pressing social need created

113 Hartman, *op. cit.*, 11–12.

114 Anna-Lena Svensson-McCarthy, International law of Human Rights and States of Exception – With special reference to the Travaux Préparatoires and Case-Law of the International Monitoring Organs (The Hague/Boston/London, Martinus Nijhoff Publishers, 1998), at 49.

115 OHCHR/IBA Human Rights Manual, 814.

by the pandemic".[116] For him, what can be done under the framework of permissible restrictions, should be preferred unless available options prove insufficient during COVID-19. This is also clearly the approach adopted by the HRC, in its Statement on derogations from the Covenant in connection with the COVID-19 pandemic. The Committee states that, "States parties should not derogate from Covenant rights or rely on a derogation made when they are able to attain their public health or other public policy objectives by invoking the possibility to restrict certain rights".[117] Therefore, a State is obliged to consider possibilities offered by the limitation clauses "prior to taking the more drastic step of derogation".[118]

E. Conclusion

The present contribution focused on the international human rights framework applicable to state of emergencies. Human rights law primarily provides for two types of regimes that states can invoke in cases of emergency: derogations and limitations. The present contribution introduced derogation and limitation clauses under human rights treaties, focusing on the ECHR with comparative references to the ICCPR. The paper then provided various arguments in favour and against emergencies in particular in regard to the current pandemic.

Diverging legal responses of states to the same global problem demonstrates the clear lack of consistency regarding derogations thereby undermining the usefulness of the concept. International human rights law, through limitation clauses, already gives states a certain degree of discretion in balancing competing rights. Limitation clauses shape themselves according to circumstances which would mean that the proportionality assessment will take into account the pandemic whether under the limitation or derogation clauses. The concept of emergency suggesting that certain human rights obligations can be "switched off" albeit temporarily should be avoided, as there doesn't appear to be much added value of the derogations. In conclusion, derogations from human rights obligations at the time of public health emergencies, including the current COVID-19

116 Martin Scheinin, COVID-19 Symposium: To derogate or not to derogate?' (6 April 2020) *Opinio Juris*, available at: http://opiniojuris.org/2020/04/06/covid-19-symposium-to-derogate-or-not-to-derogate/.

117 UN HRC, CCPR/C/128/2 (30 April 2020).

118 Daniel O'Donnell, Commentary by the rapporteur on derogation (1985) 7 *Hum Rts Q* 23.

pandemic, is neither necessary nor desirable considering that the existing limitation clauses in international law gives states sufficient freedom to deal with challenging circumstances in a legitimate way.

Le Système Juridictionnel Luxembourgeois face à la Pandémie du COVID-19. Contribution à l'Analyse du Contrôle juridictionnel et de l'Accès à la Justice en Temps de Crise Sanitaire

Fatima Chaouche, Séverine Menétrey
Université du Luxembourg

Judicial review may be carried out by civil or administrative courts as well as criminal courts when dealing with penalised violation of emergency legislation/measures. The highest courts, especially the constitutional court (or a court with an equivalent jurisdiction), where these exist in the country, should also be involved. This court must have the power to order interim measures, on request by either a substantial number of minority MPs or the Head of State[1].

« Que peut le droit »? – La question au cœur du projet de recherche ProLaw est également posée par Jean-Paul Jean en *incipit* de son étude intitulée « les systèmes de justice face à la pandémie du COVID-19 »[2]. L'état d'urgence, les mesures d'exception et la prolifération des textes émanant le plus souvent de l'exécutif sont autant de facteurs qui appellent un contrôle juridictionnel accru pour garantir les droits et libertés individuels et l'État de droit[3]. La fonction de rendre justice est une composante fondamentale de l'État de droit[4]. Durant l'état de crise, l'accès à la justice se révèle être une nécessité impérieuse alors que les pouvoirs publics se dotent de

---

1 Interim Report On The Measures Taken In The EU Member States As A Result Of The COVID-19 Crisis And Their Impact On Democracy, The Rule Of Law And Fundamental Rights Adopted by the Venice Commission at its 124th online Plenary Session (8–9 October 2020), n°78.

2 J.-P. Jean, « Les systèmes de justice face à la pandémie du COVID-19 », https://www.leclubdesjuristes.com/blog-du-coronavirus/que-dit-le-droit/les-systemes-de-justice-face-a-la-pandemie-du-covid-19/.

3 Voy. not. A. Denizot, « COVID-19 : entre droit de la peur et peur du droit », *RTD Civ.*, 2020, p. 703; E. Debout, « Mesures d'urgence sanitaire et valeurs de l'Union européenne », *R.A.E, L.E.A.*, 2020/1, p. 41.

4 V. Donier & B. Laperou-Scheneider, *Accès au juge : quelles évolutions?*, Bruxelles, Bruylant, 2013; *L. Heuschling, État de droit, Rechsstaat, Rule of Law,* coll. « Nouvelle Bibl. de thèses », vol. 16, Paris, Dalloz, 2002.

pouvoirs extraordinaires[5]. La pandémie a néanmoins également conduit, dans un premier temps, et dans certains systèmes, à une réduction de l'activité juridictionnelle[6]. Si l'examen du fonctionnement des tribunaux en temps de crise sanitaire paraît anecdotique, technique voire rébarbatif, il est nécessaire pour mesurer l'effectivité de l'accès à la justice mais aussi les possibilités d'exercer un contrôle juridictionnel sur les mesures adoptées. « Courts have a vital function during and after the pandemic, in particular to ensure judicial scrutiny of emergency legislation and to provide an effective remedy against excessive emergency measures in individual cases. Uninterrupted access to courts is also required in other urgent legal matters, and to uphold access to justice in general »[7].

Champ de l'étude : le système juridictionnel luxembourgeois – La réorganisation de l'activité des cours et tribunaux a varié selon les systèmes et selon les juridictions elles-mêmes. Certes les pays limitrophes ont procédé à des aménagements comparables, mais avec des pratiques différentes notamment dans l'exercice des recours ce qui rend une approche comparée sur le contrôle juridictionnel et l'accès à la justice face à la pandémie de COVID-19 délicate. Pour un panorama comparatif, le lecteur peut se référer au tableau mis à jour par la Commission européenne sur le site e-justice[8]. La Commission européenne pour l'efficacité de la justice met à disposition des données analogues pour les États membres du Conseil de l'Europe[9]. Les données ne sont néanmoins ni systématiques ni parfaitement à jour et sont difficilement analysables, de manière

5 Voy. X. Kramer et al., Access to justice in time of Corona », https://www.Conflictoflaws.net.

6 Voy. pour la Cour de justice : M.-A. Gaudissart, « La Cour de justice de l'Union européenne face à la crise sanitaire », *R.A.E, L.E.A.*, 2020/1, p. 97 et pour des études comparées : B. Krans, A. Nylund, C. Piché & al, « Civil Justice and COVID-19 », (2020) https://www.researchgate.net/publication/340965353_Civil_Justice_and_Covid-19; OSCE, « The Functioning of Courts in the COVID-19 Pandemic », https://www.osce.org/files/f/documents/5/5/469170.pdf; Global Access to Justice, « Impacts of COVID-19 on Justice Systems », http://globalaccesstojustice.com/impacts-of-covid-19/; S. Chardenoux et al., « Justice and Challenges in Times of Pandemic in Europe », MEDEL, juin 2020.

7 OSCE, « The Functioning of Courts in the COVID-19 Pandemic », https://www.osce.org/files/f/documents/5/5/469170.pdf.

8 https://e-justice.europa.eu/content_impact_of_the_covid19_virus_on_the_justice_field-37147-fr.do?clang=en. Avec un tableau comparatif de l'incidence de la pandém ie de covid-10 sur les procédures civiles.

9 https://www.coe.int/en/web/cepej/compilation-comments.

comparée, à ce stade[10]. « La complexité intrinsèque d'une approche comparée résulte aussi de la nécessité d'intégrer d'autres paramètres externes essentiels comme par exemple la perception du monde politique ou l'organisation centralisée ou déconcentrée de l'État héritée de l'histoire, qui permettent de mieux comprendre les différences fondamentales du niveau de confiance dans les institutions et le rapport à la décision publique en France et en Allemagne, analyse qui s'applique aussi en matière de droit et justice »[11]. Aussi sans écarter les pratiques juridictionnelles d'autres systèmes, en particulier la France et la Belgique (et plus ponctuellement d'autres pays lorsque les données sont disponibles ou ont fait l'objet d'un traitement analytique[12]), l'étude se focalise sur le fonctionnement du système juridictionnel luxembourgeois[13], principalement pendant la pandémie et les enjeux auxquels celui-ci a dû faire face après la première phase de confinement[14]. Elle repose sur une analyse des textes réglementaires et législatifs et sur la jurisprudence ainsi que sur la pratique des tribunaux et des acteurs de la justice au Luxembourg. L'étude porte principalement sur le fonctionnement de la justice civile et commerciale et dans une moindre mesure pénale. Le fonctionnement de la justice administrative est également envisagé mais davantage sous l'angle du contrôle

10 Voy. pour un instantané comparatif : B. Krans, A. Nylund, C. Piché & al, « Civil Justice and COVID-19 », (2020) https://www.researchgate.net/publication/340965353_Civil_Justice_and_Covid-19.

11 J.-P. Jean, Les systèmes de justice face à la pandémie du COVID-19, https://www.leclubdesjuristes.com/blog-du-coronavirus/que-dit-le-droit/les-systemes-de-justice-face-a-la-pandemie-du-covid-19/.

12 Voy. pour le Royaume-Uni, N. Byrom et al., « The Impact of COVID-19 Measures on the Civil Justice System », Justice Civil Council, mai 2020; pour le Québec, S. Chaffai-Parent & C.Piché, « La justice au temps de la Covid », Rapport de l'Institut québécois de réforme du droit et de la justice, 15 juin 2020.

13 Sur les nombreuses études, voy. not. J.-P. Jean, « Les systèmes de justice face à la pandémie du COVID-19 », https://www.leclubdesjuristes.com/blog-du-coronavirus/que-dit-le-droit/les-systemes-de-justice-face-a-la-pandemie-du-covid-19/; OSCE, « The Functioning of Courts in the COVID-19 Pandemic », https://www.osce.org/files/f/documents/5/5/469170.pdf; Global Access to Justice, « Impacts of COVID-19 on Justice Systems », http://globalaccesstojustice.com/impacts-of-covid-19/; S. Chardenoux et al., « Justice and Challenges in Times of Pandemic in Europe », MEDEL, juin 2020.

14 Le texte avait initialement pour objet d'étudier les mesures prises pendant la phase du premier confinement de mars 2020 à septembre 2020. Par souci d'actualisation, des données postérieures ont été ajoutées.

juridictionnel que celui de l'« aménagement des modalités procédurales » pour reprendre l'expression du législateur[15].

Qui décide du fonctionnement de la justice?- La question de savoir qui a le pouvoir de décider de la manière dont le système juridictionnel doit réagir face à la pandémie COVID-19 est cruciale et instructive en elle-même de l'équilibre des pouvoirs en temps de crise. Dans certains pays, les décisions sur la manière d'organiser les tribunaux pendant et après la pandémie ont été prises par le gouvernement, avec ou sans consultation du pouvoir judiciaire. Dans d'autres, ce sont les autorités judiciaires elles-mêmes telles que les conseils de la magistrature ou les juges eux-mêmes qui ont adopté des mesures. Enfin dans d'autres pays, les mesures ont été définies dans la législation et les lois de procédure[16]. Bien souvent il y a eu combinaison ou plus exactement succession d'interventions et de décisions. C'est le cas au Luxembourg où dans un premier temps les juridictions ont paré au plus pressé, rattrapées ensuite par des règlements grand-ducaux avant que l'intervention législative ne devienne une exigence constitutionnelle.

Pouvoir d'exception et contrôle juridictionnel – L'étude porte à la fois sur l'analyse des règles et des pratiques mais aussi sur l'exercice des recours et les décisions rendues. Derrière les règles procédurales se cachent

15 Voy. Règlement grand-ducal du 25 mars 2020 portant suspension des délais en matière juridictionnelle et adaptation temporaire de certaines autres modalités procédurales, http://data.legilux.public.lu/eli/etat/leg/rgd/2020/03/25/a185/jo; èglement grand-ducal du 29 avril 2020 portant adaptation temporaire de certaines modalités procédurales en matière pénale, http://data.legilux.public.lu/eli/etat/leg/rgd/2020/04/29/a341/jo; Loi du 20 juin 2020 portant prorogation de mesures concernant la tenue d'audiences publiques pendant l'état de crise devant les juridictions dans les affaires soumises à la procédure écrite, certaines adaptations de la procédure de référé exceptionnel devant le juge aux affaires familiales, la suspension des délais en matière juridictionnelle, et d'autres modalités procédurales, http://data.legilux.public.lu/eli/etat/leg/loi/2020/06/20/a523/jo; Loi du 20 juin 2020 portant adaptation temporaire de certaines modalités procédurales en matière pénale, http://data.legilux.public.lu/eli/etat/leg/loi/2020/06/20/a542/jo; Loi du 25 novembre 2020 http://legilux.public.lu/eli/etat/leg/loi/2020/11/25/a932/consolide/20201223; Loi du 19 décembre 2020 portant adaptation temporaire de certaines modalités procédurales en matière civile et commerciale, http://data.legilux.public.lu/eli/etat/leg/loi/2020/12/19/a1056/jo; Loi du 19 décembre 2020 portant modification de la loi modifiée du 20 juin 2020 portant adaptation temporaire de certaines modalités procédurales en matière pénale, http://data.legilux.public.lu/eli/etat/leg/loi/2020/12/19/a1046/jo.

16 Voy. OSCE, « The Functioning of Courts in the COVID-19 Pandemic », https://www.osce.org/files/f/documents/5/5/469170.pdf, p. 11.

toujours la réalisation du droit. Or cette réalisation contentieuse du droit parait d'autant plus importante que le pouvoir tend à se concentrer entre les mains du pouvoir exécutif[17]. A ce titre il convient de préciser que, au Luxembourg, l'article 32, para. 4, de la Constitution reconnaît au pouvoir règlementaire, représenté symboliquement par le Grand-Duc, le droit de déroger au cadre juridique existant par voie réglementaire pour une période ne pouvant excéder trois mois[18]. L'état de crise a été déclenché en date du 18 mars 2020 pour une durée de dix jours. Il a été confirmé et sa durée prorogée pour une période de trois mois par la loi du 24 mars 2020 portant prorogation de l'état de crise déclaré par le Règlement grand-ducal (ci-après « RGD ») du 18 mars 2020 portant introduction d'une série de mesures dans le cadre de la lutte contre le virus COVID-19. Dans ce contexte, le pouvoir règlementaire a adopté une série de règlements grand-ducaux en vue de faire face à la « crise » et à l'« urgence » induites par la propagation du coronavirus[19]. Le pouvoir règlementaire a justifié, au sein du préambule de ces règlements, qu'il convenait, au nom des « intérêts vitaux de la population », d'adopter des mesures urgentes dans des délais contraints que le processus législatif habituel n'aurait pu respecter[20]. L'ur-

---

17 La Constitution emploie le terme de « crise internationale ». Voy. E. Stoppioni, « The Protection of Health Must Take Precedence: Testing the Constitutional State of Crisis in Luxembourg », 29 avril 2020, https://verfassungsblog.de/the-protection-of-health-must-take-precedence-testing-the-constitutional-state-of-crisis-in-luxembourg/; V. Bruck, « L'état d'urgence contre l'État de droit démocratique », Septembre 2017, https://www.forum.lu/wp-content/uploads/2017/09/376_Bruck.pdf.

18 Constitution, Art. 32, par. 4 : « Toutefois, en cas de crise internationale, le Grand-Duc peut, s'il y a urgence, prendre en toute matière des règlements, même dérogatoires à des dispositions légales existantes. La durée de validité de ces règlements est limitée à trois mois ». Sur cette disposition voy. V. Bruck, « L'état d'urgence contre l'État de droit démocratique », Septembre 2017, https://www.forum.lu/wp-content/uploads/2017/09/376_Bruck.pdf.

19 Règlement grand-ducal du 3 avril 2020 portant modification du règlement grand-ducal du 1er avril 2020 portant dérogation aux articles L. 322–2 et L. 326–1 à L. 326–12 du Code du travail; Règlement grand-ducal du 17 avril 2020 portant modification du règlement grand-ducal modifié du 18 mars 2020 portant introduction d'une série de mesures dans le cadre de la lutte contre le COVID-19. Règlement grand-ducal du 29 mai 2020 portant modification du règlement grand-ducal modifié du 18 mars 2020 portant introduction d'une série de mesures dans le cadre de la lutte contre le COVID-19. Règlement grand-ducal du 12 juin 2020 portant dérogation aux dispositions des articles 3, 6, 7 et 9 de la loi du 1er août 2019 concernant les mutuelles.

20 Extrait du préambule du règlement grand-ducal du 18 mars 2020 portant introduction d'une série de mesures dans le cadre de la lutte contre le COVID-19 :

gence de l'action gouvernementale permet ainsi de prendre toutes mesures jugées nécessaires puisqu'il est admis que l'exécutif puisse, pour ne pas être gêné dans son action, déroger aux lois existantes et réglementer dans des domaines usuellement réservés au pouvoir législatif. Le pouvoir réglementaire étant traditionnellement subordonné au domaine de la loi, le voilà, en pleine crise sanitaire, émancipé de ses contraintes systémiques. En plus de contenir le pouvoir de la Chambre des députés, l'adoption de règlements grand-ducaux conformément à l'article 32, para. 4, de la Constitution habilite le gouvernement à ne pas requérir l'avis du Conseil d'État qui est, sauf urgence, de rigueur pour l'adoption des règlements exécutant lois ou traités[21]. Dans ces conditions le contrôle juridictionnel se présente comme un des derniers contre-pouvoirs face à la police administrative en action depuis le début de la crise du COVID-19. Comme l'a souligné Edoardo Stoppioni, « the state of crisis is a Pandora box that, once opened, is difficult to close. Now that Luxembourg has solidly anchored this culture in its Constitution, the Parliament and the judges need to remain alert and defend the rule of law »[22]. Pourtant et bien que l'accès à la justice

« Considérant que le virus dit « Coronavirus », désigné par « COVID-19 » et déclaré comme constituant une pandémie par l'Organisation mondiale de la Santé, a pris une ampleur et une rapidité telles qu'il y a lieu de le considérer comme constituant une menace réelle pour les intérêts vitaux de la population qui nécessite la prise de mesures urgentes et immédiates qui sont devenues indispensables afin de protéger la population et que, partant, il y a crise; Considérant que l'Organisation mondiale de la Santé insiste dans ses recommandations de limiter les contacts entre les personnes physiques afin de contenir la propagation du COVID-19; Considérant que les différentes mesures réglementaires introduites se limitent à ce qui est indispensable et strictement nécessaire et qu'elles sont adéquates et proportionnées au but poursuivi et conformes à la Constitution et aux traités internationaux; Considérant que les mesures réglementaires dérogent à des lois existantes, modifient leur dispositif actuel voire introduisent de nouvelles mesures, y compris dans les matières réservées à la loi; Considérant que le recours à la procédure législative ordinaire pour l'adoption de ces mesures indispensables ne permet pas d'assurer leur mise en œuvre immédiate; Considérant que la Chambre des Députés est dans l'impossibilité de légiférer dans les délais appropriés et que, partant, il y a urgence ».

21 Art. 1, para. 1, loi du 16 juin 2017 sur l'organisation du Conseil d'Etat. Voy. A. Durdu, « Le Conseil d'État, gardien des droits et libertés fondamentaux » in *La défense des droits et libertés au Grand-Duché de Luxembourg*, Bruxelles, Éditions Larcier, 2020, p. 127.

22 E. Stoppioni, « The Protection of Health Must Take Precedence: Testing the Constitutional State of Crisis in Luxembourg », 29 avril 2020, https://verfassungsblog.de/the-protection-of-health-must-take-precedence-testing-the-constitutional-state-of-crisis-in-luxembourg/.

a été dans une large mesure garanti, le contrôle juridictionnel des mesures n'a pas eu lieu. Les mesures destinées à lutter contre la pandémie d'une manière générale et les mesures intéressant le fonctionnement de la justice en particulier n'ont fait l'objet d'aucun recours. Cette absence de contrôle de légalité interroge parce qu'il contraste avec les recours juridictionnels exercés en France, en Belgique, en Allemagne et ailleurs en Europe où émerge un « contentieux-covid ». Les explications demeurent cependant très hypothétiques à ce stade. En « temps normal », le contrôle de légalité des règlements grand-ducaux sont strictement encadrés et que la voie de l'exception est étroite. De même le contrôle de constitutionnalité des lois est réduit, la Cour constitutionnelle ne pouvant être saisie que par voie préjudicielle[23]. En outre, elle ne peut être saisie selon une procédure d'urgence que sa loi organique méconnait. En « temps de crise » aucun outil de contrôle n'a été mis en œuvre. Le maigre « contentieux-covid » porte sur des contestations individuelles de sanctions pécuniaires pour défaut de conformité aux règles sanitaires (port du masque essentiellement). L'explication ne saurait résider dans le fonctionnement des institutions pendant la crise et tient sans doute à la culture consensuelle du pays. Alors que les juridictions (en particulier administratives) françaises et belges ont pu être taxées, sans doute à tort, de chambres d'enregistrement, les juridictions luxembourgeoises sont restées bien silencieuses faute de saisine. Néanmoins les quelques décisions rendues -quoique fort éloignée de tout contrôle objectif de légalité- accordent une protection particulière aux droits et libertés des individus[24].

Structure – L'objectif de l'étude est de dresser un panorama du fonctionnement des juridictions judiciaires, administratives et constitutionnelle (I). S'il en ressort que l'accès à la justice a été maintenu, ce constat tranche avec l'étendue très limitée du contrôle juridictionnel (II). Cette situation conduit à s'interroger, en conclusion, de manière plus prospective sur l'incidence de ce fonctionnement de crise sur l'avenir de la justice au Grand-Duché de Luxembourg.

---

23 Voy. C. Sauer, *Contrôle juridictionnel des lois au Luxembourg*, Bruxelles, Larcier, 2019; J. Gerkrath (Dir.), *Les 20 ans de la Cour Constitutionnelle: Trop jeune pour mourir*!?, Pasicrisie Luxembourgeoise, 2018.

24 Voy. Trib. adm, 27 novembre 2020, n° 45263 du rôle. Voy. N. Sadler, « La garantie des Droits et Libertés par les juridictions ordinaires » in *La défense des droits et libertés au Grand-Duché de Luxembourg*, Bruxelles, Éditions Larcier, 2020, p. 163.

A. *Le fonctionnement du système juridictionnel luxembourgeois pendant la crise sanitaire liée au COVID-19*

L'aménagement du fonctionnement des juridictions dans les premiers temps de la crise a d'abord été le fait des juridictions elles-mêmes (I). Le pouvoir exécutif a rapidement repris la main en adoptant une série de règlements grand-ducaux qui ont dû ensuite être repris ou adaptés par le biais législatif (II). Beaucoup de textes pour rien? Sans doute pas pour rien mais à l'emballement (naturel) des premiers mois succède un fonctionnement adapté mais semble-t-il stabilisé des juridictions (III).

I. *D'un aménagement individualisé par les juridictions …*

Dès le début de la crise sanitaire, la continuité des activités juridictionnelles n'est précisée par aucun texte, elle finit par se présumer.

Premièrement, le RGD du 18 mars 2020, qui est à l'origine de diverses mesures en vue de lutter contre la COVID-19, ne retient pas expressément les institutions judiciaires dans la liste des activités essentielles maintenues dans le contexte des limitations de déplacement adoptées à destination du public. Tout au plus, la continuité de leurs activités pourrait être associée à la notion globale de « services publics nécessaires au bon fonctionnement de l'État » reprise à l'article 5 du règlement précité. Ce manque de précision contraste avec un arrêté ministériel belge du 18 mars 2020[25] dans lequel « les institutions de la Justice et les professions y liées : les maisons de justice, la magistrature et les institutions pénitentiaires, les institutions de protection de la jeunesse, les experts judiciaires, les huissiers, le personnel judiciaire, traducteurs-interprètes [et] avocats » font partie des personnes et services nécessaires à la protection des « besoins vitaux de la Nation et des besoins de la population »[26].

Deuxièmement, il convient de noter que bien avant l'intervention du pouvoir règlementaire dans l'aménagement de certains délais devant les

---

25 Belgique, Arrêté ministériel du 18 mars 2020 portant des mesures d'urgence pour limiter la propagation du coronavirus COVID-19, Annexe à l'arrêté ministériel du 18 mars 2020.

26 J. Englebert, *Service nécessaire à la Nation, la Justice ne pouvait pas être confinée, Analyse critique des mesures prises par le Collège des cours et tribunaux en vue de garantir le service de la Justice nonobstant le confinement et de l'arrêté royal n° 2 du 9 avril 2020*, Anthemis, 2020.

juridictions nationales[27], qui intervient le 25 mars 2020, l'organisation des activités juridictionnelles est avant tout le fait de prises de position individuelles de la part des juridictions concernées.

Qu'il s'agisse de circulaires, de lettres à l'attention du Bâtonnier ou encore de notes de service[28], ces interventions, qui s'intensifient à compter du 12 mars 2020, remanient et assouplissent les procédures applicables devant les juridictions nationales pour assurer le maintien de leurs activités. Là aussi, ces prises de position individuelles contrastent avec les directives prises par le Collège des cours et tribunaux belge, organe porte-parole des institutions judiciaires belges. En effet, contrairement à l'émission d'instructions particulières de la part de chaque juridiction luxembourgeoise (ou du moins de la majorité d'entre elles), le monde judiciaire belge a fait le choix de communiquer des directives pour l'ensemble des tribunaux et cours concernés par la voix d'un organe représentatif assurant ainsi la diffusion de directives par la voix d'un seul interlocuteur[29]. Du côté luxembourgeois, une consolidation des plans de continuité des différentes juridictions luxembourgeoises est tentée par la publication d'un arrêté ministériel du 16 mars 2020. Il y est précisé l'organisation des audiences des juridictions judiciaires pour la période allant du 16 mars au 3 avril 2020. Voilà, en somme, la première confirmation règlementaire de la continuité des instances judiciaires. Cet arrêté ministériel, modifié par un arrêté du 6 avril 2020, entérine essentiellement les choix formulés individuellement par les juridictions judiciaires dans des circulaires et notes internes témoignant de la nécessité de communiquer de manière uniforme sur l'ensemble de ces aménagements.

Les circulaires et notes internes émises par certaines juridictions révèlent la précarité de certaines dispositions à l'aune d'une évolution défavorable du contexte sanitaire. En effet, les communications issues de certaines juridictions nationales vont, dans un premier temps, tenter de contenir la visite des tribunaux et cours aux seules situations où la présence des avocats est requise. Cette exigence se traduit, par exemple, par une réorganisation des formes de dépôts des recours (et pièces) pour les parties au procès.

---

27 Notamment via le règlement grand-ducal du 25 mars 2020 portant suspension des délais en matière juridictionnelle et adaptation temporaire de certaines autres modalités procédurales.

28 L'ensemble de ces circulaires et notes est accessible sur le site internet du Barreau de Luxembourg.

29 Cette absence de voix représentative du monde judiciaire serait-elle due à l'absence d'un organe représentant les intérêts de la justice au Luxembourg, dont notamment le très attendu Conseil national de la justice?

Ainsi, dès le 12 mars 2020, une circulaire commune[30] prise par le tribunal d'arrondissement de Luxembourg[31] et le Barreau de Luxembourg informent les avocats qu'ils sont priés de ne plus se présenter physiquement au greffe, les invitant à assurer l'envoi de leurs documents par voie postale. En outre, la circulaire précitée indique que toute communication avec le secrétariat au sujet des pièces déposées est rendue possible à partir d'adresses électroniques spécifiquement mises en service pour l'occasion. Dans le même sens, les juridictions administratives publient un avis dans lequel elles invitent les avocats à ne plus se présenter au secrétariat du greffe pour le dépôt de leurs recours et pièces. Désormais, ces documents doivent être déposés à l'entrée du bâtiment des juridictions administratives, aménagée à l'occasion pour la réception de ces pièces, ou envoyés par courrier postal[32]. Dans une note explicative du 6 avril 2020, le président du Tribunal administratif admet, à titre complémentaire et dérogatoire, le dépôt des requêtes par voie électronique[33].

L'aménagement de ces formes de dépôt est accompagné du maintien de certaines audiences dans des domaines jugés essentiels tandis que, de manière assez soudaine, plusieurs audiences de plaidoiries sont déprogrammées jusqu'à nouvel ordre. Dans la circulaire commune du Tribunal d'arrondissement de Luxembourg et du Bâtonnier, il est clairement rappelé que la présence des avocats est maintenue pour certaines audiences ou convocations particulières pour les procédures de mise en état devant les chambres civiles du Tribunal d'arrondissement. Devant les chambres commerciales, les avocats qui entendent se présenter à des affaires sont tenus d'en informer le greffe pour des raisons organisationnelles.

Toutefois, dès le lendemain[34], une instruction de service rédigée au nom du président du Tribunal d'arrondissement annonce un report des audiences de plaidoirie des chambres civiles et commerciales et indique le maintien de certaines audiences, notamment dans le contexte des assignations en faillites. Le même jour, une lettre du juge aux affaires famil-

30 Circulaire du 12 mars 2020 commune au tribunal d'arrondissement de Luxembourg et au Barreau de Luxembourg.

31 Chambres civiles et commerciales et tribunal des référés. Accessible sur le site du Barreau de Luxembourg.

32 Juridictions administratives, Avis à tous les avocats concernant les mesures afin de minimiser le risque de transmission de COVID-19.

33 Tribunal administratif, Cabinet du Président, 6 avril 2020. Accessible sur le site du Barreau de Luxembourg.

34 Tribunal d'arrondissement de Luxembourg, Information de service COVID-19 pour garantir la continuité du service du tribunal d'arrondissement de Luxembourg, 13 mars 2020. Accessible sur le site du Barreau de Luxembourg.

iales[35], qui relève également du Tribunal d'arrondissement, précise que les audiences entre le 16 mars et le 20 avril 2020 sont annulées au regard de l'impossibilité d'assurer le respect des mesures sanitaires du fait de la promiscuité dans les salles d'attente et d'audience. Exceptionnellement, il y est annoncé que les audiences de référé exceptionnels et de violence domestiques seront maintenues avec l'assurance que la distance de deux mètres sera observée pour les participants à ces audiences. Des précisions complémentaires sont prises dans un lettre du 16 mars 2020 par le juge des affaires familiales quant au dépôt de requêtes et pièces[36].

Dans un courrier du 16 mars 2020 adressé au Bâtonnier[37], le Tribunal d'arrondissement de Diekirch prend également acte de la situation sanitaire et fait état de la liste des audiences décommandées tout en maintenant l'ouverture de son guichet pour l'accueil du public dans certaines matières (renonciation à succession, aveu de faillite, etc.). Toujours dans l'optique de limiter le nombre de personnes dans les salles d'audience, le Bâtonnier, s'adressant aux avocats assistant aux audiences de mises en liberté, va jusqu'à leur suggérer de les assurer sans la présence de détenus afin de réduire, autant que possible, le nombre de personnes devant être présente[38].

Au regard de l'évolution de la situation sanitaire, des audiences qui avaient été indiquées comme maintenues, notamment dans le cadre de référé, sont reportées contrairement aux précisions apportées quelques jours auparavant. Ainsi, les audiences maintenues par la circulaire du 13 mars 2020 du Tribunal d'arrondissement sont fixées à une date ultérieure par une information de service modificative du 16 mars 2020[39]. Aussi bien dans cette dernière communication que dans une circulaire de la justice de paix de Luxembourg du 17 mars, des plaidoiries sont, toutefois, maintenues par exception pour les « affaires très urgentes » selon la justice de paix et pour les affaires « justifiant d'une urgence particulière » devant le Tribunal d'arrondissement de Luxembourg.

---

35 Lettre du juge aux affaires familiales adressée au Bâtonnier le 12 mars 2020. Accessible sur le site du Barreau de Luxembourg.

36 Lettre du juge aux affaires familiales adressée au Bâtonnier le 16 mars 2020. Accessible sur le site du Barreau de Luxembourg.

37 Lettre du tribunal d'arrondissement de Diekirch adressée au Bâtonnier le 16 mars 2020. Accessible sur le site du Barreau de Luxembourg.

38 Présence éventuelle d'un interprète ou encore d'officiers de police accompagnant le détenu.

39 Tribunal d'arrondissement de Luxembourg, Information de service COVID-19 pour garantir la continuité du service du tribunal d'arrondissement de Luxembourg, 16 mars 2020. Accessible sur le site du Barreau de Luxembourg.

Il résulte clairement de ces notes de service que c'est le juge des référés et le juge de paix qui déterminent, souverainement, les affaires qui entrent dans ces catégories et en informent les parties concernées[40]. On assiste ainsi, de manière surprenante, au fait que certaines de ces communications fixent la continuité d'un type de contentieux, jugé essentiel sur le fondement de critères inconnus et cela à la discrétion de tribunaux et cours auprès desquels ce type de contentieux est dévolu. S'il n'est pas contesté que les affaires impliquant des cas de violence domestique doivent être promptement traitées, on aurait pu s'interroger sur le caractère impérieux des assignations en faillite et les liquidations de société qui ont été maintenues en priorité dans le cadre de l'organisation des audiences de plaidoiries. On pourrait également déplorer le passage, dans une note de service, au juge unique dans des affaires qui nécessitent traditionnellement une composition plus élargie[41].

Du côté des juridictions administratives, aucune communication particulière ne fait état de la suspension des audiences. En effet, « l'avis à tous les avocats » publié par les juridictions administratives laissent entendre le maintien des audiences puisque la note indique que « l'accès aux salles d'audience (...) restera garantie »[42]. Cette compréhension de la situation est, toutefois, nuancée par une note publiée par le Président du Tribunal administratif annonçant, notamment la reprise des audiences de plaidoiries de la première chambre du tribunal à compter du 20 mars et la mise en place, « en cas de besoin » d'audiences de plaidoiries de référé et d'audiences de plaidoiries pour le contrôle d'office des affaires de rétention administrative.

---

40 Tribunal d'arrondissement de Luxembourg, Information de service COVID-19 pour garantir la continuité du service du tribunal d'arrondissement de Luxembourg, 16 mars 2020. Accessible sur le site du Barreau de Luxembourg; voir aussi Circulaire du 17 mars 2020, Juge de paix directeur, Accessible sur le site du Barreau de Luxembourg; voir aussi Lettre de la justice de paix d'Esch-sur-Alzette adressée au Bâtonnier, 19 mars 2020. Accessible sur le site du Barreau de Luxembourg.

41 Voir notamment, « Ces audiences [les affaires commerciales introduites selon la procédure orale, les assignations en faillite, etc.] sont assurées par un seul magistrat pour les besoins de la gestion du premier appel, respectivement par trois magistrats en cas de nécessité de plaidoiries, extrait de l'information de service COVID-19 pour garantir la continuité du service du tribunal d'arrondissement de Luxembourg émise par le Tribunal d'arrondissement de Luxembourg le 13 mars 2020. Accessible sur le site du Barreau de Luxembourg.

42 Juridictions administratives, Avis à tous les avocats concernant les mesures afin de minimiser le risque de transmission de COVID-19.

L'étude des différentes communications émises par les juridictions judiciaires et administratives met en évidence une gestion organisationnelle mouvante liée à l'évolution de la crise sanitaire. Elles apparaissent dès lors naturellement imprécises et contradictoires réclamant parfois d'être lues en combinaison d'autres notes publiées antérieurement. Alors que certaines audiences de plaidoiries sont maintenues selon des critères d'urgence, qui ne sont pas davantage précisés, un grand nombre d'audiences sont décalées jusqu'à nouvel ordre.

Les communications individuelles des juridictions témoignent de leur capacité d'adaptation dans l'usage des moyens de communication électroniques. Si le dépôt des mémoires par voie électronique en est la preuve parfaite, alors que ce moyen de dépôt était absent des règles de procédure écrites avant la survenance de la pandémie, il semble également que l'usage des nouvelles technologies a été favorisé en vue d'assurer la prise de délibérés. En effet, dans une déclaration adoptée lors de l'assemblée générale de la Cour supérieur de justice du 16 mars 2020, la Cour de cassation suggère d'organiser des délibérés dans les affaires où un projet d'arrêt est disponible par « mail, face-time, WhatsApp, etc. »)[43].

II. À l'aménagement des modalités procédurales par le pouvoir exécutif… puis législatif

« Afin de garantir le fonctionnement du service public de la justice pendant l'état de crise, tout en endiguant le virus COVID-19 et en protégeant tous les acteurs du monde judiciaire, un certain nombre de règlements grand-ducaux ont été adoptés afin d'adapter les textes existants »[44] (1). Ces règlements -dont les effets devaient cesser au plus tard à l'expiration du délai de trois mois suivant l'entrée en vigueur de la loi du 24 mars 2020- ont dû néanmoins être repris ou adaptés par des lois d'abord jusqu'au 31 décembre 2020 puis au-delà (2).

43 Cour supérieure de Justice, Déclaration adoptée à l'assemblée générale de la Cour du 16 mars 2020. Accessible sur le site du Barreau de Luxembourg.

44 Exposé des motifs du projet de loi n°7587.

1. *Les règlements grand-ducaux de mars-avril 2020 portant suspension des délais en matière juridictionnelle et adaptation temporaire de certaines autres modalités procédurales*

Première intervention du pouvoir réglementaire affectant les juridictions nationales, le RGD du 25 mars 2020 a instauré la suspension de certains délais devant les juridictions judiciaires, administratives, militaires et constitutionnelles pendant la durée de l'état de crise[45]. Si cette suspension générale des délais, du fait de son application indifférenciée aux « délais prescrits dans les procédures », a eu le mérite d'unifier les règles de suspension des délais afin d'harmoniser le fonctionnement des tribunaux et cours qui étaient, jusque lors régi par des règles distinctes, ce qui pouvait laisser à craindre une confusion dans le fonctionnement des institutions judiciaires luxembourgeoises. Cependant l'expression « délais prescrits dans les procédures » trop vague a dû être précisée et le RGD du 25 mars 2020 a fait l'objet de précisions par voie de différents règlements respectivement en date du 1er, 17 et 29 avril 2020. Ces modifications successives ne rendent pas l'ensemble très lisible en dépit d'une version consolidée des textes. Comme l'a résumé Thierry Hoscheit, « l'objectif poursuivi était que les justiciables et leurs plaideurs ne se trouvent pas confrontés aux conséquences résultant de l'expiration d'un délai survenue au cours d'une période agitée pendant laquelle les études d'avocat, la vie des particuliers et des entreprises et les communications entre avocats et leurs clients étaient perturbées du fait des mesures de confinement imposées par ailleurs par le RGD du 18 mars 2020 portant introduction d'une série de mesures dans le cadre de la lutte contre le COVID-19 dans ses versions successives »[46]. La suspension des délais « prescrits dans les procédures » visés dans le RGD s'applique à tous les délais de procédure y compris les délais régissant le cours des procédures (comme les délais de mise en état); et les délais régissant l'introduction des voies de recours. Spécialement, le texte précisait que la suspension joue même pour les délais préfix (régissant

45 Sur les délais procéduraux en temps de crise, voy. S. Amrani-Mekki, « La part du droit (et de la justice) dans l'angoisse contemporaine – la computation des délais », Procédures n° 5, Mai 2020, étude 15; H. Croze, « Comment gérer les délais pendant la période d'urgence sanitaire? », *Procédures* n° 6, Juin 2020, 2. Comp. sur l'inadaptabilité des délais en droit européen, M. Vautravers, « La coopération judiciaire en matière civile et commerciale en temps de crise au sein de l'Union européenne », *Obs. Brux.*, juin 2020, p. 34.

46 Th. Hoscheit, « Interrogations sur la fin de l'état de crise constitutionnelle », *J.T.L.*, août 2020, n°72, p. 99.

les voies de recours) alors que ceux-ci sont en principe insusceptibles de suspension. Il s'agit bien d'une suspension (et non pas d'une interruption) de ces délais : ce qui signifie que le temps écoulé avant le début de la crise reste comptabilisé (article 1 (1)). Selon le (2) de l'article 1er, les délais pour agir en première instance n'étaient en revanche pas suspendus mais prorogés dans les termes suivants : s'ils viennent à échéance pendant la crise, il y a prorogation de deux mois après la fin de la crise et s'ils viennent à échéance dans le mois suivant la fin de la crise, il y a prorogation d'un mois à partir de l'échéance initialement prévue. Cette solution adoptée dans le RGD du 1er avril 2020 est venue combler une lacune du règlement du 25 mars. Elle était d'autant plus souhaitable qu'il n'était pas possible de faire assigner à personne. En outre le même article 1er (3) prévoyait que la suspension des délais ne s'applique pas aux délais de comparution, ni en matière de droit des étrangers et d'hospitalisation des personnes souffrant de troubles mentaux (la matière pénale connait également d'importantes exceptions[47]). Tandis que le (4) prévoyait que « dans les cas d'urgence

---

47 L'article 2 prévoit une liste d'exceptions importantes avec des entrée en vigueur variable : Art. 2. (1)La suspension des délais prévue à l'article 1 er ne s'applique pas :

1° aux délais prévus par les articles 39 et 93 du Code de procédure pénale;
2° aux délais, prévus par l'article 116, paragraphe 8, du Code de procédure pénale, d'un jour à partir de celui de l'ordonnance ayant accordé la mise en liberté dans le lequel le procureur d'État doit interjeter appel, et de dix jours après qu'appel a été formé dans lequel la chambre du conseil, la chambre correctionnelle ou la chambre criminelle de la Cour d'appel doit statuer sur l'appel du procureur d'État;
3° au délai, prévu par l'article 127, paragraphe 6, alinéa 1, du Code de procédure pénale, de huit jours ouvrables au moins avant celui fixé pour l'examen par la chambre du conseil dans lequel le dossier est mis à la disposition de l'inculpé et de la partie civile ainsi que de leur avocat;
4° aux délais, prévu par l'article 133, paragraphe 5, du Code de procédure pénale ainsi que par des lois spéciales, dans lequel appel doit être formé contre les ordonnances du juge d'instruction ou de la chambre du conseil;
5° aux délais, prévus par les articles 203 et 222 du Code de procédure pénale, dans lesquels appel doit être formé contre les jugements de la chambre correctionnelle ou criminelle du tribunal d'arrondissement;
6° au délai prévu par l'article 9, paragraphe 4, alinéa 3, de la loi modifiée du 8 août 2000 sur l'entraide judiciaire internationale en matière pénale;
7° au délai prévu par l'article 26, paragraphe 4, alinéa 3, de la loi du 1er août 2018 portant transposition de la directive 2014/41/UE du Parlement européen et du Conseil du 3 avril 2014 concernant la décision d'enquête européenne en matière pénale;

et sauf en matière pénale, les tribunaux peuvent, à titre exceptionnel, à la demande d'une partie, déroger à la suspension des délais prévue au paragraphe 1 du présent article, par décision d'administration judiciaire après avoir demandé la position écrite ou orale de la ou des autres parties au procès ». L'expression « dans les cas d'urgence » vise certainement les référés. Elle reste cependant très vague : s'agit-il de tous les référés? Existe-t-il d'autres hypothèses que le référé? L'article 4 du RGD du 17 avril 2020 prévoyait que « pour les situations urgentes liées à la pandémie de COVID-19, la requête en référé exceptionnel en obtention de mesures provisoires visée à l'article 1007–11 peut être introduite en l'absence d'une saisine du juge aux affaires familiales par une requête au fond » et précisait que cette requête pouvait « être introduite par voie électronique ». Ces mesures devaient toutefois prendre fin deux mois après la fin de l'état de crise[48].

L'article 2 (4) du RGD consolidé prévoyait que « si, dans le cadre d'une instance pendante, les parties sont représentées par des avocats, ou si le tribunal l'ordonne, les communications et notifications visées au présent

---

8° aux délais prévus par les articles 41 à 43 de la loi modifiée du 18 février 1885 sur les pourvois et la procédure en cassation.

Les exceptions à la suspension des délais prévues au point 1° s'appliquent à partir de l'entrée en vigueur du présent règlement grand-ducal.
Les exceptions à la suspension des délais prévues aux points 2° à 8° s'appliquent à partir de l'entrée en vigueur du règlement grand-ducal du 17 avril 2020 portant modification de l'article 2 du règlement grand-ducal modifié du 25 mars 2020 portant suspension des délais en matière juridictionnelle et adaptation temporaire de certaines autres modalités procédurales.
S'agissant du point 3°, dans les dossiers dont la chambre du conseil est saisie, mais dans lesquels elle n'a pas encore statué à la date d'entrée en vigueur du règlement grand-ducal du 17 avril 2020 portant modification de l'article 2 du règlement grand-ducal modifié du 25 mars 2020 portant suspension des délais en matière juridictionnelle et adaptation temporaire de certaines autres modalités procédurales, un nouveau délai de huit jours ouvrables commence à courir à partir de la date d'entrée en vigueur précitée.
S'agissant des points 4° à 8°, les délais non encore venus à échéance avant la date d'entrée en vigueur du règlement grand-ducal du 17 avril 2020 portant modification de l'article 2 du règlement grand-ducal modifié du 25 mars 2020 portant suspension des délais en matière juridictionnelle et adaptation temporaire de certaines autres modalités procédurales, sont prorogés, et un nouveau délai de même durée que le délai initial commence à courir à partir de la date d'entrée en vigueur précitée.

48 Cette disposition ne se retrouve pas dans la version consolidée du RGD du 25 mars 2020. Voy. article 5 de la loi du 20 juin 2020.

paragraphe sont faites par voie électronique via le greffe ». L'usage de ces échanges électroniques sur lequel nous reviendrons est d'autant plus remarquable qu'il a toujours été le grand absent du droit des procédures au Luxembourg.

Outre l'aménagement des délais et des modes de communication, le règlement du 25 mars 2020 a instauré des dérogations à la comparution des parties, dans des matières que le règlement a pris le soin de délimiter, privilégiant ainsi les échanges écrits entre le ministère public et les parties au procès, notamment en appel. L'écrit et l'absence de comparution des parties et de parution de leurs mandataires étaient rendu nécessaires pour limiter les contacts physiques et le risque de prorogation. Elles posent moins de difficultés en matière civile qu'en matière pénale pour laquelle les cas étaient minutieusement énumérés à l'article 2 du RGD consolidé du 25 mars 2020. Cette *déformalisation* de la procédure pénale a été précisée dans le RGD du 29 avril 2020 portant adaptation temporaire de certaines modalités procédurales en matière pénale qui prévoit toute une série d'adaptation notamment le recours à la voie électronique pour les perquisitions et saisies, mais aussi des auditions y compris des audioconférences[49]. De même l'assistance par avocat prévu à l'article 3–6 du Code de procédure pénale était aménagée pour tenir compte des risques sanitaires et éviter les contacts physiques.

2. *Les lois successives portant adaptation temporaire de certaines modalités procédurales en matière civile, commerciale et pénale*

Les aménagements réglementaires aux règles procédurales ont été repris et précisés par deux lois du 20 juin 2020 portant prorogation de certaines mesures applicables devant les juridictions nationales l'une en matière civile et l'autre en matière pénale jusqu'au 31 décembre 2020 inclus[50]. Ces

---

49 Règlement grand-ducal du 29 avril 2020 portant adaptation temporaire de certaines modalités procédurales en matière pénale, http://data.legilux.public.lu/eli/etat/leg/rgd/2020/04/29/a341/jo.

50 Loi du 20 juin 2020 portant prorogation de mesures concernant la tenue d'audiences publiques pendant l'état de crise devant les juridictions dans les affaires soumises à la procédure écrite, certaines adaptations de la procédure de référé exceptionnel devant le juge aux affaires familiales, la suspension des délais en matière juridictionnelle, et d'autres modalités procédurales. Loi du 20 juin 2020 portant adaptation temporaire de certaines modalités procédurales en matière pénale. Comp. sur les mesures adoptées en France, N. Fricero, « Comment restaurer l'activité juridictionnelle : transférer les litiges à une autre juridiction

lois ont été pour l'une abrogée et pour l'autre adaptée par deux lois du 19 décembre 2020[51].

La prolongation législative des aménagements réglementaires est une nécessité constitutionnelle, mais la loi du 20 juin 2020 ne se contente pas de reprendre à son compte les règlements. Outre des dispositions plus ponctuelles sur les assemblées générales des barreaux et de la chambre des notaires et sur la déclaration de recouvrement de nationalité, la loi n'a repris les dispositions réglementaires que dans la mesure de leur nécessité. On peut ainsi lire dans l'exposé des motifs du projet de loi n° 7587 que « Au vu de la levée progressive des mesures de confinement et en vue d'une reprise des activités, le seul maintien temporaire de mesures et jugées utiles et nécessaires dans le cadre de la stratégie de reprise et de sortie de crise est proposé. Pour voir si et comment elle doit être maintenue, chaque mesure prise pendant l'état de crise a été analysée par rapport à sa finalité première en la mettant en balance avec les droits fondamentaux auxquels elle dérogerait le cas échéant, afin de garantir le plein respect du principe de proportionnalité ».

Concernant les délais, la loi du 20 juin 2020 ne reprend pas les dispositions relatives à la suspension des délais de procédure. « La mesure ne s'imposait plus après trois mois de crise ayant permis de réorganiser les flux de travail. Il en résulte que la suspension ne joue, en vertu de l'article 32, paragraphe 4, alinéa 4, de la Constitution, que pendant la durée de validité du règlement grand-ducal modifié du 25 mars 2020, soit concrètement jusqu'à l'expiration de l'état de crise constitutionnelle »[52]. Par contraste, l'aménagement des délais d'action en première instance qui étaient prorogés par le RGD du 29 avril 2020 (applicable rétroactivement

---

et aménager la tenue des audiences », *Procédures*, mai 2020, p. 13; N. Chifflot, « La continuité du service public de la justice judiciaire au temps du COVID-19 », *Procédures*, mai 2020, p. 4; L. Cadiet, « Procédure civile et covid-10 acte II : de l'exception au principe? », *JCL G*, Juin 2020, 715, p. 1084; S. Amrani Mekki, « La procédure civile réécrite sous contraintes sanitaires », *Gaz. Pal.*, 28 avr. 2020, p. 63. Et en Belgique, B. de Coninck et al., « La procédure civile en période de COVID-19 », *J.T.*, 2020, p. 330.

51 Loi du 19 décembre 2020 portant adaptation temporaire de certaines modalités procédurales en matière civile et commerciale, http://data.legilux.public.lu/eli/etat/leg/loi/2020/12/19/a1056/jo; Loi du 19 décembre 2020 portant modification de la loi modifiée du 20 juin 2020 portant adaptation temporaire de certaines modalités procédurales en matière pénale, http://data.legilux.public.lu/eli/etat/leg/loi/2020/12/19/a1046/jo.

52 Th. Hoscheit, « Interrogations sur la fin de l'état de crise constitutionnelle », *J.T.L.*, août 2020, n°72, p. 99.

au 26 mars 2020) est nécessairement maintenu dans la loi du 20 juin 2020 dont l'article 6 prévoit que : « Les délais, légaux ou conventionnels, qui gouvernent l'introduction des procédures en première instance devant les juridictions judiciaires, administratives et militaires, y compris les délais de prescription extinctive, les délais préfix, de forclusion ou de déchéance ainsi que les délais qui gouvernent l'introduction des recours gracieux sont prorogés comme suit : – les délais venant à échéance pendant l'état de crise, tel que prorogé par la loi précitée du 24 mars 2020, sont reportés de deux mois à compter de la date de la fin de l'état de crise; – les délais venant à échéance dans le mois suivant la fin de l'état de crise, prorogé par la loi précitée du 24 mars 2020, sont reportés d'un mois à compter de leur date d'échéance ». Cette disposition soulève d'importantes questions pratiques de computation des délais selon la date retenue de la fin de la période de crise constitutionnelle[53]. Les applications *ratione temporis* sont d'autant plus délicates qu'en matière de délais chaque jour compte[54]. L'article 7 de la loi du 30 juin prévoit notamment que les demandes de déroga-

---

53 Sur ce sujet, voy. Th. Hoscheit, « Interrogations sur la fin de l'état de crise constitutionnelle », *J.T.L.*, août 2020, n°72, p. 97. Th. Hoscheit sur le point précis de l'article 6 de la loi du 20 juin 2020 relève que « La question de savoir si la date du 24 juin 2020 est ou non incluse dans la période de crise constitutionnelle a trois implications essentielles. La première implication concerne le régime juridique de la prorogation applicable à un délai qui vient à expiration le 24 juin 2020. Si cette date est incluse dans la période de crise constitutionnelle, le délai est prorogé, en vertu du point 1 de l'article 6, de deux mois, soit jusqu'au 24 août 2020. Si par contre cette date n'est pas incluse dans la période de crise constitutionnelle, le délai n'est prorogé, sur la base du point 2 de l'article 6, d'un mois seulement, soit jusqu'au 24 juillet 2020. La différence n'est dès lors plus d'un seul jour, mais d'un mois entier!
La deuxième implication concerne, dans l'hypothèse d'un délai venu à expiration le 23 juin 2020, la question de savoir s'il vient à expiration pendant ou après la période de crise constitutionnelle. Dans l'optique prise par les pouvoirs publics faisant perdurer l'état de crise jusqu'au 24 juin 2020 inclus, il n'y a aucun doute qu'il expire pendant la durée de la crise, et le délai est prorogé en vertu de la loi relai de deux mois jusqu'au 24 août 2020. Dans notre perception faisant cesser l'état de crise au 23 juin 2020, la même réponse semble s'appliquer à première vue. Mais la réponse contraire s'impose, puisqu'il faut tenir compte du jeu des règles ordinaires de computation de délais sur le délai de procédure concrètement en cause. Expirant le 23 juin 2020, soit un jour férié légal, le délai est prorogé jusqu'au prochain jour ouvrable, soit jusqu'au 24 juin 2020, et expire dès lors après la fin de la période de crise, et la loi relais a pour effet de ne le proroger que jusqu'au 24 juillet 2020. Là encore, la différence porte sur un mois », *Ibid.*, p. 100.

54 Voy. CA, 19 novembre 2020, Arrêt N° 89/20 – III – TRAV, CAL-2020-00426 du rôle, sur une péremption d'instance.

tion à la suspension des délais introduites sous l'empire du RGD modifié du 25 mars 2020 restent soumises à ce règlement. Tandis que l'article 8 prévoit que les déguerpissements sont suspendus pendant un mois à partir de l'entrée en vigueur de la loi alors qu'ils étaient purement et simplement suspendus à l'article 5 du RGD. De même mais avec des prolongations variables sont suspendus les délais de déclaration de naissance (pendant un mois), les délais pour procéder à une saisie immobilière (pendant deux mois), les délais pour les déclarations de cessation de paiement (pendant six mois)[55].

Au titre des adaptations temporelles, la loi du 20 juin 2020 prévoit une section 3 intitulée « Règles applicables à certaines requêtes en référé exceptionnel en obtention de mesures provisoires introduites pendant l'état de crise auprès du juge aux affaires familiales et aux mesures provisoires ordonnées » qui ne contient qu'un seul article pour prolonger les effets de l'article 4 du RGD du 17 avril 2020 relatif au référé exceptionnel devant le juge aux affaires familiales.

Concernant les communications électroniques, elles sont, en vertu de l'article 2 de la loi du 20 juin 2020, maintenues pour informer, dans la procédure contentieuse devant le tribunal d'arrondissement siégeant en matière civile et devant la Cour d'appel siégeant en matière civile et commerciale, « les mandataires des parties » de la composition du siège mais aussi pour permettre aux mandataires d'informer la juridiction saisie s'ils entendent ou non plaider l'affaire. « A l'issue de l'audience, les mandataires des parties sont informés par la voie électronique de la composition de la juridiction et de la date du prononcé » (article 2, 5°). En vertu de l'article 3, devant la Cour de cassation les pièces et mémoires peuvent être transmis par voie électronique « à l'adresse déterminée par la Cour de cassation »[56].

Concernant la procédure écrite et l'absence de comparution des parties, les juridictions administratives, la Cour constitutionnelle, la Cour de Cassation et les juridictions judiciaires soumises aux règles de la procédure écrite se voient reconnaitre le droit de prendre en délibéré toutes les affaires instruites pendantes sans la parution des mandataires des parties. Cette possibilité est toutefois soumise à l'accord des parties, ce consen-

---

55 Article 9 de la loi du 20 juin 2020.

56 Ces dispositions ont été prolongées par la loi du 19 décembre 2021, voy. https://justice.public.lu/fr/actualites/2020/12/possibilite-appel-courrier-electronique-publication-adresses-elctroniques.html.

tement pouvant justifier l'atteinte portée au principe constitutionnel de publicité de la justice[57].

En matière pénale, la loi du 20 juin 2020 portant adaptation temporaire de certaines modalités procédurales en matière pénale a été précisée par la loi du 24 juillet 2020. Comme en matière civile et commerciale on y trouve les recours aux technologies que ce soit pour la notification des ordonnances de perquisition, la communication avec différentes chambres notamment celle de l'application des peines, l'audition des témoins qui peut avoir lieu à distance ou encore l'appel de certaines ordonnances et de certain jugements y compris au fond[58]. Le recours à la procédure écrite en matière pénale est contre-intuitif. La loi de juillet avait précisément pour objet de renforcer l'oralité devant les juridictions répressives. La loi de juillet supprime la procédure écrite devant la chambre du conseil, tant en première qu'en deuxième instance. L'exposé des motifs justifie la nécessité de modifier la loi du 20 juin 2020 en ce qui concerne « l'importance de la procédure orale en matière pénale eu égard aux droits de la défense, la question de la motivation de l'appel lorsqu'il est interjeté par la voie écrite, ainsi que la question de la certitude de la réception de l'acte d'appel écrit par les autorités compétentes ». Et d'ajouter : « L'ensemble des modifications proposées visent donc à rechercher un équilibre entre, d'une part, assurer les droits de la défense en redonnant aux personnes concernées le droit de « voir leur juge », et, d'autre part, maintenir des modalités procédurales propices à la lutte contre la propagation de la maladie du COVID-19 par la procédure de l'appel à interjeter par la voie écrite, et en y ajoutant l'obligation d'un accusé de réception de l'acte d'appel écrit, dans un souci de sécurité juridique au profit des appelants ».

Ces modifications législatives rapprochées posent d'épineuses questions d'application de la loi dans le temps qui peuvent, à si bref délai, également poser des questions d'égalité devant la loi[59]. La loi du 24 juillet 2020 indique à cet effet que les procédures en cours au moment de son entrée

57 J. Englebert, *Service nécessaire à la Nation, la Justice ne pouvait pas être confinée, Analyse critique des mesures prises par le Collège des cours et tribunaux en vue de garantir le service de la Justice nonobstant le confinement et de l'arrêté royal n° 2 du 9 avril 2020*, Anthemis, 2020, p. 38.

58 La loi du 19 décembre 2020 portant modification de la loi modifiée du 20 juin 2020 portant adaptation temporaire de certaines modalités procédurales en matière pénale confirme en son article 3, point 2, la possibilité d'interjeter valablement appel par courrier électronique.

59 Cf Th. Hoscheit, « Interrogations sur la fin de l'état de crise constitutionnelle », *J.T.L.*, août 2020, n°72, p.97. Voy. CA, 19 novembre 2020, Arrêt N° 89/20 – III – TRAV, CAL-2020–00426 du rôle, sur une péremption d'instance.

en vigueur, restent soumises aux dispositions de la loi du 20 juin 2020[60]. Les lois de l'été 2020 ont en outre été applicables jusqu'au 31 décembre 2020. Le 19 décembre 2020 deux lois ont été adoptées. L'une en matière civile abroge la loi du 20 juin 2020 mais son contenu est identique pour le fonctionnement de la justice civile et commerciale. L'article 9 abroge la loi du 20 juin et l'article 10 prévoit une application que ces aménagements seront en vigueur jusqu'au 15 septembre 2021. L'autre loi du 19 décembre portant adaptation de certaines modalités procédurales en matière pénale a pour objet de modifier de manière mineure et de proroger la loi du 20 juin 2020 jusqu'au 15 septembre 2021. Les lois se succèdent désormais en ce sens. Ainsi par une loi du 30 juin 2021 « la loi du 19 décembre 2020 portant adaptation temporaire de certaines modalités procédurales en matière civile et commerciale, les termes '30 juin' sont remplacés par les termes '31 décembre' »[61]. De même pour la procédure pénale, la loi du 30 juillet 2021 prévoit que « la loi du 19 décembre 2020 portant adaptation temporaire de certaines modalités procédurales en matière civile et commerciale est modifiée comme suit :

1° L'article 2, paragraphe 2, point 3°, prend la teneur suivante :
   '3° à défaut d'avoir sollicité d'être entendus en leurs plaidoiries, les mandataires des parties sont réputés avoir réitéré leurs moyens à l'audience de plaidoiries et ils sont dispensés de se présenter à l'audience fixée à cette fin. Ils déposent leurs fardes de procédure au greffe de la juridiction saisie dans les deux jours ouvrables suivant celle-ci;'.
2° À l'article 10, alinéa 1er, les termes '15 septembre' sont remplacés par les termes '31 décembre' »[62].

La première modification est intéressante car elle est destinée à apporter une précision à la loi du 19 décembre 2020 rendue « nécessaire suite à

60 Sur les délais on renvoie à Th. Hoscheit, « Interrogations sur la fin de l'état de crise constitutionnelle », *J.T.L.*, août 2020, n°72, p.97.

61 Loi du 30 juin 2021 portant modification : 1° de la loi modifiée du 23 septembre 2020 portant des mesures concernant la tenue de réunions dans les sociétés et dans les autres personnes morales; 2° de la loi du 19 décembre 2020 portant adaptation temporaire de certaines modalités procédurales en matière civile et commerciale, https://legilux.public.lu/eli/etat/leg/loi/2021/06/30/a485/jo.

62 Loi du 30 juillet 2021 portant modification : 1° de la loi du 19 décembre 2020 portant adaptation temporaire de certaines modalités procédurales en matière civile et commerciale; 2° de la loi modifiée du 8 mars 2017 sur la nationalité luxembourgeoise, https://legilux.public.lu/eli/etat/leg/loi/2021/07/30/a626/jo.

une jurisprudence allant à rencontre de l'intention du législateur »[63]. Il est admis désormais que ce n'est pas le dépôt de la farde de procédure qui déclenche le fait que les mandataires sont réputés avoir réitéré leurs moyens à l'audience de plaidoiries, mais le défaut d'avoir sollicité d'être entendus en leurs plaidoiries.

Et enfin il faut ajouter la dernière loi en date : La loi du 17 décembre 2021 portant modification de la loi modifiée du 19 décembre 2020 portant adaptation temporaire de certaines modalités procédurales en matière civile et commerciale qui dispose que « L'article 10 de la loi modifiée du 19 décembre 2020 portant adaptation temporaire de certaines modalités procédurales en matière civile et commerciale est modifié comme suit :

1° À l'alinéa 1er, les termes '31 décembre 2021' sont remplacés par les termes '15 juillet 2022'.
2° À l'alinéa 3, le terme 'à' est remplacé par le terme 'et' et les termes '31 décembre 2021' sont remplacés par les termes '30 juin 2022' »[64].

Rendez-vous est donné au législateur en juin 2022 pour prolonger ce nouveau fonctionnement des tribunaux.

III. Organisation du fonctionnement pratique des juridictions

Les juridictions luxembourgeoises n'ont pas cessé de fonctionner et en dépit de certaines critiques qui ne manqueront pas d'être formulées et que nous formulerons nous-mêmes force est d'admettre que le pragmatisme l'a emporté sur l'attentisme et le légalisme sourcilleux. L'accès à la justice a été préservé dans son principe (1) malgré des atteintes à certaines règles procédurales en particulier la représentation, l'oralité et la publicité (2).

1. Un accès à la justice préservé en son principe

Les aménagements des activités juridictionnelles de l'ensemble des tribunaux et cours du Grand-Duché de Luxembourg se sont révélés nécessaires aussi bien pour assurer la sécurité du personnel et des visiteurs des juridictions qu'en vue de maintenir, dans la mesure du possible, l'activité de l'institution judiciaire en temps de crise. « Pendant les six premières

63 Voy. Le projet de loi, https://data.legilux.public.lu/file2/2021-06-11/42.
64 https://legilux.public.lu/eli/etat/leg/loi/2021/12/17/a899/jo.

semaines de la crise COVID-19, la justice a rapidement su adapter ses procédures et a ainsi pu garantir son fonctionnement au service du justiciable »[65]. Les procédures écrites n'ont guère été impactées sous réserve de la suspension des délais avec certaines exceptions et les procédures orales ont été priorisées afin d'assurer un droit effectif à être entendu. Sous cet angle, l'accès à la justice a été maintenu et garanti même si l'activité des justices de paix a été davantage perturbée que celle des tribunaux d'arrondissement en raison de la place de l'oralité dans les différentes procédures[66].

La suspension des délais avait clairement pour objectif de garantir l'effectivité du droit d'accéder à la justice. « La plupart des pays ont pris des dispositions légales spécifiques afin de proroger les délais de procédure, pour certains dans le cadre d'un état d'urgence déclaré (Espagne, France, Italie, Pologne, Portugal, Roumanie, Slovaquie, Slovénie). Au Portugal, les circonstances exceptionnelles résultant de l'épidémie conduisent à la suspension de tous les délais de prescription et des délais-butoirs. Pour d'autres, il revient au juge de décider au cas par cas comme en Lituanie où le Conseil de la magistrature a recommandé aux juges d'apprécier l'impact sur le déroulement de la procédure des mesures prises dans le cadre de l'état d'urgence sanitaire pour en tirer les conséquences »[67]. On peut rattacher à la suspension des délais la suspension des expulsions qui donne une portée plus substantielle à l'accès à la justice et témoigne de la volonté de protéger les personnes vulnérables[68].

Il convient aussi d'avoir présent à l'esprit les exceptions à cette suspension qui témoigne de la volonté d'aménager dans le temps le droit d'action mais de ne pas priver son titulaire du droit de s'adresser à un juge rapidement en particulier en matière familiale et pénale. « En matière pénale (procédure orale) les audiences de détenus ont été maintenues dans la mesure du possible. Le contentieux des chambres du conseil a été évacué sans discontinuation en appliquant la procédure écrite introduite en raison de l'état de crise. La chambre de l'application des peines a

---

65 https://justice.public.lu/fr/actualites/2020/04/debut-vacations-judiciaires-retarde.html.

66 Voy. pour un exemple devant la juridiction de travail de report *sine die* d'audience, Trib. Trav. Esch, 16 novembre 2020, 1898/20 E-TRAV-211/19.

67 J.-P. Jean, « Les systèmes de justice face à la pandémie du COVID-19 », https://www.leclubdesjuristes.com/blog-du-coronavirus/que-dit-le-droit/les-systemes-de-justice-face-a-la-pandemie-du-covid-19/.

68 Voy., TAL, 12 mai 2020, 2020TALCH14/00067, n° TAL-2020–01020 du rôle

fonctionné sans interruption et suivant le cours procédural normal »[69]. On trouve des préoccupations analogues chez nos voisins européens. « Le choix des contentieux estimés prioritaires, à traiter avec les personnels et moyens disponibles, constitue une question essentielle. Ainsi, la suspension des délais n'est-elle pas applicable dans certains cas. Les plus fréquemment cités touchent à la protection des personnes [...] En matière pénale, la Commission européenne insiste sur la nécessité pour les victimes de violences domestiques en période de COVID-19 d'avoir toujours accès à un service spécialisé confidentiel et gratuit [...] Dans tous les pays européens, le service minimum d'audiences pénales est consacré essentiellement aux personnes arrêtées ou détenues et aux poursuites visant le non-respect des mesures décidées par les autorités pour prévenir la diffusion du COVID-19 »[70].

La mise en place rapide de moyens alternatifs notamment électroniques a également contribué au maintien du service public de la justice. Il convient toutefois de souligner que les outils électroniques (surtout la possibilité de communiquer par e-mail) ne reposent sur aucune base juridique claire et présentent une très faible cybersécurité notamment en termes de données à caractère personnel[71]. Certaines adresses électroniques crées à l'occasion du COVID-19 sont d'un accès difficile sans que la confidentialité et la protection des communications soient garanties[72]. En outre, ces moyens de communication restent un mystère pour le profane et demeurent davantage au service des praticiens du droit que des justiciables occasionnels et *a fortiori* des personnes vulnérables[73]. « The right to access justice of marginalized and vulnerable groups should be taken into consideration in determining what is urgent, and in the delivery of technological solutions. Support for these individuals should continue throughout the

---

69 https://justice.public.lu/fr/actualites/2020/04/debut-vacations-judiciaires-retarde.html.

70 *Ibid.*

71 Y. Poullet, « Pandémie, numérique et droits de l'homme : un étrange cocktail! », *JDE*, 2020, p. 246.

72 Sur la communication des adresses électroniques voy. p. ex. https://justice.public.lu/fr/actualites/2020/05/justice-deconfinement-reouverture-services.html; https://justice.public.lu/fr/actualites/2020/05/adaptations-delais-numeros-telephone-utiles.html; https://justice.public.lu/fr/actualites/2020/04/plan-audiences-delais-adresses-procedures-ecrites.html

73 **Voy. la lettre ouverte du président de la CCDH au Premier Ministre en date du 27 mars 2020,** https://ccdh.public.lu/fr/actualites/2020/20200327_COVID-19_Droits_Humains.html.

pandemic and will need to adapt as courts emerge from the pandemic »[74]. En effet, en matière d'accès à la justice, c'est prioritairement aux personnes vulnérables qu'il faut accorder de l'attention, notamment par le biais de l'assistance judiciaire[75]. Pur hasard de calendrier, sur proposition de la ministre de la Justice, le Conseil de gouvernement du 20 mai 2020 a pris la décision d'augmenter le taux horaire pour les prestations d'avocats effectuées dans le cadre de l'assistance judiciaire à 96 euros et pour les avocats stagiaires à 64 euros à compter du 2 août 2020[76]. Dans la continuité, l'adaptation du contentieux familial et la mise en place d'un référé exceptionnel répond sur papier en tout cas à une préoccupation légitime. Reste que les services du juge aux affaires familiales n'ont pas pu fonctionner à plein régime, mais les audiences se sont multipliées jusqu'à fin juillet pour rattraper les retards accumulés durant la première vague.

Les statistiques pour la période allant du 16 mars 2020 au 24 avril 2020 illustrent l'activité des tribunaux : 2.491 décisions ont été rendues par la Cour d'appel, les tribunaux d'arrondissement et des justices de paix, 4.269 affaires nouvelles sont entrées aux parquets de Luxembourg et de Diekirch et 7.934 ordonnances ont été traitées par les trois justices de paix (ordonnances pénales, de paiement ou de saisie-arrêt)[77]. Ces statistiques fournies par le ministère de la justice sont elles-mêmes un indicateur important. Comme l'a souligné la Commission européenne pour l'efficacité de la justice (CEPEJ), « le bon fonctionnement des systèmes de gestion des affaires et des mécanismes de collecte de données statistiques concernant le fonctionnement des tribunaux est d'autant plus pertinent en cas de crise sanitaire »[78]. La reprise des audiences et le retour à un fonctionnement normalisé des juridictions tant judiciaires qu'administratives a commencé le 25 mai 2020 avec des adaptations tant au niveau des horaires décalés, que des aménagements des salles d'audience. Les vacances judiciaires ont été amputées de 15 jours débutant le 3 août en lieu et place du 16 juillet afin de prolonger le plan des audiences jusqu'à début août 2020. Cette

---

74 OSCE, « The Functioning of Courts in the COVID-19 Pandemic », https://www.osce.org/files/f/documents/5/5/469170.pdf, p. 12.

75 Voy. « Déclaration du CCBE sur la réactivation de la justice en Europe », https://www.ccbe.eu/fileadmin/speciality_distribution/public/documents/Statements/2020/FR_AtJ_20200515_CCBE-Statement-for-the-reactivation-of-Justice-in-Europe.pdf.

76 Règlement grand-ducal du 29 juillet 2020 modifiant le règlement grand-ducal modifié du 18 septembre 1995 concernant l'assistance judiciaire.

77 https://justice.public.lu/fr/actualites/2020/04/pandemie-justice-bilan-six-semaines.html.

78 CEPEJ, « Les leçons et défis pour le système judiciaire pendant et après le COVID-19 », 10 juin 2020, CEPEJ (2008) 8rev.

adaptation des vacances judiciaires a été pointée notamment par le CCBE comme un moyen utile pour réduire les arriérés, même si elle n'a pas fait l'unanimité dans le monde judiciaire luxembourgeois[79]. En toute hypothèse, les règles sanitaires doivent être respectées. Il semble pourtant que la mise à disposition de gel et de masques, tout comme la distanciation sociale n'aient pas toujours été garantis dans les mêmes conditions selon les salles et les compositions des chambres. En outre les mesures sanitaires ont pu porter atteinte à des règles et principes de procédure.

2. *Des atteintes à certaines règles et principes de procédure*

En pratique certaines difficultés se sont cristallisées autour du port du masque et des questions de principe se posent en matière de publicité et d'adaptation des délais dans le temps. Concernant le port du masque, après quelques passe d'armes entre Barreau et juridictions[80], la loi du 25 novembre 2020 dispose en son article 4 que « *(7) Dans les salles d'audience des juridictions constitutionnelle, judiciaires, y compris les juridictions de la sécurité sociale, administratives et militaires, l'obligation de respecter une distance minimale de deux mètres ne s'applique pas :*

1° aux parties au procès en cours, leurs avocats et leurs interprètes, ainsi qu'aux détenus et aux agents de la Police grand-ducale qui assurent leur garde;
2° aux membres de la juridiction concernée, y compris le greffier et, le cas échéant, le représentant du ministère public, si la partie de la salle d'audience où siègent ces personnes est équipée d'un dispositif de séparation permettant d'empêcher la propagation du virus SARS-CoV-2 entre ces personnes.

En faisant usage de sa prérogative de police d'audience, le magistrat qui préside l'audience peut dispenser du port du masque une personne qui est appelée à prendre la parole dans le cadre du procès en cours, pour la durée de sa prise de parole, si cette personne est en situation d'handicap ou si elle présente une pathologie et est munie d'un certificat médical »[81].

---

79 « Points de vigilance et propositions du CCBE dans le cadre de la phase de réactivation du système judiciaire à la lumière de la crise de COVID-19 », https://www.ccbe.eu.

80 Voy. la circulaire du Bâtonnier appelant à plaider sans masque et la circulaire du président de la CJ appelant à plaider avec masque et au bon sens.

81 Loi du 25 novembre 2020 modifiant :
1° la loi modifiée du 17 juillet 2020 sur les mesures de lutte contre la pandémie COVID-19;

Avec masque ou sans c'est surtout la présence des parties et en particulier le recul de l'oralité et de la publicité qui marquent la période de crise[82]. La part et l'importance de l'oralité varient selon le type de procédure et selon le type de juridictions. La procédure pénale ne saurait être comparée au contentieux administratif, tout comme la procédure devant la Cour de cassation diffère de celle suivie par la juridiction du travail, sans parler des référés. Cependant, l'image forte de l'oralité joue un rôle de premier plan en droit processuel[83] et l'oralité des débats comme leur publicité font partie des garanties formelles de bonne justice auxquelles les mesures adoptées portent incontestablement atteinte. Sur ce point, comme sur d'autres, il semblerait cependant que la crise-covid soit plus un révélateur voire un miroir grossissant de tendances ou de velléités existantes en tout cas pour la justice civile pour laquelle la prédominance de l'écrit sur l'oral est affichée dans les textes depuis la réforme de 1996[84]. Un contentieux technique (sous-entendu sérieux) nécessiterait une procédure écrite; l'oralité ne jouant véritablement que pour les affaires de plus faible importance et dans lesquelles la représentation n'est pas obligatoire. L'absence d'audience de plaidoiries dans les procédures écrites qui requiert l'accord des parties ou de leurs représentants montre bien que l'oralité n'est pas une règle essentielle de la procédure civile. Qu'en est-il du principe constitutionnel de publicité des audiences[85]? Il semble qu'il en soit de même. Bien qu'énoncé à l'article 88 de la Constitution, le principe de publicité semble plus sym-

---

2° la loi modifiée du 10 décembre 2009 relative à l'hospitalisation sans leur consentement de personnes atteintes de troubles mentaux, http://data.legilux.publ ic.lu/eli/etat/leg/loi/2020/11/25/a933/jo.

82 Voy. H. Stewart, « Procedural Rights and Factual Accuracy », *Legal Theory*, 2020, 26(2), p. 156.

83 Voy. not. E. Vergès, « Les principes de la procédure civile: notion, fonctions, évolution », in *Les principes essentiels du procès à l'épreuve des réformes récentes du droit judiciaire privé*, IRJS Éditions, Paris, 2014, p. 10; Y. Strickler, « La raison d'être et les réformes de la procédure orale », in *Les principes essentiels du procès à l'épreuve des réformes récentes du droit judiciaire privé*, p. 35; J. N. Kiesilainen, « Efficiency and Justice in Procedural Reforms: The Rise and Fall of the Oral Hearing", in *Civil Justice between Efficiency and Quality: From Ius Commune to the CEPEJ*, Antwerp, Intersentia, 2008, p. 29; C. Glasser, « Civil Procedure and the Lawyers—The Adversary System and the Decline of the Orality Principle », *The Modern Law Review*, 1993, vol. 56–3, p. 307.

84 Dans ce sens, Th. Hoscheit, *Le Droit judiciaire privé au Grand-Duché de Luxembourg*, n° 550.

85 Voy. S. Roure, « L'élargissement du principe de publicité des débats judiciaires : une judiciarisation du débat public », *Revue française de droit constitutionnel*, 2006/4 (n° 68), p. 737.

bolique qu'opérationnel, déjà avant le 18 mars 2020[86]. « L'importance d'un principe est appréciée à la lumière de sa sanction. Or la sanction du non-respect de la publicité est relative »[87]. La violation de l'exigence de publicité doit avoir porté préjudice à celui qui s'en plaint, ce qui réduit grandement les hypothèses de sanction.

On a pu craindre des difficultés particulières d'application des règles dans le temps. Thierry Hoscheit concluait ses « interrogations sur la fin de l'état de crise constitutionnelle » en recommandant « aux plaideurs de ne pas attendre les jours ultimes pour poser les actes dont l'accomplissement est enfermé dans un certain délai »[88]. Le conseil était judicieux mais il ressort de l'étude du Premier vice-président du Tribunal d'arrondissement de Luxembourg des grandes incertitudes quant à la date du 25 juin 2020. « Dans toutes les hypothèses, l'agencement des lois donne naissance à des interrogations sur le degré de sécurité juridique qu'elles procurent »[89]. Plus largement la succession et le foisonnement des lois relatives à l'aménagement ou l'adaptation temporaire des modalités procédurales entre le 20 juin 2020 et le 19 décembre 2021 ne sont pas particulièrement lisibles y compris pour les premiers acteurs judiciaires concernés[90]. Il ne semble cependant pas qu'il y ait eu d'incidents à relever.

En conclusion provisoire de cette première partie sur le fonctionnement du système juridictionnel luxembourgeois pendant la crise sanitaire liée au COVID-19, force est d'admettre que malgré des atteintes plus ou moins marquées aux principes et règles de procédure, les cours et tribunaux ont su s'adapter et la justice n'a pas cessé de fonctionner. Reste que la taille du pays et le pragmatisme de ses habitants y sont pour beaucoup. Par exemple les délais de mise en état bien que suspendus par le RGD du 25 mars 2020 semblent avoir été dans plusieurs cas respectés. Il semblerait que ces adaptations réglementaires puis législatives n'ont suscité ni indignation ni

---

86 Rappelons qu'à la différence de l'article 22 du Code de procédure civile français qui fait du caractère public des débats un principe directeur du procès, le NCPC luxembourgeois ne fait pas de la publicité un tel principe. En outre si l'accès aux décisions de justice s'est nettement améliorée celui-ci est loin d'être généralisé à toutes les chambres de toutes les juridictions judiciaires.

87 L. Cadiet, J. Normand & S. Amrani-Mekki, *Théorie générale du procès*, Themis, 2015, n° 191.

88 Th. Hoscheit, « Interrogations sur la fin de l'état de crise constitutionnelle », *J.T.L.*, août 2020, n°72, p. 100.

89 *Ibid.*, p. 97.

90 Le dépôt des conclusions et du dossiers en procédure écrite par exemple donne lieu à des applications diverses selon les chambres du Tribunal d'arrondissement.

contestation contrairement à ce qui a pu se produire chez nos voisins belge et français[91].

On a assisté à une normalisation progressive de l'accès à la Cité judiciaire, même si les dispositions « portant adaptation temporaire de certaines modalités procédurales » restent en vigueur. A titre d'exemple, depuis le le 11 janvier 2021, l'administration judiciaire a procédé à la réouverture de tous ses services en personne, mais sur rendez-vous, avec une généralisation de l'usage de l'adresse électronique[92]. L'usage de la voie électronique pour communiquer avec les juridictions et y compris pour accomplir des actes de procédure restera sans doute un acquis des dispositions covid en matière de fonctionnement des juridictions.

Reste le port du masque qui a pu constituer une pierre d'achoppement entre magistrats et avocats[93]. Mais les contestations ont été très limitées et on épinglera une décision du Tribunal de police de et à Luxembourg du 15 septembre 2021 dans laquelle l'avocat a contesté l'obligation du port du masque. Le tribunal a jugé que « la procédure judiciaire n'est pas viciée en raison du port du masque à l'audience » et « se déclare incompétent pour statuer sur sa propre capacité mentale suite à un défaut d'oxygénation lié au port du masque »[94]! Par ailleurs, il y a un assez faible « contentieux-coronavirus » avec une relative exception en matière de bail[95]. L'absence

---

91 Comp. en France, C.E., ord. 10 avril 2020, n° 439883, 439892 et 439903. Comp. en Belgique C.E., 24 novembre 2020, n° 249.019 (relevé d'office par le C.E de l'irrégularité des dispositions des arrêtés de pouvoirs spéciaux n°s 2 et 20 du Gouvernement wallon, qui concernent la suspension du délai de recours devant le Conseil d'État pendant la première vague de la pandémie Corona). Voy. infra.

92 https://justice.public.lu/fr/actualites/2021/01/reouverture-services-fermes-au-public-depuis-26-decembre.html.

93 Loi du 25 novembre 2020 : « *le magistrat qui préside l'audience peut dispenser du port du masque une personne qui est appelée à prendre la parole dans le cadre du procès en cours, pour la durée de sa prise de parole* », https://justice.public.lu/fr/actualites/2020/11/nouvelle-circulaire-cr-audiences-masque-distanciation.html. *Voy. J.* Waldron, « À vos masques : parlez! », *Man. Lawyer*, 2020/2, p. 2.

94 TP 15 septembre 2021, Jgmt 499/21.

95 Voy. TAL, 22 décembre 2021, TAL-2021–04661; TAL, 12 juillet 2021, TAL-2021–02935; TAL, 28 juin 2021, n° 2021TALCH14/00100, n° TAL-2021–00994 du rôle, *J.T.L.*, 2021/4, p. 126; JPL, 21 janvier 2021, jugement n° 204/2021; I. Corbisier, « An II de la pandémie de COVID-19 – Un point comparatif sur les tribulations du paiement du loyer dans le cadre d'un bail commercial (Luxembourg, Belgique et France) : cacophonie, solidarisme ou pragmatisme? (première partie) », *J.T.L.*, 2021/2, p. 33; L. Dimmer, « Le Bail et la COVID – retour sur les jugements rendus en la matière », *JN Immo*, 2021/2–3, p. 345. Devant les juridictions civiles, on notera une décision du TAL sur la vente de ticket par la Rockhal pour des concerts tests, TAL, 12 février, 2021, https://anon.public.lu/Déc

de contestation juridictionnelle est sans doute l'un des traits les plus marquants de cette période au Grand-Duché de Luxembourg.

B. Le faible contrôle juridictionnel sur les mesures adoptées

Si l'accès à la justice a été en son principe préservé, l'exercice effectif d'un contrôle juridictionnel sur les mesures adoptées par l'État a été en pratique extrêmement limité (I). Cette absence de contrôle de légalité doit interroger (II).

I. Un contrôle juridictionnel limité

L' « urgence » et la « crise »[96], maîtres mots de la police administrative exercée par le pouvoir exécutif dès mars 2020, mettent en évidence l'omnipotence du pouvoir règlementaire dans la gestion de la situation sanitaire. Allégés de tout contrôle institutionnel traditionnel, les pouvoirs publics ont adopté diverses mesures, inédites, en vue d'endiguer la propagation du virus. Parmi les exemples les plus marquants de ces politiques sanitaires, notons les mesures d'exception imposant une forme de confinement de la population, la distanciation sociale requise dans certains espaces publics ou encore l'obligation relative du port du masque. Ces mesures ont en commun le fait d'avoir été l'objet de vives critiques en raison de leur caractère attentatoire aux libertés individuelles des citoyens[97]. L'office du juge national, et plus particulièrement celle du juge administratif, en l'absence

---

isions%20anonymisées/Tribunal%20d%27arrondissement%20Luxembourg%20commerce/02_Chambre/2021/20210212_TALux2-TAL-2021-01243a-accessible.pdf.

96 Voir l'usage de ces termes dans l'extrait du préambule du règlement grand-ducal du 18 mars 2020 portant introduction d'une série de mesures dans le cadre de la lutte contre le COVID-19.

97 Commission consultative des Droits de l'Homme du Grand-Duché de Luxembourg, Avis sur le projet de loi n°7606 portant introduction d'une série de mesures concernant les personnes physiques dans le cadre de la lutte contre le virus SARS-CoV-2 (COVID-19), Avis 05/2020, 9 juin 2020. Pour une critique de la mesure de couvre-feu voir aussi Commission consultative des Droits de l'Homme du Grand-Duché de Luxembourg, Avis sur le projet de loi n°7683, Avis 11/2020,

du contrôle *a priori* de constitutionnalité exercé par le Conseil d'État[98], se fonde essentiellement sur un contrôle de proportionnalité des mesures prises par les pouvoirs publics par rapport aux libertés menacées. Dans ces conditions, le contrôle juridictionnel se présente comme un des derniers contre-pouvoirs face à la police administrative en action depuis le début de la crise du COVID-19. Ce contentieux administratif est pourtant limité (1). Il répond surtout à une demande de protection des droits et libertés individuelles et non à un contrôle du pouvoir exécutif (2).

1. *Un contentieux limité devant les juridictions nationales*

Le contentieux administratif issu de l'arsenal réglementaire et législatif en vue de combattre la propagation du COVID-19 est relativement modeste au Luxembourg à l'issue d premier confinement. En effet, les juridictions luxembourgeoises se sont nettement démarquées des juridictions des pays limitrophes par un nombre limité d'affaires contentieuses[99].

Alors que le Conseil d'État français comptabilisait plus de 200 ordonnances de référé au plus fort de la crise sanitaire (cinq fois plus que l'année précédente)[100], soit en l'espace de quatre mois, les juridictions administratives luxembourgeoises ont été saisies d'un nombre de recours très limité. En effet, seuls dix jugements ont été rendus par le tribunal administratif pour l'année 2020 dans le cadre des nouveaux recours introduits par les dispositions anti-Covid. Ces nouveaux recours, qui doivent être portés uniquement devant le tribunal administratif, dérogent aux règles de

---

27 octobre 2020; voir également Avis de l'ordre des avocats du Barreau de Luxembourg, Projet de loi n°7606, 4 août 2020.

98 Constitution, Art. 83*bis* : « Le Conseil d'Etat est appelé à donner son avis sur les projets et propositions de loi et les amendements qui pourraient y être proposés, ainsi que sur toutes autres questions qui lui seront déférées par le Gouvernement ou par les lois. Sur les articles votés par la Chambre conformément à l'article 65, il émet son avis dans le délai fixé par la loi. ».

99 France, Conseil d'Etat, La lettre de la justice administrative, Edition spéciale « la justice administrative pendant la crise sanitaire », n°60, juillet 2020, accessible sur le site internet du Conseil d'Etat. J-M. PONTIER, « La crise sanitaire de 2020 et le droit administratif » *in AJDA*, n°30, 2020, p. 1695.

100 France, Conseil d'Etat, La lettre de la justice administrative, Edition spéciale « la justice administrative pendant la crise sanitaire », n°60, juillet 2020, accessible sur le site internet du Conseil d'Etat. J.-M. Pontier, « La crise sanitaire de 2020 et le droit administratif », *AJDA*, n°30, 2020, p. 1695.

procédure générale qui, sauf disposition contraire de la loi[101], permettent d'interjeter appel devant la Cour administrative contre les jugements du tribunal administratif.

Pour ces nouveaux recours qualifiés « d'urgents »[102], le législateur a souhaité privilégier la célérité de la procédure au détriment d'un second degré de juridiction. Si le temps de l'urgence peut paraître difficilement compatible avec l'existence de plusieurs degrés de juridictions, cette procédure d'exception n'est toutefois pas exempte de critiques, car elle est loin de se limiter à l'impossibilité d'interjeter appel contre les jugements du tribunal administratif. En effet, les règles procédurales applicables devant la Cour constitutionnelle n'ont pas été adaptées pour répondre à un contexte de « crise ». Par suite, les juges du tribunal administratif qui voudraient saisir la Cour constitutionnelle d'une question relative à la conformité d'une loi à la Constitution nécessaire à la résolution de leurs affaires se retrouveraient enfermés dans les délais de saisine « de droit commun » de la Cour constitutionnelle[103]. S'il est vrai que l'introduction d'une question préjudicielle devant la Cour constitutionnelle suspend « la procédure et tous les délais de procédure et de prescription depuis la date de cette décision »[104], il en est à se demander si de tels délais ne seraient pas dissuasifs dans un contexte d'urgence, de sorte à alimenter une

---

101 La formulation exacte reprise à différents endroits de la loi modifiée du 7 novembre 1996 portant organisation des juridictions de l'ordre administratif est rédigée comme suit : « Sauf disposition contraire de la loi, appel peut être interjeté devant la Cour administrative contre les décisions du tribunal administratif [...] ».

102 Art. 7, point 5) de la loi 17 juillet 2020 portant introduction d'une série de mesures de lutte contre la pandémie COVID-19 : « Le tribunal administratif statue d'urgence et en tout cas dans les trois jours de l'introduction de la requête. ».

103 Art. 6, loi du 27 juillet 1997 portant organisation de la Cour Constitutionnelle : « Lorsqu'une partie soulève une question relative à la conformité d'une loi à la Constitution devant une juridiction de l'ordre judiciaire ou de l'ordre administratif, celle-ci est tenue de saisir la Cour Constitutionnelle. Une juridiction est dispensée de saisir la Cour Constitutionnelle lorsqu'elle estime que: a) une décision sur la question soulevée n'est pas nécessaire pour rendre son jugement; b) la question de constitutionnalité est dénuée de tout fondement; c) la Cour Constitutionnelle a déjà statué sur une question ayant le même objet. Si une juridiction estime qu'une question de conformité d'une loi à la Constitution se pose et qu'une décision sur ce point est nécessaire pour rendre son jugement, elle doit la soulever d'office après avoir invité au préalable les parties à présenter leurs observations. »

104 Art. 7, loi du 27 juillet 1997 portant organisation de la Cour Constitutionnelle.

réflexion nécessaire autour de l'instauration d'une question prioritaire de constitutionnalité devant la Cour constitutionnelle.

L'existence d'un contentieux limité devant le juge administratif n'est pas contredite par les décisions rendues par les juridictions judiciaires, dont nous noterons deux affaires intimement liées aux mesures sanitaires, une en matière de bail à loyer[105] et une concernant la verbalisation d'un promeneur sur le fondement d'un règlement communal[106]. Cette différence statistique, entre le contentieux français et luxembourgeois, n'est pas surprenante. Elle s'explique de prime abord par la taille du territoire et par le nombre de ses habitants, mais cet état de fait semble également trouver sa source dans des rapports sociaux apaisés entre les citoyens et les pouvoirs publics. Marqué par une culture politique bâtie sur un consensualisme roi, concrétisé par la formation de multiples gouvernements de coalition[107], le Luxembourg est également un pays où la proximité des acteurs de pouvoir et des citoyens permet une résolution informelle de nombreux litiges déchargeant de fait les juridictions du pays.

En sus des différences statistiques démontrées ci-avant dans le poids du contentieux, nous relevons que les juridictions luxembourgeoises ont été appelées à trancher majoritairement des recours en réformation introduits à l'encontre de sanctions administratives du fait d'infractions aux mesures sanitaires de la part de cafetiers et restaurateurs. Le contentieux français, notamment devant les juridictions administratives, se distingue par la diversité de la nature des litiges portés devant le juge national incluant, notamment la question de la crise sanitaire et de la réouverture des lieux de culte, le pouvoir des maires dans l'instauration du port du masque obligatoire ou encore l'usage de drones pour surveiller le respect du confinement dans la ville de Paris[108].

Parmi les affaires devant le tribunal administratif en 2020, il convient de relever que le tribunal administratif a été majoritairement saisi de recours contre des décisions du ministre de la Santé portant fixation d'une amende administrative. En effet, parmi ces affaires[109], neuf concernent des

---

105 Trib. de Paix Luxembourg, 29 juillet 2020, n°2051/20.

106 Tribunal de police Diekrich, 21 juillet 2020, n°170/2020.

107 L. Heuschling et al., « L'opposition politique au Grand-duché de Luxembourg. Regards croisés, de science juridique et de science politique, sur une démocratie consociative », in *L'opposition politique,* LexisNexis, 2016.

108 Voir aussi pour un aperçu des référés introduits devant le Conseil d'Etat français : S. HOURSON, « Aux confins du confinement », in *Droit administratif,* n°5, Lexisnexis, mai 2020, p. 3.

109 Au 4 janvier 2021.

sanctions pécuniaires infligées à des gérants de bars ou de restaurants pour non-respect des mesures sanitaires alors qu'une seule porte sur l'isolement d'un individu testé positif à la COVID-19[110].

2. *Un contentieux de la protection des droits et libertés individuels*

Malgré le nombre et la ressemblance des affaires portées devant le juge administratif luxembourgeois, ces jugements indiquent des tendances générales vers une minoration des amendes administratives prononcées à l'encontre des gérants d'établissements, voire leur annulation. En effet, sur neuf de ces affaires, quatre ont fait l'objet d'une annulation de l'arrêté ministériel portant fixation de la sanction administrative litigieuse[111], trois ont diminué le montant de la sanction pécuniaire contesté[112] et enfin deux ont intégralement confirmé la sanction ministérielle querellée[113].

Il convient de préciser que la loi du 24 juin 2020, portant introduction d'une série de mesures concernant les activités sportives, les activités culturelles ainsi que les établissements recevant du public, dans le cadre de la lutte contre la pandémie COVID-19[114], prévoyait un recours devant le tribunal administratif contre toute amende infligée pour manquement aux obligations sanitaires incombant aux gérants de restaurants et débits de boissons. Citons à titre d'exemple, l'obligation d'accueillir les clients de ces établissements à des places assises, l'observation de certaines distances de sécurité dans l'aménagement des tables ou encore le port du masque lorsque le client n'occupait plus une place assise. Pour toute infraction à ces mesures sanitaires, les gérants des établissements en question pouvaient se voir, à titre personnel, infliger une amende administrative d'un montant

110 Elles se fondent exclusivement sur la loi du 24 juin 2020 portant introduction d'une série de mesures concernant les activités sportives, les activités culturelles ainsi que les établissements recevant du public, dans le cadre de la lutte contre la pandémie COVID-19 et la loi modifiée du 17 juillet 2020 portant sur les mesures de lutte contre la pandémie COVID-19.

111 Trib. adm, 9 octobre 2020, n°45061, 1ère Chambre; Trib. adm., 7 octobre 2020, n°45051, 3ème Chambre; Trib adm., 27 novembre 2020, n°45263, 4ème Chambre; Trib. adm., 30 novembre 2020, n°45257, 2ème Chambre.

112 Trib. adm., 8 octobre 2020, n°45062, 3ème Chambre; Trib. adm., 14 octobre 2020, n°45077, 2ème Chambre; Trib. adm., 21 septembre 2020, n°44987, 4ème Chambre.

113 Trib. adm., 7 août 2020, n°44765, Chambre de vacation; Trib. adm., 28 septembre 2020, n°45012, 4ème Chambre.

114 Abrogé par la loi du 17 juillet 2020 portant introduction d'une série de mesures de lutte contre la pandémie COVID-19.

maximum de 4 000 euros[115]. Ce montant pouvait être doublé en cas de récidive.

Dans le cadre d'un recours en réformation à l'encontre de pareille sanction, le juge administratif était appelé à statuer comme juge du fond. Ce recours est semblable à ce que le droit administratif français qualifie de recours de plein contentieux et se distingue du recours en annulation dans lequel l'office du juge administratif se limite à l'annulation, partielle ou totale, de l'acte administratif faisant grief au requérant. Toujours dans le cadre d'un recours en réformation, il doit être souligné que le juge administratif se prononce sur la base du cadre juridique en vigueur au moment où il est amené à statuer.

Plus particulièrement, les recours à l'encontre de sanctions pécuniaires du fait d'infractions commises par des commerçants, artisans ou gérants d'établissements devaient être introduits trois jours à compter de la notification à personne ou de la remise à la personne de la décision portant sanction prise par le ministre de la Santé[116]. Dans les faits, l'infraction faisait en premier lieu l'objet d'un procès-verbal d'un agent ou officier de police ou de tout autre agent habilité[117]. Dans un deuxième temps, après remise d'une copie de ce procès-verbal, le contrevenant disposait de deux semaines pour soumettre au ministre ses observations écrites et pour éventuellement demander l'accès à son dossier. Enfin, sur la base de ces éléments de dossier, c'est au ministre de la Santé que revenait, en dernier lieu, le pouvoir de prononcer l'amende par voie d'arrêté. A partir de l'introduction de la requête portant opposition à la sanction litigieuse, le tribunal administratif devait statuer « *d'urgence* » dans les cinq jours. Pour des raisons de célérité de la procédure, aucun appel n'a été prévu par le législateur devant la Cour administrative d'appel.

On pourrait aisément s'associer aux critiques du Président du tribunal administratif dans la détermination des affaires relevant d'une procédure d'urgence[118]. En effet, une amende administrative prononcée à l'encon-

---

115 La loi du 24 juin 2020 portant introduction d'une série de mesures concernant les activités sportives, les activités culturelles ainsi que les établissements recevant du public, dans le cadre de la lutte contre la pandémie COVID-19, art. 3.

116 *Ibid*, art. 3.

117 Voir Art. 3, para.3, de la loi du 24 juin 2020 portant introduction d'une série de mesures concernant les activités sportives, les activités culturelles ainsi que les établissements recevant du public, dans le cadre de la lutte contre la pandémie COVID-19.

118 Voir les critiques du Président du tribunal administratif au sujet de l'adoption de mesures accélérées dans Avis du tribunal administratif, Projet de loi n°7606 et n°7607, 18 août 2020.

tre d'un restaurateur pour non-respect des mesures sanitaires constitue-t-elle une mesure administrative d'une telle gravité, voire d'une portée irréversible, au point de « mobiliser » dans l'urgence les juges de première instance contraints de se prononcer dans un délai de cinq jours? Il nous semble exister une disproportion manifeste entre l'objet de ce contentieux et l'urgence qui lui a été reconnue devant le tribunal administratif.

Dans la majorité des affaires portant sur des sanctions administratives, le juge administratif a remis en question le bien-fondé de ces infractions. A titre d'exemple, lorsque le tribunal administratif les a annulées, il s'est fondé, dans un cas, sur l'absence de notification de l'auteur de l'infraction[119], dans un autre cas, sur une violation de la procédure de constatation de l'infraction[120] et enfin, dans un dernier cas[121], le juge administratif a retenu l'abrogation des dispositions légales portant fixation de ces sanctions. Les éléments essentiels de ces affaires sont exposés dans les développements qui suivent.

Dans un premier cas[122], la gérante d'un débit de boissons a été condamnée au paiement d'une amende administrative de 8 000 euros[123] au motif que lors d'un contrôle policier, plusieurs de ses clients consommaient des boissons au comptoir et sur la terrasse de l'établissement en méconnaissance de l'obligation d'occuper des places assises ou à défaut, de l'obligation de porter un masque[124]. Lors de la constatation de cette infraction, seule la serveuse de l'établissement était présente sur les lieux et une copie du procès-verbal lui a été remis. Le tribunal administratif a annulé l'amende susmentionnée pour défaut de notification du gérant de l'établissement retenant que seuls les responsables des établissements publics visés par la loi du 24 juin 2020 disposant d'un pouvoir décisionnel devaient être qualifiés d'auteur de l'infraction. D'après le jugement, l'absence de notification à personne de la gérante de l'établissement constituait une atteinte à ses droits de la défense puisque rien n'indiquait qu'elle avait connaissance de l'infraction et pouvait utilement faire valoir sa cause.

---

119 Trib. adm., 7 octobre 2020, n°45051, 3ème Chambre.

120 Trib. adm, 9 octobre 2020, n°45061, 1ère Chambre.

121 Trib. adm., 30 novembre 2020, n°45257, 2ème Chambre; Trib adm., 27 novembre 2020, n°45263, 4ème Chambre.

122 Trib. adm., 7 octobre 2020, n°45051, 3ème Chambre.

123 Le montant de cette amende est dû à une récidive de la part de l'établissement concerné.

124 Art. 1er, para. 3, de la loi du 24 juin 2020 : « Les restaurants, débits de boissons, salles de restauration des établissements d'hébergement, salons de consommation, cantines et tout autre lieu de restauration occasionnelle sont soumis au respect des conditions suivantes : 1° ne sont admises que des places assises [...] ».

Quelques jours auparavant[125], une chambre distincte du tribunal administratif retenait une solution inverse estimant que l'absence de signature du procès-verbal par le gérant des lieux « *n'*[était] *pas nécessaire pour conférer une valeur légale audit procès-verbal* » tout en soulignant que la remise d'une copie du rapport dressant l'infraction avait été, là aussi, remis à une serveuse de l'établissement et que le gérant était dès lors « *malvenu de contester la réception du procès-verbal* »[126]. En ce qui concerne la computation des délais de recours, un jugement du tribunal du 30 novembre 2020[127] retenait, quant à lui, qu'à défaut d'avoir notifié à personne un gérant d'établissement de son avis de contravention, le délai pour contester cette sanction devant le tribunal n'avait pu commencer à courir[128]. Relevons également qu'en matière de délai de recours, le tribunal administratif[129] a jugé que ces derniers restaient préservés lorsque l'arrêté ministériel portant fixation d'une amende à l'encontre d'un gérant d'établissement n'indiquait pas correctement les voies de recours disponibles contre ledit arrêté.

Dans un second cas[130], le tribunal administratif a annulé la décision du ministre de la Santé infligeant une amende de 2 000 euros à la gérante d'un restaurant pour non-respect des règles de distanciation sociale au sein de son établissement. La police grand-ducale lui reprochait de ne pas avoir observé les distances de sécurité requises pour la disposition de ses tables[131]. Or, il s'est avéré que la matérialité des faits à l'origine de cette sanction n'a aucunement été constatée personnellement par les policiers à l'origine du procès-verbal en violation de la loi du 17 juillet 2020[132], mais reposait sur un simple appel téléphonique de l'échevin de la commune qui aurait constaté un « *attroupement* » lors d'une promenade près de ce restaurant. En complément de son témoignage, l'échevin aurait, en outre,

125 Trib. adm., 28 septembre 2020, n°45012, 4ème Chambre.

126 *Ibid.*

127 Trib. adm., 30 novembre 2020, n°45257, 2ème Chambre.

128 *Ibid.*

129 Trib. adm., 28 septembre 2020, n°45012, 4ème Chambre.

130 Trib. adm, 9 octobre 2020, n°45061, 1ère Chambre.

131 En effet, conformément à l'art. 2, al. 1er, pt. 3, de la loi du 17 juillet 2020, les restaurateurs sont tenus de disposer les tables de leur restaurant en observant une distance de sécurité d'1,5 mètre ou, à défaut de respecter cette distance, d'installer des « barrière[s] » ou des « séparations physique[s] » permettant de limiter la circulation du virus.

132 Selon l'article 11 de la loi du 17 juillet 2020 (modifiée par la loi du 24 juillet 2020), les infractions à la loi sont constatées par les agents et officiers de police de la Police grand-ducale et par les agents de l'Administration des douanes et accises à partir du grade de brigadier principal.

montré aux agents de police une vidéo de la terrasse du restaurant bondée circulant sur le réseau social *Facebook*. Dans son jugement, le tribunal a souligné que l'infraction n'avait aucunement été relevée par les agents de police puisque ces derniers indiquaient clairement dans leur procès-verbal être arrivés sur les lieux après l'heure de l'infraction alléguée. Les premiers juges ont ensuite rejeté la pertinence de la vidéo invoquée à titre de preuve au motif qu'il était impossible de déterminer la date à laquelle elle avait été filmée. Cette décision est l'illustration parfaite, bien qu'anecdotique, de l'importance d'un contrôle juridictionnel des agissements des autorités locales et nationales afin de limiter les interventions arbitraires et disproportionnées de la force publique.

Dans un troisième cas, le tribunal administratif a annulé, dans deux affaires distinctes[133], les amendes pécuniaires prononcées à l'encontre de gérants d'établissements au motif qu'une modification de la loi du 17 juillet 2020 avait abrogé les dispositions portant fixation de ces sanctions. Saisi d'un recours en réformation, le juge administratif a rappelé qu'il était tenu d'appliquer « *les éléments de fait et de droit de la cause au moment où il statue* », de sorte qu'en l'absence de dispositions transitoires, les sanctions susmentionnées étaient dépourvues de base légale justifiant, dès lors, l'annulation des arrêtés ministériels portant fixation de ces sanctions.

Les affaires portées devant le tribunal administratif démontrent également que le juge administratif, dans la lignée d'une jurisprudence constante des juridictions administratives, interprète avec souplesse les règles procédurales applicables aux types de recours admissibles dans le contexte des causes d'irrecevabilité d'un recours juridictionnel. Dans une affaire de 2020[134], le représentant de l'État soulevait l'irrecevabilité d'un recours du fait que la gérante d'un établissement se bornait à demander l'annulation de l'arrête ministériel portant fixation d'une sanction à son encontre alors que seul un recours en réformation avait été ouvert par le législateur dans cette matière. Les premiers juges ont admis la recevabilité du recours constatant que la demanderesse invoquait « des moyens de légalité » et observait « les règles de procédure spéciales » et les « délais dans lesquels le recours [devait] être introduit »[135].

La lecture des jugements rendus à ce jour par le tribunal administratif révèle également que le juge administratif est attentif à l'énumération

---

133 Trib. adm., 30 novembre 2020, n°45257, 2ème Chambre; Trib adm., 27 novembre 2020, n°45263, 4ème Chambre.

134 Trib. adm, 9 octobre 2020, n°45061, 2ème Chambre.

135 Le tribunal sur fonde sur sa jurisprudence antérieure, notamment Trib. adm., 3 mars 1997, n°9693.

des critères qu'il retient dans son analyse de la proportionnalité des sanctions retenues par le ministre de la Santé. Tel qu'il résulte de divers jugements du tribunal administratif[136], le juge administratif constate succinctement que l'amende administrative prévue par la loi du 17 juillet 2020 est « dépourvue de tout critère d'évaluation ». Par suite, il s'attarde, dans son contrôle de proportionnalité de la mesure incriminée, « [aux] circonstances concrètes du cas d'espèces et notamment en fonction du nombre d'infractions retenues, de la gravité de ces infractions, de l'attitude la personne responsable et de ses antécédents ». Issue d'un jugement du 21 septembre 2020[137], cette formulation est reprise à l'identique par la 2ème Chambre et la 3ème Chambre du tribunal administratif dans deux autres jugements portant sur des faits relativement semblables[138].

Retenons enfin qu'une affaire jugée par le tribunal administratif se démarque de la tendance majoritaire autour des sanctions pécuniaires à l'endroit de gérants de débits de boissons. Saisi d'un recours à l'encontre d'une mesure d'isolement à résidence pour une durée de dix jours renouvelable[139], le tribunal administratif s'est prononcé sur la validité de résultats contradictoires issus de tests naso-pharyngé RT-PCR[140] (« test PCR ») réalisés sur un même individu à deux jours d'intervalle. En effet, en application de l'article 7, para. 5, de la loi du 17 juillet 2020, un recours était ouvert contre l'ordonnance de mise en isolement prise par le directeur de la Santé (ou son délégué) lorsqu'un individu présentait un risque élevé de propagation du virus SARS-CoV-2. Tout recours contre cette ordonnance devait être introduit dans un délai de trois jours à partir de la notification à personne ou de la remise directe à personne de la mesure d'isolement. Là encore, le tribunal administratif siégeait en tant que juge du fond et devait rendre son jugement dans un délai de trois jours à partir de la requête introductive d'instance. Résistant à l'ensemble des moyens soulevés par le demandeur, notamment la remise en cause de la fiabilité des tests PCR, l'incompatibilité de la mesure d'isolement avec l'article 5 de la Convention de sauvegarde des droits de l'homme et libertés fondamentales ou encore une demande de saisine de la Cour constitutionnelle en vue de mesurer la

---

136 Trib. adm., 21 septembre 2020, n°44987, 4ème Chambre; Trib. adm., 8 octobre 2020, n°45062, 3ème Chambre; Trib. adm., 14 octobre 2020, n°45077, 2ème Chambre.

137 Trib. adm., 21 septembre 2020, n°44987, 4ème Chambre.

138 Trib. adm., 8 octobre 2020, n°45062, 3ème Chambre; Trib. adm., 14 octobre 2020, n°45077, 2ème Chambre.

139 Trib. adm., 24 septembre 2020, n°45008, 1ère Chambre.

140 PCR est l'abréviation en langue anglaise pour *Polymerase chain reaction.*

conformité de la mesure d'isolement avec l'article 12 de la Constitution, le tribunal a d'emblée écarté toute remise en cause de la valeur scientifique des tests PCR. De manière précautionneuse, il s'est appuyé sur le fait que le second test négatif pouvait s'expliquer par un test « *moins sensible* » et que la première analyse réalisée par le demandeur devait primer étant donné qu'elle révélait que pour les « *trois SARS-CoV-2 génomes testés* » deux ont été détectés par ses résultats biologiques. Au regard des délais pour émettre son jugement, on ne peut que comprendre la déférence du tribunal à l'égard des explications scientifiques communiquées par le délégué du gouvernement. Il semble en effet impossible dans des délais aussi courts d'exiger des contre-expertises médicales qui permettraient d'obtenir des sources complémentaires d'informations susceptibles de mieux orienter la décision du juge administratif.

3. *Une diversification du contentieux administratif à l'issue de la première vague…*

La question de la COVID-19 et des mesures prises en vue de sa lutte vont se présenter sous diverses formes devant le juge administratif dès 2021 dans une partie du contentieux qu'il a à connaître. Ainsi, dans de nombreuses affaires relatives au contentieux des étrangers, l'incidence du virus est avant abordé dans le contexte des mesures d'éloignement prises à l'encontre de certains demandeurs d'asile. En effet, dans plusieurs jugements de 2022, le tribunal administratif a jugé que le demandeur de protection internationale qui s'est intentionnellement soustrait à un test PCR nécessaire à son transfert vers un autre Etat membre, en application du règlement Dublin III, doit « être considéré comme s'étant soustrait de manière intentionnelle à l'exécution de l'éloignement organisé, se mettant ainsi encore en situation de fuite »[141]. Une autre partie du contentieux impacté par les questions de COVID-19 est celui relatif aux conditions d'octroi du chômage partiel pour certaines entreprises affectées par la crise sanitaire[142]. Enfin, on notera également un certain nombre d'ordonnances de référé introduites devant le président du tribunal administratif du fait de la crainte, par certains agents de l'Etat, de subir un préjudice grave et

141 Trib. adm., 18 mars 2022, n° 47158; voy. également trib. adm., 7 janvier 2022, n° 46851; trib. adm., 16 février 2022, n° 47010.

142 Trib. adm., 9 mars 2022, n° 45031 et trib. adm., 10 février 2022, n° 45049.

définitif après avoir été enjoint à quitter leur poste, en raison de leur incapacité à présenter un test PCR négatif ou un certificat de vaccination[143].

II. Absence de contentieux sur la légalité des mesures adoptées faute de saisine

L'absence de contentieux portant sur la légalité des règlements grand-ducaux et de lois adoptés dans le contexte de crise est frappante. Le Conseil d'État a certes exercé un contrôle *a priori* par avis sur les lois adoptées à la sortie du premier confinement, mais il n'y a pas eu ni contrôle (ni contestation du reste) des règlements grand-ducaux et des lois adoptées depuis mars 2020. Les faiblesses structurelles et institutionnelles de la Cour constitutionnelle ne permettent pas un contrôle efficace de la législation d'urgence. Contrairement à d'autres États dans lesquels les juridictions ont été saisies d'un « contentieux covid » (qu'il s'agisse d'un contentieux de la légalité ou des droits et libertés individuels), les juridictions luxembourgeoises de tous ordres confondus sont restées bien silencieuses faute de saisine. C'est vrai pour toutes les mesures y compris celles qui concernent le fonctionnement de la justice. A titre d'exemple l'article 6 de la loi du 24 juin 2020 portant introduction d'une série de mesures concernant les personnes physiques dans le cadre de la lutte contre la pandémie COVID-19 aurait pu émouvoir à plus d'un titre. Il accorde au directeur de la santé le droit de saisir le Président du tribunal d'arrondissement territorialement compétent d'une requête proposant le confinement forcé d'une personne infectée dans un établissement hospitalier ou toute autre structure appropriée. Cette ordonnance est rendue après que le Président du tribunal d'arrondissement a entendu la personne concernée, à laquelle l'ordonnance est ensuite notifiée par la Police grand-ducale. Le Président du tribunal d'arrondissement peut, à tout moment, prendre une nouvelle ordonnance, soit *d'office*, soit sur requête de la personne concernée ou du directeur de la santé, soit du procureur d'État[144]. Si on laisse de côté cet office terrifiant du juge civil, le mode de saisine tout comme le délai d'appel de 48h suivant la notification de l'ordonnance par la Police grand-ducale interroge.

---

143 Trib. adm., 1 décembre 2021, n° 46669; trib. adm., 1 décembre 2021, n° 46665 et trib. adm., 1 décembre 2021, n° 46671.

144 Cette requête peut être introduite par voie électronique @ covid19.luxembourg@justice.etat.lu.

D'une manière générale les adaptations des audiences, la suspension des délais ou encore le recours à l'introduction d'instance par e-mail n'ont pas donné lieu à contestation. Par contraste, en France, aussi bien les syndicats d'avocats que de magistrats ont demandé au juge des référés du Conseil d'État de suspendre plusieurs règles d'adaptation du fonctionnement des juridictions durant l'état d'urgence sanitaire en particulier la possibilité de recourir à la visioconférence lors des audiences mais aussi de mener des procédures sans audience. Ces demandes ont été rejetées parce que du point de vue institutionnel, le gouvernement français avait été habilité, par la loi d'urgence votée par le Parlement le 23 mars, à adapter les règles de fonctionnement des juridictions. Du point de vue plus substantiel, le juge des référés a estimé que les mesures étaient proportionnées et visaient à respecter les règles sanitaires. Il a jugé que dans la mesure où la procédure écrite sans audience pouvait, en principe, être refusée par les parties et que la contradiction était respectée il n'y a avait pas d'atteinte disproportionnée au droit à un procès juste et équitable.[145] Toujours en France, la Cour de cassation a transmis une question prioritaire de constitutionnalité relative à la possibilité de tenir des procédures sans audience, pour vérifier sa conformité au bloc de constitutionnalité (en l'occurrence avec l'article 16 de la Déclaration des droits de l'homme et du citoyen). Sans préjuger de la réponse du Conseil constitutionnel, cela signifie que la Cour de cassation française a considéré la question sérieuse et ayant une incidence sur l'issue du litige[146]. En France comme en Belgique, les conseils d'État respectifs ont été saisis en urgence de recours à l'encontre des mesures de lutte contre le COVID-19[147]. Il en va de même dans d'autres États européens comme le relève l'étude de l'OSCE[148] ou le rapport de l'Assemblée parlementaire du Conseil de l'Europe qui souligne que : « Un système judiciaire opérationnel est indispensable pour garantir la légalité des mesures d'urgence, en général comme dans les cas particuliers. L'ingérence dans un droit

---

145 Comp. en France, C.E., ord. 10 avril 2020, n° 439883, 439892 et 439903.

146 Cass. 2e civ., 24 sept. 2020, n° 19–40.056, S. Amrani-Mekki, « Constitutionnalisation du dispositif état d'urgence sanitaire », *Procédures*, n° 11, Novembre 2020, comm. 193.

147 Voy. pour la France, https://www.conseil-etat.fr/actualites/actualites/dernieres-decisions-referes-en-lien-avec-l-epidemie-de-covid-19; B. Bonnet, « Le Conseil d'Etat et le COVID-19 », *JCP*, juin 2020, 656, p. 995 et pour la Belgique http://www.raadvst-consetat.be/?page=news&lang=fr&newsitem=640.

148 Voy. notamment les décisions de la Cour constitutionnelle moldave en date du 13 avril 2020 et de la Cour constitutionnelle roumaine du 6 mai 2020, voy. OSCE, « The Functioning of Courts in the COVID-19 Pandemic », https://www.osce.org/files/f/documents/5/5/469170.pdf, p. 38.

protégé motivée par la poursuite d'un but d'intérêt général n'est autorisée que si elle est prévue par une loi appropriée. Les tribunaux notamment les cours constitutionnelles ou leurs équivalents, doivent pouvoir examiner les lois d'urgence afin de vérifier leur conformité avec le cadre juridique national et les obligations juridiques internationales de l'État. Les cours constitutionnelles et cours suprêmes de nombreux États membres ont déjà reçu et, dans certains cas, statué sur des recours relatifs aux mesures de lutte contre la COVID-19 »[149]. Et de citer de nombreux exemples : vingt requêtes pendantes devant la Cour constitutionnelle en Autriche, plus d'un millier d'affaires devant différentes juridictions en Allemagne, ... et partout des mesures suspendues ou annulées car *jugées* disproportionnées[150].

Les pouvoirs limités de notre Cour constitutionnelle prend ici tout son relief[151]. Certes la Cour constitutionnelle pourrait être saisie d'une question à l'occasion d'une affaire à l'instar du Conseil constitutionnel français qui a été saisi d'une QPC par la Cour de cassation[152]. Ce seul contrôle par voie d'exception ouvert au Grand-Duché de Luxembourg montre toutefois ses limites. Dans un contexte de crise en particulier, un contrôle de constitutionnalité *a priori* semble nécessaire[153]. Le contrôle de l'état de crise est un rôle qui est assuré ailleurs par une juridiction

149 V. Vardanyan, « L'impact de la pandémie de COVID-19 sur les droits de l'homme et l'Etat de droit », Rapport de la Commission des questions juridiques et des droits de l'homme, AS/JUR (2020) 13, p. 18.

150 *Ibid.*

151 Voy. not. C. Sauer, « Chapitre 2 – Le caractère indéfini du contrôle de constitutionnalité : Contrôle abstrait et/ou contrôle concret » in *Contrôle juridictionnel des lois au Luxembourg*, Bruxelles, Éditions Larcier, 2019, p. 247; F. Delaporte, « Le rôle croissant de la Cour Constitutionnelle » in *La défense des droits et libertés au Grand-Duché de Luxembourg*, Bruxelles, Éditions Larcier, 2020, p. 145; J. Gerkath (Dir.), *Les 20 ans de la Cour Constitutionnelle: Trop jeune pour mourir!?*, Pasicrisie Luxembourgeoise, 2018; N. Kuhn & E. Rousseaux, « La Cour constitutionnelle luxembourgeoise : dernière pierre à l'édifice des cours constitutionnelles en Europe occidentale », *Revue internationale de droit comparé*, Vol. 53 N°2, avril-juin, 2001. p. 453.

152 Cass. 2e civ., 24 sept. 2020, n° 19–40.056, S. Amrani-Mekki, « Constitutionnalisation du dispositif état d'urgence sanitaire », *Procédures*, n° 11, Novembre 2020, comm. 193.

153 Voy. en France Cons. const., 26 mars 2020, n° 2020–799 DC, Loi organique d'urgence pour faire face à l'épidémie de COVID-19, § 3; à propos de la suspension du délai dans lequel le Conseil d'État ou la Cour de cassation doit se prononcer sur le renvoi d'une question prioritaire de constitutionnalité au Conseil constitutionnel et celui dans lequel ce dernier doit statuer sur une telle question.

constitutionnelle. Comme l'a souligné le Professeur Gerkrath ce serait donc un changement radical du rôle de la Cour constitutionnel qui serait bienvenu[154]. En l'état du droit la décision de recourir à l'article 32 para. 4 de la Constitution n'est pas contestable devant les juridictions. Certes les règlements grand-ducaux peuvent être contestés devant la juridiction administrative mais dans des conditions strictes des recours administratifs notamment de délais pour agir[155]. Dans la gamme des contrôles juridictionnels, on pourrait penser aussi à l'exception d'illégalité devant les juridictions judiciaires.

C. *Conclusions prospectives sur les évolutions possibles et/ou nécessaires du système juridictionnel luxembourgeois*

La Commission européenne pour l'efficacité de la justice (CEPEJ), dans une déclaration intitulée « Les leçons et défis pour le système judiciaire pendant et après le COVID-19 » a souligné que si la pandémie du COVID-19 a incontestablement créé des défis pour les tribunaux et autorités judiciaires dans les États membres, elle invite également « à réfléchir sur les mesures innovantes à mettre en œuvre dans les systèmes judiciaires »[156]. Elle conclut par un Principe 7 « Une justice tournée vers l'avenir) » qui se lit comme suit : « La pandémie du COVID-19 a aussi été l'occasion d'introduire en urgence des pratiques innovantes. Une stratégie de transformation du système judiciaire devrait être élaborée pour tirer parti des solutions nouvellement mises en œuvre. Certains aspects du fonctionnement traditionnel des tribunaux devraient être reconsidérés (relations avec les médias, niveau d'utilisation des nouvelles technologies, renforcement du recours aux modes alternatifs de résolution des différents et en particulier à la médiation). La modernisation du système judiciaire devrait être abordée de manière positive, et toujours dans le respect des droits

---

154 J. Gerkrath dans un article paru dans le *Wort*, https://www.wort.lu/de/politik/pandemie-massnahmen-gerichtliche-kontrolle-verbessern-5fa584a7de135b92365f8e4c.

155 Voy. R. Ergec, *Contentieux administratif luxembourgeois*, Pasicrisie, Luxembourg, 2011.

156 CEPEJ, « Les leçons et défis pour le système judiciaire pendant et après le COVID-19 », 10 juin 2020, CEPEJ (2008) 8rev.

fondamentaux garantis par la CEDH[157]. Il conviendrait également de poursuivre le dialogue nécessaire entre tous les acteurs de la justice et de tirer profit des nouvelles relations créées entre les juges, les procureurs, le personnel des tribunaux, les avocats, les agents d'exécution, les notaires, les médiateurs et les experts au moment de la crise sanitaire ». Nous ne pouvons que souscrire à ces propos. La crise sanitaire a, dans le domaine de la justice comme dans d'autres servi de miroir grossissant des qualités et des défauts de chacun. En ce sens la pandémie aura sans doute un effet durable sur la justice et son fonctionnement avec un développement de la digitalisation et de la procédure écrite. Il faudrait espérer surtout que cette crise sanitaire fasse évoluer le rapport au contrôle juridictionnel de la légalité au Grand-Duché de Luxembourg[158].

Jean-Paul Jean estime que « la pandémie du COVID-19 constitue à la fois un révélateur du niveau actuel d'utilisation des nouvelles technologies dans les juridictions et un accélérateur qui va faire basculer les systèmes judiciaires vers leur usage massif, comme pour nombre d'autres secteurs de la société. Pour accélérer le retour à une situation acceptable dans les délais de jugement, le triptyque juge unique, procédure écrite, dématérialisation va transformer le rapport à la justice civile, donc aussi le métier d'avocat avec le recul de l'oralité et du rapport humain, malgré le souhait récurrent du justiciable de pouvoir s'expliquer devant son juge »[159]. Le passage au juge unique est resté marginal devant le Tribunal d'arrondissement[160], tandis que la procédure écrite – procédure de droit commun en matière civile et administrative- n'a guère soulevé de difficulté. C'est sans doute sur le terrain de la numérisation qu'il conviendra de tirer des leçons pour

---

157 Voy. L. Bianku & H. Smith, « Les droits fondamentaux et la pandémie COVID-19 » in Engel, A. *et al.* (dir.), *Annales du droit luxembourgeois : Volume 30 – 2020*, 2019ᵉ édition, Bruxelles, Bruylant, 2021, p. 15–63

158 Voy. R. Ergec & S. Menétrey, « Avis sur l'avant-projet de loi portant organisation de la Cour suprême », in *Judicial Reforms in Luxembourg and Europe*, Nomos, 2014, p. 41.

159 J.-P. Jean, « Les systèmes de justice face à la pandémie du COVID-19 », https://www.leclubdesjuristes.com/blog-du-coronavirus/que-dit-le-droit/les-systemes-de-justice-face-a-la-pandemie-du-covid-19/.

160 Les réformes récentes du droit judiciaire belge ont accordé une place de choix au juge unique bien avant la pandémie. En France en revanche au temps de la pandémie le Conseil d'Etat a censuré l'ordonnance permettant de tenir des audiences en visioconférence à juge unique à la CNDA, https://www.conseil-etat.fr/ressources/decisions-contentieuses/dernieres-decisions-importantes/conseil-d-etat-8-juin-2020-juge-statuant-seul-et-recours-a-la-visioconference-a-la-cnda. Voy. A.-M. Cohendet, « La collégialité des juridictions : un principe en voie de disparition? », *Revue française de droit constitutionnel*, 2006/4 (n° 68), p. 713.

l'avenir. Les pratiques observées au Grand-Duché de Luxembourg pendant la pandémie montrent que la numérisation jusque-là quasiment absente et le recours à la procédure écrite ont largement fait leur place et il y a fort à parier que ces tendances se renforcent et soient consacrées de manière pérenne dans les temps à venir. Sur la digitalisation le constat est universel : « The most discussed aspect of the impact of COVID-19 on courts may be the rapid increase in the use of technology to manage the workload of courts and to maintain some functioning during lockdown and in its aftermath. [...] While reluctance among judges to adapt to IT solutions and online delivery has been noted as almost proverbial in the past, the pandemic catapulted the judiciary into the age of technology. Some IT tools have been absorbed by judges enthusiastically in a number of jurisdictions, sometimes overlooking its insufficiencies for parties, and related fair trial concerns »[161]. Comme nous l'avons souligné la base juridique et la sécurité des outils électroniques mis en place au Luxembourg sont lacunaires, mais il y a ici une opportunité à saisir pour donner un coup d'accélérateur au programme « paperless justice » (JUPAL)[162]. La Justice et le Barreau sont en discussion pour la mise en place d'un greffe électronique permettant de normaliser et de sécuriser les échanges électroniques avec le greffe. L'enjeu est de pérenniser une pratique de crise en l'assortissant de garanties juridiques et technologiques. A cet effet s'est tenu le 2 octobre 2020 un atelier de travail réunissant avocats et fonctionnaires de l'administration judiciaire pour mettre en place les bases d'un « dossier judiciaire électronique, digne successeur du dossier judiciaire papier actuel »[163]. A une question parlementaire sur le programme JUPAL, la Ministre de la justice a apporté, le 28 octobre 2020, une réponse sur l'état d'avancement de chacun des volets du programme qui reste très embryonnaire[164]. L'occasion ne doit donc pas être manquée. La digitalisation n'est cependant pas limitée aux communications et la question des audiences en visio-conférence doit aussi retenir l'attention alors qu'il ne

---

161 OSCE, « The functioning of courts in the COVID-19 pandemic », https://www.osce.org/files/f/documents/5/5/469170.pdf, p. 20.

162 Voy. E. Perru, « Crise du COVID-19, avocat et 'Paperless Justice' », https://www.lexnow.lu/blog/articles-4/post/crise-du-covid-19-avocat-et-paperless-justice-36.

163 https://justice.public.lu/fr/actualites/2020/10/programme-paperless-justice-reunion-travail-barreaux.html.

164 Voy. https://chd.lu/wps/PA_RoleDesAffaires/FTSByteServingServletImpl?path=0D7F198E74F0171A6451F4C7438A7B9FB1E1B5DCCFF6A56F5D04EA52BDD1B364D8220CDAF8E150F2C12B402A88A8A4CF$36EB064D7B0688D57B9F5D8D4A9D0AFA.

semble pas que la pratique se soit imposée pendant la crise au Luxembourg contrairement à d'autres États[165]. En revanche les dispenses d'audience -en matière civile- ont semble-t-il eu un succès qui tend à se pérenniser. Le régime juridique de cette dispense n'appelle pas de commentaire tenant à d'éventuelles difficultés de mise en œuvre puisqu'il suffit de l'accord des parties pour que leur dossier soit traité par l'administration judiciaire. Pourtant au niveau théorique l'absence d'audiences doit interroger[166]. Bien sûr elle accélère le processus, mais elle creuse également le fossé social qui sépare les justiciables de la justice institutionnelle[167]. C'est une tendance qu'il est difficile de mesurer, mais cette crise sanitaire semble également renforcer la place des modes alternatifs et en particulier de la médiation qui met la présence et la parole des parties au cœur du processus. Comme l'a souligné le CCBE, « chaque pays doit trouver le juste équilibre entre les audiences traditionnelles et les mémoires écrits. Afin d'atteindre cet objectif, une discussion approfondie entre tous les professionnels de la justice concernés est nécessaire ».[168]

165 Voy. not. le site https://remotecourts.org; S. Chiodo, "Ontario civil justice refo rm in the wake of COVID-19: Inspired or institutionalized?" (15 juillet 2020), Osgoode Legal Studies Research Paper, sous presse, et disponible sur SSRN: https://ssrn.com/abstract=3686181; « Safeguarding the right to a fair trial during the coronavirus pandemic: remote criminal justice proceedings », https://www.fa irtrials.org/sites/default/files/Safeguarding%20the%20right%20to%20a%20fair%20trial%20during%20the%20coronavirus%20pandemic%20remote%20criminal%20justice%20proceedings.pdf.

166 D. Freeman Engstrom & J. B. Gelbach, « Legal tech, civil procedure, and the future of adversarialism », *University of Pennsylvania Law Review*, 2021, https://papers.ssrn.com/abstract=3551589; C. Rule, "Online dispute resolution and the future of justice", *Annual Review of Law and Social Science*, 2020, 16:1, p. 277; M. Legg, The COVID-19 pandemic, the courts and online hearings: Maintaining open justice, procedural fairness and impartiality, *Federal Law Review*, UNSW Law Research No. 20–46, (2021), https://ssrn.com/abstract=3681165.

167 Voy. V. Denault & M. L. Patterson, Justice and nonverbal communication in a post-pandemic world: An evidence-based commentary and cautionary tatement for lawyers and judges », *Journal of Nonverbal Behavior*, 2020, 4, https://doi.org/10.1007/s10919-020-00339-x.

168 « Points de vigilance et propositions du CCBE dans le cadre de la phase de réactivation du système judiciaire à la lumière de la crise de COVID-19 », https://www.ccbe.eu.

The Repressive Response of States to COVID-19 or the Duty to Health of the Superlative Citizen. An Overview of Comparative Law

Silvia Allegrezza[1]

« Le rêve de perfection transforme nos États de droit en États policiers »
M. Delmas-Marty, Le Monde, 1st March 2021

A. *Introduction*

If we were to look for a label for the last twelve months, we could refer to the year of the sanitary empire, with the pangolin as mascot.[2] The pandemic of the Sars-COVID-19 virus (Covid) has demonstrated a real paradigm shift regarding the exercise of preventive and repressive power of states, becoming more and more a general policy of sanitation.[3] While this power is normally connected with the Foucauldian alternative 'faire mourir ou laisser vivre', the need to limit the spread of the virus has focused on the protection of life for life (like 'faire vivre ou rejeter dans la mort').[4] The bio-sanitary panopticon has thus prevailed over any individ-

---

1 This contribution uses data collected and analysis conducted by a team of researchers from the University of Luxembourg, composed by Silvia Allegrezza, Lisa Urban, Georgios Bouchagiar and Leonardo Romanò, 'Sanctioning breaches of emergency measures in time of COVID pandemic: a comparative study on the interplay of administrative and criminal sanctions'. The report is to be published in June 2021 in the framework of the project 'Protection against Infection through (European) regulatory law (ProLaw)', funded by the Fonds National de la Recherche and coordinated by Stefan Braum. Although China was not included in the study, see observations of Sun Yirong, 'From SARS to COVID-19: Balance of China's Criminal law system' (2020) 12 Tsinghua China L Rev 399.

2 Didier Truchet, Avant l'Etat d'urgence sanitaire : premières questions, premières réponses, RFDA, 2020, 597.

3 Sara Brimo et Benjamin Defoort, La police générale de la salubrité à l'épreuve de l'état d'urgence sanitaire : ou l'impossible disparition de la salubrité publique locale, RDSS, 2020, 5, 848 s.

4 Michel Foucault, La volonté de savoir, 1976, p. 181.

ual right or freedom by imposing control over population in its collective dimension and over individuals as human beings. The 'naked life', as Giorgio Agamben calls it, seems emphasised over life, the life that deserves to be lived.[5] We have learnt to 'live without'[6] going out, touching, eating, drinking or smoking, schools, theatres, cinemas, friends or family.[7] We have renounced even language: the proximity of human socialisation has become 'gathering', visits 'unauthorised outings' or travelling 'forbidden trips'. We are all part of the solution in a spirit of 'superlative citizenship' where duties are presented as manifestation of altruism and citizens no longer have rights, but rather duties to health.[8]

Like a true absolute monarchy of the old regime, the empire-state of the pandemic uses all its repressive arsenal. It is the triumph of the Thanatos-politics, governance based on fear, imminent peril and collective hibernation.[9] To this end, any sanctioning policy finds its place in this construction based on the state of emergency,[10] without its legitimacy ever

5 Giorgio Agamben, Homo Sacer, VI, L'uso dei corpi, Vicenza, 2014.

6 See essays in the collective work, coordinated by Peggy Larrieu, Vivre sans, Eres, 2020.

7 For a detailed discussion on national measures interfering with and limiting a wide array of individual rights and freedoms, see: Silvia Allegrezza, Lisa Urban, Georgios Bouchagiar and Leonardo Romanò, 'Sanctioning breaches of emergency measures in time of COVID pandemic: a comparative study on the interplay of administrative and criminal sanctions' (forthcoming), referring to, among others, limitations on movement, gathering, alcohol consumption or conducting business, as well as measures on minimum distance and mask-wearing (as detected in France, Germany, Italy, Luxembourg, Singapore, Spain and the UK).

8 Patrick Zylberman, Tempêtes microbiennes. Essai sur la politique de sécurité sanitaire dans le monde transatlantique, Gallimard, 2013. Many European states treated COVID-19 as a national health emergency and relied upon legislative measures, imposing various health-related duties on the very citizen. For such measures in France, Germany, Italy, Luxembourg, Singapore, Spain and the UK, see in more detail: Silvia Allegrezza, Lisa Urban, Georgios Bouchagiar and Leonardo Romanò, 'Sanctioning breaches of emergency measures in time of COVID pandemic: a comparative study on the interplay of administrative and criminal sanctions' (forthcoming).

9 Giorgio Agamben, A che punto siamo?, L'epidemia come politica, Quodlibet, 2020. Voir aussi Lakoff A., Collier S. J. (éd.) (2008), Biosecurity interventions: Global health and security in question, New York. Lakoff, A. (2015). Global health security and the pathogenic imaginary. Dreamscapes of modernity Chicago: University of Chicago Press.

10 S. Braum, Le droit pénal au temps du cholera, Revue pénale luxembourgeoise, 7/2021, p. 1 et seq.; Jörg Gerkrath, Constitutional engineering of State of exception regimes within the European Union, p. 45 et seq. (forthcoming); Basak Baglayan, COVID stress test for the rule of law: States of emergency under

being questioned.[11] We are, therefore, witnessing a veritable anthology of administrative sanctions enacted by special laws related to the pandemic. Criminal sanctions are, in turn, mobilised in the repressive strategy,[12] 'as occasionally happens when fear and anxiety rise'.[13] This strategy uses classic offences – of common law[14] – while introducing new offences, so that nothing escapes the strategy of zero tolerance.[15] Law is replaced by order and any deviation from order is punished.

Rather than isolated reactions at state level, the repressive strategy of the pandemic testifies to a model of globalisation, where the idea of borders takes on a new acuity: the globalisation imposed by the bio-health emergency no longer implies the retreat of nation-states, but rather exaltation through models of health security[16] that are poorly coordinated, yet ultimately converging in their ultimate goals. This blossoming of the

---

international human rights law; ProLaw p. 65 et seq. (forthcoming); see also: Le COVID-19 et le droit public, RFDA, 2020, 4, 597 s.

11 As we have argued elsewhere, some states decided to choose (urgent) legislative measures, instead of the Constitution-route. The taking of such measures may, to a certain extent, ensure respect for legality, legitimacy and necessity; this, in the sense that the measures at hand have a legal basis, pursue a legitimate goal and are necessary to fulfil a specific purpose. Yet, it may come as a surprise that, even where concrete constitutional provisions on emergencies existed, some states decided not to trigger them. For Germany, Spain, Singapore and France, see: Silvia Allegrezza, Lisa Urban, Georgios Bouchagiar and Leonardo Romanò, 'Sanctioning breaches of emergency measures in time of COVID pandemic: a comparative study on the interplay of administrative and criminal sanctions' (forthcoming).

12 «Le droit pénal, en tant que phénomène social, a été et est impliqué par la covid, à la fois en tant qu'outil de contrôle social et en tant que problème social à gérer», Carlo Sotis, Le droit pénal italien à l'épreuve de la Covid : un problème à gérer plus qu'un outil de gestion, Revue de science criminelle et de droit pénal comparé 2020/4 (N° 4), 1115–1122.

13 Carlo Sotis, Le droit pénal italien à l'épreuve de la covid : un probème à gérer plus qu'un outil de gestion, RSC, 2020, 1116.

14 Voir V. Covolo, Non-respect des mesures sanitaires et contamination à la COVID-19: Quelle responsabilité pénale de droit commun?, Revue pénale luxembourgeoise, 07/21, p. 16 et seq.

15 For a thorough analysis of the combination of criminal and administrative sanctioning, as well as the criminalisation of certain behaviours, see: Silvia Allegrezza, Lisa Urban, Georgios Bouchagiar and Leonardo Romanò, 'Sanctioning breaches of emergency measures in time of COVID pandemic: a comparative study on the interplay of administrative and criminal sanctions' (forthcoming).

16 'Another highly contagious virus', as defined by Cédric Ribeyre, La procédure pénale à l'épreuve de l'état d'urgence sanitaire, Droit pénal. N. 5, mai 2020, p. 6.

nation-state occurs whilst taking charge of a common/public good[17] – public health – and is organized around repressive state powers, which become the cog in a global strategy.

To control a health emergency that is precisely international in nature, states adopt global solutions through national declinations. However, the state character and the exaltation of borders of the nation-state become a strategy of total control, rather than a real response to the challenges – or even refusal – of globalisation.

As Patrick Zylberman puts it, the 'Tempêtes microbiennes' ('microbial storms') represent a method of crisis management. After years of economic crisis, the scars of which are still visible in several European countries, the health crisis has allowed the development and even acceleration of certain control strategies in which the individual is sacrificed in the name of the community, a superlative citizenship.[18] Strengthening individual participation in exceptional measures in the name of the common war against the virus thus becomes the key to any civic participation. If this spontaneous adherence is refused, repression unleashes all its power through a panoply of sanctions.

This article aims to dissect these normative reactions through the analysis of administrative and penal sanctions adopted in several European countries.[19] Only a deep understanding of the exceptionality of current conditions will help us return to the previous situation, to overcome the emergency without leaving any trace of its passage.

---

17 M. Delmas-Marty, intervention pendant la conférence, COVID-19, nos sociétés démasquées, France Culture, 17/02/2021, https://www.franceculture.fr/conferences/palais-de-la-decouverte-et-cite-des-sciences-et-de-lindustrie/covid-19-nos-societes-demasquees.

18 Patrick Zylberman, Tempêtes microbiennes. Essai sur la politique de sécurité sanitaire dans le monde transatlantique, Gallimard, 2013.

19 The Prolaw research analysed the laws of Luxembourg, France, Spain, Italy, Germany, the United Kingdom and Singapore. In order to avoid excessive references, we will limit our legislative indications to the laws of the Grand-Duché du Luxembourg (Loi du 17 juillet 2020 portant l'introduction d'une série de mesures de lutte contre la pandémie COVID-19 et modifiant: 1° la loi modifiée du 25 novembre 1975 concernant la délivrance au public des médicaments; 2° la loi modifiée du 11 avril 1983 portant réglementation de la mise sur le marché et de la publicité des médicaments). For detailed legislative references concerning other countries, see Allegrezza, Bouchagiar, Romanò, Urban, Sanctioning breaches of emergency measures in time of COVID pandemic: the interplay of administrative and criminal sanctions, ssrn...

The legacy of the control society risks being heavy. Enforcement structures by their nature tend to take root to ensure life after the end of the emergency.

Understanding coordinates of security policies can therefore help us refuse legacy of these measures so that they remain exceptional, avoid that certain structures of surveillance and sanctioning become a structural part of our societies.

B. *Time and space: variable coordinates of health risk and punitive strategy*

Citizenship in the superlative, 'where emphasis is placed on the duties and obligations of the citizen, as well as the need to show altruism',[20] requires that every citizen be compliant. Any deviation will be punished: this is the law of biosecurity.[21]

Within this security framework, states have developed a complex architecture of interactions between criminal and administrative law. Using data obtained in the context of a comparative law study conducted by the University of Luxembourg, this contribution aims to describe the parameters used by several European and non-European countries in their work to build a punitive arsenal dedicated to Covid. The analysis is based on legislation and, to the extent possible, jurisprudence of seven countries (Luxembourg, Germany, France, Spain, Italy, the United Kingdom and Singapore) and aims to detect convergences and differences of approaches in the punitive strategy.[22]

Any national policy for the management of a health crisis includes a range of legislative and regulatory acts aimed at reducing the spread of the virus by imposing limitations on citizens' freedoms. Containment, curfews, travel restrictions, social distancing, prohibition of public gatherings and wearing of masks are the components of this strategy to which

---

20 Patrick Zylberman, Tempêtes microbiennes. Essai sur la politique de sécurité sanitaire dans le monde transatlantique, Gallimard, 2013.

21 See, long before the Covid crisis, the contributions in the volume Biosecurity interventions: Global health and security in question, sous la direction de Andrew Lakoff et Stephen J. Collier, Columbia, 2008.

22 The interest in comparative studies in this area is demonstrated by the numerous academic initiatives in this field. In addition to the Luxembourg study, the conference of the University of Bordeaux on 27 May 2021 "COVID-19 Symposium: Constitutional, political, social and health threats and challenges in France and the United Kingdom" is noteworthy.

decision-makers have linked the possibility of punishment for violations.[23] These violations form the current ocean of administrative sanctions applicable to violations of pandemic-related restrictions.

The first finding of the comparative study is the predominance, in all systems considered, of administrative sanctions, in the form of fining, aimed at making prevention policies effective through the threat of penalty. This is a very familiar mechanism, which seems almost consolidated: the order-sanction binary is insoluble. Order without the threat of sanction is deemed ineffective.

Rather than describing the behaviour that is the subject of the offence and providing for the sanction as a consequence of the violation on a case-by-case basis, the majority of States resort to the formula 'any infringement on regulations/orders/laws will be punished'.[24] This legislative technique makes it possible to cover any situation that may in practice arise, but also grants public authorities broad discretion.[25]

The punitive response to Covid is based on three key variables: time, space and the individual. While the first two are general and **abstract criteria** linked to the coordinates of the health context, the factor linked to the specific characteristics of the individual in question indicates the tendency to assign to certain categories of citizens the role – forced – of mediators of public policies.

The institutional response may therefore vary according to the presence, or even absence, of one or more of these factors.

As for the temporal factor, these twelve months of pandemic have forced us to become familiar with the variability of the parameters of

---

23 For intelligible tables mapping, illustrating and comparing relevant breaches and the intensity of sanctioning in France, Germany, Italy, Luxembourg, Singapore, Spain and the UK, see: Silvia Allegrezza, Lisa Urban, Georgios Bouchagiar and Leonardo Romanò, 'Sanctioning breaches of emergency measures in time of COVID pandemic: a comparative study on the interplay of administrative and criminal sanctions' (forthcoming).

24 Notably, all countries (under examination) sanctioned certain conducts, regardless of the legislative technique followed in defining them. See, in more detail: Silvia Allegrezza, Lisa Urban, Georgios Bouchagiar and Leonardo Romanò, 'Sanctioning breaches of emergency measures in time of COVID pandemic: a comparative study on the interplay of administrative and criminal sanctions' (forthcoming).

25 Article 2 Loi du 17 juillet 2020 portant l'introduction d'une série de mesures de lutte contre la pandémie COVID-19. In November 2020, more than 2,000 fines for not wearing a mask were recorded, https://www.wort.lu/fr/luxembourg/plus-de-2-000-amendes-pour-non-port-du-masque-5fb8ec98de135b92361aacf6, edition of 21 November 2020.

freedom that condition our lives. The time of individual and collective, professional and cultural life is now dictated by the level of risk associated with the virus. Even the appreciation of the risk knows several variables: the rate of diffusion of Covid in a given population is only one of the items of information considered by public authorities, the potential mortality related to the virus being strongly influenced by the age and the capacities of reception of the patients in intensive therapy. Therefore, the typology, intensity and duration of the measures depend on the current level of risk and hence vary over time.

The time factor has even been valued as a method of reducing virus transmission in situations outside full containment. Through the imposition of curfew measures and a maximum number of guests from outside the household, governments have attempted to reduce contact in and out of home.

The temporal flexibility of the measures is part of the emergency logic that characterises all pandemic-related regulatory work. Dictated by the real need to limit the spread of the virus, it leaves the citizen with the duty to be constantly informed about the health situation and the rules in force, which can suddenly change.

The temporal criterion, therefore, determines the intensity of the measures to be applied to the whole national territory or only certain parts. Space, the second relevant factor, plays an essential role in determining the regulatory framework in force.

It is also the legitimate need to impose as few limitations as possible that has led to the fragmentation of the territory. Any measure then becomes geography-variable. Epidemiological mapping has therefore adopted several colours: from white to grey, from orange to red, to dark red, the latter dedicated to high-risk areas established by the European Centre for Disease Prevention and Control.

Complexity of mapping increases in those countries where structure is less centralised and the legislative power on health matters follows the geographical partition. Federal states (like Germany), but also states where regions enjoy health competencies (such as Spain) or the power to establish administrative sanctions, suffer from further fragmentation of emergency policies. Dictated by the need to better 'target' the criminal response, this fragmentation increases the discretion of local legislators and public authorities in charge of control and sanctioning.[26] In contrast to the uniformity of France or Luxembourg, a heated debate has arisen in Germany or Italy between the different *Länder* or *Regioni*, which sometimes refuse any centralised coordination.[27] If the existence of the offence depends on administrative decisions, depending on the level of risk in a certain region, province or municipality, the repressive mosaic subsequently becomes fragmented. The difficulty of knowing what measures are in force increases when moving from one region to another or from one city to another, without the rigidity of the system of administrative sanctions allowing for an adequate punitive response.

C. *The individual variable: targeted responses*

The parameters of time and space are often accompanied by the individual variable. This refers to certain personal characteristics, objective or subjective, on which the applicable rules and, consequently, the possible sanctions depend.

The consideration of these characteristics can be seen as forming integral part of the sanctions, since they are determined, first of all, by objective conditions specific to the agent. The above conditions include all the hypotheses related to the exercise of certain professions or commercial activities (magazines, cafés, restaurants, hotels and so forth).[28] Every legal tradition recognises the need for special rules related to working or trading conditions.[29] The individual parameter related to professional situations pre-exists any legislation on the health crisis and depends on authorisation

26 Observation shared even in relation to the Chinese system, see Sun Yirong, 'From SARS to COVID-19: Balance of China's criminal law system' (2020) 12 Tsinghua China L Rev 411.

27 Rosaria Sicurella, Sandra M. B. Picicituo, The legal framework of the COVID-19 pandemic: the Italian response to the coronavirus outbreak, 2021, p. 8. Ralf Poscher, Dr. Katrin Kappler, The Legal Framework of the COVID-19-Pandemic in Germany.

28 Article 2 Loi du 17 juillet 2020 portant l'introduction d'une série de mesures de lutte contre la pandémie COVID-19. Violations are punishable by an administrative fine of up to 4,000 euro (Article 11 Loi du 17 juillet 2020 portant l'introduction d'une série de mesures de lutte contre la pandémie COVID-19). On the criminalisation of offenses related to the Horeca and employers, see V. Covolo (supra).

29 All countries considered by the study introduced sanitary rules for employers and the Horeca.

procedures that are easily verifiable. In other words, the health crisis has not in itself created any changes or uncertainties in the application of rules related to the personal situation of the agent.

On the other hand, the subjective dimension of the individual variable raises serious problems in both the interpretation and application of the legal texts. This second aspect is linked to the subject's knowledge of his or her state of health; that is, awareness of his or her condition – actual or potential – as a carrier of the virus.[30] If we move on from the general rules mentioned above to specific measures of isolation, quarantine or self-monitoring, it is clear that awareness or suspicion of one's own positivity to the virus plays a central role. The dividing line between these two cases is quite clear: only a positive PCR test-result leads to the application of the isolation measure.[31]

This is a decisive passage in terms of law: if the measures of confinement, curfew, prohibition of assembly or unnecessary movement are of a general and abstract nature applicable to the entire population, any limitation that follows, on the biological level, the proven positivity to the Covid, implies a decision of isolation imposed by public authorities on the infected individual.

The person concerned will be forced into isolation; the 'contact cases' will be obliged to respect quarantine or, in less dangerous cases, to place themselves under self-surveillance. The specific conditions of isolation or quarantine in the different countries studied were very different at the beginning of the epidemic, but then became more similar as the epidemic progressed, to the point that the differences are now very limited (ranging from 7 to 10 days of isolation or quarantine). As for the conditions of 'release', in each country analysed the individual can be released after a certain period of time (varying from 30 to 15 or even 10 days after the end of the symptoms or the date of the positive test for asymptomatic cases). While at the beginning of the pandemic a negative test was required before being able to go out again, the progress of scientific research has made it possible to establish that the person is no longer contagious after a certain period of time -although the virus is still present.

30 For a discussion on *mens rea*, the cognitive and voluntary element of a given conduct and its criminalisation, see: Silvia Allegrezza, Lisa Urban, Georgios Bouchagiar and Leonardo Romanò, 'Sanctioning breaches of emergency measures in time of COVID pandemic: a comparative study on the interplay of administrative and criminal sanctions' (forthcoming).

31 Article 5, 7 et 8 Loi du 17 juillet 2020 portant l'introduction d'une série de mesures de lutte contre la pandémie COVID-19.

The intervention of public authorities implies the adoption of an ordinance that targets the specific person, as well as the members of his or her household, while imposing a duty to communicate.[32] The order is therefore an integral part of the procedure. No administrative sanction can follow the finding of contamination, without a specific decision being adopted by the administration. However, any violation of this measure leads to a penal sanction for non-compliance with an order issued by a public authority.[33] The real risk does not play any role: as it is a hypothesis of a pure and simple disobedience, the absence of any contamination does not exclude the infraction.

'Contact cases', meaning the individuals at risk due to their proximity to the contagious person, are also the object of a detailed quarantine order which indicates the modalities, the duration and the conditions in which the measure will end. This essential part of the strategy of prevention and control of the spread of the virus appears problematic, because it is based on indications provided for by the individuals tested positive. It is at this point that the repressive arsenal shows its muscular side in relation to the duties of cooperation incumbent on the citizen in preventing the spread of the virus. The duty to tell the truth implies reinforced accountability, the violation of which is punishable by quite serious penal sanctions: any omission or false declaration could then be considered as a forgery, a common law hypothesis foreseen in any national system.[34]

It must be noted that the effectiveness of the preventive measure depends on the declarations made by the positive individual and the truthfulness of his or her statements. The offences of forgery provided for in the penal code of all the countries under analysis ensure that citizens actively participate in the enforcement of crisis measures through their duty to declare, tell the truth.

---

32 As for Luxembourg, it is specified 'Il vaut noter qu'il n'y a aucune distinction entre les majeurs et les mineurs, les derniers étant soumis aux mêmes règles, et menaces de sanctions, que les adultes'.

33 In Luxembourg, it is a police penalty (fine of 500 to 1,000 euro according to Article 12 Loi du 17 juillet 2020 portant l'introduction d'une série de mesures de lutte contre la pandémie COVID-19).

34 For instance, misleading declaration in self-certification can be seen as 'faux en écriture' (in Luxembourg), be punished with imprisonment from one to six years (in Italy) or trigger the imposition of administrative fines (in the UK or Spain). See in more detail: Silvia Allegrezza, Lisa Urban, Georgios Bouchagiar and Leonardo Romanò, 'Sanctioning breaches of emergency measures in time of COVID pandemic: a comparative study on the interplay of administrative and criminal sanctions' (forthcoming). See also: V. Covolo (supra).

The responsible and supportive citizen thus becomes an agent of the state in this panopticon of the health crisis. The particular seriousness of these offences is due to the fact that the policy of fight against the coronavirus depends on the authenticity of the documents and the declarations of citizens. It is therefore not surprising that the Belgian College of Public Prosecutors has issued the directive that the public prosecutor's offices proceed to a direct summons before the criminal court on the charge of forgery and the use of forgery to underline the centrality of the duties of cooperation.[35]

D. The content of administrative sanctions

Let us now move on to the content of administrative sanctions provided for in the countries that were examined. Unsurprisingly, there is again an almost absolute convergence in terms of behaviours sanctioned; violation of the wearing of masks, the duty of isolation and quarantine, the prohibition of assembly or the curfew. The amount can, on the other hand, vary considerably from one country to another: while France, Luxembourg, the United Kingdom and Italy provide for fines that cannot exceed one thousand euro (or 960 pounds), Germany authorises financial penalties of up to 25,000 euro.[36]

Despite the shared spirit of seeking efficiency that prevails in health crisis management policies, it must nevertheless be recognised that the discretionary margin left to public authorities in determining the elements of the infringement and its gravity is remarkable.

Given the flexibility imposed by the two criteria of time and geography to better pursue the objective of countering transmission of the virus, this necessarily has a negative impact on sanctions that can be imposed. The emergency measures, constantly modified, require the citizen to be informed of the constant updating of the regulatory framework. The very structure of the administrative sanction imposes this burden on the individual.

This flexibility has also pernicious consequences for the principle of equality. Citizens are differentiated geographically and temporally: the

35 See para. 5.

36 Gesetz zur Verhütung und Bekämpfung von Infektionskrankheiten beim Menschen (Infektionsschutzgesetz – IfSG), 20 July 2000, BGBl. I S. 1045 ('IPA 2000'), Section 75 (1) No. 1 https://perma.cc/B27B-36HD.

same behaviour in one city or at a certain point of time during the day can either trigger sanctioning or be perfectly legal. The parameters of this differentiation are multiple: age, health preconditions, geographical location or time interval are factors that will have to be assessed when imposing the sanction.

The scientific uncertainty on the modalities of transmission of the disease, the distance to be kept or the days necessary for the contaminated person to cease being contagious is translated into legal uncertainty, the management of which falls to the agents of the administration. Proportionality changes its face: it is no longer supposed to concretise the seriousness of the offence, but rather to integrate the level of scientific risk linked to the propagation of the virus.

Although we may all agree upon the aims pursued by the emergency legislation related to the health crisis, the fact remains that it may provoke tensions, or even twist, with regard to the principles: of legality because of its unstable content; of equality because of the variable temporal and geographical coordinates; and of proportionality based on the importance played by the health risk instead of the seriousness of the infringement of the protected interest. If we add to this uncertainties related to jurisdictional control,[37] there are enough elements to demand that the exceptional character of the measures in question be respected and that they be lifted as soon as possible.

E. *The shifting boundaries between administrative repression and penal response*

The repressive arsenal, as we have said, is not limited to administrative sanctions.

The first common feature shared by the countries observed is plurality of the axes of intervention: every country has resorted to the administrative-criminal binary, creating a highly articulated stratification of the system of sanctions. The strategy is not at all novel, but rather consolidated at the global level. The proliferation of regulations and competent authorities to deal with the requirements to control financial actors, a direct conse-

37 F. Chaouche, S. Menetrey, Le système juridictionnel luxembourgeois face à la pandémie du COVID-19. Contribution à l'analyse du contrôle juridictionnel et de l'accès à la justice en temps de crise sanitaire, p. 87 et seq. Université du Luxembourg, 2021.

quence of the financial crisis, has implied a proportional multiplication of sanctions for non-compliance.

The dominant role of administrative sanctions should therefore come as no surprise: as in the field of banking or financial regulation, the citizen guilty of pandemic-related violations has nothing in common with the usual 'criminal' and the frequency of violations implies control by a range of public authorities. However, the symbolic value of criminal law and its stigmatising effect have not been abandoned. All countries considered confirmed the role of criminalisation as an integrative strategy of zero tolerance.

The integration between the two components – administrative and criminal – is in the majority of cases based on two factors: either the scale of intensity of the infringement of the protected interest or the subjective element of the agent's awareness of his or her positivity to the virus. What implies the passage from administrative sanction to criminal is, therefore, in the first case, the seriousness of the behaviour, a factor that is part of the material element; while, in the second, it lies in the conscious state of one's own contagiousness, which is likely to mark the passage from an administrative sanction to a criminal. We will analyse both cases in detail, describing the three main categories of criminal sanctions related to Covid. Modesty and caution are required, as a stable framework and satisfactory statistics are still missing on this subject.

The first category of 'criminal law of containment' consists of offences of pure disobedience, aimed at punishing the violation of administrative measures. The specificity is linked to the fact that these contraventions exalt the ethical and authoritarian approach, where the individual as a constitutional premise is replaced by the collective duties of a new necessary morality.[38]

They are defined by the technique of referral: the incriminating provisions do not themselves describe the behaviour that has been criminalised, but merely refer to the legislation that has been adopted to deal with the health emergency as to its content. This is the case in Luxembourg,[39] Italy[40] and France.[41] The consequence is an increasingly frequent phe-

38 Carlo Sotis, Le droit pénal italien à l'épreuve de la covid : un problème à gérer plus qu'un outil de gestion, RSC, 2020, 1116, citing Massimo Nobili, L'immoralità necessaria, Il Mulino, 2003.

39 Article 2 Loi du 17 juillet 2020 portant l'introduction d'une série de mesures de lutte contre la pandémie COVID-19.

40 Article 4 of the Italian Decree No. 19 of 25th March 2020.

41 Article 3136–1 Code de la santé publique.

nomenon resulting from the explosion of the regulatory system: the so-called 'blank penal law', where the legislator, especially during the state of emergency, limits itself to establishing sanctions for the violation of any regulatory norm, sometimes without even targeting them directly and precisely. The definition of prohibited conduct is, on the other hand, ultimately left to the regulatory power, which can quickly modify the administrative measures on which it depends without being concerned with the need to update criminal offences. Because of referral, adaptation of offences to administrative rules becomes automatic.

The second factor concerns the transmission, actual or potential, of the virus to other individuals. In this case, the essential elements to be considered are the harm to life or physical integrity caused by the Covid and the subject's awareness of his or her contagious state. The offences of attempted homicide or assault and battery are concerned. As these are common law crimes, this contribution does not intend to make a detailed analysis of the subject,[42] but will limit itself to sketching some comparative reflections.[43]

As Stefan Braum has pointed out in this review, the historical roots of criminal treatment of epidemics run deep. The most recent and perhaps most interesting example in terms of criminalisation is AIDS.[44] The stigmatisation of certain categories of people and their behaviours judged to be contrary to traditional morals has resorted to the criminal law as a concrete expression of this moral judgement. Notwithstanding a certain change in morals and the new antiretroviral treatments that have made the disease non-mortal, at least in developed countries, the criminalisation of AIDS transmission is still present and widespread throughout the world. A review of the legal arguments surrounding offences related to the AIDS

42 V. Covolo (supra).

43 For a more detailed discussion on applicable provisions of the Criminal Code, see: Silvia Allegrezza, Lisa Urban, Georgios Bouchagiar and Leonardo Romanò, 'Sanctioning breaches of emergency measures in time of COVID pandemic: a comparative study on the interplay of administrative and criminal sanctions' (forthcoming), referring to, among others: unintentional homicide or injury (articles 221–6, 121–3 and 222–19 of the French Criminal Code); reckless endangerment (article 223–1 of the French Criminal Code); failure to provide for assistance (article 223–6, al. 2 of the French Criminal Code); or intentional abstention (article 223–7 of the French Criminal Code).

44 For a global overview, Glob. Comm'n on HIV and the Law: Risks, Rights & Health, https://hivlawcommission.org/report/.

epidemic offers valuable insights into the ongoing international debate.[45] In particular, the UNAIDS[46] advocates for an ongoing assessment of actual disease risk and treatment options to better target potential criminalisation responses. This is an important factor in the context of Covid, given the extreme variability in the consequences that the virus can have on different individuals, depending in particular on the clinical and age conditions of citizens.

With regard to risk assessment, the recommendation is to place greater value on the actual risk, abandoning pure disobedience as a criterion of incrimination. However, this implies abandoning the health police and enhancing the role of experts, who alone can scientifically assess the existence of a concrete risk.[47]

As for the moral element, the proof of its existence is and remains fundamental, no presumption being acceptable in this field.

The ease of propagation, the absence of stigmatising behaviours that favour transmission and the different level of mortality are of course factors that distance Covid from AIDS. Nevertheless, it is important to follow international guidelines to limit the criminal response to the most serious cases. It is true that in reality only a minority of Covid-infected individuals are at life-risk. However, the inability to implement targeted prevention results in almost total limitations on personal freedoms, which greatly expands the scope of Covid-related offenses and makes them far more widespread. Never before had we seen such an abundance of rules whose transgression is criminally sanctioned. That is why it is essential to limit the punitive response to the most serious cases, whose gravity justifies such a sanction. For example, on 23 April 2021, a man was taken into custody by the Spanish police for infecting 22 people in the island of Ibiza. Despite significant symptoms indicating the presence of the virus, the 'supercontagiador', as labelled by the media, had always refused to

45 See in more detail Allegrezza, Bouchagiar, Romanò, Urban, Sanctioning breaches of emergency measures in time of COVID pandemic: a comparative study on the interplay of administrative and criminal sanctions (forthcoming).

46 UNAIDS, 'Ending overly broad criminalization of HIV non-disclosure, exposure and transmission: Critical scientific, medical and legal considerations' (Guidance note, 2013) 2 <https://www.unaids.org/sites/default/files/media_asset/20130530_Guidance_Ending_Criminalisation_0.pdf> accessed 4 March 2021.

47 Thomas Cassuto, Crise sanitaire du COVID-19, perspectives et enjeux d'une reponse pénale, AJ Pénal, 2020, Juillet/Août, 342 s.

be tested. The offence here is that of bodily harm.[48] This is the kind of situation that the criminal law should – it seems to us – limit itself to.

The third category of criminal offences occurs when the subject omits or falsifies statements made to public authorities about his or her state of health or the people with whom he or she has been in contact. As mentioned above, the hypotheses of falsification are called upon to protect the duty to truth that is incumbent on every citizen in the context of the health strategy. All systems examined in the comparative law study make use of these offences which are already present in their respective criminal codes. Any offence of forgery is in fact heavily punished, this being the historical heritage of these incriminations in the penal codes of the countries considered.[49] The penalties provided for, are therefore very severe and the opportunities for any citizen to commit a forgery of declaration or writing are quite frequent, since the sanitary rules often presuppose active participation of the individuals. Again, it is important that the penal response is limited to the most serious cases and not influenced by the frequency of false documents or declarations, which intensifies at specific times. Another recent example: in the week of 19 to 25 April 2021, 58 people were stopped at Brussels airport because they wanted to travel abroad with a false Covid-negative test certificate; the Hal-Vilvorde public prosecutor's office reported the following Tuesday. Most of these people had a permanent address in Belgium and all were offered a transaction of 750 euros. Those who do not pay will be brought to justice and face up to five years imprisonment and a fine of up to 2,000 euro.[50] General prevention is becoming increasingly important before vacations!

As for the relationship between administrative and criminal sanctions, the relationship between the first and the second category of offences focuses precisely on the increased intensity of the infringement of the protected interest – one goes from the risk of a major circulation of the virus to the risk of a real contamination. The third category of incriminations

---

48 Arrested after infecting 22 people while telling them: 'I'm going to infect you all', El Mundo, 24 April 2021, https://www.elmundo.es/baleares/2021/04/24/6083ea9d21efa0e60d8b45ed.html

49 François Bougard et Laurent Morelle, Prévention, appréciation et sanction du faux documentaire (VIe-XIIe siècle), dans Olivier Poncet (dir.), Juger le faux (Moyen Âge – Temps modernes), Études et rencontres, 19 s.

50 Creating fake COVID-19 documents can cost you (…) Créer de faux documents COVID-19 peut vous coûter cher, RTL.be|Actualisé: 27 avril 2021, https://5minutes.rtl.lu/actu/frontieres/a/1712573.html.

is rather linked, as we have recalled, to the seriousness of the offence of forgery.

This administrative and penal binary should therefore be articulated either as a scale (of public order disturbances and consequently of sanctions) of increasing intensity or present alternative responses. In any case, double punishment should be avoided in light of *non bis in idem*.

F. Conclusions

The comparative analysis reveals more convergences than differences among the states considered. The maturity of the different systems in terms of criminal/health law remains quite limited: the multiplication of punitive responses and their different channels suggests awareness (of public decision-makers) of the repressive weakness that underpins this zero-tolerance strategy. The examples cited show how the normative framework abandons the idea that a neutral behaviour, a pure and simple violation of an administrative measure, can be excusable and not subject to penal sanctioning. This is done at the cost of twisting the principles of equality, legality and proportionality. The state is once again exalted in its role as an actor of globalisation at the cost of a marginalised Europe.[51]

The pandemic has finally brought out the omnipresence of the problems of repressive law, overcriminalisation and lack of proportionality.[52] Let us just hope that the state of exception as a crucial argument will be respected even at the end of the pandemic, when we can finally forget and refuse its legacy. As the saying goes: 'this criminal law of crisis with its unpleasant characters, but faithfully reflecting an exceptional period, these confused provisions should disappear without regret'.[53]

---

51 See dossier "L'Union européenne face à la crise de COVID-19 » de la RTDEur, 2020, 3, 481 s.

52 Terry Skolnik, 'Criminal Law during (and after) COVID-19' (2020) 43 Man LJ 145, 146.

53 Philippe Conte, Le droit pénal de crise : l'exemple du virus COVID-19, Droit pénal, n. 5, Mai 2020, p. 5.

Part 2:
Models of Pandemic Regulation

Évaluation des Mesures juridiques de Gestion de la Pandémie de COVID-19 en France

Géraldine Bachoué, Maitena Poelemans

UPPA – CDRE

A. *L'État d'urgence sanitaire, un dispositif d'exception inédit en voie de normalisation?*

« *Nous sommes en guerre* ». Tels sont les mots employés par le Président de la République Emmanuel Macron lors de son allocution télévisée le 16 mars 2020. La crise majeure que traverse la France au plan sanitaire, sans précédent depuis un siècle, a fait apparaître la nécessité de développer les moyens à la disposition des autorités exécutives pour faire face à l'urgence, dans un cadre juridique lui-même renforcé et plus facilement adaptable aux circonstances, notamment locales. Le régime de l'état d'urgence sanitaire a donc été « inventé » spécialement pour faire face à la catastrophe sanitaire liée au COVID-19 et a trouvé sa légitimité dans l'état de « guerre ».

Il a pourtant semblé, dans un premier temps -début mars 2020-, que le régime d'exception qui régirait en France la crise sanitaire sans précédent dans le monde serait le régime d'exception en cas de menaces sanitaires graves institué par la loi du 9 août 2004[1]. Elle a introduit, dans la troisième partie du code de la santé publique, un titre III intitulé « Mesures sanitaires graves » et en vertu de l'article L. 3131–1 du code, « *en cas de menace sanitaire grave appelant des mesures d'urgence, notamment en cas de menace d'épidémie* », le ministre de la santé peut, par avis motivé, prescrire « *toute mesure proportionnée aux risques courus et appropriée aux circonstances de temps et de lieu* » en vue de protéger la santé de la population.

1 Loi n° 2004–806 du 9 août 2004 relative à la politique de santé publique, JORF n° 185 du 11 août 2004.

En plus de ce régime, trois autres régimes d'exception de gestion de crises sont déjà prévus en droit français :

- *l'état de siège*, régi par l'article 36 de la Constitution est un régime décrété en conseil des ministres en cas de péril national imminent, résultant d'une guerre ou d'une insurrection armée. Il permet de restreindre les libertés publiques et de confier des pouvoirs de police accrus aux autorités militaires. Si la France a connu ce régime à plusieurs reprises avant l'avènement de la Vème République (1848, 1870, 1914, 1939), l'article 36 de la Constitution n'a fait l'objet d'aucune mise en œuvre à ce jour.
- le régime de *reconnaissance de pouvoirs exceptionnels au Président de la République*, prévu à l'article 16 de la Constitution. Parmi les pouvoirs propres du Président, celui-ci détient en effet, dans certaines circonstances, des pouvoirs exceptionnels, appelés également « pouvoirs de crise », qui lui permettent de disposer de la plénitude des pouvoirs législatif et exécutif. Des conditions très strictes sont fixées pour l'application des pouvoirs de l'article 16[2]. Les pouvoirs exceptionnels du Président n'ont été utilisés qu'une seule fois, par le général De Gaulle, du 23 avril au 29 septembre 1961, à la suite du putsch des généraux en Algérie.
- *l'état d'urgence* qui trouve son origine, en France, dans la théorie dite « des circonstances exceptionnelles », qui a connu une première traduction législative en 1955, avec la loi n° 55-385 du 3 avril[3], maintes fois modifiée depuis. Depuis la promulgation de la loi de 1955, l'état d'urgence a été déclaré six fois, notamment lors des évènements aboutissant à l'indépendance de l'Algérie, ou encore en 2015, mais fortement modifié, suite aux attentats perpétrés sur le territoire français.

Mais face à la situation inédite, a été mis en place un dispositif lui-même inédit pour répondre à une "crise" et non pas une "menace" sanitaires : « **l'état d'urgence sanitaire** ». Ce nouveau régime est prévu par la loi d'urgence n°2020-290 du 23 mars 2020[4], adoptée en seulement cinq jours

---

2 D'une part, l'existence d'une menace grave et immédiate pesant sur les institutions de la République, l'indépendance de la Nation, l'intégrité du territoire ou l'exécution des engagements internationaux de la France, et, d'autre part, l'interruption du fonctionnement régulier des pouvoirs publics constitutionnels.

3 Loi n° 55-385 du 3 avril 1955 relative à l'état d'urgence, JORF n° 0085 du 7 avril 1955, p. 3479.

4 Loi n° 2020-290 du 23 mars 2020 d'urgence pour faire face à l'épidémie de COVID-19, JORF n°72 du 24 mars 2020, texte n° 2.

qui en définit également le régime juridique. Le Gouvernement, suivi par le législateur, souhaitait un régime d'application générale, susceptible d'être mis en place chaque fois que la France se trouverait confrontée à une catastrophe sanitaire répondant à la définition posée. La dimension générale des dispositions contenues dans le titre Ier de la loi[5] explique que le nouveau régime d'urgence sanitaire ait été immédiatement codifié au titre III du livre Ier de la troisième partie du code de la santé publique, désormais intitulé « *Menaces et crises sanitaires graves* ». Le chapitre Ier, préexistant, consacré aux « menaces sanitaires », est ainsi complété par un chapitre Ier bis dédié à ce nouvel « état d'urgence sanitaire » (art. L. 3131–12 et s.).

Il est à noter que le Parlement n'a pas suivi le Gouvernement sur une application générale, à titre définitif, refusant de pérenniser immédiatement un régime d'exception aussi restrictif sur le plan des libertés sans un débat législatif poussé, débarrassé des contraintes de l'urgence de la crise dans laquelle se trouvait la France au moment de l'adoption de la loi. Le risque est encore réel que soit pérennisée la possibilité de prendre des décisions extrêmes en cas de crises sanitaires d'une grave intensité, comme la principale mesure de lutte contre la propagation du virus, à savoir le confinement de la population, rendu désormais possible pour toute catastrophe sanitaire en vertu de l'article L. 3131- 15, 2° du code de la santé publique. Une telle mesure, d'une gravité évidente, a été présentée par le Gouvernement comme une nécessité scientifique : l'épidémiologie établissait qu'elle était la seule façon de prévenir la propagation du virus. Il s'avère, avec un peu de recul, qu'elle était surtout la seule façon de la prévenir pour un État incapable, faute de moyens, de recourir à une autre stratégie sanitaire, moins attentatoire à la liberté d'aller et venir qu'un confinement généralisé et ne comportant pas les effets économiques et sociaux désastreux de ce dernier. Dans ces conditions, donner une base juridique au confinement en l'érigeant en élément principal d'un régime général de la crise sanitaire reviendrait à normaliser un procédé d'action publique mis en place pour dissimuler les déficiences de la puissance publique.

À un régime d'exception adopté en prévision d'un temps de crise dans la précipitation et sous la pression des circonstances, le Parlement a préféré un régime d'exception expérimental, atténuant ainsi le caractère nocif du projet du Gouvernement. Les articles insérés dans le code de la santé

---

5 Le titre Ier consacre en effet un nouveau régime ayant pour vocation de faire face à toute « *catastrophe sanitaire mettant en péril, par sa nature et sa gravité, la santé de la population* », telle que l'épidémie de COVID-19.

publique ont donc été applicables dans un premier temps jusqu'au 1er avril 2021[6]. Puis ce délai a été prolongé à plusieurs reprises, la dernière prévoyant sa prolongation jusqu'au 31 juillet 2022, malgré les fortes réticences du Sénat lors des débats de la dernière loi adoptée le 10 novembre 2021[7] mais sous l'acquiescement bienveillant du Conseil Constitutionnel[8] selon lequel la prorogation de l'état d'urgence sanitaire prévue par cette nouvelle loi n'a « ni pour objet ni pour effet de déclarer l'état d'urgence sanitaire lui-même ou d'en proroger l'application » (§ 6), elle maintient "*uniquement*" jusqu'au 31 juillet 2022 le cadre juridique organisant l'état d'urgence sanitaire.

I. Un nouveau régime d'exception était-il vraiment nécessaire?

Il existait pourtant, d'autres possibilités juridiques, moins attentatoires aux libertés publiques, comme par exemple, l'engagement de la police administrative générale qui pouvait s'exercer en vue de garantir la salubrité publique, à laquelle la santé publique est étroitement liée, d'autant que, dans l'hypothèse de circonstances exceptionnelles, les prérogatives ordinaires de la police administrative peuvent être étendues[9]. De même, le régime des menaces sanitaires graves, instauré en 2004, pouvait fonder l'action gouvernementale dans la lutte contre l'épidémie. À ce titre, l'article L. 3131–1 du code de la santé publique a donné leur base juridique aux premières mesures prises par le ministre de la santé, à l'instar de son arrêté du 14 mars 2020 portant diverses mesures relatives à la lutte contre la propagation du virus[10], notamment des mesures d'interdiction

6 Art. 7 de la loi.

7 Loi n° 2021–1465 du 10 novembre 2021 portant diverses dispositions de vigilance sanitaire, JORF n°263 du 11 novembre 202.

8 Cl. Constit., décision n° 2021–828 DC du 9 novembre 2021.

9 Décret n° 2020–260 du 16 mars 2020 portant réglementation des déplacements dans le cadre de la lutte contre la propagation du virus COVID-19, JORF n° 0066 du 17 mars 2020, texte n° 2. Cette piste a d'ailleurs été explorée par le Gouvernement au moment d'adopter le décret n° 2020–260 du 16 mars 2020 portant réglementation des déplacements dans le cadre de la lutte contre la propagation du virus COVID- 19, pris par le Premier ministre sur le fondement de ses pouvoirs de police générale, à l'application desquels rien, aussi bien au niveau central que local, ne s'opposait d'un point de vue juridique.

10 Arrêté du 14 mars 2020 portant diverses mesures relatives à la lutte contre la propagation du virus COVID-19, JORF n° 0064 du 15 mars 2020, texte n° 16.

des rassemblements et de fermeture de certains établissements accueillant du public.

Pourtant, l'État français ne s'est pas contenté du droit d'exception existant. Ainsi, a- t-il convenu, avec le Parlement, de bâtir un cadre législatif à la mesure de ce type d'évènements, qui puisse offrir les outils nécessaires pour y répondre. Le nouveau dispositif d'état d'urgence sanitaire, s'inspire de l'état d'urgence « classique », mais il s'en distingue en premier lieu par ses motifs, tenant à une menace majeure pour la santé de la population, et en second lieu par son régime[11].

Dans ses grandes lignes, l'état d'urgence sanitaire qui résulte de la loi du 23 mars 2020 s'avère être un régime d'exception aggravé, en ce sens qu'il donne au Gouvernement des pouvoirs juridiques particulièrement exceptionnels. Le contexte dans lequel il a pris place l'explique : l'État français se trouvait avec des capacités d'action matérielles réduites au moment où il devait pourtant répondre à une épidémie d'une extrême gravité. Mais l'état d'urgence sanitaire est aussi un régime d'exception spécifique par rapport à l'état d'urgence « classique » : cette particularité est liée à la nature sanitaire de la crise, avec cette conséquence que les données scientifiques occupent un rôle décisif dans la mise en œuvre de ce régime et dans l'action publique qui en résulte. Il apparaît donc fondamental de trouver un équilibre entre ordre public et libertés, comme entre pouvoir politique et expertise scientifique.

Un problème demeure, néanmoins : il est possible de douter de la régularité constitutionnelle de l'état d'urgence sanitaire, en l'absence d'autorisation constitutionnelle explicite permettant l'adoption d'un tel régime… La Constitution du 4 octobre 1958 ne prévoit que deux régimes d'exception : les pouvoirs exceptionnels du chef de l'État (article 16) et l'état de siège (article 36). Il ne saurait en exister d'autres. Et il aura fallu une certaine complaisance du Conseil constitutionnel face à l'urgence pour admettre que ce silence constitutionnel sur l'état d'urgence puisse être interprété comme une autorisation pour le législateur de créer, de toutes pièces, un nouveau régime d'état d'urgence sanitaire. D'autant qu'il aurait pu juger que du point de vue du droit, il existait dans le Code de la santé publique un article adéquat, approprié à la situation et au but poursuivi.

Pourtant, c'est bien sur la base de la Constitution, et plus particulièrement du onzième alinéa du Préambule de la Constitution de 1946, selon lequel la Nation « garantit à tous … la protection de la santé » que le Conseil constitutionnel a reconnu un objectif de valeur constitutionnelle

---

11 Voir annexe 3.

de protection de la santé permettant, ou tout au moins "n'excluant" pas la possibilité pour le législateur de prévoir un régime d'état d'urgence sanitaire, tout en assurant "la conciliation entre cet objectif de valeur constitutionnelle et le respect des droits et libertés reconnus à tous ceux qui résident sur le territoire de la République"[12].

II. Mise en œuvre de l'état d'urgence sanitaire et relations entre les pouvoirs de l'État durant l'état d'urgence

1. Conditions de mise en œuvre

La déclaration de l'état d'urgence sanitaire est conditionnée, au fond, par sa nature sanitaire, dont la teneur est exprimée par l'article L. 3131–12 du code de la santé publique : « *catastrophe sanitaire mettant en péril, par sa nature et sa gravité, la santé de la population* ». La formule est générale, et non exempte de risques. Les débats parlementaires prouvent qu'il était particulièrement difficile de s'accorder sur une définition plus précise.

La déclaration de l'état d'urgence sanitaire est conditionnée, sur la forme, par l'adoption d'un décret en conseil des ministres (donc signé par le chef de l'État), à l'instar de l'état d'urgence, mais sur rapport du ministre de la santé et motivé par les données scientifiques disponibles sur la situation sanitaire, lesquelles doivent être rendues publiques. Cette dernière exigence constitue un compromis par rapport au souhait de bon nombre de parlementaires que l'état d'urgence sanitaire ne puisse être déclaré qu'après l'avis du comité de scientifiques prévu par l'article L. 3131–9 du code de la santé publique, ce qui s'est concrétisé dans les faits sur la mainmise sur le droit par les médecins.

2. Nature des mesures adoptées

Le régime d'état d'urgence sanitaire a autorisé le Gouvernement à imposer un cadre réglementaire *ad hoc* destiné, au prix d'une restriction d'un nombre important de libertés individuelles, à préserver la santé des personnes sur le territoire français. L'application de ce régime s'est accompagnée d'une modification d'ampleur de la législation par la voie d'ordonnances

12 Le juge constitutionnel l'a encore rappelé lors de l'examen de la dernière loi du 10 novembre 2021, cons.4 et 5.

(article 38 de la Constitution), c'est-à-dire de mesures adoptées par le Gouvernement, sur autorisation du Parlement, dans des matières qui relèvent normalement du domaine de la loi. Le recours aux ordonnances a été justifié par la nécessité de tirer les conséquences, dans les domaines administratifs, juridictionnels, économiques, sociaux et culturels, de l'impossibilité pour la France de fonctionner comme avant le confinement. Mais le nombre de ces textes a également fait l'objet de nombreuses critiques, écartant le Parlement du processus législatif.

Une fois déclaré, l'état d'urgence engendre une extension des pouvoirs de police administrative. Il habilite ainsi certaines autorités administratives à prendre des mesures de police administrative impliquant, pour certaines libertés, des restrictions qui auraient été illégales en temps ordinaire.

Le rôle principal est tenu, au plan national, par le Premier ministre et, au plan local, par le préfet. La nature sanitaire de l'état d'urgence aurait pu faire penser que ce rôle serait joué par le ministre de la santé et l'agence régionale de santé (ARS). Mais les restrictions de libertés posées au nom de la santé publique, élément de l'ordre public général, montrent qu'il s'agit avant tout de police, dont ont la charge, au niveau national, le chef du gouvernement et, au niveau local, l'autorité préfectorale avec le maire. La police de l'état d'urgence sanitaire est une police spéciale, dont l'exercice n'exclut pas celui de la police générale, y compris des maires, lesquels doivent pouvoir aggraver les mesures décidées au niveau national, proportionnellement à ce que les circonstances locales nécessitent. Ce cumul explique, par exemple, le couvre-feu institué au départ dans certaines communes avant d'être étendu à tout le territoire.

L'étendue des pouvoirs du Premier ministre a été particulièrement débattue au Parlement. Dans le projet de loi, l'habilitation qui lui était donnée précisait sa finalité : mettre fin à la catastrophe sanitaire. Elle précisait également les libertés susceptibles d'être retreintes, à savoir la liberté d'aller et venir, la liberté de se réunir, la liberté d'entreprendre. En revanche, elle n'établissait pas le contenu des mesures à prendre : était seulement évoquée « toute mesure générale réglementaire ». Le Parlement, qui ne pouvait se satisfaire d'un tel mandat, a procédé à une longue énumération de mesures d'objet précis, lesquelles n'ont fait que reprendre les types de mesures qui avaient été adoptés pour gérer la crise sanitaire.

Enfin, la compétence du ministre de la santé a été également réduite à l'adoption de mesures réglementaires relatives à l'organisation et au fonctionnement du système de santé, pour éviter toute interférence avec le Premier ministre. Le préfet, pour sa part, peut être habilité par le Premier ministre ou par le ministre de la santé à prendre des mesures d'application de leurs décisions ou à édicter de telles mesures à leur place dans un champ géographique qui n'excède pas celui du département (art. L. 3131-17 du code de la santé publique).

3. *Règles générales d'application des mesures*

L'ensemble des mesures administratives prises dans le cadre de la police spéciale de l'état d'urgence sanitaire, notamment le confinement, a été soumis à des règles générales posées par la loi du 23 mars. Le couvre-feu a, quant à lui, été promulgué par le décret du 17 octobre 2020. Comme toute restriction des libertés, l'adoption de mesures de police est subordonnée à l'existence d'une finalité légitime et à l'exigence de proportionnalité.

Mais quelles que soient les mesures, elles présentent des traits communs. D'une part, la finalité légitime est nécessairement d'ordre sanitaire. Mais les formulations utilisées sont diverses. Lorsque le code de la santé publique justifie les décisions du ministre de la santé et certaines de celles adoptées par le Premier ministre par la nécessité de « *mettre fin à la catastrophe sanitaire* », l'identité de motif avec celui ayant justifié la déclaration de l'état d'urgence sanitaire est évidente. En revanche, rien n'est moins sûr pour d'autres mesures, relevant du Premier ministre, pour lesquelles est utilisée une formule très générale (« *aux seules fins de garantir la santé publique* », art. L. 3131-15 du code de la santé publique) ou au contraire une finalité très spécifique (art. L. 3131-15, 8°). Des dérives pourraient en résulter, comme l'a jugé le Conseil d'Etat au sujet de l'autorisation de manifester dans l'arrêt du 15 janv. 2021, CGT et autres, req. n° 441265 en jugeant que « *si le Premier ministre peut, en vertu des pouvoirs qu'il tient du 6° du I de l'article L. 3131-15 du code de la santé publique, aux fins de garantir la santé publique, réglementer les rassemblements sur la voie publique ainsi que les réunions de toute nature et, le cas échéant, les interdire, il ne pouvait légalement, sans qu'une disposition législative lui ait donné compétence à cette fin, subordonner les manifestations sur la voie publique à un régime d'autorisation.* »

D'autre part, l'exigence de proportionnalité est énoncée par la loi en des termes (un peu trop) simples : la proportionnalité s'entend « *par rapport aux risques encourus* » et est envisagée « *strictement* ». En réalité, le juge est conduit à vérifier que la mesure est adaptée, nécessaire et proportionnée au sens strict, ce qui révèle une réalité plus complexe qu'il n'y paraît dans la loi. Celle-ci précise, en revanche, les dimensions spatiale et temporelle de l'exigence de proportionnalité : adaptation aux circonstances de temps et de lieu, obligation de mettre fin aux mesures prises sans délai quand elles ne sont plus nécessaires, et disparition automatique en même temps que prend fin l'état d'urgence sanitaire.

D'un point de vue procédural, la pratique de la gestion du COVID-19 a fortement inspiré la loi sur l'état d'urgence sanitaire en liant son élément déclencheur, à savoir la nature sanitaire de la catastrophe, à l'importance des données scientifiques dans la prise de décision. La déclaration de l'état d'urgence sanitaire impose la réunion d'un comité scientifique, dont les membres ont été nommés par des décrets. Si les avis de ce comité ne lient pas leurs destinataires sur un plan juridique, leur publicité sans délai pose sérieusement la question du degré réel d'autonomie du pouvoir politique à l'égard de l'analyse de ce comité sur l'état des connaissances scientifiques à un moment donné. Ainsi, le conseil scientifique COVID-19 avait donné un avis favorable le 8 janvier 2021 à la prorogation de l'état d'urgence sanitaire et du régime de sortie de l'état d'urgence sanitaire.

D'un point de vue du contrôle, enfin, la loi du 23 mars 2020 prend exemple sur la loi du 3 avril 1955 en rappelant que les mesures adoptées au titre de l'état d'urgence sanitaire peuvent faire l'objet d'un référé-suspension ou d'un référé-liberté devant le juge administratif. Ce contrôle juridictionnel est complété par un contrôle parlementaire, mais limité aux demandes « *d'informations complémentaires* ». Le Parlement n'en a pas moins pesé sur les prérogatives gouvernementales, en particulier, en conduisant un travail d'évaluation, d'autant plus important en période de crise qu'il s'agit de s'assurer du respect du principe de légalité. Ainsi, dès la fin du mois de mars 2020, la commission des lois du Sénat a créé en son sein une mission de contrôle et de suivi des mesures prises en application de la loi d'urgence, afin de s'assurer non seulement de la finalité, de la proportionnalité et de l'adéquation des mesures et des actions conduites par le Gouvernement dans le cadre du régime de l'état d'urgence sanitaire, mais également de la pertinence des modifications opérées par ordonnances sur le fondement des nombreuses habilitations conférées au pouvoir exécutif en application de cette même loi. Ces travaux ont donné lieu à la publication de deux importants rapports d'étape[13], en avril 2020, qui ont trouvé une traduction législative dans les lois n°2020–546 du 11

---

13 Sénat, Mission de suivi de la loi d'urgence pour faire face à l'épidémie de COVID-19-Rapport d'information au nom de la commission des lois constitutionnelles, de législation, du suffrage universel, du Règlement et d'administration générale sur les 10 premiers jours d'état d'urgence sanitaire : premiers constats – Analyse des décrets et ordonnances (justice, intérieur, collectivités territoriales, fonction publique, 8 juillet 2020; COVID-19 : deuxième rapport d'étape sur la mise en œuvre de l'état d'urgence sanitaire, 29 avril 2020

mai 2020 prorogeant l'état d'urgence sanitaire et n°2020-734 du 17 juin 2020 relative à diverses dispositions liées à la crise sanitaire, ou dans des mesures adoptées par le pouvoir réglementaire.

III. Accès à la justice pendant l'état d'urgence

1. L'accès au juge constitutionnel

Le Conseil constitutionnel a eu à se prononcer *a priori* sur la loi organique du 30 mars 2020[14], votée parallèlement à la loi sur l'état d'urgence sanitaire qui suspendait jusqu'au 30 juin le délai dans lequel le Conseil d'État ou la Cour de cassation doit se prononcer sur le renvoi d'une question prioritaire de constitutionnalité (QPC) au Conseil constitutionnel et celui dans lequel ce dernier doit statuer sur une telle question. Les conditions de vote de ce texte par le Parlement n'ont pas respecté l'article 46 de la Constitution, le projet de loi organique, adopté en conseil des ministres le 18 mars, ayant été voté au Sénat dès le lendemain, avant son approbation par les députés le 21 mars.

Dans la décision qu'il a rendu le 26 mars 2020[15], le Conseil constitutionnel n'y a vu aucun problème : « *Compte tenu des circonstances particulières de l'espèce, il n'y a pas lieu de juger que cette loi organique a été adoptée en violation des règles de procédure prévues à l'article 46 de la Constitution* ». En effectuant son contrôle constitutionnel *a priori*, pour l'ensemble des lois adoptées pour mettre en œuvre et poursuivre le régime d'état d'urgence sanitaire, le juge constitutionnel français a refusé de développer un contrôle approfondi, de vérifier véritablement le respect des principes de constitutionnalité, de nécessité et de proportionnalité. Il se limite à affirmer que les mesures remplissent les conditions requises car l'objectif de parvenir à la préservation de la santé publique est d'intérêt général

Sur le fond, le Conseil constitutionnel estime que l'article unique de cette loi organique ne soulève pas de difficulté majeure. Si aucun délai court n'est imposé pour l'examen des QPC, il « *n'interdit* [pas] *qu'il soit statué sur une question prioritaire de constitutionnalité durant cette période* ». Il faut ainsi comprendre entre les lignes que le Conseil constitutionnel

---

14 Loi organique n° 2020-365 du 30 mars 2020 d'urgence pour faire face à l'épidémie de COVID-19, JORF n° 0078 du 31 mars 2020, texte n° 2.

15 Cl. Constit., décision n° 2020-799 DC du 26 mars 2020, JORF n° 0078 du 31 mars 2020, texte n° 5.

s'estime compétent pour examiner en urgence les questions portant sur la constitutionnalité de telle ou telle disposition de la loi sur l'état d'urgence sanitaire, comme il a pu le faire pendant l'état d'urgence de la période 2015–2017. En revanche, il semblerait que les autres QPC doivent attendre. Une telle situation n'est certainement pas satisfaisante.

Il n'en demeure pas moins que, par le canal de la QPC, le Conseil a eu à se prononcer sur le calendrier des élections municipales, sur les infractions pénales réprimant les manquements aux règles de confinement, ou encore sur les règles spéciales de la détention provisoire prévues dans le cadre de l'état d'urgence sanitaire. Dans ce dernier cas, il a ainsi jugé inconstitutionnelles les dispositions qui prévoyaient la prolongation de toutes les détentions provisoires expirant lors d'un premier état d'urgence sanitaire sans intervention du juge, excluant néanmoins que les décisions de placement en détention provisoire puissent être contestées[16].

2. *L'accès au juge judiciaire*

Par une circulaire du 14 mars 2020[17], la Chancellerie a autorisé chaque juridiction, service ou établissement du ministère de la justice à mettre en œuvre un « plan de continuation d'activité » (PCA). Le 15 mars, la garde des sceaux a ordonné la fermeture au public de toutes les juridictions judiciaires, sous réserve du maintien d'un accueil téléphonique pour les urgences. Bien que non mentionnées dans cette annonce, les juridictions prud'homales, commerciales et administratives ont également appliqué cette fermeture. Chaque juridiction a donc déterminé, dans son PCA, la liste des contentieux « essentiels », sur la base d'un périmètre indicatif mais non exhaustif proposé par la Chancellerie.

Il en a résulté, dans un premier temps, une déconcentration de la prise de décision qui, quoiqu'acceptable dans son principe, a laissé les chefs de juridictions établir de façon solitaire les contentieux qui devaient impérativement être poursuivis, engendrant des problèmes d'interprétation de la notion de contentieux et une confusion entre les contentieux essentiels et les contentieux urgents.

16 Cl Constit., décision n° 2020–878/879 QPC du 29 janvier 2021.

17 Circulaire du 14 mars 2020 relative à l'adaptation de l'activité pénale et civile des juridictions aux mesures de prévention et de lutte contre la pandémie COVID-19, disponible sur : https://www.legifrance.gouv.fr/download/pdf/circ?id=44946.

La commission des lois au Sénat, déjà citée, soulève notamment l'ambiguïté relative au périmètre des activités devant se poursuivre pendant la crise. En effet, seuls les contentieux essentiels, pour lesquels un déplacement en juridiction pouvait être requis, ont vu leur traitement assuré, alors que l'instruction des autres dossiers était censée se poursuivre dans le cadre du télétravail, avec toutes les limites que celui-ci suppose compte tenu des manques en équipement informatique et des lacunes des systèmes d'information, qui ont souvent rendu le télétravail impossible, en particulier s'agissant des contentieux judiciaires civils, ce qui peut interroger sur le bon fonctionnement de la justice.

Enfin, sur le plan judiciaire, priorité a été donnée au traitement du contentieux pénal, au détriment du civil, qui représente pourtant un plus grand nombre d'affaires. Dans le même esprit, les chefs de juridiction ont été invités à annuler, dans la mesure du possible, les sessions d'assises et à renvoyer les procès dans les limites du délai raisonnable et du respect des délais de détention provisoire. Toutes les audiences des contentieux considérés comme non essentiels devaient ainsi être reportées.

La crise sanitaire se prolongeant, il était nécessaire de reconsidérer le choix fait dans l'urgence et qui va au-delà de ce que les règles sanitaires imposent. Aussi, dans un second temps, les dérogations procédurales établies par les ordonnances du 25 mars 2020 et du 18 novembre 2020[18] ont simplifié l'organisation du travail tout en permettant d'éviter au maximum la présence physique en juridiction, tant pour les justiciables et leurs avocats, que pour les magistrats et les agents de greffe : restriction, voire suppression, de la publicité des débats, organisation de vidéo-audiences, simplification des formalités... Ces dérogations temporaires n'ont pas posé de problème pour les contentieux de fond de nature civile ou commerciale, où la procédure est écrite et les parties sont représentées par des avocats. Il n'en est pas allé de même pour les contentieux mettant en cause les libertés individuelles, à savoir en matière pénale. C'est ainsi que le Conseil d'Etat a jugé que les dispositions autorisant le recours à la visioconférence, sans l'accord des parties, devant les juridictions pénales criminelles ou autres que criminelles, portent non seulement « *une atteinte grave et manifestement illégale aux droits de la défense* »[19] mais également violent le droit à un

18 Ordonnance n° 2020–1401 du 18 novembre 2020 portant adaptation des règles applicables aux juridictions de l'ordre judiciaire statuant en matière pénale, JORF 280 du 19 novembre 2020.

19 CE, ord.12 février 2021, req. n°448972; 4 août 2021, n°447916, 448388, 448962, JORF du 12 août 2021, texte 73. Le Conseil d'Etat avait suspendu la possibilité de

procès équitable garanti par l'article 6 de la CESDH ce qui ne peut être justifié dans le contexte de la lutte contre l'épidémie de COVID-19[20].

3. *L'accès au juge administratif*

Au niveau procédural, depuis le 20 novembre 2020, et jusqu'à la fin de l'état d'urgence sanitaire, l'ordonnance n°2020–1402 du 18 novembre 2020 et le décret n°2020–1406 du 18 novembre 2020 prévoient que les juridictions administratives peuvent modifier les règles de procédure applicables aux affaires qu'elles traitent, pour leur permettre de poursuivre leur activité pendant l'état d'urgence sanitaire. Il est ainsi possible pour les juridictions de communiquer par tout moyen avec les parties, d'assurer le déroulement de l'audience via un moyen de télécommunication audiovisuelle ou par voie électronique, pour les juges de participer à l'audience à distance, de recourir à la procédure sans audience en référé ou à la procédure sans audience dans certains cas pour le contentieux du droit au logement opposable, de dispenser de lecture des décisions rendues en urgence dans le contentieux de l'éloignement des étrangers…

Sur le fond, compte tenu de la répartition des compétences juridictionnelles, le juge administratif a été en première ligne, notamment dans le cadre de procédures de référé-liberté ou de référé-suspension, pour l'exercice du contrôle de la légalité des mesures prises au titre de l'état d'urgence sanitaire. La première phase de l'état d'urgence sanitaire s'est caractérisée par une certaine sécurité juridique. Les recours formés contre les mesures prescrites par les pouvoirs publics, au niveau national comme au niveau local, n'ont en effet donné lieu qu'à peu d'annulations, et ce alors même que certaines d'entre elles portaient une atteinte forte aux libertés publiques comme individuelles. Ainsi, au niveau national, aucun des recours formés devant le Conseil d'État contre les mesures prescrites par le Gouvernement n'a abouti. Seuls deux arrêtés préfectoraux ont été suspendus pendant la phase de confinement, sur un total de vingt recours.

La période de déconfinement a soulevé, en revanche, des enjeux plus importants en termes de libertés publiques. Dans un contexte se caractérisant par une amélioration progressive de la situation sanitaire, plusieurs mesures restrictives de libertés imposées à la population ont

recourir à la visioconférence dans un premier temps aux assises uniquement, CE, ord.réf., 27 nov.2020, n°446712.

20 CE, ord., 5 mars 2021, n. 440037.

été jugées illégales par le Conseil d'État, en raison de leur caractère non nécessaire et non proportionné. Tel a tout d'abord été le cas de l'interdiction générale et absolue de réunion dans les lieux de culte (ordonnances du 18 mai 2020). Tel est le cas également de l'interdiction générale et absolue des manifestations sur la voie publique. Par un raisonnement similaire au premier, le Conseil d'État a en effet suspendu cette interdiction, tout en reconnaissant la complexité de faire respecter les gestes barrières dans le cadre des rassemblements sur la voie publique (ordonnance du 13 juin 2020). Avec le deuxième confinement fin octobre 2020, la règle générale du premier confinement a été remplacée par des restrictions plus nuancées : fermeture de certains commerces plutôt que d'autres, couvre-feux différenciés selon les régions…Le Conseil d'État a ainsi été amené à se prononcer sur la cohérence des mesures.

Désormais, le juge doit opérer dans un contexte évolutif, notamment marqué par l'accès progressif des populations à la vaccination et des disparités de contamination par régions et reconnaît par exemple que le maintien du couvre-feu ne porte pas une atteinte manifestement illégale aux droits et libertés des personnes rétablies après avoir contracté le COVID-19 ou ayant bénéficié de la vaccination (ordonnance du 9 mai 2021).

Durant une année -du 17 mars 2020 au 17 mars 2021- le Conseil d'État a jugé 647 recours déposés par des citoyens, associations ou organisations professionnelles qui contestaient la gestion de la pandémie par le gouvernement sur des sujets aussi variés que la fermeture des discothèques, le déroulement des épreuves d'examen, les autorisations d'entrée sur le territoire pour se marier dans le cadre de mariages binationaux... Dans 51 affaires, il a suspendu des mesures du Gouvernement ou de collectivités territoriales et/ou leur a ordonné de modifier leurs pratiques. Dans plus de 200 affaires, des avancées ont été obtenues lors des audiences, l'État a été rappelé à ses devoirs ou les mesures contestées ont été modifiées par l'administration avant la décision du juge. Mais de l'opinion majoritaire, le Conseil d'Etat a très souvent justifié les mesures prises par le Gouvernement dans le cadre de la pandémie.

En conclusion, l'insuffisance du contrôle des parlementaires a conduit le Conseil d'Etat et, dans une moindre mesure le Conseil Constitutionnel, à être saisis de manière continue par les citoyens pour apprécier les limites de l'état d'urgence sanitaire. Ces deux instances, qualifiées en temps normal de juridictions d'exception, se sont révélées des juges du quotidien en temps de crise sanitaire.

Enfin, les dispositions de l'article 8 de la Loi n°2021–689 du 31 mai 2021 relative à la gestion de la sortie de crise sanitaire organisent les conditions récentes d'accès à la justice en France dans l'optique d'une sortie de crise sanitaire et seront applicables certainement jusqu'au 31 juillet 2022. Elles se concentrent principalement sur la possibilité de restreindre les conditions d'accès aux juridictions et sur la tenue d'audiences « à distance » avec l'accord des parties devant les juridictions pénales au risque de mettre la justice judiciaire « sous cloche ».

En conclusion sur les contrôles institutionnels, l'ensemble des juridictions supérieures en France, qu'il s'agisse de la Cour de cassation, du Conseil d'État ou du Conseil constitutionnel se sont organisées, durant la période d'application de la loi sur l'état d'urgence sanitaire, pour ne plus traiter que les questions urgentes de libertés publiques ou de libertés individuelles. Une telle position de leur part est toutefois particulièrement critiquable dès lors qu'elle crée un précédent autorisant à déroger à la Constitution en fonction de circonstances exceptionnelles. Le Conseil constitutionnel s'est ainsi défendu d'une telle brèche dans l'État de droit en la justifiant par une appréciation au regard de la situation d'espèce. La crainte vient toutefois de ce que les contrôleurs aient pu lâcher prise.

IV. Stratégies pour prolonger et mettre fin à l'état d'urgence sanitaire

L'heure n'est pas encore à la disparition du virus ni à celle de l'état d'exception instauré en France. En dépit de l'échec de la tentative du Gouvernement d'instaurer un régime pérenne de gestion des urgences sanitaires, force est de constater que nous nous trouvons actuellement dans une situation qui y ressemble fort, due à la succession des lois ayant pour objet la prolongation du régime transitoire de sortie de l'état d'urgence sanitaire. Certes, la terminologie varie, en passant d'une loi portant sur la « gestion de la crise sanitaire » ou encore sur la « vigilance sanitaire », mais elles ont bien toutes vocation à faire perdurer un état dans lequel peuvent être prises des mesures limitatives des libertés individuelles et collectives à tout moment, ou tout au moins lorsque la situation sanitaire l'exige. La dernière loi en date du 10 novembre 2021 prorogeant les régimes de gestion de la crise sanitaire jusqu'au 31 juillet 2022 n'en est que la dernière illustration.

B. Une preference coercitive au nom de la protection de la santé

Depuis l'annonce par le Président de la République le 16 mars 2020 de l'instauration de l'état d'urgence sanitaire jusqu'à maintenant (30 décembre

2021), les mesures prises dans le but de réduire les contaminations ont été des plus diverses et variées. Si l'effort a été fait de « coller » le plus possible à l'évolution de la situation, il n'en demeure pas moins qu'elles ont été des plus attentatoires aux libertés individuelles. Une première liste de mesures figure de manière exhaustive aux articles 3131–15 à 3131–17 du code de la santé publique. D'autres, comme l'obligation du passe sanitaire, sont issues des différentes lois adoptées ultérieurement.

Leur degré de restriction a bien sûr varié au fur et à mesure de la recrudescence ou de l'affaiblissement du taux de contamination. Il s'agit principalement de : mesures de confinement, avec l'interdiction de tout déplacement de personne hors de son domicile à l'exception de quelques déplacements strictement indispensables, limitativement énumérés; couvre-feu; port du masque obligatoire dans les villes et/ou dans les lieux fermés; obligation de passe sanitaire dans les lieux publics; fermeture provisoire de nombreux établissements recevant du public, dont les restaurants, salles de spectacles, musées, établissements d'enseignements, magasins de vente et centre commerciaux, sauf dérogations; interdiction des rassemblements, réunions ou activités mettant en présence plusieurs personnes (le nombre a été sans cesse modifié) en milieu clos ou ouvert; mise en quarantaine, placement et maintien en isolement des personnes affectées; prolongation de plein droit des délais de détention provisoire; contrôle des prix sur certains produits, comme les gels hydroalcooliques dont le prix de vente est plafonné…

D'autres mesures, accessoires aux interdictions ou restrictions dues au confinement, ont été prises dont celles qui ont été les plus médiatisées concernent certaines mesures restreignant les droits et libertés en matière de procédure pénale prévues dans l'ordonnance du 25 mars 2020 modifiant la procédure pénale[21] et qui prévoit l'utilisation de la visioconférence sans accord des parties devant les juridictions pénales et la prolongation de plein droit des détentions provisoires, toutes deux dans le contexte d'urgence sanitaire.

---

21 Ordonnance n° 2020–303 du 25 mars 2020 portant adaptation de règles de procédure pénale sur le fondement de la loi n° 2020–290 du 23 mars 2020 d'urgence pour faire face à l'épidémie de COVID-19, JORF n°0074 du 26 mars 2020.

I. La réponse pénale et administrative aux violations des mesures adoptées

La répression, à la fois pénale et administrative, s'est concentrée dans le cas de la violation des mesures prévues aux articles L.3131 – 15 à L.3131 – 17 du code de la santé publique dans le cadre de l'état d'urgence sanitaire et celles prises par le ministre de la santé dans le cadre du pouvoir de police qu'il tient de l'art L.3131 – 1 dudit code. Ce qui veut dire que la répression a été étendue aux mesures prises dans le cadre de ce pouvoir de police spéciale et que ces dispositions, prises dans le cadre de législations d'exception, resteront dans le droit commun.

Concentrées dans un premier temps sur les violations des mesures de confinement, et en particulier les déplacements injustifiés, les peines mises en place par la loi du 23 mars 2020 sanctionnaient la première violation par une contravention de 4ème classe -135 euros- et sa réitération, dans un délai inférieur de 15 jours, d'une contravention de 5ème classe-1500 euros à 3000 euros en cas de récidive. Le fait de commettre au moins quatre violations en moins de 3 jours est constitutif d'un délit, puni d'une peine de 6 mois d'emprisonnement et de 3 750 euros d'amende. Le non-respect du port du masque, lorsque ce dernier est obligatoire, est sanctionné par une contravention de 135 euros et en cas de récidive dans les 15 jours, le montant de l'amende passe à 1500 euros. Les personnes morales ne sont pas exemptées puisqu'elles peuvent se voir infliger cinq fois le montant de l'amende prévue pour les personnes physiques. Évidemment, ce sont ces personnes qui se verront infliger des sanctions administratives comme la fermeture d'établissements recevant du public ainsi que des lieux de réunions. Le pouvoir de sanction relève du Préfet.

La loi du 10 novembre 2021 a inséré deux nouvelles infractions réprimant le recours frauduleux au passe. La première punit d'une amende de 4ème classe le fait de transmettre à un tiers un passe sanitaire authentique en vue de son utilisation frauduleuse; la seconde sanctionne par 5 ans d'emprisonnement et 75 000 euros le fait de fabriquer, utiliser, se procurer ou proposer de procurer un faux passe sanitaire. Il est à noter qu'avant le dernier avis du Conseil d'Etat du 7 octobre 2021, le projet de loi souhaitait que cette dernière sanction s'applique indifféremment aux deux types d'infraction, ce qu'il a qualifié de « manifestement disproportionné » dans le premier cas. Le Conseil Constitutionnel dans sa décision du 5 août 2021 avait déjà jugé inconstitutionnelle la disposition incluse dans le projet de loi de la même date qui prévoyait des sanctions pénales en cas de violation de l'interdiction de sortir de chez soi de la personne positive à un test Covid.

II. Des coups de canif portés aux principes de légalité et de proportionnalité

Le mécanisme de gradation des peines pénales ne ressemble à aucun régime connu dans le droit pénal français, même si les techniques permettant de prévoir ou d'aggraver les peines au fur et à mesure des manquements sont connues du droit pénal. C'est le cas, notamment, du mécanisme de la récidive légale selon lequel il ne peut y avoir récidive que si le premier manquement constaté ou « verbalisé » (selon les termes du texte d'incrimination) n'a pas été condamné définitivement. C'est d'ailleurs pourquoi le régime de la récidive ne s'applique pas aux contraventions dont la répression passe par la procédure de l'amende forfaitaire. Le paiement d'une amende forfaitaire n'équivaut pas à une condamnation et ne constitue pas une décision de justice. En effet, selon l'art. 529 du code de procédure pénale, « *l'action publique est éteinte par le paiement d'une amende forfaitaire* ». Et même si c'était le cas, en matière d'amendes forfaitaires, le contrevenant dispose au minimum de 45 jours pour payer l'amende ou la contester, délai doublé pour la contestation (90 jours) dans le cadre de la crise sanitaire. Enfin, le Code pénal ne prévoit le régime de la récidive qu'à partir des contraventions de la 5ème classe, excluant celles de 4ème classe. Nous pouvons par conséquent conclure qu'il s'agit d'un vrai régime d'exception.

La question de la conformité avec le **principe de la légalité des délits** peut également être posée tant les dispositions du texte d'incrimination de l'article L3136–1 du code de la santé publique manquent à la fois de précision puisqu'il ne fait que renvoyer aux violations des mesures prises en application des art. L3131–15 à 3131–17 du code de la santé publique qui, eux-mêmes, renvoient aux mesures prises par le 1er ministre et les préfets. Or le décret est lui-même imprécis avec des notions de « déplacements professionnels insusceptibles d'être différés », « d'achats de première nécessité », « motif familial impérieux ». Ce qui a amené le Conseil d'État à demander au Gouvernement d'apporter des précisions à ses mesures[22]. Enfin, l'aggravation de la peine est fonction de nouvelles « constatations » ou « verbalisations », notions pouvant conduire à punir une seule et même sortie pouvant être constatée ou verbalisée plusieurs fois par la contravention de la 5ème classe, voire par le délit.

Il est également légitime de s'interroger sur la conformité du régime de sanction mis en place dans le cadre de l'état d'urgence sanitaire avec **la présomption d'innocence.** En effet, de nouvelles constatations ou verbal-

22 CE, 22 mars 2020, Syndicat jeunes médecins, n°439674.

isations peuvent conduire à la contravention de 5ème classe ou au délit alors même qu'il n'est pas établi que les précédentes aient véritablement révélé le manquement proscrit. Le paiement de l'amende forfaitaire éteint les poursuites et le paiement lui-même, qui ne vaut pas reconnaissance de l'infraction, peut intervenir dans les 90 jours, soit au-delà des délais de 15 ou 30 jours prévus pour aggraver la peine en cas de nouveau manquement. Certes, le Conseil constitutionnel peut admettre des régimes de présomption de culpabilité mais les conditions ne sont pas réunies. Il faut notamment que la présomption ne revête pas un caractère irréfragable[23] et en matière de délit, que la culpabilité ne résulte pas de la seule imputabilité matérielle d'actes sanctionnés[24]. C'est pourtant le cas ici : la seule verbalisation ou constatation de l'infraction suffit à exposer à sanction et la culpabilité résulte de la seule imputabilité matérielle de ces constats ou verbalisations.

En règle générale, des difficultés pratiques sont rapidement apparues essentiellement au sujet de la verbalisation lors des déplacements des personnes. A titre d'exemple, du fait des différentes versions du décret du 23 mars 2020 ayant modifié les motifs de dérogation de sortie, la question peut se poser de la légalité d'une contravention pour un jogging à 800 m avant que le motif « faire du sport à moins de 1 km » ait été rajouté dans l'attestation de déplacement nécessaire. La question de la **rétroactivité** peut se poser dans ce cas. De même, le mécanisme d'aggravation pour récidive qui ne s'applique qu'à compter de l'entrée en vigueur du décret, soit le 24 mars 2020, pose la question de son application dans le temps lorsqu'une première verbalisation a eu lieu avant cette date.

Le Défenseur des Droits[25] a également alerté, au moment de l'adoption de la loi prorogeant l'état d'urgence sanitaire du 11 mai 2020, sur l'extension des catégories de personnes habilitées à constater les violations des restrictions imposées sur le fondement de l'État d'urgence sanitaire à des agents de toute nature, dont certains ne sont pas assermentés. Cela exige de mentionner les garanties qui entoureront les modalités de mise en œuvre de ces contrôles et leur conséquence. Ce point est d'autant plus

23 Cl. Constit., décision n°99–411 DC du 16 juin 1999, JORF n°140 du 19 juin 1999, cons. 5 et 6.

24 Cl. Constit., décision n°2011–164 QPC du 16 septembre 2011, JORF n°216 du 17 septembre 2011, texte n° 75, cons. 3 et 7.

25 Défenseur des droits, Lettre adressée ce jour aux Présidents du Sénat et de l'Assemblée nationale ainsi qu'aux présidents des commissions des lois des deux assemblées, Paris, le 2 mai 2020.

préoccupant qu'il serait définitivement inscrit dans le code de la santé publique, et non pour une durée liée à l'état d'urgence sanitaire.

Il est à noter enfin, que peuvent désormais verbaliser les infractions aux mesures de l'état d'urgence sanitaire notamment les réservistes, les adjoints de sécurité, et lorsque la contravention a lieu dans des transports publics, les agents assermentés des services de transport, comme ceux de la SNCF et de la RATP (métros et bus parisiens).

En vertu des termes de la loi, « *les mesures prescrites en application du présent article (art. L3131–15 code de la santé publique) sont strictement proportionnées aux risques sanitaires encourus et appropriées aux circonstances de temps et de lieu.* »

La question de la **proportionnalité** a été tranchée par le Conseil constitutionnel mais seulement à propos de la peine de 6 mois d'emprisonnement encourue au bout de la 4ème violation en moins de 30 jours où il a déclaré qu'en raison de la situation sanitaire, les peines n'étaient pas disproportionnées [26]. Certains auteurs ont critiqué un « relâchement du contrôle de proportionnalité »[27] en condamnant à une peine de prison pour avoir omis de sortir plusieurs fois avec son attestation ou de l'avoir renseignée, semble potentiellement démesurée.

Le deuxième rapport d'étape du Sénat sur le COVID-19[28] fait état d'un sentiment d'une appréciation parfois hétérogène, en particulier au cours des premières semaines de confinement, des comportements autorisés et de ceux qui ne le sont pas. C'est ainsi, par exemple, qu'auraient été verbalisées des personnes ne disposant pas d'un ticket de caisse à la sortie d'un supermarché, n'ayant acheté que des aliments jugés non essentiels par l'argent verbalisateur ou encore s'étant rendues à un supermarché situé à 5 km, qui n'était pas le plus proche du domicile, alors même qu'aucune règle n'interdit explicitement ces comportements.

L'imprécision du cadre réglementaire aurait rendu difficile pour les forces de l'ordre de « *procéder à une analyse critique au cas par cas des motifs allégués par les personnes contrôlées* », D'ailleurs les différentes fiches et autres directives adressées aux agents ne fournissaient que peu d'éléments

---

26 Notamment Cl. Constit., décision n°2020–846/847/848 QPC du 26 juin 2020, JORF n°0158 du 27 juin 2020, texte n° 80.

27 Vincent Sizaire, « Savoir entretenir le flou juridique », À propos de la décision du Conseil constitutionnel n° 2020–846/847/848 QPC du 26 juin 2020, *La Revue des droits de l'homme* [Online], Actualités Droits-Libertés.

28 Sénat, COVID-19 : deuxième rapport d'étape sur la mise en œuvre de l'état d'urgence sanitaire, rapport d'information n° 608, 8 juillet 2020.

pour les assister dans l'interprétation du cadre réglementaire, en particulier relatif aux déplacements dérogatoires autorisés.

Enfin, le bilan au second confinement en France (à compter du 30 octobre 2020) reste mitigé et les verbalisations « abusives » font les gros titres dans les journaux. L'imprécision des termes de l'article 3 du décret du 23 mars 2020 concernant les restrictions d'aller et venir liées au confinement explique que les forces de l'ordre disposaient d'une grande marge d'appréciation menant à des interprétations contraires au principe d'interprétation stricte de la loi pénale.

III. *Responsabilité pénale pour intention et négligence en cas de violation des mesures de confinement*

Pendant l'état d'urgence sanitaire, et en particulier le déconfinement, les maires et les employeurs, chargés de mettre en œuvre des mesures décidées par l'État, craignaient de voir leur responsabilité pénale engagée en cas d'infection de leurs administrés ou salariés au COVID-19 (notamment les enfants dans le cadre de la réouverture des écoles). A l'initiative du Parlement, le régime instauré par la loi du 10 juillet 2000, dite loi Fauchon, sur les délits non intentionnels est précisé. Un nouvel article L.3136 – 2 dans le code de la santé publique prévoit dorénavant, qu'en cas de poursuites, la responsabilité posée à l'article 121–3 du Code pénal s'apprécie "*en tenant compte des compétences, du pouvoir et des moyens dont disposait l'auteur des faits dans la situation de crise ayant justifié l'état d'urgence sanitaire, ainsi que de la nature de ses missions ou de ses fonctions, notamment en tant qu'autorité locale ou employeur*". Dans sa décision du 11 mai 2020, le Conseil constitutionnel a jugé ces dispositions conformes à la Constitution[29]. Cependant on peut s'interroger sur la légistique, notamment l'émiettement de la rédaction législative par l'effet d'un renvoi du code de la santé publique dans le contexte critiqué d'inflation des normes. Il constitue une consécration apparente de la jurisprudence mais laisse néanmoins planer un doute sur sa portée exacte dans le temps, notamment sur son caractère éventuellement plus favorable.

Parce que dans le cas de contamination du COVID-19 il est fortement improbable que le grief qui pourrait être reproché au dirigeant d'entreprise soit la cause directe du dommage subi par le salarié par exemple, la

---

29 Cl. Constit., décision n° 2020–800 DC du 11 mai 2020, JORF n° 0116 du 12 mai 2020, texte n° 2.

responsabilité dudit dirigeant ne pourra être engagée que s'il est démontré qu'il a commis une faute qualifiée, soit délibérée soit caractérisée. Il sera possible de reprocher aux chefs d'entreprise l'insuffisance de prise des mesures de prévention pour réduire le risque de contamination, mais il sera, en revanche, difficile de démontrer l'existence d'un lien de causalité entre les actes et les omissions qui leur seront reprochées et la contamination de leurs salariés tant les possibilités pour le salarié de contracter le virus à l'extérieur de son lieu de travail sont multiples. Seule la situation du « cluster » dont l'origine serait l'entreprise pourrait engager la responsabilité de cette dernière. Il s'agira alors de démontrer que l'employeur n'a pas accompli les diligences normales, à savoir la mise en place de mesures de protection des salariés.

Les modalités d'engagement de la responsabilité pénale des dirigeants en cas d'infraction non intentionnelle ne sont pas modifiées en tant que telles par l'article L 3136–2 code de la santé publique, résultant de la loi n°2020–546 du 11 mai 2020. Ce texte prévoit néanmoins une atténuation en soulignant qu'il doit être tenu compte de la situation de crise sanitaire et invite les juridictions pénales à vérifier pour engager la responsabilité du chef d'entreprise : les « pouvoirs », la « compétence » et « l'autorité « de ce dernier comme cela est déjà indiqué à l'article 121–3 du code pénal; la nature de ses « missions » et « fonctions ».

L'article 223–1 du code pénal réprimant le risque causé à autrui n'a pas semblé applicable à la situation difficile à reconnaître.

IV. Application du droit pénal et des infractions de droit commun pour faire respecter les mesures de confinement

Les restrictions apportées notamment à la liberté d'aller et venir, de réunion ou de commercer engendrent des réactions de résistance passives ou plus hostiles de la part de certaines personnes, notamment sur la voie publique. Les contrôles destinés à veiller au respect de ces différentes restrictions s'avèrent indispensables mais peuvent, néanmoins, susciter une réaction d'opposition de la part des personnes qui en font l'objet. Plusieurs infractions pourront alors s'appliquer :

- L'infraction d'outrage, de rébellion, voire de violences commises au préjudice des forces de sécurité intérieure. L'infraction de rébellion peut ainsi être retenue pour sanctionner la résistance violente à l'exécution d'office, par la force publique, des mesures prescrites dans le cadre de l'état d'urgence sanitaire.

- De la même manière, le confinement à domicile peut être de nature à aggraver les risques de violences conjugales ou sur les mineurs au sein de cellules familiales fragiles.
- Enfin, a été constatée l'émergence d'infractions commises par volonté de tirer profit de la situation de crise. Les vols avec effraction, notamment dans les pharmacies, hôpitaux, cabinets médicaux en vue de dérober masques ou gels hydro-alcooliques mais aussi les faits d'escroquerie liés à ces mêmes produits doivent donc appeler une réponse pénale déjà prévue dans le droit commun. Les reventes desdits produits pourront recevoir la qualification de recel des infractions précitées, éventuellement de travail dissimulé par dissimulation d'activité ou encore de pratique commerciale trompeuse ou de tromperie, notamment dans l'hypothèse de masques dont l'origine aurait été frauduleusement modifiée, ou de masques périmés.

Concernant l'employeur ayant exposé un salarié au risque de contamination, avec survenance d'une incapacité temporaire de travail (ITT), le ministère public peut ouvrir une enquête préliminaire pour atteinte involontaire à la vie ou à l'intégrité d'un salarié. L'infraction sera constituée si le salarié a contracté le Covid sur son lieu de travail en raison de mesures de protection inadaptées, comme l'absence de mesures d'hygiène et distanciation sociale. En cas de décès, la qualification d'homicide involontaire pourra être retenue.

Si on reprend le cas de la « mise en danger d'autrui », celle-ci peut être punie d'un an d'emprisonnement et de 15 000 € d'amende.

Le code du travail réprime également les atteintes à la santé et à la sécurité des travailleurs. Un document unique d'évaluation des risques (DUER) doit être régulièrement mis à jour, spécifiquement dans le cadre de la protection contre le Covid. À défaut, une amende de 1 500€ pour une personne physique et de 7 500€ pour l'entreprise pourra être infligée.

C. Une gouvernance éclatée de la prévention et du contrôle

I. La multiplication des autorités sanitaires pour contrôler les pandémies

Bien que la France soit déjà dotée d'un arsenal de dispositifs de toute nature pour gérer des crises, y compris sanitaires, on assiste, à partir du mois de mars 2020, à la constitution d'un nouvel ensemble de structures, d'organisations qui viennent s'ajouter aux organisations existantes, parfois même en en supplantant certaines. Très centralisée, à partir logiquement du ministère des Solidarités et de la santé dont relève de nombreux établissements de santé placés sous sa tutelle Santé publique France (SPF), la Conférence nationale de santé (CNS), l'Agence Nationale de santé (ANS), la structuration de la chaîne des autorités de santé compétentes lors de la crise sanitaire s'est également déclinée vers les structures décentralisées, et notamment les agences régionales de santé (ARS) sont amenées à travailler en lien étroit avec les préfectures. Parmi toutes les instances citées, les ARS sont celles qui sont le plus en prise avec le terrain.

Deux nouveaux organes ont été mis en place pour apporter une expertise *ad hoc* face à cette crise en particulier, afin d'éclairer la décision publique. Il s'agit pour l'essentiel des :

- **Conseil scientifique COVID-19** installé le 11 mars 2020 par le gouvernement. Il est chargé d'apporter par des avis publiés des éclairages sur *la décision publique dans la gestion de la situation sanitaire liée au coronavirus.* Le gouvernement s'est fortement appuyé sur ses avis pendant les premiers mois de la crise sanitaire en France. Mais les relations se sont distendues par la suite;
- **Comité analyse, recherche et expertise** (**Care**) créé le 24 mars 2020, pour faire face spécifiquement à la crise sanitaire provoquée par l'épidémie de COVID-19. Il est présenté comme plus *"opérationnel"* que le Conseil scientifique. Il réunit douze chercheurs et médecins. Son rôle est de "conseiller le gouvernement pour ce qui concerne les programmes et la doctrine relatifs aux traitements, aux tests et aux pratiques de 'backtracking' qui permettent d'identifier les personnes en contact avec celles infectées par le virus du COVID-19". Concrètement, cette instance conseille notamment le gouvernement sur les traitements et les tests. Il est à noter que la CNCDH (Commission Nationale Consultative des Droits de l'Homme) s'est inquiétée du manque de transparence sur les conditions de nomination des membres de ces deux autorités sanitaires ad hoc et sur les modalités de leur fonctionnement.

Les autorités sanitaires « historiques » ont été également sollicitées dans la gestion de la crise épidémique.

- **la Haute Autorité de santé** (**HAS**) créée par la loi du 13 août 2004, est une autorité publique indépendante, financée par une dotation unique de l'Assurance-maladie. Elle intervient dans trois domaines : elle certifie des établissements de santé, évalue des produits de santé en donnant des recommandations sur les médicaments qui doivent être remboursés ou non (comme elle l'a fait récemment pour certains types de tests pour le COVID-19); elle partage des recommandations concernant les pratiques professionnelles; elle intervient dans l'organisation des soins et de la santé publique.

- **Le Haut Conseil de la santé publique** (**HCSP**) est présenté comme une « *instance d'expertise indépendante* », créée par la loi du 9 août 2004 relative à la politique de santé publique et mis en place en 2007. Il a pour mission de "contribuer à l'élaboration, au suivi annuel et à l'évaluation pluriannuelle de la stratégie nationale de santé". La HAS s'occupe des pratiques. Le HCSP des aspects de politiques sanitaires.

Enfin, 2 organes purement consultatifs, aux avis non contraignants ont également pesé dans les décisions gouvernementales : l'Académie nationale de médecine et l'Institut Pasteur fondé en 1887

Il apparaît donc bien que la France a mis en place un aéropage d'organismes et d'autorités dans la gestion de la crise, au risque d'aboutir à une répartition des responsabilités et un manque de transparence quant aux décisions prises.

II. Une succession de systèmes de traitements de données

5 dispositifs d'information ont été essentiellement mis en place pour la gestion de la crise et pour lutter contre la propagation du virus, aux côtés du Health Data Hub, ou Système national des données de santé (SNDS), base nationale des données de santé qui contient l'ensemble des données de santé des Français. :

- dans un premier temps, la loi du 11 mai 2020 de prorogation de l'état d'urgence sanitaire a autorisé la création temporaire de deux fichiers nationaux :
- « **SI-DEP** », Système d'informations de dépistage qui permet la centralisation des résultats des tests réalisés par les laboratoires et certains professionnels habilités. Les données enregistrées concernent l'identification de la personne ayant fait l'objet d'un examen de biologie médicale de dépistage du COVID-19; des informations portant sur la situation du patient nécessaires pour la réalisation des enquêtes sanitaires; des coordonnées du patient; des données d'identification et coordonnées des médecins : numéro RPPS, nom, prénom, adresse du lieu d'exercice et adresse de messagerie sécurisée etc.
- « **CONTACT COVID** », SI de traçage des cas contacts et des chaînes de contamination. Les données renseignées sont les suivantes : nom, numéro de sécurité sociale, adresse, téléphone, symptômes, test de dépistage, lieu de travail, établissements (maison de retraite, crèche,

école, prison) et individus fréquentés dans les deux semaines précédant le diagnostic. Pour la mise en quarantaine, le cadre général applicable à ces mesures (suivi médical, information régulière des personnes, conditions d'hébergement...) doit être défini par décret du Premier ministre, après avis du comité de scientifiques, « en fonction de la nature et des modes de propagation » du virus. Les mesures individuelles sont prononcées par le préfet, sur proposition du directeur général de l'agence régionale de santé (ARS), au vu d'un certificat médical. Sur demande du préfet, les entreprises de transports lui communiquent les données relatives aux passagers entrants.

Les fichiers temporaires SI-DEP et CONTACT COVID mis en service par décret du 12 mai 2020 ont permis une certaine centralisation. Ces traitements de données à caractère personnel sont encadrés par un décret en Conseil d'Etat du 12 mai 2020 qui précise leurs modalités de création et de mise en œuvre. Certains dysfonctionnements de la part d'une ARS concernant la durée de conservation des données ont été constatés par la CNIL.

A l'instar de l'état d'urgence sanitaire, ces deux systèmes à vocation provisoire tardent à disparaître. La loi de novembre 2021 reporte, en effet, au 31 juillet 2022 l'échéance jusqu'à laquelle peuvent être mise en œuvre, « dans des conditions conduisant à déroger au secret médical », ces traitements de données à caractère personnel dédiés à la lutte contre la propagation de l 'épidémie du COVID-19.

- puis à côté de ces fichiers a été déployée l'application mobile « **TOUSANTICOVID** », dont le traitement est encadré par le décret n°2020–650 du 29 mai 2020 modifié. Cette application de suivi de contacts mise à disposition par le Gouvernement est basée sur le volontariat des personnes. Elle permet d'alerter les utilisateurs d'un risque de contamination lorsqu'ils ont été à proximité d'un autre utilisateur diagnostiqué ou dépisté positif au Covid. Depuis avril 2021 l'application a permis le déploiement d'un carnet numérique qui permet de stocker, de manière électronique les certificats de résultats de test de dépistage, les certificats de vaccination et les « passes sanitaires ».

L'utilisation de ces fichiers déroge aux règles de protection des données. Par exception à la règle de destruction des données trois mois après leur collecte, la possibilité de conserver certaines données sous forme pseudonymisée et aux seules fins de surveillance épidémiologique et de recherche sur le virus se trouve sans cesse prolongée. Elle prévoit également un élargissement du champ des professionnels chargés de renseigner les informations collectées dans les systèmes d'information et d'y intégrer « le professionnel de santé sur une liste prévue par décret et habilités à la réalisation des examens de dépistage virologique ou sérologique ou sous la responsabilité de ces professionnel ». Mais certaines données ont été au fur et à mesure des lois rajoutées à la liste des données devant être supprimées : les coordonnées de contact téléphonique et électronique, nom et prénoms des personnes, numéro d'inscription au répertoire national d'identification des personnes physiques et adresse.

- Le fichier « **VACCIN COVID** » doit permettre le déroulement et le suivi de la campagne de vaccination contre le coronavirus SARS-CoV-2. Son traitement est encadré par le décret n° 2020–1690 du 25 décembre 2020 et il permet à tout professionnel de santé habilité à vacciner de rechercher une personne via son numéro de sécurité sociale et d'accéder aux données et au statut vaccinal de cette personne. La Commission nationale Informatique et Libertés (CNIL) a alerté sur le fait que toute consultation illégitime peut entraîner des sanctions. Elle a également constaté que les données de traitement de ce fichier font bien l'objet d'un chiffrement et que l'accès au téléservice requiert une authentification forte.

Enfin, le fichier **Quarantaine et Isolement**, mis en œuvre conjointement par le ministre de la santé et le ministre de l'Intérieur vise à assurer le suivi et le respect des mesures individuelles lors de l'arrivée en France de personnes en provenance d'un pays confronté à une circulation particulièrement active de l'épidémie. La CNIL s'est interrogée sur la proportionnalité du dispositif dont le déploiement n'a été prévu que dans deux aéroports ce qui ne permet pas d'atteindre les objectifs fixés au départ.

III. Les droits des malades et la protection de leurs données par le contrôle de la CNIL

Le maître mot est la pseudonymisation[30] qu'il s'agisse des données collectées dans le cadre du **SI-DEP**, ou du **Système d'information « Contact Covid »** mais l'ensemble des données seront conservées par Santé Publique France désormais jusqu'au 31 juillet 2022. Quant aux données pseudonymisées du **Système d'information « Vaccin Covid »**, elles seront

30 Cette technique permet de remplacer une donnée par une autre.

conservées pendant 10 ans et sont traitées pour le suivi de la couverture vaccinale et à la mesure de l'efficacité vaccinale.

A travers une procédure de contrôle continue, la CNIL vérifie la conformité des traitements de ces fichiers avec le Règlement général de protection des données (RGPD). Dans sa dernière délibération, datant du 27 mai 2021, la CNIL a constaté que ces dispositifs sont, pour l'essentiel, respectueux des données personnelles et en conformité avec la législation. Des défaillances persistent cependant dans la prise en compte de certaines exigences du RGPD. Et l'autorité de contrôle demande au Gouvernement de produire des éléments pour évaluer pleinement l'efficacité de ces fichiers.

Conformément au RGPD et à la loi n° 78-du 6 janvier 1978 relative à l'informatique, aux fichiers et aux libertés (loi informatique et libertés) et dans les conditions prévues par ces mêmes textes, les malades disposent d'un droit d'accès, de rectification des données les concernant (art. 48 et s. LIL). Ils peuvent également, selon les dispositions de l'article 56 de la LIL, demander la limitation du traitement de leurs données et s'opposer, pour des raisons tenant à leur situation particulière, au traitement des données les concernant. L'exercice de ces droits s'effectue en adressant un courrier au délégué à la protection des données de l'ARS (Autorité Régionale de la Santé).

Les malades disposent également d'un droit d'introduire une réclamation auprès de la Commission nationale de l'informatique et des libertés (CNIL), s'ils considèrent que le traitement de données à caractère personnel les concernant constitue une violation du RGPD et de la loi informatique et libertés.

De manière générale, la CNIL assure un contrôle continu des conditions de mise en œuvre des traitements de données des fichiers SI-DEP, Contact Covid, de l'application mobile TousAntiCovid, Vaccin COVID, conformément à la loi du 11 mai 2020 prorogeant l'état d'urgence sanitaire. La CNIL rend ainsi, en la matière, un avis trimestriel adressé au Parlement.

Dans ses différents avis, la CNIL relève que tous les projets du Gouvernement comportaient des garanties, lesquelles ont été complétées pour tenir compte des recommandations de la CNIL. Les points de vérification portent notamment sur les modalités de recueil de consentement et d'information des personnes, la sécurité des systèmes d'information, les flux de données et les destinataires, ainsi que sur le respect des droits d'accès ou d'opposition des personnes. Ces constatations peuvent conduire, en cas de manquement graves ou répétés, à l'adoption de mesures correctrices, telles que des mises en demeure et/ou des sanctions. Elles permettent également d'alimenter l'avis de la CNIL destiné à compléter le rapport adressé tous les trois mois par le Gouvernement au Parlement concernant la mise en œuvre des systèmes d'information développés pour lutter contre la propagation de l'épidémie (article 11 de la loi n° 2020- 546 du 11 mai 2020 prorogeant l'état d'urgence sanitaire).

Pour l'essentiel, la CNIL constate que les dispositifs mis en place dans le cadre de la crise sanitaire (fichiers SI-DEP et Contact Covid, application TousAntiCovid) sont respectueux des données personnelles et que la plupart des préconisations qu'elle-même a formulées dans ses avis ont été prises en compte. Pour que les organismes responsables de mauvaises pratiques cessent leurs comportements défaillants, la CNIL n'a pas hésité à leur adresser une demande directe de mise en conformité dans les meilleurs délais. Elle demande en particulier que des indicateurs soient mis en place afin d'évaluer plus précisément la contribution de ces dispositifs à la gestion de la crise sanitaire.

Parallèlement, l'article 11 de la loi n° 2020–546 du 11 mai 2020 prorogeant l'état d'urgence sanitaire a instauré un Comité de contrôle et de liaison COVID-19 chargé d'associer la société civile et le Parlement aux opérations de lutte contre la propagation de l'épidémie par suivi des contacts, ainsi qu'au déploiement des systèmes d'information prévus à cet effet[31]. Ce comité est chargé, par des audits réguliers, d'évaluer, grâce aux retours d'expérience des équipes sanitaires de terrain, l'apport réel des outils numériques à leur action, et de déterminer s'ils sont, ou pas, de nature à faire une différence significative dans le traitement de l'épidémie. Il est également chargé de vérifier, tout au long de ces opérations, le respect des garanties entourant le secret médical et la protection des données personnelles.

IV. Contrôle et surveillance numériques des mesures de confinement

Dans le contexte de déconfinement suite à l'épidémie de COVID-19, de nouveaux dispositifs de caméras vidéo dites « intelligentes » ont été déployés, notamment dans l'espace public ou dans des lieux ouverts au public. En pratique, il s'agit soit de l'ajout d'une couche logicielle à des systèmes de vidéo protection préexistants, soit du déploiement de dispositifs de prise de température automatique (caméras thermiques), de détec-

31 Décret n° 2020–572 du 15 mai 2020 relatif au Comité de contrôle et de liaison COVID-19, JORF n°0120 du 16 mai 2020, texte n° 6.

tion du port de masque, de respect des mesures de distanciation sociale, etc.

Le déploiement des caméras « intelligentes » s'est accéléré avec la pandémie de COVID-19. La Régie des transports parisiens (RATP) en a installé à la station Châtelet pour quantifier le nombre de voyageurs porteurs de masque. La ville de Cannes utilise un dispositif similaire dans trois de ses marchés. De son côté, l'aéroport de Roissy- Charles de Gaulle s'est doté de 12 caméras thermiques installées à l'arrivée des vols internationaux pour détecter les passagers fiévreux. Autre méthode, l'opérateur Orange a fourni aux autorités sanitaires, et à des chercheurs, des données anonymisées pour étudier les déplacements de la population, et aider à mieux modéliser la réalité de la pandémie et du confinement en France.

Dans un document publié le 17 juin 2020, la CNIL a toutefois affirmé que les caméras « intelligentes », c'est-à-dire capables de prendre la température ou de détecter le port du masque, ne respectaient pas le cadre légal applicable à la protection des données personnelles.

Dans le même sens, le Conseil d'État, saisi par la Ligue des droits de l'Homme, a ordonné, le 26 juin, 2020 à la commune de Lisses, dans l'Essonne, de cesser l'usage des caméras thermiques déployées dans les écoles dans le cadre du COVID-19. Il a estimé que la collectivité porte une atteinte disproportionnée à la vie privée des élèves et du personnel, qui comprend le droit à la protection des données et la liberté d'aller et venir. Sans doute le problème vient-il du fait que, plus qu'un contrôle numérique des mesures de confinement, les mesures numériques portent sur l'évolution de la pandémie et le pistage des personnes malades.

D. Evaluation de la gestion de la crise sanitaire

Nous précisons, à titre liminaire, que nous ne ferons pas d'évaluation sur la gestion purement médicale de la crise sanitaire.

La création par la loi du 23 mars 2020 d'un régime d'état d'urgence *ad hoc* appelé

« état d'urgence sanitaire » pour faire face à l'épidémie peut interpeller tant il existait d'autres régimes d'exception, sans doute, moins attentatoires aux libertés publiques. Même s'il a eu comme modèle le régime d'état d'urgence de la loi du 3 avril 1955, maintes fois utilisé, il n'en demeure pas moins qu'il a permis, par simple décret pris par le Premier Ministre, de procéder au confinement du pays entier. Ce régime d'exception aggravé pose un questionnement quant à sa conformité avec la Constitution du 4 octobre 1958 qui ne le prévoit pas, même si le Conseil constitutionnel a fait preuve d'une certaine complaisance quant à la possibilité d'en créer un nouveau de toutes pièces. Très critiqué par les juristes, il n'en reste pas moins le régime étendu au 1er juin 2021, puis remplacé par un régime transitoire jusqu'au 31 décembre 2021 dans un premier temps, puis jusqu'au 31 juillet 2022. Cette **normalisation des régimes d'urgence** se pose avec d'autant plus de questionnement en France que le régime d'urgence sanitaire fait suite à l'état d'urgence terrorisme mis en place entre 2015 et 2017.

L'état d'urgence sanitaire a instauré des mesures souvent répressives dont les mesures les plus marquantes, sont le déplacement avec attestation sanctionné, dans certains cas arbitrairement et de manière disproportionnée par des sanctions pénales, la fermeture des lieux publics et la détermination du caractère « essentiel » ou « non essentiel » des commerces mais également du contentieux. Concernant les sanctions, si elles sont constituées pour l'essentiel d'amendes, elles peuvent dans les cas les plus extrêmes être converties en peine d'emprisonnement de 6 mois au risque de porter atteinte au principe de proportionnalité. L'extension des catégories de personnes habilitées à constater les violations des restrictions, à certaines non assermentées peut également interroger.

Le processus décisionnel peut être qualifié de « mille-feuille » mettant en évidence une certaine discordance. Celle-ci a caractérisé tout d'abord l'action politique priorisant une prise de décision d'abord centralisée, puis territorialisée car faisant appel aux préfets ainsi qu'aux maires, pour après être re-centralisée. La confusion a également marqué les relations inter ministérielles, certaines conférences de presse se faisant parfois autour de 4 ministres. Mais la discordance peut également qualifier le processus décisionnel au niveau médical ou sanitaire, la création de nouvelles autorités sanitaires venant se juxtaposer à celles déjà existantes ne faisant qu'aggraver le flou quant à la répartition des responsabilités et la prise de décision.

La multiplication des systèmes d'information et des fichiers concernant les malades et les personnes suspectées d'être malades a conduit la CNIL à s'interroger à plusieurs reprises sur la proportionnalité de certains dispositifs et sur le respect de la protection des données à caractère personnel dans le cas de certains traitements de fichiers. En outre, certaines expériences ont été immédiatement interdites, comme les caméras intelligentes capables de prendre la température ou de détecter le port du masque au nom de cette même protection des données personnelles.

Le 18 mai 2021, la mission indépendante chargée d'évaluer la réponse française à la crise sanitaire engendrée par l'épidémie de COVID-19 a rendu son rapport au président de la République française. Elle établit quelques constats détaillés dont l'insuffisance du niveau de préparation à la crise; la faiblesse récurrente de l'anticipation; la complexité de la gouvernance et la centralisation excessive; l'amélioration progressive du pilotage par les autorités à la faveur des acquis de l'expérience. Mais aussi le caractère remarquable de la réactivité, l'engagement et la mobilisation des acteurs et la réponse économique française jugée globalement à la hauteur du choc subi.

Democracy, Trust, and the Rule of Law in Times of Pandemic: The UK Response to COVID-19

Valsamis Mitsilegas, Santiago Wortman Jofre

A. *Introduction*

Although the UK ranks 2nd in the overall Global Health Security Index of 2019, its response to the coronavirus crisis has shown some gaps in the assessment of its readiness to face a pandemic.[1] This is especially true when comparing the results of the GHS Index with countries like Vietnam, that even though it ranks at the 50th place, has been praised as one of the countries that better responded to the COVID-19 crisis.[2]

This report will focus on four tensions that are being put forward as cutting-across the debate on the UK's regulatory response to COVID-19. First, there is a tension between parliament and the executive in the UK regarding the needs of the emergency response towards the nature of the health crisis posed by COVID-19. This tension strikes in the balance between rapid and effective reactions, marked by the scientific uncertainty about the virus and the fast pace levels of contagion, and the need to subject any decision affecting individual rights to democratic institutions. Thus, ultimately the balance narrows down to the rights of the individuals that would be affected if the government does not react quickly to the COVID-19 crisis, and the rights of the individuals that are being affected by undemocratic measures created unilaterally by the executive power.

A second tension derives from the relationship between local institutions/governments, and the central government. This tension between local and central will affect the way in which a highly centralised response to the health crisis deals with an underpinning tradition of giving high levels of discretion to local governments, which are considered the first line of defence. In this sense, when dealing with state of emergency and

1 'The Global Health Security Index' (*GHS Index*) <https://www.ghsindex.org/> accessed 15 November 2020.

2 'Infographic: The Best and Worst Rated National COVID-19 Responses' (*Statista Infographics*) <https://www.statista.com/chart/21928/approval-ratings-national-covid-19-responses/> accessed 17 November 2020.

emergencies response, the UK has always favoured local institutions as central actors, leaving the central government with the role of coordinator. While this was the case back in the mid-20th century, it is still a major assertion within modern action plans and government emergency plans, thus affecting both the executive response and the legislative task when dealing with the COVID-19 emergency.[3] Moreover, the complexity of the relationship between local institutions and central government becomes even more complex and problematic in the UK where four nations coexist under a very delicate legal balance, thus adding another level to the tension between local and central.

The third tension is very much connected to the second one, and it refers to the legal certainty of everchanging laws and regulations. While this is also connected to the first tension, and the need to have quick and effective responses, many authors have pointed out how quick responses without the due legitimacy and the required checks may detriment the effectiveness of the legal measures because of its opacity and lack of certainty.[4]

Finally, the fourth tension relates to the use of technology to help in the legal response to the COVID-19 crisis. While the UK does not have a prominent tradition on data protection, the use of certain apps and data collection form possible cases of infected people raised the question of how this data is being stored, analysed and if it can be reliable.[5] Moreover, the data protection and data usage also raise questions as to the extent of the competence of central government regarding data collection and surveillance.

Bearing in mind these four tensions will be present throughout and will cut-across numerous issues raised in this report, the presentation of

---

3 James Smith, Civil contingency planning in government (2003) 56 Parliamentary Affairs 410, 410; Rockett J.P., 'A constructive critique of United Kingdom emergency planning' (1994) 3 Disaster Prevention and Management: An International Journal 47, 48; O'Brien Geoff, 'UK emergency preparedness: A holistic response?' (2008) 17 Disaster Prevention and Management: An International Journal 232, 233.

4 Ronan Cormacain, 'Can I go to the park please dad? Everyday lessons in legal certainty in the English coronavirus regulations' (*UK Constitutional Law Association*, 15 May 2020) <https://ukconstitutionallaw.org/2020/05/15/ronan-cormacain-can-i-go-to-the-park-please-dad-everyday-lessons-in-legal-certainty-in-the-english-coronavirus-regulations/> accessed 17 November 2020.

5 See the speech of MP Theresa May in The Telegraph, *In Full: MPs debate and vote on government's lockdown restrictions* (House of Commons 2020) <https://www.youtube.com/watch?v=mCPwmcPFYRY> accessed 17 November 2020.

the topics will be divided into three parts. The first part will deal with the macro analysis of the UK's response to the Coronavirus emergency. This includes the debate around the state of emergency, as well as the government's plan to properly address the crisis. This section will aim at deconstructing the discourse and actions of the UK towards a more resilient system. Issues such as the role of central and local governments will help to clarify some of the reasons behind the side-lining of parliament in key norms and regulations as well as the lack of legal certainty or well defined and precise legal provisions. Moreover, the assessment of the initial action plan towards coronavirus and the highly important role of scientific bodies aiding the decision of the central government will evidence a sense of permanent state of emergency, which may be detrimental to an effective response. Without a sense of planning or progress to track and backup executive measures, these provisions may lose key legitimacy.

The second part will deal with the criminal law response to the coronavirus crisis. The criminalisation of new behaviours that might be contrary to public safety or against executive measures may be seen as disproportionate when considering the legitimate end, they pursue. To this extent, the second part analysis the system response to coronavirus in terms of the statutory duties and criminal law statutes that interact with the state of emergency. Issues of proportionality and legitimacy are also relevant in this part for they put forward a symbolic statement from the government regarding its priorities and the way they want to address them. Moreover, the nature of temporary criminal norms to address en emergency situation, also has great impact on the way in which society perceives criminalisation. Thus, a fast pace changing legislation added to the strive for legitimacy without proper parliamentary scrutiny and the increasing scientific doubts may amount to a legitimacy and proportionality crisis from the criminal law system.

Finally, the third part will deal with the policing, surveillance, prevention and control within the coronavirus crisis. In this sense, as opposed to past health crisis, technology has been a great aid to governments all around the globe when dealing with COVID-19. The fact that the COVID-19 crisis hit the globe at a time in history when the human mobility was at its peak, has been analysed as a key factor in relation to its impact and spread. While this mobility, and therefore the increased impact of COVID-19, appeared to be aided by technological advances in traveling, it has also been because of the technological advances that governments managed to produce a better response than it would have been years ago. In this way, the possibility of working from homes, or being able to trace contagious patience and track their social connections to advert possible asymptomatic patience, are key examples. As a cross-cutting issue, the collection and usage of data from technological aids has always been a concern, even in those governments without a strong tradition on data protection, such as the UK.

B. Macro Analysis

I. State of Emergency in the UK: The Quest for Resilience

The way in which the UK responds to emergency situations has been under development since post war times. The aftermath of the second world war and the fear of renewed and deadlier hostilities during the cold war lead the UK to enact the Civil Defence Act 1948.[6] Up until the new millennium, the state of emergency planning was mostly focused on war and post-war scenarios, with special care for civil defence and the consequences of war. The Civil Defence Act 1948 then placed upon a designated Minister, mainly the Secretary of State for the Home Department,[7] the function of taking "(…) such steps as appear to him from time to time to be necessary or expedient for civil defence purposes".[8]

Until 1983, the obligations placed upon the local authorities by the Civil Defence Act 1948 were broadly general and mainly directed towards keeping the essential services running even during wartimes.[9] Moreover, there were no obligations placed upon local authorities to generate protocols and update prevention systems since most of their obligations lied on maintaining services and collecting intelligence on the result of hostile attacks.[10] The Home Office review of the UK's civil defence in 1981,[11] and the failure to perform notorious defence military exercises, such as the "Operation Hardrock",[12] lead to The Civil Defence (General Local

6 Smith (n 3) 410.

7 Civil Defence Act 1948 s 9(2). The Act established that the said Minister was to be designated by Order in Council. However, in absence of such order, the minister was interpreted to be the Secretary of State.

8 ibid 1.

9 Lexa Hilliard, 'Local government, civil defence and emergency planning: Heading for disaster?' (1986) 49 The Modern Law Review 476, 476/477.

10 'The Civil Defence (General Local Authority Functions) Regulations' (Home Office 1974) S.I. 1974/70 s 4 <https://www.legislation.gov.uk/uksi/1974/70/contents/made>..

11 Hilliard (n 9) 477.

12 'Bad day at Hard Rock' [1982] *New Statesman* 6.

Authority Functions) Regulations of 1983. These new regulations imposed to every council in the UK and Grater London Councils, the duty to review and revise plans in accordance with the Civil Defence Act 1948 as well as train an appropriate number of staff.[13]

During the 80s and 90s, a series of civil emergencies created a window of opportunity to seek change and revise the laws of emergency. More importantly, there was a shift in priorities since the Civil Defence Act 1948 did not have a definition of emergency nor did of disaster,[14] as it was mainly concentrated on the hazards of war and post war scenarios. The end of the Cold War washed away the fear of an imminent new armed conflict and therefore the civil defence provisions lost part of their impetus. Moreover, other civil emergencies such as the King's Cross Underground fire of 1987, the Clapham Junction rail crash of 1988 and the Hillsborough disaster of 1989, among others,[15] took over the centre of political debate. These civil emergencies evidenced the need to expand the scope of prevention to include other types of disasters that were foreseeingly more pressing. To that extent, the Home office presented two major reviews of the UK's emergency plan in 1989, and 1991 which appeared to show that Government "(…) have finally accepted the need for peacetime disaster preparedness".[16]

The review of 1989 created the figure of the Civil Emergencies Adviser who was in charge of assisting "(…) with operational responsibilities to achieve the 'highest standards of coordination and compatibility' between their contingency plans".[17] The new position was filled at the time by an air vice Marshall, Mr. David Brook, which emphasised the strong military connection.[18] The review maintained the core structure of the UK's emergency planning by reassuring the local institution's role as first in line and principal in charge of the response. As it was stated by Parker and Handmer, the British approach to emergency planning was still "(…) characterised by a lack of policies, especially explicit national policies providing

13 'The Civil Defence (General Local Authority Functions) Regulations' (Home Office 1983) S.I. 1983/1634 s 4 <https://www.legislation.gov.uk/uksi/1983/1634/resources>.

14 Terms that are normally used interchangeably.

15 Smith (n 3) 410; O'Brien Geoff and Read Paul, 'Future UK emergency management: New wine, old skin?' (2005) 14 Disaster Prevention and Management: An International Journal 353, 353.

16 Rockett J.P. (n 3) 51.

17 John Handmer and Dennis Parker, 'British disaster planning and management: An initial assessment' (1991) 15 Disasters 303, 305.

18 ibid.

ambiguous signals; and legal and organisational arrangements which are flawed in a variety of important ways".[19]

The second review of 1991 took place as a response to the first report issued by the newly appointed Civil Emergencies Adviser.[20] The review carried out by the Home Secretary, Mr. Kenneth Baker, established that "Local authority civil defence planning will in future be based on the more flexible approach".[21] This new flexible approach consisted in a central guidance on handling emergencies during peacetime, "a more flexible use of civil defence grant for local authorities", and the review of the emergencies planning organisation within the metropolitan area.[22] Thus, the reviews of 1989 and 1991 did not change much of emergency planning system of the UK. The central government was still in charge of coordinating with local institutions to help them be prepared to provide appropriate responses on the ground.[23] Nevertheless, the reviews helped provide a different mindset to the objectives of the civil emergencies plans and institutions. After the reviews, the UK started planning for peacetime emergencies rather than wartime.[24]

The new millennium brought new civil emergencies needing to be address and that somehow escaped the limits of the peacetime emergency planning. The Y2K problem and the UK Fuel Blockade of 2000 turned the spotlight towards other issues such as the disruption of civil life by technological interruptions and revealed the need for a holistic reform. Thus, a major review for reform of the civil emergencies planning was set in motion in February 2001, and by October 2001 the lead department dealing with civil emergencies was the Civil Contingency Committee under the scope of the Cabinet Office.[25] This national review of the civil emergency response, powered by the terrorist attacks of 9/11, which focused the local and international efforts on terrorism, lead to what ultimately became the Civil Contingencies Act 2004.

---

19 Dennis Parker and John Handmer, 'Improving hazard management and emergency planning' in Dennis Parker and John Handmer (eds), *Hazard Management and Emergency Planning* (Routledge 2012) 266.

20 Emergency Planning Review (Hansard, 10 July 1991) 1991 cols 391–4W.

21 ibid 393W.

22 ibid.

23 O'Brien Geoff and Read Paul (n 15) 353–354.

24 Rockett J.P. (n 3) 49.

25 Hills Alice E., 'Co-ordination and disaster response in the United Kingdom' (1994) 3 Disaster Prevention and Management: An International Journal 66, 67; O'Brien Geoff and Read Paul (n 15) 354.

The Bill of 2004 implicated a major change in the structure and goals of emergencies response in the UK, with special focus on the need for resilience. The quest for resilience has always been at the backbone of every civil emergencies plan in the UK and in numerous other disciplines such as economy, ecology, etc.,[26] although now it was stressed bluntly in Statute. The Civil Contingencies Secretariat, which supports the Civil Contingencies Committee, popularly known as COBRA (Cabinet Office Briefing Room A), defined resilience as, "The ability at every level to detect, prevent, prepare for and if necessary handle and recover from disruptive challenges".[27] Thus a holistic approach to emergencies in the UK advocates for a sustainable method to foresee, prevent, react and recover from future and present disasters or emergencies.

The resilience component of the emergency plan structured by the UK has been broken down into different components that need to be taken care by the designated authorities. While this aspect of the resilience has evolved into a more complex and detailed plan of action, there are certain underpinning spirits that remained unaltered through time. In this sense, the role of the central government and the delegation and reliance on the discretion of local institutions kept its original design. As it will be developed in the next section, while the structure of the national emergency plan grew in complexity, it kept the same underlying dynamic by supporting and enabling local authorities to react as they see fit based on immediate data from the emergency. While this seems to be most effective in terms of how quick the system can respond, it might not be efficient for grand scale emergencies, such as the current COVID-19 crisis. Although the stress of resilience seems to push for proactive rather than reactive strategies, the distributed levels of governance seem to present a reactive plan of action.

II. Civil Contingencies Structure and Levels of Governance

The latest update on the Emergency and Recovery non-statutory guidance accompanying the Civil Contingency Act 2004 reveals that while in some cases the magnitude of the emergency may require a degree of support or

26 O'Brien Geoff (n 3) 237.

27 Cabinet Office Civil Contingencies Secretariat, 'Dealing with disasters' (The Stationery Office 2004) 3rd ed. For more on resilience see G O'Brien and P O'Keefe, *Managing adaptation to climate risk: Beyond fragmented responses* (Routledge 2014) ch 6.

co-ordination form the central government. However, the default position is that "Central government will not duplicate the role of local responders who remain the basic building block of the response to an emergency".[28] As Figure 1 shows, the levels of involvement of the central government would very much depend on the nature of the emergency, although it will always have the predominance of the local response.

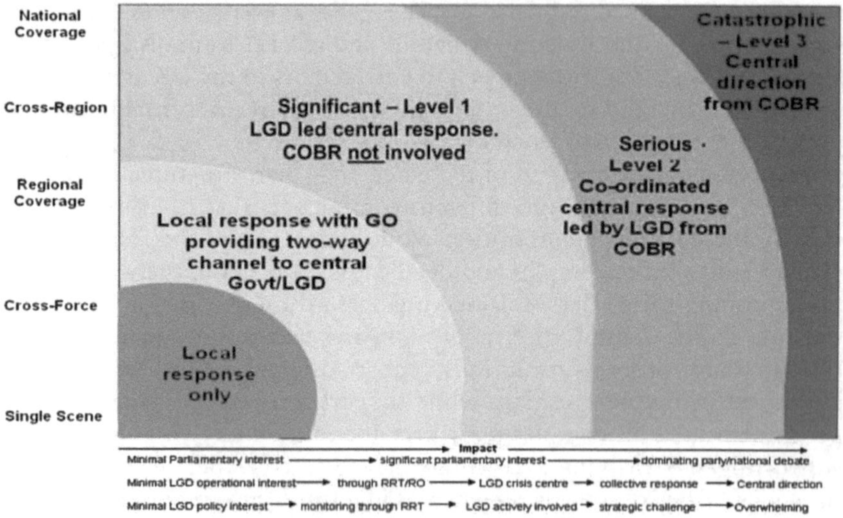

Figure 1 – Escalation of the Central Response[29]

Thus, when the crisis escalates to a catastrophic event requiring coordination form the central government, a designated Lead Government Department (LGD) would be responsible for the overall management and response.[30] In this sense, the default LGD in cases of biological hazards is the Civil Contingencies Secretariat (CCS).[31] As shown in Figure 2,

28 'Emergency Response and Recovery' (Civil Contingencies Secretariat, Cabinet Office, HM Government 2013) Non statutory guidance accompanying the Civil Contingencies Act 2004 5th ed. ch 13.

29 ibid 13.1.

30 ibid 13.2.1.

31 'List of Lead Government Departments' Responsibilities for Planning, Response, and Recovery from Emergencies' (*GOV.UK*) <https://www.gov.uk/government/publications/list-of-lead-government-departments-responsibilities-for-planning-response-and-recovery-from-emergencies> accessed 6 November 2020.

the CCS within the Cabinet Office supports the Civil Contingencies Committee also known as COBRA (Cabinet Office Briefing Room A), which constitutes the government's most important committee in terms of coordinating departments during crises.[32] According to the Institute for Government,

> "COBR's purpose is high-level co-ordination and decision making in the event of major or catastrophic emergencies, including natural disasters, terrorist attacks and major industrial accidents or disruption".[33]

Normally, COBRA meetings are chaired by senior Ministers and involve key stakeholders such as the Association of Chief Police Officers and officials from relevant departments depending on the nature of the emergency.[34] Moreover, within COBRA there is a senior decision making body, which for COVID-19 would be the National Security Council, Sub Committee on Threats, Hazards, Resilience and Contingencies, that supervises the Government's response.[35] This decision-making body meets at a Ministerial and official level when needed, and it is supported by a number of cells including communications and operations cells, Impact Management Groups, Recovery Groups, intelligence cells, etc.[36]

Furthermore, COBRA is also supported by the Scientific Advisory Group for Emergencies (SAGE), which

> "(...) is responsible for ensuring that timely and coordinated scientific advice is made available to decision makers to support UK cross-government decisions in the Cabinet Office Briefing Room (COBR)".[37]

---

32 J Vitor Tossini, 'The Cabinet office briefing rooms (COBR) – A short introduction' (18 October 2018) <https://ukdefencejournal.org.uk/the-cabinet-office-briefing-rooms-cobr-a-short-introduction/> accessed 6 November 2020; Catherine Haddon, 'COBR (COBRA)' (*The Institute for Government*, 23 January 2020) <https://www.instituteforgovernment.org.uk/explainers/cobr-cobra> accessed 5 November 2020.

33 Haddon (n 32).

34 'Emergency Response and Recovery' (n 28) s 13.4.1.

35 ibid 13.4.2.

36 ibid.

37 'About Us' (*GOV.UK*) <https://www.gov.uk/government/organisations/scientific-advisory-group-for-emergencies/about> accessed 6 November 2020.

SAGE is then in charge of providing coherent and coordinated advice while interpreting complex scientific evidence and translating it into non-technical language to support the work of the COBRA.[38]

As shown in Figure 3, at a local level, and depending on the scale of the emergency, Scientific and Technical Advisory Cells (STACs) coordinate and advice local Strategic Coordinating Groups (SCGs) and Recovery Co-ordinating Groups (RCGs) which are the first line response on the ground and the ones sin charge of managing the recovery strategy.[39] At this level, the connection between local institutions and the central government is provided by the Government Liaison Officer (GLO), which in the case of biological hazards is fulfilled by the Department for Communities and Local Government Resilience and Emergencies Division.[40] Thus, the Liaison Officer would act as the connection between COBRA and the scene.[41]

38 'Emergency Response and Recovery' (n 28) s 13.4.4. For more information on SAGE see 'Enhanced SAGE Guidance. A Strategic Framework for the Scientific Advisory Group for Emergencies (SAGE)' (Civil Contingencies Secretariat, Cabinet Office, HM Government 2012) <https://assets.publishing.service.gov.uk/government/uploads/system/uploads/attachment_data/file/80087/sage-guidance.pdf>.

39 'Emergency Response and Recovery' (n 28) s 13.4.4.

40 ibid 13.4.10.

41 ibid. To see how information flows between SAGE, STACs and SCGs, see 'Enhanced SAGE Guidance. A Strategic Framework for the Scientific Advisory Group for Emergencies (SAGE)' (n 38) 35.

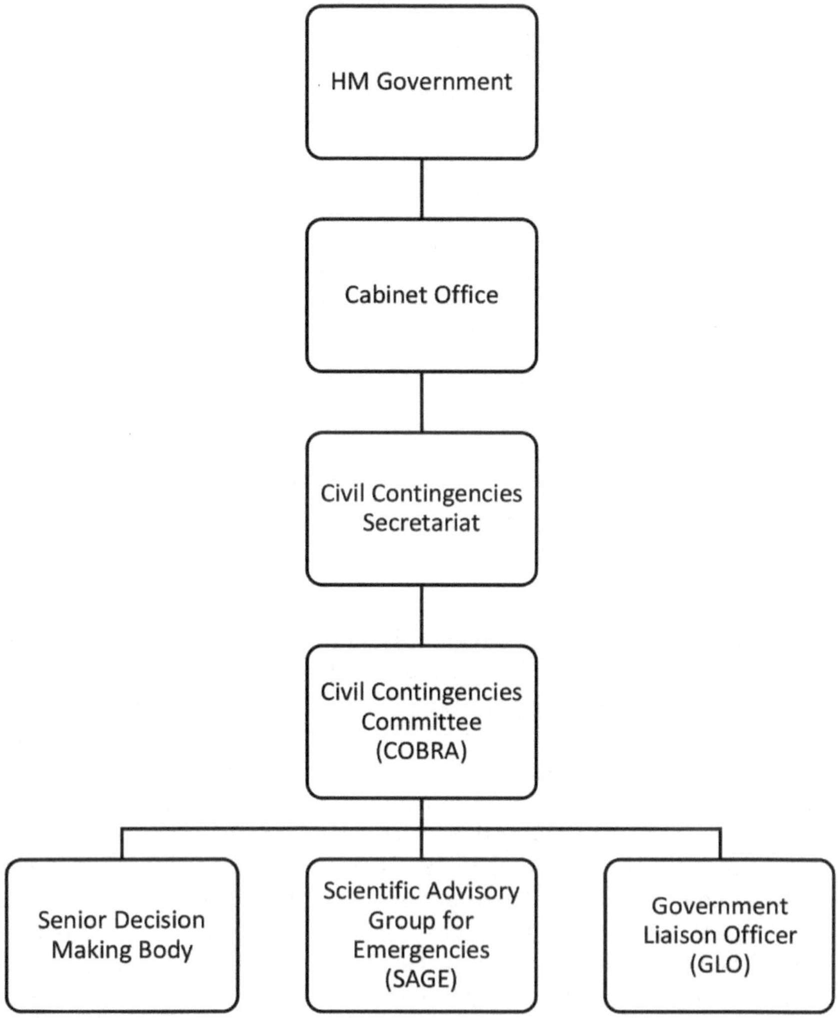

Figure 2 – Government's Central Crisis Management Structure[42]

42 'Emergency Response and Recovery' (n 28) s 13.4.

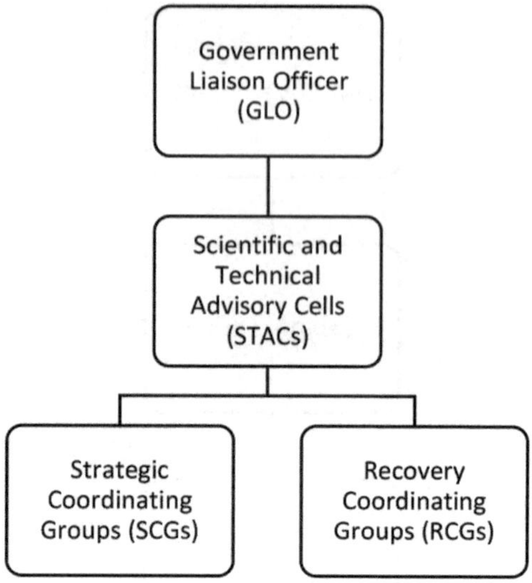

Figure 3 – Connection Between the Central Government and the Local Response[43]

Thus, as Figure 4 shows, the integral diagram of the response of the Civil Contingency Committee still bears a lot of the foundational approach towards civil defence from post-war planning. The division between the central and the local response still puts the central government in a role of cooperation and coordination while local authorities becomes the first line of defence against the immediate consequences of an emergency.

However, the COVID-19 outbreak served as a stress test to these emergency response structure and planning for it was confronted to an unprecedented biological hazard. Previous cases of biological hazards had left a heavy impact on the way in which the public administration and government of the UK handle health crisis. The Bovine Spongiform Encephalopathy (BSE) case serves as an example of the way in which the UK addressed and managed a health crisis, prising the local responses over a centralised government. Even in BSE case, the local authorities played a major role in responding to the crisis and the lessons learned involved the need to provide them with clearer guidance and a central government with statutory powers of monitoring standards of compliance and enforcement.[44]

43 ibid 13.4.10.

44 Lord Phillips of Worth Matravers, Mrs June Bridgeman CB and Professor Malcolm Ferguson-Smith FRS, 'The BSE Inquiry. Vol. 1: Findings & Conclusions'

Thus, some of the issues regarding the lack of clarity of key legal provisions might be explained by the tradition of leaving local authorities with a wide range of discretional powers, even though the nature of the emergency may have called for a different type of response.

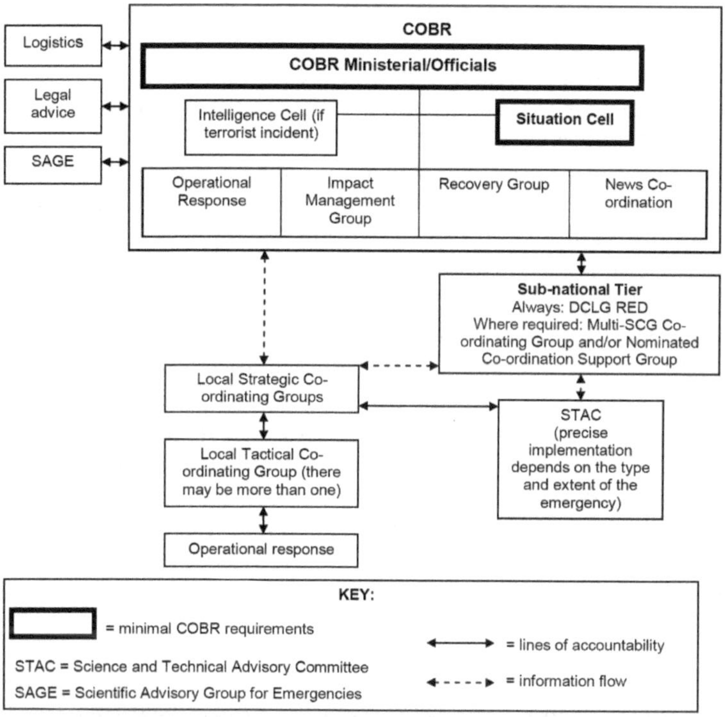

Figure 4 – Integrated Diagram of COBR response[45]

III. Executive Power and State of Emergency: speedy and changing decisions

Following the procedures described in the previous section, the PM Boris Johnson, chaired a COBRA meeting regarding the coronavirus outbreak

(Stationery Office 2000) s 1277 <https://webarchive.nationalarchives.gov.uk/20060525120000/http://www.bseinquiry.gov.uk/index.htm>; Louise Cummings, *Rethinking the BSE Crisis. A Study of Scientific Reasoning under Uncertainty* (Springer 2010) ch 8.

45 'Emergency Response and Recovery' (n 28) fig 13.2.

the 2nd March 2020.[46] Although the first response to the COVID-19 crisis was thus within the scope of the Civil Contingency Act 2004, the 25th March 2020 witnessed one of the fastest legislative responses to a health crisis in the history of the UK. The fast-tracked legislative procedure lead to the enactment of the Coronavirus Act 2002 the 25th March 2020. While many scholars agree that the speed with which the law was approved can hardly be criticised in such critical circumstances,[47] it is also true that the time frame of legislation leaves very little room for scrutiny.

The Coronavirus Act 2002 was also followed the next day by the Health Protection (Coronavirus, Restrictions) Regulations 2020 which also had analogue versions in Scotland, Wales and Northern Ireland. These regulations had a major impact on the freedom and rights of the populations, including for example the impossibility of leaving the premises of where they lived without a "reasonable excuse" (regulation 6.1 in accordance with reg. 2(4)(a), SI 2020/447). Being under the scope of Part 2A of the Public Health (Control of Disease) Act 1984, the implementation of the regulation, and the amendments that followed, were not revised by parliament. On the contrary, the Secretary of State had the prerogative of revising the regulations every 21 days with an expiry date of 6 months, which could be renewed.[48] As pointed out by Tom Hickman, "There is no evident reason why proper procedure could not be complied with and Parliament had to be bypassed".[49] In this sense, a parliamentary scrutiny regarding the scope of application of such restrictive measures would not only be more compatible with democratic values but it would also provide a very much needed legitimacy.[50]

---

46 'PM to Chair COBR Meeting on the Coronavirus Outbreak' (*GOV.UK*) <https://www.gov.uk/government/news/pm-to-chair-cobr-meeting-on-the-coronavirus-outbreak> accessed 11 November 2020.

47 David Ormerod, 'Coronavirus and emergency powers' [2020] Criminal Law Review 473, 473; UKCLA, 'Theodore Konstadinides and Lee Marsons: COVID19 and its impact on the constitutional relationship between government and parliament.' (*UK Constitutional Law Association*, 26 March 2020) <https://ukconstitutionallaw.org/2020/03/26/theodore-konstadinides-and-lee-marsons-covid-19-and-its-impact-on-the-constitutional-relationship-between-government-and-parliament/> accessed 11 November 2020.

48 The Health Protection (Coronavirus, Restrictions) (England) Regulations 2020 [SI 2020/350] s 12..

49 UKCLA, 'Tom Hickman: A very English lockdown relaxation' (*UK Constitutional Law Association*, 14 May 2020) <https://ukconstitutionallaw.org/2020/05/14/tom-hickman-a-very-english-lockdown-relaxation/> accessed 13 November 2020.

50 UKCLA, 'Tom Hickman: Eight ways to reinforce and revise the lockdown law.' (*UK Constitutional Law Association*, 16 April 2020) s 2 <https://ukconstitutionalla

Moreover, the vagueness of the terminology such as "reasonable excuse" casted doubt on the efficiency of the measure as well as the high levels of discretion left for constabularies who would be judging the reasonableness of the justification on the ground. Although new regulations such as the Health Protection (Coronavirus, Restrictions) (England) (No. 4) Regulations 2020, Section 6 provides a non-exhaustive list of possible reasonable excuses, the blurred limits of the excuse most certainly may affect the principle of legal certainty.[51]

Bypassing the Civil Contingency Act 2004 had as a consequence the disregard of parliamentary approval for new regulations in accordance with its section 26, and a high-level transfer of legislative powers to the executive branch. Furthermore, the legitimacy issues deriving from the lack of parliamentary scrutiny were also extended to the legitimacy of excessively restrictive measures as *ultra vires* from its deriving legislation.[52] In this sense, scholars asked whether the nature of the restrictions imposed by the Health Protection Regulations 2020 were "(…) within the scope of the powers conferred upon the Government by statute".[53] The Health Protection Regulations of 2020 where enacted in accordance with sections 45C(1), 45(3)(c) and 45(4)(d) of the Public Health (Control of Disease) Act 1984, and although they enable the power to make regulations, it contemplates certain limits. The focal point of concern regarding *ultra vires* restrictions is whether, when analysed holistically, the restriction 6 of the Health Protection Regulations 2020 (SI 2020/350) is a "special restriction or requirement" as stated in section 45C(4)(d) of the Public Health (Control of Diseases) Act 1984. The term "special restriction or requirement" is then analysed in section 45C(6)(a), which refers to an exhaustive list of restrictions that may be imposed by a justice of the peace according to section 45G(2), 45H(2) or 45I(2). The lawfulness of banning freedom of movement by imposing exclusion and association measures seems to be

---

w.org/2020/04/16/tom-hickman-eight-ways-to-reinforce-and-revise-the-lockdown-law/> accessed 13 November 2020.

51 Rudi Fortson, 'Open textured legislation in the times of COVID-19: 'Reasonable Excuse' and 'Legal Certainty'' (*Responding to COVID-19: Surveillance, Trust and the Rule of Law*, 2 June 2020) <https://www.qmul.ac.uk/law/research/centres-institutes/dol/cjc/responding-to-covid-19/items/open-textured-legislation-in-the-times-of-covid-19-reasonable-excuse-and-legal-certainty.html> accessed 16 November 2020.

52 David Anderson, 'Can we be forced to stay at home?' (*David Anderson QC Lawyer London UK*, 26 March 2020) <https://www.daqc.co.uk/2020/03/26/can-we-be-forced-to-stay-at-home/> accessed 13 November 2020.

53 ibid.

dependent upon the interpretation of section 45G (2) and 45G (2)(j) of the Public Health (Control of Diseases) Act 1984.[54]

Another issue that needs to be contemplated when considering the lack of parliamentary scrutiny and the extraordinary executive powers, is the fast pace changing legislation. In this sense, the coronavirus legislation can be divided into primary and secondary legislations.[55] While the primary legislation went through parliamentary debate and thus were subjected to a certain degree of democratic scrutiny, the secondary legislations where mostly enacted within executive powers by the Secretary of State.

The primary legislation in the UK, up until the time of this report, is composed of:

- Coronavirus Act 2020 (c. 7)
- Coronavirus (Scotland) Act 2020 (asp 7)
- Coronavirus (Scotland) (No.2) Act 2020 (asp 10)
- Public Health (Control of Disease) Act 1984 (c. 22)
- Public Health etc. (Scotland) Act 2008 (asp 5)
- Public Health Act (Northern Ireland) 1967 (c. 36)

The secondary legislation on the other hand, is composed of:
England

- The Health Protection (Coronavirus, Restrictions) (England) (No. 4) Regulations 2020 (S.I. 2020/1200)
- The Health Protection (Coronavirus, Restrictions) (No. 3) (England) Regulations 2020 (S.I. 2020/750)
- The Health Protection (Coronavirus, Restrictions) (No. 2) (England) Regulations 2020 (S.I. 2020/684)
- The Health Protection (Coronavirus, International Travel) (England) Regulations 2020 (S.I. 2020/568)
- The Health Protection (Coronavirus, Wearing of Face Coverings in a Relevant Place) (England) Regulations 2020 (S.I. 2020/791)
- The Health Protection (Coronavirus, Collection of Contact Details etc. and Related Requirements) Regulations 2020 (S.I. 2020/1005)
- The Health Protection (Coronavirus, Restrictions) (Self-Isolation) (England) Regulations 2020 (S.I. 2020/1045)
- The Health Protection (Coronavirus, Local COVID-19 Alert Level) (Medium) (England) Regulations 2020 (S.I. 2020/1103)

54 ibid.

55 'Coronavirus Legislation' <https://www.legislation.gov.uk/coronavirus> accessed 14 November 2020.

- The Health Protection (Coronavirus, Local COVID-19 Alert Level) (High) (England) Regulations 2020 (S.I. 2020/1104)
- The Health Protection (Coronavirus, Local COVID-19 Alert Level) (Very High) (England) Regulations 2020 (S.I. 2020/1105)

Scotland

- The Health Protection (Coronavirus) (Restrictions and Requirements) (Local Levels) (Scotland) Regulations 2020 (S.S.I. 2020/344)
- The Health Protection (Coronavirus) (International Travel) (Scotland) Regulations 2020 (S.S.I. 2020/169)
- The Health Protection (Coronavirus, Public Health Information for Persons Travelling to Scotland) Regulations 2020 (S.S.I. 2020/170)

Wales

- The Health Protection (Coronavirus Restrictions) (No. 4) (Wales) Regulations 2020 (S.I. 2020/1219)
- The Health Protection (Coronavirus, International Travel) (Wales) Regulations 2020 (S.I. 2020/574)
- The Health Protection (Coronavirus, Public Health Information for Persons Travelling to Wales etc.) Regulations 2020 (S.I. 2020/595)

Northern Ireland

- The Health Protection (Coronavirus, Restrictions) (No. 2) Regulations (Northern Ireland) 2020 (S.R. 2020/150)
- The Health Protection (Coronavirus, International Travel) Regulations (Northern Ireland) 2020 (S.R. 2020/90)
- The Health Protection (Coronavirus, Public Health Information for Persons Travelling to Northern Ireland) Regulations (Northern Ireland) 2020 (S.R. 2020/97)
- The Health Protection (Coronavirus, Wearing of Face Coverings) Regulations (Northern Ireland) 2020 (S.R. 2020/151)

The Health Protection (Coronavirus) Regulations 2020 was originally made the 10th February 2020 under the same powers conferred to the Secretary of State by the Public Health (Control of Disease) Act 1984 and was further revoked by the Coronavirus Act 2020. Moreover, and as an example of the fast pace changes, the Health Protection (Coronavirus, Restrictions) (No. 2) (England) Regulations 2020 (S.I. 2020/684) that followed the Coronavirus Act 2020 and was made by the Secretary of State the 3rd July 2020, suffered 20 changes by the 5th November 2020.[56]

This scenario gets more complex when considering the distribution of responsibilities in accordance with the devolved administrations. In this sense,

> "Major public services affected by the pandemic, in particular public health services and education, are the responsibility of the devolved administrations in Northern Ireland, Scotland and Wales. In the case of Scotland and Northern Ireland, policing and justice matters are also devolved".[57]

Although the Coronavirus Act 2020 was approved in accordance with the Sewel Convention, and thus with the consent of the devolved legislatures, it provided further and new powers to the devolved administrations.[58] These new powers included, for example, sections 11, 12 and 13 which provided indemnity for health care workers of England, Wales, Scotland and Northern Ireland. Much of what it seems chaotic and baseless, fast pace regulations may be seen as an attempt to centralise the coordination of four different governments for them to act in concert. The issue then, once again shifts towards the role of the central government and the idea that local authorities should have enough discretion to response to the immediate threat as they see fit. Such discretion relies on lifting the burden from local institutions regarding the need to double check, submit for parliamentary scrutiny or even be subjected to normal liabilities. The need for a fast response then, requires a centralised coordination but with blurred limits and vague enforcement rules, which favours discretion over foreseen consequences and action plans through the implementation of protocols.

---

56 Expert Participation, 'The Health Protection (Coronavirus, Restrictions) (No. 2) (England) Regulations 2020' <https://www.legislation.gov.uk/uksi/2020/684> accessed 15 November 2020.

57 'Coronavirus and Devolution' (*The Institute for Government*, 26 March 2020) <https://www.instituteforgovernment.org.uk/explainers/coronavirus-and-devolution> accessed 11 November 2020.

58 ibid.

IV. Side-lining of parliament: losing legitimacy through opacity

Many of the voices that favoured the lockdown measures, advocated for the idea that lockdown represented a proportionate and accurate measure to the COVID-19 emergency when considering the available scientific knowledge that was put forward to the UK's central government by the SAGE.[59] They also remark that considering the nature of the emergency and the exponential fast pace rate of contagious cases, time was a key variable to be taken into consideration when weighing the efficiency and effectiveness of restrictive measures in detriment of democratic values.[60] Thus, this intuitive claim puts forward the dilemma presented by the COVID-19 crisis where the checks and balances of democratic institutions may "(...) impair the effectiveness of the government's emergency measures by slowing down decision-making and opening the door for party politics".[61]

In this sense, most of the actions taken unilaterally, without parliamentary intervention, by the UK's government have been adopted under the claim that they were following the science.[62] This claim has been widely criticised by scientists in the UK, where they pointed out the volatility of scientific evidence in such an unknown scenario and facing a threat that has never been encountered before.[63] Moreover, the extent and limits of the concept of "science" might very well depend upon the different disciplines that are being consulted by the government under such wide umbrella. The appropriate measure might not be the same based on the evidence gathered by immunologists that the ones based on the evidence gathered by social scientists. Furthermore, political and leadership measures facing a pandemic ought to take into consideration a higher number

---

59 Jeff King, 'The lockdown is lawful: Part II' (*UK Constitutional Law Association*, 2 April 2020) <https://ukconstitutionallaw.org/2020/04/02/jeff-king-the-lockdown-is-lawful-part-ii/> accessed 16 November 2020.

60 Jeff King, 'The lockdown is lawful' (*UK Constitutional Law Association*, 1 April 2020) <https://ukconstitutionallaw.org/2020/04/01/jeff-king-the-lockdown-is-lawful/> accessed 16 November 2020.

61 Jan Petrov, 'The COVID-19 emergency in the age of executive aggrandizement: What role for legislative and judicial checks?' (2020) 8 The Theory and Practice of Legislation 71, 76.

62 Hannah Devlin and Sarah Boseley, 'Scientists criticise UK government's "following the Science" claim' The Guardian (23 April 2020) <https://www.theguardian.com/world/2020/apr/23/scientists-criticise-uk-government-over-following-the-science> accessed 18 November 2020.

63 ibid.

of variables than the ones considered by very narrow and specialised scientific research. As stated by the World Health Organisation,

> "(…) these measures can have a profound negative impact on individuals, communities, and societies by bringing social and economic life to a near stop. Such measures disproportionately affect disadvantaged groups, including people in poverty, migrants, internally displaced people and refugees, who most often live in overcrowded and under resourced settings, and depend on daily labour for subsistence".[64]

The consistent stance of the WHO regarding lockdown, encouraged governments to weigh the benefits and consequences from a broader perspective and take into consideration a higher number of variables than what specific scientific evidence may suggest.[65]

Another concern regarding the justification of the government by 'following the science', is the opacity of the claimed scientific evidence. As pointed out by Prof. Sheila Bird, former programme leader of the Medical Research Council's biostatistics unit at the University of Cambridge, the underpinning scientific evidence to such governmental measures is not evident.[66] The criticism derives from the opacity of a key aiding cell to COBRA as it is the SAGE institution. The lack of transparency regarding the members, structure, and input of this governmental organisation, taints the decision-making process with a lack of public scrutiny and thus casts doubt on its legitimacy or even its rigor.[67] As it was pointed out at the beginning of this report, such issues deepen the flimsy trust equilibrium between government and its citizens.

Other issues to take into consideration, are the lack of consensus in the scientific community regarding certain key elements of COVID-19, and

64 'Coronavirus Disease (COVID-19): Herd Immunity, Lockdowns and COVID-19' <https://www.who.int/news-room/q-a-detail/herd-immunity-lockdowns-and-covid-19> accessed 14 November 2020.

65 'Reality Check: No, the WHO Didn't Reverse Its Position on Coronavirus Lockdowns' (*Global News*) <https://globalnews.ca/news/7398396/coronavirus-lockdown-who-reality-check/> accessed 18 November 2020; Nicky Ryan, 'FactFind: Has the World Health Organisation Changed Its Position on Lockdowns?' (*TheJournal.ie*) <https://www.thejournal.ie/world-health-organisation-lockdowns-5237323-Oct2020/> accessed 18 November 2020.

66 Devlin and Boseley (n 62).

67 ibid.

the risks and consequences of relying too much on scientific backup.[68] On this last point for example, it seems as if 'following the science' diverted the responsibility and accountability towards an unknown and undetermined scientific community, rather than towards democratically elected officials, who were appointed to fulfil a decision-making role in peace and emergency situations.[69] This dynamic and shift in responsibilities and functions would change democratic values of governance for a technocratic model of governance.[70]

Much of the legitimacy issues brought by the lack of parliamentary scrutiny were evidenced in the debate of the House of Commons regarding the second lockdown measures of 2020. In this opportunity, MP Sir Graham Brady started his speech by pointing out that,

> "(...) we are being asked today to take away the fundamental freedoms of nearly 68 million people in this country. (...) Can I just say that three hours debate on such a massive intervention taking away liberty shows how little we value the liberty of our constituents, it is not good enough, it should have been at least a day of debate before we took such extreme action".[71]

Furthermore, the UK enacted 91 out of 102 laws and regulations related to the coronavirus crisis by June 2020 without proper parliamentary scrutiny.[72] This was made through a negative procedure by which the law does not need Parliamentary approval to become law, but the House of Commons or Lords can pass a motion within a specified period of normally 40 days to annul the statutory instrument.[73] However, this remedy has

---

68 Cormac Mac Amhlaigh, 'Legitimacy in the time of Coronavirus' (*Verfassungsblog*, 17 April 2020) <https://verfassungsblog.de/legitimacy-in-the-time-of-coronavirus/> accessed 20 November 2020.

69 Stephen Thomson and Eric C Ip, 'COVID-19 emergency measures and the impending authoritarian pandemic' [2020] Journal of Law and the Biosciences 19 <https://doi.org/10.1093/jlb/lsaa064> accessed 16 November 2020.

70 ibid 20.

71 The Telegraph (n 5) pt 01:33:18.

72 Harry Yorke and Dominic Penna, 'More than 90 Coronavirus laws and rules imposed without parliamentary scrutiny' *The Telegraph* (17 June 2020) <https://www.telegraph.co.uk/politics/2020/06/17/90-coronavirus-laws-rules-imposed-without-parliamentary-scrutiny/> accessed 18 November 2020.

73 'Negative Procedure - MPs' Guide to Procedure - UK Parliament' <https://guidetoprocedure.parliament.uk/collections/PtBJuBiU/negative-procedure> accessed 18 November 2020.

not been used since 1979.[74] Additionally, eight regulations were passed through an affirmative procedure which requires laws to be approved by Parliament within 28 to 40 days or they would be revoked.[75] Again, showing the extreme rareness of these events, the last time an instrument was revoked was in 1978.[76]

These expedite decision-making from the executive power may seem to be justified by the ever-changing scenario of the coronavirus crisis, and the changing conclusions of the scientific community provided by a hectic research dynamic. Nevertheless, side-lining parliamentary scrutiny may have a direct effect on the outcome of these measures, which are highly dependable on the voluntary compliance of all members of society. Disparities in the way in which people obey the emergency laws may seriously affect the efficiency of them since every individual may exponentially spread the virus.

In this sense, it is not entirely clear that the dilemma which presents quick decisions as correlating with efficient decisions, is entirely true. An interesting point to explore is how side-lining parliamentary scrutiny, as the utmost expression of deliberative democracies, may derive in the opacity of the decision-making process of the executive power. This may also derive in the lack of legitimacy of key regulatory responses to COVID-19,[77] which ironically may be the ones most desperately needing high levels of voluntary compliance.[78] Keeping key checks and balances of highly important decisions and extreme measures such as the ones that are being taken as a result of the coronavirus crisis, may help improve their efficiency. Likewise, it becomes a crucial element when analysing trust in government and decisive institutions such as the judicial system. Setting the pace and pushing democratic institutions to fulfil their functions and engage in thorough debates in times of emergency will also help the dialectic process of weighing the vast amount of social interests at stake. This connects with the idea that governmental decision making should also be transparent and balancing higher number of variables than specialised scientific research.

74 ibid.

75 Yorke and Penna (n 72).

76 'Affirmative Procedure - MPs' Guide to Procedure - UK Parliament' <https://guidetoprocedure.parliament.uk/collections/9CcpWjdj> accessed 18 November 2020..

77 Cormacain (n 4).

78 Petrov (n 61) 76/77.

V. Permanent state of emergency

The initial Coronavirus Action Plan contemplated four phases that were expected to change as a response to the amount of COVID-19 positive cases and the threat posed by it. The four phases were:

> "**Contain**: detect early cases, follow up close contacts, and prevent the disease taking hold in this country for as long as is reasonably possible
> **Delay**: slow the spread in this country, if it does take hold, lowering the peak impact and pushing it away from the winter season
> **Research**: better understand the virus and the actions that will lessen its effect on the UK population; innovate responses including diagnostics, drugs and vaccines; use the evidence to inform the development of the most effective models of care
> **Mitigate**: provide the best care possible for people who become ill, support hospitals to maintain essential services and ensure ongoing support for people ill in the community to minimise the overall impact of the disease on society, public services and on the economy".[79]

In this sense, the action plan did not contemplate a sustainable solution as according to the scientific evidence available at the time, there wasn't a foreseeable transition out of the state of emergency.

The 11th May 2020, the government published a recovery strategy which was updated the 24th July 2020, and where the Prime Minister gave a hopeful foreword. In its statement the PM sustained that the first coronavirus action plan from March 2020 was the right decision with the available scientific data at the time.[80] As he asserted that the UK had begun to "(…) beat back the virus",[81] the recovery plan foresaw three stages of recovery. The first stage was considered as the departure stage which aimed at clarifying the updated situation by the time the recovery plan was released.[82] The stage acknowledged the ease of the COVID-19 positive cases and the im-

---

79 'Coronavirus Action Plan: A Guide to What You Can Expect across the UK' (Department of Health & Social Care 2020) s 3.9 <https://www.gov.uk/government/publications/coronavirus-action-plan>.

80 'Our Plan to Rebuild: The UK Government's COVID-19 Recovery Strategy' (Cabinet Office 2020) Command Paper number CP 239 <https://www.gov.uk/government/publications/our-plan-to-rebuild-the-uk-governments-covid-19-recovery-strategy/our-plan-to-rebuild-the-uk-governments-covid-19-recovery-strategy> accessed 18 November 2020.

81 ibid.

82 ibid 1.1.

pact that lockdown measures were having in other areas of society such as the economic and social life. The second stage was named as the 'smarter controls' phase, and it aimed at replacing the existing measures for smarter measures and balancing the rest of social areas affected by the coronavirus crisis, such as the mental health consequences, economic, etc.[83] Finally, the third stage was named "reliable treatment", and stated that "(…) rolling out effective treatments and/or a vaccine will allow us to move to a phase where the effect of the virus can be reduced to manageable levels".[84]

Thus, the third stage relied heavily on a hypothetical effective treatment or vaccine. This made it hard for the public eye to see a sustainable transition out of the state of emergency in the near future. The quest for the vaccine indeed did not arrive on time and by November 2020 a new lockdown had to be imposed, although this time it was subjected to parliamentary debate. Nevertheless, the regression also evidenced some major issues regarding the action plan, the recovery plan and the public feeling of a permanent state of emergency. The concern raised by this permanency has been proved in other areas such as terrorism, where maintaining high threat levels for too long may derive in desensitisation of the public.[85]

Finally, the differences between the responses and planning of the four nations within the UK has also created some tensions, not only in the relationship between local and central governments but also in terms of the feasibility of the UK's plan.[86] Thus, while England enacted the second lockdown measures by November 2020, Wales eased their restrictions on the 9th November.[87] As stated at the beginning of this report, the nature of the COVID-19 pandemic requires a unified and coordinated response from the central government which by the second wave of the virus, was already under serious doubts and pressure.

83 ibid 3.1.

84 ibid 3.2.

85 Philip Kirby, 'The End of the Rainbow?' (2013) 158 The RUSI Journal 54, 58/59.

86 'Coronavirus: The Challenges for Devolution' (UK in a changing Europe, 9 April 2020) <https://ukandeu.ac.uk/coronavirus-the-challenges-for-devolution/> accessed 20 November 2020; 'Coronavirus and Devolution' (n 57).

87 'Covid: The New Lockdown Rules for England, Wales, Scotland and Northern Ireland' *BBC News* (17 November 2020) <https://www.bbc.com/news/explainers-52530518> accessed 18 November 2020.

C. Systemic Analysis

From a systemic point of view, COVID-19 and its containment measures had a two-fold impact on the criminal law system. On the one hand, the new reality had a strong impact on the whole criminal justice system, from criminalisation to procedure and punishment. On the other hand, it had an impact on the world and operations of criminals and criminal enterprises, whether professional or opportunistic.

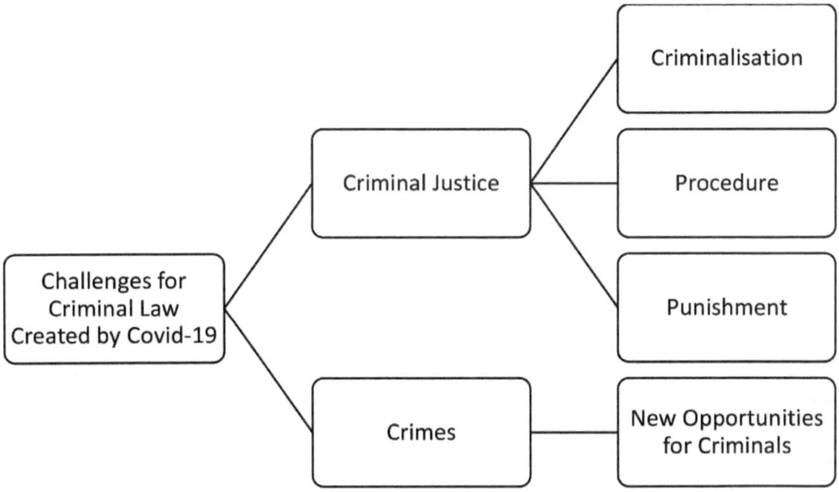

Figure 5 – COVID-19 Challenges at a Systemic Level

Regarding the criminalisation, the fast pace contagion of the pandemic and the quick identification of spreading behaviour required a fast criminalisation of a whole new number of conducts that were not considered criminal before the pandemic. Furthermore, from a procedural point of view, the COVID-19 emergency created serious difficulties in the delivery of justice. The judicial system required a series of adjustments since, for example, the physical presence of people in trial became highly limited. It also required long-lasting traditions to adapt to new realities such as for example the need to question witnesses through video conferences. The technology became both a solution, for it enabled distant social interaction, and a hurdle, for the limitations of present times may potentially interfere with the criminal procedure. This had huge consequences for the criminal justice system which faced a great deal of pressure and, in some cases for example, had to be more lenient towards less serious offences.[88]

Another way in which the criminal procedure was affected by the COVID-19 crisis, was the dilemma it created within the prison system. On the one hand, individuals that were convicted and spending time in prison before the pandemic became a vulnerable group and the government could no longer guarantee their safety if an outbreak appeared within the prison. On the other hand, the criminalisation of new behaviour casted doubt on the reasonability of sending COVID-19 related offenders to overcrowded prisons, thus increasing the risk on their lives and the lives of others.

Furthermore, the pandemic world scenario created further opportunities for criminals.[89] New criminal behaviours raised from the new social dynamics created by measures tending to contain the pandemic. Therefore, for example, lockdown and the need to use technology daily from our homes created new opportunities for cybercriminals to increase their success during phishing attempts.[90] Equally surging partly because of the COVID-19 containment measures, offences such as domestic abuse has experienced a 7.6 % of increase when compared to previous 12 months.[91] The lockdown has in some cases trapped a victim of domestic abuse with the abuser, and in others exposed the domestic abuse situation that was covered by the daily social life.

This section will thus focus on the systemic level of the UK's coronavirus response, specially referring to the normative response in general and the criminal law response in particular. The analysis ordered in accor-

88 Jamie Grierson, 'Suspects to avoid criminal charges in UK during COVID-19 crisis' *The Guardian* (14 April 2020) <https://www.theguardian.com/law/2020/apr/14/suspects-to-avoid-criminal-charges-in-uk-during-covid-19-crisis> accessed 30 November 2020.

89 Paul O'Hare, 'Covid in Scotland: How has the pandemic affected crime levels?' *BBC News* (13 November 2020) <https://www.bbc.com/news/uk-scotland-54916511> accessed 30 November 2020; Kevin Pratt, 'UK citizens urged to beware COVID-19 scammers' (*Forbes Advisor UK*) <https://www.forbes.com/uk/advisor/personal-finance/2020/11/27/uk-citizens-urged-to-beware-covid-19-scammers/> accessed 30 November 2020; 'The COVID-19 crisis has created the perfect storm for the illicit trade industry' (*Politics Home*, 26 November 2020) <https://www.politicshome.com/members/article/the-covid19-crisis-has-created-the-perfect-storm-for-the-illicit-trade-industry> accessed 30 November 2020.

90 Helen Warrell and Nic Fildes, 'Cyber criminals exploit Coronavirus disruption' [2020] *Financial Times* <https://www.ft.com/content/cbe2b35a-66d2-11ea-a3c9-1fe6fedcca75> accessed 30 November 2020.

91 O'Hare (n 89).

dance with the topics and categories presented in Figure 5. It will also be crossed by the trust in the decisions of government as well as the assessment of proportionality, impact and rationality of such measures in the pandemic context. The new regulatory measures and criminal provisions might be presented from a different perspective when analysing the legitimacy of the pursued end and the accuracy of the chosen means. Moreover, an impact assessment would also be idyllical when trying to understand the social benefits of such restrictive measures. This point will be related to the lack of transparency and accountability of the decision-making process from the centralised government without a proper parliamentary scrutiny.

I. Statutory Duties and Offences

At the time of writing this report, the Crown Prosecution Service in the UK released 19 guidelines related to coronavirus.[92] From those 19 guidelines, 2 were related to the Coronavirus Act 2020 and 17 were related to the different regulations passed by government. Thus, the statutory duties and offences can be divided into those that are contemplated in the Coronavirus Act 2020 and those that are enforced by executive regulations.

92 'Prosecution Guidance | The Crown Prosecution Services 'C' <https://www.cps.gov.uk/prosecution-guidance> accessed 1 December 2020.

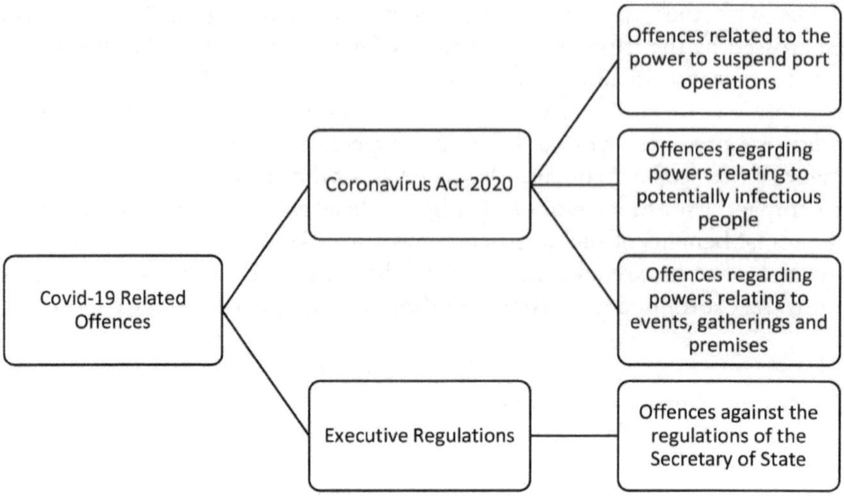

Figure 6 – Diagram of COVID-19 Related Offences

Regarding the Coronavirus Act 2020, it contains 9 sections with specific offences and 2 sections regarding particular procedural provisions. The three procedural provisions refer to the temporary disapplication of disclosure offences in Scotland (section 34), the suspension of offence relating to signing of declaration for cremations in Scotland (schedule 14, section 8), and the modification of the section 22(11A) of the Prosecution of Offences Act 1985 (power of Secretary of State to set time limits in relation to preliminary stages of criminal proceedings) by limiting the cases in which the trial on indictment is considered to start, to those circumstances in which the jury is sworn to consider the issue of guilt or when a plea of guilt is accepted (schedule 24, section 12). The 9 sections containing the statutory offences may be divided into three sub-categories. The first category contains those offences related to the power to suspend port operations (schedule 20, section 6). The second category refers to the powers relating to potentially infectious people in England, Scotland, Wales and Northern Ireland (schedule 21, section 23, section 45, section 67, and 88 respectively). Finally, the third category involves powers relating to events, gatherings and premises in England, Scotland, Wales and Northern Ireland (schedule 22, section 9, section 21, section 32, and section 44, respectively).

Conversely, the offences contemplated in executive norms respond to the different Health Protection Regulations and lockdown measures including, for example, the tier system in England, Scotland, Wales and Northern Ireland.[93] Moreover, the offences within a certain regulation will change depending on, for example, the local tier regulation.[94] As an example of the offences contemplated by executive regulations, section 8 of the Health Protection (Coronavirus, Restrictions) (No. 2) (England) Regulations 2020 establishes that,

"(1) A person who without reasonable excuse contravenes a requirement in regulation 4, 5, 6(10), (11) or 7 commits an offence.
(2) A person who obstructs, without reasonable excuse, any person carrying out a function under these Regulations, including any person who is a relevant person for the purposes of regulation 7, commits an offence.
(3) A person who, without reasonable excuse, contravenes a direction given under regulation 7, or fails to comply with a reasonable instruction or a prohibition notice given by a relevant person under regulation 7, commits an offence.
(4) An offence under this regulation is punishable on summary conviction by a fine (…)".

Same as the offences within the executive regulations, the offences under the Coronavirus Act 2020 aim at securing compliance with its provisions. For example, the offences related to the power to suspend port operations, punish those behaviours that contradict the regulations of the schedule on port operations. The same legislative technique is used throughout the rest of the offences, where the law states more or less the same formula, mainly that,

> "A person commits an offence if the person fails without reasonable excuse to comply with a prohibition, requirement or restriction imposed on the person by a direction issued under this Part of this Schedule" (Schedule 22, section 9 of the Coronavirus Act 2020).

---

93 'Covid: What Are the New Tiers and Lockdown Rules in England, Scotland, Wales and Northern Ireland?' *BBC News* (3 December 2020) <https://www.bbc.com/news/explainers-52530518> accessed 8 December 2020.

94 'Coronavirus: Local Coronavirus Regulations Tier 3 | The Crown Prosecution Service' <https://www.cps.gov.uk/legal-guidance/coronavirus-local-coronavirus-regulations-tier-3> accessed 4 December 2020; 'Coronavirus: Health Protection (Coronavirus, Restrictions) (No.2) (England) Regulations 2020 | The Crown Prosecution Service' <https://www.cps.gov.uk/legal-guidance/coronavirus-health-protection-coronavirus-restrictions-no2-england-regulations-2020> accessed 4 December 2020.

As stated by the Crown Prosecution Service (CPS), the difference between the Coronavirus Act 2020 offences and the Health Protection (Coronavirus) Regulations offences rests in that the former mainly refers to "(…) potentially infectious persons who refuse to co-operate with the police or public health officers, when they are required to be screened for COVID-19", and the latter provides a legal test to "(…) whether someone has a reasonable excuse for being outside their home".[95] Although this elements might be within the core differences between the two categories of offences, the CPS view on these differences may be interpreted as an over-simplification of the width and height of the coronavirus related offences.

II. Criminalisation, Over-criminalisation, and Legal Certainty

This section deals with the debates surrounding the legal certainty of COVID-19 related measures, including statutory offences and executive regulations. Fast pace legislative technique triggered by the need to provide a swift response to an unprecedented and quickly volatile health crisis does not provide fertile ground for clear and precise laws. Thus, the main questions aimed to address in this section are whether the citizens perceive they know the rules or whether they could reasonably be expected to know the rules. The answer to these questions would be hypothesised from the quality (and quantity) of the norms as well as their drafting technique. Moreover, the issues of legality and legitimacy will appear once again in relation to the parliamentary scrutiny of the criminal law response to COVID-19.

As it was hinted in previous sections, the statutory duties and offences related to the coronavirus emergency in the UK are spread across numerous provisions in the four nations which constitute the UK. Thus, the offences have three levels of complexity including their constant change and update, their diverse sources (whether an Act or a Regulation), and their different jurisdictions (England, Scotland, Wales, and Northern Ireland). Moreover, the pressing need for a quick response and the need to enforce highly restrictive measures, such as lockdown, turned the UK government towards the most widespread enforcement mechanism, punishment. As

95 'CPS Announces Review Findings for First 200 Cases under Coronavirus Laws | The Crown Prosecution Service' <https://www.cps.gov.uk/cps/news/cps-announces-review-findings-first-200-cases-under-coronavirus-laws> accessed 4 December 2020.

stated by Jennifer Collins, "there is comfort in the familiar".[96] As explained in previous sections, the criminal law reaction to the pandemic has witness a massive creation of offences with renewed powers and discretion to law enforcement and criminal justice agents. The result may require an assessment of proportionality and rationality in those cases in which coronavirus related offences are given priority and labelled as horrific,[97] while other offences are being discharged as less serious to reduce pressure on the judicial system.[98]

It may also be argued that in the case of a pandemic emergency, there is a special need to reassure the validity of the norm by increasing the level of punishment and securing its enforcement.[99] The punishment thus communicates the validity of the norm and reassures the rule of law. A highly prioritised punishment with increased sentences for aggravating circumstances related to coronavirus offences, thus sends the message that reducing those behaviour is a number one priority for society.

The view on the need to reassure the norm through punishment and communicate its high level of priority is confirmed by the CPS guidelines and the position of law enforcement agents.[100] Moreover, the views of law enforcement and judiciary agents reveal a high-level preventive discourse, by which the justification of unprecedented powers to retrain individual rights is the need to contain and thus prevent the spread of the virus to keep society safe. As it was asserted by the CPS Director of Legal Service, Gregor McGill, "The coronavirus pandemic (…) has resulted in the criminal justice system being given exceptional powers to help keep us all safe".[101] In the same way, the National Police Chiefs' Council chair, Martin Hewitt, stated that,

96 Jennifer Collins, 'Coronavirus and the spread of crime control' (*UK Constitutional Law Association*, 28 April 2020) <https://ukconstitutionallaw.org/2020/04/28/jennifer-collins-coronavirus-and-the-spread-of-crime-control/> accessed 20 November 2020.

97 'CPS brings Coronavirus criminals to justice | The Crown Prosecution Service' <https://www.cps.gov.uk/cps/news/cps-brings-coronavirus-criminals-justice> accessed 20 November 2020.

98 Grierson (n 88).

99 Günther Jakobs, 'Imputation in criminal law and the conditions for norm validity' (2004) 7 Buffalo Criminal Law Review 491.

100 'CPS Brings Coronavirus Criminals to Justice | The Crown Prosecution Service' (n 97).

101 'CPS Announces Review Findings for First 200 Cases under Coronavirus Laws | The Crown Prosecution Service' (n 95).

> "These were unprecedented circumstances in which officers were presented with new powers within days of them being announced. This has all been done at pace and everyone in the Criminal Justice System has had to deal with a new body of legislation, which has undoubtedly led to some confusion".[102]

This reveals not only that legal certainty is indeed an issue for society due to the complexity and density of the coronavirus legislation, but that is also a problem for law enforcement agents and judicial operators that find it hard to keep up and stay updated.

Moreover, as it was stated by the CPS on a review of the coronavirus-related prosecutions, all 44 procedures under the Coronavirus Act 2020 finalising in March & April were found to be unlawful by May 2020 (Table 1).[103]

Number of cases finalised (March & April)	**Number incorrectly charged**	
Health Protection Regulations: 187 cases	Withdrawn	7
	Returned to Court	5
	Total	**12**
Coronavirus Act: 44 cases	Withdrawn	31
	Returned to Court	13
	Total	**44**

Table 1 – Number of Cases ending in March & April that were Incorrectly Charged

As shown in Table 2, the same happened with the cases finalising in September. After the review of the CPS, out of the 26 offences charged under the Coronavirus Act 2020, all of them were found to be unlawful.[104]

102 ibid.

103 ibid; 'All Prosecutions under New Coronavirus Act Unlawful, Review Finds' (*The Independent*, 15 May 2020) <https://www.independent.co.uk/news/uk/home-news/coronavirus-act-unlawful-prosecutions-review-uk-a9516566.html> accessed 9 December 2020.

104 'September's Coronavirus Review Findings | The Crown Prosecution Service' <https://www.cps.gov.uk/cps/news/septembers-coronavirus-review-findings> accessed 17 December 2020.

Number of cases finalised (September)	Number incorrectly charged	
Health Protection (Coronavirus, Restrictions) Regulations: 122 cases	Withdrawn	11
	Returned to Court	4
	Total	**15**
Coronavirus Act: 26 cases	Withdrawn	22
	Returned to Court	4
	Total	**26**

Table 2 – Number of Cases ending in September that were Incorrectly Charged

The steady trend of unlawful prosecutions shows the extent and consequences of legal uncertainty, even for police officers, and the constrains of coronavirus on criminal procedures. While the CPS statistics predated some of the Health Protection Regulations, the exponential growth of the number of laws and regulations on coronavirus related issues and the vagueness of non-exhaustive lists of 'reasonable excuses' not to comply with them, may explain the fact that government did not do better later in the year.[105]

Furthermore, most of the offences contemplate the caveat of being justified in case of having a 'reasonable excuse' not to comply with the prohibition, requirements or restrictions imposed by the norm. While in some cases the law shifted towards a more detailed explanation of what constitutes a 'reasonable excuse' and contemplated a non-exhaustive list of possible excuses, the term is far from being respectful of the principle of legal certainty.[106] Thus the complexity of a diverse and multi-layered source of coronavirus related offences (Coronavirus Act 2020 and executive regulations), is complemented by a rather vague legislative technique.

The concept of 'reasonable excuse' in the coronavirus regulations was characterised by the literature as broad and vague.[107] Acknowledging the criticism, government provided a non-exhaustive list of possible reasonable excuses that not only did not help clarify the core concept of 'reasonable

105 'Government refuses to bolish Coronavirus law used unlawfully in every prosecution' (*The Independent*, 28 June 2020) <https://www.independent.co.uk/news/uk/home-news/coronavirus-law-government-cps-lockdown-unlawful-prosecutions-a9577371.html> accessed 9 December 2020.

106 Fortson (n 51).

107 Tom Hickman, 'The use and misuse of guidance during the UK's Coronavirus lockdown' [2020] SSRN 32, 19/20.

excuse',[108] but contributed to the lack of legal certainty. This may also be explained by the local/central dichotomy embedded in the UK's response to civil emergencies tradition. Leaving enough discretion for local authorities or law enforcement agents to be able to make a decision on the spot without pressure or consequences, may lead to individuals having to risk authorities disagreeing with them on what constitutes a reasonable excuse.[109] Thus, the subjectivity of the interpretation on what constitutes a 'reasonable excuse', may lead to legal uncertainty, which may lead to an unequal enforcement of the law, which ultimately undermines the trust in government and the legitimacy of the norm.

The 'reasonable excuse' justification may also be explained by the uncertainties faced by the government in such an unprecedented health emergency. The impossibility of weighing a large number of variables in an *ex-ante* analysis of the consequences of the coronavirus norms and regulations may have contributed to their vagueness. Leaving room for adjustment at further levels of government also presents the advantage of leaving the decision-making responsibility to those how have more and more recent information. This point of view thus criticises the consequentialist approach to law-making. If the law is being judged from a utilitarian point of view on the benefits and values that brings to society, the lack of information in the COVID-19 crisis prevents an accurate prediction of the benefits and consequences. For example, as recognised by the WHO, while lockdown may be beneficial for short-term containment of the virus, it may have devastating long-term consequences for economies.[110] Thus the impossibility to foresee and weigh consequences beforehand may explain the broad and vague legislative technique.

Additionally, the over-criminalisation that appeared as a result of prohibiting new behaviours against coronavirus regulations were not the only means of abuse of criminal law during the COVID-19 emergency. In this sense, traditional offences were also found to be reinterpreted to encompass coronavirus-related offences. As an example, offences such as assault found a broaden interpretation by which it was applicable to those cases were the perpetrator coughed or spitted on the victims (namely,

108 Tom Hickman, Emma Dixon and Rachel Jones, 'Coronavirus and civil liberties in the UK' (2020) 25 Judicial Review 151, s 16.

109 ibid 17.

110 'Coronavirus Disease (COVID-19): Herd Immunity, Lockdowns and COVID-19' (n 64).

law enforcement agents or healthcare workers).[111] The CPS referred to the charging of old offences of assault under section 1(1) and 1(2) of the Assaults on Emergency Workers (Offences) Act 2018, and showed *inter alia* the case of Bevan Burke who breached the terms of his licence and while doing so, coughed at police officers and told them he hoped they died from the virus. Burke's sentence was "(…) 42 weeks in prison for two counts of assaulting an emergency worker and assault by beating".[112] In other cases, the sentence was increased by the aggravating circumstances of an offender who in his course of perpetration a theft, made racist statements in relation to coronavirus, which amounted to racially aggravated harassment.[113]

Overall, the criminalisation of new behaviour against coronavirus laws and regulations has not been the only area of criminal law affected by an overreaction of the legal system. The new interpretation of old offences appears also as an added behaviour that needs to be taken into consideration by law enforcement agents and judicial officials. This great new workload for the police force and judicial system may have contributed to the lack of legal certainty. The system faced an unknown and unprecedented threat which reflected upon the uncertainty of government on how to overcome it (in some countries the lack of knowledge was even recognised by the president),[114] and was evidenced by the enactment of broad and vague laws and regulations.

III. Criminal law to restrict movement

The proportionality of restrictive measures may seem questionable since a proper ponderation of the means to a legitimate end has not been analysed democratically through parliament for most of the regulations enacted until October 2020. In the BSE outbreak precedent of 1997,[115] restrictive

111 Terry Skolnik, 'Criminal law during (and after) COVID-19' (2020) 43 Manitoba Law Journal 145, 153.

112 'CPS Brings Coronavirus Criminals to Justice | The Crown Prosecution Service' (n 97).

113 Collins (n 96).

114 'Inside Macron's Coronavirus War' (*POLITICO*, 12 April 2020) <https://www.politico.eu/interactive/inside-emmanuel-macron-coronavirus-war/> accessed 8 December 2020.

115 Guardian Staff, 'BSE Crisis: Timeline' *The Guardian* (26 October 2000) <https://www.theguardian.com/uk/2000/oct/26/bse3> accessed 14 November 2020.

measures on importation and meat consumption may have seemed proportionate and democratically adopted at a domestic and EU level. While the level of propagation and lack of clear scientifical evidence at the beginning of the COVID-19 crisis might have justified an over-criminalisation and the adoption of over-restrictive measures, it started to be less and less justified as more scientifical evidence was gathered. The proportionality issue also required weighing the trade off when imposing an extreme measure as a freedom restriction.

Moreover, the relaxations of the first lockdown in England for example, questioned much of the privileges safeguarded by such measures. The relaxation of the first lockdown measure in England included activities such as picnics, tennis, golf, country outings, etc, which raised the question of the elitist nature of the measures.[116] Another questioned aspect of the laws to restrict movement in the UK, was that it was clear from the start that it did not constitute a sustainable long-term solution to the emergency. The measures aimed at delaying the pace of propagation and thus giving healthcare services the time to deal with the overload demand.[117] Again, the lack of available data and certainty over a number of variables made it hard for central governments to weigh the pros and cons of such restrictive measures. Thus, many members of government and the public in general remained skeptical about the effectiveness of lockdown measures and cast doubt on stressing out the collateral damage.[118]

The impact on the legitimacy of these measures was also fostered by the lack of parliamentary scrutiny. The fact that the lockdown measures were accompanied by offences aiming at securing the compliance of the regulations without having the assessment of parliament also casted doubt on the legitimacy of these criminal law provisions. Considering criminal law as the most restrictive rules on individual rights. They ought to be enacted and implemented with utmost care. This care may be considered as requiring the minimum benchmark of a democratic assessment where

116 UKCLA, 'Tom Hickman' (n 49).

117 'Our plan to rebuild: The UK Government's COVID-19 recovery strategy' (n 80) fig 1.; Explanatory memorandum to 'Coronavirus: Health Protection (Coronavirus, Restrictions) (No.2) (England) Regulations 2020 | The Crown Prosecution Service' (n 94).

118 Jemima Kelly, 'Why are we really in lockdown?' (17 April 2020) <http://ftalphaville.ft.com/2020/04/15/1586943153000/Why-are-we-really-in-lockdown--/> accessed 8 December 2020.

all affected parts can have a deliberation on the necessity, rationality and proportionality of such restrictive measures.[119]

IV. Impact on Criminal Procedure and Debates on Punishment

The coronavirus crisis also brought some debates around the proportionality and rationality of coronavirus-related criminal laws and restrictions in relation to punishment and prisons, as well as on the impact on criminal procedure. In this sense, the debate can be divided in two.

On the one hand, the coronavirus crisis brought the debate surrounding the release of convicted criminals that were serving sentences in prison. The main idea behind this debate was that because of the close nature of prisons and the fact that many where overcrowded or not clean enough,[120] the government was no longer able to guarantee the physical safety of inmates. The premise was that in case of a certain outbreak within the premises of a prison, the vulnerability of inmates was particularly high.[121] This debate sparked several points regarding the need to make criminals serve the sentences of their convictions and the right of convicted criminals to basic safety health requirements.[122] While releasing convicted criminals at an early stage may jeopardise the victims, and the general public, views on justice, some voices put forward the need to leave behind old theories of punishment and focus on restorative justice initiatives.[123] This would require working on the relationship between offenders and victims and thus reduce the need for excessive punishment.

---

119 Carlos Santiago Nino, *The constitution of deliberative democracy* (Yale University Press 1996) 219.

120 'Prisoners locked up for 23 hours due to Covid rules is "dangerous"' *BBC News* (20 October 2020) <https://www.bbc.com/news/uk-54607813> accessed 8 December 2020.

121 Jamie Grierson Home affairs correspondent, 'Covid cases in prisons in England and Wales double in October' *The Guardian* (13 November 2020) <https://www.theguardian.com/society/2020/nov/13/covid-cases-in-prisons-in-england-and-wales-double-in-october> accessed 8 December 2020.

122 Karthik Sivashanker and others, 'COVID-19 and decarceration' (2020) 369 BMJ m1865, 1.

123 'Opinion: Thousands of prisoners may be exposed to Coronavirus – We need to release them all' (*The Independent*, 21 May 2020) <https://www.independent.co.uk/voices/coronavirus-uk-prison-covid-19-probation-a9525601.html> accessed 8 December 2020.

In this regard, the chairman of the Sentencing Council, Lord Justice Holroyde, stated that,

> "The Sentencing Council is aware of and understands the concerns that many people have about the effect the COVID-19 emergency is having on conditions in prisons and the potentially heavier impact of custodial sentences on offenders and their families. There are well-established sentencing principles which, with sentencing guidelines, are sufficiently flexible to deal with all circumstances, including the consequences of the current emergency. These principles are familiar to judges and magistrates and were reaffirmed by the Lord Chief Justice when giving the judgment of the Court of Appeal in the case of *Manning*. (…) Each case must of course be considered on its own facts, and the court has an obligation to protect the public and victims of crime. Judges and magistrates must make their independent decisions as to what sentence is just and proportionate in all the circumstances of each individual case".[124]

The case of *Manning* involved a guilty plea to four counts of sexual activity with a child, contrary to section 9(1) of the Sexual Offences Act 2003 (counts 1 to 4), and one count of Causing or inciting a child to engage in sexual activity, contrary to section 10(1) of the same Act (count 5).[125] In this opportunity, the court established a precedent in which the COVID-19 emergency could and should be taken into consideration when measuring the appropriate punishment. In this sense, the Court said that,

> "We would mention one other factor of relevance. We are hearing this Reference at the end of April 2020, when the nation remains in lock-down as a result of the COVID-19 emergency. The impact of that emergency on prisons is well-known. We are being invited in this Reference to order a man to prison nine weeks after he was given a suspended sentence, when he has complied with his curfew and has engaged successfully with the Probation Service. The current conditions in prisons represent a factor which can properly be taken into account in deciding whether to suspend a sentence. In accordance

---

124 'The pplication of sentencing principles during the COVID-19 emergency – Sentencing' <https://www.sentencingcouncil.org.uk/news/item/the-application-of-sentencing-principles-during-the-covid-19-emergency/> accessed 17 December 2020.

125 *Regina v Christopher Manning* [2020] EWCA Crim 592 (Court of Appeal Criminal Division).

> with established principles, any court will take into account the likely impact of a custodial sentence upon an offender and, where appropriate, upon others as well. Judges and magistrates can, therefore, and in our judgment should, keep in mind that the impact of a custodial sentence is likely to be heavier during the current emergency than it would otherwise be. Those in custody are, for example, confined to their cells for much longer periods than would otherwise be the case – currently, 23 hours a day. They are unable to receive visits. Both they and their families are likely to be anxious about the risk of the transmission of COVID-19".[126]

The principle of taking into consideration the state of emergency when deciding on the length of the custodial sentence, was confirmed in *Jones* and recently (November) in *Taylor*, where the length of the sentence was reduced from 8 to 6 months, and from immediate detention to detention suspended respectively, when taking into consideration the COVID-19 situation.[127] The scope of the considerations and leniency established in *Manning* where furthered narrowed down by following precedents. After Jones, the court was also called to decide an appeal on similar grounds in the case of *Randhawa*, although in this opportunity the sentence was delivered before the COVID-19 lockdown. In this case the court decided that the sentencing reduction has no application in cases where the sentence took place before the lockdown measures.[128] Further clarifying the limits of the leniency, the Court of Appeal established in *Whittington* that,

> "The more serious the offence, and the longer the sentence, the less the pandemic can weigh in the balance in favour of a reduction unless there is clear, cogent and persuasive evidence of a disproportionately harsh impact on the prisoner. Over the course of a long sentence the period of time during which the prisoner is subject to lock down because of the pandemic might be quite short in relative terms. It is for prison governors to do what they can to alleviate the worst adverse effects".[129]

---

126 ibid 41.

127 *Regina v Paul Anthony Jones* [2020] EWCA Crim 764 (Court of Appeal (Criminal Division)) [19]; *Regina v Thomas James Taylor* [2020] EWCA Crim 1630 (Court of Appeal Criminal Division) [10/11].

128 *Regina v Kaljit Kaur Randhawa* [2020] EWCA Crim 1071 (Court of Appeal Criminal Division) [15].

129 *Tyler Whittington v The Queen* [2020] EWCA Crim 1560 (Court of Appeal (Criminal Division)) [30].

This debate in the UK led to the intention of making early release of low-risk prisoners under certain surveillance requirements such as electronic tags.[130] Although the aim was to release around 4,000 inmates, the Common Justice Committee mentioned that no more than 18 prisoners were released by 20th April 2020.[131] The issue becomes even more worrying since the victims of COVID-19 in prisons are not only prisoners but prison workers and ultimately society, since the prison walls are not able to contain the virus. As a focus of infection, prisons have the potential of being a bastion for propagation. Moreover, the debates around prisons also presented the diminished rights of prisoners with yet another hurdle, since for example prison visits were also affected by the tier restrictions, being suspended in tier 3 areas.[132] This widens the levels of social isolation for inmates, who now can only be contacted through email, voicemail or letter, and collides with their basic human rights.[133]

On the other hand, the debate also reached the issue of new convictions on coronavirus-related offences and the proportionality of sending them to serve prison sentences. While doing so would be consistent with the idea that more punishment reassures the validity of the norm, it would be detrimental for overcrowded and unsanitary prisons in a coronavirus context. Furthermore, the crisis has also affected the activity of the judicial system which as a consequence has convicted less people than previous years,[134] with suspected offenders of less serious crimes even avoiding criminal charges.[135]

In this sense, criminal procedure law has been under a stress test in relation to how much long-lasting traditions can be accommodated to the new coronavirus regulations. Issues such as questioning witnesses or even the public presence in trials had to be adapted to the new possibilities. Moreover, judicial officers where restricted in their possibility of attending

---

130 'Coronavirus: low-risk prisoners set for early release' *BBC News* (4 April 2020) <https://www.bbc.com/news/uk-52165919> accessed 8 December 2020.

131 Francis Pakes, 'Coronavirus: why swathes of prisoners are being released in the world's most punitive States' (*The Conversation*, 20 April 2020) <http://theconversation.com/coronavirus-why-swathes-of-prisoners-are-being-released-in-the-worlds-most-punitive-states-136563> accessed 8 December 2020.

132 'Coronavirus (COVID-19) and Prisons. Guidance for Families and Friends of People in Prison in England and Wales during the Coronavirus Pandemic.' (*GOV.UK*, 2 December 2020) <https://www.gov.uk/guidance/coronavirus-covid-19-and-prisons> accessed 8 December 2020.

133 ibid.

134 Pakes (n 131).

135 Grierson (n 88).

court or even doing basic presential tasks. In this sense, as an example, in *GP* the Court of Appeals had to decide on how COVID-19 might have affected the work of the jury.[136] Although in this particular case the Court of Appeals reached the conclusion that the state of emergency did not affect the jury, the fact that it was a matter of appeal serves as an example of the judicial concerns raised by the state of emergency.

Contrary to other jobs, while some judicial activity may enable distant engagement, others require workers to be present in the courtroom. Tasks such as questioning witnesses or assessing evidence require a certain degree of immediacy that has been challenged by the social distancing measures.[137] Courtrooms also tend to have very limited capacity, thus not being able to accommodate under the new measures the amount of people that would normally fit in such a small and confined space. Jury trials in such context may pose unresolvable challenges.[138] Likewise, the extent of the use of technology required a more through debate that the one presented until the coronavirus crisis. Accepting evidence that has been produced and evaluated with different rules of social distancing may not be fully compliant with defence rights and may require some thorough debate and consideration. As a consequence, criminal procedure rules have changed or have been amended virtually every month since the outbreak of the coronavirus emergency.[139]

V. Criminals also Adapt

Finally, a central issue for law enforcement agents, policy makers and law makers, has been the new trends in criminal behaviour forced by the new rules of society. This change in social interaction created a new playground for criminals that were used to operate in different contexts, with different

---

136 *Regina v 'GP'* [2020] EWCA Crim 1056 (Court of Appeal Criminal Division) [36/37].

137 Owen Bowcott Legal affairs correspondent, 'Has Coronavirus changed the UK justice system for ever?' *The Guardian* (24 May 2020) <https://www.theguardian.com/law/2020/may/24/has-the-uk-justice-system-been-changed-for-ever-by-the-coronavirus> accessed 9 December 2020.

138 ibid.

139 'Announcements from the Criminal Procedure Rule Committee' (*GOV.UK*) <https://www.gov.uk/guidance/announcements-from-the-criminal-procedure-rule-committee> accessed 9 December 2020; 'Criminal Procedure Rules' <https://www.justice.gov.uk/courts/procedure-rules/criminal> accessed 9 December 2020.

dynamics and opportunities. Much as the rest of society, criminals had to adapt to a new normality.

In this sense, the UK's 2020 trends in police recorded crime saw an annual decrease of 4 %.[140] The substantial fall was mainly focused on the months from April to June which may be explained by the increased amount of time that people spent in lockdown, thus reducing the crime opportunities in public spaces.[141] As stated by the office for National Statistics,

> "Overall, theft offences fell by 15 % in the year ending June 2020. There were also falls in robbery offences (10 % decrease), sexual offences (7 % decrease) and criminal damage and arson (8 % decrease)".[142]

Nevertheless, offences such as homicide increased 9 % (6 % corresponds to the Essex lorry deaths case),[143] drug offences raised 21 %,[144] and cases of domestic abuse increased 21 % (with a 9 % increase in the period from April to June 2020 when compared to April to June 2019).[145] Moreover, the Office for National Statistics noticed that there was an increased demand for domestic abuse-related services, such as specialised helplines or websites, during the lockdown period.[146]

Other such as fraud and computer misuse, for example, also showed a trend of increasing cases although they had different outputs depending on the reporting bodies. In this sense, while the centre Action Fraud reported a 4 % rise in fraud offence, the UK Finance organisation reported a 44 % rise and CIFAS reported a 4 % decrease. As mention by the Office of National Statistics, these reports need to be interpreted in the context of the coverage and fraud types in which each reporting body focuses.[147]

Overall, as stated by the Office of National Statistics,

---

140 Nick Stripe, 'Crime in England and Wales: Year Ending June 2020' (Office for National Statistics 2020) Statistical Bulletin 10 <https://www.ons.gov.uk/peoplepopulationandcommunity/crimeandjustice/bulletins/crimeinenglandandwales/yearendingjune2020#toc> accessed 6 December 2020.

141 ibid.

142 ibid.

143 'Essex Lorry Deaths: "Every Cog" in People Smuggling Plan "in the Know"' *BBC News* (2 December 2020) <https://www.bbc.com/news/uk-england-essex-55158353> accessed 7 December 2020; Stripe (n 140) 10.

144 Stripe (n 140) 10.

145 ibid 21.

146 ibid.

147 ibid 23.

> "The coronavirus (COVID-19) pandemic is likely to have had differential effects on trends in fraud and computer misuse offences. For example, Action Fraud reported that the increase in "online shopping and auctions" fraud (to 70,403 offences) could be accounted for by the increase in online shopping whilst the decrease in "other advance fee" fraud (to 25,418 offences) could be attributed to reduction in holiday fraud figures as fewer holidays were booked".[148]

Moreover, regarding domestic abuse for example, and as stated by the director of the UK Safer Internet Centre, David Wright, 60 % of peopled that survived domestic abused reported that the abuses got worse during the pandemic.[149] Therefore, the regulations aiming at containing and controlling the COVID-19 emergency created a particular set of circumstances that produced a new set of problems and criminal behaviour that responded to the new circumstances. Although the health crisis caused by the pandemic created new opportunities for criminals, it also created a different social context that might foster worsen versions of pre-pandemic crimes.

Overall, this change in the criminal context both from the new opportunities and the exaltation of old conducts, created a need for law enforcement agents and judiciary officials to redistribute priorities and relocate resources in a very fast pace. Moreover, the actors involved in the emergency response needed to overcome the issues of legal certainty and the enforcement of new offences from the Coronavirus Act 2020 and the Health Regulations in a very short period. This led back to the idea that legal certainty did affect trust in government not only for the lack of certainty on the lawfulness of pre-pandemic common behaviour, but also because government representatives such as law enforcement agents were also uncertain of the rules in place. This might also be another variable that could explain the undermining of trust in government and the doubts on the legitimacy of governmental measures due to their lack of transparency and lack of clarity on the means, ends, proportionality and rationality of COVID-19-related measures.

148 ibid.

149 '"Revenge porn new normal" after Cases Surge in Lockdown' *BBC News* (16 September 2020) <https://www.bbc.com/news/technology-54149682> accessed 7 December 2020.

VI. Key Points

As a summary, the analysis at the systemic level regarding the criminal law response of the UK to the Coronavirus emergency can be narrowed down to the following points:

- The coronavirus emergency has affected both the way in which government and the judicial system address and relate with the new measures that tend to contain and mitigate the effects of the pandemic.
- Regarding government, the emergency has triggered an over-legislation and over-criminalisation of new behaviours that aim at enforcing the new rules to face the health emergency. The number of new regulations that are created and updated at a very fast pace also challenge the limits of legal certainty. The same can be said of the vague legislative technique used by government due to the uncertainties presented by the virus. Thus, justifications such as having a 'reasonable excuse' to avoid compliance with regulations only serve to foster legal uncertainty and evidence a governmental lack of clarity.
- The lack of parliamentary scrutiny has also raised concern regarding the proportionality and legitimacy of highly restrictive measures such as lockdowns. Involving parliament in such decisions would benefit the decision-making process by providing more transparency as well as legitimacy. Moreover, as opposed to scientific bodies such as SAGE, parliament would involve a dialectic process of deliberation, thus enabling different social interests to be weighed and assessed before enacting extreme measures.
- Regarding the punishment, the coronavirus crisis has challenged the proportionality and rationality of custodial sentences when considering the risks of incrementing the prison population during a pandemic. Moreover, courts acknowledged that a prison sentence during a pandemic constitutes a harsher punishment than in normal times. It has also increased the seriousness of traditional offences such as assault, thus resulting in lengthier sentences for aggravated circumstances according to the COVID-19 context. For example, the case of spitting on law enforcement agents while being arrested or saying racist phrases in relation to coronavirus during a theft.
- Moreover, the CPS review of the prosecutions under the Coronavirus Act 2020 has shown that none of the charges have been lawful, thus strengthening the evidence of legal uncertainty.
- Finally, the coronavirus emergency has created new opportunities for criminals provided by a new set of social relationships. The rules and

measures that tend to contain and mitigate the impact of the virus, also pushed criminals to adapt in a constantly changing scenario where the uncertainty may serve as an advantage for criminal enterprises. The cases of new types of fraud or cybercrimes serve as examples.

D. *Policing, Prevention and Control Analysis*

The third level of analysis of the present report focuses on the surveillance and policing reactions to the COVID-19 crisis. As presented in previous sections this level of analysis will be cut across by the central debates on data collection, data usage, surveillance techniques and privacy in the UK's emergency response to COVID-19. Issues such as transparency of decision-making processes that use a vast amount of data collected individuals will also be presented as a core issue within policing, surveillance, and technology.

From the postal espionage crisis of 1844 to the modern international controversies on the extent of data processing and storing, the British history of surveillance and intelligence may provide some answers to the nature of the problems faced today.[150] In this sense, as stated by authors like David Vincent,

> "(...) the nineteenth century was inventing a problem which the early twenty-first is struggling to resolve. It was always possible through postal espionage for one country to open the mail of citizens of another. As the Report from the Secret Committee on the Post Office established, this had been practised at least since Elizabethan times and it was the essence of the request by the Austrian government in 1844. But the arrival of electronic and then digital networks, and the growing presence of private companies in their management, have vastly compounded the potential for the narrative of national liberty to collide with the realities of international surveillance".[151]

Offering a narrative of national liberty and national security based on the importance of information and data, MP Theresa May followed the PM in the parliamentary debate on the new lockdown on the 4th November 2020,

150 David Vincent, 'Surveillance, privacy and history' (*History & Policy*, 1 October 2013) <http://www.historyandpolicy.org/index.php/policy-papers/papers/surveillance-privacy-and-history> accessed 15 December 2020.

151 ibid.

pointing out that, "(…) just as Ministers are making tough decisions, so is Parliament, and Parliament will make better decisions if it is fully and properly informed".[152] Moreover, the former PM continued to assess the use of data of the new government and pointed out the Texas sharpshooter fallacy in which the government is basing their policy. She pointed out that, "(…) for many people it looks as though the figures are being chosen to support the policy, rather than the policy being based on the figures".[153] In a call for transparency she urged the need to know the methodology and the details behind the scientific models that are stirring the policy decisions of government.[154] She also reassured the need to make available that data for parliament to weigh all the costs of the pandemic and the policy measures and make a democratic judgment of the appropriate policies. In this sense, she asserted that,

> "There is a lack of data on the costs of the decisions being made: costs in non-covid treatment in the NHS, and in non-covid deaths; costs in domestic abuse; costs in mental health, with possibly more suicides; and of course costs to the economy, with jobs lost, livelihoods shattered, businesses failing and whole sectors damaged. What sort of airline industry will we have as we come out of this? What sort of hospitality sector will there be? How many small independent shops will be left? The Government must have made that assessment, so let us see it and make our own judgments".[155]

The issues raised by the former PM have been debated along this report and have been presented as the consequences of lack of transparency and lack of parliamentary scrutiny. The tensions between central government, parliament and local authorities becomes evident in debates such as the one held for the lockdown restrictions of the second wave of COVID-19.

The debates surrounding the rationality, proportionality and necessity of such restrictive coronavirus measures is not only concerned with the need to make democratic decision even in emergency context, but also on the way in which government collects, and uses data. As it was pointed out in section one, much of the decision-making and policy-making process in the UK showed technocratic features. This means that bodies that aid

---

152 The Telegraph (n 5) s 00:47:50.

153 'Public Health: 4 Nov 2020: House of Commons Debates' (*TheyWorkForYou*) <https://www.theyworkforyou.com/debates/?id=2020-11-04e.331.0> accessed 9 December 2020.

154 ibid.

155 ibid.

policy-making groups within government play a decisive role in skewing the emergency policy towards certain measures. The problem with this epistemological process of arriving to public policies aiming to contain and solve the coronavirus emergency, is that the bodies that provide highly relevant input such as SAGE, are not being democratically scrutinised or held accountable for their methods. In this sense, the input provided by bodies and agencies like SAGE impact not only in the type of policies implemented by government, but also on the type of message sent by government. Thus, relationship of trust built between government and society will be very much dependent on the type and quality of the message transmitted by government. While a strong position of leadership may be required, flawed decisions based on obscure methodologies may undermine trust in government and doom any valuable effort to overcome the civil emergency.

In this context, policing and surveillance play a key role in responding to data and collecting data, respectively. The difference between policing and surveillance can be seen in the difference between law policing and high policing. While the first refers to the activity of 'agents in uniform' and the law enforcement contact with the community, the latter refers to intelligence led policing and the collection of valuable data to drive public policies and low policing.[156] As it was stated by Brodeur, the *raison d'être* of high policing is national security, thus being highly implicated in the coronavirus emergency response since government highlighted it as a threat to national security.[157] In the case of terrorism for example, Figure 7 shows the different agencies and actions involved in each side of low and high policing.

---

156 Jean-Paul Brodeur, 'High and low policing in Post-9/11 Times' (2007) 1 Policing: A Journal of Policy and Practice 25.

157 Kevin Rawlinson, '"This enemy can be deadly": Boris Johnson Invokes Wartime Language' *The Guardian* (17 March 2020) <https://www.theguardian.com/world/2020/mar/17/enemy-deadly-boris-johnson-invokes-wartime-language-coronavirus> accessed 9 December 2020; 'Health Secretary Sets out Government "battle Plan" for COVID-19' (*GOV.UK*) <https://www.gov.uk/government/news/health-secretary-sets-out-government-battle-plan-for-covid-19> accessed 9 December 2020.

Agency		*Action*	*Activity category*
Military		War; overseas interventions; domestic interventions in civil emergencies such as freeing hostages	**Beyond policing' (violent control)**
Security services: MI5, MI6, GCHQ		Intelligence collection and application; disruption	
The Special Branch and Counter-terrorism specialists		Intelligence collection and application; disruption; arrest and prosecution	
Criminal Investigation Dept (CID)		Investigation, arrest and prosecution	**'High policing'**
Uniformed policing	Response	Intelligence collection; reassurance; and arrests	**'Low policing'**
	Nighbourhood	Community intelligence collection and reassurance; managing community tensions	
Multi-agency activity		Integration, empowerment, and de-radicalisation	
Civilian communities		Responsibilised empowerment; informal control, diversion and intelligence	**'Beyond policing' (disciplinary governance)**

Figure 7 – The continuum of UK state counter-terrorism apparatus[158]

This continuum is reflected upon the coronavirus emergency as a dichotomy between the low policing response driven by high policing data and the opacity of the use of scientific evidence by the central government. The overall strategy of government has been to keep policing proactive rather than reactive, thus aiming at preventing measures.[159] In this sense, the use of technological advances to gather data and predict possible focuses of conflict or risk has been key in setting the strategy to cope with coronavirus. However, the quick pace of the coronavirus emergency and the need for a swift response has also relegated the constitutional aspects of surveillance and security. The lack of parliamentary scrutiny has also been missing in terms of assessing the impact of coronavirus policing and surveillance in the individual privacy right and mobility of UK citizens.[160]

158 F Furedi, *Invitation to terror: The expanding empire of the unknown* (Bloomsbury Academic 2009) fig 21.1 <https://books.google.fr/books?id=bLgzPwAACAAJ>.

159 Collins (n 96).

160 Niovi Vovoula, 'Prevention, surveillance, and the transformation of citizenship in the "Security Union": The Case of Foreign Terrorist Fighters' in Ulrich Sieber

In such a chaotic context the coronavirus emergency has evidenced the need to have constitutional controls over the way in which private data and metadata is collected, stored and used.[161]

I. Surveillance, tracing, tracking and the use of technology

One of the issues that triggered a constitutional debate in the UK was the use of technology for surveillance and policing purposes.[162] The concerns comprehend the use of technology to gather and process private data and metadata, as well as the use of technology such as drones to ensure surveillance and enforce coronavirus regulations more effectively.[163]

The use of technologies to address the coronavirus emergency raises the question of proportionality and necessity in relation to the trade off on privacy. In this sense, governments have been relying on technological advances to be able to collect data in real time and be able to predict risks and trends in the way in which the virus propagates.[164] The use of surveillance thus represents to the government an effective channel of information that is required to increase the number of variables that can be used to predict trends and risks. As in any statistical analysis, multivariable predictions tend to increase the chances of finding stronger correlations when more variables are available to include in a multivariable analysis

---

and others (eds), *Alternative systems of crime control* (Duncker & Humblot 2018) 325.

161 Valsamis Mitsilegas, '"Security Law" and preventive justice in the legal architecture' in Ulrich Sieber and others (eds), *Alternative systems of crime control* (Duncker & Humblot 2018) 214/215.

162 Collins (n 96); 'Ensuring data privacy as we battle Covid 19 (*OECD*) <https://www.oecd.org/coronavirus/policy-responses/ensuring-data-privacy-as-we-battle-covid-19-36c2f31e/> accessed 9 December 2020; Rajeev Syal, 'UK Contact-tracing app could fall foul of privacy law, government told' *The Guardian* (7 May 2020) <https://www.theguardian.com/world/2020/may/07/uk-coronavirus-contract-tracing-app-could-fall-foul-of-privacy-law-government-told> accessed 9 December 2020; 'UK Coronavirus app "must respect privacy rights"' *BBC News* (23 March 2020) <https://www.bbc.com/news/technology-52003984> accessed 9 December 2020.

163 'Coronavirus: Peak district drone police criticised for "Lockdown Shaming"' *BBC News* (27 March 2020) <https://www.bbc.com/news/uk-england-derbyshire-52055201> accessed 9 December 2020.

164 'Covid 19 Surveillance' (*GOV.UK*) <https://www.gov.uk/government/publications/covid-19-surveillance/covid-19-surveillance> accessed 9 December 2020.

model.[165] This becomes especially true for social variables. Thus, the use of technological apps and software enables governments and scientists to enlarge the data sample, therefore increasing the chances of having more accurate predictions and overall knowledge of the COVID-19 phenomenon.

To this extent, the elephant in the room seems to be how to distinguish personal from coronavirus related data, and how much of the coronavirus related data is actually relevant to achieve the legitimate end of enhancing the knowledge on the coronavirus emergency.

Moreover, there seems to be a need to distinguish between preventive data collection and reactive data collection. As an example, a UK initiative on reactive data collection may be seen in the adaptation of facial recognition AI that was originally intended for preventing terrorist attacks, to measure body temperature and spot victims of coronavirus in Bristol Airport.[166] A similar thing happened at Bournemouth Airport.[167] The same can be said about the collection of metadata such as location, to attack on outbreaks and see whether someone was in contact with an infectious person.[168] In this case, for example, Professor Jon Crowcroft, from the Alan Turing Institute, warns that,

> "Inevitably, there are caveats to producing this sort of technology, and limitations. Privacy is a big one. Any app system and accompanying database must be designed with comprehensive, user-centric privacy policies built in".[169]

---

165 Alan Agresti, *Statistical methods for the social sciences* (5th Edition, Pearson Education Limited 2018) ch 10.

166 Alan Tovey, 'Facial recognition system dapted to spot Coronavirus victims' *The Telegraph* (27 April 2020) <https://www.telegraph.co.uk/business/2020/04/27/thermal-camera-identification-system-prepares-companies-life/> accessed 9 December 2020.

167 'Will thermal cameras help to end the lockdown?' *BBC News* <https://www.bbc.com/news/av/business-52479043> accessed 9 December 2020.

168 Mark Sweney and Alex Hern, 'Phone location data could be used to help UK Coronavirus effort' *The Guardian* (19 March 2020) <https://www.theguardian.com/world/2020/mar/19/plan-phone-location-data-assist-uk-coronavirus-effort> accessed 9 December 2020; 'Coronavirus: government using mobile location data to tackle outbreak' (*Sky News*) <https://news.sky.com/story/coronavirus-government-using-mobile-location-data-to-tackle-outbreak-11960050> accessed 9 December 2020.

169 Sweney and Hern (n 168).

Other initiatives both from private actor (for example King's College London and the science company ZOE, or Palantir),[170] and government,[171] have been putting forward the use of apps to collect health data and metadata that would be used only for health reasons and under the protection of European Standards of GDPR. The issue surrounding data protection and privacy also becomes a high priority to initiatives that require the engagement of a vast amount of the general public. Convincing a high number of members of society that the app will safeguard their privacy by using a minimum, not personal, amount of data would potentially secure more users.[172] Nevertheless, the level of democratic scrutiny and accountability remains obscure in relation to the extent of the 'minimum' data collected and the models behind the use of such data.

The issue becomes more complex when the data is surrendered by mobile network providers.[173] The amount of sensitive data and metadata collected has the potential to have a huge impact on civil liberties, with mass surveillance collecting some information that might be relevant for the coronavirus emergency, and a lot of other sensitive information that might not be relevant. The question then lies on how would government, high policing bodies, and scientific advisors be able to distinguish, before breaching privacy, relevant form irrelevant data.

Another issue is the way in which these technologies are being use and the how the usage affects the social behaviour of a community. As an example, the use of drones for surveillance and the message conveyed by the government on the importance of following the restrictions regulations, have fostered a culture of naming and shaming.[174] The consequences of forwarding policing activities to citizens of members of the civil society,

---

170 'About This Research' <https://covid.joinzoe.com/about> accessed 9 December 2020; 'Palantir provides Covid19 tracking software to CDC and NHS, pitches european health agencies' (*TechCrunch*) <https://social.techcrunch.com/2020/04/01/palantir-coronavirus-cdc-nhs-gotham-foundry/> accessed 9 December 2020.

171 'NHS Covid app: privacy notice' (*GOV.UK*) <https://www.gov.uk/government/publications/nhs-covid-19-app-privacy-information/nhs-test-and-trace-app-early-adopter-trial-august-2020-privacy-notice> accessed 9 December 2020.

172 ibid; 'About This Research' (n 170)..

173 Shona Ghosh, 'Privacy activists ear the UK might spy on its own citizens to tackle COVID-19. Here's what we know.' (*Business Insider*, 26 March 2020) <https://www.businessinsider.com/explainer-coronavirus-uk-phone-tracking-2020-3> accessed 9 December 2020.

174 Amelia Tait, 'Pandemic shaming: Is it helping us keep our distance?' *The Observer* (4 April 2020) <https://www.theguardian.com/science/2020/apr/04/pandemic-shaming-is-it-helping-us-keep-our-distance> accessed 9 December 2020.

would encompass unforeseen consequences and foster the polarisation of views on the coronavirus emergency. In an era of high polarisation with high levels of misinformation, and a coronavirus emergency that requires individuals acting in concert, such measures may provide the perfect storm to undermine the efforts to effectively address the coronavirus emergency.

II. Privacy and data protection

Although enhancing the available data may be seen as a legitimate end, there are limits that need to be taken into consideration specially when dealing with sensitive information. The proportionality assessment on how to handle the collision between the need to improve the knowledge on the coronavirus emergency and the individual right to privacy requires a democratic debate.

Similar concerns to the ones raised regarding surveillance for crime prevention efforts can be put forward in relation to surveillance and the use of personal data for the prevention or containment of the coronavirus emergency. Moreover,

> "The impact of state intervention on the individual is intensified when one considers the potential of combining personal data from different databases collected for different purposes in a landscape of blurring of boundaries and interoperability (…) in order to create a profile of risk or dangerousness".[175]

In this sense, as stablished by the Court of Justice in the join cases of Tele2 and Watson,[176] the data and metadata serves the purpose of providing contextual information for profiling individuals. The content of the communication thus becomes demoted to a background issue.

In Tele2, the Court of Justice established that,

> "The fact that the data is retained without the subscriber or registered user being informed is likely to cause the persons concerned to feel that their private lives are the subject of constant surveillance".[177]

175 Mitsilegas (n 161) 210.

176 Joined Cases C-230/15 and C-698/15, Tele2 Sverige and Watson, judgement of 21.12.2016, para. 99.

177 Ibid., para. 100.

This argument flags the concerns regarding the constant feeling of being watched and under scrutiny, thus resembling the Benthamian panopticon idea of surveillance.[178] In this sense, the fears regarding privacy and data in modern ages serve to induce "(...) a state of conscious and permanent visibility that assures the automatic functioning of power".[179]

The debate regarding the clash between the legitimate end of helping to better inform policies and government decisions in the fight against coronavirus ought to require clearer standards and rules regarding the extent and limit of privacy breach. In this sense, the proportionality and rationality of the measure would be better received by public and the civil society if there was a more transparent and comprehensive plan contemplating the use of sensitive data collected through surveillance technologies as the ones described in this section. In an open letter, several self-labelled 'responsible technologists' warned that,

> "It is not yet clear how data will be collected, or used, within the legal framework. Nor what technical safeguards will be used. We are also concerned that data collected to fight Coronavirus could be stored indefinitely or for a disproportionate amount of time, or will be used for unrelated purposes".[180]

In this sense, as pointed out by Yuval Noah Harari, "Asking people to choose between privacy and health is, in fact, the very root of the problem".[181] The apparent dichotomy should not be one since government and parliament should be able to provide alternative solutions that are less detrimental to individual right. Transparency in the decision-making process and proper democratic deliberation ought to ensure an adequate balance. In times when the emergency requires global unity,[182] profiling and fostering naming and shaming behaviour could very much diminish national efforts to contain and overcome the coronavirus emergency.

---

178 Michel Foucault, *Discipline and punish. The birth of the prison* (Second Vintage Books Edition, Vintage Books a Division of Random House 1995) 200.

179 ibid 201.

180 Rachel Coldicutt, 'Open letter: Contact tracking and NHSX' (*Medium*, 27 March 2020) <https://rachelcoldicutt.medium.com/open-letter-contract-tracking-and-nhsx-e503325b2703> accessed 10 December 2020.

181 Yuval Noah Harari, 'Yuval Noah Harari: The world after Coronavirus | Free to read' (20 March 2020) <https://www.ft.com/content/19d90308-6858-11ea-a3c9-1fe6fedcca75> accessed 10 December 2020.

182 ibid.

III. Faith in technology, trust in government and hope for users

As stated by the literature on the relationship between trust and legitimacy, the former may be defined as a subjective judgement made by a trustor, regarding the likelihood of a trustee behaving within certain expectations and values under circumstances of uncertainty.[183] Thus, trust requires three elements: a trustor, a trustee, and a behaviour that the former wishes from the latter.[184] The uncertainty of the trustor regarding the aftermath, provides trust with a certain degree of requiring faith.[185] Trust involves a certain degree of acceptance of our interpretations and a suspension of our awareness of the unknown, or unknowable, which makes it a separate category from knowledge or ignorance.[186]

Legitimacy on the other hand, although it has also been subject of a dense literature and its multiple definitions exceed the scope of this report,[187] it can be seen from an etymological point of view as making something lawful or declaring something to be lawful.[188] Nevertheless, legitimacy will be addressed in this section as the "(…) belief that authorities, institutions, and social arrangements are appropriate, proper, and just".[189]

Applied to the coronavirus emergency, both trust and legitimacy become core concepts that ought to be regarded as the cornerstone of the governmental response to COVID-19. Considering the degree of uncertainty faced by the public, government and the scientific community, faith in technology and the power of innovation enables society and economies to subsist despite the uncertainty. As opposed to passed health emergen-

183 Jonathan Jackson and Jacinta M Gau, 'Carving up concepts? Differentiating between trust and legitimacy in public attitudes towards legal uthority' in Ellie Shockley and others (eds), *Interdisciplinary Perspectives on Trust: Towards Theoretical and Methodological Integration* (Springer International Publishing 2016) 53 <https://doi.org/10.1007/978-3-319-22261-5_3>.

184 ibid.

185 Guido Möllering, 'The nature of trust: From Georg Simmel to a theory of expectation, interpretation and suspension' (2001) 35 Sociology 403, 414..

186 ibid.

187 Julian V Roberts and Mojca M Plesnicar, 'Sentencing, legitimacy, and public opinion' in Gorazd Mesko and Justice Tankebe (eds), *Trust and Legitimacy in Criminal Justice. European Perspectives* (Springer 2015) 34.

188 'Legitimate | Origin and meaning of legitimate by Online Etymology Dictionary' <https://www.etymonline.com/word/legitimate> accessed 15 December 2020.

189 Tom R Tyler, 'Psychological perspectives on legitimacy and legitimation' (2005) 57 Annual Review of Psychology 375, 376.

cies, the key distinctive feature of the modern coronavirus emergency is the level of technological development reached by humankind. When compared the Coronavirus crisis with other health crisis such as the Spanish flu, the main distinctive feature is the depth of understanding of the problem and the speed to which humankind arrived at that knowledge. A quick understanding of the problem enables society to adopt social behaviours to counter act or prevent the effects of viruses. An example of this may be found in the simple procedure of thoroughly washing hands, which was adopted in the 19th century thanks to the scientific understanding of microorganisms.[190] A great deal of this unprecedented achievements have been reached thanks to technology.

Therefore, society and humankind place a great deal of faith and trust in the technological edge to face the pandemic. However, technology by itself does not constitute neither a solution nor a threat. To become part of the solution or the problem, technology requires development, implementation, users, policy and governmental support, etc. Thus, according to authors like Pagliari, the questions that are facing trust challenges in the coronavirus emergency may be summarised into a non-exhaustive list of eight categories: technology, privacy policies, usefulness, optionality, fairness, people, institutions, and users.

---

190 Harari (n 181).

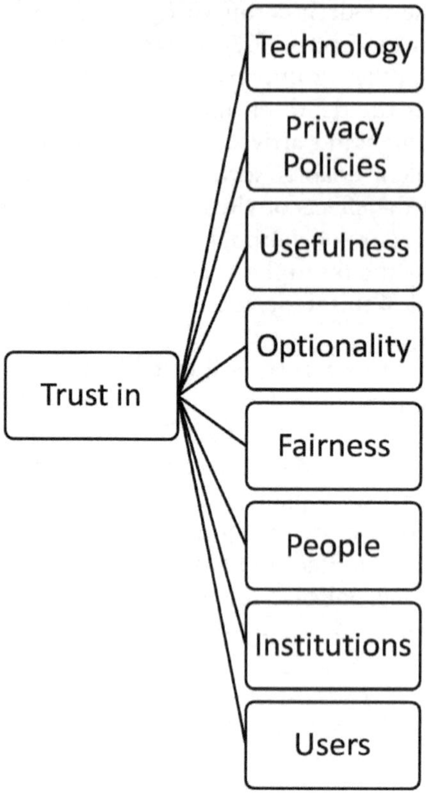

Figure 8 – Diagram regarding categories of trust[191]

Regarding technology, questions of trust can be related to its safety, reliability, accountability, side-effects, etc. The questions in this category focus on the trust people place in technology considering the levels of uncertainty surrounding its design, functionality, and unintended consequences. The trust in privacy policies on the other hand, refers to the data that serves as input and output of the technology. These questions relate to surveillance and concerns regarding a hypothetical and unintended mission creep. Fears regarding the role of anonymity and the objectives of

191 Claudia Pagliari, 'The ethics and value of contact tracing apps: International insights and implications for Scotland's Covid-19 response' (2020) 10 Journal of Global Health <http://www.jogh.org/documents/issue202002/jogh-10.020103.htm> accessed 14 December 2020.

technologies may also correlate with a lack of specialised knowledge from society and a lack of adequate explanation from the specialised community. Trust in the usefulness of the technology to address the coronavirus emergency is very much related to questions of proportionality.[192] The questions regarding the usefulness aim at untangling the relationship between the legitimate aim of coping with the coronavirus emergency and the mean provided by technological developments. Thus, the trust here relates to a level of scepticism on the capabilities of technology to properly address the core issues of the emergency. Moreover, there is also a level of call for accountability and weighing the risks on privacy against the uncertainty of a technological development accurate enough to solve the emergency. The questions of trust regarding optionality refer to the voluntary nature of technology and the possibility of people being able to opt out. Trust in the fairness of technology also refers to the concerns regarding unintended consequences of data collection. The issues raised by this category also relate to the proportionality of the technology as well as the possibility of it leading to discrimination, alienation, exploitation, and coerciveness. The category of people on the other hand, refers to the trust placed on people behind the technology such as developers or shareholders. The questions around this category relate to possible conflicts of interest, or transparency regarding goals and ambitions. The category on institutions address the concerns regarding the organisations and corporations in charge of delivering the technology and the policy around it. Finally, the questions related to users address the issue of individuals misusing technology in a way that could harm or create inconveniencies to others.[193]

Overall, trust in government and technology is intrinsically related to issues of legitimacy and democracy. In the UK, the sense of disregard of proper democratic procedures may have contributed to the damaged legitimacy of the measures adopted by government during the coronavirus emergency. Moreover, the lack of transparency in certain decision-making processes and the inputs that drive those decision, may have also contributed to the scepticism and mistrust of the general public. Mission creep in terms of mass surveillance and misuse of data, poses a real threat to the general public and the legitimacy of democratic institutions.

---

192 Tomáš Sobek and Josef Montag, 'Proportionality test' in Alain Marciano and Giovanni Battista Ramello (eds), *Encyclopedia of Law and Economics* (Springer New York 2018) <https://doi.org/10.1007/978-1-4614-7883-6_721-1>.

193 Pagliari (n 191).

IV. The Use of Contact Tracing

Contact tracing can be defined as,

> "(…) one way of trying to control and track the spread of the virus. It involves notifying individuals when they have come into contact with others who may have been exposed to the COVID-19 virus and giving them appropriate advice, for example to get tested and or to self-isolate, in order to minimise the further spread of the virus".[194]

This procedure may be done manually or digitally. Regarding the former, tracing the spread of the virus requires people to fill in forms and submit sensible information about themselves. This information may be their names, locations, who they were in contact with, for how long were they in contact, etc.[195] While the information is submitted by the person itself, whether by completing a form at a restaurant, bar, etc., or by filling a form online, it would still be processed and stored digitally.[196]

On the other hand, digital ways of performing contact tracing include the use of programmes or applications software in smartphones, which trace proximity between users through Bluetooth technology. In this sense,

> "When two people come within a certain distance of each other, their phones exchange 'tokens' (unique identifying numbers) that have been allocated to each phone. The app stores a list of the tokens belonging to all contacts they have made over a given period. If an individual begins to show symptoms of COVID-19, or tests positive for the virus, the app is notified. It can then alert other users that they may be at risk of infection if the infected person's token is stored in their phone".[197]

---

194 Joint Committee on Human Rights, 'Human Rights and the government's response to COVID-19: Digital contact tracing' (House of Commons and House of Lords 2020) Third Report of Session 2019–21 s 4 <https://publications.parliament.uk/pa/jt5801/jtselect/jtrights/343/34304.htm#_idTextAnchor001> accessed 10 December 2020.

195 Joint Committee on Human Rights, 'The Government's response to COVID-19: Human rights implications' (House of Commons and House of Lords 2020) Seventh Report of Session 2019–21 s 162 <https://publications.parliament.uk/pa/jt5801/jtselect/jtrights/265/26502.htm> accessed 14 December 2020.

196 ibid.

197 Susie Wright, 'Contact tracing apps for COVID-19' <https://post.parliament.uk/contact-tracing-apps-for-covid-19/> accessed 10 December 2020.

As it was stated in previous sections (4.1), the data collected using apps often requires a high number of users engaging with the software.[198] Some studies have suggested the epidemic could be supressed with "(…) 80 % of all smartphone users using the app, or 56 % of the population overall".[199] Although this level of uptake has not been reached in other parts of the world,[200] and that 12 % of the UK smartphones do not have the required technology to support the app,[201] the UK government might have been encouraged by the level of social acceptance of contact tracing apps. According to a study, 65 % of British citizens agreed with using contact tracing apps in smartphones.[202]

After implementing the contact tracing app on the 24th September 2020 in England and Wales, governmental sources state that by the 27th September 2020, 10 million people downloaded the app.[203] While this might not be a good start to achieve the 80 % benchmark aimed at the beginning of the trials, some studies suggest that "(…) a well-staffed manual contact tracing workforce combined with 15 % uptake of an exposure notification system could reduce infections by 15 % and deaths by 11 %".[204] Thus, although high levels of uptake may not be needed to generate an impact on the Coronavirus emergency, the level of acceptance in the aftermath of the implementation of contact tracing apps may suggest a damaged social trust.[205]

---

198 ibid.

199 Robert Hinch and others, 'Effective configurations of a digital contact tracing app: A Report to NHSX' (2020) 3 <https://cdn.theconversation.com/static_files/files/1009/Report_-_Effective_App_Configurations.pdf?1587531217>.

200 Stephanie Findlay, Richard Milne and Stefania Palma, 'Coronavirus contact-tracing apps struggle to make an impact' (18 May 2020) <https://www.ft.com/content/21e438a6-32f2-43b9-b843-61b819a427aa> accessed 15 December 2020.

201 Wright (n 197).

202 Helen Warrell, 'Majority in UK support use of mobile phones for Coronavirus contact tracing' (17 April 2020) <https://www.ft.com/content/1752affb-24dc-4ad9-8503-78f9ce1adca9> accessed 15 December 2020.

203 'NHS COVID-19 app has been downloaded over 10 million times' (*GOV.UK*) <https://www.gov.uk/government/news/nhs-covid-19-app-has-been-downloaded-over-10-million-times> accessed 15 December 2020.

204 'New research shows tracing apps can save lives at all levels of uptake | University of Oxford' <https://www.ox.ac.uk/news/2020-09-03-new-research-shows-tracing-apps-can-save-lives-all-levels-uptake> accessed 14 December 2020.

205 Alex Hern UK technology editor, 'Contact-tracing pp for England and Wales "Hampered by loss of public trust"' *The Guardian* (21 September 2020) <https://www.theguardian.com/world/2020/sep/21/covid-coronavirus-contact-tracing-app-hampered-lack-trust> accessed 15 December 2020.

Engaging with the app would mean users needing to download the software and enable certain features, such as activating Bluetooth, or enabling access to health information stored in other apps, such as the health app in iPhone. In the UK, the contact tracing app for the COVID-19 emergency was called *NHS COVID-19* and was put forward by the NHSX. The NHSX defines itself as,

> "(...) a joint unit bringing together teams from the Department of Health and Social Care and NHS England and NHS Improvement to drive the digital transformation of care".[206]

However, even if participation remains voluntary, it is important to note that any consent given by citizens to take part in mass tracing systems must be meaningful: the European Court of Justice has noted that such consent would be undermined if citizens did not have a real choice of objecting to the processing of their personal data.[207] In this context, it is paramount that governmental pressure to participate in the system does not lead to discrimination, stigmatisation and dangerous distinctions between 'good' and 'bad' citizens in the eyes of the state. This becomes especially true with the current discourse on 'civic duties' of 'saving lives' exacerbating the potential of stigmatisation. A push towards uncritical mass surveillance may lead to a two-way erosion of trust between citizens and the state. On the one hand, the generation of mistrust from the state to citizens who do not participate in tracing systems either by choice or by lack of access to technology may lead to the exclusion of and discrimination against these citizens in key areas of everyday life, including commerce, work and travel. On the other hand, the potential of the trust of citizens towards the state being eroded is significant.[208]

Another issue regarding privacy rises form the available options of data storage and sharing, especially regarding the data collected by contact tracing apps. These apps have a real time preventive nature and aim at identifying through the use of location, whether a person was in contact with someone infected or potentially infected. After identifying proximity,

---

206 'Home' (*NHSX*) <https://www.nhsx.nhs.uk/> accessed 14 December 2020.

207 C-291/12 Michael Schwarz v Stadt Bochum: for further analysis see this European Law Blog.

208 Valsamis Mitsilegas, 'Responding to COVID-19: Surveillance, trust and the rule of law - School of Law' (26 May 2020) <https://www.qmul.ac.uk/law/news/responding-to-covid-19/items/responding-to-covid-19-surveillance-trust-and-the-rule-of-law.html> accessed 10 December 2020.

the app can suggest some measures such as testing or self-isolation.[209] The privacy issues with these apps is the way in which data collected may be stored and/or shared. In this respect, there are two models for storing and sharing information: centralised or decentralised. The first one refers to those cases in which data is "(...) stored locally on an individual's phone and as little data as possible is shared with the NHS".[210] The latter refers to those cases in which "(...) data is shared with a central server managed by the authority which carries out data processing and/or storage".[211]

The centralised model may present some advantages in terms of accuracy or effectiveness as for example creating hotspots and letting hospitals prepare before the surge of cases in a certain area. On the other hand, the decentralised model would be more protective of individual privacy rights and would minimise the risk of privacy breaches.[212] The preference for the latter has also been confirmed by the European Parliament and the European Data Protection Board (EDPB).[213] Moreover, there are also contingency risks that need to be taken into consideration since, for example, a centralised model would also create greater incentives for criminals to hack into the software.[214] Public trust in technology was challenging before the COVID-19 outbreak, and so far there haven't been indicators suggesting this has changed.[215] Moreover, the trends suggest that the challenges have been intensified.[216] Thus, a transparent democratic debate should be able to weigh the rights at stake and protect the individual privacy rights while at the same time reassuring a maximum health protection.

Regarding the choice between a centralised or a decentralised model, the UK has changed its way of dealing with data processing and storing throughout the pandemic. The centralised model also poses the challenge of unintended threats such as the use of data, that was initially collected to fight coronavirus, for other purposes. Another unforeseen consequence may also be that the identifiers used for individuals can serve as permanent

209 Wright (n 197); Matt Burgess, 'Everything you need to know about the new NHS contact tracing app' [2020] *Wired UK* <https://www.wired.co.uk/article/nhs-covid-19-tracking-app-contact-tracing> accessed 10 December 2020.
210 Joint Committee on Human Rights (n 194) para 6.
211 ibid.
212 ibid.
213 ibid.
214 ibid 7.
215 'Trust and technology: Critical for success during COVID-19' <https://www.kpmg.us/growth-strategy/trust-and-technology.html> accessed 10 December 2020..
216 ibid.

records.[217] The mission creep contingency was not properly addressed by government when it chose a centralised model at the beginning of the emergency.[218] As it was stated by some authors, the Minister of State for Health and the Secretary of State showed a 'dismissive attitude' towards privacy and data protection by thinking of them as 'barriers' or 'bureaucracy'.[219] Moreover, the weighing of risk factors versus benefits was not held democratically, being decided single-handedly by the executive power.

Although more countries were increasingly inclined to adopt a decentralised model,[220] the first signs of trials in the Isle of Wight showed a preference for the centralised model.[221] However, international pressure as well as from the Joint Committee on Human Rights (JCHR) from the House of Commons and the House of Lords, might have helped in government's change of mind.[222] The roll-up of the app was therefore delayed, and the decision was made to shift from a centralised model to a decentralised model developed by Apple and Google.[223] The shift in models was highly welcomed by the JCHR, who also raised concern regarding the lack of legislation defining what data should be collected, for how long should it be stored and when should it be deleted.[224] The JCHR also put forward the need to enact a ban on contact tracing data being

217 Joint Committee on Human Rights (n 194) s 7.

218 ibid.

219 'The Failure of the UK's centralised COVID-19 contact-tracing app by Oliver Butler' (*blogdroiteuropéen*, 24 September 2020) <https://blogdroiteuropeen.com/2020/09/24/the-failure-of-the-uks-centralised-covid-19-contact-tracing-app-by-oliver-butler/> accessed 15 December 2020.

220 'Coronavirus contact-tracing: World split between two types of app' *BBC News* (7 May 2020) <https://www.bbc.com/news/technology-52355028> accessed 15 December 2020.

221 'Coronavirus: Health minister says app should roll out by winter' *BBC News* (17 June 2020) <https://www.bbc.com/news/technology-53083340> accessed 15 December 2020.

222 Joint Committee on Human Rights (n 195) s 157.

223 Herbert Smith Freehills LLP-Miriam Everett, Hannah Brown and Katie Collins, 'UK switches to decentralised approach to contact tracing app | Lexology' <https://www.lexology.com/library/detail.aspx?g=14e8a3ee-f931-4f1f-b2a4-b35fb8b24aa2> accessed 15 December 2020; 'UK Virus-Tracing App Switches to Apple-Google Model' *BBC News* (18 June 2020) <https://www.bbc.com/news/technology-53095336> accessed 15 December 2020; Joint Committee on Human Rights (n 195) s 157.

224 Joint Committee on Human Rights (n 195) s 167.

shared for any other reason than to fight the Coronavirus emergency, thus expressly addressing concerns over a mission creep.[225]

Nevertheless, as stated by the JCHR,

> "Manual contact tracing is the main component of the UK's test, track and trace system. This still involves data being collected; indeed, that data is arguably more sensitive than that collected by the app".[226]

Thus, to be effectively protecting privacy and individual rights, the call for legislation on the matter should also include data collected through manual contact tracing methods.

The lack of clarity regarding the legal intricacies of these apps and the huge consequences that they may have for society, could also account for the scepticism of society. Taking into consideration that 4 out of 10 persons in the UK trust government to protect data, and that almost the same proportion are willing to share data with it,[227] much needs to be done to remedy mistrust. The issue has also been raised by civil society and watchdogs,[228] who have even submitted a pre-action legal letter to the health secretary of the UK, Matt Hancock, and the Department of Health and Social Care.[229] As pointed out by Dr. Richard Milne, from the University of Cambridge Trust and Technology Initiative,

> "In the UK, there is significant trust in the NHS and its use of data for care. In contrast, there's scepticism about secondary uses of data, and particularly the use of health data by the private sector, and less faith that companies will act in a way that encapsulates the interests of the general public. (...) With this in mind, the current situation is not ideal for the development of trustworthy data practices. COVID-19 surveillance introduces new forms of data into discussions, data that most people have not previously considered as relevant to their health

---

225 ibid.

226 ibid 168.

227 European Data Journalism Network, 'COVID-19 has served as the pretext for widespread surveillance' (*European Data Journalism Network*) <https://www.europeandatajournalism.eu/News/Data-news/COVID-19-has-served-as-the-pretext-for-widespread-surveillance> accessed 10 December 2020.

228 'Blog: Data protection considerations and the NHS COVID-19 app' (22 September 2020) <https://ico.org.uk/global/data-protection-and-coronavirus-information-hub/blog-data-protection-considerations-and-the-nhs-covid-19-app/> accessed 10 December 2020.

229 'UK test and trace system accused of breaching privacy' (*Privacy International*) <http://privacyinternational.org/es/node/4101> accessed 10 December 2020.

or that of others, which are collected or generated by companies with little prior interaction with the health system, and are being used by governments in an emergency situation".[230]

Therefore, the right to privacy should be broadly defined to include data collection and storage as well as usage and transfer.[231] Furthermore, new measures and the use of new technology should be critically scrutinised on a case-by-case basis, to ensure full compliance with legality and proportionality.[232] A proper democratic assessment of legality, proportionality and rationality becomes more pressing when considering that there is no evidence to sustain that the use of contact tracing data is an effective technology to enhance the pandemic response.[233] This casts doubt on the proportionality and necessity of contact tracing technologies,[234] thus reassuring the need to debate and assess on a case-by-case bases the conducive nature of each new measure or a new technology. This would also be a way of taking out of obscurity the decision-making process and the scientific methodology driving COVID-19-related laws and regulations.

E. Concluding Remarks

This report analysed the regulatory response of the UK to the present Coronavirus emergency. Issues regarding the effects of COVID-19 on the rule of law and trust of citizens in government, technology and the judicial system had been common denominators at all levels of analysis. It is important to bear in mind that the analysis will always fall short since the object of study is essentially a moving target and is subjected to constant and rapid change, especially since the emergency is ongoing.

---

230 Richard Milne, 'Trust and trustworthiness in COVID-19 data' (*Trust & Technology Initiative*, 15 April 2020) <https://www.trusttech.cam.ac.uk/research-agendas-and-perspectives/covid-19-trust-technology-society-research-perspectives/trust-and> accessed 10 December 2020.

231 'Developing a global privacy regime in the age of mass surveillance: Four key principles' (*openDemocracy*) <https://www.opendemocracy.net/en/digitaliberties/developing-global-privacy-regime-in-age-of-mass-surveillance-four-key-principles/> accessed 10 December 2020.

232 Mitsilegas (n 208).

233 'Covid 19 rapid evidence review' (*Ada Lovelace Institute*, 20 April 2020) 11 <https://www.adalovelaceinstitute.org/wp-content/uploads/2020/04/Ada-Lovelace-Institute-Rapid-Evidence-Review-Exit-through-the-App-Store-April-2020-2.pdf> accessed 10 December 2020.

234 ibid 12.

The report dealt with four tensions in the regulatory response of the UK, that cut-across three levels of analysis: the macro state of emergency, the systemic criminal law, and the surveillance, policing and preventing.

The four tensions underpinning the report related to the relationship between parliament and the executive power, the relationship between local authorities and central government, the issues of legal certainty regarding overarching laws and regulations and the use of technology. Moreover, throughout the report, the tensions exhibited some challenges regarding the need for trust and legitimacy in times were appropriate procedures might lead to higher risk of health vulnerability and harm. In this sense, it is worth mentioning that the state of emergency discourse seen in other countries,[235] has not been widely used in the UK. Nevertheless, the trade-offs presented in this report have not always been handled with due care and have not always been properly weighed through democratic scrutiny and proportionality assessments. Although the government has, in some cases, listened to the concerns, and rectified their actions. For example, these rectifications led to the parliamentary debate that took place when deciding the second lockdown of November 2020, or the shift from a centralised to a decentralised model of data processing and storing.

Another issue that hampered public trust related to the transparency of the methods that lead to decisions and policies enacted unilaterally by the executive power. Shielded by the argument of facing an emergency that required swift and effective responses, government showed a disregard for democratic procedures and the intrinsic value of deliberation.[236] These

235 ABP News Bureau, 'France declares State Of Emergency To battle second wave of COVID-19, imposes night curfew in 9 cities' (15 October 2020) <https://news.abplive.com/news/world/france-health-emergency-france-declares-public-health-state-of-emergency-over-covid-19-1364370> accessed 16 December 2020; Célia Belin Nicolaï Agneska Bloch, and Jérôme, 'France at war against the Coronavirus: Politics under anesthesia?' (*Brookings*, 31 March 2020) <https://www.brookings.edu/blog/order-from-chaos/2020/03/31/france-at-war-against-the-coronavirus-politics-under-anesthesia/> accessed 16 December 2020; 'State of Emergency in France may extend to spring' <https://www.aa.com.tr/en/europe/state-of-emergency-in-france-may-extend-to-spring/2014331> accessed 16 December 2020; 'What does it mean that France has extended its state of health emergency until February 2021?' (10 July 2020) <https://www.thelocal.fr/20200710/what-does-it-mean-that-frances-state-of-health-emergency-wont-be-renewed> accessed 16 December 2020; 'French parliament declares health emergency to combat pandemic' (*France 24*, 22 March 2020) <https://www.france24.com/en/20200322-french-parliament-declares-health-emergency-to-combat-pandemic> accessed 16 December 2020.

236 Nino (n 119) 101.

values may include endowing legitimacy to acts of government as well as fostering trust. The argument regarding the need to listen to science on the other hand, has been a trigger for opacity and a shift towards a technocratic decision-making process. The lack of scrutiny and transparency in relation to the role, input and output of scientific bodies such as SAGE, which assist government in their decisions has also contributed to jeopardising legitimacy and trust. This becomes especially true since government has expressed that SAGE possess a high level of influence in the decision-making process of the executive power.

Furthermore, the historical development of the state of emergency responses has influenced the UK response to the coronavirus emergency since local authorities have always been the centre of attention and responsibility in dealing with civil emergencies. In this sense, the traditional strategy of leaving enough discretion to local authorities to be able to make calls on the spur of the moment during their immediate response to a civil emergency has passed on to current ways of dealing with the coronavirus emergency. Government has traditionally taken a role of coordination and assistance to local authorities thus creating a tension between a central government aiming to show leadership and strong decision-making when facing COVID-19 and the local authorities. This tension becomes particularly strong in the UK when considering the issues of devolution and the pre-existing tension of four nations coexisting under a delicate legal balance.

The level of uncertainty created by the coronavirus emergency has also impacted on the way in which government undertook the task of regulating social behaviour to prevent the spread of the virus. This uncertainty has a two-fold dimension. On the one hand, it refers to the uncertainty of the virus itself, and on the other hand, it refers to the uncertainty of the impact the virus will have on different aspects of society. Thus, not only there was little knowledge of the virus, but there was also a lack of assessment on the way in which societies would be affected by extreme measures such as the economical impact of lockdowns, mental health problems, etc. This uncertainty may have been reflected in the vague legislative technique used by government to enact regulations that do not provide the minimum level of legal certainty required for citizens to obey by the law. This became especially problematic since the UK has appealed to overcriminalisation to force compliance with a long list of constantly changing laws and regulations, where even the PM gets confused.[237] The vague justification clause of 'reasonable excuse' to avoid criminal liability when breaking the coronavirus laws and regulations, serves as an example of lack of legal certainty.[238]

Finally, the need to create more accurate predictions to better prevent the spread and impact of COVID-19 has led to a push for more surveillance and data collection. This has raised several concerns regarding privacy rights as well as the use of data and the need to avoid a mission creep. When considering that, as opposed to past pandemics, humankind is in a better position that it was before thanks to technological advancements, the proportionality assessments and moral dilemmas become more problematic. In this sense, the tension between public trust and the use of technology by the government to address the coronavirus emergency has shown a need to have clear regulations regarding data collection, processing and storing.

---

237 'Boris Johnson "misspoke" over North East Covid restrictions' *BBC News* (29 September 2020) <https://www.bbc.com/news/uk-54342688> accessed 16 December 2020.

238 Cormacain (n 4).

Controls and Penalties in the time of Pandemic: The Constitutional State on Trial

Adan Nieto
Universidad de Castilla-La Mancha

A. *The Leviathan during a pandemic: Bewildered? Authoritarian? A watchdog? An anarchist? A libertarian?*

The COVID-19 pandemic is the first ever to be addressed with the instruments and within the boundaries of constitutional states. The legal framework applicable to COVID-19 greatly differs from that of the last great epidemic, the 1918 Spanish flu. Note that this deadly influenza pandemic spread throughout Europe near the end of World War I, a time when governments were obviously not as responsive to health issues or freedom restrictions[1]. Therefore, COVID is a "stress test" for many European countries' constitutional systems, and it provides a great chance to assess the effectiveness of the rule of law during an emergency whilst further developing pandemic regulations for the future.

A few years ago, Ulrich Beck prophetically claimed that emergencies and catastrophic events had a tremendous political potential.[2] Risk always shakes the foundations of the branches of government. Authoritarian states, like pre-1978 Spain or 19th century liberal governments, managed crises and emergency situations through exceptional legislation, i.e., states of emergency or exception, and martial law. In Germany, it is called *Ausnahmezustand*, and French law provides for the so-called *état d'exception*. Civil rights would be suspended and checks and balances would be modified, i.e., the checks and balances system would not apply as provided in liberal constitutions. So, under states of emergency, authoritarian governments would (i) implement further restrictions on fundamental rights; and (ii) concentrate all powers in the hands of the dictator. Emergency law in

1 See Álvarez Gracia V/Arias Aparicio F./ Hernandez Diez E, *Lecciones jurídicas para. la lucha contra la pandemia*, Iustel, 2020, p. 19 ss.

2 See Presno Linares M.A, *Estado de alarma y sociedad del riesgo global*, in Atienza Macias E/Rodriguez Ayuso J.F, Las respuestas del derechos a las crisis de salud pública, Dykinson, 2021, p. 15 ss.

constitutional states alters the normal functioning of the various branches of government and provides for derogations of individual rights in the interest of appropriately managing the emergency, but it does not entail a new emergency constitutional framework. States of emergency allow for restrictions, limitations and derogations, but they must be reasonable and justified under the principle of proportionality. Expanding the executive branch's powers is justified, but such "over empowerment" must be scrutinized by the legislature. Also, national-to-regional devolution of powers is reversed, and authority is centralized in the hands of the executive branch, although implementing certain joint governance mechanisms. It should be noted that it is better for national authorities to be coordinated with regional bodies than to establish hierarchical relationships between them.[3]

As could be expected, COVID-19 has triggered certain conflicts between all branches of government in Spain. The Spanish Constitutional Court recently found both states of emergency declared by the Government (and ratified by the legislature) unconstitutional. Courts of justice have overruled many of the emergency measures and provisions issued by regional governments and authorities. According to regional bodies, the national Government has overstepped their authority, encroaching upon regional authorities' decision-making powers during the emergency. Allegedly, the national Government made decisions that fell within the scope of power of regional authorities, taking credit for successes whilst letting regional governments take the political fall when measures failed. All of these clashes have occurred within a highly polarized political environment, featuring a far-right party with an increasing public presence and two major national parties that are unable to compromise or agree on basic aspects.[4]

Regardless of these clashes, some of which are circumstantial and others inherent to any crisis, the point is to come up with a legal framework successfully securing fundamental rights in times of a pandemic. Historically, emergency law has resulted from political crises, periods of civil unrest, social upheaval or threats to safety and public order. All of these are emergencies or crises requiring political responses. However, a health crisis must be addressed by relying on technical standards based on scientific knowledge. Therefore, technocracy, i.e., leaving the most important decisions in the hands of experts, could be a reasonable approach to these situations. Nonetheless, this is not a feasible approach and thus should

3 See Álvares Garcia V., *El concepto de necesidad en Derecho público*, Civitas, 1996.
4 Munoz Molina A., *La otra pandemia*, El País, 27 de septiembre de 2020.

not be considered a real option, since it would be incompatible with constitutional states. Crises and emergencies, regardless how "technical," "scientific" or "knowledge-based" they get, should be managed on the basis of political standards. Ultimately, the aim should be to strike a fair balance between the various interests at stake. Health and life are major legal interests, but they should not set aside many other rights.

One should keep in mind, however, that scientific knowledge is essential for political decision-making. But scientific arguments are often misused to underpin, impose or, better said, legitimize, many political decisions. Not being able to differentiate between the appropriate use and the misuse of science in political decision-making is the most serious attack on all citizens' right to a transparent government in the time of a pandemic.[5] Along these lines, being able to access scientific knowledge and clearly differentiating between what qualifies as essentially scientific and inherently political is directly proportional to citizens' and authorities' capacity to control and oversee the government. Courts' ability to rely on the proportionality principle for reviewing any fundamental rights restrictions depends on whether they are able to access scientific knowledge on an equal footing with the decision-maker. A similar issue arises when appointing the decision-maker. To some extent, concentrating powers in the executive branch is only justified on the grounds that it has greater access to scientific knowledge and expertise. However, this could work differently. Reasonably, the most knowledgeable authority should be the decision-maker, but if there is no access to scientific or expert knowledge, the decision-maker's decisions cannot be reviewed or controlled, and it could exercise its powers arbitrarily or disproportionately.

Emergency law during scientific crises thus requires a risk governance system that (i) allow for incorporating scientific and technical knowledge in legal decision-making; and (ii) be compatible with the separation of powers. The COVID-19 health crisis exemplifies–to an unexpected and unthinkable extent–the negative implications of not properly arranging for a smooth relationship between science and the law. Failing to come up with an efficient risk governance framework has given rise to a *bewil-*

5 See Esteve Pardo J, El desconcierto del Leviatán. Política y derecho ante las incertidumbres de la ciencia, Marcial Pons, Barcelona-Madrid, 2009; applying the theses of this work to the legal situation created by the Covid, La apelación a la Ciencia en el gobierno y la crisis del COVID-19, *Revista de Derecho público: Teoría y Método*, Vol. 2, 2020, p. 35 ss; Atienza M.., Variaciones sobre un tópico weberiano. Acerca del lugar de la ciencia en la decisión política, *Revista de las Cortes Generales*, nº 111, 2021, p. 75 ss.

dered Leviathan. This giant monster is throwing fists around supported by the rule of law, but it is blindfolded, because it is not walking on firm scientific ground. The first section of this report tackles this issue from a cross-cutting approach, discussing the impact of the pandemic on the constitutional checks and balances system.

Nonetheless, this is not the only concern raised by the pandemic for the constitutional state. Other than the debate around decision-*makers* and decision-*making*, there is an essential decision to make: which fundamental rights must be limited or restricted. Most of us had never experienced such major restrictions on our fundamental rights, but certain groups, e.g., the elderly living in nursing homes or inmates, have been hit hardest. From a comparative law perspective, health emergency legislation worldwide evidences that certain rights will be clearly–and often severely–limited by anti-covid measures, i.e., freedom of movement and free enterprise (also referred to as the freedom to conduct a business). Along with this twofold core, there are additional rights and freedoms directly or indirectly affected by anti-covid measures, including the freedom of assembly and of association and religious freedoms. We must discuss how to protect these other fundamental rights, since the restrictions thereon are not usually governed by emergency legislation. As shown below, in Spain, at first, it became a widely accepted claim that the freedom of assembly (and, more specifically, the right to demonstrate) had become suspended, as a result of the limitations imposed on freedom of movement.

From a *de lege ferenda* perspective, there are additional debates triggered by the COVID-19 pandemic that also involve clashes and conflicts between fundamental rights and other legal interests. First, it is worth examining the legal response to fake news in social media: Can we impose criminal penalties on fake news writers? Should there be regulations requiring social media owners to control and filter fake news stories as with hate speech? Are information, news literacy and fact checking the only tools against fake news and disinformation? Second, we could discuss the use of artificial intelligence (AI) and big data for, *inter alia*, find Covid cases nearby. When the pandemic began, some scholars predicted that COVID-19 was a testing ground for the government to become a watchdog relying on data mining and AI. This would give rise to a new *surveillant Leviathan*, different from Foucault's panopticism, where surveillance was limited to specific spaces and institutions. We will not address it in this report, but the mandatory vaccination debate is worth noting in this context.[6]

Finally, this report delves into how to ensure that anti-Covid measures are effective and, more specifically, the role of criminal law and criminal justice. Throughout this long pandemic period we have already experienced two completely opposite approaches to enforcement and compliance. At first, compliance was left in the hands of law enforcement authorities. Police officers watched citizens closely–it was oppressive at some points–and were entitled to impose administrative and criminal penalties. The unlawful or criminalized behavior, i.e., the administrative infringement or criminal offence, was "disobedience to authority." This approach actually expanded law enforcement surveillance and broadened police officers' scope to interpret and define the applicable legal framework. Criminalizing "disobedience to authority" requires watching, reviewing or controlling law enforcement officers' law enforcement action (repetition intended). At a later stage of the COVID-19 pandemic, and particularly after the spread of the Omicron variant, governments have started to emphasize individual responsibility and accountability (also, "self-responsibility" or "self-reliance"). Some commentators have rightly pointed out that this might be a turn towards an *anarchist* or *libertarian Leviathan*; the motto would be: if you can and have the means, stay at home, lock yourself down and work remotely. Promoting individual responsibility is essential, but failing to implement mandatory Covid prevention measures entails exposing or leaving unprotected the most vulnerable segments of the population.[7]

B. *Background for non-Spanish readers: a regulatory overview of the COVID-19 pandemic*

The Spanish legal system has two tiers or levels when it comes to addressing health emergencies. The first level–ordinary emergencies–is provided in Organic Act 3/1986 on Public Health (LOMESP). Article 3 LOMESP empowers health authorities to "adopt any measures necessary to control (i) infected persons or positive cases; (ii) any persons who are or have been

---

6 See Cierco Seira C., La vacunación contra el Covid y sus principales debates jurídicos, *Afduam, Extraordinario (2021), Tomo I*, p. 309 ss.; ibid., La vacunación obligatoria y su eventual proyección sobre la Covid *El Cronista del Estado Social y Democrático de Derecho*, núm. 23, 2021.

7 See Simon P., *El Leviatán anarquista*, El País, 27.12.2021

in contact therewith; and (ii) the surroundings, as well as any measures considered necessary in case of risks of infection." This is a paramount example of an emergency law provision: it is open-ended and loosely worded, and it also grants discretionary powers to health authorities with the aim of addressing future (and unpredictable) situations.[8]

Unlike other rules that broadly govern general emergencies[9] with a centralizing approach, the LOMESP is a devolving or non-centralizing provision that does not alter the distribution of powers between national and regional authorities. Indeed, the competent health authorities to implement these emergency measures are regional bodies, namely regional government presidents. In certain regions, implementing the LOMESP requires adopting enabling or empowering regional provisions.

The second level–regarding extraordinary emergencies–is based on Article 116 of the Spanish Constitution, which governs the state of exception, state of emergency and state of siege. We have noticed that other constitutional systems do not regulate these states in which governments are empowered to be able to put through policies that they would normally not be permitted to do, for the safety and protection of their citizens. This is the case with the United Kingdom, the United States or Switzerland; even when they do provide for exceptional legal frameworks, they do so differently. For example, in times of crisis, the French Constitution allows "extraordinary powers" to the President. Article 36 regulates the "state of siege" (*état de siège*). Finally, an Act of 3 April 1955 allows the proclamation, by the Council of Ministers, of the "state of emergency" (*état d'urgence*). Article 116 of the Spanish Constitution (SC) includes a more comprehensive regulation. First, it provides for three different exceptional states or exceptional legal frameworks: (i) state of exception; (ii) state of emergency; and (iii) state of siege. Second, it specifically empowers authorities and bodies to declare these states and provides for the relationship between the executive and the legislature. And, finally, Article 116 SC clearly establishes that the Spanish legislature or *Cortes Generales* should continue to run normally, with no disruptions.[10]

Organic Act 4/1981 on the states of emergency, exception and siege (LOAES) implemented Article 116 SC. One of the most prominent aspects

---

8 See Álvarez Garcia V/Arias Aparicio F./Hernandez Diez., *Lecciones jurídicas para. la lucha contra la pandemia*, op. cit., p. 23 ss.

9 See Ley 17/2015 del Sistema Nacional de Protección Civil; Ley 36/2015 de Seguridad Nacional,

10 See Perz Royo J./Carrasco Duran M., *Derecho constitucional*, 16 Ed, 2018, Marcial Pons, p. 845 ss.

of LOAES is whether the underlying rationale or approach is purpose-based (*tesis causalista*) or rights-based (*tesis gradualista*). In fact, Constitutional Court Judgment 148/2021, the first Covid-related ruling, addresses this matter. According to the purpose-based rationale, the defining feature of these exceptional states or frameworks is that each of them come in response to specific conditions or circumstances and that they should be declared on specific grounds. The state of emergency would apply in case of natural disasters, health crises or significant disruptions to essential services. Article 4(c) LOAES expressly mentions pandemics as an example of health crises. States of exception would be enforced during civil unrest. The state of siege would apply to political crises, i.e., if Spain's independence or sovereignty was threatened. Consequently, under the purpose-based approach, in times of Covid the Spanish Government could only enforce the state of emergency, and not the states of exception or siege.

Advocates of the rights-based approach, which was finally upheld by the Constitutional Court in Judgment 148/2021, focus on the potential restrictions on individual rights and freedoms. They emphasize that, under the state of emergency, fundamental rights cannot be suspended, but only limited. The difference between limiting and suspending fundamental rights has thus become a key issue. So, in the view of rights-based advocates, the lockdown adopted by Spain's Government during the first state of emergency actually qualified as a suspension of fundamental rights, which therefore could only be enforced under a state of exception.[11]

This debate is really about legitimacy and oversight, including parliamentary control and judicial review, regarding decisions severely affecting fundamental rights. In order to fully understand this controversy, we should further discuss the LOAES. It is for the Government to declare the state of emergency issuing a decree that should remain in force during a 15-day period without any parliamentary involvement. During this 15-day period, the Spanish legislature could request information for the sake of political scrutiny or control, but it is not entitled to revoke the state of emergency. In a nutshell: under Spanish law, unlike the other exceptional legal frameworks, the state of emergency does not require parliamentary approval at first. The state of emergency decree expires after

11 The bibliography that has been generated by the state of alarm is enormous, a state of the art in Domenech Pascual, Dogmatismo contra pragmatism. Dos maneras de ver las restricciones de derechos fundamentales impuestas con ocasión de la Covid 19, *InDret 4.2021*, p. 345 ss.

a 15-day period, after which a new law extending the emergency must be voted by the *Cortes Generales*. Note that the Spanish Parliament (*Cortes Generales*) may amend the Government's decree as it sees fit. Regarding judicial review, note that the limitations and restrictions established by the state of emergency cannot be challenged either in the *Cortes Generales* or before the courts of justice. The only court that has jurisdiction to hear any claims against these limitations and restrictions is the Constitutional Court following an unconstitutionality appeal. As noted above, the provision declaring the state of emergency is a decree, i.e., a regulatory (non-statutory) provision under Spanish law. However, its effects are as if it was a statutory provision, and that is why it is not subject to judicial review by ordinary courts of justice. Nevertheless, keep in mind that under a standard emergency framework, limitations and restrictions imposed by regional or national authority are subject to judicial review by ordinary courts of justice.

Organic Act 4/1981 on the states of emergency, exception and siege (LOAES) fails to regulate the duration of any extensions of the state of emergency after parliamentary approval. Accordingly, both the Government and the legislature enjoy a broad scope of discretion that matches the inherent unpredictability of crises and disasters. However, in Judgment 183/2021, the Spanish Constitutional Court criticized that Parliament authorized a 6-month long state of emergency, from October 2020 to May 2020. After parliamentary approval, terminating the state of emergency is no longer within the Parliament's scope of power; rather, it is a Government prerogative.

Finally, it is worth highlighting the effects of the state of emergency on the relationships between national and regional government authorities.[12] States of emergency are presidential and centralizing, although they do have some elements that allow for flexibilization. Declaring a state of emergency is an exclusive power of the national Government, but regional governments are entitled to request that "regional states of emergency" be declared. Also, after declaring the state of emergency, whether with a national or regional scope, the national Government may delegate its emergency management powers to a minister or to the president of a regional government.

Having discussed the core elements of the regulatory framework, it is worth noting that COVID-19 management strategies have been back

12 See Velasco Caballero F./ Lopez De Castro L., Distribución territorial del poder durante la pandemia, *Afduam, Extraordinario (2021), Tomo I*, p. 61 ss.

and forth between ordinary health emergency legislation (LOMESP) and exceptional or extraordinary legal frameworks, i.e., the state of emergency under the LOAES.[13]

After the first Covid cases in February 2020, the pandemic was left in the hands of regional health departments under Article 3 LOMESP. The most stringent measures were (i) perimeter closures for towns with high incidence rates; or (ii) hotel lockdowns for infected patients. Subject to the rules and regulations applicable at the time, such restrictive actions required prior judicial approval, just like other rights restrictions implemented by public authorities that affect citizens individually. Not a single judge or court questioned these measures.

On 14 March, the Government declared the first state of emergency, thereby changing the regulatory framework altogether. At this point, the LOAES made its appearance. Royal Decree 463/2020 implemented the state of emergency, thus prompting a shift from ordinary emergency law to an extraordinary emergency framework. After 15 days, the Spanish *Cortes Generales* extended the state of emergency (see Royal Decree 476/2020 of 27 March). All parties voted in favor of this extension. Then, at the Government's request, parliament approved six additional extensions of the state of emergency. The first extensions were for 15-day periods, but the sixth one lasted a whole month.[14] This first state of emergency ended on 21 June. The most significant social distancing measures were stay-at-home orders, but they were not equally stringent or strict throughout this long period. The strictest or most stringent stage was the so-called "super lockdown" during the first week of April 2015.[15] After May, the

13 For more details, see Álvarez Garcia V./Arias Aparicio F./ Hernandez Diez e., *Lecciones jurídicas para. la lucha contra la pandemia*, p. 199; Domenech Pascual G., Dogmatismo contra pragmatism. Dos maneras de ver las restricciones de derechos fundamentales impuestas con ocasión de la Covid 19, p. 351 ss.

14 Royal Decree 476/2020, of 27 March, extending the state of emergency declared by Royal Decree 463/2020, of 14 March. The extension was until 12:00 am of 12 April 2020. Royal Decree 487/2020, of 10 April, provided for an extension until 12:00 am of 26 April 2020. Then, Royal Decree 492/2020, of 24 April, set out an additional extension until 12:00 am of 10 May 2020. Royal Decree 514/2020, of 8 May, extended the state of emergency until 12:00 am of 24 May 2020. Royal Decree 537/2020, of 22 May, further extended the state of emergency until 12:00 am of 7 June 2020. See also Royal Decree 555/2020, of 5 June, extending the state of emergency until 12:00 am of 21 June 2020.

15 Royal Decree-Law 10/2020 regulating recoverable paid leave for employees that do not provide essential services, to reduce population mobility in the fight against COVID-19.

"de-escalation" stage began.[16] Progressively, provincial authorities began to loosen COVID-19 restrictions.

The President delegated its emergency management duties to a "crisis cabinet" made up of the President himself and the Ministers of Health, Defence and Internal Affairs. So, Spain's state of emergency was a centralized one, triggering a major change in the standard allocation of powers between regional and national bodies. Centralization does not mean no dialogue between government levels. Indeed, government officials and regional presidents met on a regular basis. At first, there were no significant conflicts or disputes, but they appeared as the de-escalation stage kept moving forward. There was a clash between (i) regional presidents calling for a return to normalcy as soon as possible; and (ii) the national Government, which refused to loosen the restrictions and allow regional governments to further de-escalate and ease anti-covid measures. As a result, some regions claimed that they were being treated unfairly and unequally. During the parliamentary approval process of the state of emergency's last extension there was greater opposition. Whereas almost all parties voted in favor of the first two extensions, the next ones raised concerns. Opposition parties and even some coalition members refused to support the extensions. Consequently, the Government went through a parliamentary struggle to further extend the state of emergency.

The first party to break consensus was far-right Vox, which on 28 April 2020 filed an unconstitutionality appeal against the state of emergency decrees. The arguments revolved around the aforesaid debate between purpose-based advocates and rights-based advocates. The appellants (i.e., Vox's legal counsel) raised the claim that the state of emergency entailed a suspension–and not a mere limitation–of fundamental rights. So, it could not be adopted by enforcing a state of emergency framework, but only under a state of exception. In sum, in the political arena, the first state of emergency resulted in a major dispute between the national Government and regional leaders and, most certainly, among the various political parties. At the time, Spain's Covid incidence or prevalence rate was as low as 5.87 per 100,000 population, and the Spanish President even stated that Spain "had beaten Covid" and that the country could return to a near-normal situation.

Within this context, there was another turn of events. After the state of emergency, the ordinary emergency framework appeared, i.e., Organic

16 COVID-19 De-escalation Plan adopted by the Council of Ministers on 28 April 2020.

Act 3/1986 on Public Health (LOMESP). LOMESP provisions, which were broad and open-ended, had to be supplemented by national pieces of legislation. For instance, the Government passed legislation on (i) the mandatory use of face masks in public spaces; or (ii) reduced seating capacity at certain venues or premises.[17] The return to standard emergency regulations, i.e., the so-called "new normalcy" or "semi-normalcy," entailed leaving the pandemic in the hands of regional authorities. Spain's Government started to play a secondary or subordinate role.

This new environment prompted a legal debate regarding the interpretation of the abovementioned Article 3 LOMESP. According to some scholars and commentators, this provision only allowed for adopting *individualized* contention and social distancing measures. Put differently, in their view it only allowed for action targeting specific Covid-infected individuals and their close contacts. According to this approach, Article 3 LOMESP did not entitle regional health authorities to close down entire towns (perimeter closures) or adopt Covid-related measures affecting the rights and freedoms of an undetermined number of people. Some commentators, on the other hand, considered that Article 3 LOMESP did empower public authorities to implement non-individualized measures with a broad and undetermined scope. The final clause of Art. 3 provides that health authorities may adopt "any measures considered necessary in case of risks of infection," thus empowering public authorities to implement such non-individualized measures with a broad and undetermined scope.[18]

Lawmakers embraced the latter interpretation, as Spain passed Act 3/2020 of 18 September. This piece of legislation was adopted really quickly, right when the strictest interpretation seemed to be gaining ground in the case law. Act 3/2020, which includes additional provisions on the justice system during the pandemic, provides for a significant amendment to the Administrative Jurisdiction Act (*Ley de la Jurisdicción Contencioso Administrativa*). The judicial review of anti-covid measures set out in Art. 3 LOMESP is left in the hands of regional high courts, thus requiring the prior approval by each region's regional high court of any measures considered "urgent and necessary for public health [by regional governments] although limiting or restricting fundamental rights if they do not target specific addressees or have an undetermined scope." This created a regional

17 Decreto Ley 21/2020 de medidas urgentes de prevención, contención y coordinación para. hacer frente a la crisis sanitaria ocasionada por el COVID-19.

18 See Domenech Pascual, Dogmatismo contra pragmatism. Dos maneras de ver las restricciones de derechos fundamentales impuestas con ocasión de la Covid 19, p. 355 ss.

judicial review system led by the most prominent judicial bodies in each region.

Despite lawmakers' efforts for clarifying the legal situation, early in the Fall of 2020 there were various regional courts' rulings[19] emphasizing that regional authorities were not entitled to provide for broad, open-ended measures or lockdowns. These rulings relied on Art. 3 LOMESP to support their arguments. Other courts issued judgments suspending specific anti-covid measures on the grounds that they were unreasonable or disproportionate. Simultaneously, there was a major political clash between the Region of Madrid (ruled by the opposition party) and the national Government. The Madrid Regional Government–duly empowered to manage the COVID-19 pandemic–refused to meet the Ministry of Health's requirements in order to trigger more restrictive measures given the increase in covid cases. As a result, the national Government began to manage the pandemic in the Region of Madrid declaring an *ad hoc* state of emergency for various towns and cities therein.

In parallel with these clashes and disputes, as 2020 was coming to an end, there was a sharp rise in Covid cases. Some regional presidents wanted to impose more severe restrictions, particularly curfews, in order to force citizens to stay at home in the evening and at night. However, based on the case law that regional high courts were establishing in connection with Art. 3 LOMESP, curfews and stay-at-home orders raised major concerns, and it was unlikely that courts would approve these stringent measures.

The national Government's response to the uncertainty created by a bunch of contradictory rulings led to another turn of events. National authorities, after declaring a new state of emergency under Decree 926/2020 of 25 October, went back to applying the extraordinary emergency framework. Nevertheless, this new state of emergency was very different from that of March 2020. In the first place, it was a decentralized state of emergency. Decree 926/2020 laid down a set of social distancing measures (curfews, stay-at-home orders, the temporary closure of restaurants, bars, enter-

19 Court Order 32/2020, of 22 October, issued by the Basque Regional High Court upholding the Government ban on gatherings of more than 6 people. See also the court orders issued by the Madrid and Aragón Regional High Courts. See a critical view of these court orders in the following works by Velasco Caballero F., *El TSJ del País Vasco no ratifica los límites a las reuniones*; *El TSJ de Madrid no ratifica los confinamientos por falta de autorización lega*l; and *El TSJ de Aragón deniega la ratificación de medidas sanitarias para. la Almudia de Doña Godina* (https://francis covelascocaballeroblog.wordpress.com/)

tainment and recreation venues, and perimeter closures and lockdowns for entire regions) that were enforced by regional governments based on the spread of COVID-19 in each region. As a result, certain regions mandated very strict measures, e.g., stringent temporary closures of restaurants and curfews, whereas others–remarkably, the Region of Madrid–were much more lenient. Note that the fundamental rights limitations during the second state of emergency were a lot less restrictive than during the first one.

The second state of emergency was long. As mentioned before, during the first state of emergency the national Government would seek extensions in parliament every 15 or 30 days. However, Decree 926/2020 sought parliamentary approval for a 6-month state of emergency, specifically until 9 May 2021. The LOAES, as pointed out above, does not include any provisions on the duration of states of emergency or on the frequency with which parliament has to authorize extensions. Additionally, as noted before, after the Spanish legislature approves the state of emergency, only the national Government can decide to terminate it, even if the *Cortes Generales* consider that the extension requirements are no longer fulfilled. Therefore, many claimed that authorizing a 6-month state of emergency was unconstitutional.

Yet again, far-right Vox members of parliament (MPs) raised these arguments and filed an unconstitutionality appeal against the second state of emergency. The appeal was also critical of the broad delegation of powers made by the Government to regional authorities for the application and enforcement of social distancing measures.

From 9 May 2021 until now, we have gone back to ordinary emergency law, i.e., Art. 3 LOMESP and regional governments handling the pandemic. Currently there is a decentralized approach to COVID-19, and additional states of emergency are very unlikely. Spain's national Government is almost out of the picture when it comes to managing the pandemic. In fact, it played a secondary role when Coronavirus cases fueled by the highly transmissible Omicron variant were skyrocketing in late December 2021. The Government neither sought to pass additional pieces of legislation. There are some calls for a new Act on Pandemics to settle the existing legal concerns. Note that there are a lot more legal issues and concerns than the ones discussed herein. Nevertheless, such a new piece of legislation does not seem to be on the Government's political agenda.

Legally speaking, although with certain political implications, the Spanish Constitutional Court handed down two rulings on the state of emergency largely upholding the claims of far-right Vox in its appeals. Constitutional Court Judgment 148/2021, of 14 July, found lockdowns and stay-at-home orders unconstitutional, and they were the leading measures of the first state of emergency. Constitutional Court Judgment 183/2021, of 27 October, declared the second state of emergency unconstitutional, on the grounds that both (i) the 6-month parliamentary extension authorized in Parliament; and (ii) the delegation of powers to regional presidents were contrary to the *Constitución Española*. The Constitutional Court delivered these rulings in the midst of a great controversy about whether the Court is politicized. One should keep in mind that, at the time, most of the Constitutional Court justices' terms had expired because the two major political parties were unable to compromise on the appointment of new members.

C. *Deciding and controlling: the "how" matters more than the "who"*

First, it is worth discussing the impact of the COVID-19 pandemic on the checks and balances system. To that end, we must examine the role of each branch of government regarding both (i) the decisions on rights restrictions; and (ii) the control and review thereof.

The Spanish legislature has gone back and forth, from refusing to pass legislation, to putting on a big show on the media.[20] This contrasts with the underlying rationale of the constitutional provisions governing the various exceptional states. Historically speaking, states of emergency were literally an "exception" to the constitutional order, which would be superseded by a different framework. The Spanish Constitution departs from this approach, particularly regarding the state of emergency, which qualifies as a less exceptional legal regime that could be considered closer to civil protection rules than to traditional exceptional frameworks. Although the Spanish Parliament should have played a more prominent role both during the state of emergency and in managing the pandemic, it did not.

During such a long pandemic, legislatures have had more than enough time to pass legislation to manage this health crisis with increased legal certainty and greater safeguards. Shockingly, at times of "expedited lawmaking," legislatures fail to modify health emergency law in spite of its obvious shortcomings. When Spain passed the ordinary (1986 LOMESP) and extraordinary (1981 LOAES) emergency legislation, lawmakers probably did not think that extremely restrictive measures like stay-at-home

20 See Aguafo Renedo C. Gobierno y parlamento en la emergencia sanitaria, *Afduam,, Extraordinario (2021), Tomo I*, p. 49 ss.

orders and lockdowns would be necessary to tackle pandemics. Also, note that, back then, the national-to-regional devolution process provided in the 1978 Constitution had barely started. By approving the second state of emergency and extending it for an additional 6 months, what the Spanish legislature actually did was allowing the Government to adopt a temporary Act on Pandemics, addressing decentralization issues (and the allocation of powers) along with the implementation of anti-covid measures, since some courts questioned that such restrictive measures could be adopted under ordinary emergency legislation. The purpose of states of emergency should not be to cover aspects or make up for measures that must be subject to ordinary health emergency laws.

However, the Spanish Parliament's inactivity during the pandemic has more to do with its poor legislative performance over the last few years, particularly since the 2008 crisis. A distinct feature of the Spanish legal system is the proliferation of the so-called "royal decree-law."[21] These pieces of legislation, which can only be found in Spain and Italy, are aimed at *exceptionally* enabling the Government to adopt regulatory provisions, i.e., decrees, with the same effects as statutory provisions (i.e., with the force of a law) that should be subsequently ratified in Parliament. These provisions are only meant for emergency conditions. Obviously, this does not mean that the Spanish Parliament no longer has legislative activity. During this Covid health crisis, the *Cortes Generales* have adopted provisions on euthanasia, LGTBQ+ rights or education. Also, there is parliamentary debate on employment legislation, sex-related crime or the General Budget Act. Nevertheless, there has been no lawmaking activity whatsoever regarding the country's main issue over these two years. During the COVID-19 pandemic, MPs have put on quite a performance in Parliament that looked more like political show business (*Politainment*), with huge theatrical discussions and no real political debate or lawmaking. Almost no political parties have submitted amendments to the public health legislation. There was only a legislative proposal for a new Act on Pandemics and the draft was rejected.[22]

Admittedly, the Spanish Parliament's scrutiny of the executive has not been outstanding. In addition to turning the so-called "Government control sessions" into some sort of farce, parliamentary oversight was seriously

---

21 See Huergo Lora A., *Estado de alarma en el país de los decretos leyes*, 13. Junio. 2020, https://almacendederecho.org/.

22 See also the Draft Organic Act 3/1986 modifying Organic Act 4/1981, of 1 June, on the states of emergency, exception and siege. However, this initiative did not even become a bill because it was rejected by the remaining parties.

diminished because the Spanish Parliament regulations did not provide for remote meetings. During the first three weeks of the state of emergency, some commentators claimed that the *Cortes Generales* were "hibernating," and that there had been a "parliamentary eclipse."[23] Such inactivity is contrary to Article 116(5) SC, under which states of emergency should not disrupt parliamentary activity. Aside from this three-week "hibernation," by allowing for a 6-month state of emergency the Spanish legislature shot itself in the foot regarding its oversight duties. It also waived its obligation to scrutinize the Government by providing that the *only* control over the executive would be for the President to report to Parliament every two months and on a monthly basis to the Parliamentary Health Committee. However, such loose oversight was not effective. The Government, as set out in the decree ratified by Parliament, had delegated its crisis management powers to regional governments, empowering them to implement rights restrictions and anti-covid measures based on the evolution of the pandemic. The decentralization under the state of emergency has revealed an additional (and significant) gap. The Spanish Senate, constitutionally defined as a "territorial chamber," has no powers vested upon it under exceptional legal frameworks, and regional parliaments neither have any specific oversight powers.

Given the lack of parliamentary control over the executive, it is somewhat understandable that the role of the judiciary and the Constitutional Court was strengthened. Courts have not been deferential to national and regional government authorities, but claiming that the COVID-19 pandemic has been managed by judicial authorities would be a huge overstatement. On the one hand, as noted before, some regional courts questioned the interpretation of Art. 3 LOMESP as set out in a statutory provision in order to allow for non-individualized rights restrictions with a broad and undetermined scope. But, on top of that, judicial authorities have often relied on the proportionality principle to revoke or invalidate anti-covid measures that limited fundamental rights. These decisions are really shocking, because (i) as soon as the Supreme Court had the chance to rule on this matter, it pointed out that judicial review had to be "extremely limited" (Supreme Court Judgment of 24 May 2021); and (ii) the review on grounds of proportionality has to be performed based on empirical data that are not always accurate. Therefore, according to the Constitutional Court, judicial authorities must be deferential to lawmakers, and they

23 See Solozabal Echevarria J.J, El estado de alarma y el Derecho de crisis en nuestro sistema constitucional, *Afduam, Extraordinario (2021), Tomo I*, p. 27 ss.

should only invalidate blatantly unreasonable or disproportionate measures.

After repealing the core of the state of emergency decrees, the Constitutional Court also became a key player in this pandemic. The Constitutional Court's case law seeks to clarify the distribution of powers between (i) the national Government; (ii) regional governments; and (iii) the Spanish Parliament. In a nutshell: the Constitutional Court's arguments focus on whether or not the restrictions on freedom of movement are overly stringent. To that end, it breaks down restrictions into three different categories. First, the Court refers to ordinary restrictions that could be adopted under an ordinary or standard emergency framework by regional authorities and subject to judicial review; these are the least stringent restrictions. Second, there are exceptional restrictions, limiting fundamental rights, which should be implemented by the national Government under a state of emergency and subject to prior parliamentary approval and, in some cases, also subject to judicial review by the Constitutional Court. Third, there are even more stringent restrictions, i.e., those that can only be adopted under the state of exception. Note that, in Spain, unlike the state of emergency, the *estado de excepción* requires prior parliamentary approval. These are "overly stringent" restrictions which, according to the Constitutional Court, qualify as a suspension of fundamental rights and not a limitation.[24]

Ultimately, the Court's stance is based on the assumption that the greater the restriction on a fundamental right, the greater the need for enhanced legitimacy in decision-making. Thus, in the Court's view, (i) the national Government's legitimacy under the state of emergency is greater than that of regional government authorities; and (ii) simultaneously, the Parliament has more legitimacy than the national Government. This "legitimacy ranking" is not only based on who makes the decision, but also on who reviews the decision and oversees decision-makers, since the

---

24 Various commentaries on these judgments can be seen at Domenech Pascual P. Dogmatismo contra pragmatismo, p. 377 ss; Presno Linera M., El estado de alarma en crisis, *Revista de las cortes generales*, nº 111, 2021, p. 219 ss.; Atienza M., La importancia de la ponderación. a propósito de la sentencia del tribunal constitucional español sobre la pandemia, *Silexx*, 4.11.2021 (https://www.si-lex.es/ https://www.si-lex.es/); Aragon M., ¿Alarma o excepción?, *Diario del Derecho*, 6 de julio 2021(https://www.iustel.com//diario_del_derecho/noticia.asp?ref_iustel=121 3081&popup); Cruz Villalón P. Destripando al Tribunal Constitucional, 23 julio 2021, *El País*; Garcia Roca A., Constitucionalidad de la alarma, *El País*, 12 de julio de 2021; Quadra Salcedo T., Rompiendo el consenso constitucional, *El País*, 22 julio 2021.

underlying assumption is that the Constitutional Court's review is more effective than that of regional high courts, and that parliamentary scrutiny is better than judicial review.

Most likely, the Constitutional Court's line of case law draws significant criticism, but it certainly does not give rise to an authoritarian emergency framework. Under truly authoritarian emergency law, the national Government would have been attributed broader powers and judicial review would have been loosened for the sake of effectiveness. However, the Constitutional Court's line of case law could be considered a centralist doctrine, since it disempowers regional governments. The difference between the regional and national levels lies exclusively in the stringency of the restriction, not in the existence or assessment of the emergency situation. The Constitutional Court emphasizes that the national Government enjoys a broad margin of appreciation when assessing a health crisis and declaring a state of emergency. In this case, constitutional review would be limited to "imaginary," "hypothetical" or "almost unthinkable" cases within the Spanish constitutional framework.

Nevertheless, regional health authorities have been another *de facto* key player. The first state of emergency, with a significantly centralizing effect, focused on effectiveness and not on safeguards, and evidenced that national authorities were "rusty" and "out of shape." In fact, due to the national-to-regional devolution of powers in health-related matters, national bodies no longer had any experience in health emergencies. During the first state of emergency, there were some disputes, but not really about effectiveness. Rather, these disputes were about who paid the political price (and took the credit) of anti-covid measures. In spite of these conflicts, the relationship between national and regional authorities was mostly cooperative, and it has been fairly smooth thanks to the creation of a specific body, i.e., the Inter-territorial Health Council. Throughout this time, regional and national legal frameworks have operated without any major disruptions or disputes.

So, the main constitutional debate in Spain revolves around legitimacy. This debate has taken place in fairly traditional terms, i.e., claiming that the only source of legitimacy is representative democracy. Within this context, parliaments always have the highest degree of legitimacy, over governments, and governments have greater legitimacy than the judiciary because they make decisions under participatory mechanisms and subject to parliamentary scrutiny. Judicial authorities are only considered legitimate as long as they act in accordance with the law (i.e., with constitutional and statutory provisions). Therefore, if there is scientific uncertainty, courts of justice must be deferential to lawmakers. When there are clear, undisputed, empirical or science-based solutions, expert evidence can play a role in judicial review. Otherwise, if courts cannot rely on meaningful scientific arguments, judicial review should not just turn into a science lecture. Within contexts of uncertainty, the judiciary can only admit that there is an asymmetry between the standard of conduct (addressed to public authorities) and the standard of judicial review.[25] Therefore, as concluded by the Spanish Supreme Court, it is best to exercise limited judicial review over lawmakers.

This approach to the debate, through the lens of traditional constitutional law, is misguided. On the one hand, it entails disregarding that, during the COVID-19 pandemic, two additional sources of legitimacy have emerged[26]. One of them is the so-called output legitimacy, which is performance or effectiveness-oriented. This is why, at some point, nobody has questioned the joint governance arrangements between national and regional authorities. Decision-makers and decision-making powers do not matter as long as decisions are effective. The other significant source of legitimacy that has arisen during the pandemic is the so-called knowledge-based or technical legitimacy. Citizens have accepted individual rights restrictions not so much because the decisions stemmed from democratically elected bodies, but because they relied on more meaningful and extensive scientific knowledge[27].

This new source of legitimacy fuels the debate about how law and science come together. As pointed out before, the way law and science are articulated is key when it comes to drafting an Act on Pandemics. Administrative law scholars have already come up with various mechanisms for bringing together legal and scientific frameworks. First, it is worth examining the precautionary principle governing the interaction between law and science within contexts of scientific uncertainty, e.g., in the field of food law and food safety.[28]As for the management of covid-related

---

25 See Arroyo Jimenez L., *El control judicial del poder en situaciones de incertidumbre*, 4 Enero 2022, https://almacendederecho.org/.

26 See with references about the different forms of legitimacy Munoz De Morales M., *El legislador penal europeo: racionalidad y legitimidad*, Civitas, 2018.

27 See Miro Llinares F., *Hechos en tierra de normas: Una introducción epistemológica a la relevancia de la realidad fáctica en el Derecho penal*, en Suárez López, J. M., Barquín Sanz, J., Benítez Ortúzar, I. F., Jiménez Díaz, M. J., Sáinz Cantero Caparrós, J. E. (Coords.). Estudios jurídicos penales y criminológicos en homenaje a Lorenzo Morillas Cueva., Dykinson, 2018.

28 Esteve Pardo J., *El desconcierto del Leviatan*, op. cit, p. 141 ss.

risks, we are probably not facing a context of scientific uncertainty; we are mostly confronted with prevention needs. The main issue is assessing or weighing the costs and benefits of certain anti-covid measures that have been found effective by the experts.

In any event, what matters is not the difference between prevention and precaution, but rather the methodology implemented in those areas where the precautionary principle applies. Indeed, the precautionary principle entails implementing further and more sophisticated decision-making procedures, seeking that decision-makers be forced to provide a more extensive and meaningful reasoning. EU Regulation 178/2002 laying down the general principles and requirements of food law aptly exemplifies this. The decision of banning a given food additive, for instance, can be broken down into two distinct stages: (i) risk assessment; and (ii) risk management. Stage (i) is based on strictly scientific criteria and should be conducted by independent specialized agencies. In the EU, the European Food Safety Authority performs a risk assessment relying solely on scientific standards[29]. Then, the decision-making body issues a political decision following a cost-and-benefit analysis. This decision-making procedure, which emphasizes legal reasoning and the separation of decision-making levels, is based on transparency. Also, this procedure separates scientific and political arguments, and the underlying transparency allows for disclosing and sharing scientific knowledge.

In Spain, fundamental rights restrictions during the pandemic, whether stemming from Parliament, local governments, or regional authorities, should be based on a similar decision-making procedure as that governing those sectors subject to the precautionary principle, like food law. Similarly, the review or scrutiny, whether conducted by ordinary courts, the Constitutional Court, or national and regional legislatures, should be based on the legal rationale used by the courts when applying the precautionary principle. Such review should pay careful attention to procedural aspects, legal reasoning, and decision-making, not focusing as much on the very substance of the restrictive measure.

One of the main shortcomings of Spain's approach to the pandemic has been the lack of transparency regarding the scientific knowledge justifying and underpinning political decision-making. Nobody ever disclosed the members of the expert panel that was supposed to be advising the

---

29 See Hospes O./Hadiprayitno ed., *Governing food security. Law, politics, and the right to food*, Wageningen Academic, European Institute for Food Law series nº 5, p. 161 ss

Government or the panel's reports or remarks. Obviously, we assume that this "expert panel" was not an independent agency and that it made decisions through appropriate procedures, which is a pre-requirement for the scientific and political assessment stages to be clearly differentiated. Individual rights restrictions and political narratives definitely required underlying knowledge-based or technical legitimacy. Otherwise, these restrictions would seem unreasonable or unjustified and there would be no agreement on whether or not to comply with them. This is why decision-makers have been repeatedly raising scientific criteria and standards, although without openly disclosing these criteria and providing them in the abstract. There have been attempts to fulfil scientific standards simply by producing documents from international organizations. However, these supporting documents do not suffice to meet the reasoning requirements–i.e., the duty to give reasons–necessary for political decision-making in contexts of uncertainty.

So, the constitutional debate on fundamental rights restrictions must not revolve around "decision-makers" and "reviewers," and let alone around the difference between suspending and limiting rights (which is a moot debate) or the essence of individual and undetermined restrictive measures. Such debates are absurd and misguided, as evidenced by the serious interferences with the freedom of movement of two specific groups of people: older adults living in nursing homes; and inmates.

Locking the elderly in their rooms in nursing homes for weeks, no visitors allowed, qualifies as suspending or limiting their freedom of movement? Is it a restriction with a broad and undetermined scope, or an individualized restrictive measure targeting a specific (and vulnerable) group? Such a radical lockdown of nursing homes was adopted by regional presidents within the framework of ordinary legislation, i.e., as an individualized fundamental rights restriction which was subsequently upheld–without much questioning–by regional high courts. Authorities barely gave any supporting reasons or justifications. This has also been the case with restrictions on inmates. There have been exceptional restrictions regarding prison leaves, permits, communications, solitary confinement, or the suspension of in-prison training programs. These measures have been adopted through non-statutory, low-rank provisions, such as circular notes issued by the General Directorate for Prisons.[30]

---

30 See Rodriguez Yague C., COVID-19 y prisiones: un desafío no sólo sanitario y de seguridad, también humanitario, *Revista General de Derecho Penal*, 33, 2020.

The main issue regarding fundamental rights protection in times of a pandemic is not about decision-*makers* but decision-*making*. Probably, it is not for the most democratically representative body to decide. Rather, decision-making powers should be placed in the hands of any decision-makers who are able to make quicker, better-informed decisions and who have the ability to follow through and manage those decisions. Only decision-making procedures resembling precautionary law allow for issuing reasonable, proportionate, transparent, and duly reasoned decisions. Accordingly, judicial review would not have to focus on the final content or substance of the decision, but rather on whether the applicable procedural requirements and the duty to give reasons have been fulfilled. Courts must be more or less deferential to lawmakers depending on the degree of fulfillment of these duties and requirements. Regardless, even if the judicial review focuses on the merits of the decision, under a strict interpretation of the proportionality test, judicial scrutiny is only possible if (i) courts have access to the same knowledge and criteria as decision-makers; and (ii) the decision-making body has also performed a "transparent impact assessment," disclosing the costs and benefits attached to the relevant decision or measure.

D. The COVID- 19 pandemic and fundamental rights

The COVID-19 pandemic has shown that many public authorities, relying on very diverse empowering provisions and entitlements–not necessarily emergency law–have mandated rights restrictions. For instance, see the restrictive measures implemented in prisons and nursing homes. On top of that, we witnessed indirect restrictions on fundamental rights as a result of anti-covid action. Particularly during the first wave, there was a heated debate about the right to demonstrate and religious freedom. Both aptly exemplify the alarming lack of protection of certain fundamental rights that at first did not seem at risk of being restricted.

The right to demonstrate was questioned in the context of the labor day rallies promoted by labor unions.[31] Most of these demonstrations were scheduled by unions and complied with the applicable safety measures

31 See about this question Garcia Garcia L., Libertad religiosa en tiempos de coronavirus, *Afduam, Extraordinario 2021, Tomo I*, p. 127 ss; Perez Alvarez S. *Restricciones a la libertad religiosa durante la crisis sanitaria del COVID-19*, Atienza Macias E/ Rodriguez Ayuso, J.F (dir), Las respuestas del derecho a las crisis de salud pública, Dykinson, 2021, p. 295 ss.

preventing the spread of COVID: the demonstrators would drive their car around wearing a face mask. The state of emergency provisions do not allow for expressly limiting freedom of assembly (i.e., the right to demonstrate). Thus, the standard rules on demonstrations still apply. So, even during a pandemic, no authorization is required to demonstrate other than reporting the scheduled demonstration to the competent authority, who might modify some aspects or otherwise ban the demonstration on very specific grounds (public order). The competent authority is the Government delegate, i.e., a Government representative for each region. If such Government delegate deems appropriate to ban or modify certain aspects of the demonstration, e.g., the place or the date, it can only do so on "sufficient objective grounds," leaving no reasonable doubt that the demonstration would interfere with other constitutional rights and interests at stake. Therefore, it does not suffice to give reasons; the standard of reasoning requires that there be no doubt. And, when in doubt, the right to demonstrate enjoys a favorable presumption (*favor libertatis*).

Under this legal framework, the competent authorities prohibited most labor day rallies on May 1, 2020. As a result, labor unions filed complaints before the relevant regional high courts. Except in one case, courts upheld the ban on demonstrations. The Constitutional Court followed suit immediately, rejecting the appeal brought by a labor union. The Constitutional Court's arguments were based on the precautionary principle and the prevailing scientific uncertainty: "Given the current stage of scientific research, within this changing environment, it is impossible that there be a high degree of certainty as to how covid is transmitted (...)." Such a "significant and inapprehensible" uncertainty leads the Constitutional Court to prohibit demonstrations.[32]

So, applying the precautionary principle seems appropriate, but only if there is a specific procedure for implementing restrictions based on a framework that smoothly brings together law and science. Outside of this legal framework, relying on the precautionary principle–as the Constitutional Court does–leaves fundamental rights completely unprotected.

The external dimension of religious freedom covers practicing or attending acts of worship, i.e., any acts with religious meaning. In-person attendance at masses was prohibited for most of the first state of emergency, since it was not allowed to walk on public walkways to go to church. In

32 See Presno Linera M., *El estado de alarma en crisis*, p. 180 ss; Rodriquez Pinero M., Estado de alarma y derecho de manifestación del sindicato. *Derecho de las relaciones laborales*, 2020, 6, p. 673 ss.

other words, Decree 463/2020 did not prohibit attending mass *per se*, but it did impose attendance restrictions (see Art. 18). However, it was unclear if people were allowed to go to places of worship (Art. 11). Religious ceremonies were subject to strict surveillance by law enforcement officers. In fact, the police even interrupted some masses. Organic Act 4/1981 on the states of emergency, exception and siege (LOAES) does not enable public authorities to interfere with religious freedom, but, as discussed above, these religious rights and freedoms were undermined *de facto*. The same applies to another external expression of religious freedom like funeral wakes. At some points during the pandemic, authorities banned funeral wakes and receptions, and only three people were allowed to attend burial ceremonies. These restrictions on funeral wakes, receptions and burial ceremonies were implemented by authorities at different levels, including the Minister of Health empowered by Decree 462/2020[33] and several regional authorities. For the most part, these were no supporting arguments or a meaningful legal reasoning to justify these measures. Authorities simply referred, in broad terms, to the health crisis or a health emergency. Courts have ruled on the constitutionality of these provisions only in certain cases. In this context, judicial review is based on the proportionality principle but, yet again, any proportionality assessments become really complex because courts of justice do not have access to meaningful scientific information and data.

We can most certainly learn a lesson from the restrictions on the right to demonstrate and religious freedom: pandemic rules should be applicable to any public authority implementing health prevention measures, but also if such measures interfere with fundamental rights. Trying to limit rights that could be affected by anti-COVID measures on an *ex ante* basis is impossible. Ultimately, the pandemic affected individual rights altogether, i.e., the whole sphere of fundamental rights. In order to further elaborate on this, we will discuss if it is necessary to implement anti-fake news legislation in the time of a pandemic, assuming that it would most certainly interfere with freedom of expression. Similarly, we inquire about whether or not AI-based prevention systems, restricting the right to privacy and maybe undermining personal data protection, should be more widely used.

---

33 See Order SND/298/2020, of 29 March, establishing exceptional measures regarding funeral wakes and receptions to limit the spread of COVID-19. Then, these restrictions were relaxed under Order SND/386/2020 of 3 May and Order 399/2020, of 9 May

One of the most concerning aspects of the pandemic has been the spread of fake news through social media, including information that is in stark contradiction with medical fact and scientific criteria, potentially misleading the population and jeopardizing health and safety. In the political arena, there has been no discussion about enacting anti-fake news legislation, despite that fake news have contributed to create anti-vaccination movements[34]. The EU is also against implementing measures for preventing the spread of fake news, and advocates that the companies that own and manage social media voluntarily put in place self-regulation mechanisms to remove fake news stories. This approach has been proven totally ineffective. WHO officials have even claimed that there is an *infodemic* in parallel to the COVID-19 pandemic. According to them, there is a massive flow of fake news and information, neither verified nor fact-checked, that makes it hard to be appropriately informed about current affairs because it is extremely complicated to find reliable and accurate sources. An avalanche of misinformation and inflammatory content, contrary to medical fact and data disseminated by public authorities, keeps spreading worldwide. It took social networks way too long, including Facebook, to remove the various fake news stories posted and shared on various profiles. Also, note that self-regulation was not as effective regarding fake news written Facebook can Flin Spanish or Italian as it was for English fake news stories.[35]

Given the circumstances, future pieces of legislation on pandemics may need to include some sort of anti-fake news provisions, which will most certainly affect freedom of expression. This anti-fake news framework would have a limited scope, i.e., it would only be applicable during the pandemic. This is similar to the current French Act on Fake News, which only tackles or acts against fake news stories published prior to an election. Anti-fake news measures need not be criminal penalties. The German model, based on fines, can also be effective.[36] Obviously, regardless of the approach, any forms of punishment imposed on fake news should be subject to judicial review. The focus should not be on whoever publishes or posts fake news stories, but rather on companies managing communication and information services, who should filter any fake news that can

---

34 See Avaaz, *How Facebook can Flatten the Curve of the Coronnavirus Infodemic*, 15 April 2020, in www.secure.avaaz.org.

35 See Guerini T., La tutela penal della Libertà di manifestazione del pensiero nell'epoca delle fake news e delle infodemie, *DisCrimen*, 16.5.2020., p. 13 ss.

36 A comparative analysis in Guerini T., *Fake news e diritto penale*, Giapachilli, 2020, p. 53 ss.

be dangerous to citizens' health and safety, relying on an independent authority with oversight and control powers subject to *ex post* judicial review.

Just like freedom of expression could be subject to certain restrictions in the future, so could be personal data and the right to privacy if we allow for a greater presence of AI mechanisms and systems.[37] In Spain, these mechanisms were barely used at the early stages of the pandemic. The most important provision in this regard was an order issued by the Health Minister,[38] requiring that a computer app be created within the framework of the European strategy called "Pan-European Privacy Preserving Proximity Tracing Project."[39] The purpose was twofold: (i) providing pandemic-related information and advice to citizens; and (ii) allowing persons with Covid symptoms to test themselves, in order to reduce the workload of public health services and make them more available. So, the first app was *Asistencia Covid*,[40] enabling the geolocation of users' data in order to verify if users are within a specific region, i.e., a very large area. The aim is not to control citizens. In fact, this app ultimately has a statistical purpose and, more specifically, it seeks to understand how people move around and the availability of each province's health services. Additionally, *Radar Covid* was created.[41] It scans for infected persons nearby and notifies users of any close contacts. Since it uses bluetooth services for location and tracing, *Radar Covid* is not as invasive as other apps using our cell phone's gps. A second type of app based on big data is *Data COVID-19*. This application seeks to study and track mobility during the health crisis. It cross-references data from mobile operators anonymously and in an aggregated manner.

---

37 See Pinar Manas J.L., *La protección de datos durante la crisis del coronavirus*, Consejo General de la Abogacía Española, 20 de Marzo 2020; Rodriguez Ayuso J.F., *Cumplimiento de la normativa de protección de datos personales en estado de alarma por parte de las Administraciones públicas*, in Atienza Macias E/Rodriguez Ayuso J.F (dir), Las respuestas del derechos a las crisis de salud pública, Dykinson, 2021, p. 89 ss.

38 Order SND/297/2020, of 27 March, tasking the State Secretariat for Digitalization and Artificial Intelligence under the Ministry of Economic Affairs and Digital Transformation, to implement certain actions to manage the COVID-19 health crisis.

39 https://www.pepp-pt.org/.

40 https://asistencia.covid19.gob.es/. Martinez, Ricard, *Protección de datos y geolocalización en la Orden SND/297/2020*, available at https://hayderecho.expansion.com/2020/03/31/proteccion-de-datos-y-localizacion-en-la-orden-snd-297–2020/.

41 https://radarcovid.gob.es/

Nobody has raised major objections against these measures,[42] and they are in accordance with the applicable EU[43] and domestic[44] provisions. These IA-based measures are in line with the guidelines issued by the Spanish Data Protection Agency (AEPD).[45] Remarkably, the AEPD expressly stated that "[t]his emergency cannot entail a suspension of the fundamental right to personal data protection. But also, data protection regulations should not be used to hinder or otherwise limit the effectiveness of measures implemented by the competent authorities, particularly health bodies, in their fight against the pandemic" (emphasis added). It is worth noting that there has been no talk about the need for defining exceptional limits or boundaries on the right to personal data protection. In other words, the right to personal data protection has not been weighed against the rights to life and health, and let alone has there been discussion about using big data and AI techniques with control purposes. Taking the perspective of the legality principle, as required by the ECtHR's case law, these measures could be based on Organic Act 3/1986 on Public Health (LOMESP).

In fact, Spain is considered a country where big data and AI are underdeveloped and underused. There were much more advanced mechanisms that could have been used for medical purposes without jeopardizing the right to personal data protection. Indeed, these instruments should ensure anonymity and provide for all possible safeguards so that sensitive data (e.g., those included in diagnostic apps) not be used for implementing restrictions on social rights or as biometric passports to justify restrictions

42 A Spanish data protection service provider (i.e., a private company) file a complaint before the Spanish Data Protection Agency against the app *Radar Covid.* See Voz Populi.

43 Regulation (EU) 2016/679 of the European Parliament and of the Council, of 27 April 2016, on the protection of natural persons with regard to the processing of personal data and on the free movement of such data.

44 Organic Act 3/2018, of 5 December, on Personal Data Protection.

45 Spanish Data Protection Agency (AEPD). See the AEPD Report of 26 March 2020 on self-test apps and webs (https://www.aepd.es/es/prensa-y-comunicacion/notas-de-prensa/aepd-apps-webs-autoevaluacion-coronavirus-privacidad) and the Report drafted by the AEPD's legal department (https://www.aepd.es/es/documento/2020-0017.pdf). These reports are in line with the report issued by the European Data Protection Board (EDPB) on 20 March 2020. Available at: https://edpb.europa.eu/news/news/2020/statement-edpb-chairprocessing-personal-data-context-covid-19-outbreak_en

on citizens' freedom of movement.[46] However, I do feel that (in Spain, at least) the Orwellian nightmare will not come true any time soon.

E. Punitive law: halfway between disobedience and self-regulation

The pandemic has not given rise to a new exceptional punitive or criminal law framework. At first glance, this could be considered a positive aspect. Historically, criminal law applicable under emergency conditions has always been more stringent and subject to fewer safeguards than standard criminal justice systems. However, one of the most concerning aspects of how Spanish authorities managed the COVID-19 pandemic is precisely the application and enforcement of punitive law.

To realise the enormous lack of legal certainty that has accompanied the use of punitive, criminal and administrative law during the pandemic, it is enough to look chronologically at the different scenarios that have followed one after the other. During the first state of alarm, from March to June 2020, the government opted to sanction breaches of the containment measures and especially that of confinement through criminal and administrative offences of disobedience. Decree 463/2020 limited itself to making a normative referral, merely stating that non-compliance or resistance to the orders of the authority would be sanctioned in accordance with ordinary legislation. This reference could theoretically be implemented in two ways. The first was to understand that the applicable legislation was health legislation. The severity of these penalties depends on the level of risk that this non-compliance generates for health. The second option was to understand that the infringement of the containment measures, whether those contained directly in Decree 463/2020 or those adopted by the health authorities on the basis of the powers conferred on them, constituted an infringement of disobedience. This interpretation was the one chosen by the government. The Ministry of the Interior instructed the police that breaches of the rules of confinement were to be punished as disobedience to authority.[47]

---

46 See, Cotino Hueso L., *Inteligencia Artificial y vigilancia digital contra la COVID-19 y contra la privacidad. El diablo está en los detalles*, IEEE.ES, 36/2020, regarding the anti-covid measures that should be adopted in order to maximize the potential of AI mechanisms whilst avoiding data protection risks.

47 See Cano Campos T.. Sanciones administrativas, in *Afduam, Extraordinario (2021), Tomo I*, p. 225.

From the point of view of legal theory this interpretation is absurd, it is one thing to break a rule and another to disobey a specific command of the authority addressed to a specific person or group of citizens. However, this interpretation was probably adopted for two reasons. First, because it reinforced the very important police activity in the first months of the pandemic. The police authorities also specified, with a great deal of discretion, the different grounds on which it could or could not be exempted. Thus, for example, the police drew up lists indicating what was or was not understood to be basic necessities or assessed which was the nearest commercial establishment and the one to which the citizen had to go, whether he liked it or not. The choice of disobedience offences, rather than public health-based offences, meant that police supervision was strengthened as much as possible as the main tool in the fight against the pandemic. Disobedience offences safeguard the principle of authority and therefore require a certain degree of resistance by the offender to comply with the order of the authority. If the discovery of an offence already constitutes disobedience, it is in fact the supervisory function that is being protected. It is enough for the police to detect a citizen who breaks the confinement or any other containment measure for there to be an offence, without the need for express resistance.[48]

The choice of the disobedience route also provided more general prevention and therefore deterrence. The typical elements of disobedience offences are easier to prove and the police report, describing the circumstances of the act, has a very important weight among the evidential material of the process. Furthermore, the typology of offences with which disobedience is sanctioned allows not only for administrative sanctions, but also criminal sanctions. The demarcation line between the two offences is also purely quantitative and therefore difficult to draw. Even if in the end the judges do not consider the existence of an offence of disobedience to be proven, the fact that the investigation is initiated as a criminal offence alone makes it more effective as a preventive measure. Fortunately, judges very soon closed the way to the use of the offence of disobedience, restricting it to those cases where there was a specific order from the police and a repeated refusal to comply with it. For this reason most of the administrative sanctions imposed were annulled. In the field of criminal sanctions,

48 See Maroto Calatayud M., Desobediencia y creación policial del Derecho, *in Afduam, Extraordinario (2021), Tomo I,* p. 211.

except in an isolated case resulting from a sentence of conformity, there are no sentences for the crime of disobedience.[49]

Now that the state of alarm has ended, the situation has "normalised" as far as the law on penalties is concerned. The shadow of the offences of disobedience disappears. The peculiarity of this phase is the concurrence of different sanctioning orders to punish the various containment measures in force in this phase. State health regulations are the most important source, but other precepts can also be found in legislation on transport, prevention of occupational hazards, etc. Many regions have also set up their own specific regulations, and local legislation also allows the use of sanctions imposed by municipal bodies in certain cases. The most important precept is, in any case, art. 2 c) of the LGSP, which punishes with fines of up to 3,000 € the infringement of any health regulation that has no or little impact on the health of the population.

This situation is not acceptable from the point of view of legal certainty and equality. The penalties, without any justifiable reasons, varied from one region to another, with no clear criteria to determine when the state or regional regime applies. Article 2 c) of the LGSP, in addition to being absolutely indeterminate in terms of the nature of the offence, leaves an excessive margin of discretion in the hands of the administration when it comes to determining the sanction. The new state of alarm of 25 October 2020, Decree 926/2020 also lacks sanctioning provisions. However, in this third moment, the possibility of using disobedience offences has been forgotten, and the framework described above continues to be used.

The rulings of the Constitutional Court 148/2021 and 183/2021 declaring the most important rule of both states of alarm unconstitutional have meant a new turn of the screw, increasing the lack of legal certainty.[50] STC 148/2021 basically obliges the annulment of all sanctions imposed for infringing confinement, even when there has already been a final judgement. There is no ex officio annulment, and citizens who wish to annul their fines must use an administrative procedure that is likely to cost more than the fine. More doubts exist about the sanctions to be annulled under STC

---

49 See Dopico Gomez Aller J.*¿Puede calificarse como delito de desobediencia grave a la autoridad (art. 566 del Código penal) el mero incumplimiento de la prohibición de circular por las vías públicas durante el periodo de confinamiento?*, en Brito Siso C./ Martoto Calatayud M./ Guías Sectoriales COVID-19. Icam.es, 2020; Roca Agapito L., Las normas no se desobedecen, se infringen, *Diario La Ley*, num. 9632, 2020; Ramon Ribas E., *Desobediencia y estado de alarma*, Tirant lo Blanch, 2021

50 Cfr. Aparicio E., *Efectos de la sentencia del TC sobre el derecho de alarma en los procedimientos sancionadores,* 20 Julio 2021, http://almacendederecho.org.

183/2021, the TC has not been at all precise on this point, leaving the discussion open.

The use of sanctioning law during the pandemic, apart from the above, requires further reflection on the motives that lead citizens to comply with containment measures. Social psychology and, in the field of criminal law, criminology have for years been pointing out the limits of a strategy based on deterrence. Compliance is influenced by several factors. Emotional deterrence would, for example, emphasise the subject's fear of contagion or of spreading the disease to others. Social influence would emphasise society's moral judgement of the offender or the extent to which compliance is widespread. If everyone wears masks, in public spaces and at low density, even if the measure is absurd, one will end up wearing it if one fears being socially singled out by others. Procedural and substantive legitimacy is also important. Sanctions that citizens perceive as fair, and which are also used by the criminal justice system and police forces in a fair manner, are more likely to be adhered to.[51]

In view of the various factors outlined above, the question would be for future situations, what weight should be given to the imposition of sanctions to ensure compliance with protective measures. Although the studies that have been done are not conclusive, and at some points give contradictory results, the fact is that disuasion only works at a reasonable cost if efforts are made to ensure that citizens internalise the content of the rules, and this are clear and coherent. This cannot be said of many of the containment measures adopted that meet these objectives. Perhaps confinement during the spring of 2020 or the mandatory wearing of masks in enclosed spaces did, but from this point onwards the law on penalties has probably had to be overused. In the future, enforcement of containment measures should probably be managed in a more multidisciplinary way, including educators, sociologists, communicators, designing more complex strategies than those based on deterrence and relying more on the responsibility of citizens. Indeed, in the later waves of the pandemic, police oversight and law enforcement pressure is very different from the earlier waves.[52]

---

51 See Gomez Bellvis A.B, La disuasión en el estado de alarma, *Indret, nº 1, 2022*, incluiding an empirical study. Also for a more theoretical perspective, Hierro L., Sobre la eficacia de las normas de emergencia, *Afduam, Extraordinario (2021), Tomo I,* p. 191 ss.

52 Similary in relation to the vaccine, Cierco Seira C, *La vacunación contra la COVID-19 y sus principales debates jurídicos,* p. 321 ss.

F. Conclusions: a few lessons for future pandemics

From a legal point of view, the important thing to learn from this pandemic are the experiences that we must learn in order to deal with future pandemics, which, according to experts, are quite likely. The current legal framework, at least in Spain, can be improved. These improvements are especially important to increase the protection of fundamental rights and, beyond that, their generic capacity to act. As has been stated, the cornerstone is the reform of the decision-making mechanisms for the adoption of restraint measures. They need to be more transparent and scientifically based, based on an agency composed of independent experts. These experts should come from various fields of knowledge, not only health sciences, but also behavioural sciences, economics, etc. Fundamental rights can be excessively limited when the usual decision-making procedures are used in situations governed by the precautionary principle or scientific uncertainty. In this context, judicial control, based on the principle of proportionality, is not effective. There is always a risk of moving from political to judicial crisis management.

Such a procedure would bring more technical legitimacy to containment measures, which would influence citizens' compliance. Deterrence through sanctions, and police supervision, are not feasible strategies when it comes to controlling thousands of micro-behaviours. Communication strategies that increase voluntary compliance by citizens are necessary.

The Legal Framework of the COVID-19 Pandemic in Germany

*Ralf Poscher, Katrin Kappler**

A. Introduction

Germany already had a legal framework in place for dealing with infectious diseases before the current COVID-19 pandemic, with the Infection Protection Act (*Infektionsschutzgesetz*) at its heart. This law enables the country's health authorities to adopt measures deemed necessary to effectively combat pandemics. Consequently, the authorizations outlined in this law have been used as a legal basis for the measures thus far taken during the COVID-19 pandemic. As the pandemic continued, the law was amended several times to broaden the scope of the measures authorities were allowed to take in response to the situation at hand. A limit to the scope of measures and type of amendments that can be made to the law is provided by the Infection Protection Act itself as well as the German constitution: A survey of the most recent case law would appear to show that this has been considered to be a reliable legislative limit even during these exceptional circumstances. In addition, German data protection laws have been of importance. This became particularly apparent during the design phase of the various coronavirus tracing apps. This report presents the legal framework that Germany has used to fight the pandemic.

B. Facts: Reconstruction of the Pandemic in Germany

After the pandemic was first reported in China and the Chinese authorities sealed off Wuhan and other cities during the course of January 2020, on 27 January 2020, the first person was tested positive in Germany (a man who had business-related contact with an infected woman).[1] While

---

* Ralf Poscher is a Director of the Max Planck Institute for the Study of Crime, Security and Law. Katrin Kappler is a postdoctoral researcher at the Institute.

1 https://www.aerztezeitung.de/Medizin/Erster-Coronavirus-Fall-in-Deutschland-406139.html (last accessed 16.12.2021).

only a few more cases were reported over the following days, a district in North Rhine-Westphalia registered a strong spread of the virus for the first time in mid-February, which could eventually be traced back to a large carnival gathering.[2] At the beginning of March 2020, the return of holidaymakers, especially from Austrian ski resorts, led to a massive increase in the number of detected cases, especially in southern Germany. The epidemic peaked in Germany towards the end of March 2020, with more than 6,000 new infections being recorded in a single day.[3]

To avoid confusion among the individual actors in the pandemic, the distribution of competences between the federal government and the states (*Länder*) should be briefly explained here: The federal government has legislative competence for measures against infectious diseases. Consequently, the Infection Protection Act is a federal law. In principle, the *Länder* are responsible for implementing the requisite measures under the Infection Protection Act.[4] The *Länder* have enacted most of the measures through legal ordinances (*Rechtsverordnungen*), which are implemented by state authorities.[5] Due to the widespread nature of the coronavirus, the *Länder* have increasingly cooperated with their state counterparts and the federal government. Throughout the initial phase of the pandemic, the *Länder* and the various health authorities made uncoordinated, individual decisions based on the Infection Protection Act.[6] The *Land* of Bavaria proved to be a "motor for development" during this period, and it was the first state to impose a curfew.[7]

As events unfolded, state and federal crisis management began to operate in a more coordinated fashion. On 22 March 2020, the federal government and the states unanimously agreed on the enactment of contact restrictions in the form of ordinances (known locally as the first "lock-

---

2 https://www.zeit.de/wissen/gesundheit/2020-03/coronavirus-ausbreitung-zeitverlauf-landkreise-staedte-karte (last accessed 16.12.2021).

3 https://www.rki.de/DE/Content/InfAZ/N/Neuartiges_Coronavirus/Situationsberichte/2020-03-28-de.pdf?__blob=publicationFile (last accessed 16.12.2021).

4 The Basic Law rule of Art. 30 applies, according to which the exercise of all state powers and the fulfillment of state tasks is a matter of the *Länder*, see Walus, DÖV 2010, 127 (129).

5 For an initial overview, see Kingreen, in: Handbuch Infektionsschutzrecht, 2nd edition 2022 (forthcoming), Chapter 1, para. 107.

6 Kingreen, in: Handbuch Infektionsschutzrecht, 2nd edition 2022 (forthcoming), Chapter 1, para., 24.

7 https://www.thelocal.de/20200320/bavaria-becomes-first-german-state-to-impose-lockdown.

down").[8] Unnecessary social contacts were to be avoided; some *Länder* allowed contact with one person from outside the primary household, others prohibited even this.[9] In particular, visits to hospitals and nursing homes were banned. In public spaces, a minimum physical distance of 1.5 meters had to be maintained between people from outside the primary household. All facilities that were deemed non-essential were closed. In addition to educational and cultural institutions, this closure affected almost all trade and service companies, as well as restaurants, hotels, sports facilities, and playgrounds.[10] Public events, meetings, and religious services were prohibited. These measures were initially limited to two weeks. Bavaria and North Rhine-Westphalia even passed their own infectious disease laws.[11]

As the number of new infections decreased, the measures from the first lockdown were slowly relaxed. By mid-April 2020, while the federal government and the states agreed to extend contact restrictions, they also agreed to gradually reopen schools and daycare facilities. In addition, certain retailers were able to reopen under strict conditions. Further easing, in particular for visiting arrangements in hospitals and nursing homes, for universities and colleges, and for cultural facilities and mass sporting events followed in May. Bars and clubs remained closed. The social distancing rules and the obligation to wear a mask in situations where the minimum distance could not be maintained continued to apply. Contacts in public spaces also had to be further restricted. In mid-April the infection rate was around 2,000 new infections per day, during the summer months it further dropped to less than 1,000 new infections per day.[12]

---

8 The results of the Federal-*Länder* agreement are available in English at: https://www.bundesregierung.de/resource/blob/975226/1733914/fa51a075a455ada58bb478c0561b43f7/2020-03-23-beschluss-laender-statement-kanzlerin-eng-data.pdf?download=1 (last accessed 16.12.2021).

9 Poscher, in: Huster/Kingreen, Handbuch Infektionsschutzrecht, 2nd edition 2022 (forthcoming), Chapter 4 para. 133 et seq.

10 Kingreen, in: Handbuch Infektionsschutzrecht, 2nd edition 2022 (forthcoming), Chapter 1, para. 25 et seq.; Kaiser/Hensel, Federal Republic of Germany: Legal response to COVID-19, in: King et. al., The Oxford compendium of national legal responses to COVID-19, Oxford 2021, para. 74 et seq., available at: https://oxcon.ouplaw.com/view/10.1093/law-occ19/law-occ19-e2.

11 https://www.verkuendung-bayern.de/files/gvbl/2020/07/gvbl-2020-07.pdf (last accessed 16.12.2021); https://recht.nrw.de/lmi/owa/br_bes_text?print=1&anw_nr=2&gld_nr=%202&ugl_nr=2121&val=5136&ver=0&aufgehoben=N&keyword=&bes_id=5136&show_preview=1 (last accessed 16.12.2021).

12 https://www.rki.de/DE/Content/InfAZ/N/Neuartiges_Coronavirus/Situationsberichte/2020-08-31-de.pdf?__blob=publicationFile (last accessed 16.12.2021).

While coordination between the federal government and the *Länder* had worked well during the first lockdown and most politicians agreed that the measures were reasonable and proportionate, coordination became much more difficult during the following period. This was due to the fact that the infection rates developed differently in the various federal states. As a result, the *Länder* began to once again adopt measures on their own, which in some cases led to considerable deviations in different states.

In June 2020 a COVID-19 tracing app was released. During the summer months it was decided that the schools would reopen after the summer holidays. Private travel was not prohibited but remained discouraged. After infectious disease experts had already issued warnings in the summer months about a second wave of infection approaching Germany, a rapid development in infection rates could be observed from October onwards and, with the onset of winter, new infection rates remained consistently high. Even in this second wave of infection with up to 24,000 new infections per day, cooperation between the federal and state governments remained difficult. Again, this can partly be attributed to the different developments in the individual *Länder*. Nevertheless, one should also note that all the *Länder* had high infection rates. Due to these high infection rates, the *Länder* again adopted stricter measures in consultation with the federal government. In general, only five individuals from two households were allowed to meet. Non-essential travel had to be avoided, and overnight accommodation was only available for business trips, not for tourist trips. Since the infection rates continued to be constantly high, the federal government and the *Länder* agreed to a second lockdown on 13 December 2020.[13] The retail sector closed, with exceptions for shops selling daily necessities. These measures were intended to apply until at least 10 January 2021. However, special rules applied around Christmas and New Year's Eve. For this period, the *Länder* were able to allow gatherings of up to four people from the immediate family circle beyond one's own household (plus younger children) as an exception to the otherwise applicable contact restrictions. For New Year's Eve, a nationwide ban on large gatherings was implemented. In addition, the *Länder* continued to adopt their own different regulations. In Baden-Württemberg, for example, only gatherings of two households were allowed.

---

13 The results of the telephone conference between the federal government and the *Länder* are only available in German: https://www.bundesregierung.de/resource/blob/997532/1827366/69441fb68435a7199b3d3a89bff2c0e6/2020-12-13-beschluss-mpk-data.pdf?download=1 (last accessed 16.12.2021).

In spite of these measures, infection rates continued to rise, with more than 1,000 deaths per day recorded for the first time on 29 December 2020.[14] The situation did not ease with the onset of 2021, likely also as a result of the various virus mutations. The federal government favored the continued application of already enacted measures, especially contact restrictions and curfews, but refrained from actions such as obligatory work-from-home measures or compulsory testing. Many of the states, however, have continued to push for an end to the nationwide lockdown. Coordinating measures has thus become even more problematic. In particular, the federal government was dissatisfied with the regulations in many *Länder* and reacted by amending the Infection Protection Act to enable the unilateral implementation of measures without the intervention of the *Länder*.

Meanwhile, a societal schism has emerged. In mid-April 2021, for example, 49 percent of the population was in favor of tougher measures,[15] while large "*Querdenker*" ("lateral thinking") demonstrations continue to take place in protest against the measures. In this context, the Federal Office for the Protection of the Constitution (*Bundesamt für Verfassungsschutz*) announced that "*Querdenker*" are now being monitored nationwide.[16] In addition, the impression is growing that the measures have not been thought through by political decision-makers. This can be illustrated by just one example: Travelling abroad remains possible, even without compulsory testing, if it is not to a designated risk area. Travelling within the country, on the other hand, has been all but impossible because hotels remain closed to tourists as of May 2021.

Despite these inconsistencies, the infection numbers have been falling since the beginning of May. This is probably due to a variety of reasons, including the fact that fears of overcrowded intensive care units resulted in greater precaution among the population and more people have been vaccinated.[17] Therefore, the measures have been relaxed since June, e.g., contact restrictions were eased and restaurants were allowed to open for

---

14 https://www.rki.de/DE/Content/InfAZ/N/Neuartiges_Coronavirus/Situationsberichte/Dez_2020/2020-12-30-en.pdf?__blob=publicationFile (last accessed 16.12.2021).

15 https://de.statista.com/statistik/daten/studie/1117657/umfrage/corona-krise-umfrage-zu-aktuell-geltenden-corona-massnahmen/ (last accessed 16.12.2021).

16 https://www.tagesschau.de/inland/verfassungsschutz-querdenker-103.html (last accessed 16.12.2021).

17 See https://www.sueddeutsche.de/gesundheit/corona-infektionen-trendwende-modellierungen-1.5284545?reduced=true (last accessed 16.12.2021).

tested, recovered or vaccinated people. The concrete measures depend on the individual incidence rate of the region. Nevertheless, some obligations continue to exist, e.g., the obligation to wear a face mask indoors.

The vaccinations initially led to an easing of the situation. Subsequently, however, another question came into the focus of the federal government, namely how to encourage unvaccinated people to get vaccinated.[18] The vaccination campaign had begun to significantly slow and less and less people were getting vaccinated. In August 2021, the federal and state governments therefore agreed that the states make access to care facilities, indoor catering, hotels and public events conditional on vaccination, recovery or testing. At the same time, it was agreed that free testing for citizens was to be abolished.[19] The intent was to increase the pressure on the unvaccinated.

Germany had been in an epidemic situation of national scope (*Epidemische Lage von nationaler Tragweite)* since March 2020. This classification, made by the Bundestag, was a condition for the measures taken during the pandemic. In September 2021, the newly constituted Bundestag decided not to renew the epidemic situation of national scope.[20] Even beforehand, the still-acting Federal Minister of Health, *Jens Spahn*, had expressed the view that there was no reason to extend the epidemic situation of national scope.[21] In November 2021, the infection numbers rose dramatically again and the pandemic reached a new peak in Germany. In some federal states, the 7-day incidence was at times over 1000, and hospitals were at the limit of their capacity.[22] It was also at this time that the new virus variant *Omikron* emerged, which raised concerns about even greater increases in the number of infections.[23] Vaccination rates increased during this period. While the epidemic situation of national scope was not reintroduced, in order to slow down the rapid spread of the virus several previously used

18 Kingreen, in: Huster/Kingreen, Handbuch Infektionsschutzrecht, 2nd edition, 2022 (forthcoming), Chapter 1, para. 44.

19 https://www.baden-wuerttemberg.de/de/service/presse/pressemitteilung/pid/keine-kostenlosen-corona-tests-mehr-ab-dem-11-oktober-2021/ (last accessed 16.12.2021).

20 See further: Kingreen, *Epidemie ohne epidemische Lage, VerfBlog,* 2021/10/22, https://verfassungsblog.de/epidemie-ohne-epidemische-lage/ (last accessed 16.12.2021).

21 https://www.tagesschau.de/inland/spahn-neuinfektionen-101.html (last accessed 16.12.2021).

22 See further: Kingreen, in: Kingreen/Huster; Handbuch Infektionsschutzrecht, Chapter 1 para. 46.

23 https://www.rki.de/DE/Content/InfAZ/N/Neuartiges_Coronavirus/Virusvariante.html (last accessed 16.12.2021).

measures were reintroduced or expanded. For example, compulsory home office and free testing were made possible again. In addition, the focus of these new measures is to ensure that access to certain services is only granted to vaccinated or recovered persons. Even measures that require a test in addition to proof that a person is vaccinated or recovered are permissible. Despite the increase in infections, the closure of hotels, restaurants and supermarkets has been ruled out. In addition, schools and universities are also to remain open.

C. *Constitutional Framework*

In addition to the political debate, a legal debate has developed. The Infection Protection Act, which only a few researchers had previously addressed, has become the focus of heightened academic debate. Numerous commentaries and manuals were published in a short time.[24] Moreover, the courts have also made a large number of decisions on coronavirus-related measures and the Infection Protection Act.[25] The focus was not only on individual questions of the Infection Protection Act but also on the limits set by the constitution (Germany's Basic Law).

I. *Competencies*

The first important constitutional issue is the delimitation of competences between the Federation and the *Länder*. German law distinguishes between legislative competence and administrative competence. Whereas legislative competence describes the competence to enact laws, administra-

24 See for example: Kießling, Kommentar IfSG, 2020; 2nd edition 2021; Eckart/Winkelmüller, Infektionsschutzrecht Kommentar, 2020; Huster/Kingreen, Handbuch Infektionsschutzrecht, 2021; 2nd edition 2022. Even a separate journal was launched, the CoVuR.

25 Kaiser/Hensel, Federal Republic of Germany: Legal response to COVID-19, in: King et. al., The Oxford compendium of national legal responses to COVID-19, Oxford 2021, para. 43 et seq., available at: https://oxcon.ouplaw.com/view/10.1093/law-occ19/law-occ19-e2.

tive competence refers to the competence to implement and execute the law.[26] As a rule, the *Länder* are responsible for implementing the laws.[27]

In the pandemic, federalism has come under increased pressure. Surveys have demonstrated that a majority of Germans are critical of federalism and would like to further empower the federal government.[28]

Two examples in particular show that the fundamental distribution of power set out in the constitution was not always upheld: On the one hand, decisions were regularly made by the Conference of Minister Presidents, which meant that the *Länder* should at least adopt similar regulations.[29] On the other hand, it became increasingly clear during the pandemic that not all *Länder* were willing to toe the line of the federal government. In order to make stricter uniform federal measures legally possible, the Infection Protection Act was thus amended. The regulation in § 28b Infection Protection Act contained two core elements. Firstly, measures came into force immediately when the infection incidence value of 100 was reached. Thus, no enforcement act was required. Secondly, the federal government itself had the possibility to enact more far-reaching measures by means of ordinances.[30] From a constitutional point of view, this is possible – at least if the limits of the constitution, especially those of Art. 80 Basic Law – are respected. Whether this is politically appropriate is not a legal question. But it should be noted that a uniform federal government regulation is not automatically the best solution, because a federal approach – despite all its disadvantages – allows a more flexible approach, adapted to the respective infection situation in each of the states. The validity of this provision was limited in time. It therefore expired at the end of July 2021. There were several claims against the norm, but the Federal Constitutional Court ultimately declared it constitutional.[31]

---

26 Walus, DÖV 2010, 127 (128–129).

27 Poscher, in: Huster/Kingreen, Handbuch Infektionsschutzrecht, 2nd edition 2022 (forthcoming), Chapter 4 para. 41.

28 Gallon, Informeller Föderalismus statt öffentlicher Deliberation: Oder: Warum die Öffentlichkeit bei der Bund-Länder Koordination in der Pandemiebekämpfung beteiligt werden sollte, VerfBlog, 2021/2/09, https://verfassungsblog.de/informeller-foderalismus-statt-offentlicher-deliberation.

29 § 28b (6) of the Infection Protection Act.

30 This also raises complicated legal issues, which are discussed under IV. C. 1.

31 BVerfG, BeckRS 2021, 36514.

1. Historical background and legislative power

Legislative responsibility for laws dealing with infectious diseases (*Infektionsschutzrecht*) lies with the federal government. Thus, the Basic Law follows the tradition of German constitutional law. For example, both the 1871 Reich Constitution and the Weimar Constitution attributed the power to pass legislation in this field to the federal level.[32] The Basic Law currently regulates the legislative competences attributed to the Federation: In principle, legislative competence lies with the *Länder* (Art. 70 Basic Law). The federal government is only authorized to act if the Basic Law explicitly regulates this. In this regard, the Basic Law distinguishes between the exclusive competences of the Federation (Arts. 71, 73) and the competing legislative competences (Art. 72). In the latter cases, the *Länder* are responsible only insofar as the federal government has not exercised its legislative competence. Dealing with infectious diseases falls under the competing legislative competences (Art. 74 (1) no. 19), but the federal government has made use of its competency through the enactment of the Infection Protection Act. Therefore, the *Länder* may only issue laws that do not contradict the federal rules.

Nevertheless, the states of Bavaria and North Rhine-Westphalia passed their own Infection Protection Acts. This raises the question as to how far the blocking effect of the federal Infection Protection Act extends. In general, the scope of the blocking effect of a federal law does not result from the interpretation of the legislative competence but must be determined on the basis of an interpretation of the federal law. The decisive question is therefore to what extent the federal legislature wanted to make a final provision. Especially with the latest amendments to the Infection Protection Act, the federal government has made it clear that it wants to regulate the matter conclusively. Therefore, there is no longer any room for the regulations of the *Länder* – they are unconstitutional.[33] The Bavarian Infection Protection Act has meanwhile already expired (without ever having been applied).[34] The North Rhine-Westphalia Infection Protection Act is scheduled to expire at the end of 2022.[35]

---

32 Hess, Seuchengesetzgebung 2009, 222 et seq.

33 Poscher, in: Huster/Kingreen, Handbuch Infektionsschutzrecht, 2nd edition 2022 (forthcoming), Chapter 4 para. 13.

34 Kingreen, in: Huster/Kingreen, Handbuch Infektionsschutzrecht, 2nd edition 2022, Chapter 1 para. 96.

35 § 22 Infection Protection and Powers Act of North Rhine-Westphalia.

2. *Administrative Competence*

Administrative competence lies generally with the *Länder*. This follows from the rule in Art. 83 of the Basic Law. The *Länder* then determine the authorities responsible for the specific measures (historically, this has mostly been done by means of ordinances).

At the same time, however, the federal government has the option of setting up independent federal authorities in order to be able to implement the infectious disease law itself. This possibility was used when founding the Robert-Koch-Institute. The Institute's main task is research and knowledge transfer to the *Länder* through recommendations, information, and data evaluation (§ 5 Infection Protection Act). It also operates as a reference point for European and international health protection organizations. The Institute does not impose rules itself. However, it is possible that other decision-makers will link legal consequences to the Institute's assessments. A classic example of this has been the classification of coronavirus risk areas. The classification as a risk area is made after joint analysis and decision by the Federal Ministry of Health, the Federal Foreign Office, and the Federal Ministry of the Interior. For persons entering Germany who stayed in a risk area at any time within the last ten days prior to entry, there was an obligation to isolate in accordance with the respective quarantine regulations of the responsible *Länder*. In addition, the Federal Ministry of Health decreed a compulsory test for those entering from risk areas.[36]

In the version of the Infection Protection Act that applied before the pandemic, the Federal Ministry of Health only had limited powers. At that time, § 5 regulated Federal-state coordination in the event of an epidemic, and it was then specified in an administrative regulation that the Federal Minister of Health should be involved. This has changed fundamentally: Through a legal amendment during the pandemic, the legislature granted the Federal Ministry of Health additional powers, for example, to take measures to ensure the supply of medical products by means of a legal ordinance. In doing so, it is also possible to deviate from existing laws, even from the Infection Protection Act itself. These new powers have been widely criticized by legal scholars, in particular because they no longer ade-

---

36 The original text of the ordinance is available at: https://www.bundesgesundheitsministerium.de/fileadmin/Dateien/3_Downloads/C/Coronavirus/Verordnungen/Testpflicht_Risikogebiete_VO_BAnz_081120.pdf (last accessed 16.12.2021).

quately respect the separation of powers.[37] Through these changes, the legislature has mainly tried to create an emergency right for epidemics, which is not provided for in the constitution, as the next section will show.[38] The regulations are therefore partly unconstitutional.[39]

II. No Emergency Provision

It should first of all be noted that the German constitution does not recognize any health emergency. It only provides for a state of emergency in cases of national defense.[40] In the spring of 2020, there were political reform considerations to introduce a pandemic emergency, but these considerations were not implemented.[41]

However, § 5 of the Infection Protection Act created a law with powers for the Federal Minister of Health similar to a state of emergency. The aim of this provision is to grant the Minister a kind of emergency competence as soon as the *Bundestag* has determined an epidemic situation of national importance (*Epidemische Lage von nationaler Tragweite*). The Minister can then take a variety of measures on the basis of ordinances and orders and even deviate from existing law. Such a construction is not generally unconstitutional. However, the German constitution does provide a limit on such powers of regulation in Art. 80 Basic Law, which is reached here. Art. 80 Basic Law states that the federal government, a federal minister, or the *Länder* may be authorized by a law to issue ordinances. This provision serves to relieve the legislature and is based on efficiency concerns, which are vital in an emergency situation.[42] But this is limited to specific instances.[43] The constitutionally enshrined principles of democracy and the

---

37 Gärditz/Abdulsalam, GSZ 2020, 108 (114); Katzenmeier MedR 2020, 461 (462 et seq); Mayen, NVwZ 2020, 828 (833 et seq.).

38 Poscher, in: Huster/Kingreen, Handbuch Infektionsschutzrecht, 2nd edition 2022 (forthcoming), Chapter 4 para. 26 et seq.

39 Heinig/Kingreen/Lepsius/Möllers/Volkmann/Wißmann, JZ 2020, 861 (867 et seq.).

40 Art. 115a of the Basic Law.

41 See the reporting at: https://www.lto.de/recht/nachrichten/n/corona-handlungsfaehigkeit-gesetzgeber-bundestag-ueberlegungen-aenderung-grundgesetz/ (last accessed 16.12.2021).

42 Ossenbühl, in: Isensee/Kirchhof, Handbuch des Staatsrechts Bd. 5, § 103 para. 11 et seq.

43 Art. 80 (1) Basic Law.

separation of powers must not be undermined by such actions.[44] Yet, with the new regime, the division of power is no longer respected. Especially, the relationship between law and regulation is reversed. Ordinances typically have the task of giving concrete form to laws. The new regulations in § 5, however, are so broad that even laws can be restricted by ordinances issued by the Federal Minister of Health. This procedure is typical of an emergency regime.[45] Nevertheless, the German constitution does not provide for such a regime. Thus, the regulations are unconstitutional.[46] This is still true after the latest changes, even though they are moving in the right direction.[47] Whereas the power to differ from the Infection Protection Act itself was overruled, the competence to issue regulations deviating from other federal laws remained.[48] Still, the norms continue to apply until the Federal Constitutional Court has found them unconstitutional.

III. Judicial Review

Judicial control has proven to be a reliable instance in the pandemic. Judicial review of the pandemic measures took place primarily before the administrative courts. Since most of the measures were enacted by ordinances, the abstract review of the law (*Normenkontrolle*) is the most relevant legal remedy. In such instances, the courts examine whether the ordinance is compatible with higher-ranking law, i.e., also with fundamental rights. If the court finds that parts of the ordinance or the entire ordinance is unlawful, it shall be repealed. The effect is therefore not only *inter partes* but *erga omnes*. The Federal Constitutional Court is only competent if all other legal remedies have been exhausted. The situation is different, however, if no ordinance has to be issued but the measures come into force di-

---

44 Poscher, in: Huster/Kingreen, Handbuch Infektionsschutzrecht, 2nd edition 2022 (forthcoming), Chapter 4 para. 27; Kingreen, in: Handbuch Infektionsschutzrecht, 2nd edition 2022 (forthcoming), Chapter 1 para. 57, 127 et seq.

45 Poscher, in: Huster/Kingreen, Handbuch Infektionsschutzrecht, 2nd edition 2022 (forthcoming), Chapter 4 para. 27.

46 Gärditz/Abdulsalam GSZ 2020, 108 (114); Katzenmeier MedR 2020, 461 (462 et seq.); Mayen NVwZ 2020, 828 (833 et seq.).

47 Poscher, in: Huster/Kingreen, Handbuch Infektionsschutzrecht, 2nd edition 2022 (forthcoming), Chapter 4 para. 30.

48 Kaiser/Hensel, Federal Republic of Germany: Legal response to COVID-19, in: King et. al., The Oxford Compendium of National Legal Responses to COVID-19, Oxford 2021, para. 20, available at: https://oxcon.ouplaw.com/view/10.1093/law-occ19/law-occ19-e2.

rectly, as is the case with the old version of § 28b Infection Protection Act, where measures came into force immediately when the infection incidence value of 100 was reached. Here, the Federal Constitutional Court is responsible as the first and at the same time last instance.Since court proceedings regularly take a long time, there is the possibility of interim legal protection both before the administrative courts and before the Federal Constitutional Court. This was central in the judicial review of the pandemic measures. In these proceedings, the case is not examined comprehensively but rather summarily.[49] The courts may only issue a temporary order if this is urgently required to avert serious disadvantages, to prevent imminent violence, or for another important reason for the common good.[50] The Federal Constitutional Court makes an impact assessment and examines whether the disadvantages that would arise if an interim injunction were not granted but the application were successful on the merits outweigh the disadvantages that would arise if the requested interim injunction were granted but the application were not successful on the merits. Only in the main proceedings do the courts finally decide whether the statutory instrument is lawful/constitutional. The courts have primarily reviewed the extent to which the measures in the legal ordinances are proportionate, i.e., suitable, necessary, and appropriate. In particular, suitability and necessity have been the core aspects of the coronavirus-related judicial review. That said, when conducting such reviews the courts – as well as the politicians – were confronted with knowledge deficits. Legally, this is solved by granting the legislature a broad prerogative to assess the measures. The courts have also regularly referred to this. As knowledge about the pandemic grew, judicial control became more intensive.[51] However, there are also decisions in which the judges assessed the knowledge deficits differently and took the view that they are better able to assess the situation and scope of the pandemic than the legislature. This can sometimes lead to problems, because divergent decisions among the courts become more frequent and

49 Kaiser/Hensel, Federal Republic of Germany: Legal response to COVID-19, in: King et al., The Oxford compendium of national legal responses to COVID-19, Oxford 2021, para. 46, available at: https://oxcon.ouplaw.com/view/10.1093/law-occ19/law-occ19-e2.

50 § 32 of the Act on the Federal Constitutional Court (BVerfGG) and § 47 (6) of the Code of Administrative Court Procedure (VwGO).

51 Kaiser/Hensel, Federal Republic of Germany: Legal response to COVID-19, in: King et al., The Oxford compendium of national legal responses to COVID-19, Oxford 2021, para. 46, available at: https://oxcon.ouplaw.com/view/10.1093/law-occ19/law-occ19-e2.

the prerogative of assessment is not sufficiently protected. This is all the more true if the decisions are made in interim legal protection judgments.[52]

In October 2021, a first decision was handed down in a main proceeding (*Hauptsacheverfahren*): The Bavarian Higher Administrative Court ruled that the curfew imposed in March 2020 was unlawful because the state could have imposed contact restrictions as a milder, but equally suitable, measure.[53] The Federal Constitutional Court ruled otherwise in its November 2021 decisions, rejecting several constitutional challenges to contact restrictions, curfews and school closures.[54]

IV. Basic Rights as Limits

1. Right to life and physical integrity as a key right

The right to life and physical integrity has been a key legal issue in the pandemic. It is well established in German constitutional law that not only must the state may not interfere with them, but it also must actively protect them under certain circumstances.[55] For this reason, the rights also serve to justify restrictions on other rights and freedoms, as was frequently the case during the pandemic. However, what is often overlooked in the political and legal debate is the fact that the right to life and physical integrity does not always take precedence over civil liberties. It was argued by journalists and politicians – especially at the beginning of the pandemic – that the protection of life and health was an absolute priority and that stringent measures were therefore indispensable. This is too simplistic and legally untenable. Apart from the emphasized position of human dignity as a right that cannot be restricted, the Basic Law does not recognize any hierarchical relationships between human rights and the right to life.[56] It is therefore always necessary to weigh up the various conflicting rights.

52 Poscher, in: Huster/Kingreen, Handbuch Infektionsschutzrecht, 2nd edition 2022 (forthcoming), Chapter 4 para. 118.
53 VGH Bayern, COVuR 2021, 739.
54 BVerfG, BeckRS 2021, 36514; BeckRS 2021, 36492.
55 BVerfGE 46, 160 (164 et seq.); 77, 170 (214); 85, 191 (212); 115, 25 (44 et seq.).
56 Kingreen, in: Handbuch Infektionsschutzrecht, 2nd edition 2022 (forthcoming), Chapter 1, para. 64.

2. *Conflicting freedoms*

To protect the right to life and physical integrity, far-reaching measures have been adopted that interfere with various other freedoms.

a) General Right to Personality (Art. 2 (1) in conjunction with Art. 1 (1) Basic Law)

Over time the Federal Constitutional Court has, through its case law, developed a comprehensive and multifaceted right to personality, subject to proportionate limitations provided by law, which is derived from a combined reading of Art. 2 (1) in conjunction with Art. 1 (1) of the Basic Law. Recognized sub-categories of this right include (and which are relevant to our analysis here) the general freedom of action, sometimes in the form of a right to personal self-determination, which in general encompasses the freedom to act as one pleases. It also encompasses the protection of outer and intimate spheres of personality and private life, which also protects the freedom to socially interact with others. This outer sphere of private life was limited by the contact restrictions and/or prohibitions. The general freedom of action was limited, for example, by the obligation to wear a medical face mask. These restrictions were considered to be proportionate by the courts. The argument was that wearing a mask is a building block in the fight against the pandemic and that this is supported by scientific evidence.[57] In the opinion of the courts, the legislature's margin of discretion in implementing such measures was therefore not exceeded.[58]

b) Freedom of movement (Art. 11 (1) Basic Law) and freedom of the person (Art. 2 (2) Basic Law)

The German constitution provides for both a right to freedom of movement and freedom of the person. The demarcation between the two fundamental rights is a recurrent source of dispute.[59] The very scope of the pro-

---

57 OVG Lüneburg, Beschl. v. 6.7.2020 – 13 MN 238/20, BeckRS 2020, 15929, para. 8 et seq.

58 OVG Münster, Beschl. v. 30.4.2020 – 13 B 539/20, BeckRS 2020, 9246, para. 18 et seq.

59 Kunig, in: Münch/Kunig, GG, Art. 2 para. 74; Starck, in: v. Mangoldt/Klein/Starck, GG, Art. 2 para. 74.

tection afforded by Art. 2 (2) (freedom of the individual) is controversial: While it is often understood as freedom to visit or stay in a place which is in itself accessible (factually and legally),[60] it is sometimes more strongly associated with an element of state coercion,[61] according to which it is only intended to protect against restrictions whose enforcement is threatened by direct coercion not only under the general conditions of administrative enforcement law but also in a qualified manner, which could be discussed with regard to the initial restrictions imposed by the coronavirus regulations.[62] In any case, the Infection Protection Act itself assumes that injunctions under § 28 (1) can affect the freedom of the person, since it mentions Art. 2 (2) of the Basic Law among the restricted fundamental rights. It is therefore preferable that the demarcation between the two fundamental rights should be based on views that emphasize the protective purpose of Art. 11 Basic Law. It aims to protect the taking of residence and domicile within the territory of the Federal Republic of Germany. Moreover, Art. 11 Basic Law aims to protect citizens against prohibitions on choosing a place to settle within Germany and to make this place the center of their personal life.[63] The protective purpose must be considered in each individual case.

This demarcation was particularly relevant in the case of the coronavirus curfews. These usually stated that public spaces could only be entered with a valid reason (*triftiger Grund*). On this basis, the curfews partially enacted in Germany did not tend to regulate freedom of movement.[64] It was prohibited to stay in a public space: What was not covered by the regulation, however, was the question of where persons stayed whilst avoiding public spaces. For example, there was no restriction on staying at one's place of residence.[65]

In addition, the question arises whether the curfews were a deprivation of liberty. Especially the distinction between house arrest and curfew is not trivial, because both curfew and house arrest obliges people to stay

---

60 BVerfGE 105, 238 (248).

61 Di Fabio, in: Maunz/Dürig, GG, Art. 2 Abs. 2 para. 30 et seq.; Schulze-Fielitz, in: Dreier, GG, Art. 2 Abs. 2 para. 98; Kingreen JURA 2020, 1019 (1023).

62 Kingreen, in: Handbuch Infektionsschutzrecht, 2nd edition 2022 (forthcoming), Chapter 1, para. 71 et seq.

63 Poscher, in: Huster/Kingreen, Handbuch Infektionsschutzrecht, 2nd edition 2022 (forthcoming), Chapter 4 para. 133 et seq.

64 However, some legal scholars argue differently, see for example: Siegel, NVwZ 2020, 577 (578).

65 Poscher, in: Huster/Kingreen, Handbuch Infektionsschutzrecht, 2nd edition 2022 (forthcoming), Chapter 4 para. 139.

in a specific place.[66] If curfews are considered a deprivation of liberty, special justification requirements apply to the infringement on fundamental rights. In particular, a judge must then decide on the measure (judicial approval – *Richtervorbehalt*).

Both the contact bans and the curfews were considered lawful by the courts. The courts argued that the reduction of social contacts would contribute to the containment of the virus.[67] It was also pointed out by the German Constitutional Court that all contact restrictions and curfews contained exceptions and were therefore proportionate.[68]

The discussion was further intensified by the newly introduced § 28b of the Infection Protection Act, which established a night curfew as soon as the incidence value was higher than 100 for three days in a row. This curfew was the starting point for a large number of constitutional complaints, many of which were filed on the day the new regulations came into force.[69] Legal scholars have put forward both formal and substantive reasons against the regulation, especially the proportionality of the night curfew was cast into doubt.[70] However, the Federal Constitutional Court did not classify the norm as unconstitutional.[71] Firstly, the Court's impact assessment in the interim legal proceeding was in favor of the state.[72] It explicitly left open whether the norm is formally and substantively constitu-

---

66 Poscher, in: Huster/Kingreen, Handbuch Infektionsschutzrecht, 2nd edition 2022 (forthcoming), Chapter 4 para. 138. Further on house arrests: Gusy in: v. Mangoldt/Klein/Starck GG Art. 104 para. 22; Kingreen/Poscher Grundrechte, 2021, § 10 para. 572.

67 BayVerfGH, NVwZ 2020, 785 (787 et seq.); VG Ansbach, COVuR 2020, 150 (152 et seq.).

68 BVerfG Beschl. v. 7.4.2020 – 1 BvR 755/20, BeckRS 2020, 5317, para. 11.

69 https://www.deutschlandfunk.de/bundesverfassungsgericht-viele-beschwerden-und-eilantraege.1939.de.html?drn:news_id=1251731 (last accessed 16.12.2021).

70 In the legislative process, two legal scholars took a clear position: Möllers, Stellungnahme zum Entwurf eines Vierten Gesetzes zum Schutz der Bevölkerung bei einer epidemischen Lage von nationaler Tragweite BT-Drucksache 19/28444, https://www.bundestag.de/resource/blob/834614/9ace24a12b228c12a677f4b05aec4865/19_14_0323-2-_Prof-Dr-Moellers_-viertes-BevSchG-data.pdf; Kießling, Stellungnahme als geladene Einzelsachverständige für die öffentliche Anhörung im Gesundheitsausschuss des Deutschen Bundestages am 16.4.2021 https://www.bundestag.de/resource/blob/834718/f9d7dff3462d982b089359365a45624a/19_14_0323-6-_ESV-Dr-Andrea-Kiessling_-viertes-BevSchG-data.pdf (last accessed 16.12.2021).

71 BVerfG, BeckRS 2021, 9842.

72 BVerfG, BeckRS 2021, 9842, para. 21.

tional.[73] In particular, the judges ruled that it is not clear that the night curfew is manifestly unsuitable, unnecessary, or inappropriate to combat the pandemic. According to the judges, this also applies with regard to the link to the incidence value of 100. Thus, the Federal Constitutional Court decisively focuses on the broad assessment prerogative of the legislature.[74]

In the decisions of the Federal Constitutional Court from November 2021, the approach outlined above was also confirmed in the main proceedings.[75] The Federal Constitutional Court argued that curfews were not deprivations of liberty, basing its reasoning primarily on the fact that curfew restrictions were a less intense infringement of fundamental rights. However, it is not convincing to focus (solely) on the intensity of the interference. The fundamental difference between curfews and imprisonment or house arrest is rather that in the case of deprivations of liberty, the state knows where the person is and has access to the person at all times.[76] The Federal Constitutional Court was therefore correct in reaching the result that there is no deprivation of liberty. A person is only deprived of his or her liberty if the person has to stay in a specific, narrowly defined place. However, the curfews were structured differently: People were not obliged to stay in a certain place (e.g., in their own homes), but were not allowed to stay in public places.[77]

c) Religious Freedom

The Court regularly pointed out that, when adopting measures during the COVID-19 pandemic, religious freedom was often not sufficiently considered. Art. 4 of the Basic Law obliges the state to respect religious activities and to safeguard the free development of the religious freedom of its citizens. Freedom of religion in this sense includes the freedom of confession and the freedom of worship.[78] The Basic Law does not provide any explicit restrictions. Thus, interferences with freedom of religion can only be justified by conflicting constitutional law.

---

73 BVerfG, BeckRS 2021, 9842, para. 27.
74 BVerfG, BeckRS 2021, 9842, para. 33.
75 BVerfG, BeckRS 2021, 36514.
76 Poscher, in: Huster/Kingreen, Handbuch Infektionsschutzrecht, 2nd edition 2022 (forthcoming), Chapter 4 para. 138.
77 See further: Poscher, in: Huster/Kingreen, Handbuch Infektionsschutzrecht, 2nd edition 2022 (forthcoming), Chapter 4 para. 139.
78 Korioth/Augsberg, Religion and the Secular State in Germany, 320 (322).

This right to religious freedom was affected in many ways by the pandemic measures, in some cases by explicit bans on religious festivals but also, more generally, by the contact restriction requirements. At the beginning of the pandemic, the Federal Constitutional Court even considered a ban on physical liturgical services over Easter to be constitutional, even though it called for a strict time limit to be placed on the ban and for it to be continuously reviewed.[79] However, as knowledge on how to contain the virus grew, the Court emphasized that, in view of the special protection of freedom of religion in the Basic Law, a general ban on religious gatherings without exception is incompatible with the Basic Law.[80] Therefore, the possibility had to exist for religious communities to apply for exceptions, e.g., if an adequate hygiene concept had been developed.

The former regulations did not prohibit religious gatherings and worship at Christmas. However, for a church to open it had to develop hygiene concepts in compliance with the rules for social distancing. Under the current case law, such a regulation is compatible with the Basic Law. Physical liturgical services were also possible over the subsequent Easter insofar as the requisite hygiene concepts were in place. The same now applies to gatherings during Ramadan: religious gatherings are possible, but there were strict requirements in most of the *Länder*.

d) The Right to Freedom of Assembly

The measures enacted in the COVID-19 pandemic have severely restricted the rights of assembly.

The freedom of assembly guaranteed by the German Basic Law is not only conceived as a particularly important right in a modern democracy but also as a right to collective personal development.[81] The concept of assembly must, in light of its importance, be broadly interpreted.[82] In contrast to the freedom of religion, the freedom of assembly can be restricted by law for other reasons than just conflicting constitutional rights. Accordingly, there are special assembly laws in place which provide for authorizations for prohibitions and conditions.

---

79 BVerfG NJW 2020, 1427 (1428), para. 14; BVerfG, BeckRS 2020, 5584, para. 15 et seq.

80 BVerfG, NVwZ 2020, 783 (785).

81 Höfling, in: Sachs, GG, 9th edition 2021, Art. 8 para. 8 et seq.

82 Gusy, in: von Mangoldt/Klein/Starck, GG, 7th edition 2018, Art. 8 para. 18 et seq.

Even during the pandemic, the freedom of assembly was used frequently in Germany, e.g., in protests about asylum policy or even about the coronavirus measures themselves. For example, several thousand people met for *Querdenken* demonstrations in Berlin, Munich, and Frankfurt.

Almost all of the *Länder* imposed bans on assembly, in some cases without any exceptions.[83] In some cases, the ordinances of the *Länder* contain explicit assembly bans, in others the bans resulted from contact restrictions on gatherings in for public spaces, which only allowed for a few people from a very small circle to meet. Insofar as these bans on assembly were meant as outright bans or were understood or applied in this way by the authorities, they were usually overruled by the courts as disproportionate.[84] The courts instructed the authorities to first ensure that the protection against infection was maintained by imposing appropriate conditions. At any rate, some assembly organizers had themselves contributed to ensuring effective protection against infection, often with creative ideas such as distance bands; in some cases they even went beyond the protective measures provided for in the coronavirus ordinances.[85] Accordingly, such demonstrations were able to take place.

As laws in Germany exist on the basis of which assemblies can be prohibited, the question concerning their relationship with the Infection Protection Act has been raised by legal scholars. This conflict is also reflected in the individual assembly bans, which were based partly on the Infection Protection Act and partly on the right of assembly. Some argue that the laws derived from the Infection Protection Act are more specific (leges speciales) and therefore apply instead of the more general assembly laws.[86] Measures against assemblies can also be taken on the basis of the newly inserted § 28a of the Infection Protection Act. At the same time, however, the assembly authority (*Versammlungsbehörde*) can also issue conditions and/or ban assemblies in agreement with the health authorities. This interaction is also partly reflected by the legal regulations of the *Länder*, as in some cases the authorities are required to act in concert, and in others, the

83 For example, in the states of Baden-Württemberg, Berlin, Brandenburg, or Hamburg, see for the original wording of the ordinances: § 3 Abs. 2 S. 1 CoronaVO BW v. 22.3.2020 (GVBl. 135); § 1 Abs. 1 SARS-CoV-2-EindmaßnV Bln v. 22.3.2020 (GVBl. 220); § 1 Abs. 1 S. 1 SARS-CoV-2-EindV Bbg v. 22.3.2020 (GVBl. 1), § 2 Abs. 1 S. 1 SARS-CoV-2-EindämmungsVO Hmb v. 2.4.2020 (GVBl. 181).

84 BVerfG, NJW 2020, 1426 et seq.; BVerfG, NVwZ 2020, 711 et seq.

85 OVG Magdeburg, BeckRS 2020, 8016, para. 13 et seq.

86 Lindner, in: Schmidt, COVID-19, 3rd edition 2021, § 18 para. 56.

assembly authorities have been allowed to issue exceptions to assembly bans.[87]

e) Right to School Education (Art. 2 (1) in conjunction with Art. 7 Basic Law)

Pupils were severely affected by school closures during the pandemic. In its November 2021 decisions, the Federal Constitutional Court derived a right to school education from Article 2 (1) in conjunction with Article 7 (1) of the Basic Law.[88] This right is intended to guarantee a minimum standard of school education and is based on the corresponding guarantees of international treaties, in particular Article 19 of the ICCPR and Article 28 of the Convention on the Rights of the Child.[89] In addition, the influence of the case law of the ECtHR, which has previously shaped the right to education, for example with regard to non-discriminatory access to education, is evident.[90] Following up on this, the right to school education also guarantees a right to equal participation in schooling and a right against restrictions on existing schooling.[91] However, the right is not intended to imply a claim to a specific design of state schools.[92] The Federal Constitutional Court affirmed an infringement of the fundamental right to school education by the banning face-to-face teaching.[93] However, this interference was deemed to be justified because the ban on face-to-face teaching was adequate, necessary and appropriate to protect life and

87 For example, this has been regulated in Hamburg, Mecklenburg-Vorpommern, and Bremen; see for the original wording: § 10 Sars-CoV-2-EindämmungsVO Hmb v. 30.6.2020 (GVBl. 365); § 8 Abs. 3 Corona-Lockerungs-Lvo M-V v. 7.7.2020 (GVBl. 518); § 2 Abs. 5 Covvo Brem v. 5.8.2020 (GVBl. 798).

88 BVerfG, BeckRS 2021, 36492.

89 See further: Poscher/Rux/Langer, Das Recht auf Bildung, 2009; Wrase, Ein Beschluss mit weitreichenden Folgen: Das Recht auf schulische Bildung nach der Schulschließungs-Entscheidung des Bundesverfassungsgerichts, VerfBlog, 2021/12/05, https://verfassungsblog.de/ein-beschluss-mit-weitreichenden-folgen/.

90 Wrase, Ein Beschluss mit weitreichenden Folgen: Das Recht auf schulische Bildung nach der Schulschließungs-Entscheidung des Bundesverfassungsgerichts, VerfBlog, 2021/12/05, https://verfassungsblog.de/ein-beschluss-mit-weitreichenden-folgen/.

91 BVerfG, BeckRS 2021, 36492 para. 53.

92 BVerfG, BeckRS 2021, 36492 para. 53.

93 BVerfG, BeckRS 2021, 36492 para. 74 et seq.

health.[94] As a result, the school closures were found to be in accordance with the constitution. Nevertheless, the Federal Constitutional Court has ruled for the future that the prohibition of face-to-face teaching is not justified in all circumstances because, at least in the case of longer periods, the state must create alternative provisions that guarantee a minimum standard of school education.[95]

3. General principle of equality derived from Art. 3 as an additional limitation

The German constitution also contains a general principle of equality in Art. 3 Basic Law. Art. 3 basic Law contains the general principle of equality in paragraph 1 and special equality clauses in paragraph 3 as well as specially designed guarantees of equality for men and women in paragraph 2.

A look at the case law relating to the coronavirus measures shows that the general principle of equality must be observed when assessing the legality of a measure. In a whole number of judgments, the courts questioned not the protective measures as such but the differentiations which the executive had either made or not made in their scope of application. In some cases, the courts assessed the regulations as being too broad, as a result of which inherently unequal situations were inadmissibly treated as equal. Although business closures and event prohibitions were considered possible in principle, some courts considered that some closure orders were too general.[96] For example, the administrative court in Bremen found that the blanket ban on events of any kind in closed rooms with more than 250 people present violated the fundamental rights of a career fair organizer in accordance with Art. 12 (1) of the Basic Law and Art. 3 (1), because a general prohibition regardless of the infection occurrence and special features of different event formats did not allow for the necessary differentiations and was therefore unconstitutional.[97]

In some cases, however, the regulations were considered to be not general enough. In these cases, the courts criticized the fact that the same matters were treated differently. This argument mostly played a role with regard to the exceptions to restrictions provided for in the ordinances. The administrative court of Hamburg, for example, was not convinced by the

---

94 BVerfG, BeckRS 2021, 36492 para. 77 et seq.

95 BVerfG, BeckRS 2021, 36492 para. 177.

96 BVerfG, BeckRS 2020, 6938, para. 13.

97 VG Bremen, BeckRS 2020, 21981, para. 41.

closure of amusement arcades without exception, as the authorities did not show that they pose a higher risk of infection than restaurants that were re-opened with hygiene concepts.[98] Similarly, the Higher Administrative Court of Berlin-Brandenburg found that shut-down laws that differentiated between restaurants and shisha bars were an unjustified unequal treatment of substantially identical situations.[99] A violation of Art. 3 was also discussed when shops larger than 800 m^2 had to remain closed, while smaller operators were permitted to re-open. The authorities argued that the distinction was justified because the social distancing and hygiene rules could be better respected and controlled in smaller shops. Some courts found this to be a permissible, justified distinction, while others found these measures to be an impermissible unequal treatment of similar situations.[100]

D. *Infectious Disease Law (Infektionsschutzrecht)*

Infectious Disease Law includes all regulations that govern the state's handling of infectious diseases. This area of the law is cross-sectional and encompasses many overlapping areas, such as security law, state liability law, criminal law, and data protection law. As previously noted, the core of this area of law in Germany is the Infection Protection Act. The Infection Protection Act regulates measures to prevent and control infectious diseases, including COVID-19. It is applicable irrespective of whether the state is dealing with an epidemic or a pandemic. The only question is whether an infectious disease within the meaning of the Infection Protection Act is present. The Infection Protection Act differentiates between surveillance, prevention, and control. This distinction is used to cover different stages before and during the development of an epidemic or a pandemic.

Thus, the Infection Protection Act shows some of the same characteristics of the doctrinally well-developed general police law which originated in the 19th century.[101] The Infection Protection Act could be regarded as a differentiation of the general police law that was used to handle epidemics in the 19th century. In terms of structuring infection protection

98 VG Hamburg, BeckRS 2020, 9916, para. 14 et seq.

99 OVG Berlin, BeckRS 2020, 9917, para. 13, 17, 11; OVG Berlin, BeckRS 2020, 9919, para. 14, 18.

100 OVG Bremen, BeckRS 2020, 18788, para. 32 et seq.

101 Other legal scholars, however, argue that infectious disease law is closer to risk prevention, see e.g., Engels, DÖV 2014, 464 (467 et seq.).

in surveillance, prevention, and control, it mirrors the structure of general police codes which also distinguish between preparation, investigation, and the control and aversion of a danger.[102] Another structural feature that the infectious disease law shares with the general police law is its use of general and specific powers.[103] The general clause authorizes unspecified measures and reflects the fact that not all measures can be specifically regulated. However, as soon as a measure is specifically regulated, it can no longer be based on the general clause. In the course of the current pandemic, one of the main legal issues was whether and for how long measures could still be based on the general clauses of the Infection Protection Act.[104] Furthermore, the internal structure of the powers of the Infection Protection Act can be mapped onto the doctrinal structure underlying general police powers.[105] The police codes of the *Länder* contain the basic model of the regulatory structures and dogmatic principles on which other policing is based. The general doctrinal structure of these powers consists of five main elements:

1. the specification of the goods to be protected, in general public security and order;
2. the type of threat, in general a concrete or abstract danger;
3. types of responsibility, in general responsibility for one's actions or state of affairs;
4. non-guilt-based norms of attribution;
5. proportionality-based restrictions on the measures police can revert to in order to control and avert danger.

This basic structure can therefore also help to systematize and interpret the standards of the Infection Protection Act. This does not mean that the Infection Protection Act only repeats the terms and measures of security law. Rather, the different elements of the general police law structure are tailored to the specific dangers of infectious diseases. For this reason, standard terms of the general police law, such as danger or responsibility, do

102 Poscher, in: Huster/Kingreen, Handbuch Infektionsschutzrecht, 2nd edition 2022 (forthcoming), Chapter 4 para. 50.

103 Gärditz/Abdulsalam, GSZ 2020, 108 (111); Gusy, GSZ 2020, 101 (103); Schwarz, JA 2020, 321 et seq.; Kießling, Coronavirus, Masern und die Grundrechte, VerfBlog, 2020/3/02, https://verfassungsblog.de/coronavirus-masernund-die-grundrechte/.

104 Papier, DriZ 2020, 180 et seq.; Gärditz/Abdulsalam, GSZ 2020, 108 (114).

105 Poscher, in: Huster/Kingreen, Handbuch Infektionsschutzrecht, 2nd edition 2022 (forthcoming), Chapter 4 para. 50 et seq.

not necessarily appear in the Infection Protection Act but are replaced by infection-specific terms. Nevertheless, these specific terms can be interpreted and systematized by linking them to similar categories in the general police law.[106]

I. Surveillance

The measures used to monitor the occurrence of infections belong to the category of risk prevention measures. The system is essentially based on reporting obligations. These notification requirements apply not only to diseases with epidemic potential but also to suspected cases and to the detection of pathogens.

Under § 15 of the Infection Protection Act the Federal Ministry of Health is authorized to extend the obligation to report other diseases or pathogens by statutory order – regularly with the approval of the *Bundesrat*. On the one hand, the reporting obligations for persons and institutions obliged to report are accompanied by limitations of fundamental rights, as they apply not only to other public bodies but also to private healthcare employees and professionals, examination centers, and laboratories. On the other hand, the reporting obligations are associated with limitations of the fundamental rights of those persons whose data must be reported to the health authorities according to § 9 of the Infection Protection Act.[107]

II. Prevention

The fourth section of the Infection Protection Act deals with the prevention of infectious diseases, thus distinguishing it from the control of these diseases, which is regulated in the fifth section. Preventive measures are intended to halt the outbreak of an infectious disease.[108] The boundary between measures to prevent and control infections therefore does not follow the concept of risk: Prevention and control cover different risks, preventing the risk of a contagious disease spreading from a source of infec-

---

106 Poscher, in: Huster/Kingreen, Handbuch Infektionsschutzrecht, 2nd edition 2022 (forthcoming), Chapter 4 para. 3 et seq., 50 et seq.

107 Müllmann, in: Kießling, IfSG, 2nd edition 2021, § 9 para. 1.

108 Müllmann, in: Kießling, IfSG, 2nd edition 2021, Vorb. § 6, para. 1 et seq.

tion to humans and combating the risk of people who are already infected from further spreading the disease. As long as a source of infection has not yet led to the transmission, infection control measures are governed by § 16 et seq. of the Infection Protection Act; after an infectious disease has begun to spread §§ 24 et seq. of the Infection Protection Act are relevant.

The section on prevention contains a general clause (*Generalklausel*) in § 16 that provides the central basis for concrete action. This provision empowers the competent authority to take the necessary measures to avert the dangers threatening the individual or the general public. This is accompanied by authorizations for surveillance and investigation measures (§ 16 (2)) or for the destruction of objects if they present a risk of infection (§ 17).[109]

With regard to the COVID-19 pandemic, this means that the measures intended to counteract the spread of the disease could not and cannot be based on §§ 16–19 of the Infection Protection Act. It would have been different, for example, if the authorities had discovered a source of infection in animals – like in China – and then tried to prevent transmission to humans.

III. Control

Once an infectious disease has broken out, it is no longer a question of preventing its outbreak but of combating its further spread. This is the subject of the fifth section of the Infection Protection Act. This section also operates with a general clause and standard powers (*Standardermächtigungen*). General clauses determine general requirements for a large number of measures that have not yet been specified in detail. Standard powers, on the other hand, set conditions for a specific measure, such as isolation in § 30 of the Infection Protection Act. All measures in the COVID-19 pandemic have been adopted on the basis of this section.

1. General Clause

Throughout the COVID-19 pandemic, the section of the Act covering the control of an infectious disease has been paramount. The general clause of § 28 was particularly relevant. § 28 provides – analogous to § 16 – that au-

---

109 Mers, in: Kießling, IfSG, 2nd edition 2021, § 17, para. 1 et seq.

thorities may take all necessary protective measures if and to the extent that they are necessary to prevent the spread of infectious diseases. A prerequisite for the facts of the case is therefore that an infectious disease exists and that it is designated as such by the Infection Protection Act. If such a disease exists, the authorities may take all necessary protective measures, i.e., it is granted discretionary powers. On the basis of this law, various measures were taken, such as bans on leaving the household or on social contacts.

a) Amendments to the general clause during the pandemic

The general clause was amended twice during the coronavirus pandemic. In March 2020, the general clause was supplemented with examples of very intensive fundamental rights interventions, such as a nightly curfew.[110] In November, the legislature included a large number of the measures previously taken within the context of the coronavirus pandemic into § 28a of the Infection Protection Act. In so doing, it made use of the regulatory strategy thus far pursued under the Infection Protection Act and identified these measures as mere examples that could be enacted under the general clause of § 28 (1) of the Infection Protection Act. In this way, the Infection Protection Act continues to deviate from the regulatory technique that is customary in security law, namely defining standard measures as independent authorizing elements. Nevertheless, this difference should not be overemphasized. Especially in the case of the coronavirus pandemic, the frequent use of the general clause has been borne out of the fact that it is still not entirely clear which control measures are successful under which conditions. The fact that the regulations are designed as examples of applications of the general clause does not affect their exclusiveness. A deviation from the measures and conditions provided for in § 28a of the Infection Protection Act as examples cannot be arbitrarily justified as an unnamed case of application of the general clause. With § 28a of the Infection Protection Act, the legislature has indicated which measures it considers permissible under which conditions. Therefore, authorities cannot order comparably intensive interventions under different conditions. Just as, prior to the introduction of § 28a of the Infection Protection Act, it was not possible to order isolation or a prohibition of activities without considering the special requirements of the standards powers. This could only be different

110 See e.g., Guckelberger, NVwZ-Extra 9a, 1 et seq.

if – as was the case at the beginning of the coronavirus pandemic – completely unexpected circumstances arise that make it necessary to take similarly serious measures to avert very serious dangers before the legislature is able to create standard powers with special requirements. However, this does not fundamentally differ from the relationship between the general clauses of security law and the independent standard measures usually provided for there.[111]

b) Possibility to homogenize the measures nationwide

After the federal government expressed frustration concerning the way in which the individual states were applying the pandemic controls, it elected to reform the Infection Protection Act once again and introduced a § 28b. The essence of this amendment was that numerous measures came into force immediately when the incidence value of 100 is reached on three days in a row. These intrusive measures (e.g., nightly curfew) have been the focus of much legal and political discussion. It is significant that the regulations came into force immediately when the incidence value of 100 was reached three days in a row. The law was thus self-executing.[112] This regulatory technique has rarely been used in German law with respect to the protection of personal liberty (Art. 2 (2) Basic Law). The Basic Law assumes that, as a rule, interventions to fundamental rights are made *on the basis* of a law, i.e., the executive acts on the basis of a given law.[113] Interventions directly by law are the exception. In the context of this debate on § 28b Infection Protection Act, the nightly curfews have drawn particular criticism from legal scholars. Such curfews directly interfere with Art. 2 (2) Basic Law, which means that formal and substantive requirements are necessary to ensure their constitutionality. From a formal point of view, it is first of all important that Art. 2 and Art. 104 Basic Law only permit interferences *on the basis* of a law but not *by* a law. This means that an executive

111 Poscher, in: Huster/Kingreen, Handbuch Infektionsschutzrecht, 2nd edition 2022, Chapter 1 para. 76.

112 Kießling, Stellungnahme als geladene Einzelsachverständige für die öffentliche Anhörung im Gesundheitsausschuss des Deutschen Bundestages am 16.4.2021, 2, https://www.bundestag.de/resource/blob/834718/f9d7dff3462d982b089359365a45624a/19_14_0323-6-_ESV-Dr-Andrea-Kiessling_-viertes-BevSchG-data.pdf (last accessed 16.12.2021).

113 See Sommermann, in: von Mangoldt/Klein/Starck, Grundgesetz Kommentar, 7. Auflage 2018, Art. 20 para. 273 et seq.

act would be required here as well. This diminishes the legal protection for those affected, because legal action cannot be taken against a measure but only against the law itself. In addition, this means that the Federal Constitutional Court acts as the only court of jurisdiction here. This is, at the very least, problematic with regard to the guarantee of legal protection (Art. 19 (4) Basic Law). Moreover, problems arose concerning the clarity and determination of the norm. There is no official announcement of the individual measures. This means that the population itself had to study the numbers to find out whether the incidence value of 100 has been reached three days in a row. The measures only apply after the following day, meaning that citizens also need to keep this in mind when trying to figure out whether the additional restrictions are in force. This has inevitably resulted in great uncertainty about what measures apply where and when, which is untenable. However, this law was limited in time and has since expired. Furthermore, the Federal Constitutional Court declared this law to be in line with the constitution.[114] All objections to the law were deemed unavailing. The Court conceded that the wording speaks in favor of the view that an executive act is required. However, the Court believed that as a consequence of regarding legislative acts already as infringements, such infringements must in principle be justifiable. This argumentation, however, is circular and therefore not convincing. The fact that even laws that do not require an act of implementation can restrict a person's freedom does not mean that they must also be permissible.[115] In addition, the court affiermed the definiteness of the norm and regarded the limited legal protection against infringements of personal liberty directly through legislatives acts as unproblematic.[116]

In addition, § 28b (6) empowers the federal government to adopt further measures in ordinances. This is constitutionally possible because the limits of Art. 80 Basic Law have been observed, in particular because it has been explicitly stipulated that the *Bundestag* and *Bundesrat* must agree to the ordinances. But there is, again, a problem of legal protection, because no administrative court review of norms is possible against legal ordinances; only declaratory actions for the non-existence of the obligations arising from the respective legal ordinance can be made.[117] However, this

114 BVerfG, BeckRS 2021, 36514.

115 Poscher, in: Huster/Kingreen, Handbuch Infektionsschutzrecht, 2nd edition 2022 (forthcoming), Chapter 4 para. 140.

116 BVerfG, BeckRS 2021, 36514, para. 135 et seq.

117 Möllers, Stellungnahme zum Entwurf eines Vierten Gesetzes zum Schutz der Bevölkerung bei einer epidemischen Lage von nationaler Tragweite BT-Druck-

means that the decision is only effective inter partes and the legal ordinance cannot itself be annulled by the administrative courts.

c) Proportionality and the aim of the measures

In addition, even if the authority acts on the basis of the general clauses and is granted discretionary powers, it cannot act without limits. There are general limits which must be respected. In addition to the principle of certainty, the principle of proportionality is particularly relevant here.[118] The requirements that arise from the principle of proportionality with regard to the individual protective measures are largely measure-specific. They will be different for face mask requirements than for general assembly bans.

However, some aspects of the proportionality analysis are important for almost all measures. One such aspect relates to the permissible purpose of the protective measures. In view of the far-reaching measures to combat the pandemic, it has been argued by legal scholars that their permissible goal cannot be to save as many people as possible from infection and associated damage because this would lead to an absolutization of these legal interests at the expense of other fundamental freedoms.[119] Rather, the permissible purpose of the protective measures can only be to keep the infection process under control to the extent that it does not lead to the potential overload of the health system.[120] It is understandable, in view of the far-reaching measures that have been taken to combat the coronavirus, to look for starting points in order to be able to put a stop to the infection protection dynamic. On the one hand, the Basic Law not

---

sache 19/28444, 2 et seq., https://www.bundestag.de/resource/blob/834614/9ace24a12b228c12a677f4b05aec4865/19_14_0323-2-_Prof-Dr-Moellers_-viertes-BevSchG-data.pdf; Kießling, Stellungnahme als geladene Einzelsachverständige für die öffentliche Anhörung im Gesundheitsausschuss des Deutschen Bundestages am 16.4.2021, 7, https://www.bundestag.de/resource/blob/834718/f9d7dff3462d982b089359365a45624a/19_14_0323-6-_ESV-Dr-Andrea-Kiessling_-viertes-BevSchG-data.pdf (last accessed 16.12.2021).

118 Guckelberger, NVwZ-Extra 9a, 1 (10 et seq.).

119 Lepsius, Vom Niedergang grundrechtlicher Denkkategorien in der Corona-Pandemie, https://verfassungsblog.de/vom-niedergang-grundrechtlicher-denkkategorien-in-der-corona-pandemie.

120 Lepsius, Vom Niedergang grundrechtlicher Denkkategorien in der Corona-Pandemie, https://verfassungsblog.de/vom-niedergang-grundrechtlicher-denkkategorien-in-der-corona-pandemie (last accessed 16.12.2021).

only does not recognize a prohibition on the protection of life and health but, on the contrary and according to the largely undisputed case law of the Federal Constitutional Court, the state has a duty (derived from fundamental rights) to actively protect life and health.[121] On the other hand, the limitation is also not convincing in terms of its substance: It categorically excludes any protective measure in cases involving a slowly but steadily advancing wave of infections that will affect large parts of the population without ever overloading the health system.

Thus, limits to the measures must be found in other dogmatic elements of the principle of proportionality. Case law on the coronavirus measures shows that, in particular, the courts have critically examined the necessity of the protective measures. This is hardly surprising, as the authorities were extremely tested in the first few months of the pandemic and, when in doubt, opted for far-reaching and blanket-like restrictions rather than finely tuned and differentiated measures. With increasing experience and a growing knowledge of how the virus spreads, some of the measures have since proven to be excessive and have been corrected by the courts. In addition, the appropriateness test was also relevant, in which various fundamental rights positions were reconciled.[122] For example, it was pointed out that the freedom of assembly is a high good of the German constitution; consequently, bans without the possibility of exception are unconstitutional. The authorities picked up on this and implemented other measures, which proved to be (at least partially) lawful.[123]

d) Specific conditions for certain intervention-intensive measures

The Infection Protection Act in § 28a (2) provides specific requirements for particular measures. The prohibition of meetings and religious/ideological gatherings (§ 28a (1) no. 10 of the Infection Protection Act), restrictions on leaving the country (§ 28a (1) no. 3 of the Infection Protection Act), and bans on visits by relatives to retirement and nursing homes and hospitals

---

121 Poscher, in: Huster/Kingreen, Handbuch Infektionsschutzrecht, 2nd edition 2022 (forthcoming), Chapter 1 para. 110.

122 Kaiser/Hensel, Federal Republic of Germany: Legal response to COVID-19, in: King et. al., The Oxford compendium of national legal responses to COVID-19, Oxford 2021, para. 46, available at: https://oxcon.ouplaw.com/view/10.1093/law-occ19/law-occ19-e2.

123 Poscher, in: Huster/Kingreen, Handbuch Infektionsschutzrecht, 2nd edition 2022 (forthcoming), Chapter 1 para. 114 et seq.

(§ 28a (1) no. 15 of the Infection Protection Act) are only permissible if the effective containment of the spread of the pandemic would be significantly endangered. On the one hand, this clarifies that these measures are only permissible as the ultima ratio due to the high intensity of the limitations vis-à-vis the fundamental rights as well as the constitutional significance afforded to the fundamental rights positions affected by these limitations. On the other hand, a qualified threat to contain the pandemic is also required, which can probably be measured by the infection incidence rate.

2. *Standard powers*

It is important to note that no measures can be taken under this general clause if they are more specifically regulated by the Infection Protection Act, such as surveillance (§ 29), isolation (§ 30), and prohibition of professional practice (§ 31).

Surveillance is considered to be a control measure, although surveillance alone cannot obviously prevent infections. Surveillance is primarily ensured through access rights for the authorities. Property, rooms, installations, and facilities as well as means of transport may be entered. The purpose of this surveillance is to allow the authorities to adapt preventive measures. Moreover, surveillance is also carried out, for example, through physical examinations.

The oldest and most important control measure is isolation.[124] Until May 2020, this legal measure was still called quarantine.[125] By renaming it, the German legislature reacted to the distinction in medicine, which distinguishes between isolation of sick individuals and quarantine of suspected infectious diseases. The measure is designed to apply to both cases. However, it does not refer to "quarantine for the entire population." Such a measure would be a curfew, which cannot be based on § 20 but only on § 28, 28a of the Infection Protection Act.

In addition, § 31 of the Infection Protection Act empowers the authorities to prohibit professional activities. This is to prevent certain groups of persons from spreading diseases at work.

---

124 Kießling, in: Kießling, IfSG Kommentar, 2nd edition 2021, § 30 para. 1.
125 Kießling, in: Kießling, IfSG Kommentar, 2nd edition 2021, § 30 para. 4.

IV. Criminal law and administrative offense

Criminal law and the law on administrative offences have so far played a minor role in combatting the coronavirus. However, the Infection Protection Act also contains criminal offences and administrative offences: Violations of contact and other restrictions laid down by the *Länder* in statutory ordinances are considered to be an administrative offence (according to § 73 (1a) No. 24 of the Infection Protection Act) if the respective ordinance threatens to impose a fine. A fine (or even imprisonment) is possible if a contact restriction or hygiene regulation of a legal ordinance of the *Länder* is deliberately violated and, as a result, the disease COVID-19 or the pathogen SARS-CoV-2 has demonstrably been spread (§ 74 of the Infection Protection Act). Moreover, a fine or imprisonment can be imposed on anyone who contravenes a specific individual order (e.g., from a health authority to comply with certain hygiene regulations in a restaurant (§ 75 (1) No. 1 of the Infection Protection Act)). The *Länder* have adopted catalogues of fines for various infringements. Concerning the catalogue of the state of Berlin, it was clarified in court that such catalogues are only legal if they have been adapted to the current situation and comply with the principle of legal certainty of Art. 103 (2) Basic Law.[126] According to Art. 103 (2), no act may be punished if it has not previously been defined as a criminal offence by law and provided with a threat of punishment. The norm itself contains several legal principles, namely the requirement of certainty, which includes the definition of the offence (nullum crimen sine lege) and the definition of the threat of punishment (nulla poena sine lege), as well as the prohibition of analogy, the prohibition of customary law, and the prohibition of retroactivity.[127] The clarity of some provisions was also the subject of rulings by the Federal Constitutional Court in November 2021; the judges declared the provisions to be sufficiently clear.[128]

In addition, the criminal law is applicable if a dangerous bodily injury occurs, which is generally considered to be the case when a person demonstrably and intentionally infects another person with a virus (including COVID-19).[129] A person commits an offense if they are symptomatic. If no symptoms of the coronavirus have yet occurred, it is still unclear whether an intentional infection can be considered as dangerous bodily injury.

---

126 VGH Berlin, BeckRS 2020, 9726, para. 18 et seq.

127 Radtke in BeckOK GG, 49th edition 2021, Art. 103 para. 18.

128 BVerfG, BeckRS 2021, 36514, para. 151 et seq.

129 See Zitzelsberger, in: Esser/Tsambikakis, Pandemiestrafrecht, 2020, § 2 para. 47 et seq.

In the case of HIV transmission, for example, German courts have ruled that dangerous bodily injury is possible even without symptoms. However, it remains controversial whether this case law is also applicable to the coronavirus.[130]

E. Data Protection: Health data protection law (Gesundheitsdatenschutzrecht)

Data protection law is complex. This is already evident from the interdependencies in the multi-level system. The term describes a system in which individual states no longer make decisions in isolation but are integrated into a political system in which decisions are made at several levels. European Union law in particular has an immense influence on German data protection law.

I. Interaction between infectious disease law and data protection law on the national and international level

The coronavirus pandemic has witnessed a convergence between infectious disease law and data protection law.[131] While enhanced data processing may mean that other, far-reaching measures may not need to be taken, such data processing also creates privacy risks. As noted, German law in this field has been strongly shaped by European law. At the level of the European Union, the fundamental right to privacy is based not only on the right to respect for private and family life under Art. 7 of the Charter of Fundamental Rights of the European Union (CFR) but also on the specific right to the protection of personal data under Art. 8 CFR.

Under the Basic Law, the right to informational self-determination under Art. 2 (1) in conjunction with Art. 1 (1) applies. In 1983, the Federal Constitutional Court announced this right to informational self-determination.[132] This right protects against the collection and processing of personal data by the state.[133] This follows from the fact that the Federal Constitutional Court developed this right as a special manifestation of the gen-

130 Lorenz/Oğlakcıoğlu, in: Kießling, IfSG, 2nd edition 2021, Vor § 73 ff., para. 18 et seq.

131 Kühling/Schildbach, in: Huster/Kingreen, Handbuch Infektionsschutzrecht, 2021, 203 (207).

132 BVerfGE 65, 1 (41 et seq.).

133 BVerfGE 78, 77 (84).

eral right of personality and, in continuation of the previous concretizations of this right – protection of privacy, right of reply, right to resocialization, or protection against self-incrimination – defined it in very general terms. The right to informational self-determination is therefore a summary of all aspects of personality protection relating to information about the personality and especially about the privacy of the individual.[134]

In German academic debate, the right to informational self-determination is increasingly viewed critically. The main issue here is the autonomy of the right to informational self-determination. It is not clear what the right to data protection is about and what the right protects substantively.[135] Fundamental rights usually protect a specific liberty or equality interest.[136] However, the object of protection is not clear here; for example, data cannot be controlled like property[137] – a right that the Federal Constitutional Court has upheld for a long period of time. The property approach has been criticized as naïve in our contemporary, technologically-interconnected and socially-networked reality because personal data is exchanged at all levels all of the time.[138] At the same time, data collection can be so harmless that it cannot yet be regarded as an infringement of fundamental rights.[139] This right is not intended to protect against data collection as such but rather to prevent the exercise of fundamental rights from being adversely affected by data collection or data processing.[140] Therefore, it is not an equal right but a modification of already existing fundamental rights. The same applies to Art. 8 CFR. In the debate on the threats posed by data transfer in the COVID-19 pandemic, this approach would also lead to differentiated results, because not the right to informational self-determination is relevant but the rights behind it. This also raises the question of the risks that actually emanate from the coronavirus tracing apps. This would possibly even enable a more effective design of the app with faster contact tracing. Nevertheless, this is not reflective of the law as it stands; thus, the case law of the Federal Constitutional Court should be taken as a reference point.

---

134 Rixen in Sachs, GG, 9th edition 2021, Art. 2 para. 72 et seq.
135 Poscher, in: Miller, Privacy and Power, 2017, 129 (131).
136 Poscher, in: Miller, Privacy and Power, 2017, 129 (131).
137 Marsch, Das europäische Datenschutzgrundrecht, 2018, 98 et seq.; Albers, Rechtstheorie 33 (2002), 61 (81).
138 Poscher, in: Miller, Privacy and Power, 2017, 129 (133).
139 Poscher, in: Miller, Privacy and Power, 2017, 129 (133).
140 Poscher, in: Miller, Privacy and Power, 2017, 129 (133).

II. Concrete conflict situations

1. Reporting obligations

The reporting obligations already described in detail interfere with the protection of the right to informational self-determination. The reporting system of the Infection Protection Act is structured to occur at several tiers. First, a report is made by the responsible persons (doctor, etc.) to the responsible health department (§ 6 et seq.). Then the report is passed on to the authorities of the *Länder* (§ 11), who then pass the information to the Robert-Koch-Institute. Under certain circumstances reports can also be made to the WHO or EU agencies. The processing of the data is legal under Art. 9 (2) General Data Protection Regulation (*DSG-VO*); under data protection law, there is also an obligation to delete the data as soon as it is no longer needed (Art. 17 (1) (a) General Data Protection Regulation). Interference with the right to informational self-determination needs to be justified. In terms of proportionality, the infectiousness and the severity of the associated disease(s) must be considered because these factors have a decisive influence on the risk to public health.[141]

2. Data processing in accordance with the Infection Protection Act

The investigative measures than can be undertaken in accordance with § 25 and § 16 (2) Infection Protection Act are not without complications as both paragraphs provide for far-reaching investigative powers, for example the right for authorities to receive information from doctors who are released from their obligation to maintain confidentiality.[142] This data processing does not require the consent of the person concerned, because Art. 9 (2) I General Data Protection Regulation expressly permits such processing. The law requires that appropriate and specific measures must be taken to safeguard the rights of the data subject. In addition, the Infection Protection Act itself requires in § 16 (1) that the data may only be processed for the purposes of the Act itself. These conditions must be taken seriously because of the excessive powers of the measures.

---

141 Kühling/Schildbach, in: Huster/Kingreen, Handbuch Infektionsschutzrecht, 2021, 203 (241).

142 Kühling/Schildbach, in: Huster/Kingreen, Handbuch Infektionsschutzrecht, 2021, 203 (216).

3. *Obligation of private parties to collect data*

In order to protect against infection, the *Länder* can also oblige private individuals to record contact data.[143] This applies in particular to restaurants and cafés, operators of fitness studios, or hairdressers. In the case of an infection, the data can be viewed by the authorities in order to inform contacts and take further actions. As sensitive health data are involved, data protection law provides strict conditions that must be respected. Constitutional requirements must also be complied with, especially the right to informational self-determination. This is particularly problematic because of the requirement of parliamentary approval (*Parlamentsvorbehalt oder Wesentlichkeitstheorie*). According to the case law of the Federal Constitutional Court, this means that the legislature itself must make all essential decisions in fundamental normative areas, especially in the area of the exercise of fundamental rights.[144] Due to the high bar set by the Federal Constitutional Court with regard to the right to informational self-determination, it is uncertain whether the rules of the *Länder* are constitutional.[145] It would therefore make sense to supplement the Infection Protection Act with a legal provision that allows contact data to be recorded by means of state ordinances.[146] So far, however, this has been classified as a lawful measure by the courts.[147]

4. *Coronavirus tracing apps*

During the pandemic, contact tracing via smartphone apps was quickly identified by numerous governments as a means to limit the spread of the pandemic. It was also evident that the legal arrangement in Germany meant that such apps could be designed to comply with data protection law.[148] The German government has so far developed two different apps. In April 2020, a coronavirus data donation app was developed first, followed by a coronavirus warning app in June. Both apps have different

143 This was done mainly through legal ordinances based on the general clause.

144 BVerfGE 33, 1 (10 et seq.).

145 Kühling/Schildbach, in: Huster/Kingreen, Handbuch Infektionsschutzrecht, 2021, 203 (244 et seq.).

146 Ibid.

147 See for example OVG Münster, BeckRS 2020, 21590, para. 62 et seq.

148 Haschert, in: Schmidt, COVID-19, 3rd edition 2021, § 24 para. 29 et seq.

target groups and different approaches to pandemic control. They are both voluntary.

The data donation app only covers a small target group and contains very sensitive data used for infection monitoring. Voluntarily provided data are used to identify sources of infection. Fitness wristbands or smartwatches are used to measure data such as pulse, blood pressure, and sometimes body temperature. In addition, participants provide data such as age, gender, and postcode. Global positioning data and location are not recorded. Although these data do not allow for the detection of infections, they are used for monitoring purposes. If the sample is large enough, at least potential sources of infection can be identified and further measures taken. Despite these sensitive health data, such an app is legally permissible as long as it is based on consent. The voluntary nature of the app makes sure of this. Compulsory use of an app would be inadmissible from a fundamental rights perspective.[149]

The coronavirus warning app has a far broader scope. It is aimed at the population at large and designed to contain the spread of the pandemic by tracing contacts. This app has attracted far more attention. The purpose is quick and easy contact tracing. It is designed to determine the potential risk of infection for individual users in order to interrupt infection chains. The app works via Bluetooth and changing IDs for the users. If one app user is close enough to another app user and one of them later tests positive (and enters this via the app, which is also voluntary), the other user is notified via the app. Information about the contact person who is infected is not transmitted. The problem here is the inherent notification delay, meaning that chains of infection cannot be tracked as effectively as desired. Due to the voluntary nature of the app, the data protection requirement to consent also exists here. Some experts have argued that because tracing apps only work if a large enough segment of the population uses the app, political and social pressure to do so means that use of the app is no longer considered voluntary. However, this notion is not at all comparable to a compulsory app and would only hold true if the state were to create incentives through the app, such as a rule that restaurant visits are only possible if the app is used.

Apps have also been used in the private sector, e.g., the hospitality industry. Here, however, consent is also required for reasons of data protection. One app that has received considerable attention in this context

149 Kühling/Schildbach, in: Huster/Kingreen, Handbuch Infektionsschutzrecht, 2021, 203 (248 et seq.).

is called Luca. Interestingly, the Luca app is no longer solely used in the private sector. Rather, health authorities have also opted to use the app. This raises legal questions, including compliance with the right to informational self-determination. The major difference between the coronavirus warning app and the Luca app is that the former does not require any personal data at all. With the Luca app, users have to provide some data about themselves and actively use the app, e.g., by recording their location.[150] With this data, health authorities can contact them if necessary. In practice, this means that health authorities can issue measures against individual persons based on the data provided by the Luca app; this is not possible with the coronavirus warning app. It should however be noted that health authorities can also access data from the Luca app only with the individual's consent.[151] This fact initially placated criticism of the app as the apparent privacy concerns were seen to be not as drastic as initially thought. Nevertheless, criticism once again intensified after the source code of the app was published, thereby revealing a number of security vulnerabilities in the app. The Federal Office for Information Security (BSI) was initially supposed to comprehensively examine and evaluate the Luca app, but the Federal Ministry of the Interior prevented such an examination. The importance of the app is decreasing because the coronavirus warning app has been redesigned so that contact tracking works just as well; in the meantime, even QR codes which were originally designed solely for the Luca app can now be scanned.[152]

5. Transmission and further use of data

During the pandemic it was reported that lists of infected persons were being forwarded to the police by health authorities in some of the *Länder*. This data transfer was based on the idea that police officers should be protected against infection. In the absence of a legal basis, such transfers are illegal. However, transfers of this nature raise the fundamental question of whether contact details gathered for the purpose of the fight against the coronavirus may be passed on when criminal offences have taken place and the contact details provided by the tracing data could be useful in

150 Stroscher/Schomberg, ZD-Aktuell 2021, 05138.

151 Stroscher/Schomberg, ZD-Aktuell 2021, 05138.

152 https://www.tagesschau.de/inland/corona-warn-app-luca-101.html (last accessed 16.12.2021).

identifying the culprits. This primarily concerns crimes that are not related to the coronavirus measures, e.g., when police are looking for witnesses to an assault.

F. Conclusion and Outlook

Germany already had a legal system in place to combat pandemics before the outbreak of COVID-19. On the basis of the general clause, numerous measures could be adopted to contain the infection, although not all of them were proportionate. However, the pandemic has also shown that judicial review in Germany is well designed and effective. During the second wave of the pandemic, the German legal framework proved to be a good basis for combating the pandemic. Nevertheless, numerous amendments to the Infection Protection Act were made in order to make the far-reaching measures used to combat the pandemic compatible with the constitution. Like the pandemic itself, this has been an ongoing process. Some of these reforms were important and effective, because they created legal certainty. However, other reforms – especially § 5 of the Infection Protection Act – are likely unconstitutional. At the same time, however, judicial control has worked quite well. The courts regularly curtailed overreaching measures. In so doing, the courts developed a legal framework to guide the actions of the legislature and state authorities. In addition, data protection and privacy laws have, on the whole, proved resilient. With its decisions in November 2021, the Federal Constitutional Court – albeit belatedly – provided policymakers with a constitutional orientation to counter the pandemic in the future, even if not all of the explanations presented were convincing. Within this system, tracing apps, for example, have been developed. At the same time, it must be emphasized that the pandemic has also revealed the partly failed conception of the right to informational self-determination. This misunderstanding has resulted in the apps not working to their full extent.

The Legal Framework of the COVID-19 Pandemic: The Italian Response to the Coronavirus Outbreak[1]

Rosaria Sicurella, Sandra M. B. Picicuto

A. *Preliminary Remarks*

Little more than two years have passed since the entire world has started talking about the COVID-19 pandemic, and one point at least makes the unanimity of Scholars and decision makers: the pandemic has deepened economic, social and juridical problems, urging to be handled promptly and effectively. In no time, we've moved from normal to an emergency situation, thus paving the way for a partial departure from state of law well-grounded mechanisms, and the triggering of state of emergency new dynamics.

In this context, traditional topics already discussed at length in the past have suddenly become pivotal in solving real cases. Among the most sensitive is the one involving the conflict of laws and the hierarchy of sources. This issue has never been fully solved through a systematic interpretative criterion, also due to some partial and not fully implemented Constitutional reforms. In the legal context of the pandemic, this is a leading problem, also in the light of an inconsistent legislative production. Constitutional principles and values certainly set a benchmark. However, given that they do not provide for specific behavioral directions and that they have to be balanced against each other, judges are the one called to set the balance between opposing instances in the concrete case.

The Italian Government has faced the COVID-19 crisis in the name of the so-called *precautionary constitutionalism*, recognizing a leading role to the right to health, in whose interest all the other rights and goods can be limited. A number of restrictive measures and behavioral duties – supported by relevant sanctions – have been introduced by means of law

1 The present contribution is the result of a joint study of the authors. Rosaria Sicurella is responsible for drafting paragraphs 0 (Preliminary remarks), and 2 (Repressive measures); Sandra Maria Benedetta Picicuto is responsible for drafting paragraphs 1 (Constitutional issues) and 3 (The impact of the coronavirus crisis on criminal proceedings and punishment).

decrees and ordinances of the Ministries, so limiting most of the freedoms and fundamental rights. The Parliament has lost its leading role, given that its long and complex procedures did not fit with the strict timeline required to face the emergency. Nevertheless, a whole re-centralization of the power has not been recorded, although the Government has taken most of the fundamental decisions. Indeed, the Regions (and, at least at the beginning, also the cities) have had the power to introduce, by means of Regional and City Majors' ordinances, restrictive measures based on the specific needs and features of the Regions, who were very fluid during the pandemic.

The pandemic situation has inevitably also affected the criminal justice system. The various legal texts hastily launched in Italy have laid down a large set of preventive and punitive measures, only later being rationalized. As for the impact on the *reserve of law*, that has been affected, especially in the first period of the pandemic, by the massive use of law decrees issued by the Government, it should be noted that this choice – and the related loss of the Parliament's leading role – seems justified it the light of the reasons of necessity and urgency on which law decrees are grounded. However, some points stay quite critical: the unclear succession of norms, the usage of the so-called "chain deferment" and "in blank criminal law provisions", the new role of Region Presidents and City majors as legislators, providing for incrimination duties as well.

Moreover, one cannot but critically assess the "hypertrophic, generalized and undifferentiated usage of Criminal Law", aiming at criminalizing several illicit conducts who would have required a distinguished evaluation. At the beginning, the simple violation of the Governmental measures has led to – at least in theory – a criminal reaction. Indeed, the Italian Government has opted for pursuing prevention by means of Criminal Law, using the threat of Criminal Law sanctions to prevent the infection spread. In this sense, it could be affirmed that the Italian first reaction preferred intimidation to accountability, while some other European Countries haven't used sanctions at first, suggesting measures to prevent the virus spread to their citizens instead.

In the context of the pandemic, the "criminal law of the coronavirus" is called to respond to multiple needs: not only the need to protect vulnerable people, but also the need for a reasonable evaluation of antisocial behaviour perpetrated in a state of necessity, together with the need to attentively consider the possibility to select adequate criteria to assess criminal responsibility of political decision-makers and administrative authorities, and also the need for special consideration for the conduct of health workers overwhelmed by the emergency.

On the one side, social distance compromised the fragile balance involving needy and poor people. For example, some temporary employees and occasional workers lost their income without the assistance of any social security cushion. Furthermore, the amount of homeless increased while a reduced number of people has been able to offer them assistance. In this context, in which some legal assets and fundamental rights have been challenged – first of all, the crimes against property – the institution of "state of necessity" may play a role.

With respect to the position of political decision-makers, administrative authorities, and health companies, while recognizing the merits for the full engagement of the most, one cannot but blame the evident unreadiness and improvidence of some of them when called to manage the Covid pandemic, that was possible to somehow predict at least some months earlier. Though, the complexity of the assessment the culpability for crimes against the person or against public safety – due to cognitive or organizational lacks and to the discretionary nature of the political decisions taken by institutional subjects – prompts for the highest caution in taking the path of criminal justice in order to assess the organization of health care and possible liability. Here the question has arisen about the criteria to be followed to assess their legal/criminal responsibility, in addition to the political one.

Assumptions and limits within which hospitals and welfare institutions could incur the "criminal offenses of the pandemic", or those resulting from tragic choices to deal with the emergency, follow the regime of administrative liability introduced by legislative decree 231/2001. Nevertheless, given that the main actors in the pandemic treatment have been the healthcare workers and the administrators of the National Healthcare System, along with local administrators, it should be mentioned that these individuals – whose conduct reflects the liability of their organizations – cannot trigger any corporate criminal liability under legislative decree no. 231/2001, given that non-economic public bodies are not subject to legislative decree no. 231/2001.

However, in terms of public and political debate, the main issue has concerned the suitability of the classical criterions to evaluate the liability of the healthcare workers for involuntary offences, under article 590-*sexies* of the Italian Criminal Code (ICC), dedicated to "criminal responsibility for negligent homicide or personal injuries in the health sector". The turning point has been such an exceptional situation requiring specific precautionary norms, given that COVID-19 was a brand-new scientific phenomenon, demanding a specific criterion to evaluate the causal link between the violation of the precautionary norm and the event (i.e. death or damage). However, the crucial topic of the level of tolerance to be adopted in evaluating healthcare workers' mistakes turned much more sensitive in the framework of the pandemic, in which these workers have been called to face a new phenomenon involving tragic choices as well. Furthermore, and above all, in such a short period of time, it has been impossible to elaborate, adopt and implement suitable guidelines; the latter being established by article 590-*sexies* as the turning point of healthcare workers criminal responsibility regime. Hence, the COVID-19 pandemic cannot be faced following stable guide-lines yet: the origin of the virus is still unknown, as well as how harmful it can be and its relationship with external factors (such as pollution); furthermore, scientists are still adjusting the treatment, aiming at discovering the perfect one, and they are also still studying the spread of the virus and the protection offered by the vaccine, both in terms of time and strength. The National System for Guidelines has created a page dedicated to the Corona Virus Disease in the best practices' section (that is subsidiary to the guide-lines' one). Be that as it may, the provision in art. 590-*sexies* has appeared difficult to fit with many of the situations occurred in the pandemic; thus stimulating the idea of the application of article 452 ICC, addressing the offence of unintentional epidemic, with respect to situations in which a "position of guaranty" is considered to have been violated by these workers.

Moreover, establishing health workers' unintentional liabilities also implies the assessment of whether the conduct of the health workers can be deemed, in some cases, unavoidable or not otherwise demanded as a consequence of an organizational faults of the healthcare local and National authority. In this case, it should be assessed if there is any causal link between these organizational faults, the healthcare workers and the harmful event. This assessment has been made very challenging by such a massive pandemic, given that there have been neither pre-existing experimentation, nor scientific evidence in this field.

This being understood, it has to be discussed how Criminal Law can and should address the conduct of the healthcare workers operating in such a new and difficult pandemic framework, under a situation of necessity that can imply tragic choices.

Against this background, and the awareness of the existence of a set of risks that appears to be impossible to neutralize even by using the maximum diligence, the Italian lawmaker has finally decided for the introduction of two new provisions especially tailoring criminal responsibility of the Health workers all along the period officially established by the Government as "state of emergency" because of the COVID-19 epidemic (the Italian Government declared the state of emergency of 31st January 2020).

In drafting these provisions, the legislature was confronted with the concurrent need to somehow "shield" the healthcare workers, on the one side, while not disregarding the need to adequately protect, also through criminal law measures, patients' life and health, on the other. Indeed, the ignited debate, at a political and also academic level, perfectly showed the crucial challenge of conceiving more flexible general standards aiming at limiting criminal responsibility to serious negligence exclusively, while avoiding the risk of introducing provisions derogating general principles and standards, that could significantly impact the overall system of criminal justice.

The provisions adopted by the Italian lawmaker have gained a diffused consensus among Scholars. However, we will probably need some time to discover whether the way followed by the Italian lawmaker adequately fits these needs. Finally, what we have to be aware, is that the COVID-19 pandemic has created an unprecedented global situation of culpable risk, in which a partially unknown virus is intertwined with irresponsible human behaviour, generating new precautionary rules that have redefined our own lifestyle.

B. *Constitutional issues*

It is unequivocal that, during the pandemic, some fundamental freedoms have been suspended or limited in the name of public health. According to the Italian Constitutional Court, all the fundamental rights complement each other, and no one prevails on the others[2]. Therefore, rights and principles have to be constantly balanced and the equilibrium point has to be set under the criteria of proportionality and rationality. In other words, it should be verified and confirmed that the same result could not have been reached through different means, less invasive to the rights than the one adopted. Furthermore, limitations have to be temporary[3].

---

2 *See*, among others, Italian Constitutional Court no. 85 of 2013 and no. 58 of 2018 on the Ilva case. In the latter, referring to the right to health, the Court held that "no right is tyrant".

3 On this requirement, *see*, among others, Italian Court of Cassation no. 15 of 1982, according to which fundamental rights' restrictions are acceptable only if limited in time.

Moving on to the concrete scenario under analysis, it has to be noted that the restrictive measures, originally established for limited periods of time, have been repeatedly extended, following the pandemic tendency. Consequently, their compliance with the criteria of proportionality, rationality, and temporariness has been questioned more and more stringently, also in the light of the relation between the measure adopted and the advantage in terms of public health[4].

It has been said that we are fighting a war against a tiny, invisible enemy and that we are living in exceptional times. Beyond any journalistic portrayal, making these measures fit in the constitutional framework is a very sensitive operation.

I. The Constitutional framework

1. State of exception vs state of emergency

First of all, it has to be clear that the Italian Constitution does not explicitly provide for a state of emergency[5], and all the more reason for a state of exception, referring to necessity, extraordinariness and urgency arising from certain facts, instead.

In case of war, the "necessary power" is provided to the Government under article 78 of the Constitution, specifically addressing the state of war formally declared by the Parliament. This provision clearly refers to war and, consequently, cannot be applied to other, unknown, emergencies.

---

4 *See* M. D'Amico *I diritti fondamentali alla prova dell'emergenza sanitaria da Coronavirus: profili sostanziali*, BioLaw Journal – Rivista di BioDiritto, no. 3/2020, p. 31.

5 On the lack of a state of emergency discipline in the Italian Constitution, *see* C.Ianello, *Riflessioni su alcune conseguenze ordinamentali prodotte dall'emergenza covid: dalle limitazioni delle libertà costituzionali alla riemersione del sistema parallelo di amministrazione extra ordinem*, Osservatorio sulle fonti, no. 1/2021, available on http://www.osservatoriosullefonti.it; and F.Pallante, *Pandemia, sicurezza, democrazia*, Questione Giustizia, 6 December 2021, available on www.questione giustizia.it.

In the framework of the pandemic, some Authors have pondered on the introduction of an emergency clause in the Italian Constitution that may be useful to face similar circumstances in compliance with the Constitutional identity of the State. Such a clause should be based on a situation of emergency which urges the State to face it by means of exceptional tools. *See G. De Minico, Costituzionalizziamo l'emergenza?*, Osservatorio sulle fonti, fasc. speciale, 2020, available on http://www.osservatoriosullefonti.it.

Furthermore, the Italian Constitution provides the Government with specific tools, the law decrees, to be adopted in case of necessity and urgency and to be later ratified by the Parliament within 60 days. Law decrees seem to be the legislative instrument designed to face difficult times such as the pandemic ones. Despite this, they have not been the only legislative solution adopted to face the Coronavirus outbreak, for two main reasons. Firstly, the legislative procedure for the adoption of law decrees, that involves the Parliament, takes a pretty long time, even if it is shorter than the one concerning ordinary laws. Secondly, although "exceptional" in nature, law decrees are a legislative tool commonly used by the Government in its everyday activity[6].

The legal basis of the state of emergency related to the Coronavirus outbreak has to be found somewhere else, then.

Under article 24 of legislative decree no. 1 of 2018 (also known as Civil Protection Code), the Government is able to declare the statutory state of emergency during which civil protection orders can be adopted "*in derogation to any current provision, within the limits and with the methods indicated in the resolution on the state of emergency and in compliance with the general principles of the legal system and the European Union rules*"[7].

Following the World Health Organization's declaration of the state of emergency, dated 30th of January 2020, the National state of emergency has been formally declared by the Board of Ministry on the 31st of January 2020, under article 7, paragraph 1, letter c) of the Civil Protection Code, according to which "*National emergency related to calamitous events arising from nature or human activities those, due to their intensity or length, have to be faced immediately, through extraordinary powers and means to be used within limited period of time under article 24*".

In conclusion, it can be said that the provisions adopted to face the pandemic fill in the democratic order, although some of them are extraordinary in nature. Despite the vivid debate arose around the topic, the

---

6 On the misuse of law decree *see* M.D'Amico, *supra*, and A. Algostino, *Costituzionalismo e distopia nella pandemia di COVID-19 tra fonti dell'emergenza e (s)bilanciamento dei diritti*, in *Costituzionalismi.it*, no. 1/2021, p. 1.

7 The scope of civil protection orders is debated. According with the Civil Protection Code, these orders aim at coordinating the civil protection operations, also waiving the ordinary law, within the scope of the state of emergency and in compliance with the general principle of the legal system and the EU. Orders are provided by the Prime Ministry even through the Chief of the Civil Protection Department.
On the relevant aspects of the Civil Protection Code see M. Cavino *COVID-19. Una prima lettura dei provvedimenti adottati dal Governo*, in Federalismi.it, osservatorio emergenza COVID-19, 18 March 2020, available on www.federalismi.it.

Italian legislation has been shaped within the Constitutional boundaries, consequently being no room for debating on a state of exception meant as a suspension of the judicial order[8]. Nevertheless, it is very clear that preventing the virus transmission has been the main priority of the Government, whose action has been inspired to the safeguard of private and public health rather than individual freedoms. In this regard, a suspension of the rule of law might be recorded, but, if it is the case, it has been still in line with the Constitution, given that it has been temporary, proportionate, and functional to the legal order itself.

2. *Executive power and emergency provisions. Sources of law. The role of Parliament*

The framework of sources addressing the Coronavirus outbreak is complex[9]. Along with the already mentioned constitutional background and the role of law decrees, some sources were used to face the pandemic.

The framework has been originally settled by law decree no. 6 of 2020 (converted into law no. 13 of 5 March 2020), providing for "specific measures to manage the Coronavirus pandemic". This decree was later repealed by the decree no. 19 of 2020, aiming at rearranging and simplifying the pandemic legal structure.

Law decree no. 6 of 2020 conferred to the Prime Ministry the power of introducing all the necessary measures to limit the virus transmission and manage the emergency by means of the "decrees of the Prime Ministry"[10]. Some strict measures were, then, introduced on a local level, in the areas

8 However, it has been held that the chain of law decrees e decrees of the Prime Ministry fits in the hierarchy of the sources only under a formal point of view, given that a new legal order has been created in practice. *See* G.De Minico, *supra*.

9 For an overview, *see* G.Mobilio, *La decretazione d'urgenza alla prova delle vere emergenze. L'epidemia da COVID-19 e i rapporti tra decreto-legge e altre fonti*, Osservatorio sulle fonti, fasc. speciale, 2020, p. 351, available on http://www.osservatoriosullefonti.it.

10 For a first overview on this legislative instrument, *see* M. Cavino, *La natura dei DPCM adottati nella prima fase di emergenza COVID. Lettura di Corte cost. n. 198/2021*, Federalismi.it, 3 November 2021, p. 81, available on www.federalismi.it; and L. Conte, *La reazione allo stato di emergenza Covid nella prospettiva del sistema delle fonti*, Studium Iuris, 2020, p. 991.

where Covid had a wider impact at first (so called "red zone"), while more general ones were applied in the other areas of the Country[11].

The following law decree no. 19 of 2020 has improved (and better specified) the power of the Prime Ministry of introducing restrictive measures besides the red zones. This latter decree is more compliant with the legality principle than the previous one, given that it has specifically listed the measures at the disposal of the Prime Ministry and removed the opening clause according to which he would have been able to adopt any further "measure to limit and manage the pandemic"[12], not better identified. Furthermore, according with the decree, all the measures had to be commensurate with the actual risk and implemented for a limited period of time. In addition, a technical-scientific committee has been required to release opinions on the technical issues, also regarding the suitability and proportionality of the measures to be implemented. Finally, the central government has been entitled to the leading role and the main source of law has begun the decree of the Prime Ministry. Nevertheless, the role of the Regions has been recognized as well, given that the opinions or the proposals of their presidents have to be taken into consideration (*see* paragraph 1.1.3 below).

On the other hand, presidents of the Regions and city mayors have been entitled of the ordinance power[13] in case of extreme necessity and urgency and while a decree of the Prime Ministry has not been adopted on that matter yet.

---

11 For a first comment on the law decree no. 6 of 2020 *see* M.Cavino, *COVID-19. Una prima lettura dei provvedimenti adottati dal Governo, supra*, and G. L Gatta, *Un rinnovato assetto del diritto dell'emergenza COVID-19 più aderente ai principi costituzionali, e un nuovo approccio al problema sanzionatorio: luci ed ombre nel d.l. 25 marzo 2020, n. 19*, Sistema Penale, 26 marzo 2020, available on www.sistemapenale.it.

12 This clause, in article 2 of the decree no. 6 of 2020, has been considered as a white proxy to the Prime Ministry, so challenging the principle of legality. In particular, the most sensitive topic has regarded the limitation of fundamental rights whose, according with the Italian Constitution, can be governed by the Parliament only. Nevertheless, such a wide proxy could have been understood in the light of the exceptional situation the decrees aimed at managing. Indeed, the decree no. 6 of 2020 has been introduced during the very first stage of the pandemic, when the broader powers seemed necessary to face the new phenomenon; later on, the decree no. 19 of 2020 narrowed the Prime Ministry's powers specifically listing the appropriate measures.

13 Under article 32 of law no. 833 of 1978, article 50 of legislative decree no. 267 of 2000, and article 117 of legislative decree no. 276 of 2000.

Continuing the analysis of the pandemic legal framework, article 32 of law no. 833 of 1978 has to be mentioned as well. This source provides the Ministry of Health with a peculiar power to deliver orders on hygiene and public health matters enforceable to the whole State or to part of it. These measures can be implemented only in the meantime a decree of the Prime Ministry has to be adopted and in case of necessity and urgency[14]. Finally, Civil Protections orders have had a role too, as well as regional and local orders.

All in all, the exceptional powers mentioned above are still in line with the legality principle, according to which orders are not limited by the law (they can also be in contrast with it) but only by the principles of the legal system and the Constitution. The emergency power regulation is then grounded on the legality principle, as already mentioned in paragraph 1.1.1 above, although some unusual legal instruments have been used to face a new situation requiring a centralized and quick decision process[15].

Nevertheless, in the framework depicted above the Parliament seems to have lost its leading role[16], given that the main source of law has been the decree of the Prime Ministry, that is not subject to the Parliament control. Furthermore, to prevent the spread of the virus within the Parliament, the Parliament itself has reduced its functioning, limiting the amount of parliamentarian accessing the premises through agreements between the parties to reduce the attendees still guaranteeing the minimum number of

---

14 Article 2, paragraph 2, law decree no. 19 of 2020: "*In the meanwhile the Decrees of the Prime Minister are adopted, and producing effects until that time, in case of necessity and urgency in relation with situations suddenly developed, restrictive measures can be adopted by the Ministry of Health under article 32 of the Law no. 833 of 1978*".

15 E Raffiotta, *Sulla legittimità dei provvedimenti del governo a contrasto dell'emergenza virale da coronavirus*, BioLaw Journal – Rivista di BioDiritto, special issue no. 1/2020, p. 95.

16 For a critic overview, *see* M. C Grisolia, *Il rapporto Governo-Parlamento nell'esercizio della funzione normativa durante l'emergenza COVID-19*, Osservatorio sulle fonti, fasc. speciale, 2020, p. 595, available on http://www.osservatoriosullefonti.it; I. Massa Pint, *La tremendissima lezione del Covid 19(anche) ai giuristi*, Questione Giustizia, 18 March 2020, available on www.questionegiustizia.it; and F. Pallante *supra*.

parliamentarians to deliberate[17]. Needless to say, the image of a reduced Parliament suggested the idea of a suspension of democracy to many[18].

3. *The distribution of legislative power: central Government vs Regions*

The coronavirus outbreak has not affected the whole national territory the same way. During the first phase of the pandemic, it has mainly affected the North of Italy and, above all, Lombardia[19] and Veneto Regions. A very first "red zone" was therefore established by the law decree no. 6 of 2020 and it covered eleven towns where a sensitive amount of COVID-19 positive patients was detected. Given the increasing spread of the virus, the red zone was later extended to the whole territory of some Regions (Friuli Venezia Giulia, Veneto, Lombardy, Piemonte, Liguria and Emilia Romagna) and, finally, a national lockdown was established by means of the decree of the Prime Ministry dated 11th March 2020.

Given the partial overlap between the different levels of governments, a debate arose on the distribution of the legislative power between central Government and Regions. This issue is specifically addressed in article 117 of the Italian Constitution, where the subjects under the legislative power of the sole central Government are listed (second paragraph), as well as the subjects under the concurrent power of the central and the Regional Governments (third paragraph); finally, the sole power of the Regional governments covers all the subjects not expressively allocated to the central government (fourth paragraph)[20].

---

17 Some further debate arose on the possibility of arranging remote discussions and remote voting sessions and on the tools to allow Covid-positive parliamentarians to express their vote. In this context, it has to be mentioned that the election of the President of the Republic took placed as well, on January 2022.

18 The idea of a reduced Parliament, staying in the background of the pandemic management, is strongly opposite to the image of a leading Parliament that the Italian Constitution depicted in case of war. *See* C.Tripodina, *La Costituzione al tempo del Coronavirus*, Costituzionalismo.it, no. 1/2020.

19 For the sake of historical accuracy: the so-called patient 0 was identified in Codogno, a small town in Lombardia, on the 21st of February 2020 – even if some research shows that the virus was actually circulating around Italy even before that date.

20 In particular, the following, relevant subjects are included within the government sole power: relationship with religious affiliations (on which, *see* paragraph 1.2.2 below), public order, general provisions on education. On the other hand, the following, relevant subjects are addressed to the concurrent power of the central and

In the light of the above, it is worth pointing out how the distribution of the legislative power has been involved by the adoption of the restrictive measures[21], challenging the principle of loyal cooperation between Government and Regions.

At the very beginning of the pandemic, as already known, the Government's restrictive measures were only applicable to the area identified, under law decree no. 6 of 2020, and their violation represented a criminal offence under article 650 of the Italian Criminal Code (*see* paragraph 2.1 below); furthermore, Regions and local entities were entitled of the ordinance power only in the meantime a decree of the Prime Ministry has to be adopted and in case of necessity and urgency. As far the Regional and local orders, whose scope of application is limited to their own territory, their role has been partially subject to the scope of the central power. To prevent different orders from overlapping, article 35 of decree no. 9 of 2020 finally established that once national orders have been served, local orders cannot be in contrast with them.

Having a closer look at the distribution of power between central and Regional governments, it should be noted that article 2 of law decree no. 19 of 2020 states that restrictive measures are adopted by means of decrees of the Prime Ministry, having heard between the others "*the presidents of the Regions where the measures have to be applied or the president of the Regions committee in case the measures have to be applied to the whole Country*". Furthermore, "*decrees of the Prime Ministry can also be adopted upon the proposal of the presidents of the relevant Regions, in case the measures have to be*

---

the regional governments: education, health care, civil protection, government of the territory. Therefore, it is clear that some of the subjects directly and deeply involved by the restrictive measures are under the concurrent legislative power already mentioned. This has implied some overlaps between the powers and some issues have eventually arose on the efficacy of the measures. On this topic, *see F.Cintiolli, Sul regime del lockdown in Italia (note sul decreto legge n. 19 del 25 marzo 2020)*, Federalismi.it, osservatorio emergenza COVID-19, 6 April 2020, available on www.federalismi.it.

21 For a complete overview, *see* M. Bignami *Le fonti del diritto tra legalità e legittimità nell'emergenza sanitaria*, Questione Giustizia, no. 2/2020, p. 11, available on www.questionegiustizia.it; V Di Capua, *Il nemico invisibile. La battaglia contro il COVID-19 divisa tra Stato e Regioni*, Federalismi.it, osservatorio emergenza COVID-19, 20 May 2020, available on www.federalismi.it; and P. Masala, *I diritti fra Stato e Regioni nell'emergenza sanitaria, a vent'anni dalla revisione del Titolo V: quali lezioni possono trarsi e quale "ribilanciamento" occorre realizzare, per una più efficace garanzia dell'eguaglianza sostanziale?*, Costituzionalismo.it, no. 1/2021, 137, available on www.costituzionasmo.it

applied only to specific regions, or on the proposal of the president of the regions' committee, in case the measures have to be applied to the whole Country".

Therefore, the legislative power of the Regions has been limited to the tight space left by the decrees of the Prime Ministry. The city majors' ordinance power has been limited as well. In other words, a recentralization of the power occurred, challenging the principle of loyal cooperation between institutions[22]. However, it was not a full recentralization given the pivotal role the Regions had in containing the virus' spread[23]. The presidents of the Regions, indeed, were able to both express their opinions before the adoption of the decrees of the Prime Ministry and propose the adoption of these decrees. On the other side, they were able to adopt their own ordinances, although only within their scope of application and without affecting neither manufacturing activities nor sectors of national interest and in the meanwhile (and until the time) of the adoption of a decree of the Prime Ministry. The city majors' ordinance power was subject to the same limits.

Despite the framework depicted above appears to be clear under a theoretical point of view, the concrete result has been confusing sometimes, due to partial overlap of the sources.

The ordinance adopted by president of the Campania Region on the 13th of March 2020 could be regarded as an example in this sense. Due to the increasing number of COVID-19 positive patients in Campania, the president of the Region released a regional ordinance providing with restrictive measures more severe than the national ones. The Administrative judges required to evaluate the ordinance's legitimacy have found that the ordinance at stake was a response to a difficult local situation and that it was not in contrast with the National provisions. Hence, comparing

---

22 On the recentralization of the power and the leading role of the Prime Ministry in managing the pandemic, *see* F.Sorrentino, *Riflessioni minime sull'emergenza* coronavirus, Costituzionalismo.it, no. 1/2020, p. 131, available on www.costituzionalismo.it

23 Regions have been involved both in the implementation of the measures and in the legislative process by means of the so called "Conference State-Regions", the main tool to coordinate the central Government and the Regions, in compliance with the principle of loyal cooperation between institutions. Although this principle was respected in theory, an authentic dialogue between the presidents of the Regions and the Prime Ministry has not always been possible, because of the urgency to adopt measures. On this, *see* E. Catelani, *Centralità della Conferenza delle Regioni e delle Province autonome durante l'emergenza COVID-19? Più forma che sostanza*, Osservatorio sulle fonti, no. 2/2020, p. 502, available on: http://www.osservatoriosullefonti.it.

the different interests at stake and considering the extremely high rate of the virus circulation within the Region, the ordinance appeared to be justified in the name of public health. Although the Court ruled for the validity of the ordinance, it should be noted that the ordinance covered also subjects under the sole jurisdiction of the central Government, that therefore should not be in contrast with the National legislation[24].

II. Constitutional interests and principles at stake

The coronavirus crisis has challenged several constitutional interests and principles. Some of them have been directly jeopardized by the restrictive measures aiming at managing the pandemic, some others by the COVID-19 vaccination. As it often happens, the goal has been a fair balance between the conflicting principles at stake, in the light of the proportionality, temporariness, and sensibleness criteria[25].

By way of introduction, it should be considered that some of the measures that can be adopted to protect individual and public health – to which article 32 of the Italian Constitution is devoted – can have an

24 For this and other similar cases, *see* V. Carlesino, *La gestione della pandemia da parte del Governo e il rapporto Stato-Regioni*, Diritto.it, 16 October 2020, available on www.diritto.it.
Another case study to be mentioned is the one concerning the Valle d'Aosta Regional law no. 11 of 9 December 2020 which introduced in that Region some measures less strict than the National ones, in order to support a partial release from the restrictions. The Italian Constitutional Court (decision no. 37 of 24 February 2021) has held that, given the global nature of the pandemic, the relevant preventive measures have to be adopted by the central Government and, in the name of public interest and health, they cannot be mitigated by the other level of governments. For a comment on this decision, *see* M.Gola, *Pandemia, Stato e Regioni: quando la 'materia' non basta (nota a Corte Costituzionale n. 37/2021)*, Giustizia insieme, 19 maggio 2021, available on www.giustiziainsieme.it; G.Lavagna, *Il COVID-19 e le Regioni. Uso e "abuso" delle ordinanze* extra ordinem *dei Presidenti regionali*, Federalismi.it, 14 July 2021, p. 94, available on www.federalismi.it; and A. Lucarelli, *La gestione dell'emergenza da COVID-19 tra regole uniformi, istanze di autonomia ed incertezza negli strumenti normativi*, Giurisprudenza Costituzionale, vol. 66, no. 2/2021, p. 465.

25 On the impact of the Coronavirus pandemic on fundamental rights in the EU *see* European Union Agency for Fundamental Rights, *Coronavirus pandemic in the EU – fundamental rights implications*, available on www.fra.europa.eu; and, for a comparative analysis, L.Cuocolo, (edited by), *I diritti costituzionali di fronte all'emergenza COVID-19. Una prospettiva comparata*, Osservatorio emergenza COVID-19 updated to 5 May 2020, available on www.federalismi.it.

impact on Constitutional rights and freedoms such as the freedom of movement (article 16), the freedom of assembly (article 17), the religious freedom (article 19), the right to education (articles 9, 33 and 34), personal freedom (article 13), as well as the right to work and the Public Administration functioning (articles 4 and 97 respectively). The whole pandemic regulation has been inspired to the safeguard of public and individual health[26]: during the peaks of the virus spread, most of the other rights have been restricted in the name of health, while during the descending phases of the curve, economic reasons influenced the government's decision[27]. Some of these aspects are discussed in the paragraphs below.

1. *Conflicting freedoms: personal freedom, freedom of movement and freedom of assembly*

The measures implemented to prevent the transmission of the virus (e.g. lockdown, quarantine orders, social distance) have affected some fundamental rights.

From March 2020 on, some provisions have had a negative impact on the citizens' freedoms. The freedom of movement has been restricted, quarantines orders seized, social events suspended, restaurants, bar, shops, universities and schools closed; even the industrial production has been suspended, except for the fundamental one[28]. Both National and local

---

26 On the concept of individual and public health in the Italian Constitution, *see* C. Ianello, *supra*. The Author specifies that, instead of balancing health and freedom, balancing constitutional freedom and the safeguard of public health (meant as a public interest) should be more appropriate.
On the leading role of the right to health during the pandemic *see* also F.Grandi, *L'art. 32 nella pandemia: sbilanciamento di un diritto o "recrudescenza" di un dovere?*, Costituzionalismo.it, no. 1/2021, p. 82, available on www.costituzionalismo.it.

27 G.De Minico *supra*.
On the balancing of rights, in the light of the predominant right to health and keeping in mind the principle of solidarity and the economic background, *see* A. Ruggeri, *L'emergenza sanitaria, la solidarietà dimezzata e... l'uovo di Colombo*, Consulta Online, 26 February 2021, available on https://www.giurcost.org/editori ali/.

28 By way of example, article 2 of decree no. 6 of 2020 has provided, between the others, the following preventive measures to be applied to the whole National territory: meetings and social events of any kind (including cinemas and theatres) have been suspended; museums closed; special preventive measures adopted in bar, restaurants and shops; sport events and competitions suspended, with the exception of the professional ones, to be hold behind closed door; schools and

lockdowns have been ordered, splitting Italy into areas with different restrictions on the basis of parameters concerning the virus spread and the capability of the health care system to manage the patients. Therefore, some fundamental freedoms have been limited to face the pandemic.

Speaking about fundamental rights, it is first of all important to be mentioned that, under article 13 of the Italian Constitution, personal freedom is inviolable and can be limited only by the judicial authorities by means of justified orders and in cases and within the limits provided by the law. Moreover, under article 16 of the Constitution, the freedom of movement can be limited for health care or security reasons. It is worth mentioning that, during lockdown, the freedom of movement has been suspended rather than just limited. Furthermore, under article 17 of the Constitution, meetings and assemblies in public places can be forbidden for security and public safety reasons. Preventive measures limited private meetings as well. Religious freedom and data protection have been affected as well, as shown in paragraphs 1.2.2 and 1.2.5 below.

Quarantine orders and the prohibition to leave the house have deeply affected both personal freedom and freedom of movement, respectively relevant under the already mentioned article 13 and 16 of the Italian Constitution as well as article 2, Protocol 4 ECHR and article 5 ECHR[29].

---

universities' activities suspended and switched to remote learning; Covid-positive individuals and individuals under quarantine order have been ordered to remain in their place; red zone's inhabitants have not been able to move in and out their area, with the exceptions of movements for justified reasons such as work, necessity and health.

29 Some Authors held that quarantine orders have mainly affected personal freedom, before of the freedom of movement. They also challenged the right to health, given that quarantine orders can be compared to mandatory health treatment, relevant under article 32 of the Italian Constitution. L. Cuocolo, *I diritti costituzionali di fronte all'emergenza COVID-19: la reazione italiana*, in L. Cuocolo (edited by), *I diritti costituzionali di fronte all'emergenza COVID-19. Una prospettiva comparata*, Osservatorio emergenza COVID-19 aggiornato al 5 maggio 2020, p. 13, available on www.federalismi.it.

On the contrary, the Italian Constitutional Court has recently stated that mandatory quarantines orders only affect the freedom of movement, and not personal freedom. These restrictive measures do not represent a form of physical coercion. They are generally applied for public health reasons to an undefined group of people characterized by having tested positive for COVID-19. These are the main points of the Constitutional Court decision dated 8th April 2022, as shared by the Court Information Office. *See Corte costituzionale: le disposizioni sulla quarantena obbligatoria costituiscono una limitazione della libertà di circolazione e non della libertà personale (comunicato stampa)*, Sistema Penale, 11 April 2022, available on www.sistemapenale.it.

They have affected fundamental freedoms to the point of being compared with detention[30]. It follows that, given the relevance of the interests at stake, quarantine discipline should have been addressed by precise laws, rather than a sequence of vague decrees, providing standards to make it fit in the limitation of fundamental rights, preventing any negative outcome.

Restrictions to movement have been implemented as well, banning flights from risk areas abroad and limiting the possibility of movement also within Italy, by means of increasing restrictions until the National lockdown. Movements justified by working reasons or necessity have been allowed, until a gradual release from the restrictions. These have clearly affected the freedom of movement and, even if all the measures have been introduced by decrees fitting in the pandemic legal framework, a certain level of confusion in the sequence of the sources can be reported as well.

Moving back from the freedoms challenged by the restrictive and preventive measures to the big picture, it has to be considered that all the measures have been implemented to prevent the collapse of the whole society. Indeed, in the name of public health, the sacrifice of individual freedoms and rights has been functional to the protection of collective rights. As often with fundamental rights, the issue has turned to be the fair balance between them, keeping in mind the principle of necessity (i.e. the sacrifice of certain rights can be justified by the concrete circumstance) and proportionality (i.e. the situation cannot be dealt with by less invasive measures)[31].

All in all, considering the violent and unexpected outbreak of the Coronavirus pandemic, the adoption of unusual and restrictive measures seems reasonable. The challenge here is avoiding that these exceptional measures – justified by the circumstances – become permanent.

---

30 Significantly, quarantine has been defined as *"the most extreme use of government power over people who have committed no crime"*. P.J Price, *A Coronavirus Quarantine in America Could be a Giant Legal Mess*, The Atlantic, 16 February 2020.
For an comment on the matter, *see* also G. L. Gatta, *I diritti fondamentali alla prova del Coronavirus. Perché è necessaria una legge sula quarantena*, Sistema Penale, 2 April 2020, available on www.sistemapenale.it.

31 F. De Stefano, *La pandemia aggredisce anche il diritto?*, Giustizia Insieme, 2 April 2020, available on www.giustiziainsieme.it.

2. *Religious freedom*

The right to religious freedom has been affected by the Coronavirus measures as well[32], in particular in relation to the suspension of public religious ceremonies.

Between the other sources addressing the matter, the main has certainly been article 2, paragraph 1, letter v) of the Decree of the Prime Ministry dated 8th of March 2020, according to which "*The churches' opening is subject to the adoption of preventing measures capable of avoiding mass gathering, in the light of the dimensions and features of buildings and able to guarantee at least 1-meter social distance between attendings. Religious and civilian ceremonies are suspended, including funerals*". Special restrictions have later been adopted for Easter celebrations and funerals as well. Later on, starting from May 2020, some protocols have been signed to gradually come back to regular ceremonies, subject to the Coronavirus spread, the adoption of preventing measures and any general restrictions[33].

The provisions addressing and limiting the religious freedom have challenged article 19 of the Italian Constitution, granting the religious freedom, article 7 of the Constitution, according to which the Roman Church and the State of Italy are independent and sovereign, and article 8 of the Constitution, granting the religious freedom to all the religions. As far as the relationship between the Roman Church and the State of Italy is concerned, the so-called Patti Lateranensi, recalled under article 7 of the Constitution, have to be mentioned as well: they regulate the relationship between the two parties, and any amendments to them has to be agreed by both of them.

The decision of the State to suspend religious ceremonies – beyond the reasonableness of the measure[34] – has deeply affected a core activity of the Church, crossing the line of the Church competences. Despite this, it can be argued that the State had the power to one-sidedly suspend

---

32 *See* L Cuocolo, *I diritti costituzionali di fronte all'emergenza COVID-19: la reazione italiana*, *supra*; and G. Macri, *La libertà religiosa alla prova del COVID-19. Asimmetrie giuridiche nello "stato di emergenza" e nuove opportunità pratiche di socialità*, Stato, Chiese e pluralismo confessionale, no. 9/2020, p.23, available on www.statochiese.it.

33 On the measures adopted, *see* M. Madonna, *La libertà religiosa ai tempi del coronavirus tra diritto e letteratura*, 9 November 2020, on www.fondazionefeltrinelli.it

34 It has also been challenged by the emeritus president of the Constitutional Court, A. Baldassarre, who provocatively compared the right to go the church to the one to go to the supermarket.

ceremonies because religious freedom gives up to public health. On the other side, it could be sustained that any hierarchy between constitutional principles could be drawn because the relationship with the Church is strictly ruled under Patti Lateranensi and article 7 of the Constitution: any one-sided decision on religious issues would then be in breach of them[35]. Even though the Italian Episcopal Conference later agreed with the State decision, supporting it and so avoiding raising the issue of competences, the matter at stake is very sensitive in the light of the relationship between the two parties, becoming an important precedent in this field.

3. *Right to education*

The restrictive measures to prevent the Coronavirus spread also affected the right to education, one of the main aspects of the personality right, guaranteed by the Constitution.

Considering both the premises (often made up of small classrooms for numerous students) and the public transportation system used by most students to reach schools, online lessons have been preferred to in-person ones during the peaks of the pandemic. This has caused some problems both on the professors' side and on the students one, given the different teaching method that had to be shaped on the way and the technological gap to be filled.

Even if some measures have been implemented to come back to in-person classes (e.g. facial masks, social distance and body temperature check through thermoscans at the entrance), during the whole state of emergency in-person classes have been replaced by remote learning and vice-versa often, following the pandemic trend.

Although remote learning has allowed education to go on during difficult times, it is clear that it has strongly affected the quality of the school experience, not only in terms of education quality but also in terms of personal development and opportunities, raising inequality issues as well.

---

35 For an in-depth overview on the opposite arguments, *see* S. Nitoglia, *Covid e libertà religiosa*, 8 June 2020, on www.l-jus.it

4. *Individual health and public health*

It has already been mentioned that some fundamental rights have been limited in the name of the right to health.

Article 32 of the Italian Constitution defines health as a fundamental right of the individual and a collective interest, so including both the individual and the public aspect of it. The two sides are on the same level, and any of them can be undermined by the other[36].

Although in the Italian health system a central role is played by the individuals and their right to health within the limit of their freedom, the pandemic has brought the attention to the solidarity principle and, then, to the role of individual health in the framework of public health. Indeed, public health is generally grounded on individual self-consciousness, but some forms of enforcement may be extraordinarily necessary. Therefore, the Coronavirus outbreak stressed the already existing link between individual and public health, as the National Committee for Bioethics pointed out[37]. This may be easily understood. Given the strong interaction characterizing our society, individual health produces effects on the collective ones. In practical terms, everyone preventing to catch the virus avoids the virus spread. Consequently, in the light of the principle of solidarity, even individuals less exposed to the coronavirus' bad consequences (such as young people) should be required to adopt preventing measures not only to protect themselves but, above all, to protect all the other, weaker individuals they could infect. This is the reason behind some of the limitations to fundamental principles already mentioned above.

On the other side, it has to be mentioned that the triumph of public health over the individual one has afflicted the individual health care, both in terms of prevention of other diseases[38] and in terms of curing pre-existing ones[39], given that the national healthcare system has been mainly

---

36 B. Caravita, *L'Italia ai tempi del coronavirus: rileggendo la Costituzione italiana*, Federalismi.it, 18 March 2020, available on www.federalismi.it.

37 https://salutogenesi.org/media/attachments/2020/06/22/comitato-nazionale-per-la-bioetica.pdf

38 On the prevention side, according with the National Observatory for cancer screenings, between January and May 2020 there have been around one million of screening less than usual, due to the pandemic. Data available on https://www.fondazioneveronesi.it/magazine/articoli/oncologia/screening-oncologici-in-ritardo-a-causa-del-covid-19.

39 On the chronic disease management side, the scenario is even worse: it has been estimated that visits, exams, and surgeries have been cancelled to two patients on five, on average, and some specialized center (such as the one for sclerosis in

focused on COVID-19 prevention and treatment. The deficiency recorded on both sides has also affected the amount of avoidable deaths due to the lack of (or the delay of) cares: indeed, on the one hand, the healthcare system has not been working properly because most of its resources have been dedicated to COVID-19 and, on the other hand, patients entitled to healthcare have procrastinated because of the fear of becoming infected during their stay at the hospital.

Finally, further issues concerning public health and fundamental rights have to be discussed in relation to the COVID-19 vaccine. On this, see paragraph 1.2.6 below.

5. *Technologies to prevent the spread of the virus*

All the restrictive measures and the limitations discussed above have one point in common: prevention. Preventing the spread of COVID-19 seems to be the best weapon to fight against the virus, indeed.

Technologies played a pivotal role in this context, both allowing some activities to be performed from home (e.g. remote learning and working from home) and tracing the spread of the virus, with the goal of limiting contacts and exposures[40].

For this reason, decree no. 28 of 2020, then converted into law by law no. 70 of 2020, has introduced into the Italian legal system the tracing app called *Immuni*, available since the 8th of June 2020[41]. Nevertheless, *Immuni*

Cagliari, Sardinia) have been converted into COVID-19 hospitals, closing their doors to their usual patients whose care was deeply afflicted. Some data, along with the protest of the relevant associations, are available on https://www.ansa.it/canale_saluteebenessere/notizie/medicina/2020/10/13/covidper-pazienti-cronici-e-rari-difficolta-e-ritardi-cure_e361ea25-1588-4637-9d49-05c563afbd0f.html.

40 The main goal is spotting positive subjects and alerting people who got in close touch with them. Although this kind of tracing has been immediately implemented by means of traditional methods, the use of technology can make a difference. Quoting the WHO, "*you cannot fight a fire blindfolded. And we cannot stop this pandemic if we don't know who is infected*" (WHO, media briefing, 16th of March 2020).
For an overview on this topic, *see C. Caramdi, Contact tracing ed emergenza sanitaria. "Ordinario" e "straordinario" nella disciplina del diritto al controllo dei dati personali*, Nuova Giurisprudenza Civile Commentata, no. 3/2020.

41 For a first comment on the Law, see *C. Caramdi*, C. Tabarrini *supra.* For the sake of completeness, please note that the first Italian source of law on tracing app has been article 14 of Decree no. 14 of 2020, followed by article 17*bis* of Decree no. 18 of 2020.

– as well as other tracing apps in other Countries – brought some debates around its impact on fundamentals rights. Hence, tracing apps collect personal data (including sensitive ones, such as health data[42]), affecting not only the right of privacy but eventually some other fundamentals rights, such as the freedom of movement and association. A balance between the interests at stake has to be set, then, even in the light of the EU General Data Protection Regulation, that states that privacy protection can be limited under certain conditions, including public health in case of pandemics (article 9 and 23 of GDPR)[43]. Therefore, the protection of privacy can be limited by either supranational and national detailed provisions[44] to guarantee public health when it is necessary[45], under article 9 and 23 of GDPR.

In other words, in case Member States implement tracing apps they have to strictly regulate them by law, within the GDPR limits[46]. Furthermore, the European Data Protection Board (EDPB) provided Member

42 These are a peculiar kind of personal data, according with article 4 no. 15 of GDPR (*'data concerning health' means personal data related to the physical or mental health of a natural person, including the provision of health care services, which reveal information about his or her health status*") and with recital no. 35 ("*Personal data concerning health should include all data pertaining to the health status of a data subject which reveal information relating to the past, current or future physical or mental health status of the data subject. This includes information about the natural person collected in the course of the registration for, or the provision of, health care services as referred to in Directive 2011/24/EU of the European Parliament and of the Council (1) to that natural person; a number, symbol or particular assigned to a natural person to uniquely identify the natural person for health purposes; information derived from the testing or examination of a body part or bodily substance, including from genetic data and biological samples; and any information on, for example, a disease, disability, disease risk, medical history, clinical treatment or the physiological or biomedical state of the data subject independent of its source, for example from a physician or other health professional, a hospital, a medical device or an in vitro diagnostic test*").

43 For a complete outlook of the GDPR framework *see* G. Amore, *COVID-19 e protezione dei dati personali*, on Studium Iuris, no. 10/2020 and G Della Morte, *La tempesta perfetta. COVID-19, deroghe alla protezione dei dati personali ed esigenze di sorveglianza di massa*, SidiBlog, 30 March 2020.

44 See also article 52 of the ECHR and 2002 ePrivacy Directive.

45 It is worth pointing out that the European Commission (notice dated 17th of April 2020) has stressed on the principle of necessity under article 9 and 23 of GDPR. The principle of necessity strictly involves an evaluation on the national health system, given that the tracing is subject to the identification of Covid positive subjects and that its contacts, spotted by the app, have to be looked after by the health system too.

46 On the effectiveness of a European tracing app, implemented by all the member States, see S. Crespi, *Applicazione di tracciamento* Immuni *tra normative nazionale*

States with a formal declaration and some guidelines[47] on tracing in the context of the pandemic, highlighting the relevance of privacy protection.

As far as the Italian regulation implementing *Immuni*[48] is concerned, it clearly fits with the first requirement, being regulated by a specific national provision: decree no. 28 of 2020, converted into law by law no. 70 of 2020[49]. It should be noted that the Italian legislation focuses more on the proportionality principle than on the necessity one. The decree strengthens on the relevance of tracing to safeguard public health. It provides for users to be fully informed before they launch the app, and the alert system is based on the devices' proximity (still remaining anonymous) rather than on GPS technology. Furthermore, the decree limits the scope of application of data collected through *Immuni*, that cannot be used for any further scope than the ones related to the public health, ruling out any mass surveillance. Nevertheless, data could be used, anonymously, for statistics

---

e diritto UE in materia di protezione dei dati personali, on Freedom Security Justice, no. 3/2020 p. 49.

47 Available on https://edpb.europa.eu/

48 For the sake of clarity, some context on how *Immuni* operates can be of help.
Given the precarious balance between fundamentals rights in which *Immuni* operates, its functioning complies with some requirements (some of them have been suggested by the European Commission with the notice dated 17th of April 2020): i) downloading the app has to be on a voluntary basis, with no negative consequence on people not downloading it; ii) *Immuni* operates on the basis of the Bluetooth Low Energy technology rather than the GPS one. Bluetooth seems to minimize the impact on privacy, working on contact tracing rather than on location tracing; iii) data are also stored on a national, central server. On the contrary, EU suggested to encrypt data and store them on the mobile device rather than on central servers (on the debate arose on this matter, *see* C. Blengino, *Tecnologia di sorveglianza e contenimento della pandemia*, Questione Giustizia, no. 2/2020); iv) the Ministry of Health is the data controller and cooperates with the Civil protection, the National Institute of Health, the Ministry of the Economy, and Sogei S.p.A. (the company offering the servers); v) adequate, relevant and necessary data are the only ones that can be collected within the scope of *Immuni*; vi) data can be stored of a limited period of time. According with the law, the Ministry of Health is called to determine the relevant period of time, established in 14 days.
For an overview on tracing app in the framework of GDPS and Constitutional values, *see* D. De Falco *La politica del tracciamento dei contatti e dei test per COVID-19 alla luce delle ultime direttive OMS: nessun ostacolo giuridico impedisce di utilizzare il "modello coreano" anche in Italia*, Federalismi.it, osservatorio emergenza COVID-19, 28 March 2020, available on www.federalismi.it.

49 According with some scholars, a specific law, exclusively addressing the tracing app, would have been better than the one adopted, that regulates *Immuni* between other Covid-related topics. On this, see S. Crespi, *supra.*

and research purposes, but only in relation to public health (article 6, § 3 of the decree). In compliance with the proportionality principle, moreover, data can be collected and stored only for a limited period of time[50], under article 6, § 6 (nonetheless, the period of time does not appear to be strictly established, being subject to the declaration of the state of emergency).

In conclusion, the introduction of tracing apps is a step forward in the privacy evolution, moving from the original right to be let alone to the new role of the individual who cooperates with the others to safeguard fundamental rights. Privacy is no longer a "negative right", aimed at defending the individual sphere; the new concept of privacy is a complex one in which personal data are made available to pursue public goals[51].

6. *COVID-19 vaccine*

The COVID-19 vaccine release has represented a beacon of hope through the storm of the pandemic. Nevertheless, some issues have arisen both in terms of distributive justice and of conflicting freedoms.

A first debate has arisen on how to distribute the vaccine in case there would have been less doses than people wanting to receive them[52]: a logical and rational criterium had to be identified, indeed, to deal with the scarcity of the resources. The Constitution has been considered as a compass even in this case. Starting from article 32 of the Constitution,

---

50 The period of time was firstly set up to the 31st of December 2020, subject to the declaration of the state of emergency. The relevant period of time has been later extended.

51 On this new concept *see* C. *Camardi*

52 On this, see G. Battarino, *Prime riflessioni sui criteri costituzionalmente fondati di distribuzione dei vaccini anti Sars-Cov-2*, Questione Giustizia, 24 November 2022, available on www.questionegiustizia.it; and R. Romboli, *Aspetti costituzionali della vaccinazione contro il COVID-19 come diritto, come obbligo e come onere (certificazione verde COVID-19)*, 6 September 2021, Questione Giustizia, available on www.questionegiustizia.it.
Under a broader point of view, the limited amount of available doses involves the production and distribution of vaccines and, eventually, the vaccine patent. This topic is still more sensible if we think to the distribution on the worldwide scale, in particular with regard to less developed Countries. *See C. Bertolino "Certificato verde COVID-19" tra libertà ed eguaglianza*, Federalismi.it, 16 giugno 2021, available on www.federalismi.it; and A. Cauduro, *Il diritto al vaccino. Il ritardo delle imprese farmaceutiche: i rimedi*, Giustizia Insieme, 9 marzo 2021, available on www.giustiziainsieme.it.

granting the protection of health, it could be inferred that healthcare workers should receive the vaccine first, in order to guarantee the normal functioning of the healthcare system[53]. Also, police force and law enforcement agencies should have a priority line, as well as all the workers providing the Country with essential facilities and services. Finally, fragile people and people exposed the most to COVID-19 should receive the vaccine on a priority basis too.

From the above overview, it is clear that the topic of distributive justice is at the meeting point of some constitutional interests. Once again, it is a matter of balance. Therefore, according to some scholars[54], the Parliament should have addressed the distributive justice matter, by means of ordinary law, while the executive power and the relevant commissioners should have only dealt with its practical implications.

Another point to be discussed is whether COVID-19 vaccination may be mandatory[55] or not. Once again, the individual right to health interacts with public health and other freedoms.

In Italy, COVID-19 vaccination has been (and still is) elective. Nevertheless, a vaccination certificate (the so-called "green pass")[56] has been required to perform most of the everyday activities: the lack of vaccination strongly limited most of the fundamental freedoms, making it basically necessary to conduct a normal life, although still not mandatory[57].

In this sense, it could be affirmed that making the vaccine certificate the condition of exercising some individual rights was an implicit way to induce the population getting their vaccine. This mechanism could be considered not fully in line with the Constitution: indeed, our system allows

53 It should be noted that, anyway, not all the healthcare workers are exposed to the virus the same way, nor their service is directly linked to the COVID-19 treatment. Hence, a distributing order could have been drawn even within the same class.

54 G.Betarrino, *supra*; N. Rossi, *Il diritto di vaccinarsi. Criteri di priorità e ruolo del Parlamento*, Questione Giustizia, 4 January 2021, available on www.questionegiustizia.it.

55 According with article 32 of the Constitution and case law (*see* e.g. Court of Cassation no. 5 of 2018), health treatments can be mandatory in case they are functional to keep safe not only the interested individual but also the others. This being understood, it can be said that, under certain circumstances, vaccination may be mandatory and this would be in line with the Italian Constitution.

56 Introduced by article 3 of law decree no 105 of 2021.

57 The regulation of the green pass certificate has been amended several times. For the sake of completeness, it is worth point out that the certificate could have been released also on the basis of a negative Covid test or following recovery, even if the certificate's validity has not always been exactly the same in all these scenarios.

vaccination to be mandatory, but does not foresee any form of moral/soft suasion that induces citizens getting their vaccine on an elective (but not spontaneous) basis, using the limitation of other fundamental rights as a leverage[58].

C. *Repressive measures*

Generalities

A topical question of the assessment in the concrete case of criminal law responsibility in situations where collective fears and feelings are at stake is the one of searching the right criminal law response, still avoiding the risk of using criminal law to channel the collective emotions by a 'vigilantistic' approach and turning the justice system into a travesty of justice, as well as the opposite risk of a general leniency because of the massive dimensions of the phenomenon, and the many difficulties of establishing relevant facts and proving individual involvement in them.

---

58 *See* C. Bertolino *supra*. For a critic overview: L.Brunetti *La Costituzione può obbligare, ma non costringere: sulla incostituzionalità degli attuali divieti come mezzo per incentivare la vaccinazione anti COVID-19 (cd. green pass)*, in Forum di Quaderni Costituzionali, no. 3/2021, p. 492, available on: www.forumcostituzionale.it. For this latter Author, the balance between the right to health and other rights has been already made in article 32 of the Italian Constitution: therefore, fundamental rights cannot be further restricted to induce citizens getting their vaccine. Furthermore, the possibility to obtain a temporary green pass through a negative COVID-19 test cannot be considered a fair alternative to vaccination.
On making the vaccination mandatory and on the potential liability of the State for not have made it mandatory, *see* A.Ruggeri, *Ancora in tema di obbligatorietà del vaccino contro il COVID-19 e della responsabilità per la sua mancata introduzione*, Giustizia insieme, 11 October 2021, available on www.giustiziainsieme.it.
In the decision of keeping the vaccination elective, some people see an attempt to limit the State liability in case of damages descending from the vaccine.
A further and vivid debate has arisen on the suspension of not vaccinated workers, in case the vaccine certificate was required to access the work facilities. *See* C. Della Guistina, *La vaccinazione contro il COVID-19 tra facoltà ed obbligo nel rapporto di lavoro subordinato. Riflessioni giuspubblicistiche*, Federalismi.it, 28 July 2021, available on www.federalismi.it; and L.Taschini *Il vaccino anti Covid nel rapporto di lavoro. Riflessioni a partire dall'ordinanza cautelare del Giudice del lavoro di Messina*, Giustizia Insieme, 16 February 2021, available on www.giustiziainsie me.it. For the sake of completeness, it also has to be mentioned that for certain categories of workers (such as the workers of the healthcare system) vaccination has been made mandatory.

The situation of pandemic has produced an enormous impact on the Italian criminal justice system. Great attention needs to be paid not only to the criminal law provisions introduced by the various legal texts adopted during the very first wave of the pandemic (beginning of March 2020) and establishing criminal sanctions with respect to violation of specific measures adopted to contain the spreading of the virus (*see* paragraph 2.1 below) – that appears to be quite critical with respect to both the principle of legality and that of effectiveness, and because of that they were progressively repealed, except for the figure of violation of quarantine (*see* paragraph 2.2 below), –, but also, and above all, to relevant preexisting offences, such as the offence of epidemic (articles 438 and 452 ICC, or the various offences related to forgery (articles 483 ff. ICC) for which evident dangers appear of analogical application, or extensive interpretation disregarding the full meaning of some of the essential elements of the offence (and because of that risking to result in concrete applications *praeter* or *contra legem* even). Moreover, also classical criminal law offences such as negligent homicide or personal injuries have been impacted by the emergency situation. The crucial issue of the assessment of individual responsibility especially of some categories of people – medical and other health workers, employers, competent public authorities – has ignited the public debate about the need to introduce *ad hoc* criminal provisions, as the consequence of properly taking into consideration the exceptional situation in which these people have acted, but facing the concrete risk that the situation drives to systemic changes in the structure and dynamics of the general categories, especially as regards the assessment of the causality link and the negligent behavior (*see* paragraph 2.3 below). Moreover, the vaccination campaign, involving a massive number of people in a very limited length of time, opened a new chapter with respect to the need to deal with the responsibility of the health workers responsible for the vaccine administration, that has ended up in an occasion for a rethinking of criteria to be followed when dealing with the individual responsibility of the whole medical and health personnel with respect to facts produced all along the period of the "state of emergency" (*see* paragraph 2.4 below).

I. Criminal provisions establishing criminal sanctions with respect to violation of specific measures adopted to contain the spreading of the virus

The various legal texts adopted following the official declaration of the state of emergency established a significative set of sanctions to support the several measures adopted to contain the spreading of the virus. In this respect, however, it is to be stressed the progressive change of attitude towards the strict necessity of criminal sanction instead of non-criminal ones (especially administrative sanctions, though with a punitive effect/impact) that can be detected looking at what has been named as the "coronavirus legal framework" as a whole. Indeed, only the first Law-Decree adopted by the Government on the 23rdFebruary 2020, the Law Decree no. 6, (converted in Law on the 5th of March 2020) established the violation of all the measures of containment as a criminal offence. The legal texts which followed provided for administrative sanctions, except for the violation of the absolute prohibition to leave home for anyone subject to quarantine following He/She was identified as positive to COVID-19 which is confirmed as a criminal offence.

According to article 3, par. 4, of the Law Decree no. 6 of 2020, the violation of the many detailed measures established to contain the spread of the virus, especially affecting the ordinary freedom of movement, but also the freedom of association, religion and the other personal freedom already discussed above, under paragraph 1.2, as well as the performance of non-essential activities[59]– is sanctioned in accordance with article 650 ICC (the offence of "Inosservanza dei provvedimenti dell'Autorità" – *Failure to comply with Authorities' measures*). According to article 650 ICC,

> "*Anybody who does not comply with a measure legally given by the Authority in reason of justice, public safety, public order or hygiene, will be sentenced, if the act does not amount to a more serious offence, to criminal detention [arrest] for up to three months, or to pay a fine of up to two hundred and six euro.*"

Even though the provision in 650 ICC has always been considered by Criminal Law Scholars as a very critical one regarding the conformity to the principle of legality and, especially, of legislature's exclusive power to establish criminal offences (article 25 2nd par. of the Constitution), the Constitutional Court by its decision no. 168/1971 confirmed it does not violate the Italian Constitution (provided that some punctual requirements

59 Between the others, the prohibition to move in to and out of town, the suspension of public events and reunions both in public and private places; the suspension of nursery service and school activities (including school trips); the closing of museums; the suspension of public exams and services, except for the essential ones; the orders for quarantine with active surveillance for people fulfilling certain requirements; the suspension of some working activities and businesses; the prescription of wearing face masks to access to most of the available services; the limitation to access to close places and public transportation.

are met: a) the measure was adopted in the exercise of a power/duty provided for by the law; and b) the law establishes "by sufficient specification" the scope and conditions of the Public Authority's provision establishing the measure). However, a serious doubt about the effectiveness of this solution was expressed also by the judiciary because of the alternative sanction of the arrest or the payment of a fine, so that the offence can be extinguished by oblation, under article162-*bis* ICC.

A different legal qualification of the violation of the containment measures was also envisaged by some prosecutors, who have referred to the more serious offence established in article 260 of the Health Act (*Testo unico delle leggi sanitarie – TULS*, introduced through the King's Decree on 27 July 1934, nr. 1265), according to which

> *"Anybody who does not comply with a measure legally given with the aim to stop the encroachment or the spreading of an infectious disease of man will be sentenced to criminal detention for 3 up to 18 months, and to pay a fine of € 500,00 up to € 5.000,00".*

Indeed, starting from the Legislative Decree nr 19/2020, this qualification has been adopted with respect to the violation of the absolute prohibition to leave home for anyone subject to quarantine provided He/She has been identified as positive to COVID-19.

The Law Decree no. 19 of the 25th of March 2020 (converted into Law no. 35/2020) has significantly improved the quality of provisions introduced to face the risks linked to the spreading of COVID-19, in terms of clarity of their contents – and especially the list of measures to be adopted at national or local level –, as well as of proportionality of the sanction provided for in case of violation. In particular, article 4 replaced the exclusive reference to the criminal offence in article 650 ICC provided for in the Legislative Decree 6/2020 with a more articulated system of sanctions. While "ordinary" violations of the various containment measures listed in article 1 paragraphs 1 and 2 are provided exclusively with accessory administrative fines (from 400 euros up to 3.000 euros, finally reduced to a maximum 1.000 euros when converted in law)[60], the specific violation of the absolute prohibition to leave home for anyone subject to quarantine provided He/She has been identified as positive to COVID-19 (in article 1 para. 2 e))

60 As expressly provided for in article 4 of the Decree no. 19/2020, the administrative offences will be subject to the provisions established in Law no. 689 of 1981 (establishing the legal framework for any administrative offence with a punitive affect), and especially provisions dealing with *mens rea* requirements (article 3), excuses/justifications (article 4), and participation/conspiracy (article 5).

(the so called "mandatory quarantine", to be distinguished from the "fiduciary or precautionary quarantine" that can be established by Health Authorities with respect to any individual having been in contact with a person identified as positive to COVID-19, or anyone arriving Italy from abroad, for which only and administrative sanction is provided for in case of violation – as established by article 1, para. 2, lett. *d*, and article 4, paragraph 1, of the Law Decree nr. 19/2020) –, is punished by referring to the offence established in article 260 TULS, whose sanctions are aggravated by article 4, paragraph 7, of the Law Decree, which provides for a criminal detention for 3 up to 18 months, *and* the payment of a fine of € 500,00 up to € 5.000,00".

As for the issue arising from the change of legislation, and especially the change of the legal nature of the sanctions provided for all the measures of containment (except for the violation of the mandatory quarantine), according to article 4, paragraph 8

> *"the provisions replacing criminal sanctions with administrative sanctions apply also to violations committed before the entry into force of the present decree, but in these cases the minimum applies of half value of the relevant administrative sanctions".*

This explicit statement was necessary in order to comply with the *favor rei* principle, since it was a special temporary law- the Law Decree 6/2020 – the legal basis for the previous legislative provisions; for which, according to article 2, paragraph 5, ICC the general rule of the *abolitio criminis* provided for by article 2, paragraph 2, ICC does not apply.

Moreover, according to article 4, paragraph 1 of the Decree no. 19/2020, the application of criminal sanctions provided for in article 650 ICC, or in any other provision especially dealing with special legislative competence conferred (to Central or Local Authorities) in reason of health (as for article 260 TULS) is expressly excluded; while the legal qualification as a criminal offence (other than the abovementioned ones) remains open; something that is of a particular relevance with respect to the criminal offence of *negligent epidemic, forgery, negligent homicide or personal injuries by negligence* (*see* paragraph 2.3.1 and 2.4).

The main features of this system of sanctions were also confirmed by the Law Decree no. 33/2020. More precisely, article 2, paragraph 1, expressly refers to administrative sanctions provided for in article 4 of the Decree no. 19/2020 with respect to the violation of the (more limited list of) measures of containment, while in paragraph 3 it refers to the criminal offence in article 260 TULS – provided that the violation cannot be established as a more serious offence – with respect to the violation of the mandatory quarantine established by the Health Authority when the person has been identified as positive to COVID-19.

II. *The criminal offence of violation of the mandatory quarantine. Criticalities about compliance with constitutional principles*

As mentioned above, both the Law Decrees no. 19/2020 and 33/2020 punish the violation of the mandatory quarantine by referring to the criminal offence in article 260 TULS. As far as the legal description of the illicit conduct is concerned, a slight – but significant – difference can be pointed out. Indeed, article 1, paragraph 2 lett. e) of the Decree no. 19/2020 refers to the violation of the "absolute prohibition to step away from home", while article 1, paragraph 6 of the Decree no. 33/2020 refers to the "ban of mobility from home".

Indeed, as outlined especially by some scholars, the choice for the legislature (Government) to use a different terminology should logically be considered as a redefinition of the scope of the offence. More precisely, the reference to the ban of "mobility" would require for the offence to be established that the person not only stepped away from home, but also "circulated", so creating the conditions to an easing of the spreading of the virus. This reading would achieve a better compliance with the principle of offensiveness and the use of criminal sanctions as *extrema ratio*.

However, following both legal texts, the sanctioned conduct stays in two assumptions: the fact of being identified as positive to COVID-19; and, because of that, the fact of being the addressee of an absolute prohibition to step away (or to move) from home in reason of being subject to quarantine.

Two main critical issues arise:

a) whether it is the law itself (the Law Decree and then the Decree of the Prime Minister – DPCM) to be considered as the source of the limitation of personal freedoms affected by the quarantine, or whether it requires an individual provision issued by the competent Administrative Authority (that offers judicial remedies against it);
b) whether the quarantine affects the freedom of movement (on the national territory) exclusively, that according to article 16 of the Italian Constitution, can only be ordered for health or security reasons through a legal provision addressed to all the citizens (reserve of law); or whether it also affects personal freedom that according to article 13 of the Constitution can be restricted, in the cases and following the

conditions provided for by the law, through a motivated decision of the judicial authority (reserve of jurisdiction).

The first question (under letter (a) above) seems to have been solved by article 1, paragraphs 6 and 7, of the Decree no. 33/2020, stating that "the quarantine is ordered by a provision from the Health Authority", clearly aiming at solving the doubts that arose under the previous Decree – which was silent about the topic. This second position was shared by some distinguished scholars[61], while very much criticized by most, both academics and practitioners. Indeed, when converted in law (22 May 2020), article 1, paragraph 2, lett. e) of the Law Decree 19/2020 was amended by the express reference to the quarantine to be ordered by the town mayor (as the local Health Authority).

The sensitive question then has arisen with respect to the violation of the mandatory quarantine before the Law Decree was converted into law (and modified on this point), where the necessary requirement for the criminal offence of violating the mandatory quarantine of an individual provision was missing. According to the general rules this would get to the exclusion of the criminal offence for those individuals who were accused without an *ad hoc* provision.

In conclusion, the criminal offence under article 260 TULS would result in being non-applicable for violation of the mandatory quarantine when a previous individual provision by the competent Health Authority has not been adopted.

As for the second critical question (under letter (b) above), this remains unsolved. Indeed, following the opinion of a large number of scholars and practitioners (among others, Gatta, Natale), the general provisions in the Law Decree no. 33/2020, while improving the previous legal context with respect to the express provision of the competent administrative authority and the procedure to be followed to order the mandatory quarantine, nevertheless violate the principle of "reserve of jurisdiction". Indeed, a judicial decision is not required. Responding to the arguments opposed by some Scholars and practitioners (Luciani, Bignami), the majority points out that:

- the material content of the quarantine order essentially coincides with the one of the home detentions.(see § 1.2.1 above);

61 M.Luciani *Il sistema delle fonti del diritto alla prova dell'emergenza*, in *Rivista AIC*, n. 2/2020, pp. 126–127.

- the Italian Constitutional Court, in the past, has considered as falling in the scope of the principle of reserve of jurisdiction those situations where the restrictions to the personal freedom were less serious (though joined with social blame and moral stigma) [e.g., reprimands under Tulps (Constitutional Court, no. 11/1956); identification procedures implying personal inspections (Constitutional Court, no. 30/1962); the expulsion order from the Country (Constitutional Court, no. 105/2001 and 222/2004); blood tests to collect evidence during the invistagation phase (Constitutional Court no. 238/1996); the order to appear before the relevant office or police station during the time of sports events for people subject to the DASPO measure (Constitutional Court no. 143 and 193 of 1996 and 144 of 1997); personal security measures (referring to non-detention one, the expulsion order from the Country for the foreign, Constitutional Court no. 58/1995). Personal preventive measures have been included under the guarantees provided by article 13 of the Constitution too: Constitutional Court no. 419/1994, on the so called "soggiorno cautelare" preventive measure (article 25-*quarter* of the Law Decree no. 306/1993), ruled that the measure – as it is concretely ruled and applied – certainly represents a restriction of personal freedom and not only a restriction of the freedom of movement and staying; therefore it is covered by article 13 of the Constitution;
- the need for a judicial control cannot be excluded especially as regards the precautionary quarantine, where the many limitations are ordered with respect to persons who are not identified as positive necessarily but were in strict contact with people identified as positive, or they enter in the Italian territory from abroad. Here the effective justification of the sensitive limitations of the personal freedoms relies on more ambiguous conditions; so that the person subject to these limitations should be able to e.g. argue before a judicial authority about whether He/She was indeed in "strict contact" with a person identified as positive. In this case, the concerned person can go before the Administrative Court, but this would not stop the absolute prohibition to move from home, without the guarantees established in article 13 of the Italian Constitution;
- the same extensive approach to the guarantees established in case of restrictions to the personal freedom is followed by the European Court of Human Rights when interpreting article 5, § 1, lett. e) ECHR referring to the "lawful detention of persons for the prevention of the spreading of infectious diseases, of persons of unsound mind, alcoholics or drug addicts or vagrants" as one of the situations allowing limitations to per-

sonal liberty (provided they are ordered "in accordance with a procedure prescribed by law"). In particular, the European Court has considered that the measure of isolation decided to contain the spreading of an infectious disease is to be considered as a deprivation of freedom, regardless of the fact that it is to be executed in hospital or at home)[62].

In conclusion, the lack of judicial control with respect to the limitations of personal liberty implied by any measure of quarantine gives rise to serious doubts of violation of the guarantees enshrined in article 13 of the Constitution, and because of that about the existence itself of the criminal offence for violation of the quarantine. This will most probably lead the judge who first will face this accusation to bring the case before the Constitutional Court, that will definitively decide about this offence.

III. New issues and problematic aspects and/or innovative interpretation of preexisting offences

The criminal offences described above are all conceived as subsidiary ones, then to be set aside when a more serious criminal offence can be established. Among these, the first to be considered is that of *epidemic* (*see* paragraph 2.3.1 below), but also offences dealing with *false documents* come at stake (*see* paragraph 2.3.2 below). The classical offences of negligent homicide or personal injuries by negligence were also deeply affected, in particular with respect to medical personnel and health workers in general; something that has ended up finally with the introduction of two new provisions, establishing specific criteria, more favorable to the offender, to assess the negligence in relation to cases of death of patients during the state of emergency. They are listed in a specific paragraph below.

62 ECHR 25 January 2005, *Enhorn v. Sweden*, req. nr. 56529/00, dealing with the case of a Swedish citizen affected by HIV having been addressed by a decision of the Administrative judge with a measure of 3 months of sanitary /Health isolation (which was then further prorogated) following the violation of some prescriptions of the competent doctor.

1. The criminal offence of epidemic

According to article 438 ICC the offence of epidemic is established by

> "*Anybody who causes an epidemic by spreading pathogenic germs*".

In the intentional form the offence is provided for to be sentenced to life imprisonment, while in the negligent one (article 452 ICC) – the most relevant one in the present situation – is punished with criminal detention from one up to five years. According to the wording of article 438, in case of death of more people, the death penalty applies. However, following the abolition of the death penalty in Italy, by means of article 1, para. 2, of the Lieutenant's Legislative Decree no. 224, adopted on the 10th August 1944, replacing the death penalty with life imprisonment, no more distinction can be drawn with the situation of the offence of 'simple' epidemic only creating the danger of death of more people.

As for the negligent form of epidemic producing the death of more people, the punishment to be applied is still debatable. According to the original wording of article 452 paragraph 1 ICC, the negligent form of offences that in the intentional form are punished with the death penalty are punished with criminal detention from three up to twelve years. Following the opinion of some scholars, article 1 of the Legislative decree 224/1944 (replacing the death penalty with life imprisonment) only concerns these provisions that directly refer to the death penalty. This is not the case in article 452, paragraph 1, which refers to death penalty only indirectly (establishing the punishment from 3 up to 12 years for offences that in the intentional form are punished with death penalty). According to this opinion, the entry into force of the Law Decree 224/1944 will have as a consequence the implicit repeal of the provision in article 452.

However, while the wording of art. 1 Law Decree 224/1944 remains problematic, the solution of a repeal of article 452 paragraph 1 would lead to an unreasonable conclusion when comparing the situation of a negligent epidemic followed by the death of several persons (possibly punished with the light sentence of 1 year of detention up to 5 years) and the negligent homicide when provoking the death of more people (for which the agent can be sentenced to up to 15 years of detention); though the important difference with regard to the link between the rule of diligence and the death cannot be neglected.

Following that, the interpretative solution of a punishment of three up to 12 years seems to stem from a coherent and systematic interpretation of the code.

Three crucial questions arise when applying this offence to the actual situation, with important consequences on the assessment of individual responsibility:

1. whether the person infected can be considered as "author" of the offence of epidemic, following a strict interpretation of the wording of article 438 ICC;
2. whether the offence can only be established through a commissive conduct, or it can also be realized through a failure to act (by people holding a warranty position).
3. whether a causality link can be established between the conduct of a single person with the further development of the spreading of the disease;

As for the first question (1), the positive answer relying on the assumption that not only who "holds" the pathogenic germs (e.g. a scientist experimenting new chemical pathogenic germs) is the author of the offence of epidemic, but also an infected person because of the fact that He/She is the "container" of the pathogenic germs is supported by the clear position taken by the Supreme Court (even though not sitting in plenary) in its decision nr 1065/2019, dealing with a case of HIV multiple contagions following multiple unprotected sexual intercourses (for what the Court has nevertheless excluded that the offence of epidemic could apply). Stepping away from the different position taken by the appeal judge, the Italian Supreme Court stated that article 438 ICC makes no distinction about possible conducts of spreading the virus, and in particular it does not require any physical or space "otherness" between the germs that are spread and the person who spreads them. Moreover, according to the Supreme Court (which on this point recalls the position of the same (sitting in plenary) in the decision nr 576/2008 about a case of civil damages following contaminated blood transfusion) the very substance of the offence of "epidemic" stays on the "uncontrollable diffusivity" of the disease and its "rapid development with respect to an undetermined number of people"; something that results being the logical conclusion having in mind that in the Italian criminal code the one of epidemic is an offence affecting "public safety". This cannot be found in case of HIV contagion, while on the contrary it perfectly fits to the present situation of pandemic.

As for the second question (2), according to the opinion of most scholars and practitioners, the offence can be established by both a commissive conduct or a failure to act; so interpreting the reference to the "spreading of pathogenic germs" in a way does not require a commissive conduct necessarily. This reading draws a much wider scope for this offence, since it can be established following a failure to act in a way that would have contained the circulation of the virus by who holds a warranty position: competent public authorities; elderly housing Directors; employers[63]. Here the crucial question arises about the need for a correct definition of the scope of the "warranty position" *(posizione di garanzia*"), which according to Italian criminal law is an essential element for responsibility of failure to act, in order to avoid any automatic imputation of criminal responsibility to the holder of the same[64]. However, taking the above-mentioned categories of people just apart, the offence (as a failure to act) is quite hard to be established. Individual responsibility cannot rest on the assumption that provisions establishing all the various measures of containment give birth to a warranty position for any individual with respect to him/herself as a "source" of danger (of the further spreading of the disease). Indeed, the violation of the containment measures cannot automatically imply the violation of the warranty position to avoid the spreading of the pathogenic germs, since it is necessary to assess also the collective dimension and the social contacts triggering the concrete danger of a further spreading of the virus. Following these arguments, the individual conduct of epidemic – as a failure to adopt the necessary measures to stop or contain the circulation of the virus – could be only established with respect to an individual having been identified as positive to COVID-19 (through a molecular test) and having circulated and been in contact with other people.

As for the third question (3), it is to be preliminarily outlined that according to the majority of scholars, the material element of the offence of epidemic relies, in addition to the conduct, on a twofold consequence of the conduct itself: on the one side, the actual damage of having transmitted the infection (at least) to another person; on the other, the (additional) concrete risk of a further spreading of the virus, implying the assessment by the judge of the diffusive nature of the disease. While this last requirement is far from being problematic in the present case of contagion of COVID-19 looking at the critical numbers of infected (and dead) people,

---

63 One has also to consider that other forms of individual responsibility with respect to the offence of epidemic may arise by the interplay with general provisions about conspiracy/participation to the offence (by a negligent conduct, article 113 ICC. This widening of the scope of individual responsibility is to be handled very carefully.

64 M.Scoletta *Covid, risorse scarse e profili di responsabilità da reto degli enti sanitari*, in G. Lo Sappio (edited by), *Scelte tragiche, Quaderni del Dipartimento jonico*, 2021, p. 198 ff.

the assessment of the fact that the individual conduct has "caused" the transmission of the virus recalls the crucial question of establishing the causal link between a single human conduct and a 'macro-event' where different concurring 'preconditions' of the same occur. Difficulties arise especially with respect to the assessment of the link of causality as it concerns the component of concrete danger (additional to the single contagion), that is to say the assessment about whether the conduct has concretely contributed to the progressing or the improvement of the strength of the disease. On this point, epidemiological analysis could be of great help, at least in theory, while in practice their relevance is to be largely reduced because of the difficulty to agree on a solid methodology concerning the choice of data to be analyzed, as well as the standards to compare. Moreover, many difficulties arise from the way through which the transmission has been realized, and then the individual conduct (deserving the punishment), because of scientists' diversity of positions on the capacity of transmission of the infection of the various materials (plastic, metal, paper, clothes, etc.), or the duration of the incubation period (from 3 up to 14 days), or even the maximum distance for the transmission (1, one and half or two meters). So that the tracing of contagion, whenever possible, will hardly be conclusive to establish individual responsibility "beyond any reasonable doubt".

It follows that a causality link with the development or the strengthening of the contagion is finally impossible to prove (so called, *probatio diabolica*) with respect to individual conduct in general, while it could be imagined with individual conduct of special categories of people whose decisions have a large-scale effect, such as the competent Public Authorities or the Employer (with respect to the workplace He/She is responsible for). With respect to these people, when assessing their personal responsibility, the focus needs to be put on the concrete application of standards and criteria to establish a negligent behavior, and the scope of the warranty position on them, in case of failure to act (on this point *see* paragraph 2.3 below).

As for the argument that, looking at the situation of the on-going epidemic, the individual conduct, though contributing to the spreading and circulation of the virus, did not really "cause", it is considered to be easily solved. Indeed, this very restrictive reading would collide with the nature of the epidemic itself, relying on the circulation and spreading of the virus, and not on the initial 'triggering' of the same exclusively.

2. *The criminal offences related to forgery and the use of false documents.*

All the legal texts dealing with the containment measures affecting the freedom of circulation refer also to special situations (expressly listed in the same legal texts) allowing to derogate from the general restrictions to mobility. It is on the individual to prove the fact of being in presence of one of the situations listed. However, no special criminal provisions have been introduced with respect to the case of false declarations. Neither the Law Decrees expressly refer to any of the existing provisions in the criminal code (articles 483 ICC ff.).

It is the Directive no. 14606, issued by the Ministry of Interiors on the 8th March 2020 and addressed to competent public authorities (*Prefetti*), that statues that one may comply with the requirement to prove to be in one of the situations of derogation by producing a "self-certification", as provided for in articles 46 and 47 of the Decree of the President of the Republic of 28 December 2000, n. 445 (also by filling the forms provided for by the Police or other Controlling Public Force).

Following this directive, any false declaration in the form can give rise to the offense of forgery, or the offence of false declaration to a public official (article 495 ICC), together with the special offence in article 76 of the Decree of the President of the Republic nr 445/2000.

However, evident criticalities arise from this conclusion, especially with respect to the evident risk of an application by analogy of the above-mentioned criminal provisions.

Concerning article 483 ICC, since it is not a legal provision, nor an administrative act with effects for all citizens to refer to the "self-certification" with respect to the statement about the reasons justifying the individual mobility – but a text internal to the administration exclusively, with no effects on individuals –, in the opinion of some scholars[65], false declarations in the form about the reasons of mobility cannot be qualified as "self-certification" that can only concern data that can be obtained also by consulting the public registries or already at the disposal of the public administration. Consequently, false declarations about the reasons put to justify the mobility from home cannot be assumed as falling in the scope of the criminal offenses in articles 76 of the Decree of the President of

65 On this issue, *see* A.F Masiero, *Reati di falso e autocertificazione durante l'emergenza COVID-19: tra ricerca dell'effettività e simbolismo*, Sistema penale, 2021, p. 137 ff.; M. Pelissero *Covid 19 e diritto penale pandemico. Delitti contro la fede pubblica, epidemia e delitti contro la persona alla prova dell'emergenza sanitaria*, Rivista italiana di diritto e procedura penale, 2020, p. 537 ff.

the Republic 445/2000 and 483 ICC. A different view is expressed by some other Scholars arguing on the wording of article 47 of the Decree of the President of the Republic no. 445/2000, that in paragraph 3, refers to "any situation, personal qualities and facts not covered by article 46 [...]". The combined reading of articles 47, paragraph 3, and 76 of the Decree of the President of the Republic could lead to consider the false declaration in the form as falling in the scope of the offence in article 483 ICC.

However, well-established jurisprudence only considers article 483 ICC as applicable when the document can be qualified as an "official document", and objective facts are at stake, while mere intentions are not relevant. Consequently, false declarations in the form about the reason allowing the mobility would not be relevant to establish the offence in article 483 ICC. On this point, a clear position by the Supreme Court is highly desirable. At present, it is interesting to mention the position taken by a judge responsible for the investigations (Giudice per le indagini preliminari del Tribunale di Milano), who has confirmed the exclusion of the offence in case of false declaration about the reason of the mobility, and also about the place of destination. On the contrary, article 483 ICC could apply with respect to indication of the place of origin/departure, to be considered as an "objective fact" and not a mere intention.

Concerning article 495 ICC, dealing with false declarations to a public official, according to the exact wording of the provision, only false statements about "personal identity, status and own or other qualities" may give rise to criminal responsibility. Following that, according to the opinion of some scholars only false declaration about the fact of being addressed by an obligation of quarantine, or of not being positive to Covid may be covered by the wording of article 495 ICC when referring to "other qualities". However, this reading is far from convincing the unanimity or even the majority of criminal law Scholars.

A crucial question has arisen since in its last version the form circulated from the Government expressly referred also to article 495 ICC in case of false declarations with respect to any of the data in the form. Such a reference unduly qualifies as a criminal offence a 'mere' violation of the measure (that is of administrative nature), at least for information other that the ones related to personal identity, status or other personal or others qualities. According to the opinion of some scholars, out of the situations covered by article 495 ICC, that is to say declarations concerning identity, status or other qualities, such a solution can even affect the principle of *nemo tenetur se detegere*, though it essentially applies in the context of the proceedings.

IV. *Criticalities about the 'classical' offences of negligent homicide and personal injuries by negligence*

Very sensitive questions have arisen with respect to the assessment of criminal responsibility of some categories of people – medical and other health workers, elderly residence directors, employers, competent public authorities – in case of death or serious injuries as a consequence of COVID-19. More precisely, the criminal justice system is shaken up by the many different inputs when trying to channel in the assessment of criminal responsibility the two main dynamics of the request for the necessary "indulgence" when assessing criminal responsibility of people on the front line in the containment of the contagion, on the one side, and the need to recognize such a responsibility whenever the fatal consequence could have been avoided if the person would have acted following the right standards of diligence and prudence, as indicated by the well-established good practices and the best scientific literature.

Indeed, significant criticalities have been detected with respect to the 'general' provision in article 590-*sexies* of the ICC (introduced by Law n. 24 adopted on the 8th of March 2012), dealing with non-intentional homicide or injury by health workers[66], when focusing especially on the criteria to be followed in order to assess the link of causality and the negligent behavior in the special circumstances of the COVID-19.

Concerning the question about the assessment of the link of causality, the idea has been put to refer to the so-called "epidemiological causality"[67], which however appears to be quite problematic when assessing individual criminal responsibility. Indeed, the assessment of the link of causality cannot but be left to the discretion of the judiciary – and in particular the discretion to be employed when considering the single concrete facts in a context where well-established knowledge about causality does not simply exist, and we experience a variety of concurrent "causes" of the contagion, leading usually to the exclusion of criminal responsibility as the

---

66 Article 590-*sexies* ICC:
"*If the conducts relevant under articles 589 and 590 ICC have been performed within the framework of healthcare activities, the punishments there established are applied, apart from what established in the second paragraph.*
In case the event has happened because of malpractice, the author has not to be punished if he has respected the guidelines established and published under the law, or, if there are not guidelines, the best practices, as long as they are suitable for the case at stake".

67 M.G Margano, *Brevi note sulla prova della causalità nel contagio da Covid 19*, Cassazione penale, 2020, p. 3106 ff.

consequence of the impossibility to conclude that the objective element of the offence (conduct plus event plus the causality link between the two) can be established "beyond any reasonable doubt".

As for the qualification of the conduct as negligent, the question has arisen of the possible function to be played by the many detailed measures of containment introduced by the special Covid legislation (that were not adopted following the provision in article 590-*sexies* referring to "the (relevant)guiding lines selected and published according to the law", or "the good practices " in the medical sector, and especially the question whether and when they can be considered as exhaustive, and then excluding the reference to the general standards to establish negligence or not (specific negligence v. general negligence).

More precisely, as it was stressed by some Scholars and practitioners, the possibility for the health workers, all along the pandemic, to rely on the provision in article *590-sexies,* comma 2, to achieve the exclusion of his/her criminal liability, would have resulted being extremely difficult, according to the strict interpretation of the same provision by the Supreme Court's Grand Chamber (Corte di Cassazione, Sez. U, n. 8770, 21/12/2017, case Mariotti,). In this decision, the Court stated that healthcare workers cannot be held liable under article 589 and 590 ICC in case of: a) non-serious malpractice referred to the execution; b) compliance with the recognized guidelines and best practices; c) previous evaluation of the adequacy of the recommendation of the guide-lines in the concrete case.

Consequently, such a restricted area of unpunished unintentional conduct does not fit with the scenario of a new virus and the relevant state of emergency in which healthcare workers have been called to work (above all, during the first phase of the pandemic where experimental and off-label drugs have been used, also keeping in mind the direct liability of medical doctors and the institute of the informed consent.

Against this background, an intense discussion was launched since the very beginning of the spreading of the virus (March-July 2020), on the need for a "legal shield" especially for conducts of the category of health workers, in addition to the provision in article 54 ICC establishing the "necessity" as a general justification from criminal responsibility. Indeed, article 54 ICC being applicable only to illicit conduct, its scope of application in the situation of Covid appears to be quite limited. It can apply, for instance with respect to the conduct of the health worker that found him/herself in a situation of "conflict of duties", since, He/She had decided to use the unique ventilator at his/her disposal for one of the more patients arriving at the hospital, so provoking the death of the others. On the contrary, the state of necessity cannot cover those situations where, because of the extreme stress following the overburdening of hospitals, the worker has committed a little error which has nevertheless provoked death or personal injuries[68].

Proposals for the introduction of special grounds to exclude criminal responsibility of health workers for negligent homicide or serious personal injuries have been put by some members of the Parliament from different political parties in the framework of the "conversion" procedure[69] of the Law Decree nr 18, adopted on 17th March 2020 (the so called Decree "*Cura Italia*")[70].

However, none of these proposals has been accepted finally by the Parliament (Law No. 27, adopted on 24 April 2020), while provoking an ignited debate also because they were suspected of aiming at introducing an excuse having an extremely large scope (excluding not only criminal responsibility but also the civil one and even responsibility for financial losses) to be then extended also to other categories, and especially to the heads of the competent public administration offices.

Apart from this last consideration, many criticisms have been expressed by scholars and practitioners about the approach and the wording of the proposals, and even before that, about the need for such provisions. In par-

68 For a deep analysis on this point, *see* the various contributions in G.Losappio, (ed), *Scelte tragiche*, *supra*.

69 According to article 77 of the Italian Constitution, the Law Decrees adopted by the Government "in case of necessity and urgency" are considered as having no effects since their adoption, unless they are "converted" in a law of the Parliament within 60 days of their entry into force.

70 One of the main proposals discussed (drafted by On. Mallegni and Sicari): stays: "*1-bis. Per tutta la durata dell'emergenza epidemiologica da COVID-19 di cui al decreto-legge 23 febbraio 2020, n. 6 e ai provvedimenti attuativi, l'esercente una professione sanitaria o il soggetto abilitato a norma dell'articolo 102 del decreto-legge 17 marzo 2020, n. 18, non è punibile per i reati di cui agli articoli 589 e 590 del codice penale quando il profilo di colpa sia determinato da indisponibilità di mezzi o il soggetto abbia agito in situazione di urgenza allo scopo di salvaguardare la vita o l'integrità del paziente. Nei casi contemplati dal precedente periodo, qualora l'evento si sia verificato a causa di imperizia, in deroga a quanto previsto dall'articolo 590-sexies, secondo comma, del codice penale, la punibilità è sempre esclusa*". A second proposal (by On. Marcucci and others) was drafted as follows: "*3. Fermo quanto previsto dall'articolo 590-sexies del codice penale, per tutti gli eventi avversi che si siano verificati od abbiano trovato causa durante l'emergenza epidemiologica COVID-19 di cui alla delibera del Consiglio dei ministri del 31 gennaio 2020, la punibilità penale è limitata ai soli casi di colpa grave. La colpa si considera grave unicamente laddove consista nella macroscopica e ingiustificata violazione dei principi basilari che regolano la professione sanitaria o dei protocolli o programmi emergenziali eventualmente predisposti per fronteggiare la situazione in essere, tenuto conto di quanto stabilito dal comma 2.*"

ticular, while recognizing the emergency situation as a special burden and an exceptional stress especially for health workers, the doubts expressed deal essentially with the_risk of systemic derogations that could also imply radical changes with respect to the general categories of criminal law. According to this view, the introduction of special provisions addressing criminal responsibility of health workers in the context of COVID-19 pandemic would result in further confusing the quite recent (and still debated) general regulation of health workers criminal responsibility (enshrined in article 590-*sexies)* while being able to cover only very few situations. Moreover, in addition to the technical drafting difficulties, the idea of a "shield" to protect the conduct of some categories of people would also appear to be problematic since it clearly relies on the assumption that the criminal law system is unable to face the present situation – simply because of its exceptional gravity and the emergency it has followed – and the many proceedings that can be expected involving health workers (especially but not exclusively). Then there is the idea that the system can only face "ordinary" situations. Furthermore, according to some Scholars, the supposed need for a shield hides somehow the idea that these people have acted in a kind of generalized negligence or at least a widespread shallowness, while hindering at the same time the possibility of properly identifying and punishing conduct that results being patently negligent[71].

V. *The special provisions dealing with health workers' criminal responsibility in the context of COVID-19 epidemic.*

Following the solicitations especially coming from practitioners and professional associations, while taking into consideration the criticism expressed by some Scholars, Italian legislature finally came up with the introduction of two new provisions, Articles 3 and *3-bis* of the Law Decree n. 44/2021, then converted in law n. 76/2021, the first dealing with criminal liability of health workers in charge of vaccine administration; the second aiming at establishing special criteria to assess individual responsibility of health workers for non-intentional homicide and injury in the context of COVID-19 pandemic.

The two favorable norms, both temporary and characterized by the logic of the emergency, correspond to two different legal models to limit the healthcare workers' liability. Article 3, concerning the sole administration

71 F.Palazzo, *Pandemia e responsabilità colposa*, Sistema penale, 2020.

of vaccine, fully relieves criminal liability (it has been defined as a "liability lockdown"). Article 3bis concerns all the healthcare activities related to the pandemic and reshapes the border of criminal liability, limiting it only to serious negligence.

Both provisions establish a more lenient regime of criminal responsibility than art. *590-sexies,* par. 2, so that they will apply retroactively (to facts committed before the entry into force of the law n. 76/2021, but after the declaration of the state of emergency), following the *favor rei* principle.

Then, what is now at stake is the very nature of these forms of exclusion of individual responsibility, and the consequences which follow.

As for the exclusion of criminal responsibility of the healthcare workers charged with anti- COVID-19 vaccination, requiring that the death or injury, occurred during the vaccination campaign, be the consequence of the administration of the vaccine in a way complying with the data provided in the trade license released by the relevant authorities and in the vaccination guidelines published on the Ministry of Health website, the position taken by the Supreme Court seems to be in favor of qualifying this situation as a ground for excluding the *mens rea* (applying also in the case that the author was mistaken in assuming that He/She was complying with the official indications about the administration of the vaccine) that implies the existence of a causal link between the inoculation and the death or damages suffered, apart from any unintentional blame (even if serious) in case all the other indications have been observed[72].

As for the scope of application, the provision expressly refers to the "administration" of the vaccine. However, the inoculation (i.e. a mere injection) could hardly cause damage relevant under a Criminal Law perspective. Quite the opposite, the procedure preceding the inoculation is more sensitive, dealing with the activity of *triage,* on the one side, and the collection of the informed consent of the patient about possible negative side effects of the same, on the other. It is at this stage that the new provision seems to achieve its goal, whenever the death or injury is linked to the administration of the vaccine, though it was realised following the indications by the producer. The express reference in the rubric to the health workers (*"responsabilità sanitaria"*) appears to keep the possibility out to apply this provision as a ground to exclude the responsibility of all the categories of people of the "vaccine supply chain": from the producer

---

72 Corte di Cassazione, Ufficio del Massimario, Relazione su novità normativa, n. 35/2021.

to the authorities who authorized the usage and established the procedures (i.e. kind of vaccine, age limit, and so on).

As for the provision dealing with *negligent homicide and personal injuries by negligence* in the context of the COVID-19 pandemic, it results in a ground for excluding criminal responsibility of_health workers (in the period of Covid 19 pandemic, as established by Government's official statement) whenever their conduct, having produced the death or injury, is realised by "non serious" negligence. It is worth mentioning the effort of the legislature to guide the judge when assessing whether in a concrete case negligence can be considered to be serious or not, by referring in the same legal text to elements of the factual situation, and stating that: "For the purposes of evaluating the culpability's level, the judge has to keep in mind, between the factors able to exclude the seriousness, the scarcity of scientific knowledge on the Covid desease and the relevant treatment, and the scarcity of human and material resources available in relation to the amount of patients, besides the lower level of experience and technical skills of the healthcare workers not specialised in facing the pandemic".

Unlike the provision dealing with the responsibility in case of vaccine administration, which implies that lack of any form of negligence (since it requires that the vaccine be administrated in compliance with the precautionary indications of the producer), the provision in article *3-bis*, establishing that only the serious negligence hypothesis has to be punished, as ruled in the case law too for cases of emergency or very complicated cases under the rule of article 2236, Italian Civil Code, should be applied only in cases of slight negligence, and not in cases where there is no negligence at all, that are relevant under article 43 co. 3 ICC. On the other side, such a limitation of the healthcare workers' liability to slight negligence cases allows the legal protection in cases of fraud or serious negligence (that cannot be justified neither in the emergency scenario). This rule does not apply to the hypothesis of unintentional epidemic (article 438 and 452 ICC). Tough, this offence can be applied only in specific cases, given that it raises some issues on the concrete causal link and on the alternative legal behavior side; as it was shown in paragraph 2.3.1 above.

It is worth stressing the reference made to the fact that the offence is to be originated in the context of the COVID-19 pandemic ("che trovano causa nella situazione di emergenza"). This expression is to be kept distinguished from the "state of emergency" strictly referring to the official statement of the Government. By doing so, the Italian legislature in 2021 has meant to avoid the mere chronological limit to the epidemic period, so that, in order to exclude the criminal responsibility of the health workers, it is not required that the conduct occurred during the lapse of time covered by the declaration from the Government of the state of emergency, but they have to rely on a situation of "urgency", in the sense of a situation of "hurry" that may have affected the ordinary process leading to the conduct; something which results being perfectly in line with the rationale of the provision of this ground for excluding criminal responsibility. Indeed, this wording allows to cover not only facts connected to Covid-related pathologies, but facts concerning non Covid-related pathologies, provided that these facts occurred (or were aggravated) because of the lowering of the level of medical assistance following the priority given to the need to fight against the COVID-19 pandemic. Finally, in this perspective, the provision focuses on the impact of the situation of emergency on the health workers ordinary *modus operandi*, that has to be taken into consideration when assessing whether the expected diligence was possible to be exercised in the concrete case.

2.6 *Criminal responsibility of the employer*

With respect to criminal responsibility of the employer, the special legal provisions adopted seem to regulate this situation[73]. According to article 29 bis of the Law Decree nr 23 of 8 April 2020 establishing "Obligations on the employers to protect from the risk of contagion from Covid 19", the employers "*comply*" with the general obligation in article 2087 of the civil code – requiring the head of business to adopt all the necessary measures according to the nature of the activity, and also the experience and the technique, in order to protect physical integrity and moral personality of the workers – by adopting all the measures of containment indicated in the Protocol concluded by the Government and the social partners on 24th April 2020 (including the amendments and integrations covered by article 1, para. 4, of the Law Decree 16th May 2020). The various measures of containment, then, adopted at national and/or local level, and also the provisions established in the framework of the agreements concluded between management and labor (the two parties of the industry), as suggested by the Law Decree 19/2020, and then established as mandatory for the reopening of all the activities following the easing of the lockdown by article 1, para. 14, of the Law-Decree 33/2020, are considered as concrete application in the situation of the pandemic of the general obligation

73 V.Valentini, *Organizzazione del lavoro e responsabilità punitivo-penali da contagio: a che punto siamo?*, Archivio penale, 2021, p. 2 ff.

established in article 2087 of the civil code. More precisely, according to article 1, para. 15, of the Law Decree no. 33/2020, the set of the precautionary measures provided for in the safety protocols – including also measures requiring a revision of the whole organization of the activities – is to be taken as the basis to assess the negligent nature of the employer's conduct. According to the prevailing practitioners' opinion, the obligation on the employer to revise, when necessary, the whole organization of the activities also implies the obligation to revise the so-called "Risk Assessment Document" and updating it with respect to the specific risks of contagion arising in the concerned sector of activity. This reading is supported also by the wording (as well as the well-established jurisprudence) of articles 2 and 28 of the law-decree nr. 81/2008 referring to a "global evaluation" of any risk for the health and safety of the workers and the identification of all the necessary measures to prevent such risks, and also provide with a planning of measures aimed at improving the level of workers' health and safety in the medium and long term.

Following that, the general obligation in article 2087 of the civil code would come at stake 'only' when: a) the employer is confronted with a different risk (than contagion for Covid); b) further well-established knowledge about infection with COVID-19 shows the need for different measures to be adopted in order to contain the spread in the workplace.

Having said that, the risk nevertheless remains of an obligation to comply with 'unrealistic' general standards of diligence whenever the relevant measure of containment results to be too wide or not perfectly fitting with the concrete case.

D. *The impact of the coronavirus crisis on criminal proceedings and punishment*

The coronavirus crisis has deeply affected the administration of criminal justice. On the one hand, it has produced effects on hearings, mainly in relation to their organization – turning most of them into remote hearings – and on their length- suspending the statute of limitation. On the other hand, it has brought some debates around punishment and prison.

I. Remote Justice

Criminal law proceedings have been rearranged and accommodated to the needs arising from COVID-19[74]. In this context, IT played a leading role: a computerization process of criminal proceedings has been implemented to face the crisis, indeed[75].

However, remote hearings jeopardize some fundamental principles of the Italian criminal procedure, such as the immediacy and the oral development of the proceedings[76], possibly having an impact on the way evidence is admitted into the proceedings and shaped before the Court by means of cross-examination. In this context, the risk of obtaining a hurried justice seems too high to be justified, even in the name of the pandemic[77]. Although remote justice could produce positive effects in terms of the efficiency of the system and allowed justice to function during the pandemic, it has to be kept in mind that in-person hearings have been structured to guarantee the best possible "search for the truth", in respect of the parties' rights. The system can be implemented, of course, but its fundamental principles cannot be waived.

---

74 Article 83 of decree no. 18 of 2020 has been the first source of law addressing the reorganization of the judicial system to face the Coronavirus crisis.

75 The computerization process has already had a concrete impact on some steps of the proceedings, such as summons and filings, which have been switched from hard papers to digital files. Furthermore, given that in-person hearings attendance (and some related activities, such as questioning witnesses) has been no longer considered safe, also considering the limited capacity of the courtrooms, remote hearings have been arranged.
Hopefully, such a computerization could also lead to positive results in terms of efficiency. On this future perspective, *see* L.Giordano *Il processo penale a distanza ai tempi del Coronavirus*, Dir. pen. proc., 2020, p. 920; and F. Tripodi *Il processo penale post-Covid: rispettare la Costituzione, facendo di necessità (qualche) virtù*, Forum di Quaderni Costituzionali, no. 2/2020, p. 296 available on www.forumcostituzionale.it.

76 On this critical issue *see* E.Amodio, E.M Cataliano, *La resa della giustizia penale di fronte alla bufera del contagio*, Sistema Penale no. 5/2020, p. 267, available on www.sistemapenale.it; and M. Daniele, *l'immediatezza in crisi. Mutazioni pericolose ed anticorpi accusatori*, Sistema Penale, 15 febbraio 2021; available on www.sistemapenale.it.

77 F. Vergine, G. Micheli, *Emergenza epidemiologica da COVID-19, efficienza e processo penale*, Il Processo, no. 3/2020, p. 843.
The risk of lowering the criminal proceedings' guarantees in the attempt of preventing the spread of the virus is increased by the nonuniform application of the measures between Courts. *See* G.Spanger, *Il processo penale al tempo del COVID-19*, Studium Iuris, no. 12/2020, p. 1461.

Be that as it may, the measures adopted[78] have guaranteed the administration of justice during the pandemic. Among the other measures[79] that have to be mentioned are, at least, the arrangement of remote hearings for the cases that could not be postponed[80], the deferral of the hearings that could be postponed (suspending the statute of limitation as well, as discussed below in paragraph 3.2 below), the possibility for imprisoned people to remotely attend the hearings by means of videoconferences specifically regulated by the Ministry of Justice, and the online filing of documents, briefs and instances, allowed by articles 23 and 24 of Decree no. 137 of 2020[81].

---

78 An in-depth analysis of these measures is provided by G.Castiglia, *Udienze e termini processuale penale in regime di pandemia di COVID-19*, Sistema Penale, no. 5/2020, p. 325, available on www.sistemapenale.it; and L.Giordano *supra.*

79 In addition to the ones listed, the following has to be mentioned, at least. It has been possible to held by means of videoconference questionings under article 294 of the Italian Criminal Procedure Code (according to which the person subject to the application of a precautionary measure has to be interrogated immediately and, in any case, within 5 days from the application of the measure), regulated by the same protocols mentioned above. On the suspension of this strict period of time *see* Supreme Court of Cassation, no. 28936 of 2020. According with the decision at stake, the suspension provided by article 83 of decree no. 18/2020 (on which *see* paragraph 3.2. below) is not applicable to questioning under article 294 of the ICPC. For a first comment to this decision *see* V.Gramulia, *Interrogatorio di garanzia e legislazione dell'emergenza COVID-19 (art. 83, co. 2 d.l. n. 18/2020): tra garanzie difensive e tutela della salute collettiva*, Sistema Penale, 17 November 2020, available on www.sistemapenale.it.

80 The activities have been regulated by specific protocols between the Court, the Prosecutor's Office, and the Bar Association, on the basis of decree no. 11 and 18 of 2020. Law no. 27 of 2020, incorporating the decree no. 18 of 2020, has formally recognized the protocols mentioned above, allowing some further hearings to be performed remotely, via videoconference. The scope of application has been limited by decree no. 28 of 2020, however. In particular, final discussion hearings and hearings in which parties' examination are held cannot be performed remotely, unless the parties agree.
For the sake of completeness, the resolution of the Italian Supreme Council of the Magistracy (*Consiglio Superiore della Magistratura, CSM)* has to be mentioned as well. In this resolution, dated 4 November 2020, the Supreme Council provided its judges and prosecutors with some guidelines to deal with the emergency.
On this topic *see*C. Gallo, *Prima lettura delle nuove linee guida del CSM in materia di emergenza Covid (delibera 4.11.2020)*, Giustizia Insieme, 9 November 2020, available on www.giustiziainsieme.it; and C. Gallo, *Emergenza sanitaria e organizzazione degli uffici. Il ruolo dell'autogoverno*, Giustizia Insieme, 3 November 2020, available on www.giustiziainsieme.it.

81 It can happen by means of certified emails or through a new online portal committed to remote criminal proceedings. See M.Agostini, M. Petrini, *Decreto legge*

II. The suspension of the statute of limitation

Strictly related to the deferral of hearings due to the pandemic is the suspension of the statute of limitation.

Due to the difficulties the judicial system has faced in relation to the coronavirus crisis (for an overview on the need of reorganizing hearings and all the other activities *see* paragraph 3.1 above), article 83 of the decree no. 18 of 2020 has suspended the statute of limitation with the aim of preserving pending criminal proceedings[82]. The suspension has been based on article 159 of the Italian Criminal Code, according to which particular provisions[83] can establish the suspension in addition to the other reasons to suspend, as specifically listed.

The suspension of the statute of limitation collided with two main principles: the right to trial within reasonable time and the principle of non-retroactivity of unfavorable criminal laws.

If the first issue could easily be solved in the light of the exceptional crisis arising from the pandemic, some thoughts should be shared to figure the second issue out. Indeed, suspending the statute of limitation, thus extending the length of the proceedings, could produce unfavorable effects on the people subject to the investigations/trials in relation to facts

---

Ristori, disposizioni emergenziali per l'esercizio delle attività giurisdizionale, Giustizia Insieme, 30 October 2020, available on www.giustiziainsieme.it; and M.Bozzaorte, *Decreto legge Ristori, il deposito telematico degli atti penali: significative novità e sconsolanti conferme*, Giustizia Insieme, 30 October 2020, available on www.giustiziainsieme.it.

Nevertheless, the Supreme Court of Cassation has limited the scope of application of the provision at stake. For a first comment to this decision (no. 32566 of 2020) *see* L.Agostino *Art. 24 del decreto "ristori": l'interpretazione restrittiva della Cassazione in tema di deposito telematico degli atti durante il periodo emergenziale*, Sistema Penale, 2 December 2020, available on www.sistemapenale.it.

82 Article 83 of the above-mentioned decree originally established that the suspension period had to be applied since the 9th of March 2020 until: i) the 11th of May 2020, for proceedings whose hearings have been set later than the 11th of May (so called "first phase of postponement"); ii) the 30th of June 2020, for proceedings whose hearings have been set later than the 30th of June (so called "second phase of postponement"); iii) the 31st of December 2020, for proceedings pending before the Supreme Court of Cassation and fulfilling certain requirements.
The provision was later amended and prorogated by article 36 of law decree no. 23/2020, converted into law by law no. 40/2020.

83 It is worth mentioning that this is not the first time that unpredictable situations led to the suspension of the statute of limitation. For example, it happened in 2009, due to the terrible earthquake that shook the Italian Region Abruzzo.

performed before the suspension was provided. Therefore, the suspension may be inconsistent with the principle of non-retroactivity of unfavorable criminal laws regulated under article 25 and 117 of the Italian Constitution in relation to article 7 of the ECHR and article 2 of the Italian Criminal Code.

Nevertheless, suspending the statute of limitation appears a reasonable and concrete solution to the delay the legal system was (and is still) subject to because of the coronavirus outbreak. Hence, the suspension aims at preserving the regular development of pending proceedings and, as a consequence, it is supposed to be applied retroactively.

Despite this concrete and solid argument, the theoretical outlook may suggest a different conclusion, consistent with the principle of non-retroactivity. According to case law[84], indeed, the statute of limitation is a substantial rather than a procedural legal institute: hence, it is strictly bound to the non-retroactivity principle[85].

The matter at stake was addressed by the Italian Constitutional Court on the 18th of November 2020 with the decision no. 278. The decision of the Court clearly stated that the suspension under the Decrees no. 18 and 23 of 2020 is not inconsistent with the non-retroactivity principle nor with the supranational principles at stake.

In a nutshell, the Court[86] has steadily restated the principle of non-retroactivity of unfavorable criminal laws ("*it represents an unconditioned*

---

84 Between the others, Constitutional Court no. 393 of 2006; Constitutional Court no. 115 of 2018 and Court of Cassation no. 9494 of 2018 (in the context of the so called "Taricco saga")

85 For an incisive overview on the statute of limitation's nature and on the arguments and interests at stake, *see* G.L Gatta "*Lockdown" della giustizia penale, sospensione della prescrizione del reato e principio di irretroattività: un cortocircuito*, Sistema Penale, 4 May 2020, available on www.sistemapenale.it; G.L Gatta, *Il corso della giustizia e il corso della prescrizione del reato durante l'emergenza COVID-19*, Sistema Penale, 4 May 2020, available on www.sistemapenale.it; and R. Bartoli, *Irretroattività e prescrizione: proposta di una soluzione in attesa della Corte costituzionale*, Sistema Penale, 12 October 2020, available on www.sistemapenale.it.

86 For a complete comment on the decision, *see* M. Montempelli, *Emergenza COVID-19 e ragionevole durata del processo penale*, Sistema Penale, 13 January 2021, available on www.sistemapenale.it; G.M Flick, *Emergenza e sospensione della prescrizione: una scelta problematica della corte costituzionale*, Cassazione Penale, no. 1/2021, p. 44; G.L Gatta, *Emergenza Covid e sospensione della prescrizione del reato: la Consulta fa leva sull'art. 159 c.p. per escludere la violazione del principio di irretroattività ribadendo al contempo la natura sostanziale della prescrizione, coperta dalla garanzia dell'art. 25, co. 2 Cost.*, Sistema Penale, 26 December 2020, available on www.sistemapenale.it; and R.Bartoli, *Con una finta la consulta aggira il problema*

value, not subject to any balance with other values") as well as the substantial nature of the statute of limitation, hence being subject to the non-retroactivity principle. After that, the Court has stated that the suspension provided under article 83 of the decree is a general hypothesis of suspension for needs of public health and that the suspension there provided has to be included within the range of article 159 of the Italian Criminal Procedure Code (as a specific provision suspending the proceedings, in line with the principle of legality). Given the above, the Court has ruled out the possibility of a violation of the non-retroactivity principle in the light of article 159 ICPC, given that "*at the time the fact was performed, the author knew or was able to know that if the proceeding is suspended under a provision providing for it, the statute of limitation will be suspended as well*"[87].

Therefore, the suspension has to be deemed legitimate and applicable to the proceedings regarding facts performed before the decrees provided for the suspension. Furthermore, the Court has acknowledged that the suspension could have a negative impact on people under investigation/indicted people, but it also stated that it affects in the same way even the other parties of the proceedings, including the victims.

A strongly related matter has been later addressed by the United Section of the Supreme Court of Cassation. The question concerned the suspension of the proceedings pending before the Supreme Court of Cassation. The United Section was required to establish whether the suspension has to be applied either exclusively to the proceedings filed to the Court Office within the range of time established (from the 9th of March to the 30th of June) or to all the proceedings pending during that period of time. On the 26th of November 2020 the Supreme Court ruled that the suspension has to be applied exclusively to the proceedings pending and filed within the prescribed range of time,[88] without prejudice to the other provisions

---

della irretroattività/retroattività della sospensione della prescrizione connessa al Covid, Sistema penale, 8 February 2021, available on www.sistemapenale.it.

87 This last argument raises some issued. Indeed, if it is true that article 159 ICPC providing for suspension was pre-existent, it is also true that the specific hypothesis of suspension due to the pandemic was a completely new scenario. Given that it was not possible to neither imagine this scenario before the pandemic outbreak, at the time the facts were performed, the Court reasoning should have been more focused on retroactivity/non retroactivity of this specific hypothesis, instead of simply reconduct it into article 159 ICPC. *See* R.Bartoli *Con una finta la consulta aggira il problema della irretroattività/retroattività della sospensione della prescrizione connessa al Covid*, *supra*.

88 For a first comment to the decision, *see F. Lazzari, La decisione delle Sezioni unite sui presupposti per l'operatività della disciplina emergenziale di sospensione della pre-*

of the decree, given that the suspension operated *ex lege* with regard to the proceedings whose hearings were scheduled in the period of time the decree pinpointed.

III. The effect of the coronavirus on imprisonment and release

The coronavirus outbreak has had a strong impact on people that were serving sentences in prison. In addition to the possibility of remotely attending the hearings involving them (on which, *see* paragraph 3.1 above) and to the chance to meet visitors during prison visits, the main issue has been how to keep prisons safe and clean, preventing the virus spread within the premises[89].

The matter is extremely delicate, above all in the light of the situation of overcrowding that affects the Italian premises and of the obsolescence of most of the structures, and it is worth mentioning that same insurrections have broken out within the prisons for this reason, eventually causing the death of some inmates[90].

Four main decrees have attempted to deal with this situation during the pandemic[91]. At the very beginning, isolating the premises by "closing the prisons' doors", seemed to be the best approach to prevent the virus

scrizione nei procedimenti davanti alla Corte di cassazione (informazione provvisoria), Sistema Penale, 30 November 2020, available on www.sistemapenale.it.

89 At the following link, a report on the prisons' condition updated to the coronavirus outbreak, https://sistemapenale.it/pdf_contenuti/1599505938_xvi-rapporto-antigone-carcere-italia-fase-2-covid.pdf.

90 For a general outlook, *see E.Dolcini, Carcere e COVID-19: una cronistora dal decreto 'cura Italia' al 'decreto ristori'*, Rivista italiana di diritto e procedura penale, no. 1/2021, p. 3; G.L Gatta, *Carcere e coronavirus: che fare?*, Sistema Penale, 12 March 2020, available on www.sistemapenale.it.
The topic is extremely sensitive both under a political and social point of view, affecting people living inside and outside prisons, as the constant interest of the National Authority for imprisoned people has shown.

91 Between the others, the main sources have been: decree no. 18 of 2020, followed by decrees no. 28 and 29 of 2020 and decree no. 56 of 2021. G. L Gatta, *Emergenza COVID-19. Il testo del decreto "cura Italia": detenzione domiciliare (con braccialetto elettronico) per pene anche residue non superiori a 18 mesi (fino al 30 giugno), licenze straordinarie per i semiliberi e rinvio delle udienze dopo il 15 aprile (salve eccezioni)*, Sistema Penale, 4 May 2020, available on www.sistemapenale.it. For a comment to the measures, *see* also E.Dolcini, G.L Gatta, *Carcere, coronavirus, decreto 'cura Italia': a mali estremi, timidi rimedi*, Sistema Penale, 20 March 2020, available on www.sistemapenale.it.

from going inside. In this context, visits have been switched into remote meetings, voluntary work has been limited as well as all the opportunities for inmates to go out of the premises.

Soon after, a different approach has been adopted, reducing the amount of new people going into the prisons and increasing the amount of imprisoned going out of prisons, using alternative measures to detention and special leaves[92].

Although these measures have been improved and implemented during the pandemic, they have not been able to drastically reduce the overcrowding that affects the Italian prisons[93] and that represented the main risk factor for the spread of the virus[94].

Even these exceptional provisions have been brought to the attention of the Constitutional Court. In particular, the question raised concerned the proceeding to monitor and, in case, withdraw the home detention granted to people serving sentencing for major offences. According with article 2 of the decree no. 29 of 2020, the Court granting home detention in relation to the coronavirus crisis has to check on the measure's grounds fifteen days after granting it and, later on, once a month. In case of a negative evaluation on the reasons to commute the prison sentence into house arrest, the Court has to immediately withdraw the order, without

---

92 Home detention brought some debates around the possibility offered to people convicted for mafia-related crimes and subject to strict detention to serve their sentence out of prison given their health condition. Also in this case, a balance between health conditions, punishment and crime prevention had to be reached. The matter has been later issued by decree no. 28 of 2020, establishing a specific procedure to address the cases involving people convicted for mafia-related crimes. The relevant requirements have been examined by the Italian Constitutional Court (decision no. 245/2020). According with the decision, the requirements settled by law no. 70 of 2020 for mafia-related crimes do not lower the standard concerning the right to health of certain inmates, given that they are the result of the balance between individual health and public order.
On this, *A. Della Bella*, *Emergenza Covid e 41 bis: tra tutela dei diritti fondamentali, esigenza di prevenzione e responsabilità politiche*, Sistema Penale 1 May 2020, available on www.sistemapenale.it.

93 F. Gianfilippi, *Il contrasto all'emergenza epidemiologica in carcere nel D. L. "Ristori"*, Diritto penale e processo, no. 2/2021, p. 190.

94 In this sense, G. Giostra, *Disinnescare in modo sano la bomba-virus nelle carceri*, Sistema Penale, 22 March 2020, available on www.sistemapenale.it, in which the Author complains about the previous missed opportunities to reduce the overcrowding that is the origin of most of the problems affecting the imprisonment system. To contain the transmission of the virus within prisons, the Author suggests reducing the flow of people going into prisons and to improve the flow of people going out of prisons.

properly involving the party's counsel. The Constitutional Court has addressed this point on the 22nd of July[95], returning the file to the judge who raised the question in order to let him check whether the matter was still at stake in the light of law no. 70 of 2020 which converted the above-mentioned decree into law, amending it. Indeed, according to law no. 70, the original article 2 of the decree has been replaced by article 2-*bis*, providing counsels with full access to the files concerning the withdrawal proceeding. For the sake of completeness, it is worth mentioning that a new constitutional question has been raised by the same Court after that the evaluation suggested by the Constitutional Court has been performed. The new question also related to the right of defense in the withdrawal process[96]. The Constitutional Court addressed this second question on the 4th of November 2020 holding the question not founded[97] because the withdrawal procedure was not in contrast with the rights of defense.

Be that as it may, as is often the case with such a sensitive topic, it should be noted that the pandemic could have been a great opportunity to re-think the Italian imprisonment system, finally making detention the last resort, as it should have originally been.

---

95 For a first comment *see* E, Andolfatto, *Un'ordinanza interlocutoria della Consulta sul "decreto antiscarcerazioni"*, Sistema Penale, 1 August 2020, available on www.siste mapenale.it.

96 For a complete outlook on the whole constitutional issue *see* J. Della Torre, *Il Magistrato di sorveglianza di Spoleto non demorde: il "d.l. antiscarcerazioni" di nuovo alla Consulta*, Sistema Penale, 23 September 2020, available on www.sistemapenal e.it.

97 For a short notice on the Court decision *see* F.Lazzeri, *Infondate le questioni di legittimità della disciplina "anti-scarcerazioni" come modificata dalla l. 70/2020*, Sistema Penale, 6 November 2020, available on www.sistemapenale.it; and *La sentenza della Corte costituzionale sulla legittimità della disciplina anti-scarcerazioni adottata nell'emergenza covid (d.l. 29/2020 e l. 70/2020)*, Sistema Penale, 25 November 2022, available on www.sistemapenale.it.

Legal Communitarianism and Pandemic Regulation in Singapore

Li-ann Thio[*]

A. Introduction: From Pandemic Regulation to Endemic Management

Since the first COVID-19 case was detected on 23 January 2020 until the first quarter of 2022, Singapore, has been both lauded and criticised for its approach towards pandemic management. This has been characterised as a "crucible of fire for this generation of Singaporeans,"[1] being primarily a "public health crisis,"[2] coupled with the need to sustain a globally integrated economy and international transport hub, and to mitigate the fears, tensions and fatigues affecting the Asian city-state's population of 5.7 million people.

Singapore's top ranking in Bloomberg's Covid Resilience Ranking in April 2021 did not last, with the advent of the Delta wave variant in May 2021.[3] It plummeted to 39th place by October 2021, hitting peaks of 5000 infections per day. This was disconcerting, given the low fatality rates of just 29 deaths Singapore had known by end 2020. Singapore rebounded to 18th place[4] in December 2021, when the Omicron variant arrived, when it was incrementally opening up its borders to international travel, while maintaining conservative regulatory measures domestically. Health official warnings in early January 2022 that the highly transmissible Omicron wave could entail 15,000 cases a day[5] came to past, with Singapore facing

---

* Ph.D. (Cantab); LL.M. (Harvard Law); B.A. Hons (Oxon); Barrister (G.I.) Provost Chair Professor, National University of Singapore

1 '2022 a 'time of transition' for Singapore, with economic recovery and expansion of travel expected: PM Lee', ChannelNews.Asia.com (CNA), 31 Dec 2021

2 Senior Minister Tharman Shanmugaratnam, 'Learning from crisis', Speech, 2021 Administrative Service Appointment and Promotion Ceremony, 29 March 2021

3 'The rapid rise of the Delta variant and how it is shaping Singapore's Covid-19 fight', CNA.com, 18 June 2021.

4 '19 spots up: Singapore's stellar recovery on Bloomberg's Covid resilience ranking', *The Independent* (Singapore), 23 Dec 2021

5 'Impending Omicron wave could mean up to 15,000 cases a day in Singapore: MOH official', *Today* (Singapore), 5 Jan 2022

hitting a peak of 26000 cases mid-February.[6] As most people had mild symptoms, they were told to recover at home and seek treatment from their primary care physician as needed, [7] reserving hospitals for acute cases. The fear of an overwhelmed healthcare system has consistently driven government efforts to protect both lives and livelihoods.[8]

Originally, when the virus was largely an unknown, the government adopted a 'zero COVID-19' elimination strategy, which focused on containment through contact tracing, social distancing measures, quarantine and treatment; the option of "flattening the infection curve" by "letting the disease burn through the population until herd immunity developed" was rejected, to avoid the prospect of high fatalities in the thousands, especially amongst the vulnerable elderly.[9] The chief goal was to keep the rate of community infections down.[10]

In mid-2021, the government announced a pivot towards 'living with COVID-19', [11] where the virus would be treated as endemic, like influenza, which accounts for 600-800 annual deaths.[12] This was anchored upon the National Vaccination Programme, inaugurated in December 2020, offering free and voluntary vaccinations for all citizens and permanent residents. The focus shifted from 'test, trace, quarantine' to 'test, trace, vaccinate', supplemented by border controls.

As of 18 February 2022, Singapore attained one of the world's highest vaccination rates, with 94% of the eligible population fully vaccinated and 65% boostered. Singapore has had 661,198 in total cases, with 975 total deaths.[13] This shift came with realising the impossibility of entirely stamping out highly infectious variants and thus, given the high vaccination

6 'Daily COVID-19 cases cross 26,000 mark: MOH introduces new measures to reduce strain on healthcare system', CNA.com, 22 Feb 2022

7 'More COVID-19 Omicron patients in S'pore can isolate at home', *Straits Times* (Singapore), 16 Feb 2022.

8 'Singapore in 'more resilient position' due to higher vaccination rate, says PM Lee', *Business Times* (Singapore), 8 Aug 2021.

9 Prime Minister Lee Hsien Loong, Speech, Debate on the motion of thanks to the President, (2 Sept 2020).

10 Darius Lee 'COVID-19 in Singapore: Responsive communitarianism and the legislative approach to the 'most serious crisis; iince Independence', (2020) SJLS 630-664; see also Li-ann Thio, 'Singapore and Pandemic Regulation' Report which discusses pandemic regulation up to December 2020.

11 Gan Kim Yong, Lawrence Wong, Ong Ye Kung, 'Living normally with COVID-19': *Straits Times* 24 June 2021

12 Voo, Lim & Tam, 'Commentary: Does Singapore seem more anxious about death from COVID-19 than from other causes?' CNA.com, 19 Oct 2021.

13 See the MOH website at https://www.moh.gov.sg (visited 25 Feb 2022).

rates, it was time to "trust that the high immunity levels will do their jobs."[14]

In the pandemic's early days, the original plan to keep schools and business running with the necessary precautions was scrapped and a nation-wide 'Circuit Breaker' (CB) or partial lockdown was imposed from 7 April to 1 June 2020. An "elevated set of safe distancing measures"[15] (SDM) sought to reduce social interactions in public and private, in hopes of curbing rising local infection rates. Singapore borders had by then been shut to foreign travel and only essential services, such as providing food and essential health items, were allowed to operate.[16] Work from Home (WFH) became the new norm, and educational institutions shifted to full home-based online learning.

Since then, the government has sought to cautiously implement a calibrated, phased re-opening of the economy and society, navigating between the extremes of total lockdown and removing all restrictions on a 'Freedom Day'. The goal was to remain "nimble" and "able to adapt"[17] to new developments. In the pandemic's first year, three phases of reopening with approximate dates were announced as the operating roadmap, until an effective vaccine was available.[18]

Initially, the liberalisation of control measures was tied to the capacity to perform contact tracing effectively, to ringfence and quarantine the infected or potentially infected. Specifically, the take-up rate for technological innovations developed under the 'Smart Nation' government initiative, such as TraceTogether, a smartphone app. This operates by Bluetooth to identify other nearby phones which have installed the app, tracking when one is in close proximity with other persons, including timestamps. This form of digital contact tracing, introduced in March 2020, reduced the time consumed in the labour intensive process of contact tracing by interviewing patients from 4 days to less than 1.5 days.[19] The government also distributed through community centres a free TraceTogether token,

---

14 'They had the vaccines and a plan to reopen. Instead They Got Cold Feet', *New York Times* 8 Oct 2021

15 MOH, 'Circuit breaker to minimise further spread of COVID-19', 3 April 2020

16 A comprehensive list of 'essential services' is maintained on the Singapore GoBusiness website .

17 'Staying nimble against COVID-19 instead of setting trigger points like case numbers', *Straits Times* 10 Jan 2022

18 MOH, 'End of circuit breaker, phased approach to resuming activities safely' 19 May 2020.

19 Smart Nation Singapore, "Digital contact tracing" at https://www.smartnation.gov.sg/combating-covid-19/digital-contact-tracing.

for those not having a smartphone or who chose not to download the app because of privacy concerns.

Later, reopening was tied to vaccination rates, to minimise "the incidence of severe illness and death."[20] Experts considered a minimal 80% vaccination rate was needed to attain COVID-19 herd immunity.[21] However, the meeting of this target in August 2021 did not immediately see restrictions relaxed. Indeed, restrictions were tightened to slow down transmission rates mere weeks after announcements they would be relaxed, spurred by infection clusters like the July 2021 Jurong Fishery Port cluster. Many were frustrated by these actual or perceived policy flip-flops.[22]

The importance of managing not only the virus but also emotions and the collective psyche posed additional challenges. As Singapore sought to safely reopen society, including progressively increasing quarantine-free international travels without triggering significant loss of life or overwhelming the healthcare system, the Prime Minister (PM) urged Singaporeans to adjust their mindsets and not be "paralysed by fear." Vaccinations had made COVID-19 a manageable endemic disease for the vast majority, except for seniors.[23] Nonetheless, when faced with infection surges, the choice to scale back the easing of safety measures reflects the government's risk averse disposition, in order to buy time to better understand the new variant, identify and slow its spread, to ramp up healthcare capacity and to get more people vaccinated. [24] By the third quarter of 2021, vaccination-differentiated safe management measures (VDS) were introduced, to promote more vaccinations. As VDS measures became more extensive and onerous, to the point of effectively presenting a 'jab or job' situation, the 'communitarian' nudge became a more 'authoritarian' shove, as some chose to get vaccinated under duress, which caused disquiet in some quarters.

Despite its deserved reputation for efficient, technocratic governance, underlain by commitment to the formal rule of law[25] which preserves

20 MOH, Para 21, 'Preparing for our transition towards Covid resilience', 6 Aug 2021.

21 '80% of S'pore's population needs to be vaccinated to achieve herd immunity against COVID-19: Chief health scientists', *Straits Times*, 17 Dec 2020.

22 'Frustration, hopelessness: Dealing with COVID-19 fatigue in another round of tighter restrictions' CNA.com., 5 Aug 2021

23 'PM Lee calls on Singaporeans to 'not be paralysed by fear', be able to live with COVID-19 as endemic disease', *Today*, 9 Oct 2021.

24 'Singapore among earliest countries to accept Omicron not threatening nationally: Professor Fisher', *Financial Express* (India), 29 Dec 2021

25 Thio Li-ann, 'Between apology and apogee, autochthony: The Rule of Law beyond the rules of law in Singapore, (2012) SJLS 269.

the sanctity of commercial contracts and property rights, the government acknowledged its shortcomings in pandemic management. This includes the clumsy initial execution of home recovery protocols (HRP) and the failure to act swiftly to prevent the growth of migrant worker clusters, which erupted in April 2020 in purpose-built dormitories housing 200,000 people living in close quarters, housing some 12 to 20 men in each room.[26]

Globally, the accumulation of executive powers for pandemic regulation has sparked concerns about the state of constitutional government, rule of law and health of civil liberties. However, a strong executive wielding expansive discretionary powers is a familiar feature in the Singapore constitutional landscape, where the ruling People's Action Party (PAP) government has been in power since Independence in 1965 and is well known for its top-down interventionist managerial governance style. Today, this is qualified by a more participatory, consultative approach to government. Although their share of the national vote declined, the PAP won 83 of 93 elective seats during the July 2020 'pandemic' General Elections. It operates within a dominant party system where emphasis is placed on political constitutionalism and responsive government, where control of executive abuses draws internally "from Parliament and the Executive itself in upholding high standards of public administration and policy."[27] Judicial review is available to uphold constitutional supremacy, but the courts, as a facet of the separation of powers and co-equality, [28] view the executive as collaborative partners in the project of good government, where they play "a supporting role by articulating clear rules and principles" by which "the Government may abide and conform to the rule of law."[29] The courts have rejected proportionality review,[30] and generally apply a reasonableness test in rights adjudication,[31] They view their role primarily as vindicating personal rights, rather than expounding upon public policy, to avoid acting as a second legislative chamber.

26 'Singapore's cramped migrant worker dorms a 'perfect storm' for rising coronavirus infections, *South China Morning Post*, 6 April 2020.
27 Chan Sek Keong, "Judicial review – From angst to empathy" (2010) 22 SAcLJ 469 at 477, [29].
28 *Tan Seet Eng v AG* [2016] 1 SLR 779 at [90]
29 Chan, *supra* note 27.
30 *Chee Siok Chin v Minister for Home Affairs* [2006] 1 SLR(R) 582 at [87].
31 Li-ann Thio, 'Principled pragmatism and the 'third wave' of ommunitarian judicial review in Singapore' in Jaclyn L. Neo (ed.), *Constitutional Interpretation in Singapore: Theory and Practice* (Routledge, 2016), 75-116

This essay examines the implications of these matters in the context of Singapore, a non-liberal democracy based on the Westminster parliamentary system, which identifies as a communitarian polity[32] whose normative orientation elevates community interests above the self, and where rights are not trumps but apprehended in tandem with "moral and social obligations"[33] and the common good. This domestic expression of the 'Asian values' discourse has been criticised as an apology for authoritarian power and statist values. This danger, where appeals to the collective are concerned, always subsists. But there is also the possibility that a commitment to communitarianism may be authentic, an autochthonous expression of a community-oriented socio-political culture where shared public norms are developed through forms of consensus-seeking through "dialogue, tolerance, compromise,"[34] and implemented through persuasion and mediation. Social harmony and relational solidarity is prized and adversarial litigation and aggressive lobbying frowned upon, in favour of more reconciliatory social engagement modalities.[35] However, while hortatory methods and 'soft law' standards inform social relations, the government also considers that "rules and penalties are necessary", but "not enough"[36] - reflecting a brand of what may be called 'legal communitarianism.' This emphasises the instrumental role of law as a tool for effective governance, as part of a culture of authority, while appreciating the importance of clear rules and judicial review in sustaining a culture of legality.

Communitarian tenets were evident in pandemic management. In tandem with Singapore's healthcare and technological capacities, as well as deep financial reserves, the Prime Minister in November 2021 attributed the success of Singapore's pandemic management to an 'all of society'

---

32 Li-ann Thio, "We are feeling our way forward, step by step": The Continuing Singapore Experiment in the Construction of Communitarian Constitutionalism in the 21st Century's First Decade in *Constitutionalism in Asia in the Early Twenty-First Century*, Albert Chen ed. (Cambridge University Press, 2014) at 270-294.

33 *Taw Cheng Kong v. Public Prosecutor* [1998] 1 SLR(R) 78 at [54].

34 Sundaresh Menon, 'The Rule of law: The path to exceptionalism' (2016) 28 SAcLJ 413 at [24]

35 Government leaders have noted that "Street protests, lobbying" are not integral parts of the Singapore system, while courts have agreed with the government that Singapore political culture knows no place for investigative journalism which carries a political agenda: Law Minister K Shanmugam, Speech, New York State Bar Association Rule of Law Plenary Session (28 Oct 2009); *Review Publishing v Lee Hsien Loong* [2010] 1 SLR 52 at [272].

36 Speech, para 18, Lee Hsien Loong (PAP Secretary General), People's Action Party Convention, 28 Nov 2021 (text available: www.pap.org.sg)

effort, encompassing the effective political leadership, competent public service and Singapore's socially disciplined "high trust" society which is able to sustain solidarity and social resilience, integral to "our Singapore spirit" as "one united people." [37] This was reflected in public-private partnerships, which worked to set up Community Care facilities at the Expo conference centre in 2020 when Singapore was "overwhelmed with our first wave of infection."[38] The private sector also contributed to the war against COVID-19 by manufacturing needed equipment like masks or safe swabbing booths. [39] This trust manifested in three ways.

First, in the 'vertical' trust the people have towards the PAP government, based on its track record, democratic[40] and performance legitimacy, to see the republic through the crisis, to ensure food and medical supplies. PM Lee thought this trust facilitated the people's ready acceptance of government recommendations to get vaccinated in order to protect themselves and their families.[41] This resonates with the view in the government-authored shared values white paper,[42] a kind of quasi-constitutional preamble, that the neo-Confucian concept of "government by honourable men" or "君子" (*junzi*) who are duty-bound to do right for the people , having their "trust and respect" suited Singapore more than the liberal distrust of government. He thought this distrust fueled vaccine hesitancy and resistance in Europe and the US.[43] Trust was sustained insofar as the rule of law virtue of equal protection was observed, where rules like wearing masks applied to all, from ministers to road-sweepers. The undermining of public trust by foreign government leaders who abused their privileged position by ignoring general rules was cast as anti-models.[44] Clearly, the

37 Finance Minister Lawrence Wong, Para 319, Singapore Budget 2022 Speech (Charting our New Way Forward Together), at https://www.mof.gov.sg/singaporebudget/budget-2022/budget-statement/h-conclusion#Conclusion.

38 Wong, *ibid.*, para 320.

39 *Supra*, note 9.

40 Due by April 2021, general elections were called during the pandemic in July 2020 when the situation was relatively stable as the PM sought "a fresh five-year mandate" necessary to overcome future challenges. The PAP secured 61.2% of the popular vote: 'Singapore calls for Elections despite Pandemic', *New York Times* 23 June 2020.

41 Para 10, *supra*, note 36.

42 Para 41, shared values white paper (Cmd 1 of 1991, Singapore Parliament).

43 Para 11, *supra*, note 36.

44 Para 17, *ibid. E.g.* Boris Johnson's Lockdown Partygate'. *The New Yorker*, 11 Jan 2022; 'Biden, other politicians chided for lapses in mask protocols', *Las Vegas Review Journal* 28 Oct 2021. In contrast, Singapore's Prime Minister was seen

government appreciates that public confidence is needed to secure popular cooperation to generate tolerance for intrusive crisis management measures and to enhance their efficacy through personal responsibility.

Second, horizontal trust by which "we can treat people as honourable citizens who are responsible," who will take care of themselves and others through good personal hygiene in public places and observe safe-distancing measures even when no one is checking, flowing from "that sense of solidarity with others."[45]

Last, a trust in the intangible "collective spirit as one people" able to "work with, and not against one another;"[46] this may be described as 'communitarianism as solidarity,' reflected in the 'Singapore United' slogan.[47]

During the pandemic's first year, the government was able to "secure widespread cooperation from the people" in accepting restrictive measures including "mandatory social distance, the wearing of face masks, 14-day periods of quarantine and size limits on public gatherings."[48] The government was seen as acting mostly "sensibly and responsibly", adopting temporary reversible laws to augment its powers and refraining from "capitalizing on the crisis to roll back civil liberties and democratic processes." [49] A sense of care for the people was reflected in promises that "no one will be left behind", that the needy and vulnerable would be helped, and jobs would be saved and created.[50]

However, the introduction of harsher measures towards the voluntarily unvaccinated people in the latter half of 2021, the sense this minority was being demonized, threatened the "unity of purpose and hearts", perceived as crucial for surviving the crisis.[51] Those raising concerns over

---

wearing two masks at a public meeting: 'PM Lee seen wearing 2 masks at Jakarta ASEAN Summit, Netizens call him "Kiasi", sporeuncensored.com, 25 April 2021

45 Para 18, supra, note 36.

46 *Ibid.*

47 *e.g.* K Shanmugam, Second Reading, COVID-19 Bill, 94 Singapore Parliamentary Debates Official Reports (SPR), 7 April 2020; Prime Minister's Office (PMO), Singapore, "PM Lee Hsien Loong on the COVID-19 situation in Singapore on 12 March 2020" ("We are SGUnited…we do not leave anyone behind.")

48 *Daniel De Costa Augustin v AG* [2020] SGCA 60 at [2].

49 Kevin YL Tan, Singapore's regulatory response to COVID-19, The Regulatory Review, 15 June 2020 at https://www.theregreview.org/2020/06/15/tan-singapore-regulatory-response-covid-19/.

50 'No one will be left behind': PM Lee urges S'poreans to stay united as we face 'crisis of our generation', 26 May 2020, Mothership.sg

51 'Update 'on the COVID-19 situation in Singapore by PM Lee Hsien Loong, 9 Oct 2021

vaccine safety and efficacy contrary to the official public health narrative were aggressively rebuked; challenging VDS measures as unreasonable and disproportionate, and not necessarily science-based, were largely ignored, whether raised before Parliament or by civil society in cyberspace. Some consider such measures as repressive bullying, effectively jeopardizing the livelihood of unvaccinated workers barred from entering their workplaces as part of Work Vaccination Measures. This authoritarian turn can cause alienation and increased vaccine skepticism and hesitancy, where genuine concerns go unanswered or are shut down.[52] An 'us versus them' divide has opened up, where some citizens and even health journalists have called for harsher treatment of the unvaccinated who are seen as holding the majority hostage by delaying 'reopening'; even the Health Minister has labelled the voluntarily unvaccinated 'free-riders.'[53] This may be described as a brand of 'communitarianism as muscular majoritarianism' , where a minority group is blamed for harming the interests of the overwhelming (vaccinated) majority, and their concerns ridden roughshod through measures adopted in the name of the greater good.[54]

B. *Legal framework, health policy and governance/culture*

Extraordinary times call for extraordinary measures - this was evident in the passage of multiple fiscal stimulus packages which required independent presidential concurrence[55] where these drew down on past national reserves. In the 2020-2021 period, pandemic budget expended some $53.7 billion dollars for protecting jobs, stabilising businesses and immediate financial assistance.

---

52 Susan Pennings & Xavier Symons, 'Persuasion, not coercion or incentivisation, is the best means of promoting COVID-19 vaccination' (2021) 47(10) Journal of Medical Ethics 710-711 at 711 ("[P]eople may be more willing to undergo the small risk of vaccination against COVID-19 if they perceive that public health professionals and the government treating them with respect, as equal citizens to be persuaded, rather than inferiors to be coerced.")

53 Health Minister Ong Ye Kung, Opening Remarks, COVID-19 Multi-Ministry Taskforce Press Conference, 21 Jan 2022 at [18].

54 Lee Kwok Weng, 'Forum: Make COVID-19 jab mandatory, except for the ineligible, *Straits Times,* 23 Nov 2021

55 'Coronavirus: S'pore's survival and existence at stake, draw on reserves needed to take care of people, says President,' *Straits Times*, 22 May 2020.

On 22 January 2020, the government set up a Multi-Ministry Taskforce (MTF)[56] to coordinate the national response to the virus, originally co-chaired by the Health and National Development Minister.[57] The next day, a Chinese tourist became Singapore's first COVID-19 case. The MTF gave regular press briefings to communicate policies and their rationale, to promote transparency and guidance. The Ministry of Health's (MOH) website provided a centralised site containing information about updated safe management measures, health protocols and resources, to promote accessibility to all relevant rules and advisories.[58]

In November 2020, the government created and co-opted the expertise of the 14 Member Expert Committee on COVID-19 Vaccination (EC19V),[59] in developing vaccination strategy. True to its technocratic bent, the government characterises its decision-making as "based on data, evidence and science."[60] While referring to World Health Organisation (WHO) advisories [61]and the best practices of states like Israel and the United States, it recognizes that WHO can be behind the curve, as in failing to recognise asymptomatic transmission until June 2020 and advising against wearing masks which engender a false sense of security. The Prime Minister candidly acknowledged that in taking WHO's recommendations, it mistakenly advised the public not to wear masks unless one was feeling unwell from January to April 2020; in hindsight, it would have been wise to recognize that unlike SARs, the coronavirus could be transmitted by asymptomatic individuals. Individuals could have been encouraged to wear reusable masks earlier, saving surgical masks (in the face of shortages)

56 MOH of Health, Singapore, "Multi-Ministry askforce on Wuhan Coronavirus: Terms of reference and
composition" (27 January 2020).

57 As of February 2022, it is co-chaired by three ministers: Finance Minister Lawrence Wong, Health Minister Ong Ye Kung and Trade and Industry Minister Gan Kim Yong.

58 Singapore has the second highest rate of internet penetration in Southeast Asia, 88.4% as of mid 2020: Statistica, Internet Usage in Singapore - Statistics and Facts, 14 Oct 2020 at https://www.statista.com/topics/5852/internet-usage-in-singapore/.

59 'Top experts in healthcare, science appointed to committee to make recommendations on Singapore's COVID-19 vaccination strategy', *Straits Times* 13 Nov 2020

60 'No silver bullet': Nimble, evidence-based approach to deal with new COVID-19 variants, says Lawrence Wong, *Today,* 30 Nov 2021

61 *E.g.* Singapore adheres to WHO's case definition for classifying COVID-19 deaths, excluding non-pneumonia fatalities: '22 new COVID-19 infections in Singapore, lowest daily figure in nearly 6 months', CAN.com, 7 Sept 2020.

for healthcare workers.[62] Singapore makes its own scientific judgments and does not blindly accept all WHO recommendations, including WHO warnings against treating COVID-19 as endemic. [63]

I. Legislative Framework

Although article 150 of the Constitution authorises a state of emergency where "the security or economic life of Singapore is threatened", the government in the face of rising COVID-19 infections in March-April 2020 chose not to adopt emergency legislation which has a 6 months shelf-life, nor to invoke pre-existing statutory provisions which authorize public health emergencies, triggering powers to regulate movement in and out of declared restricted zones[64]. Instead, it built on the existing legal architecture, anchored in the 1976 Infectious Diseases Act ("IDA"), which was amended after the 2003 SARs crisis to strengthen the provisions for serving legally binding Home Quarantine Orders, breach of which is an offence. The IDA established a framework for contact tracing, surveillance, health education and enforcement; it makes it an offence for someone who knows or suspects he is a "case or carrier or contact" of a scheduled infectious disease, including COVID-19, to expose other persons to the risk of infection by his presence or conduct in a public place.[65] It imposes penalties of up to $10,000 and 6 months imprisonment for first time offenders. The Immigration Act provided powers to enforce border controls and prohibit anyone suffering from an infectious disease which would pose a community threat from entering Singapore.[66]

---

62 'I would rather overreact than underreact': PM Lee on thinking behind COVID-19 circuit breaker in ST book, *Straits Times* 20 Jan 2022

63 'WHO warns not to treat COVID-19 as endemic: Should Singapore be concerned?', *Straits Times*, 17 Jan 2022.

64 Section 17A, Infectious Diseases Act 1976. With effect from 28 Feb 2020, COVID-19 was included in the First and Second Schedule of the IDA, making it an offence for a person who suspects he is a carrier of an infectious disease like Covid to expose other persons to risk of infection by his conduct in any public place.

65 Section 21A, Infectious Disease Act; Covid -19 was added to the First and Second Schedule of the Act from 28 Feb 2020.

66 Section 8(3)b, Immigration Act (Cap 133, Rev Ed 2008)

The centrepiece COVID-19 (Temporary Measures) Act ("CTMA"), was adopted at breakneck speed after three readings[67] held on 7 April 2020, providing the basis for elevated SDM during the CB. Meant to last a year, it has since been extended until April 2023.[68] Its penalties are pegged to those in the IDA.

With the PAP's parliamentary majority, the passage of any bill or constitutional amendment,[69] which requires a simple and two-thirds majority respectively, is a foregone conclusion. Urgent bills attract only minimal parliamentary scrutiny and do not accommodate public consultation. The CTMA is wide-ranging, addressing health and economic shock issues, including government intervention into private contracts, contrary to the rule of law and sanctity of contract. Temporary and targeted interventions, such as providing temporary relief for the non-performance of specific contractual obligations and tax remissions, were justified in terms of fairness and economic longevity in a time of closed borders and temporarily shut down businesses, to safeguard "the economic structure for common good."[70] The Minister was empowered to regulate access to places of business, work and worship, which restricts the article 14 right to assembly and association, and the article 15 right of religious freedom. Premises providing essential services continued to operate subject to precautionary measures.

To complement the IDA and to make SDM legally binding, where these were previously based on ministry advisories,[71] Part 7 of CTMA empowers the Minister under section 34 to make regulations or 'control orders' for "preventing, protecting against, delaying or otherwise controlling the incidence or transmission of COVID-19 in Singapore" where there was a "serious threat to public health" and a need to supplement existing law. [72] Such control orders were to be presented to Parliament as soon

---

67 'Necessary for Singapore to fast-track COVID-19 laws amid unprecedented situation: Lawyers', CNA 13 April 2020.

68 Section 2, COVID-19 (Temporary Measures) (Amendment) Bill (No 7 of 2022) provides "Part 7 remains in force until the end of 8 April 2023."

69 E.g. in May 2020, article 64 of the Constitution was amended to allow Parliament to sit in a location other than Parliament House if Parliament "resolves that it is or will be impossible, unsafe or inexpedient for Parliament to sit and meet in one place."

70 Law Minister K Shanmugam, 'COVID-19 (Temporary Measures) Bill', 94 Singapore Parliament Reports, 7 April 2020

71 *E.g.* Ministry of Manpower, 'Advisory on safe distancing measures at the workplace' 13 March 2020

72 Section 34, COVID-19 (Temporary Measures) Act 2020 (No 14 of 2020).

as possible after publication in the Gazette; the minister is duty-bound under section 34(6) CTMA to publish these orders "so as to bring it to the notice of" all affected persons, crucial to the rule of law virtue of law being "capable of guiding the behaviour of its subjects."[73] This goes beyond the general requirement to publish delegated legislation in the gazette,[74] as it gravitates towards the higher standard of actual rather than constructive notice. Parliament can by resolution annul or amend the control order.

Subsidiary legislation based on the CTMA provided for alternative meetings for societies, unions and companies, regulation of foreign employee dormitories, financial reliefs, religious gatherings and sporting events, for example, which has implications for constitutional guarantees of religious liberty (art 15) and freedom of movement (art 13). In particular, the COVID-19 (Temporary Measures) (Control Order) Regulations 2020, adopted the same day as CTMA was enacted, contains most of the penal provisions and movement restriction rules, which were not thoroughly scrutinised. Acting with "reasonable excuse" is a defence to liability: s34(7).

Section 3A of the Regulation mandated wearing masks by all above 6 years of age outside one's place of residence; through regulatory carve-outs or "unrules"[75] it identified instances where the rules were dispensed with, such as driving a car, dental treatment or engaging in strenuous physical exercise like jogging but not walking. It detailed circumstances where face shields could be worn instead: section 3B. To minimize contact between people, all social gatherings in public or private spaces were disallowed under section 6. Persons were "urged" to stay home, but the control order would always allow people to go out for "good and necessary reasons" [76] such as buying groceries, recreation or seeking medical treatment.

Section 4(4) regulates the number of visitors to one's place of residence, which has variously ranged between 2, 5 and 8. Individuals in public places were required to keep at least one metre away from other persons

---

73 Joseph Raz, 'The rule of law and its virtue' in *The authority of law: Essays on law and morality* (OUP 1979) at 214

74 Section 23, Interpretation Act (Cap 1)

75 Unrules "allow regulators to ensure that certain actors can avoid otherwise applicable obligations - but without completely removing the rules, as with deregulation." Cary Coglianese, 'Obligation alleviation during the COVID-19 crisis', The Regulatory Review, 20 April 2020 at https://www.theregreview.org/2020/04/20/coglianese-obligation-alleviation-during-covid-19-crisis/ See also Cary Coglianese, Gabriel Scheffler, Daniel Walters, 'Unrules', (2021) 73 Stanford Law Review 885

76 Health Minister Gan Kim Yong, Second Reading, COVID-19 (Temporary Measures) Bill, 7 April 2020 at [21]

under section 7, though pragmatic exceptions were made for public transport passengers who were to wear masks, not talk on the phone or to other commuters to avoid spreading droplets in an enclosed space. [77] However, as train and bus stations are crowded places, this exception may not intuitively chime with the rationale of avoiding close contact. The Regulations also stipulate safe management measures for various enterprises and retail shopping centres, including observing capacity limits, cleaning protocols and implementing entry controls to facilitate contact tracing of every customer: Part 3A. The previous WFH recommendation now carried legal force for section 11 non-permitted enterprises. Where workers are on site, safety measures must be observed, such as not cross-deploying them (section 13).

The rules also reflect cultural considerations, such as permitting grandchildren to be brought daily to their grandparents' residence for informal childcare under section 4(3)(c), reflecting the nature of inter-generational families. Enforcement officers in ensuring compliance with control orders may direct individuals or groups not to enter or leave any premises or to direct businesses to stop or to limit access to the premises.

The Singapore government chose not to resort to extraordinary laws, preferring the "legislative model" of dealing with COVID-19 "by enacting ordinary statutes that delegate special and temporary powers to the executive."[78] Conferring broad discretionary powers on ministers precludes the need to seek legislative approval for potential policies and measures and raises rule of law concerns. Nonetheless, these are couched as temporal powers, underscoring their exceptional nature and the expectation they will expire after the pandemic. The speed with which legislation and regulations can be enacted or adopted, without robust scrutiny, gives rise to fears of executive abuse of powers, with the chief restraint being that of governmental responsibility, sensibility and the desire to sustain public trust.

---

77 'Coronavirus: Commuters must wear masks on buses, trains and refrain from talking', *Straits Times* 20 May 2020

78 John Ferejohn & Pasquale Pasquino, 'The law of the exception: A typology of emergency powers' (2004) 2(2) ICON 210-239 at 217.

II. Soft Administrative Law and Executive Interpretation of Rules

Aside from formal regulatory methods and legal sanctions, Singapore also deployed informal and voluntary regulatory modalities. While legislation placed many ministry advisories and guidelines on a legal footing, the open-ended formulation of some COVID-19 regulations and the scope of the exceptions, coupled with the suddenness of policy changes, caused confusion. People began to call for clarification over these gray areas, such as by sending letters to the press.

Government agencies, as part of the executive branch, began to issue interpretations to clarify such issues, which appear to have some legal force. These may be termed a sort of 'soft administrative law', that is, the elaboration of standards by administrative agencies lacking formal powers to issue determinative readings of rules, but whose pronouncements provided guidance and gave rise to expectations of compliance, functioning to all intents and purposes like legal rules. For example, Regulation 13F required activities involving personal interactions not critical to business operations to be cancelled during the control period; it was unclear what 'non-critical' events were, and in response, government agencies advised this would include welfare activities or celebratory festivals.[79] Although not explicitly stated in the COVID-19 regulations, the National Environment Agency provided guidelines that if someone smoked in public, masks must be worn after smoking is completed. While not formally binding, these advisories exert some degree of compliance-pull, as quasi-rules, subject to no formal oversight.

III. Health Policy - An Overview

Although there is no constitutional right to health, [80] the government has adopted a human welfare approach towards safeguarding public health and managing the pandemic. From its earlier experience with the

79 'F&B businesses come to grips with new circuit breaker measures, but some unsure what to do', CNA.com, 22 April 2020.

80 Singapore is not party to the International Covenant on Economic Social and Cultural Rights which contains a right to health, though it has acceded human rights treaties like the Convention for the Elimination of all forms of Discrimination Against Women and Convention on the Rights of the Child, which contain health rights for women and children.

SARs pandemic in 2003, it put in place legislation[81] and a set of competences and response capabilities, upgrading medical facilities, stockpiling medical equipment, building isolation hospitals and the cutting-edge National Centre for Infectious Disease (NCID), completed in 2019, which has advanced research and pandemic-level treatment facilities. [82]

The government was proactive in *ensuring* that masks, ventilators, personal protection equipment for healthcare workers were secured; [83] it entered into advance purchase agreements to ensure Singapore was near the front of the vaccine queue,[84] and actively sources for anti-viral drugs and therapeutics.[85] The government was able to provide enough vaccines for all by the third quarter of 2021.

It sought by investing in cold-chain storage and logistics requirements to become Southeast Asia's vaccine distribution hub[86] and has strengthened its vaccine manufacturing capacity by encouraging pharmaceutical companies developing the mRNA vaccines like Moderna and BioNTech to establish a local presence, further strengthening Singapore's position as a leading biomedical sciences hub[87] and to ensure future vaccine access.[88] It has also invested in research efforts to produce medical technology such as a "swab-bot", new swab designs and tests kits with faster delivery of results than standard Polymerase Chain Reaction tests.[89]

---

81 Wayne Arnold, 'In Singapore, 1970's law becomes weapon against SARS', *New York Times* 10 June 2003.

82 'New centre to bolster Singapore's infectious disease management', *Straits Times*, 16 Jan 2019.

83 'Singapore looking at new sources, local manufacturing for essential supplies such as masks', CAN.com, 19 Feb 2020

84 Singapore in multilateral initiative to secure COVID-19 vaccine doses', *Straits Times*, 26 July 2020; PM Lee Hsien Loong. 'On the COVID-19 Situation in Singapore' PMO, 14 Dec 2020.

85 'Merck and Singapore sign deal on COVID-19 antiviral pill, Reuters, 7 Oct 2021; 'Singapore receives its first batch of Pfizer's Paxlovid pill for COVID-19 treatment', CNN.com, 12 Feb 2022.

86 'Singapore races to become Southeast Asia's vaccine distribution hub', Nikkei Asia, 9 Dec 2020

87 'Moderna announces expansion to SG', msn.com, 16 Feb 2022

88 'Vaccine maker Moderna to incorporate Singapore subsidiary', *Business Times*, 16 Feb 2022; 'Vaccine maker BioNTech to set up regional HQ, manufacturing site in S'pore', *Straits Times*, 10 May 2021

89 'Singapore develops novel COVID-19 swabs to address global and local shortage', Biospectrum Asia 15 July 2020; 'Singapore-made COVID-19 swab test robot could reduce healthcare workers' risk of infection', CAN.com, 21 Sept 2020; 'New COVID-19 test kit by DSO and A*Star cuts testing time by half,' *Straits Times*, 18 July 2020

When the virus first hit, measures were taken to *promote* health through public educational efforts such as a washing hands guide; the newspapers carried health advisories to support the government messaging of maintaining personal hygiene, wearing masks in public and safe distancing. This has been described as participating in "the state's public relations performance" within "an authoritarian context of news production".[90] Responding to the "latest scientific evidence",[91] it reversed its policy and stopped discouraging mask-wearing as others could be protected by your keeping "your droplets to yourself."[92] It also decided to *provide* four surgical masks to each Singapore household in February 2020, to alleviate public anxiety,[93] and continued with future reusable mask distribution exercises, enabling people to meet what had become a legal obligation to wear masks in public. [94]

Health-related financial reserves enabled the government to implement free and aggressive community testing,[95] allowing the swift identification and isolation of cases, to prevent community transmission. To ease public anxiety, the government also committed to covering COVID-19 related hospital bills for all Singapore residents and Long Term Pass Holders and to subsidise medical treatment for respiratory infections through the Public Health Preparedness Clinics.

The government has consistently sought to expand healthcare capacities by providing a "layered set of healthcare facilities customized to patient needs,"[96] whether critically or mildly ill, or asymptomatic. To prevent hospitals from being overwhelmed and to reserve space for severe cases needing to be warded in Intensive Care Units (ICU) or requiring oxygen sup-

---

90 Satveen Kaur-Gill, 'The COVID-19 pandemic and outbreak inequality: Mainstreaming reporting of Singapore's migrant orkers in the margins', Frontiers in Communication, 30 Sept 2020 at https://www.frontiersin.org/articles/10.3389/fcomm.2020.00065/full.

91 MOH, 'Continued stringent implementation and enforcement of circuit reaker measures', 14 April 2020.

92 PMO, "PM Lee Hsien Loong on the COVID-19 situation in Singapore on 3 April 2020.

93 'Singapore is building up mask stockpile, but people should not take availability of masks for granted: Chan Chun Sing', *Today*, 22 May 2020

94 "Singapore to distribute 'better' reusable face masks to households" CAN.com 6 May 2020; 'Spore residents begin collecting 2 free reusable masks each from Temasek', *Strait Times*, 21 Sept 2020

95 COVID-19 tests to be offered to more than 45,000 hawkers, cleaners and food delivery workers, *Today*, 15 Oct 2020.

96 Ministerial Statement, Health Minister Gan Kim Yong, Second update on whole of Government response to COVID-19', 4 May 2020 at [39].

plementation, community care facilities (CCFs) and community recovery facilities were set up in holiday resorts, conference facilities and even army camps, with the help of government bodies, private companies as well as the Singapore Armed Forces, to handle patients with mild symptoms or recovering patients still needing to stay in isolation. [97] This approach avoided excessive strain being placed on hospital wards and maintained a 'buffer' to handle any sudden case upsurges.

As vaccination rates rose and because infected persons suffered mostly mild symptoms, the nation pivoted to a Home Recovery protocol (HRP), which became the default mode of care by September 2021.[98] The unvaccinated and elderly were still admitted to hospitals or CCFs. Those on the HRP protocol who tested positive for COVID-19 would receive an SMS with a link to provide details to start the 10-day home recovery; they would be issued an isolation order and their household members would have to register themselves online as close contacts, whereupon they would receive an electronic quarantine order via SMS and be required to do a self-administered Antigen Rapid Test (ART) and report the results daily by 12pm. Free ART kits may be collected at a Regional Screening Centre near one's residence.

Telemedicine facilities were made available, as well as a 'home buddy' tasked to answer non-medical related questions. The MOH sent 'care packs' including an oximeter to help monitor blood oxygen levels, and medication was also sent to homes. Those on home recovery needed to maintain a daily regimen of monitoring their temperature, pulse rate and blood oxygen saturation; leveraging on technology, this information was to be submitted daily by 10am to a website (Home Recovery Vitals Diary). General Practitioners were later given more autonomy in deciding whether a patient was a suitable candidate for the HRP or needed to be sent to a hospital.

To facilitate the shift to a 'nation of testing' and encourage a pervasive practice of testing as a form of self-monitoring and facet of social responsibility, the government has distributed free ART kits to households, and has actively sourced cheaper and affordable kits available at general

---

97 'Community care facilities for COVID-19 patients with mild symptoms will double bed capacity to 20,000 by end-June,' *Today* 28 June 2020.

98 'Buddy system, ART tests: What does home recovery mean for COVID-19 patients in Singapore?' *Straits Times*, 23 Sept 2021

retailers;[99] individuals are urged to keep these at hand in their homes.[100] Individuals receiving Health Risk Warnings or Health Risk Alerts from the MOH through SMS are instructed on the frequent testing regime to follow, and may collect a pack of 3 ART self-tests kits from some 100 islandwide vending machines.

People, including the fully vaccinated, are "strongly encouraged" to self-test regularly with ART kits before attending large-scale events or visiting vulnerable people, as well as in case they think they have been exposed but do not have acute respiratory symptoms. [101] The government has also leaned on the private sector to go beyond the 14-day regular rostered testing for workers in higher risk settings by adopting a "vaccinate or regular test regime", as part of the new norm at the workplace.[102]

In addition, regular self-testing may be supplemented by taking a self-paid fast and easy test at 20 Quick Test Centres (QTC) from 1 October 2021; a person who tests positive should then visit a Swab-and-Send Home Clinic for a Government funded PCR test to confirm their infection status. Less intrusive test kits, such as breathalyzers deployed at checkpoints, are also being developed and piloted, as are new testing methods like wastewater surveillance at housing estates. Regular testing and "the social consciousness to get ourselves tested regularly" was thought crucial in transiting to the new normal, as enforcement action *per se* did not suffice.[103]

To prevent general clinics from being swamped by people who had tested positive via an ART kit but had mild or no symptoms, and who wanted to be registered in the system, the government arranged for people to take a fully government funded supervised self-administered ART at QTCs, where their positive infection results could be uploaded on the

---

99 MOH, Antigen rapid test kits venting machines deployed slandwide and updates to home recovery and travel classifications', 17 Sept 2021; 'Flowflex ART kits available at $4.90 each at Unity and FairPrice outlets', *Straits Times* 10 Dec 2021. This is about a third of what other kits cost.

100 Lawrence Wong, 95 Singapore Parliament Reports, 26 July 2021, Fifth Update on Whole-of-Government Responses to COVID-19.

101 MOH, Paras 13-14, 'Maintaining heightened alert to minimise risk of transmission as we re-open safely', 10th June 2021

102 COVID-19: People strongly encouraged to self-test regularly as a matter of 'social responsibility', says Lawrence Wong CNA.com 3 Sept 2021. The government will only subsidise the twice weekly ART kit testing for the medically ineligible.

103 Lawrence Wong, 95 Singapore parliament reports, 26 July 2021, Fifth update on whole-of-government responses to COVID-19.

HealthHub mobile application within 30 minutes.[104] This app allows citizens to access their individual health records, which the government has centralized control over.

The state subsidised national vaccination programme (NVP) commenced in December 2020. In response to concerns about vaccine safety, the government mantra was that the benefits of being vaccinated outweighed the risks of vaccination. At present, the government underwrites the costs of three vaccines: Pfizer, Moderna and Sinovac, all approved under the Pandemic Special Access route allowing the emergency use of vaccines in a pandemic situation. This was a consideration in not making vaccination mandatory.[105] The Health Sciences Authority (HSA) in February 2022 granted Novavax's non mRNA vaccine interim authorisation.[106]

Healthcare workers and staff were prioritized in the vaccination drive, followed by the elderly who were at greater risk of severe infections, as well as workers in high-risk settings, such as construction and process industries, including migrant workers. People were invited via SMS to make a booking at a vaccination centre.

To assuage vaccine injury fears and promote higher vaccine coverage, the government set up a Vaccine Injury Financial Assistance Programme (VIFAP) for those "very rare instances" where a person vaccinated under the NVP suffers serious side effects, as medically accessed.[107] This is in addition to existing healthcare financing and insurance schemes, and provides a "one-time good-will financial assistance": up to $225,000 is awarded at the top tier (death or severe permanent disability), $10,000 for the middle tier (admitted to intensive care but who recover) and $2000 where hospitalisation and medical intervention is required. Each claim must be evaluated by a MOH appointed independent clinical panel and unsuccessful applicants are given reasons, and may seek a reassessment if there is new supporting medical information.[108] Sinopharm vaccinations may be administered by private clinics but this is not subsidised by the

---

104 'Quick test centres to allow supervised antigen rapid tests, infection record to be updated within 30 minutes' *Today*, 15 Feb 2022; MOH, Supervised self-administer antigen rapid test available at test centres' 15 Feb 2022

105 Ong Ye Kung, 95 SPR, 26 July 2021 Ministerial Statements, Fifth update on whole-of-Government responses to COVID-19

106 'Novavax's Nuvaxovid COVID-19 vaccine granted interim authorisation in Singapore', CNA.com, 14 Feb 2022

107 Vaccine injury financial Assistance Programme for COVID-19 vaccination at www.moh.gov.sg/covid-19/vaccination/vifap

108 '296 patients qualified for COVID-19 vaccine injury payouts as at Dec 31: MOH', *Straits Times* 7 Jan 2022.

government or covered by VIFAP. By August 2021, some 144 applicants reportedly received VIFAP assistance, including awarding $225,000 to a 16-year old boy because he suffered a cardiac arrest after his first dose.[109] The MOH clarified that the local incidence rate of myocarditis remains low "at 0.48 per 100,000 doses."[110]

Acting cautiously, the Expert Committee on COVID-19 vaccination (EC19V) initially recommended that sub-groups like pregnant women, the immunocompromised and adolescents under 16 years of age should not be vaccinated until there was sufficient data pointing to their safety and efficacy. Following the science, these groups were cleared for vaccination after the EC19V reviewed global and local data, in June, July and December 2021 respectively. [111] However pregnant women were encouraged to discuss the risks and benefits with their doctors to make an informed decision, given that less data existed for this group.[112] While some parents were enthusiastic about vaccination for their children, others were concerned about the long-term effects or adverse reactions. The government noted it had no plans to require vaccination as a condition for attending schools and urged parents to make the right decision for their children,[113] warning that they could suffer from severe post-infection complications and require ICU care, and that vaccination would afford them protection against the virus. [114]

The HSA in its November 2021 safety report noted that of the 9.95 million mRNA COVID-19 vaccine doses administered as of 31 October 2021, 13,334 reports of adverse events were received.[115] As of 31 December, the small number of 296 patients qualified for VIFAP assistance.

---

109 'Highest financial aid of $225k paid to two patients for serious side effects from COVID-19 vaccine: MOH', *Straits Times*, 17 Aug 2021

110 MOH, 'Positive progress for 16 year old who had an out of hospital cardiac arrest after COVID-19 Vaccination, 16 August 2021

111 'Severely immunocompromised people can now get COVID-19 jabs in S'pore' *Straits Times*, 28 July 2021; 'Spore sets up paediatric vaccination centres; one can jab 1000 children a day', *The New Paper* (Singapore), 17 Dec 2021. 'Vaccination needed to protect kids from possible exposure to COVID-19, risk of severe complications: Janil', *Straits Times*, 20 Dec 2021

112 'Pregnant women, cancer patients on active treatment can get COVID-19 jabs', *Straits Times*, 1 June 2021

113 Chan Chun Seng, 'Vaccination for primary school students and possibility of VDS for preschools and primary schools, 95 SPR 1 Oct 2022

114 'Children below 12 starting to form majority of COVID-19 cases admitted to hospitals: MOH', CNA.com, 21 Jan 2022

115 '200 suspected 'adverse events' reported out of 854, 268 COVID-19 booster shots administered: HSA', *Today*, 16 Nov 2021

Strenuous efforts were made to make it "even more convenient" for the elderly to get vaccinated, reflecting the human rights concern for vulnerable social groups. Mobile vaccination teams were deployed to heartland areas to vaccinate less mobile seniors; [116] home visits for the elderly immobile could be arranged. [117] From July 2021, seniors over 60 could walk into any vaccination centre without an appointment to receive vaccination.[118] The Health Promotion Board launched a "Let's Get our Seniors Vaccinated" programme on 13 August 2021, offering $30 vouchers to help referrers cover costs, such as accompanying seniors to vaccination centres. After a fortnight, some 550 seniors were successfully referred for their first dose.[119] As of January 2022, seniors above 60 had been vaccinated in the high 90%.[120]

Mental health issues became prominent during the pandemic; after initially not including psychological treatment as an "essential service" which could operate during the CB, the government did a volte-face following public calls from mental health professionals detailing client stress in trying to work from home.[121] Programmes like the 24-hour National Care hotline received extra support and online mental health resources.[122] A new inter-ministerial agency called the COVID-19 Mental Wellness Taskforce was convened to assess the psycho-social impact of the pandemic and to ensure all had access to quality mental healthcare.[123] This reflects a salutary holistic appreciation of public health and a willingness to allocate resources to address the problem.

---

116 MOH, 'Bringing COVID-19 vaccination to the heartlands for seniors' , 15 July 2021.

117 'PM Lee's address on the COVID-19 situation in Singapore', CNA.com, 31 May 2021

118 MOH, 'No rior Apapointment needed at Moderna vaccination centres' 2 Aug 2021.

119 MOH, 'Vaccination incentive', 14 Sept 2021

120 MOH, Para 34., 'Response to Omicron Wave', 10 Jan 2022.

121 'Society must recognise potential mental health crisis following COVID-19, says Singapore doctor', *Today*, 10 July 2020

122 23,000 people called National Care Hotline with issues such as mental health, marriage, family: Desmond Lee, *Today*, 8 July 2020.

123 'Task force to tackle mental health needs amid pandemic' *Straits Times*, 11 Oct 2020

IV. Governance by Effective Communication, Persuasion, Empathy and Trust

In a pandemic, effective communication is key to sustaining public trust both in terms of substance and style. It is necessary to address the public's fears and to prepare the public for what is coming next, through clear, concise policy directions and advice through both "traditional and social media on a near daily basis."[124] The political leadership needed to sustain its moral authority to persuade the people to trust in its programme, through leading by example, to "close the emotional distance between us" in addressing the medical and "psychological battle" ahead. [125] Ministers took a three-month pay cut to demonstrate empathetic solidarity with the financially struggling;[126] they were always seen wearing masks in public and were vaccinated early to demonstrate their belief in vaccine safety. The Prime Minister spoke sympathetically of the "painful adjustments"[127] required by safe distancing to keep "our families safe" and frequently thanked Singaporeans for their "trust and support" in complying with "tough and painful measures." [128] The Prime Minister made various televised addresses to reassure the public that there were enough food supplies,[129] or to persuade seniors to comply with measures restricting social gatherings. During the first weekend of the CB, he identified as a senior citizen in urging older Singaporeans to stay at home, given their greater vulnerability to the virus.[130] Exhortation rather than diktat and legal sanction was resorted to promote conformity with new social norms, through utilizing a medium which would reach a broader range of people than a government gazette. [131]

The political leadership also demonstrated awareness of the public's frustrations, anxieties and fatigue, particularly where the momentum to-

---

124 Gan, *supra*, note 86. at 356.

125 Health Minister Gan Kim Yong, Statement at Parliament, On the Update on Whole-of-Government Response to COVID-19, 25 March 2020.

126 'PM and ministers to take three-month pay cut in solidarity with Singaporeans coping with coronavirus', *Straits Times* 26 March 2020

127 PMO, "PM Lee Hsien Loong on the COVID-19 situation in Singapore on 3 April 2020"

128 *Supra*, note 37.

129 'PM Lee Hsien Loong on the COVID-19 situation in Singapore on 8 February 2020'.

130 PMO, "PM Lee Hsien Loong on the COVID-19 situation in Singapore on 10 April 2020".

131 PMO, 'PM Lee Hsien Loong's remarks in English, Malay and Chinese on the Coronavirus Disease 2019 (COVID-19) situation in Singapore',3 April 2020.

wards relaxing restrictions was thwarted by their reinstatement in facing infection surges. While Singapore governance is known for its technocratic efficiency, the pandemic presents a moving target. While seeking to give hope to the people, the government cautioned of the need to remain flexible as it may be necessary "to tap the brakes again", to return to heightened alert or even a CB if ICU cases rise sharply,[132] to "protect our healthcare system and healthcare workers."[133]

Public trust is sustained when the government is seen to be responsive and reasonable in formulating and adjusting policy. Compassion also inspires confidence, as where the government calibrates regulation in response to appeals, as well as the gentle intercession of the President, [134] such as relaxing an initial CB prohibition on home bakers, which would deprive many Muslim minority home businesses of a vital income source in the Ramadan season.[135]

The government demonstrated a relational approach towards religious leaders, particularly where strict curbs had to be placed on religious practices, which limits the article 15 religious freedom guarantee. This is based on fostering good-will and warm ties between political and religious leaders, to preserve religious harmony and avoid contentious relations.[136]

Rather than just imposing legal restrictions, given that article 15 is subject to public health exceptions, government ministers meet with representative religious groups like the Inter-Religious Organisation (IRO) to brief and update them on the COVID-19 situation, in seeking their cooperation. For a time, all religious services were mandatorily suspended and strict group size limits applied to using places of worship for essential rites like funerals and weddings. The government adopted a persuasive tone in 'asking' religious leaders to advise their followers to adhere to social distancing measures. In solidarity, many religious groups pivoted to support the national effort and "the religious needs of their followers"[137]

132 'Govt won't rule out return to circuit breaker or heightened alert if COVID-19 cases in ICUs rise sharply: Lawrence Wong', *Today*, 6 Sept 2021

133 'Protect the vulnerable, secure Singapore's future', *Straits Times*, 9 Oct 2021.

134 'How Singapore's president spoke up for home businesses amid pressure to ease tighter circuit breaker rules', *South China Morning Post*, 9 May 2020.

135 'Coronavirus: Minister addresses concerns over curbs on home-based bakers', *Straits Times*, 28 April 2020.

136 Jaclyn Neo & Shazny Ramlan, 'COVID-19 and Religious Organisations: Constitutional Environment and Organisational Choices' RSIS Interreligious Relations Issue 24, 1 June 2021

137 MCCY Minister Grace Fu, Speech 'Religious solidarity amid COVID-19', 28 April 2020 at [4], [10].

by adapting religious practices through e-learning and live-streaming worship services. The Islamic Religious Council (MUIS) stated the azan (call to prayer) could be performed at home; a fatwa was issued stating that the suspension of Friday prayers could be religiously justified in emergency situations,[138] and mosques also produced online Islamic teaching.[139] When religious services progressively resumed, these were subject to precautionary measures pertaining to physical proximity, duration of services and intensity of expression like singing which could produce contagious droplets. For example, singing by worshippers with masks was precluded, and common items like prayer mats and books were not to be shared.[140] In this regard, the government acknowledged the importance of religious activities to the lives of many Singaporeans and the need through relaxing restrictions to "help support Singaporean's spiritual needs."[141]

The government adopted a harsher posture and policies against unvaccinated Singaporeans by requiring all events, regardless of size, to implement vaccination differentiation safe management measures (VDS) from 1 Feb 2022. This effectively meant that only the vaccinated could attend congregational services. Rather than aggressive lobbying, religious leaders took the road of quiet diplomacy to extract concessions. For example, a Catholic church adopted a supplicatory posture in communicating their view that all parishioners have the right to worship, regardless of their vaccination status.[142] They extracted the modest allowance of having 5 masked unvaccinated worshippers observing safe distancing at private worship meetings with one vaccinated religious worker. The government justified this on the basis of the "prevailing permissible group size of five for social gatherings" at private homes.[143] It would have been unreasonable and disheartening if VDS measures failed to reasonably accommodate an important constitutional right. Notably, the government has taken a more

---

138 MUIS, Fatwa Statement on precautionary measures in dealing with COVID-19, 24 March 2020

139 MUIS, 'Media Statement on extension of temporary closure of mosques, 16 March 2020

140 Updated safe management measures for religious ctivities, 25 Jan 2022, Ministry of Culture, Community and outh and crisis preparedness for religious organisations

141 'Health Minister Gan Kim Yong: 'All religious organisations can host up to 100 for services', *Straits Times*, 24 Sept 2020

142 'Churches appealing for concessions for unvaccinated worshippers when new COVID-19 rules kick in on Feb 1', *Straits Times* 20 Jan 2022

143 'Unvaccinated people can continue attending private worship in groups of up to 5 from Feb 1', *Straits Times*, 26 Jan 2022.

unyielding stance towards other groups which have publicly called for changes to VDS, discussed below.

To counter false rumours and misinformation, the public was urged not to share unsubstantiated information and to refer to reliable sources like the MOH website.[144] Individuals who spread misinformation during the CB through Facebook posts, which may have sparked another round of panic buying, have been charged for communicating false messages under the Miscellaneous Offences (Public Order and Nuisance Act) and sentenced to 4 months imprisonment for a post taken down after 15 minutes. This indicated the gravity with which the government considered false messaging during a pandemic.[145] The government also has not hesitated to invoke powers under the Protection from Online Falsehoods and Manipulation Act (POFMA),[146] such as issuing Correction Directions (CD) to Facebook posts containing what the government considers a 'false statement of fact.' This requires the poster to put up a correction notice that what has been posted contains a falsehood and to prominently place a link in that location to a government website, Factually.sg., which contains corrective information. It has been argued that this unduly restricts free speech under article 14, or is a form of compelled speech. Internet intermediaries may also be issued a General Correction Order (GCO) which requires them to communicate a correction notice to all users in Singapore that a false statement of fact has been made on their platform. The Minister must be satisfied that the falsehood pertains to specific grounds, such as being prejudicial to security or public health and that public interest warrants the issuance of POFMA orders.

The Court of Appeal in The Online Citizen v Attorney-General[147] held that since the statement-maker is not required to take down the post, free speech is not restricted; a CD merely constrains the statement maker who can maintain the original text of the published material, provided the correction notice is inserted within the published material. In a sense, this constitutes an online right of reply; judicially determined false speech is valued lowly, given there is no human right to communicate misinformation. CDs have been issued to Facebook posts falsely claiming COVID-19

---

144 Gov.sg, "Clarifications: Misinformation, rumours regarding COVID-19, 23 April 2020

145 'COVID-19: Taxi driver jailed 4 months for posting false information about closure of supermarkets, food outlets" *Today*, 27 May 2020.

146 Thio Li-ann, Public Law in *Law and Technology in Singapore*, Phang, Chesterman and Goh eds., (Singapore: Academy Press, 2021) at 577-626

147 [2021] SGCA 96

deaths, that COVID-19 vaccines were more dangerous than other vaccines in causing death and injury, that the Omicron variant is vaccine resistant, and ivermectin could safely prevent and treat COVID-19, for example.[148] Facebook and Twitter have also complied with GCOs to communicate to all Singapore end-users of their platforms that communications about a Singapore COVID-19 variant was a falsehood.[149]

The Prime Minister noted that a key difference between the 2003 SARs crisis and the COVID-19 crisis was the prevalence of social media; he was glad that POFMA was available to deal with falsehoods "fomenting FUD - fear, uncertainty and doubt", by providing swift corrections to allay public panic and preserve confidence in pandemic measures. Critics have argued this is a one-sided exercise of power, relying on ministerial self-discipline not to abuse broad discretion, although there are remedies in the form of appealing to the Minister and High Court, as well as general judicial review. Ultimately, a CD may be seen to be justified from the free speech rationale of arguments from truth and democracy; it relies on the citizen acting as a rational person who will access and read alternative points of view and make up his own mind.

V. *Carrots and Sticks: Enforcement and Sanctions, Incentives and Internalisation*

1. *Enforcement and Sanctions (and shoves)*

Fast-changing COVID-19 rules and policies have been confusing, with certain dining-in rules so complex parliamentarians observed an "advanced degree" was needed to navigate them.[150]

---

148 "Wuhan virus: Government will not hesitate to use Pofma on fake news regarding viral outbreak, says Iswaran" *Today*, 26 January 2020; 'Pofma correction direction issued to Goh Meng Seng over false claims about Omicron variant', *Straits Times* 4 Dec 2021. MOH, Para 4, Issuance of Correction Direction under the POFMA on Falsehoods on COVID-19 Vaccines, 29 Nov 2021; Issuance of Correction Direction under the Protection from Online Falsehoods and Manipulation Act on Falsehoods on Effectiveness of COVID-19 Vaccines and Clarifications on Ivermetin, MOH News Highlight, 24 Oct 2021.

149 'POFMA directive issued to Facebook, Twitter, SPH Magazines over 'Singapore variant' of COVID-19 Falsehood', CNA.com, 20 May 2021

150 He Ting Ru, Speech, debate on ministerial statement for support easures for phase two (Heightened Alert) and Phrase Three (Heightened Alert), 27 July 2021

To give Singaporeans time to become familiarised with the rules, a graduated approach towards imposing COVID-19 related penalties was adopted. During the early days of the CB for example, advisories and stern written warnings were issued rather than legal sanctions. After about a week, fines[151] were imposed in "egregious cases"[152] and breaching safe distancing rules in full sight of the public was legally prosecuted. After the CB when gatherings were capped at 5, where "enough time has transpired" for the relevant actors to know the safe distancing rules, a stricter enforcement method was adopted, even for first time offenders.[153] In August 2020, a restaurant was fined $2000 and suspended for 10 days for allowing 20 people to gather in a private locked room, which an Enforcement Officer (EOs) discovered during a spot check. [154] EOs assisted by Safe Distancing Ambassadors patrolled popular public spaces and did not hesitate to issue fines to large groups of people ignoring the rules. [155] An impromptu New Year's celebration at Clarke Quay by unmasked participants is being investigated, criticized by then MTF as a "potential superspreading event," a lapse in "civic responsibility".[156]

People failing to abide by Singapore COVID-19 laws and who breach SDM, Stay Home Notices (SHN) or Quarantine orders have had their foreign work permits revoked and been deported.[157] The sight of photographs of expats from Britain, the US and Austria meeting to drink in groups during the CB at Robertson Quay sparked considerable ire; the Prosecution sought a custodial sentence for their "audacious" actions conveying the impression that Singapore laws could be "belittled with impunity", demonstrating "blatant disregard" for personal and public safety.[158] They were

---

151 Ministry for the Environment and Water Resources (MEWR), "More than 2,900 Stern warnings and 40 fines ssued for failure to comply with elevated safe distancing measures" (10 April 2020).

152 MEWR, "Stiffer penalties for breach of safe distancing measures from 12 April 2020" (12 April 2020).

153 MOH, 'Calibrated adjustments in stabilisation phase, 8 Nov 2021.

154 MEWR, "Stiffer penalties for breach of safe distancing measures from 12 April 2020" (12 April 2020).

155 'Sentosa, East Coast Park crowds show complacency 'may have set in', says Masagos who warns of increased enforcement' *Today,* 22 July 2020

156 'Authorities looking into 'potential superspreading event' at Clarke Quay after crowds purportedly gathered for impromptu New York Countdown', *Today,* 2 Jan 2022

157 12 people deported, barred from re-entering Singapore after flouting COVID-19 circuit breaker rules, CNA.com, 13 July 2020

158 *PP v Neil Gordon Buchan et al* (25 June 2020), District's Court – URA-000105-2020-1 & Ors at [12] https://www.statecourts.gov.sg/cws/Resou

fined up to $9000 and had their work passes revoked for breaking the law for the "frivolous purpose of drinking and chatting."[159] The judge did not think imprisonment warranted for first-time offenders whose "deplorable" conduct took place over the relatively short span of an hour. This was comparable to the $4500 fine imposed on local Francis Soh for breaching Regulation 6 prohibiting social gatherings; he had flaunted an hour-long gathering held at his cousin's house on Facebook, stating: 'we are having an illegal gathering…so what?'[160] People involved in social gatherings within enclosed spaces, investigated by the police on anonymous tip-offs were fined about $3000.[161] An element of proportionality in sentencing is evident insofar as offences of long duration attracted custodial sentences, such as in a case where three men took a planned overnight camping trip of some 27 hours at an outlying islands during the CB.[162]

To underscore the importance of compliance with COVID-19 regulations, the Immigration Authority took harsh action against those falsifying travel histories or breaching SHN requirements, through cancelling passports, [163] deportation[164] or terminating permanent residency status. [165]

2. *Incentives, Inducement, and Internalisation*

Apart from legal sanctions, the government has deployed 'carrot and stick' measures to induce certain behavior, including nudging or shoving people towards getting vaccinated through vaccine differentiation measures which discriminate on the basis of vaccination and only permit vaccinated indi-

---

rces/Documents/BriefGroundsofDecision-PPvNeilGordonBuchanAndOthers.pdf.

159 'Singapore expats who flouted circuit breaker rules fined up to US$6,400, work passes revoked', *South China Morning Post* 25 June 2020

160 'So what?': Man who posted about dinner gathering during circuit breaker fined S$4,500, *Today* 20 May 2020

161 'Woman fined for gathering with 14 other people at Chinese New Year celebration last year,' CNA.com, 7 Feb 2022.

162 'Fine, jail for trio who camped on Ubin amid virus', *Straits Times*, 16 June 2020

163 Immigration and Checkpoints Authority, "Singapore citizen's passport cancelled, investigated for possible offences for breaching stay-home notice requirements" (29 March 2020)

164 Immigration and Checkpoints Authority, "British national deported for falsely declaring his travel history at The Family Justice Courts" (26 April 2020).

165 'COVID-19: 2 to be charged under Infectious Diseases Act, 1 stripped of PR status', *Yahoo News Singapore*, 26 Feb 2020.

viduals from accessing selected premises, activities and events, discussed below.

An example of a financially based inducement relates to how Singaporeans disregarding a 18 March 2020 travel advisory[166] to defer all travel would from 27 March, be charged the full costs of serving a SHN issued under the IDA, as well as expenses incurred for testing, amounting to $2200.[167] Additionally, they would incur unsubsidised rates at public hospitals if admitted for suspected COVID-19 within 14 days of their return, as they "risk the lives of other Singaporeans and residents when they return."[168]

The broad acceptance and internalisation of COVID-19 restrictive measures such as mask-wearing is evident in the reproach directed, both online and offline, at people caught breaching safe-distancing measures. Facebook sites dedicated to calling out flouters like SG Covidiots emerged, with some 14,000 members.[169]

A viral video of an unmasked woman declaring she was 'sovereign' and above the law, arguing heatedly with passers-by, earned the Law Minister's public rebuke; she was charged with breaching COVID-19 regulations, fined $2000 and sentenced to two weeks in prison. [170] Letters to the press pointed out that people walking slowly or doing light exercise were flouting the rules by not wearing masks.[171] Acts of citizen vigilantism with racist overtones took place where self-appointed public health guardians filmed and sought to harass unmasked strangers, as where a person demanded that an old Indian couple walking without masks run, as Regulation 2(a) exempts mask-wearing when "jogging or running but not walking," as forms of strenuous exercise.

---

166 Singaporeans advised to defer all travel abroad amid heightened risk of imported COVID-19 cases, CNA.com, 18 March 2020; MOH, "Tighter measures to minimise further spread of COVID-19" (24 March 2020); MOH, "Expansion of the enhanced stay-home notice requirements to all countries" (8 April 2020).

167 Gov.sg., 'Updates to border measures for travellers entering Singapore: Changes to stay-home notice arrangements and COVID-19 testing', 15 June 2020.

168 'Returning Singapore residents from UK, US to serve stay-home notices at hotels', CNAcom, 25 March 2020

169 'Singapore's Covid-snitches harass and shame strangers in racially charged videos', Coconuts Singapore, 17 April 2020

170 'Sovereign' woman pleads guilty to breaching COVID-19 rules, gets two weeks' jail and fine', *Straits Times*, 7 May 2021

171 Vedha Thiagarajan, 'Tighten rules on mask-wearing for those not doing strenuous exercise', *Today*, 19 July 2020

One Alan Tham who breached his SHN and boasted on Facebook about how he left his home to go eat *bak kut teh* (pork rib soup) was not only chastised by his friends; Tham was investigated and charged under section 21A of the Infectious Diseases (COVID-19 Stay Orders) Regulation 2020,[172] on the Law Minister's specific request, who noted that many Singaporeans were "upset" at hearing reports of returning travelers disregarding SHNs by going out to bars and restaurants. He encouraged members of the public to provide information to the police about people flouting SHN, to be investigated.[173] Tham was given a deterrent 6 months imprisonment sentence for his "socially reprehensible" behavior.

The Environment Minister urged citizens to facilitate enforcement by providing "as many actionable details" as possible of breaches of safe distancing rules, to the police or using the Oneservice mobile application.[174] This proved popular, attracting some 700 reports within two days of launching the feature.[175] This culture of snitching flowed (perhaps to ugly extremes) from the communitarian emphasis on the mutual responsibilities of all towards the safety of others, rather than the demand for rights.

VI. *Legal and Political Accountability*

1. *Judicial Review*

While judicial review to challenge COVID-19 measures was available and indeed classified as "essential and urgent" [176] applications during the CB period, this did not, at least in 2020, serve as a major check over pandemic regulations insofar as these allegedly violated constitutional liberties. It

172 The offence relates to exposing other persons "to the risk of infection by his presence or conduct in any public place" where a person knows or suspects he is a case, carrier or contact of a scheduled infectious disease: *Public Prosecutor v Alan Tham Xiang Sheng*, 23 April 2020, Brief Sentencing Remarks, SC-902973 (Available at statecourts.gov.sg); 'S'porean man who breached SHN to eat bak kut teh jailed for 6 weeks', mothership.sg, 23 April 2020.

173 'Shanmugam: Police to investigate S'porean man who flouted SHN to eat bak kut teh', mothership.sg, 25 March 2020

174 Masagos Zulkifli, 15 April 2020, https://www.facebook.com/masagos/posts/1475009695993376.

175 'As OneService reports against safe distancing offenders increase, some frontliners get assaulted' Asiaone 16 April 2020

176 See Supreme Court of the Republic of Singapore, *Registrar's Circular No. 4 of 2020* (5 April 2020).

is not a suitable remedy for short-term orders like 14 day SHN issued to overseas returnees. In 2020, there was only one failed public law suit, conducted by videoconference, alleging that restrictions on elections held during the pandemic, such as the ban on physical rallies, contained in the Parliamentary Elections (COVID-19 Special Arrangements) Act (Act 21 of 2020) impinged upon the right to vote. [177]

Various judicial review applications against vaccination differentiation measures were brought in 2021 and remain pending, as discussed below.

2. *Political Accountability*

a) A Confusing Multiplicity of Rules and Policies

Some degree of political accountability through the institutions and processes associated with political constitutionalism was achieved. Within and without Parliament, criticisms about complicated SDM rules and the difficulty the people and business faced in keeping up with frequent policy changes, stressing citizens and healthcare workers alike, were levied. A doctor in a blog post spoke of the bewildering effect of 3 different criteria on boosters being disseminated within a 2-week period.[178] Efforts have since been made to streamline COVID-19 rules and regulations, to do away with "complicated flow charts",[179] so that people can understand not just the letter but "spirit of the rules", enabling them to exercise individual responsibility and "do their part to help manage the pandemic."[180] SDM have been simplified to five parameters (group sizes, mask-wearing, workplace requirements, safe distancing and capacity limits) within which measures can be relaxed or tightened to meet new variants. Signaling a confident step towards living with COVID-19, the government in February

177 *Daniel De Costa Augustin v Attorney-General* [2020] SGCA 60

178 A confused population cannot pull together to fight the COVID-19 pandemic, *Straits Times*, 6 Oct 20-21. This related to a direction given to general practitioners on 14 September 2021 that those above sixty could receive a booster jab if their primary vaccination regime was complete 180 days ago; on 17 September this was stated to be 150 days and on 24 September 143 days if the MOH has invited the person to take the booster via SMS.

179 'COVID-19 healthcare guidelines to be drastically simplified, all S'poreans on home recovery will get care: PM Lee', *Straits Times*, 9 Oct 2021.

180 Health Minister Ong Ye Kung, Opening Remarks, COVID-19 Multi-Ministry Taskforce Press Conference, 16 Feb 2022.

2022 announced it would be scrapping safe-distancing rules in mask-on settings, as part of a wider "reset" of restrictions that had grown unwieldy over time.[181]

Future plans are laid out in Parliament, as are the beneficial impact of COVID-19 regulatory measures. For example, the Finance Minister noted during his 2022 Budget speech that vaccination efforts averted an estimated 8000 deaths during the Delta wave of August-December 2021.[182]

b) Service lapses and the Home Recovery Protocol

Public feedback and criticism is something a responsive government addresses. Much was directed at the initial poor execution of the Home Recovery Programme (HRP)piloted in August 2021, which became the default care arrangement for all COVID-19 positive patients, given the milder nature of the virus where 98% of patients are asymptomatic; those clinically unsuitable are sent to hospital or treatment facilities to recover. From 6 January 2022, primary care doctors exercised grater autonomy in deciding whether to prescribe an individual as a Protocol 1, 2, or 3 case, depending on severity of symptoms and health status. Protocol 3 cases are identified by the MOH as a close contact of an infected person and must take ART tests and upload the results at go.gov.sg/agsubmit; if this is negative after Day 7, no further test is needed. If a person is well but tests positive, they should isolate at home for 72 hours and then take an ART, exiting isolation when this is negative. If a person is unwell and tests positive, they are to see a doctor, and the MOH will contact them on recovery procedure. They will be discharged in 10 days if vaccinated, 14 days if unvaccinated/partially vaccinated, and the TraceTogether alert will be automatically removed on discharge. Protocol 2 rests on an honesty based system, which needs the "cooperation, the civic-mindedness and the sense of self-responsibility" of everyone.[183]

---

181 'Singapore's move to streamline COVID-19 rules signals confidence in living with virus: observers', *Business Times*, 16 Feb 2022

182 '5 highlights from MOF's report on the impact of past key COVID-19 Budget measures', *Straits Times* 17 Feb 2022.

183 Ong Ye Kung, Vaccination for primary chool students and possibility of VDS for preschools and primary schools, 95 SPR 1 Oct 2022

People eligible for HRP did not need to go to hospital but in an advisory[184] were told they should immediately self-isolate from other household members in a separate room 'preferably with an attached bathroom'; none of the household members could be over 80 years or in a vulnerable group, e.g. be pregnant or have multiple comorbidities and would receive a Health Risk warning within 48 hours. Technology was leveraged upon to get people comfortable with home recovery, in the form of telemedicine and a phone hotline to a Home Recovery buddy to address non-medical issues. [185]

However, the government did not appear to fully appreciate the impracticality HRP posed to many people, and had to revise this, as more than 1 million Singapore families live in public housing flats with 2-4 rooms. Further, many households had a person over eighty and if they recovered at home, the implication would be that all in the household must wear masks during the 10-day recovery period, later reduced to 7. While the HRP originally applied to the fully vaccinated aged 50 or younger, this was later extended to those up to 69 years, but dropping the reference to the attached bathroom. Furthermore, HRP implementation faced operational failures, as where close contacts of infected persons were only contacted some 8-9 days after the relevant encounter, showing a lack of preparedness. People were unable to contact health officials on hotlines for advice on their specific situations and were without guidance. The SG Quarantine Order Support Group emerged on Telegram, for people to share their experiences.[186] There were long lag times between testing positive and being taken to a recovery facility. Parliamentary questions about the failures in implementing the HRP were raised,[187] and addressed, with the government acknowledging service lapses; persons with vulnerable family members were assured they could go to an isolation facility to recover. [188]

Parliament is the forum where the government has been called to account for policy U-turns such as abruptly limiting those permitted to wear

---

184 MOH, Paras 9-12, Antigen rapid test kits venting machines deployed islandwide and updates to home recovery and travel classifications', 17 Sept 2021

185 Eligible for Home Recovery Programme at https://www.covid.gov.sg/unwell/hrp.

186 'This is poor planning': COVID-19 home recovery patients voice confusion, frustration over what to do', *Straits Times*, 23 Sept 2021; '

187 Issues with COVID-19 home recovery programme being ironed out: Ong Ye Kung', *Straits Times*, 4 Oct 2021

188 COVID-19 healthcare guidelines to be drastically simplified, all S'poreans on home recovery will get care: PM Lee', *Straits Times*, 9 Oct 2021.

face-shields instead of masks.[189] The government was candid about the "rough edges"[190] of its regulatory approach; on hindsight, it would have required the earlier wearing of face masks, given that infected persons could be asymptomatic, and would have taken a more aggressive precautionary approach towards managing migrant worker dormitories.

c) Redressing the Mismanaged Migrant Workers Cluster

Parliament provides the venue for the government to explain how governance gaps have been redressed, such as the initial mishandling of the migrant worker clusters which erupted in April 2020 in crowded dormitories, but which was brought down to single digits by October 2020.[191]

The government gazetted some dorms as isolation areas, quarantining migrant workers in their rooms. This gave rise to complaints and concerns about their mental health, poor ventilation, unsanitary toilets and poor food quality, which NGOs helped to publicise. Infected workers and their close contacts were isolated and received medical care, while healthy workers were moved into temporary accommodations in army camps and cruise ships, to reduce the numbers in existing dorms. The government also partnered with religious groups and NGOs to meet the worker's psychological and spiritual needs. Employers were required to continue to pay migrant workers salaries during the CB,[192] with government subsidies, and an app was developed to monitor the health status of foreign workers, through requiring foreign workers to self-report their temperatures and any flu-like systems. Required regular rostered testing was introduced, as a tool to enable workers to get back to work. New dormitories with better

---

189 Minister Gan explained that after the CB period, more personal interactions required full face masks to be worn as face shields did not provide adequate coverage, given the gaps between the shield and face: Ministerial Statement, Government's Plans in our Continuing Fight against COVID-19 Pandemic, 94 SPR, 5 June 2020

190 *Supra*, note 37.

191 '47 per cent of migrant workers in Spore dorms have had a COVID-19 infection, says Manpower and Health Ministries', *Straits Times*, 15 Dec 202; 'All migrant worker dorms, including standalone isolation blocks, cleared of COVID-19: MOM, *Today*, 19 Aug 2020

192 Ministry of Manpower (MOM), 'Advisory on salary payment to foreign workers residing in dormitories', 11 April 2020.

living conditions and able to meet disease response needs were built.[193] Government attention and efforts have thus been purposefully directed at improving the living standards of foreign workers in Singapore, in response to the emergence of the problem and public feedback.[194]

d) Trace Together and Privacy Concerns

Singapore has utilised technology to aid in pandemic management. For example, deploying pilotless drones which track anomalies such as large gatherings and streams footage back to the police[195] and robotic dogs to issue social distancing warnings in public parks[196] has facilitated SDM observance. The ability to upload ART testings online also facilitates public health monitoring.

However, the fears of technology abuses and the surveillance state have also arisen, in relation to the Trace-Together app developed by the Government Technology Agency and launched in March 2020. Singapore was the first country to deploy a national COVID-19 smartphone Bluetooth app to expedite its advanced contact tracing system. Manual contact tracing, used during the SARs era, could not handle the sheer volume of COVID-19 cases. The app works by exchanging short-distance Bluetooth signals with nearby users. Privacy concerns were raised when these tracing apps and wearable devices were first announced on 5 June 2020, eliciting a petition opposing the device which gained 30,000 signatures within 3 days.[197]

---

193 'Plans to overhaul housing for foreign worker unveiled', *Straits Times*, 2 June 2020

194 'The long, challenging journey to bring COVID-19 under control in migrant worker dormitories', CNA, 12 Sept 2020

195 'Coronavirus: Singapore uses pilotless drones for social distancing monitoring', *South China Morning Post*, 6 Aug 2020

196 Singapore's Smart City Response to COVID-19, ARC Advisory Group Blog, 28 Aug 2020 at https://www.arcweb.com/blog/singapores-smart-city-response-covid-19.

197 Petition: All that is stopping the Singapore government from becoming a surveillance state is the advent and mandating the compulsory usage of such a wearable device," the petition stated. "What comes next would be laws that state these devices must not be turned off [and must] remain on a person at all times - thus sealing our fate as a police state." Saira Asher, 'TraceTogether: Singapore turns to wearable contact-tracing Covid tech', BBCnews.com 4 July 2020

Strenuous efforts were taken to assuage public fears through ministerial assurances[198] that it was not a tracking device but a partly decentralised data collection system to be used exclusively for protecting citizens during a public health crisis.[199] Proximity data was stored locally on the phone in an encrypted format for 25 days (accounting for the 14 day incubation period of the virus), and then automatically purged, rather than on a central server. [200] Other built-in safeguards including prompting users to deactivate its functionality when a disease outbreak ends, to allay fears of entrenched, continuing surveillance. Users will only be asked to share these records when contacted by MOH as part of contact-tracing investigations. If they refuse, they may be prosecuted under the IDA.[201] A similar protocol applies to Tracetogether tokens[202] where the device must be physically handed over to the authorities to extract data where the user becomes infected. Although only mandatory for migrant workers living in dormitories, the government urged Singaporeans to participate in this brand of community-driven contact tracing, as its efficacy improves, the higher the adoption rates;[203] this would bolster confidence in "opening up and resuming more activities"[204] for larger gatherings such as conferences and business events.

On the basis of these representations, which reflected the government's acknowledged responsibilities as public data custodian, people downloaded the app or used the token. The hope was to get a 70% participation rate,[205] in order to progress to the next phase of reopening. By the first

198 'Contact-tracing device will not track location; people can use TraceTogether if they prefer, says Vivian Balakrishnan', *Straits Times*, 8 June 2020.

199 Huang Weixian, "Contact tracing app is safe, secure and needed as Singapore opens up" *Straits Times* 13 June 2020; see also Darius Lee, "Transparent rules needed on use of contact tracing data" *Straits Times* 12 June 2020.

200 'TraceTogether presents chance for Singapore to restore track record on data privacy and security', *Today,* 8 Oct 2020.

201 'Singapore launches TraceTogether mobile app to boost COVID-19 contact tracing efforts,' CNA.com, 20 March 2020

202 'TraceTogether token collection to be expanded to 100 more locations across Singapore', *Straits Times,* 4 Oct 2020

203 Health Minister Gan Kim Yong, Ministerial Statement, On the update on whole-of-Government response to COVID-19, 25 March 2020 at [36]

204 'COVID-19: Home-based workers may return to offices in cohorts, work-related events with up to 50 people allowed', *Today*, 23 Sept 2020.

205 '70% of Singapore residents participating in TraceTogether programme: Vivian Balakrishnan', CNA.com, 23 Dec 2020

quarter of 2021, some 90% of residents were using TraceTogether.[206] It was later made mandatory from 1 June 2021, becoming the sole method for digital check-ins to places like shopping malls, workplaces, schools, gyms and places of worship. This technology has reportedly helped identify 75 people who had to be placed under quarantine, but which manual tracing was likely to have missed.[207]

However, it transpired that the minister in charge of the Smart Nation initiative had committed an oversight, which he admitted before Parliament in January 2021. He had not realised that Tracetogether data was not exempt from the police power under section 20(1A) of the Criminal Procedure Code to order anyone to produce 'data' to facilitate investigation or trial proceedings. The minister apologized, promising the police would judiciously use such data only for serious offences. This sparked public outrage,[208] which critics characterised as a betrayal of trust.[209] Some people declared they would delete the TT app.[210]

Moved by this, the Minister accepted full responsibility and at the next parliamentary sitting in February 2021, introduced a new law on a certificate of urgency, which allows a bill to be put through three readings in one sitting. [211] This law confined the use of TraceTogether data to seven categories of "serious offences", including murder and terrorism.[212] A parliamentarian's suggestion of publishing disclosure reports to help the public understand how data was being used beyond contact-tracing was also adopted.[213]

---

206 'Budget debate: Contact tracing process shortened with almost 90% of S'pore residents using TraceTogether', *Straits Times*, 26 Feb 2021

207 'Tracetogether token or app mandatory at malls, workplaces, schools from June 1', *Straits Times*, 22 April 2021

208 Clarification by Minister for Foreign Affairs, 95 Singapore Parliament Report, 5 Jan 2021 Issue No 15.

209 'Sporeans are feeling betrayed because of TraceTogether. The govt needs to restore trust', Mothership.sg, 9 Jan 2021

210 'Some TraceTogether users upset with Govt's revelation on police access to data, say they'll use it less,' *Today* 7 Jan 2021; '350 people asked for their contact tracing data to be deleted', *Straits Times*, 3 Feb 2021; 'More than 1,100 users have deregistered from TraceTogether: Vivian', *Straits Times* 11 May 2021.

211 95 Singapore Parliament Report, 2 Feb 2021 (COVID-19 Temporary Measures (Amendment)) Bill.

212 'Bill restricting use of TraceTogether data for serious crimes passed by Parliament' CNA.com, 2 Feb 2021.

213 'Parliament passes bill specifying use of TraceTogether, SafeEntry data by Police', *Today*, 3 Feb 2021

This episode resulting in a ministerial *mea culpa* was a lesson in transparency, of admitting rather than doubling down on errors. It appears to have gone some way to assuage privacy concerns; although some 350 people wrote in to request that their TraceTogether data be deleted over the past month, which the minister regretted, he noted that a further 390,000 had come on board the TraceTogether programme. This reflects a broad trust in the digital tool for pandemic management, and in the police to act lawfully. This is distinct from the liberalism of fear rooted in distrust and suspicion of public authorities and reflects the brand of responsive democracy which is a facet of Singapore political constitutionalism in Singapore. Nonetheless, some opposition politicians for fear of government overreach maintained the view the police should not be able to use Tracetogether data, and that public trust in public health measures had been eroded. [214]

C. *Vaccinations and Discrimination/Differentiation: The Law and Politics of Regulation, Reception and Resistance*

I. *Regulation and Reception*

Vaccines were seen as a "game changer"[215] and have become central to the Singapore pandemic management model, seen as the way to the 'new normal' of a Covid resilient nation.

Authorities indicated that restrictions would be relaxed after hitting the 80% milestone, which it did in August 2021, giving Singapore the highest rate of complete vaccinations according to Reuters.[216] By February 2022, over 94% of the eligible population had been fully vaccinated and 67% had received booster shots, introduced in September 2021, on the recommendation of the Expert Committee on COVID-19 Vaccination (EC19V)).[217] MOH provided that from 14 February 2022, boosters are required to maintain fully vaccinated status (270 days or 5 months after the

---

214 'TraceTogether: PAP MPs say proposed legislation addresses concerns; PSP suggests data should only be used for contact tracing', CNA.com 11 Jan 2021.

215 PMO, PM Lee Hsien Loong, 'Update on the COVID-19 situation in Singapore, 9 Oct 2021.

216 'Singapore fully vaccinates 80% of population against COVID-19', Reuters, 29 August 2021

217 'Singapore starts booster shots as Covid cases hit 1 year high', Nikkei Asia, 14 Sept 2021. The MOH stated that the recommendation for the elderly and immunocompromised to be boosted was aligned with measures adopted in

last dose of the primary vaccination series).[218] The government prefers the experimental mRNA vaccines on the basis of their apparent effectiveness. In December 2021, the government said that full vaccination status could not last perpetually with the vaccines offering waning protection, but was contingent on boosters. It also reduced the exemption from VDS of the recovered from 270 to 180 days, stemming from concerns of heightened reinfection risk posed by the Omicron variant and the rapid decline in protection acquired through past infections, from 1 January 2022, encouraging the recovered to take mRNA booster shots.[219] This shows the broad powers of the executive and co-opted expert committees. The VDS are a powerful mechanism to induce people to take the booster, even if this is a multi-year requirement, where the long-term effects of novel are not fully known.

Vaccine skepticism persists, despite the official position that NVP vaccines are safe and efficacious, a view advanced by the legacy media. Concerns are mainly expressed on social media outlets like Telegram, some being raised before Parliament by opposition politicians. Despite reaching its vaccination milestones, in the face of new variants, there has been no significant relaxing of COVID-19 restrictions. Indeed, the government has adopted harsher measures against the voluntarily unvaccinated, while maintaining concessions for the involuntary unvaccinated, in its push to expand vaccine coverage to optimise COVID-19 resilience.

Originally, vaccine differentiation safe management measures (VDS) were introduced to induce more vaccinations, albeit framed in terms of protecting the unvaccinated from infection and severe illness. These greatly restricted free movement, with the steady extension of the range of socio-economic activities the unvaccinated were prohibited from engaging in.

These measures were justified on the basis that the vaccinated had a lower risk of getting infected and transmitting the virus.[220] The MOH in a written answer to a parliamentary question dated 14 September 2021 rejected the criticism that VDS was discriminatory, stating that with a "very high level of vaccination, reaching or approximating herd immunity,

---

Israel and Germany: MOH, 'Strengthening our tools to achieve covid resilience, 3 Sept 2021

218 COVID-19 booster shot needed to maintain fully vaccinated status from Feb 14: MOH', CNA.com 5 Jan 2022

219 MOH, 'Preparing for the omicron variant' 14 Dec 2021

220 'Perks for those vaccinated against COVID-19 not meant to be discriminatory; Ong Ye Kung' *Straits Times*, 1 July 2021

it is possible to remove the differentiated measures." It was estimated this would happen in case 80% of the population were vaccinated,[221] although no time frames were given, thus creating uncertainty.

The government tried the 'carrot' of offering perks to the vaccinated, such as the privilege of overseas travel without having to serve SHN, or exemptions from the Pre-Event Test (PET) for events like weddings or live performance. Private firms offered modest discounts to promote vaccination.[222] The Health Minister asserted that VDS were not meant to discriminate but served public health purposes as the nation moved towards "a sense of normality."[223] The premise of VDS may be problematical insofar as vaccines go towards ameliorating the severity of infection rather than transmissibility of the virus[224] and could transmit the virus. Nonetheless, the MOH asserted that vaccination provided "significant protection" against infection and helps "to reduce the severity of the disease and onward transmission."[225]

VDS measures were introduced in August 2021, where up to 5 fully vaccinated people could dine in restaurants, while the limit was 2 for non-vaccinated people. Stronger attempts to 'nudge' people towards vaccination were introduced in October 2021 when the voluntarily unvaccinated were not allowed to dine in anywhere, which had some success. [226] Vaccinated persons could make hospital visits without the need for a self-paid pre-visit COVID-19 test. This lacks medical sense insofar as the vaccinated may be infected and also carry transmissible viral loads. [227] The unvaccinated needed a negative self-paid PET test to enter shopping malls and other VDS settings to access services like banking, medical and dental treatment, getting haircuts and childcare.

---

221 *Supra*, note 21.

222 'New deals and discounts for those vaccinated against COVID-19 in Singapore', *Straits Times*, 21 Aug 2021

223 Vaxxed or vexed: What will life for the unvaccinated be like in Singapore', *Straits Times*, 21 Aug 2021

224 Acharya et al, 'No significant difference in viral load between Vaccinated and Unvaccinated Asymptomatic and Symptomatic Groups infected with SARs-CoV-2 Delta Variant' (29 Sept 2021) at https://www.medrxiv.org/content/10.1101/2021.09.28.21264262v1.

225 MOH, 'Updates on Local Situation and Heightened Alert to Minimise Transmission, 14 May 2021

226 'More getting COVID-19 shots since VTL news and dine-in ban for unvaccinated', *Business Times*, 12 Oct 2021

227 MOH, 'Vaccination-differentiated approach for visitors at all hospitals', 16 Aug 2021

The requirement of a negative PET, valid for only 24 hours, was extended to the workplace effective 1 January 2022. These costs add up, at $20-30 per test. The medically ineligible (involuntarily unvaccinated) were exempted from these requirements. VDS measures were expanded to all national libraries and community centres from 1 December 2021, restricting entry only to the fully vaccinated to "further reduce the risk of transmission in such settings."[228]

The turning of the screws proceeded apace with the decision that from 1 January 2022, only fully vaccinated individuals, the medically ineligible and children under 12 could enter VDS settings, in removing the previous 'concession' of allowing the unvaccinated to get a PET and show a negative test. Later clarifications stated that the unvaccinated could access 'standalone' supermarkets and seek medical clinics in malls, as it would be unthinkable to cut off citizens from basic services in the name of protecting the unvaccinated.[229] VDS measures were extended, from 1 February 2022, to all indoor sports facilities, hotels and institutes of higher learning.[230] Even with 96% of the eligible population fully vaccinated, the government still insisted on getting more vaccinated and boosted in the face of the Omicron variant.[231] Cutting off the unvaccinated from social life exacts a social cost, compounding their isolation and harming their mental health, which was apparently discounted,[232] as some letters to the press noted with concern.[233]

The government decided to underwrite all COVID-19 medical bills of Singaporeans, Permanent Residents and long-term pass holders, to ally public anxiety when COVID-19 was "an emergent and unfamiliar disease." This approach is to continue until things stabilise but as of 8 December 2021, the voluntarily unvaccinated would have to foot their own COVID-19 medical bills should they be hospitalized, which could

---

228 MOH, Para 10, Updates in Safe Management Measures, 22 Nov 2021

229 Unvaccinated workers, people seeking medical and childcare services can enter shopping malls', CNA.com, 13 Oct 2021

230 'Vaccination checks to be expanded from Feb 1 to all indoor sports facilities, institutes of higher learning, hotels' *Today*, 14 Dec 2021

231 MOH, Para 9, Extension of primary series vaccination to children aged 5-11 years and booster vaccinations to all individuals aged 18 to 29 years', 10 Dec 2021

232 MOH, Para 23, Calibrated adjustments in stabilisation phase, 8 Nov 2021

233 Tan Sek Jen, Forum: Don't ignore mental health of unvaccinated, especially youngsters', *Straits Times*, 14 Oct 2021

amount to $25,000 before applicable medical subsidies.[234] This move sent "important signal" for all eligible persons to get vaccinated,[235] as with VDS, the government was taking a "stronger stance" against the unvaccinated who "disproportionately contribute to the strain on our healthcare resources."[236]

The government enlisted private sector assistance in its vaccination drive, as a fully vaccinated workforce would ensure a safe environment for all. [237] An August 2021 advisory released by the Tripartite Partners (the government, National Trade Unions Congress and Singapore National Employers Federation) offered 'guidelines' urging employers to ensure workers were vaccinated or tested regularly, providing them time off to get their jabs and recover. To further pressurise employers, companies could check their workforce's vaccination rate online at the Workforce Vaccination Checker.[238] Employers could now require unvaccinated employees (excluding the involuntarily unvaccinated) to bear any costs of testing only affecting them, though they were urged to come to reasonable arrangements with pregnant employees when it came to sharing testing costs, although pregnant staff were "strongly encouraged" to be vaccinated. Employers were "under no circumstances" to terminate an employee's service on grounds of vaccination status alone, although vaccination could be required of potential hires. [239] Taking its cue from a 2 July 2021 advisory that companies could make worker vaccinations compulsory in higher-risk setting, Jetstar Asia became the first air carrier to do so.[240]

VDS measures was criticised as discriminatory, given that vaccinated and unvaccinated alike face the same infection risks, and the vaccinated

---

234 COVID-19 patients who are unvaccinated by choice could face $25,000 bill before subsidies says MOH, CNA.com, 12 Nov 2021

235 'COVID-19 patients who are unvaccinated 'by choice' will have to pay their own medical bills from Dec 8', CNA.com, 8 Nov 2021

236 'COVID-19 patients unvaccinated by choice to pay for own treatment from Dec. 8, 2021, mothership.sg, 8 Nov 2021

237 MOH, Para 25, 'Preparing for our ransition towards Covid resilience' 6 August 2021

238 MOM, Updated advisory on COVID-19 vaccination at the workplace 23 Oct 2021 (updated 27 Dec 2021).

239 'Must employers pay for tests for unvaccinated staff who have to report to the workplace?' *Straits Times*, 26 Oct 2021

240 'Vaxxed or vexed: What will life for unvaccinated be like in Singapore?' *Straits Times*, 21 August 2021

might pose a bigger transmission threat if asymptomatic.[241] As of 17 October 2021, 96% of workers were vaccinated, with 113,000 unvaccinated workers. Further, an October 2021 advisory departed from the August one, adopting a more hardliner stance in stating Singapore must take "strong steps" to protect the involuntarily unvaccinated, and that a fully vaccinated workforce would pose lower risks to employees' lives. While employers can allow the unvaccinated to work from home, the advisory indicated this could be harmful both to one's career and impede organizational performance.

The harshest measure by far relates to the Workplace Vaccination Measures announced on 23 October, that from 1 January 2022, all unvaccinated individuals would not be allowed to return to the workplace as the option of doing a PET with a negative result was withdrawn.[242] Employers could redeploy such workers to jobs which could be done from home, adjusting remuneration commensurate with job responsibilities, place them on no pay leave on mutually agreeable terms, or, as a last resort, terminate their employment in accordance with the employment contract. If an employee was dismissed because he could not be present at the workplace, this would not constitute wrongful dismissal. This departs from the August 2021 advisory that employers should not threaten, penalize or terminate unvaccinated employees.

Without vaccination status, the unvaccinated can lose their jobs, which is disproportionate and out of step with the 'shift to endemic' mindset, considering the high vaccination rates and Omicron's milder impact. The advisory states that by not coming to the workplace, unvaccinated employees "are protected from being exposed to the threat of the virus." It "urged" the remaining 2% of employees to get vaccinated in order to help society and the economy reopen safely, to "protect" their well-being and "avoid any impact to their jobs and livelihoods."[243] This rings a little hollow given the negative impact of such measures on the physical and mental well-being of those affected, as well as dashing their economic security. Al-

---

241 'Unvaccinated workers count cost of not getting jabbed as COVID-19 workplace rules loom', *Today*, 26 Aug 2021

242 MOM, *supra*, note 238. This has been argued to be wholly unreasonable: Dominic Chan, 'The voluntary nature of COVID-19 vaccination and the nreasonableness of barring workers from workplace (20 Dec 2021): https://www.movetheneedlesg.com/post/the-voluntary-nature-of-covid-vaccination-and-the-unreasonableness-of-barring-workers-from-workplace.

243 Para 6b,13, 'Updated advisory on COVID-19 vaccination at the workplace', 23 Oct 2021

though cast in the persuasive language of "urge", this effectively transcends a nudge and is a shove towards making a decision to get vaccinated under duress, a *de facto* mandate short of legal compulsion. Thus, pandemic management has wrought an insalubrious situation where employers can discriminate against current and prospective employees on grounds of vaccination status, creating second-class citizens.

The vaccine-centric MOH was criticized for acting "more like the marketing agency" for pharmaceutical companies "than an independent regulator."[244] Not all decisions appeared to rest on 'science' as opposed to political judgment. For example, when faced with the new Omicron variant in November 2021, Health Minister Ong Ye Kung rejected arguments that vaccinations should be halted in favour of waiting for a new vaccine. He insisted on the necessity of "insurance" in the form of "existing vaccines", as there was a "good chance" these would work against Omicron.[245] Even if the Omicron variant was less severe, he thought it untimely to "gamble" by removing VDS "on the "hunch" that Omicron may be less severe for the infected unvaccinated."[246]

The strong government pro-vaccination narrative has emboldened private citizens, journalists and government parliamentarians[247] to call for mandatory vaccinations as a civic duty,[248] such that $500 fines would be incurred under the IDA for failing to get a mandated vaccine. Letters to the press have urged that the unvaccinated not be allowed into public places, noting that a "vaccine certificate is already built into the TraceTogether app."[249] The unvaccinated have been demonized as irresponsible, selfish and anti-social for holding back the reopening of society, and urged to

---

244 John Atkinson, Open Letter to Prime Minister Lee, 12 December 2021, Facebook at https://m.facebook.com/story.php?story_fbid=1249147566647388&id=100074386432580.

245 Health Minister Ong Ye Kung, Opening Remarks, paras 23-26, COVID-19 Multi-Ministry Taskforce Press Conference, 30 Nov 2021

246 'Now's not the time to gamble and remove vaccination differentiation measures: Ong Ye Kung', *Today*, 21 Jan 2022.

247 Senior Minister of State (Defence), Heng Chee How, 95 SPR, 27 July 2021, Ministerial Statements, Support Measures for Phase Two (Heightened Alert) and Phase Three (Heightened Alert) and Support Measures for Phase Two (Heightened Alert),

248 ' 'Forum: Set deadline for getting jabs and have more restrictions for those who miss it', *Straits Times* 22 Sept 2021; 'Forum: Don't hesitate to vaccinate, don't hesitate to mandate', *Straits Times*, 17 Sept 2021

249 'Forum: Bolder carrot-and-stick approach needed to accelerate COVID-19 vaccine roll-out', *Straits Times*, 5 July 2021

look beyond "principles and rights to the greater good of society."[250] There have been emotive calls to punish and ostracise the unvaccinated, stirring hostility towards a group holding an unpopular view which obstructs the NVP. [251]

This bodes poorly for sustainable democracy or relational well-being, as the issue is framed in terms of 'us versus them', between the interests of the unvaccinated minority and that of the vaccinated majority who chose vaccination to protect themselves and others, [252] which is socially divisive. This discounts the possibility that the unvaccinated may have strong reasons for not being vaccinated or ignores a possible policy of respecting a person's agency in making personal and familial health decisions, as in the case of Japan.[253] Indeed, public health concerns could be met by simply reinstating the PET requirement for entry into VDS settings.

Nonetheless, without dismissing it out of hand, the government has stated that it has no plans to make vaccinations mandatory, as the vaccines were not fully registered and admitted only for pandemic use. [254] Even the Health Minister described the unvaccinated as free riders[255] or a group that "disproportionately make up the bulk of severe and ICU cases", straining the healthcare system.[256] He rejected the argument that the number of the unvaccinated, some 120,000 as of January 2022, was low and did not sustain a public health threat warranting VDS. The healthcare system would be overwhelmed if say, some 5800 of the 120,000 unvaccinated contracted Covid. This was "not a small number" given that at its peak,

250 'Forum: Make COVID-19 jab mandatory, except for the ineligible', *Straits Times*, 23 Nov 2021

251 'Actor Hossan Leong gets pushback for tweeting SG is held hostage by the unvaccinated', *The Independent*, 13 Sept 2021; 'Forum: Time to rely on stronger measures rather than just persuasion', *Straits Times* 19 July 2021.

252 Alex Yam, 95 SPR, 24 July 2021 (Fifth update on Whole of Government Responses to COVID-19)

253 Aaron Kheriaty, 'Japan's Vaccination Policy: No Force, No Discrimination', Brownstone Institute, 14 Dec 2021.

254 'No plans for mandatory COVID vaccinations in Singapore: MOH' *Yahoo News*, 24 Sept 2021

255 Health Minister Ong Ye Kung, Opening Remarks, MTF Press Conference, 21 Jan 2022 at [18]

256 Calibrated Adjustments in Stabilisation Phase, 8 Nov 2021. In particular, seniors, who account for 1.5% of the population accounted for two-thirds of individuals needing ICU care or who have died: MOH, Para 3, Protecting the Vulnerable, Securing our Future', 9 Oct 2021

"our maximum ICU occupancy was 176;" this scenario would be avoidable if the unvaccinated had just "chosen to take their jabs instead."[257]

Originally the presumption was the unvaccinated should prove they were not a threat to others by taking self-funded ARTs. This makes it safer to be around the unvaccinated with a negative ART test, as asymptomatic vaccinated individuals can be carriers. This is reflected in the advice given to the vaccinated to minimise social interactions insofar as they could be infected and asymptomatic, unwittingly bringing this "home to seniors."[258] Thus visitors to households with unvaccinated persons or vulnerable elderly are "strongly encouraged" to test themselves before visiting.[259]

Taking away even this option reveals the punitive nature of VDS measures[260] which cannot be justified in terms of healthcare concerns. It also presumes that refusing to get vaccinated is morally wrong, deserving punishment, which is something requiring broad public debate, rather than mere assumption by office-holders. Indeed, the government acknowledged that from the public health standpoint, the voluntarily and involuntarily unvaccinated should be treated alike, both being equally vulnerable, as distinct from permitting medically ineligible persons to be tested before joining social events. Nonetheless, the medically ineligible were extended concessions to be able to dine in restaurants or enter malls; their personal agency was respected, while they were advised to minimize their social activities and use their concession "judiciously."[261]

This reflects a tripartite social 'caste' system composing the socially responsible vaccinated, the faultless medically ineligible, and the 'irresponsible' unvaccinated subject not to concession but sanction, through paternalistic strong-arming exacted through social shaming, curbing free movement and the prospect of job loss. The rationale of seeking not to compromise "the well-being of the vulnerable members of our community"[262] is disquieting, as the stigmatizing and punitive exclusion from social

257 'Now's not the time to gamble and remove vaccination differentiation measures: Ong Ye Kung', *Today*, 21 Jan 2022

258 MOH, Para 9, 'Further precautionary easures to protect our vulnerable elderly from COVID-19 surge', 18 July 2021

259 MOH, para 6, 'Resuming our transition towards Covid resilience', 20 Nov 2021

260 Health Minister Ong Ye Kung, 95 SPR, 24 July 2021 (Fifth update on Whole of Government Responses to COVID-19)

261 MOH, Para 29, Calibrated adjustments in stabilisation phase, 8 Nov 2021 at https://www.moh.gov.sg/news-highlights/details/calibrated-adjustments-in-stabilisation-phase_8Nov2021.

262 Ibid., para 36.

and economic life will negatively impact anyone. Indeed, there are reports that some succumbed to taking the vaccination because they felt like "a social outcast" and wanted to regain "a sense of freedom."[263] The attempt to direct opprobrium or public censure against the unvaccinated may also be inferred by contrasting their treatment with the government's rejection of a proposal by a parliamentarian that the people involved in the Karoake or KTV cluster of July 2021, foot their own medical costs. These people had gone to many lounges, where hostesses mingle between groups, leading to a cluster in July 2021 which caused actual communal harm in delaying reopening plans. [264] The Health Minister said that while many were upset at their "irresponsible behavior", the government still "had a public responsibility to ensure that everyone receives the medical care they need", and that a punitive approach could discourage the miscreants from coming forward for testing or to hide from contact tracers.[265]

This does not seem sensible, compared to the willingness of the unvaccinated to be socially responsible by taking ART tests at their own costs before entering VDS settings, an option now removed.

Short of imposing a difficult to police mandate which would seriously undermine social trust in excluding unvaccinated citizens from "the normal activities of life", VDS measures operated as a 'stick' by "making it painful for the unvaccinated", through the stress of being 'othered', deprived of modern life conveniences and potentially their livelihood. While there is no constitutional right to work, this is a fundamental interests and its loss carries serious economic as well as mental health consequences. The VDS is easier to enforce than forcible vaccination. The Health Minister of State admitted that VDS were "in a way" a workaround the mandate option, an attempt "to try and get around some of that problem, to expose different segments of the population to different risks." [266]

While the political costs of discriminating against the unvaccinated is relatively minor given their lack of political clout, the size of the 'unvacci-

263 'Singaporeans, whether vaccinated or refusing to be jabbed, feel a social divide over coronavirus', *South China Morning Post*, 16 Sept 2021

264 MOH, Updates on Phase 3 (Heightened Alert) Measures, 16 July 2021

265 'Penalising those involved in KTV cluster 'would cost us more in the long run: Ong Ye Kung', *Yahoo News*, 26 July 2021

266 Janil Puthucheary (Senior Minister of State for Health), Ministerial Statement, 'Update on ICU and Hospital Capacity', 95 SPR 1 Nov 2021. Notably, the paper of record did not mention this admission and only mentioned that mandatory vaccinations were not a straightforward course of action: 'Complicated to make COVID-19 vaccines in Singapore mandatory: Janil Puthucheary', *Straits Times*, 1 Nov 2021

nated' can vary as vaccination status is now contingent on participation in the booster programme. The government can easily change the definition of fully vaccinated status through subsidiary legislation[267] in accordance with its reading of the science, to determine who has "cleared status"[268] needed to use facilities subject to VDS. Centralised control is facilitated by the TraceTogether smartphone app and token, which indicates vaccinated status, now a precondition for participation in social life and amenities.

II. Resistance

The unvaccinated and other concerned citizens have received or viewed these VDS measures as discriminatory, involving government overreach in not being a necessary public health differentiating measure. The vaccinated majority seems to support VDS measures, by dint of complying with them.

Those resisting vaccination and their allies have concerns about ignored alternative treatments, like Ivermectin. The HSA has warned people not to self-medicate with it, as it is not approved for treating or preventing COVID-19.[269] A more pressing concern is with the safety and efficacy of novel, experimental vaccines. Reluctance is fueled by reports from abroad and anecdotal evidence of persons suffering strokes, heart inflammation, organ failure and bell palsy, for example; local incidents of such adverse reactions are shared through websites[270] and social media channels like Telegram groups which collate this information, as well as of reports of

---

267 First schedule, Infectious Diseases (Mass Gathering Testing for Coronavirus Disease 2019) Regulations 2021.

268 'Fully vaccinated' status expires after 365 days, MOH to review this as more data becomes available', mothership.sg, 12 Nov 2021. Under rule 9 Infectious Diseases (COVID-19 Access Restrictions and Clearance) Regulations 2021 (s 273/2021), individuals are not to enter a "restricted place" if they lack a "cleared status" as defined under rule 6.

269 Health Sciences Authority, 'Advisory on the use of ivermectin for COVID-19', 5 Oct 2021. The press reported that a female retiree was hospitalized after she was persuaded to take ivermectin to protect herself from COVID-19: 'Grandmother hospitalized after taking ivermectin to 'protect herself' against COVID-19', *Straits Times*, 4 Oct 2021. The illegal sale of ivermectin can attract a $50,000 fine or 2 years imprisonment under the Health Products Act.

270 'Gym buddies and siblings' health took a turn for the worst after Pfizer Jab' Voice of Wilderness, https://vow.sg/suspected-vaccine-injured-among-young-adul ts/.

people suffering non-life threatening side effects like eczema, shingles and irregular menses *e.g.*, SG Suspected Vaccine Injuries Channel." [271]

While the government acknowledges the risks associated with vaccination, such as myocarditis, anaphylaxis and pericarditis and other allergic reactions like rashes, these are described as rare and small, with symptoms expected to subside within a few days.[272] The official position is that overall, the benefits outweigh the known risks in relation to Pfizer, Moderna and Sinovac vaccines.[273] The MOH asserts that the experts in the form of the HSA and EC19V have assessed vaccines to be safe and efficacious, that medical teams are equipped to treat adverse reactions and medical professionals are bound to report such incidents.[274] The EC19V in response to reports of how younger men receiving mRNA vaccinations have suffered myocarditis and pericarditis issued a warning to avoid strenuous physical activity for one week post-vaccination and to be wary of difficulty breathing or abnormal heartbeats.[275]

Concerns have also been raised about the lack of transparency with respect to vaccine injury and the need for this to be clearly defined, with set times for compensation payouts; further, the government rather than the injured party should bear the onus of proving the vaccine did not cause the injury, rather than the injured being told by a government appointed panel of experts that their injuries were unrelated to their vaccination.

With the legacy media generally supporting the government's public health policies, dissenting voices have sought to articulate alternative views they feel have been shut out of the official narrative, using such available

271 The big Read in short: COVID-19 'info war' - it's not just the virus wreaking havoc', *Today,* 12 June 2021

272 The Health Sciences Authority stated this in relation to Pfizer vaccine. The Expert Committee on COVID-19 Vaccination issued a statement urging all medically eligible persons to be vaccinated, starting with groups subject to greater risks (healthcare workers and the elderly), but that vaccinations should remain voluntary. 'HSA grants interim authorisation for Pfizer-BioNTech COVID-19 vaccine in Singapore', *Business Times*., 14 Dec 2020.

273 'HSA grants interim authorisation for Pfizer-BioNTech COVID-19 vaccine in Singapore', *Business Times*., 14 Dec 2020; 'HSA grants interim authorisation for Moderna Vaccine in Singapore' Press Release 3 Feb 2021; 'HSA grants interim authorisation for Sinovac-CoronaVac vaccine in Singapore', Health Sciences Authority Press Release 23 Oct 2021;

274 MOH, Issuance of correction directions under the protection from online falsehoods and manipulation act on falsehoods on COVID-19 vaccination', 15 April 2021

275 'Spore teen who suffered cardiac arrest after COVID-19 jab undergoing rehab, gets $225k in financial assistance', *Straits Times,* 16 Aug 2021

means as websites, open letters, social media posts and e-petitions. These views have ranged from conspiracy theories to reasoned arguments, such as against VDS. While these open letters have been posted on other websites, they did not get traction or attention from mainstream media.[276] Websites such as that of "Truth Warriors" and individuals which challenge vaccine efficacy, advocate for alternative treatments or which "falsely" exaggerate[277] the dangers of Covid vaccines and discourage people taking them have received POFMA CDs. Groups of doctors who issued public letters warning of the risks of unstudied and unknown long-term effects of mRNA vaccines for adolescents, addressed to parents, were swiftly lambasted by "aghast" government officials as "unscientific and unprofessional",[278] promoting misinformation and scaremongering, prompting 11 of 12 doctors to retract one such letter. [279] An EXC19V member slammed this and similar letters as "fake science on social media,"[280] even group chat organisers see their role as being "a sounding board to surface alternative views."[281] Petitions calling for an Outpatient Home Treatment Plan[282] developed by international critical care doctors and providing cheap antiviral drugs like

---

276 E.g. Dominic Chan, 'A nuanced analysis of Vaccination-Differentiated Safe Management Measures, 2 November 2021, reposted by the truthwarriors at https://www.truthwarriors.info; Dominic Chan, 'The voluntary nature of Covid vaccination and the unreasonableness of barring workers from workplace, 29 Dec 2021 at movetheneedlesg.com

277 POFMA correction directions issued to Cheah Kit Sun, Goh Meng Seng over COVID-19 vaccine falsehoods, CNA.com, 29 Nov 2021

278 'Aghast and disappointed': Koh Poh Soon Slams doctors for spreading myths, untruths in open letter on COVID-19 vaccine', *Today*, 22 May 2021; Expert committee hits back at open letter by 12 S'pore doctors saying mRNA COVID-19 vaccine not safe & not effective for those aged 12-15. Mothership.sg, 22 May 2021.

279 MOH, Expert Committee on COVID-19 Vaccination endorses extension of use of Pfizer-BionTech COVID-19 vaccine in individuals aged 12 to 15 years and longer dosing interval for MRNA vaccines', 18 May 2021

280 'Infectious disease expert David Lye calls out misinformation about COVID-19 vaccines', *Straits Times*, 7 June 2021; 'MOH responds to call to delay COVID-19 jabs for schoolboys, says benefits outweigh risk', *Straits Times*, 29 June 2021

281 Quoting Mr Jake Goh, who runs a Telegram group: 'The big read: Conspiracy theories, scientific misinterpretations, plain ignorance abound in COVID-19 infodemic', CNA.com, 14 June 2021; 'Infectious diseases expert David Lye calls out misinformation about COVID-19 vaccines', *Straits Times* 7 June 2021.

282 'A Petition to Battle Plan Against COVID-19: The 3rd Front', by Citizens against Covid 19, 16 June 2021 athttps://www.truthwarriors.info/l/a-petition-to-battle-plan-against-covid-19-the-3rd-front/ . Original petition at Petition Battle Plan Against COVID-19: The 3rd Front (ipetitions.com)

ivermectin have also been roundly criticized by experts on government affiliated bodies as lacking evidence of effectiveness or being 'anti-science,' even where there is lack of universal consensus on the 'science', as science takes times where experimental vaccines are concerned.

Petitions have been made calling for an apology from Singapore Press Holdings, for the socially divisive tone in a Straits Times article authored by Salma Khalik, where she stated that since unvaccinated people faced a higher risk of getting infected and spreading the disease, society had the right to protect itself from harm by requiring the former to get tested before participating in social events. She advocated that the government withdraw subsidies and insurance coverage for the voluntarily unvaccinated, since their refusal to vaccinate was "tantamount to a self-inflicted injury." [283] Alternative perspectives or the value of medical self-determination were not discussed.[284] The matter took a judicial turn through proceedings against Khalik under section 15 of the Protection from Harassment Act, for making two false statements in her 7 August 2021 article,[285] in the hopes of securing a correction order. In a sworn affidavit, Khalik submitted that her statements were that of opinion, not fact and the petitioners asked that opinions should be clearly labelled and that both sides of the story be presented.[286]

Other petitions have sought policy changes, and called for the dropping[287] or calibration of VDS measures to protect the unvaccinated/unboosted from losing their jobs[288] as well as to prohibit the unvaccinated

283 'Only fair to protect vulnerable in Spore against COVID-19 spread by unvaccinated people' *Straits Times* 7 August 2021

284 Salma Khalik, 'Eligible individuals who refuse COVID-19 vaccine endanger themselves and others', *Straits Times* 24 Feb 2021

285 This stated "It is only fair to protect vulnerable in S'pore against COVID-19 spread by unvaccinated people" and "People who are not vaccinated face a much higher risk of getting infected and spreading the disease." This was reported on the Healing the Divide website on 9 Nov 2021: We Are Suing SPH – Healing The Divide at https://healingthedivide.cc/2021/11/09/wearesuingsph/.

286 Petition: SPH to Apologise and Terminate Salma Khalik's Employment for Stating "Not statement of Fact", https://www.change.org/p/mr-khaw-boon-wan-sph-to-apologize-terminate-salma-khalik-s-employment-for-stating-non-statement-of-fact?redirect=false (2901 signatures)

287 An online petition calling for the termination of VDS measures gained 10,000 signatures in 2 weeks: 'Divergent lives from Tuesday for the vaccinated and unvaccinated in Spore', *Straits Times*, 9 Aug 2021

288 Petition · Remove or Re-Calibrate VDS Measures & Protect The Unvaccinated/Unboosted From Losing Jobs · at https://www.change.org/p/remove-or-re-cali

from entering malls.[289] Some of their concerns have been taken up by opposition politicians through Facebook posts or even through parliamentary adjournment motions, such as the plea of Jaime Wong, a tennis coach who shared that with effect from 15 January 2022, she was unable to enter her tennis school and continue her profession as she was unvaccinated; having willingly accepted VDS measures barring her from malls and taking twice weekly ART tests, she was at a loss with the rationale of being barred from her workplace.[290]

Opposition MPs have pointed out that vaccination policies were socially divisive, discriminatory and disrespectful towards individual autonomy in making medical decisions. Further, that it was "unthinkable and illogical" to ruin livelihoods on grounds of vaccination.[291] Although they made the point that having doubts about vaccination is "not unreasonable", that the effect of VDS measures on personal livelihoods was "too harsh", the official response elicited simply pointed to the unvaccinated consuming a disproportionate amount of medical and hospital resources, including expensive therapeutics; even if 1% of the currently unvaccinated group of 48,000 workers caught Covid, this would "tax our ICU bed capacity."[292]

Those who dissent against vaccines or who are hesitant towards vaccination have organized groups, e.g. Healing the Divide (HTD), a self-described group of "intelligent vaxxers." The founder, Iris Koh, started a petition addressed to the Prime Minister entitled "Do not let vaccination status divide us", attracting 15993 signatures.[293] Apart from expressing concerns about social divisions, calling for the end to VDS measures and for an independent board to verify whether injuries and death are caused by the vaccines, the petition called for 'constructive dialogue'

---

brate-vds-measures-protect-the-unvaccinated-unboostered-from-losing-jobs (9184 signatures)

289 Petition · Don't Allow unvaccinated people to enter malls in Singapore! at ·https://www.change.org/p/lee-hsien-loong-don-t-allow-unvaccinated-people-to-enter-malls-in-singapore (1077 signatures)

290 Hazel Poa, Vaccine differentiated safe management measures, 95 SPR, 10 Jan 2022

291 Leong Mun Wai, 'Drop vaccination discrimination, please respect personal autonomy', Facebook, 12 Nov 2021 at https://www.facebook.com/leongmwofficial/posts/322420099693951.

292 Rahayu Mahzam (Parliamentary Secretary, Minister of Health), Vaccine differentiated safe management measures, 95 SPR, 10 Jan 2022.

293 Petition · Do not let vaccination status divide us. · Change.org

and citizen involvement in discussing public health safety issues.[294] HTD subsequently held online townhalls ("United we stand for Choice", 31 October 2021) and posted videos ("Remembering those we love and lost") which Youtube, as censor, subsequently removed for apparently violating Youtube's medical misinformation policy. The MOH welcomed this, in characterising the HTD channel as a source of misleading information[295] and the group as adopting "an anti-vaccination stance," a descriptor chorused by mainstream media.[296] The prospect of the two behemoths of government and technological companies like Youtube or Facebook in a kind of public-private partnership possessing the power as information gatekeepers to control the public narrative should alarm those who value viewpoint diversity, which appreciating the damage misinformation can cause.

Iris Koh received some notoriety as an alleged purveyor of misinformation: she was reportedly under police investigations in November 2021 for allegedly obstructing public servants from discharging their duties by apparently urging some 2700 people via Telegram to overwhelm various ministry hotlines under the guise of giving feedback on VDS; this provoked anger on the part of some netizens and the official criticism that such tactics would deny genuine callers the opportunity to seek help. [297] In January 2022, MOH filed a police report against HTD for purportedly telling parents to overwhelm medical staff at paediatric vaccination centres

294 'Do not let vaccination status divide us', at Petition · Do not let vaccination status divide us. · Change.org https://www.change.org/p/prime-minister-of-singapore-lee-hsien-loong-do-not-let-vaccination-status-divide-us?source_location=search_index&algorithm=promoted&original_footer_petition_id=&grid_position=2&pt=AVBldGl0aW9uAJCkygEAAAAAYcNkzXWKi50yNmQ2ZjliZg%3D%3D.

295 MOH, Removal of Content from Youtube Channel for Violating Com.munity Guidelines' 7th Nov 2021 at https://www.moh.gov.sg/news-highlights/details/removal-of-content-from-youtube-channel-for-violating-community-guidelines_7Nov2021.

296 Content from anti-vaccination YouTube channel removed for violating guidelines, *Straits Times*, 8 Nov 2021

297 Natasha Meah, 'Anti COVID-19 vaccine group founder, husband, under police probe for allegedly instigating people to overwhelm public hotlines, Today, 25 Nov 2021; Isabelle Liew, 'Couple linked to anti-vaccine group investigated for instigating others to flood public hotlines', *Straits Times*, 25 Nov 2021; Louisa Tang, 'Judge denies bail for Healing the Divide founder Iris Koh after 'appalling belligerence' including tearing up charge sheet=.' *Today*, 31 January 2022

with questions.[298] Koh was also charged with allegedly conspiring with a medical practitioner to fraudulently represent that some people had been vaccinated by submitting false COVID-19 vaccination records. [299]

There is clearly a cost to disagreeing publicly with the official public health narrative, particularly in a deference society where harmony is prized as is the impulse to conformity. These episodes show the limits of political checks in terms of government responsiveness and accommodation where it comes to core aspects of health policy, on which they are unyielding.

Where petition fails, the last resort is had to judicial review; even where the prospects of success are mild, the 'performative' aspect of seeking to hold the government accountable for unreasonable policies or alleged rights violations carries political value.

To date, there have been at least three applications for judicial review, brought between November 2021- February 2022. The first was brought on behalf of Iris Koh,[300] the second by Lim Tean, an opposition politician who posted news on his Facebook account of an application by 6 people seeking to quash certain COVID-19 directives.[301] The third group of 5 applicants disassociated themselves from previous meetings and court proceedings, declaring their sole intent was to ensure taking vaccines was a personal choice within a country where "everyone feels that they are part of the Singapore conversation and the Singapore family."[302]

These applications relate to alleged violations of constitutional guarantees of life and personal liberty, including the right to livelihood (article 9), equality (article 12), freedom of movement (article 13), right of peaceful

---

298 Healing the Divide founder Iris Koh, doctor charged with conspiracy to submit fake COVID-19 vaccination records; MOH investigating clinic, *Today*, 23 Jan 2022

299 Doctor gets more serious charge of lying to MOH that woman was vaccinated against COVID-19, Today, 25 Jan 2022

300 'Founder of 'Healing the Divide' anti-vax group engages lawyer M Ravi to start legal proceedings against S'pore govt', Mothership.sg 14 Nov 2021.

301 'Statement filed in the Judicial Review Proceedings Brought by the 6 Applicants to Quash Directives of the MTF, MOM and MOH, Lim Tean, 28 December 2021 at https://www.facebook.com/PeoplesVoiceSingapore/posts/46849718464 5524 . This challenged the 23 October 2021 MTF directive that employers could terminate the employment of unvaccinated employees and the 8 November 2021 directive that the unvaccinated by choice would have to bear the medical costs of any treatment.

302 Loy Hwa Wei, Statement before Commencement of Court at VDS Judicial Review (wordpress.com)

assembly at the workplace (article 14), and religious freedoms (article 15). Various policies have also been challenged on grounds of administrative reasonableness. This shows that when government actions are perceived as over-reaching or abuses of power, rights consciousness is provoked. This happens even within communitarian settings which often prioritise responsibilities over rights, where most people have not had the chance to consider their civil liberties before the swathe of intrusive COVID-19 regulations made them feel "the bridle of government around our throats."[303]

D. *Concluding thoughts*

It appears the government's pandemic management has the overwhelming support of Singaporeans, who are moved by appeals to solidarity and the greater good, who accept prioritizing the interests of the national community over that of individuals, who trust in the government or who are at least 'nudged' by the carrots and stick approach anchored in the VDS regime. In an era where pandemic-induced divides and distrust are globally increasing, according to polls like the Edelman Trust barometer, Singapore apparently bucks the trend, given the strong levels of trust in the ethics and competence of government and business, which helps maintain social cohesion.[304]

However, not all is quiet on this Asian front and it appears that trust is fraying at the edges, even if resilience rather than social resentment remains dominant. The state has actively advanced a vision of what it means to be a good citizen in a pandemic, and by default, a bad citizen, utilizing laws and other social shoves or inducements to shape behavior and articulating an ever-growing list of social duties. The good citizen gets vaccinated and boostered, observes safe distancing measures, does not spread misinformation, wears a mask and takes personal responsibility in relation to personal hygiene, self-testing and not exposing the vulnerable to possible infection. The good citizen follows the latest health protocol and does not seek hospital or medical treatment if infected with mild symptoms, to preserve healthcare capacity. The bad citizen fails to do these things and is subject to harsh VDS which represent to them a turn to the

303 Brigid Delaney, 'The pandemic has forced 'safe, comfortable' Australians to confront human rights. So what's next?' *The Guardian* (UK), 3 Dec 2021

304 S'pore's COVID-19 story: In the same storm, in different boats, but going the right way?, *Straits Times*, 22 Jan 2022

authoritarian, both by their governors and non-governmental voices. This provokes social rifts, where there is a shift from solidarity to singling out small, politically insignificant groups for blame. As stated by an applicant for judicial review:

> It is unreasonable to fail to consider the harms and/or detrimental effects to the social, economic, mental, spiritual and/or emotional wellbeing of the Applicants (both as individuals, and as part of the class of the unvaccinated population) arising from or associated with the imposition and continued imposition of VDS and/or WVM. Such harms include...the denial or restriction on the freedom of movement, the denial and/or restriction to access to the goods, services, events, activities and/or opportunities provided at such prohibited places, and also exposure, both individually as Applicants and as part of the class of the unvaccinated population, to alienation, segregation, marginalization, ridicule, contempt and/or avoidance by or from the rest of society, effectively making them into 2nd class citizens and/or a new substratum of society...

The Singapore approach of legal communitarianism as applied to pandemic management may thus be seen as a salutary tale of how effective governance can ward off or manage pandemic harms, or as a cautionary tale of how a dominant majority can oppress a weak minority, spotlighting the importance of rights as correctives of asymmetries of power. This reflects the eternal constitutionalist conundrum articulated by Madison in the Federalist No. 51, of first enabling the government to control the governed, and then obliging the government to control itself.

Bibliography

Ackerman B., The Emergency Constitution, The Yale Law Journal 113 (2004), p. 1029ff.

Agamben G., A che punto siamo?, L'epidemia come politica, Quodlibet, 2020.

Agamben G., Homo Sacer, VI, L'uso dei corpi, Vicenza, 2014.

Agamben G., Homo sacer. Die souveräne Macht und das nackte Leben, 2019.

Agamben G., State of Exception, University of Chicago Press 2005, 111 p.

Agostini M., Petrini M., 'Decreto legge Ristori, disposizioni emergenziali per l'esercizio delle attività giurisdizionale', Giustizia Insieme, October 2020.

Agresti A., Statistical Methods for the Social Sciences (5th Edition, Pearson Education Limited) 2018

Albrecht P.-A., Kriminologie – Eine Grundlegung zum Strafrecht, 4. Auflage.

Allegrezza S., Le réponse répressive des Etats face à la Covid ou le devoir à la santé du citoyen superlatif. Un aperçu de droit comparé, Revue pénale luxembourgeoise.

Amhlaigh C. M., 'Legitimacy in the Time of Coronavirus' (Verfassungsblog, 17 April 2020) <https://verfassungsblog.de/legitimacy-in-the-time-of-coronavirus/> accessed 20 November 2020.

Amodio E., Catalano E. M., 'La resa della giustizia penale di fronte alla bufera del contagio', Sistema Penale, 2020.

Amrani Mekki S., « La procédure civile réécrite sous contraintes sanitaires », Gaz. Pal., 28 avr. 2020.

Amrani-Mekki S., « Constitutionnalisation du dispositif état d'urgence sanitaire », Procédures, n° 11, Novembre 2020, comm. 193.

Amrani-Mekki S., « Constitutionnalisation du dispositif état d'urgence sanitaire », Procédures, n° 11, Novembre 2020, comm. 193.

Amrani-Mekki S., « La part du droit (et de la justice) dans l'angoisse contemporaine – la computation des délais », Procédures n° 5, Mai 2020, étude 15.

Anderson D., 'Can We Be Forced to Stay at Home?' (David Anderson QC Lawyer London UK, 26 March 2020).

Andolfatto E., 'Un'ordinanza interlocutoria della Consulta sul "decreto antiscarcerazioni"', Sistema Penale, August 2020.

Aparicio E., "Efectos de la sentencia del TC sobre el derecho de alarma en los procedimientos sancionadores",20 Julio 2021.

Armstrong M., 'Infographic: The Best and Worst Rated National COVID-19 Responses' (Statista Infographics), November 2020.

Baglayan B., Fahner J. H., 'One Can Always Do Better' (2017) 17 Hrlr 2.

Bartoli R., 'Irretroattività e prescrizione: proposta di una soluzione in attesa della Corte costituzionale', Sistema Penale, October 2020.

Battarino G., 'Prime riflessioni sui criteri costituzionalmente fondati di distribuzione dei vaccini anti Sars-Cov-2', Questione Giustizia, November 2022.

Bianku L. and Smith H., « Les droits fondamentaux et la pandémie COVID-19 » in Engel, A. et al. (dir.), Annales du droit luxembourgeois : Volume 30 – 2020, 2019e édition, Bruxelles, Bruylant, 2021.

Bonnet, « Le Conseil d'Etat et le COVID-19 », JCP, juin 2020, 656, p. 995 et pour la Belgique http://www.raadvst-consetat.be/?page=news&lang=fr&newsitem=640.

Bontempelli M., 'Emergenza COVID-19 e ragionevole durata del processo penale', Sistema Penale, January 2021.

Bougard F., et Morelle L., Prévention, appréciation et sanction du faux documentaire (VIe-XIIe siècle), dans Olivier Poncet (dir.), Juger le faux (Moyen Âge – Temps modernes), Études et rencontres.

Bowcott O., 'Has Coronavirus Changed the UK Justice System for Ever?,' The Guardian, 24 May 2020

Braum S., Le droit pénal aux temps de Choléra, Revue pénale luxembourgeoise, 7/2021.

Brimo S. et Defoort B., La police générale de la salubrité à l'épreuve de l'état d'urgence sanitaire : ou l'impossible disparition de la salubrité publique locale, RDSS, 2020.

Brodeur J.P, 'High and Low Policing in Post-9/11 Times', (2007).

Bruck V., « L'état d'urgence contre l'État de droit démocratique », Septembre 2017, https://www.forum.lu/wp-content/uploads/2017/09/376_Bruck.pdf.

Brunetti L., 'La Costituzione può obbligare, ma non costringere: sulla incostituzionalità degli attuali divieti come mezzo per incentivare la vaccinazione anti COVID-19', Forum di Quaderni Costituzionali, 2021.

Burgess M., 'Everything You Need to Know about the New NHS Contact Tracing App', Wired Up, 2020.

Butler O., "The Failure of the UK's Centralised COVID-19 Contact-tracing App", blogdroiteuropéen, 24 September 2020.

Byrom N. et al., « The Impact of COVID-19 Measures on the Civil Justice System », Justice Civil Council, mai 2020.

Caballero V., F./Lopez de Castro L., Distribución territorial del poder durante la pandemia, Afduam, Extraordinario (2021).

Cadiet L., J. Normand & S. Amrani-Mekki, Théorie générale du procès, Themis, 2015, n° 191.

Cadiet L., « Procédure civile et covid-10 acte II : de l'exception au principe? », JCL G, Juin 2020, 715.

Camardi C., Tabarrini C., "Contact tracing ed emergenza sanitaria. "Ordinario" e "straordinario" nella disciplina del diritto al controllo dei dati personali", Nuova Giurisprudenza Civile Commentata, no. 3/2020.

Cano Campos T., " Sanciones administrativas, in AFDUAM", Extraordinario (2021).

Caravita B., "L'Italia ai tempi del coronavirus: rileggendo la Costituzione italiana", Federalismi.it, March 2020.

Cassuto T., Crise sanitaire du COVID-19, perspecitves et enjeux d'une reponse pénale, AJ Pénal, 2020, Juillet/Août.

Cavino M., "COVID-19. Una prima lettura dei provvedimenti adottati dal Governo", Federalismi.it, March 2020.

Cavino M., "COVID-19. Una prima lettura dei provvedimenti adottati dal Governo",Federalismi.it, 2020

Cavino M., "La natura dei DPCM adottati nella prima fase di emergenza Covid. Lettura di Corte cost. n. 198/2021", Federalismi.it, November 2021.

Chaffai-Parent S., Piché C., « La justice au temps de la Covid », Rapport de l'Institut québécois de réforme du droit et de la justice, 15 juin 2020.

Chardenoux S. et al., « Justice and Challenges in Times of Pandemic in Europe », MEDEL, juin 2020.

Cheng I., 'COVID-19: Singapore looking at new sources, local manufacturing for essential supplies such as masks', 2020.

Chifflot N., « La continuité du service public de la justice judiciaire au temps du COVID-19 », Procédures, mai 2020.

Chiodo S., "Ontario Civil Justice Reform in the Wake of COVID-19: Inspired or Institutionalized?" (15 juillet 2020), Osgoode Legal Studies Research Paper, sous presse, et disponible sur SSRN: https://ssrn.com/abstract=3686181.

Cintioli F., "Sul regime del lockdown in Italia (note sul decreto legge n. 19 del 25 marzo 2020)", Federalismi.it, April 2020.

Coghlan N., "Dissecting COVID-19 Derogations" (5 May 2020) Verfassungsblog, https://verfassungsblog.de/dissecting-covid-19-derogations/.

Cohendet A.-M., « La collégialité des juridictions : un principe en voie de disparition? », Revue française de droit constitutionnel, 2006/4 (n° 68).

Coldicutt R., 'Open Letter: Contact Tracking and NHSX', Medium, 27 March 2020.

Collins J., 'Coronavirus and the Spread of Crime Control' (UK Constitutional Law Association, 28 April 2020.

Conte P., Le droit pénal de crise : l'exemple du virus COVID-19, Droit pénal, n. 5, Mai 2020, p. 5.

Corbisier I., « An II de la pandémie de COVID-19 – Un point comparatif sur les tribulations du paiement du loyer dans le cadre d'un bail commercial (Luxembourg, Belgique et France) : cacophonie, solidarisme ou pragmatisme? (première partie) », J.T.L., 2021/2.

Cormacain R., 'Can I Go to the Park Please Dad? Everyday Lessons in Legal Certainty in the English Coronavirus Regulations' (UK Constitutional Law Association, 15 May 2020).

Cotino H. L., " Inteligencia Artificial y vigilancia digital contra la COVID-19 y contra la privacidad. El diablo está en los detalles », 2020.

Covolo V., Non-respect des mesures sanitaires et contamination à la COVID-19 : Quelle responsabilité pénale de droit commun?, Revue pénale luxembougeoise, 07/2021.

Criddle C., Kelion, L. 'Coronavirus Contact-Tracing: World Split between Two Types of App', BBC News, May 2020.

Criddle C., "Revenge Porn New Normal" after Cases Surge in Lockdown' BBC News, September 2020

Criddle E. J., "Protecting Human Rights During Emergencies: Delegation, Derogation, and Deference", in M. Ambrus and R.A. Wessel (eds.), Netherlands Yearbook of International Law 2014.

Criddle E.J., 'Human Rights, Emergencies and Rule of Law', in Human Rights Quarterly (April 2010).

Croze H., « Comment gérer les délais pendant la période d'urgence sanitaire? », Procédures n° 6, Juin 2020, 2.

Daes E.-I.A.,"The Individual's Duties
to the Community and the Limitations on Human Rights and Freedoms Under Article 29 of the Universal Declaration
of Human Rights: A Contribution to the Freedom of the Individual Under Law" (1983), E/CN.4/Sub.2/432/Rev.2.

De Coninck B. et al., « La procédure civile en période de COVID-19 », J.T., 2020.

De Falco D., Maddalena M. L., 'La politica del tracciamento dei contatti e dei test per COVID-19 alla luce delle ultime direttive OMS: nessun ostacolo giuridico impedisce di utilizzare il "modello coreano" anche in Italia', Federalismi.it, March 2020.

De Minico G., "Costituzionalizziamo l'emergenza?", Osservatorio sulle fonti, 2020.

De Stefano F., "La pandemia aggredisce anche il diritto?", Giustizia Insieme, April 2020.

Dearden L., 'Government Refuses to Abolish Coronavirus Law Used Unlawfully in Every Prosecution' (The Independent, 28 June 2020.

Debout E., « Mesures d'urgence sanitaire et valeurs de l'Union européenne », R.A.E, L.E.A., 2020/1.

Delaney B., 'The pandemic has forced 'safe, comfortable' Australians to confront human rights. So what's next?' The Guardian (UK), Dec 2021.

Delaporte F., « Le rôle croissant de la Cour Constitutionnelle » in La défense des droits et libertés au Grand-Duché de Luxembourg, Bruxelles, Éditions Larcier, 2020.

Deleuze G., Postskriptum über die Kontrollgesellschaften, in: Folkers/Lemke, p. 127 et seq.

Della Bella A., 'Emergenza Covid e 41 bis: tra tutela dei diritti fondamentali, esigenza di prevenzione e responsabilità politiche', Sistema Penale 1 May 2020.

Della Giustina C., 'La vaccinazione contro il COVID-19 tra facoltà ed obbligo nel rapporto di lavoro subordinato. Riflessioni giuspubblicistiche', Federalismi.it, July 2021.

Della Morte G., 'La tempesta perfetta. COVID-19, deroghe alla protezione dei dati personali ed esigenze di sorveglianza di massa' SidiBlog, March 2020.

Delmas-Marty M., Intervention pendant la conférence, COVID-19, nos sociétés démasquées, France Culture.

Denault V. and Patterson M.L., « Justice and Nonverbal Communication in a Post-pandemic World: An Evidence-Based Commentary and Cautionary Statement for Lawyers and Judges », Journal of Nonverbal Behavior, 2020, 4, https://doi.org/10.1007/s10919-020-00339-x.

Denizot A., « COVID-19 : entre droit de la peur et peur du droit », RTD Civ., 2020.

Desierto D. A., Necessity and National Emergency Clauses: Sovereignty in Modern Treaty Interpretation Account (Brill 2012), 252.

Developing a Global Privacy Regime in the Age of Mass Surveillance: Four Key Principles' (openDemocracy), 10 December 2020.

Devlin H., and Sarah Boseley, 'Scientists Criticise UK Government's "following the Science" Claim' The Guardian (23 April 2020).

Di Todaro F., "Screening oncologici in ritardo a causa del COVID-19", Magazine, 2020.

Diaz Crego M., Kotanidis S., States of emergency in response to the coronavirus crisis: Normative response and parliamentary oversight in EU Member States during the first wave of the pandemic, EPRS | European Parliamentary Research Service, 04–12–2020, 60 p.

Dimmer L., « Le Bail et la Covid – retour sur les jugements rendus en la matière », JN Immo, 2021/2–3.

Dolcini E., Gatta G. L., 'Carcere, coronavirus, decreto 'cura Italia': a mali estremi, timidi rimedi', Sistema Penale, March 2020.

Donier V. and Laperou-Scheneider B., Accès au juge : quelles évolutions?, Bruxelles, Bruylant, 2013

Durdu A., « Le Conseil d'État, gardien des droits et libertés fondamentaux » in La défense des droits et libertés au Grand-Duché de Luxembourg, Bruxelles, Éditions Larcier, 2020.

Dyzenhaus D., L'état d'exception, in M. Troper, D. Chagnollaud (eds.), Traité international de droit constitutionnel, T. II, Distribution des pouvoirs, p. 739 ff.

Dyzenhaus D., States of Emergency, in Michel Rosenfeld, Andras Sajo (eds.), The Oxford Handbook on Comparative Constitutional Law, Oxford 2012, p. 442ff.

Dzehtsiarou K., "Article 15 derogations: are they really necessary during the COVID-19 pandemic?" (2020) 4 E.H.R.L.R 359.

D'amico M., "I diritti fondamentali alla prova dell'emergenza sanitaria da Coronavirus: profili sostanziali", BioLaw Journal, 2020.

Englebert J., Service nécessaire à la Nation, la Justice ne pouvait pas être confinée, Analyse critique des mesures prises par le Collège des cours et tribunaux en vue de garantir le service de la Justice nonobstant le confinement et de l'arrêté royal n° 2 du 9 avril 2020, Anthemis, 2020.

Ergec R. and Menétrey S., « Avis sur l'avant-projet de loi portant organisation de la Cour suprême », in Judicial Reforms in Luxembourg and Europe, Nomos, 2014.

Ergec R., Contentieux administratif luxembourgeois, Pasicrisie, Luxembourg, 2011.

Feldman W., Theories of Emergency Powers: A Comparative Analysis of American Martial Law and the French State of Siege, Cornell International Law Journal, vol. 38, no. 3, 2005, pp. 1021–1048

Ferejohn F., Pasquino P., 'The law of the exception: A typology of emergency powers', International Journal of Constitutional Law (2004).

Fernandez G.B., 'Within the Margin of Error: Derogations, Limitations, and the Advancement of Human Rights' (2019) 92 Phil. L.J., 5–6.

Findlay S., Richard Milne and Stefania Palma, 'Coronavirus Contact-Tracing Apps Struggle to Make an Impact',18 May 2020.

Fitzpatrick J. M., 'Human Rights in Crisis the International System for Protecting Rights During States of Emergency', (University of Pennsylvania Press, 1994), at 29.

Fortson R., 'Open Textured Legislation in the Times of COVID-19: 'Reasonable Excuse' and Legal Certainty" (Responding to COVID-19: Surveillance, Trust and the Rule of Law, 2 June 2020).

Foucault M., Die Geburt der Biopolitik, in: Folkers/Lemke, p. 115 et seq (p. 116).

Foucault M., In Verteidigung der Gesellschaft, Vorlesung vom 17. März 1976, in: Folkers/Lemke, p. 88 et seq. (p. 92).

Foucault M., La volonté de savoir, 1976.

Foucault M., Recht über den Tod und Macht zum Leben, in: Folkers/Lemke (Eds), Biopolitik, p. 65 et seq. (p. 69).

Foucault M., 'Discipline and Punish. The Birth of the Prison', Second Vintage Books Edition, Vintage Books a Division of Random House, 1995.

Fraenkel E., The Dual State: A Contribution to the Theory of Dictatorship, (orig. in German 1943), The Lawbook Exchange, Ltd., Reprint 2010, 266 p.

Freeman Engstrom D. and Gelbach J.B., « Legal Tech, Civil Procedure, and the Future of Adversarialism », University of Pennsylvania Law Review, 2021, https://papers.ssrn.com/abstract=3551589.

Fricero N., « Comment restaurer l'activité juridictionnelle : transférer les litiges à une autre juridiction et aménager la tenue des audiences », Procédures, mai 2020.

Furedi F., Invitation to Terror: The Expanding Empire of the Unknown (Bloomsbury Academic), 2009.

Gallo C., 'Prima lettura delle nuove linee guida del CSM in materia di emergenza Covid (delibera 4.11.2020)', Giustizia Insieme, November 2020.

Gallon J.,“Informeller Föderalismus statt öffentlicher Deliberation”,Verfassungsblog, February 2021.

Gan Kim Y., Lawrence Wong, Ong Ye Kung, ‘Living normally with COVID-19’, Straits Times, June 2021.

Garcia A. V., /Arias Aparicio F./Hernandez Díez E., “Lecciones jurídicas para la lucha contra la pandemia” Iustel, 2020.

Garcia A. V., “El concepto de necesidad en Derecho público” Civitas, 1996.

Garibaldi O. M., ‘General Limitations on Human Rights: The Principle of Legality’ (1976) 17 Harv Int'l L J 503.

Gatta G. L., ‘Carcere e coronavirus: che fare?’, Sistema Penale, March 2020.

Gatta G. L., ‘“Lockdown” della giustizia penale, sospensione della prescrizione del reato e principio di irretroattività: un cortocircuito’, Sistema Penale, May 2020.

Gaudissart M.-A., « La Cour de justice de l’Union européenne face à la crise sanitaire », R.A.E, L.E.A., 2020/1.

Gerkath J. (Dir.), Les 20 ans de la Cour Constitutionnelle : Trop jeune pour mourir!?, Pasicrisie Luxembourgeoise, 2018.

Gerkrath J. (Dir.), Les 20 ans de la Cour Constitutionnelle : Trop jeune pour mourir!?, Pasicrisie Luxembourgeoise, 2018.

Gerkrath J., Constitutional Engineering of exception regimes within the European Union.

Gerkrath J., https://www.wort.lu/de/politik/pandemie-massnahmen-gerichtliche-kontrolle-verbessern-5fa584a7de135b92365f8e4c.

Gerkrath J., The Figure of Constitutional Law of the ‘Integrated State’: The Case of the Grand Duchy of Luxembourg, EuConst 2014.

Ghosh S., ‘Privacy Activists Fear the UK Might Spy on Its Own Citizens to Tackle COVID-19. Here’s What We Know.’, Business Insider, 26 March 2020.

Giostra G., ‘Disinnescare in modo sano la bomba-virus nelle carceri’, Sistema Penale, March 2020.

Glasser C. « Civil Procedure and the Lawyers—The Adversary System and the Decline of the Orality Principle », The Modern Law Review, 1993, vol. 56–3.

Gola M., “Pandemia, Stato e Regioni: quando la ‘materia’ non basta (nota a Corte Costituzionale n. 37/2021)”,Giustiziainsieme, 2021.

Gramuglia V., ‘Interrogatorio di garanzia e legislazione dell'emergenza COVID-19 (art. 83, co. 2 d.l. n. 18/2020): tra garanzie difensive e tutela della salute collettiva’, Sistema Penale, November 2020.

Grandi F., ‘L’art. 32 nella pandemia: sbilanciamento di un diritto o “recrudescenza” di un dovere?’, Costituzionalismo.it, 2021.

Greene A., Permanent States of Emergency and the Rule of Law. Constitutions in an Age of Crisis, Hart Publishing, Oxford 2018, 256 p.

Greene A., ‘Derogating from the European Convention on Human Rights in response to the coronavirus pandemic: if not now, when?’ (2020) 3 E.H.R.L.R 262–276.

Grierson J., Home affairs correspondent, 'Covid Cases in Prisons in England and Wales Double in October' The Guardian,(13 November 2020).

Grierson J., 'Suspects to Avoid Criminal Charges in UK during COVID-19 Crisis' The Guardian (14 April 2020).

Grisolia M. C., "Il rapporto Governo-Parlamento nell'esercizio della funzione normativa durante l'emergenza COVID-19", Osservatorio sulle fonti, 2020.

Gross O., 'Once More unto the Breach: The Systemic Failure of Applying the European Convention on Human Rights to Entrenched Emergencies' (1998) 23 Yale J Int'l L 437.

Gross O., Law in Times of Crisis. Emergency Powers in Theory and Practice, 2006

Grote R., Regulating the State of Emergency – The German Example, Israel Yearbook on Human Rights, 2003, p. 151ff.

Guerini T., "La tutela penal della Libertà di manifestazione del pensiero nell'epoca delle fake news e delle infodemie", DisCrimen, 16.5.2020.

Gómez Bellvís A.B, " La disuasión en el estado de alarma, Indret,", 2022.

Harari Y. N, 'Yuval Noah Harari: The World after Coronavirus | Free to Read, 20 March 2020.

Hartman J.F., 'Derogation from Human Rights Treaties in Public Emergencies--A Critique of Implementation by the European Commission and Court of Human Rights and the Human Rights Committee of the United Nations' (1981) 22 Harv Int'l L J.

Heinig/Kingreen/Lepsius/Möllers/Volkmann/Wissman, Juristenzeitung (JZ), 2020, p 861 et seq. versus Hase, Juristenzeitung (JZ) 2020.

Helfer L. R., 'Rethinking Derogations from Human Rights Treaties' (2021) ASIL Editorial Comment, 24.

Hennebel L., Tigroudja H., Traité de droit international des Droits de l'Homme, Paris, Pedone 2016.

Hern A., UK technology editor, 'Contact-Tracing App for England and Wales "Hampered by Loss of Public Trust', The Guardian, 21 September 2020.

Heuschling L. et al., « L'opposition politique au Grand-duché de Luxembourg. Regards croisés, de science juridique et de science politique, sur une démocratie consociative », in L'opposition politique, LexisNexis, 2016.

Heuschling L., État de droit, Rechsstaat, Rule of Law, coll. « Nouvelle Bibl. de thèses », vol. 16, Paris, Dalloz, 2002.

Hickman T. R., Between Human Rights and the Rule of Law: Indefinite Detention and the Derogation Model of Constitutionalism, Modern Law Review, 2005.

Hickman T., 'A Very English Lockdown Relaxation' (UK Constitutional Law Association), 14 May 2020.

Hickman T., Eight Ways to Reinforce and Revise the Lockdown Law.' (UK Constitutional Law Association), 16 April 2020.

Hickman T., Emma Dixon and Rachel Jones, 'Coronavirus and Civil Liberties in the UK' (2020).

Hickman T., 'The Use and Misuse of Guidance during the UK's Coronavirus Lockdown' [2020].

Hilliard A., 'Local Government, Civil Defence and Emergency Planning: Heading for Disaster?' The Modern Law Review, 476/477, (1986).

Hills Alice E., 'Co-ordination and Disaster Response in the United Kingdom' (1994).

Hinch R., and others, 'Effective Configurations of a Digital Contact Tracing App: A Report to NHSX' (2020).

Hoscheit Th., Le Droit judiciaire privé au Grand-Duché de Luxembourg, n° 550.

Hoscheit Th., « Interrogations sur la fin de l'état de crise constitutionnelle », J.T.L., août 2020, n°72.

Hourson S., « Aux confins du confinement », in Droit administratif, n°5, Lexisnexis, mai 2020, p. 3.

Hovius B., 'The Limitation Clauses of the European Convention on Human Rights: A Guide for the Application of Section 1 of the Charter' (1985) 17 Ottawa L Rev 213.

Huergo L. A.,"Estado de alarma en el país de los decretos leyes", 13. Junio. 2020.

Huster S., Kingreen T., "Handbuch Infektionsschutzrecht", 2022.

Ianello C., "Riflessioni su alcune conseguenze ordinamentali prodotte dall'emergenza covid: dalle limitazioni delle libertà costituzionali alla riemersione del sistema parallelo di amministrazione extra ordinem", Osservatorio sulle fonti, 2021.

Jackson J., Jacinta M Gau, 'Carving Up Concepts? Differentiating Between Trust and Legitimacy in Public Attitudes Towards Legal Authority' in Ellie Shockley and others (eds), Interdisciplinary Perspectives on Trust: Towards Theoretical and Methodological Integration,(Springer International Publishing), 2016).

Jakab A., German Constitutional Law and Doctrine on State of Emergency – Paradigms and Dilemmas of a Traditional (Continental) Discourse, German Law Journal 2005, p. 453.

Jakobs G., 'Imputation in Criminal Law and the Conditions for Norm Validity' (2004).

Jean J.-P., « Les systèmes de justice face à la pandémie du COVID-19 », https://www.leclubdesjuristes.com/blog-du-coronavirus/que-dit-le-droit/les-systemes-de-justice-face-a-la-pandemie-du-covid-19/.

Jemima K., 'Why Are We Really in Lockdown?' (17 April 2020).

Jimenez A., " El control judicial del poder en situaciones de incertidumbre" 4 Enero 2022.

Kaiser A.B, Hensel R., "Federal Republic of Germany: Legal Response to COVID-19", Oxford Constitutional Law, 2021.

Kaur-Gill S., 'The COVID-19 Pandemic and Outbreak Inequality: Mainstreaming Reporting of Singapore's Migrant Workers in the Margins', Frontiers in Communication, 30 Sept 2020.

Kessedjian C., Public Order in European Law, Erasmus Law Review, 2007.

Khalik S., 'Eligible individuals who refuse COVID-19 vaccine endanger themselves and others', Straits Times, Feb 2021.

Kiesilainen J.N., « Efficiency and Justice in Procedural Reforms: The Rise and Fall of the Oral Hearing", in Civil Justice between Efficiency and Quality: From Ius Commune to the CEPEJ, Antwerp, Intersentia, 2008.

King J., 'The Lockdown Is Lawful: Part II' (UK Constitutional Law Association, 2 April 2020).

King J., 'The Lockdown Is Lawful' (UK Constitutional Law Association, 1 April 2020).

Kingreen T., "Epidemie ohne epidemische Lage", Verfassungsblog, October 2021.

Kirby P., 'The End of the Rainbow?' The RUSI Journal, (2013).

Konstadinides T., and Marsons L.: "COVID-19 and Its Impact on the Constitutional Relationship between Government and Parliament.' (UK Constitutional Law Association, 26 March 2020).

Kramer X. et al., « Access to Justice in Time of Corona », https://www.Conflictoflaws.net.

Krans B., Nylund A., Piché C. & al, « Civil Justice and COVID-19 », (2020) https://www.researchgate.net/publication/340965353_Civil_Justice_and_Covid-19.

Kuhn N. and Rousseaux E., « La Cour constitutionnelle luxembourgeoise : dernière pierre à l'édifice des cours constitutionnelles en Europe occidentale », Revue internationale de droit comparé, Vol. 53 N°2, avril-juin, 2001.

Kurohi K., "New centre to bolster Singapore's infectious disease management", The Straits Time, 2019.

Lai L., ''This is poor planning': COVID-19 home recovery patients voice confusion, frustration over what to do', The Straits Times, January 2022.

Lakoff A. and Collier S. J., Biosecurity Interventions: Global Health and Security in Question, Columbia, 2008.

Lakoff A., (2015). Global Health Security and the Pathogenic Imaginary. Dreamscapes of Modernity Chicago: University of Chicago Press.

Lakoff A., Collier S. J. (éd.) (2008), Biosecurity Interventions: Global Health and Security in Question, New York.

Lam L., 'COVID-19: Woman fined for gathering with 14 other people at Chinese New Year celebration last year', CNA, February 2022.

Larrieu P., Vivre sans, Eres, 2020.

Lazzeri F., 'La decisione delle Sezioni unite sui presupposti per l'operatività della disciplina emergenziale di sospensione della prescrizione nei procedimenti davanti alla Corte di cassazione (informazione provvisoria)', Sistema Penale, November 2020.

Lebret A., COVID-19 pandemic and derogation to human rights, (4 May 2020), Advanced access publication, Journal of Law and the Biosciences, 1–15.

Lee D., 'COVID-19 in Singapore: 'Responsive Communitarianism' and the Legislative Approach to the "Most Serious Crisis" Since Independenc', Singapore Journal of Legal Studies, 2020.

Legg M., "The COVID-19 Pandemic, the Courts and Online Hearings: Maintaining Open Justice, Procedural Fairness and Impartiality", Federal Law Review, UNSW Law Research No. 20–46, (2021), https://ssrn.com/abstract=3681165.

Lemke M., What does state of exception mean? A definitional and analytical approach, Zeitschrift für Politikwissenschaft (ZPol), 2018, pp. 373–383.

Lucarelli A., "La gestione dell'emergenza da COVID-19 tra regole uniformi, istanze di autonomia ed incertezza negli strumenti normativi", Giurisprudenza Costituzionale, 2021.

Luciani M., 'Il sistema delle fonti del diritto alla prova dell'emergenza', Rivista,2020.

Madonna M., "La libertà religiosa ai tempi del coronavirus tra diritto e letteratura", Fondazione Feletrinelli, November 2020.

Marzano M. G., 'Brevi note sulla prova della causalità nel contagio da Covid 19', Cassazione penale, 2020.

Masala P., "I diritti fra Stato e Regioni nell'emergenza sanitaria, a vent'anni dalla revisione del Titolo V: quali lezioni possono trarsi e quale "ribilanciamento" occorre realizzare, per una più efficace garanzia dell'eguaglianza sostanziale?", Costituzionalismo, 2020.

Masiero A. F., 'Reati di falso e autocertificazione durante l'emergenza COVID-19: tra ricerca dell'effettività e simbolismo', Sistema penale, 2021.

McGoldrick D., 'The interface between public emergency powers and international law', International Journal of Constitutional Law 2, (2004), 380–429, 388.

Meah N., 'Anti COVID-19 vaccine group founder, husband, under police probe for allegedly instigating people to overwhelm public hotlines, Today, 25 Nov 2021.

Menon S., 'The Rule of Law: The Path to Exceptionalism', Singapore Academy of Law Journal, 2016.

Milanovic M., "European Court decides A and others v. United Kingdom" (19 February 2009) EJIL:Talk, available at: https://www.ejiltalk.org/european-court-decides-a-and-others-v-united-kingdom/.

Milne R., 'Trust and Trustworthiness in COVID-19 Data' (Trust & Technology Initiative), 15 April 2020.

Mitsilegas V., 'Responding to COVID-19: Surveillance, Trust and the Rule of Law – School of Law', 26 May 2020.

Mitsilegas V., "Security Law" and Preventive Justice in the Legal Architecture' in Ulrich Sieber and others (eds), Alternative systems of crime control (Duncker & Humblot), 2018.

Mobilio G., " La decretazione d'urgenza alla prova delle vere emergenze. L'epidemia da COVID-19 e i rapporti tra decreto-legge e altre fonti", Osservatorio Sulle Fonti, 2020.

Molloy S., "COVID-19 and Derogations Before the European Court of Human Rights" (10 April 2020) Vervassungsblog, available at: https://verfassungsblog.de/covid-19-and-derogations-before-the-european-court-of-human-rights/.

Momtaz R., 'Inside Macron's Coronavirus War', Politico, April 2020.

Munoz de Morales M., " El legislador penal europeo: racionalidad y legitimidad", Civitas, 2018.

Munoz M. A., “La otra pandemia”, El País, 27 de septiembre de 2020.

Möllering G., ‘The Nature of Trust: From Georg Simmel to a Theory of Expectation, Interpretation and Suspension’, 2001.

Möllers C., “Stellungnahme zum Entwurf eines Vierten Gesetzes zum Schutz der Bevölkerung bei einer epidemischen Lage von nationaler Tragweite BT-Drucksache 19/28444”, Bundestad, 2021.

Neo J., Ramlan S., ‘COVID-19 and Religious Organisations: Constitutional Environment and Organisational Choices’ RSIS Interreligious Relations Issue 24, June 2021.

Neuman G. L., Constrained Derogation in Positive Human Rights Regime, in Evan J. Criddle, Human Rights in Emergencies, Cambridge University Press 2016.

Ní Aoláin F., Report on the Promotion and Protection of Human Rights and Fundamental Freedoms while Countering Terrorism on the Human Rights Challenge of States of Emergency in the Context of Countering Terrorism, A/HRC/37/52 (2018).

O'Donnell D., 'Commentary by the Rapporteur on Derogation' (1985) 7 Hum Rts Q 23.

Ormerod D., ‘Coronavirus and Emergency Powers’, Criminal Law Review, (2020)O’Brien G., and Read Paul, ‘Future UK Emergency Management: New Wine, Old Skin?’ (2005).

O’Brien G., ‘UK Emergency Preparedness: A Holistic Response?’ (2008).

O’Hare P., ‘Covid in Scotland: How Has the Pandemic Affected Crime Levels?’ BBC News (13 November 2020).

Paddeu F., Waibel M., The Final Act: Exploring the End of Pandemics (July 2020) University of Cambridge Faculty of Law Legal Studies Research Paper Series, paper no. 27/2020.

Pagliari C., ‘The Ethics and Value of Contact Tracing Apps: International Insights and Implications for Scotland’s COVID-19 Response’,Journal of Global Health, 2020.

Pakes F., ‘Coronavirus: Why Swathes of Prisoners Are Being Released in the World’s Most Punitive States’,The Conversation, 20 April 2020.

Palazzo F., ‘Pandemia e responsabilità colposa’, Sistema penale, 2020.

Pardo E.J., “El desconcierto del Leviatan”, 2009.

Parker D., and Handmer J., ‘Improving Hazard Management and Emergency Planning’ in Dennis Parker and John Handmer (eds), Hazard Management and Emergency Planning (Routledge 2012).

Pennings S., Symons X., ‘Persuasion, not coercion or incentivisation, is the best means of promoting COVID-19 vaccination’, Journal of Medical Ethics, 2021.

Pernice I., Multilevel Constitutionalism and the Treaty of Amsterdam: European Constitution-making Revisited?, CML Rev. 1999, p. 703.

Perru E., « Crise du COVID-19, Avocat et 'Paperless Justice' », https://www.lexnow.lu/blog/articles-4/post/crise-du-covid-19-avocat-et-paperless-justice-36.

Petrov J., 'The COVID-19 Emergency in the Age of Executive Aggrandizement: What Role for Legislative and Judicial Checks?' (2020).

Pierré-Caps S., Constitutionnaliser l'état d'urgence?, Civitas Europa 2016, p. 141 ff, at p. 143.

Pinto M., "La tremendissima lezione del Covid 19(anche) ai giuristi", Questione Giustizia, March 2020

Piñar Mañas J.L., " La protección de datos durante la crisis del coronavirus, Consejo General de la Abogacía Española", 20 de Marzo 2020.

Pontier J.-M., « La crise sanitaire de 2020 et le droit administratif » in AJDA, n°30, 2020.

Poullet Y., « Pandémie, numérique et droits de l'homme : un étrange cocktail! », JDE, 2020, p. 246.

Presno Linares M.A., ' Estado de alarma y sociedad del riesgo global, in Atienza Macias E/ Rodriguez Ayuso J.F (dir), Las respuestas del derechos a las crisis de salud pública' Dykinson, 2021.

Price P.J., 'A Coronavirus Quarantine in America Could be a Giant Legal Mess', The Atlantic, 16 February 2020.

Rabinow P., Artifizialität und Aufklärung. Von der Soziobiologie zur Biosozialität, in: Folkers/Lemke, p. 385 et seq.

Raffiotta E., "Sulla legittimità dei provvedimenti del governo a contrasto dell'emergenza virale da coronavirus", BioLaw Journal, 2020.

Rawlinson K., '"This Enemy Can Be Deadly": Boris Johnson Invokes Wartime Language', The Guardian, 17 March 2020.

Raz J., "The Rule of Law and its Virtue' in The Authority of Law: Essays on law and morality', Oxford University Press, 1979.

Renedo A. C., "Gobierno y parlamento en la emergencia sanitaria", AFDUAM, Extraordinario, (2021).

Reynolds J., Empire, Emergency and International Law, Cambridge University Press 2017.

Ribeyre C., La procédure pénale à l'épreuve de l'état d'urgence sanitaire, Droit pénal. N. 5, mai 2020.

Rockett J.P., 'A Constructive Critique of United Kingdom Emergency Planning' (1994).

Rodriguez Y.C., "COVID-19 y prisiones: un desafío no sólo sanitario y de seguridad, también humanitario, Revista General de Derecho Penal",2020.

Rodríguez-Piñero M., 'Estado de alarma y derecho de manifestación del sindicato. Derecho de las relaciones laborales,' 2020.

Rossiter C., Constitutional Dictatorship. Crisis Government in the Modern Democracies, New Brunswick und London 2002 (1948).

Roure S., « L'élargissement du principe de publicité des débats judiciaires : une judiciarisation du débat public », Revue française de droit constitutionnel, 2006/4 (n° 68).

Royo P., J./Carrasco Duran M. "Derecho constitucional" 16 Ed, 2018.

Ruggeri A., 'Ancora in tema di obbligatorietà del vaccino contro il COVID-19 e della responsabilità per la sua mancata introduzione', Giustizia insieme, October 2021.

Ruggeri A., 'L'emergenza sanitaria, la solidarietà dimezzata e… l'uovo di Colombo' Consulta Online, February 2021.

Rule C., "Online Dispute Resolution and the Future of Justice", Annual Review of Law and Social Science, 2020.

Ryan N., 'FactFind: Has the World Health Organisation Changed Its Position on Lockdowns?' (TheJournal.ie), 2020.

Sadler N., « La garantie des Droits et Libertés par les juridictions ordinaires » in La défense des droits et libertés au Grand-Duché de Luxembourg, Bruxelles, Éditions Larcier, 2020.

Santiago C. N., The Constitution of Deliberative Democracy (Yale University Press) 1996

Santos Botelho C., COVID-19 and stress on fundamental rights in Portugal: An intermezzo between the state of exception and constitutional normality, Revista Catalana de Dret Públic, (special issue) 2020, 183–194. https://doi. org/10.2436/rcdp.i0.2020.3553.

Sauer C., Contrôle juridictionnel des lois au Luxembourg, Bruxelles, Larcier, 2019.

Sauer C., « Chapitre 2 – Le caractère indéfini du contrôle de constitutionnalité : Contrôle abstrait et/ou contrôle concret » in Contrôle juridictionnel des lois au Luxembourg, Bruxelles, Éditions Larcier, 2019

Schabas W., The European Convention on Human Rights: A Commentary, Oxford University Press 2015.

Scheinin M, 'COVID-19 Symposium: To Derogate or Not to Derogate?' (6 April 2020) Opinio Juris, available at: http://opiniojuris.org/2020/04/06/covid-19-symposium-to-derogate-or-not-to-derogate/.

Schmidt, "Rechtsfragen zur Corona-Krise"C.H Beck, 2021.

Schreuer C., 'Derogation of Human Rights in Situations of Public Emergency: The Experience of the European Convention on Human Rights' (1982) 9 Yale J World Pub Ord 113.

See S., 'Singapore's move to streamline COVID-19 rules signals confidence in living with virus: observers', Business Times, February 2022.

Seira C., "La vacunación contra el Covid y sus principales debates jurídicos", Afduam, Extraordinario, 2021.

Sheeran S.P., Reconceptualizing States of Emergency under International Human Rights Law: Theory, Legal Doctrine, and Politics (2013) 34 Mich J Int'l L 491.

Simon P., "El Leviatán anarquista" El País, 27.12.2021.

Skolnik T., 'Criminal Law during (and after) COVID-19' (2020) 43 Man LJ 145, 146.

Skolnik T., 'Criminal Law During (and After) COVID-19', Manitoba Law Journal, 2020.

Smith Freehills H. LLP, Everett M., Brown H. and Collins K., 'UK Switches to Decentralised Approach to Contact Tracing App | Lexology', December 2020.

Smith J., 'Civil Contingency Planning in Government' (2003).

Sobek T., and Josef Montag, 'Proportionality Test' in Alain Marciano and Giovanni Battista Ramello (eds), Encyclopedia of Law and Economics (Springer New York), 2018.

Sotis C., Le droit pénal italien à l'épreuve de la covid : un problème à gérer plus qu'un outil de gestion, RSC, 2020, 1116, citing Massimo Nobili, L'immoralità necessaria, Il Mulino, 2003.

Sotis C., Le droit pénal italien à l'épreuve de la covid : un probème à gérer plus qu'un outil de gestion, RSC, 2020.

Stewart H., « Procedural Rights and Factual Accuracy », Legal Theory, 2020, 26(2).

Stoppioni E., « The Protection of Health Must Take Precedence: Testing the Constitutional State of Crisis in Luxembourg », 29 avril 2020, https://verfassungsblog.de/the-protection-of-health-must-take-precedence-testing-the-constitutional-state-of-crisis-in-luxembourg/.

Strickler Y., « La raison d'être et les réformes de la procédure orale », in Les principes essentiels du procès à l'épreuve des réformes récentes du droit judiciaire privé.

Stripe N., 'Crime in England and Wales: Year Ending June 2020' (Office for National Statistics), 2020.

Svensson-McCarthy A.-L., International Law of Human Rights and States of Exception – With Special Reference to the Travaux Préparatoires and Case-Law of the International Monitoring Organs (The Hague/Boston/London, Martinus Nijhoff Publishers, 1998).

Sweney M., Hern A., 'Phone Location Data Could Be Used to Help UK Coronavirus Effort',The Guardian,19 March 2020.

Tait A., 'Pandemic Shaming: Is It Helping Us Keep Our Distance?' The Observer,4 April 2020.

Tan G., 'TraceTogether presents chance for Singapore to restore track record on data privacy and security', Today, May 2020.

Tan S.J., 'Forum: Don't ignore mental health of unvaccinated, especially youngsters', Straits Times, Oct 2021.

Tang L., 'So what?': Man who posted about dinner gathering during circuit breaker fined S$4,500', Todayonline, May 2020.

Thiagarajan V., 'Tighten rules on mask-wearing for those not doing strenuous exercise', Today, July 2020.

Thio Li-ann, 'Between Apology and Apogee, Autochthony: The Rule of Law beyond the rules of law in Singapore', Singapore Journal of Legal Studies (2012).

Thio Li-ann, 'Principled Pragmatism and the 'Third Wave' of Communitarian Judicial Review in Singapore', Constitutional Interpretation in Singapore: Theory and Practice, Routledge, 2016.

Thio Li-ann, 'Public Law in Law and Technology in Singapore, Phang, Chesterman and Goh', Singapore: Academy Press, 2021.

Thomson S., and Eric C Ip, 'COVID-19 Emergency Measures and the Impending Authoritarian Pandemic', Journal of Law and the Biosciences, 2020.

Toebes B., "Human Rights and Public Health: Towards a Balanced Relationship" (2015) 19 Int. J. Hrs. 4, 448–504.

Tovey A., 'Facial Recognition System Adapted to Spot Coronavirus Victims',The Telegraph, 27 April 2020.

Tripodi F., 'Il processo penale post-Covid: rispettare la Costituzione, facendo di necessità (qualche) virtù', Forum di Quaderni Costituzionali, 2020.

Tripodina C., "La Costituzione al tempo del Coronavirus", Costituzionalismo.it, 2020.

Truchet D., Avant l'Etat d'urgence sanitaire : premières questions, premières réponses, RFDA, 2020.

Tyler T. R., 'Psychological Perspectives on Legitimacy and Legitimation' (2005).

Valentini V., 'Organizzazione del lavoro e responsabilità punitivo-penali da contagio: a che punto siamo?', Archivio penale, 2021.

Vardanyan V., « L'impact de la pandémie de COVID-19 sur les droits de l'homme et l'Etat de droit », Rapport de la Commission des questions juridiques et des droits de l'homme, AS/JUR (2020) 13.

Vautravers M., « La coopération judiciaire en matière civile et commerciale en temps de crise au sein de l'Union européenne », Obs. Brux., juin 2020.

Vergès E., « Les principes de la procédure civile: notion, fonctions, évolution », in Les principes essentiels du procès à l'épreuve des réformes récentes du droit judiciaire privé, IRJS Éditions, Paris, 2014.

Vincent D., 'Surveillance, Privacy and History', (History & Policy), 1 October 2013.

Vincent S., « Savoir entretenir le flou juridique », À propos de la décision du Conseil constitutionnel n° 2020–846/847/848 QPC du 26 juin 2020, La Revue des droits de l'homme [Online], Actualités Droits-Libertés.

Vitor Tossini J., 'The Cabinet Office Briefing Rooms (COBR) – A Short Introduction' (18 October 2018).

Voo, Lim and Tam, 'Commentary: Does Singapore seem more anxious about death from COVID-19 than from other causes?' CNA.com, Oct 2021.

Vovoula N., 'Prevention, Surveillance, and the Transformation of Citizenship in the "Security Union": The Case of Foreign Terrorist Fighters' in Ulrich Sieber and others (eds), Alternative systems of crime control (Duncker & Humblot), 2018.

Waldron J., « À vos masques : parlez! », Man. Lawyer, 2020/2, p. 2.

Wallace S., Derogations from the European Convention on Human Rights: The Case for Reform (2020), 20 HRLR 769–796.

Wallace S., 'Derogations from the European Convention on Human Rights: The Case for Reform' (2020) 20 H.R.L.R. 769–796.

Wanye A., "In Singapore, 1970's Law Becomes Weapon Against SARS", New York Times, 2003.

Warrell H., and Fildes N., 'Cyber Criminals Exploit Coronavirus Disruption',Financial Times, [2020].

Warrell H., 'Majority in UK Support Use of Mobile Phones for Coronavirus Contact Tracing',17 April 2020.

Wee S.-L., 'They Had the Vaccines and a Plan to Reopen. Instead They Got Cold Feet', New York Times, October 2021.

Weixian H., "Contact tracing app is safe, secure and needed as Singapore opens up" Straits Times, June 2020.

Weng L.K., 'Forum: Make COVID-19 jab mandatory, except for the ineligible', Straits Times, November 2021.

Wright S., 'Contact Tracing Apps for COVID-19', 10 December 2020.

Yirong S., 'From SARS to COVID-19: Balance of China's Criminal Law System' (2020) 12 Tsinghua China L Rev 399.

YL Tan K., 'Singapore's regulatory response to COVID-19', The Regulatory Review, June 2020.

Yorke H., and Penna D., 'More than 90 Coronavirus Laws and Rules Imposed without Parliamentary Scrutiny' The Telegraph (17 June 2020).

Zylberman P., Tempêtes microbiennes. Essai sur la politique de sécurité sanitaire dans le monde transatlantique, Gallimard, 2013.

JURISPRUDENCE:

A. - NATIONAL JURISPRUDENCE:

Cass. 2e civ., 24 sept. 2020, n° 19–40.056.

Trib. adm., 3 mars 1997, n°9693.

France Cons. const., 26 mars 2020, n° 2020–799 DC.

Cl. Constit., décision n° 2020–799 DC du 26 mars 2020, JORF n° 0078 du 31 mars 2020, texte n° 5.

C.E., ord. 10 avril 2020, n° 439883, 439892 et 439903.

Cl. Constit., décision n° 2020–800 DC du 11 mai 2020, JORF n° 0116 du 12 mai 2020, texte n° 2.

Cl. Constit., décision n°2020–846/847/848 QPC du 26 juin 2020, JORF n°0158 du 27 juin 2020.

Tribunal de police Diekrich, 21 juillet 2020, n°170/2020.

Trib. de Paix Luxembourg, 29 juillet 2020, n°2051/20.

Trib. adm., 7 août 2020, n°44765, Chambre de vacation
Trib. adm., 21 septembre 2020, n°44987, 4ème Chambre.
Trib. adm., 28 septembre 2020, n°45012, 4ème Chambre.
Tribunal administratif, 7 octobre 2020, no 45051, 3ième chambre.
Trib. adm., 7 octobre 2020, n°45051, 3ème Chambre.
Trib. adm., 8 octobre 2020, n°45062, 3ème Chambre.
Trib. adm., 8 octobre 2020, n°45062, 3ème Chambre.
Tribunal administratif, 9 octobre 2020, no 45061, 1ière chambre.
Trib. adm, 9 octobre 2020, n°45061, 1ère Chambre.
Trib. adm, 9 octobre 2020, n°45061, 2ème Chambre.
Trib. adm., 14 octobre 2020, n°45077, 2ème Chambre
Trib. Trav. Esch, 16 novembre 2020, 1898/20 E-TRAV-211/19.
Trib. adm, 27 novembre 2020, n° 45263.
Trib adm., 27 novembre 2020, n°45263, 4ème Chambre.
CE, ord.réf., 27 nov.2020, n°446712.
Trib. adm., 30 novembre 2020, n°45257, 2ème Chambre.
JPL, 21 janvier 2021, jugement n° 204/2021.
Cl Constit., décision n° 2020–878/879 QPC du 29 janvier 2021.
TAL, 12 février, 2021, https://anon.public.lu/Décisions%20anonymisées/Tribunal%20d%27arrondissement%20Luxembourg%20commerce/02_Chambre/2021/20210212_TALux2-TAL-2021-01243a-accessible.pdf.
CE, ord., 5 mars 2021, n. 440037.
TAL, 28 juin 2021, n° 2021TALCH14/00100, n° TAL-2021–00994 du rôle, *J.T.L.*, 2021/4.
TAL, 12 juillet 2021, TAL-2021–02935.
CE, ord.12 février 2021, req. n°448972; 4 août 2021, n°447916, 448388, 448962, JORF du 12 août 2021.
TP 15 septembre 2021, Jgmt 499/21.
Cl. Constit., décision n° 2021–828 DC du 9 novembre 2021.
Trib. adm., 1 décembre 2021, n° 46669.
Trib. adm., 1 décembre 2021, n° 46665.
Trib. adm., 1 décembre 2021, n° 46671.
TAL, 22 décembre 2021, TAL-2021–04661.
Trib. adm., 7 janvier 2022, n° 46851.
Trib. adm., 10 février 2022, n° 45049.
Trib. adm. 16 février 2022, n° 47010.
Trib. adm., 9 mars 2022, n° 45031.
Trib. adm., 18 mars 2022, n° 47158.
Court Order 32/2020, of 22 October, issued by the Basque Regional High Court.

B. - EUROPEAN AND INTERNATIONAL COURTS

CJEU,19 March 2019, Préfet des Pyrénées-Orientales v Abdelaziz Arib, C-444/17, ECLI:EU:C:2019:220.

ECtHR, Greece v. United Kingdom *(Cyprus I)*, App. No. 176/56, 1958–1959).

ECtHR, *The Greek Case*, Application Nos. 3321/67, 3322/67, 3323/67, 3344/67 (1969).

ECtHR, *Sunday Times v. United Kingdom*, 2 E.H.R.R. 245 (1979).

ECtHR, *Lawless v. Ireland*, Application No. 332/57 (1 July 1961).

ECtHR, Ireland v. United Kingdom, 18 January 1978, application no. 5310/71, § 163.

ECtHR, *Ireland v. the United Kingdom*, (18 January 1978).

ECtHR, *Brannigan and McBride v. the United Kingdom*, (26 May 1993).

ECtHR, *Aksoy v. Turkey*, (18 December 1996).

ECHR 25 January 2005, Enhorn v. Sweden.

ECtHR, Öcalan v. Turkey, 12 May 2005, application no. 46221/99, § 179.

ECtHR, *A & Others v. United Kingdom*, Application No. 3455/05, 19 February 2009.

LEGISLATION :

A. - EU LEGISLATION:

Directive 2004/38/EC of the European Parliament and of the Council of 29 April 2004 on the right of citizens of the Union and their family members to move and reside freely within the territory of the Member States, EUOJ, L 158, 30.04.2004.

Regulation (EU) 2016/399 of the European Parliament and of the Council of 9 March 2016 on a Union Code on the rules governing the movement of persons across borders (Schengen Borders Code), OJEU, L 77, 23.3.2016.

B. - TREATY LAW:

African Charter on Human and Peoples' Rights, June 27, 1981, 21 ILM 58.

American Convention on Human Rights (1969), 1144 UNTS 123.

American Convention on Human Rights Art. 27.1, Nov. 22, 1969, O.A.S.T.S. No. 36, 1144 U.N.T.S. 123 [ACHR].

Convention for the Amelioration of the Condition of the Wounded and Sick in Armed Forces in the Field, Aug. 12, 1949, 6 U.S. I. 3114, T.I.A S. No. 3362, 75 U.N.T.S. 31.

Convention for the Amelioration of the Condition of the Wounded Sick and Shipwrecked Members of Armed Forces at Sea, Aug. 12, 1949, 6 U.S.T. 3217, 1.1.A S. No. 3363, 75 U.N.T.S. 85.

Convention for the Protection of Human Rights and Fundamental Freedoms, Art. 15.1, Nov. 4, 1950, 213 U.N.T.S. 221 [ECHR].

Convention Relative To the Protection of Civilian Persons in Time of War, Aug. 12, 1949, 6 U.S.T. 3516. T.I.AS. No. 3365, 75 U.N.T.S. 287).

European Social Charter, (1965) 529 UNTS 89.

Geneva Convention Relative to the Treatment of Prisoners of War, Aug. 12, 1949, 6 U.S.T. 3316, T.I.A S. No. 3364, 75 U.N.T.S. 135.

International Covenant on Civil and Political Rights (ICCPR) (1966), 999 UNTS 171.

International Covenant on Civil and Political Rights, Art. 41, Dec. 16, 1966, 999 U.N.T.S. 171 [ICCPR].

League of Arab States, Revised Arab Charter on Human Rights Art. 4.1 (May 22, 2004), 12 INT'L HUM. RTS. REP. 893 (2005) [Arab Charter].

Revised European Social Charter 1999, ETS 163, 529 UNTS 89.

Universal Declaration of Human Rights, Adopted and proclaimed by General Assembly resolution 217 A (III) of 10 December 1948.

C. - NATIONAL LEGISLATION

Loi organique d'urgence pour faire face à l'épidémie de COVID-19.

Gesetz zur Verhütung und Bekämpfung von Infektionskrankheiten beim Menschen (Infektionsschutzgesetz – IfSG), 20 July 2000, BGBl. I S. 1045 ('IPA 2000').

Loi n° 55–385 du 3 avril 1955 relative à l'état d'urgence, JORF n° 0085 du 7 avril 1955.

Loi du 27 juillet 1997 portant organisation de la Cour Constitutionnelle.

Loi n° 2004–806 du 9 août 2004 relative à la politique de santé publique, JORF n° 185 du 11 août 2004.

Italian Decree No. 19 of 25th March 2020.

Arrêté du 14 mars 2020 portant diverses mesures relatives à la lutte contre la propagation du virus COVID-19, JORF n° 0064 du 15 mars 2020.

Décret n° 2020–260 du 16 mars 2020 portant réglementation des déplacements dans le cadre de la lutte contre la propagation du virus COVID-19, JORF n° 0066 du 17 mars 2020.

Belgique, Arrêté ministériel du 18 mars 2020 portant des mesures d'urgence pour limiter la propagation du coronavirus COVID-19, Annexe à l'arrêté ministériel du 18 mars 2020.

Loi n° 2020–290 du 23 mars 2020 d'urgence pour faire face à l'épidémie de COVID-19, JORF n°72 du 24 mars 2020, texte n° 2.

Règlement grand-ducal du 25 mars 2020 portant suspension des délais en matière juridictionnelle et adaptation temporaire de certaines autres modalités procédurales, http://data.legilux.public.lu/eli/etat/leg/rgd/2020/03/25/a185/jo.

Ordonnance n° 2020–303 du 25 mars 2020 portant adaptation de règles de procédure pénale sur le fondement de la loi n° 2020–290 du 23 mars 2020 d'urgence pour faire face à l'épidémie de COVID-19, JORF n°0074 du 26 mars 2020.

Loi organique n° 2020–365 du 30 mars 2020 d'urgence pour faire face à l'épidémie de COVID-19, JORF n° 0078 du 31 mars 2020, texte n° 2.

Règlement grand-ducal du 3 avril 2020 portant modification du règlement grand-ducal du 1er avril 2020 portant dérogation aux articles L. 322–2 et L. 326–1 à L. 326–12 du Code du travail.

Règlement grand-ducal du 17 avril 2020 portant modification du règlement grand-ducal modifié du 18 mars 2020 portant introduction d'une série de mesures dans le cadre de la lutte contre le COVID-19.

Règlement grand-ducal du 29 avril 2020 portant adaptation temporaire de certaines modalités procédurales en matière pénale, http://data.legilux.public.lu/eli/etat/leg/rgd/2020/04/29/a341/jo.

Règlement grand-ducal du 29 avril 2020 portant adaptation temporaire de certaines modalités procédurales en matière pénale, http://data.legilux.public.lu/eli/etat/leg/rgd/2020/04/29/a341/jo.

Décret n° 2020–572 du 15 mai 2020 relatif au Comité de contrôle et de liaison COVID-19, JORF n°0120 du 16 mai 2020.

Règlement grand-ducal du 29 mai 2020 portant modification du règlement grand-ducal modifié du 18 mars 2020 portant introduction d'une série de mesures dans le cadre de la lutte contre le COVID-19.

Règlement grand-ducal du 12 juin 2020 portant dérogation aux dispositions des articles 3, 6, 7 et 9 de la loi du 1er août 2019 concernant les mutuelles.

Loi du 20 juin 2020 portant prorogation de mesures concernant la tenue d'audiences publiques pendant l'état de crise devant les juridictions dans les affaires soumises à la procédure écrite, certaines adaptations de la procédure de référé exceptionnel devant le juge aux affaires familiales, la suspension des délais en matière juridictionnelle, et d'autres modalités procédurales, http://data.legilux.public.lu/eli/etat/leg/loi/2020/06/20/a523/jo.

Loi du 20 juin 2020 portant adaptation temporaire de certaines modalités procédurales en matière pénale, http://data.legilux.public.lu/eli/etat/leg/loi/2020/06/20/a542/jo.

Loi du 20 juin 2020 portant prorogation de mesures concernant la tenue d'audiences publiques pendant l'état de crise devant les juridictions dans les affaires soumises à la procédure écrite, certaines adaptations de la procédure de référé exceptionnel devant le juge aux affaires familiales, la suspension des délais en matière juridictionnelle, et d'autres modalités procédurales.

Loi du 20 juin 2020 portant adaptation temporaire de certaines modalités procédurales en matière pénale.

Loi du 24 juin 2020 portant introduction d'une série de mesures concernant les activités sportives, les activités culturelles ainsi que les établissements recevant du public, dans le cadre de la lutte contre la pandémie COVID-19 et

Loi du 24 juin 2020 portant introduction d'une série de mesures concernant les activités sportives, les activités culturelles ainsi que les établissements recevant du public, dans le cadre de la lutte contre la pandémie COVID-19.

Loi modifiée du 17 juillet 2020 portant sur les mesures de lutte contre la pandémie COVID-19.

Règlement grand-ducal du 29 juillet 2020 modifiant le règlement grand-ducal modifié du 18 septembre 1995 concernant l'assistance judiciaire.

Ordonnance n° 2020–1401 du 18 novembre 2020 portant adaptation des règles applicables aux juridictions de l'ordre judiciaire statuant en matière pénale, JORF 280 du 19 novembre 2020.

Loi du 25 novembre 2020, http://legilux.public.lu/eli/etat/leg/loi/2020/11/25/a932/consolide/20201223.

Loi du 25 novembre 2020 modifiant :
1° la loi modifiée du 17 juillet 2020 sur les mesures de lutte contre la pandémie COVID-19;
2° la loi modifiée du 10 décembre 2009 relative à l'hospitalisation sans leur consentement de personnes atteintes de troubles mentaux, http://data.legilux.public.lu/eli/etat/leg/loi/2020/11/25/a933/jo.

Loi du 19 décembre 2020 portant adaptation temporaire de certaines modalités procédurales en matière civile et commerciale, http://data.legilux.public.lu/eli/etat/leg/loi/2020/12/19/a1056/jo.

Loi du 19 décembre 2020 portant modification de la loi modifiée du 20 juin 2020 portant adaptation temporaire de certaines modalités procédurales en matière pénale, http://data.legilux.public.lu/eli/etat/leg/loi/2020/12/19/a1046/jo.

Loi du 19 décembre 2020 portant adaptation temporaire de certaines modalités procédurales en matière civile et commerciale, http://data.legilux.public.lu/eli/etat/leg/loi/2020/12/19/a1056/jo.

Loi du 19 décembre 2020 portant modification de la loi modifiée du 20 juin 2020 portant adaptation temporaire de certaines modalités procédurales en matière pénale, http://data.legilux.public.lu/eli/etat/leg/loi/2020/12/19/a1046/jo.

Loi du 30 juin 2021 portant modification : 1° de la loi modifiée du 23 septembre 2020 portant des mesures concernant la tenue de réunions dans les sociétés et dans les autres personnes morales; 2° de la loi du 19 décembre 2020 portant adaptation temporaire de certaines modalités procédurales en matière civile et commerciale, https://legilux.public.lu/eli/etat/leg/loi/2021/06/30/a485/jo.

Loi du 30 juillet 2021 portant modification : 1° de la loi du 19 décembre 2020 portant adaptation temporaire de certaines modalités procédurales en matière civile et commerciale; 2° de la loi modifiée du 8 mars 2017 sur la nationalité luxembourgeoise, https://legilux.public.lu/eli/etat/leg/loi/2021/07/30/a626/jo.

Loi n° 2021–1465 du 10 novembre 2021 portant diverses dispositions de vigilance sanitaire, JORF n°263 du 11 novembre 202.

POLICY AND OTHER DOCUMENTS:

'Announcements from the Criminal Procedure Rule Committee' (GOV.UK) , December 2020.

'Boris Johnson "misspoke" over North East Covid Restrictions' BBC News, 29 September 2020.

'Coronavirus (COVID-19) and Prisons. Guidance for Families and Friends of People in Prison in England and Wales during the Coronavirus Pandemic.' (GOV.UK, 2 December 2020).

'Coronavirus Action Plan: A Guide to What You Can Expect across the UK' (Department of Health & Social Care 2020).

'Coronavirus and Devolution' (The Institute for Government, 26 March 2020).

'Coronavirus: Health Minister Says App Should Roll out by Winter' BBC News, June 2020)

'Emergency Response and Recovery' (Civil Contingencies Secretariat, Cabinet Office, HM Government 2013) Non statutory guidance accompanying the Civil Contingencies Act 2004 5th ed. ch 13.

'Enhanced SAGE Guidance. A Strategic Framework for the Scientific Advisory Group for Emergencies (SAGE)' (Civil Contingencies Secretariat, Cabinet Office, HM Government 2012)

'Legitimate | Origin and Meaning of Legitimate by Online Etymology Dictionary' , 15 December 2020.

'Negative Procedure – MPs' Guide to Procedure – UK Parliament'.

'New Research Shows Tracing Apps Can Save Lives at All Levels of Uptake | University of Oxford', December 2020, https://www.ox.ac.uk/news/2020-09-03-new-research-shows-tracing-apps-can-save-lives-all-levels-uptake.

'Our Plan to Rebuild: The UK Government's COVID-19 Recovery Strategy' (Cabinet Office 2020).

'The Global Health Security Index' (GHS Index) ,15 November 2020.

'UK Test and Trace System Accused of Breaching Privacy' (Privacy International) , 10 December 2020.

« Points de vigilance et propositions du CCBE dans le cadre de la phase de réactivation du système judiciaire à la lumière de la crise de COVID-19 », https://www.ccbe.eu.

« Safeguarding the right to a fair trial during the coronavirus pandemic: remote criminal justice proceedings », https://www.fairtrials.org/sites/default/files/Safeguarding%20the%20right%20to%20a%20fair%20trial%20during%20the%20coronavirus%20pandemic%20remote%20criminal%20justice%20proceedings.pdf.

2014/415/EU, Council Decision of 24 June 2014 on the arrangements for the implementation by the Union of the solidarity clause, EUOJ L 192, 1.7.2014.

Aerztezeitung,'Erster Coronavirus-Fall in Deutschland', 2020.

Avis de l'ordre des avocats du Barreau de Luxembourg, Projet de loi n°7606, 4 août 2020.

Avis du tribunal administratif, Projet de loi n°7606 et n°7607, 18 août 2020.

CEPEJ, « Les leçons et défis pour le système judiciaire pendant et après le COVID-19 », 10 juin 2020, CEPEJ (2008) 8rev.

Circulaire du 12 mars 2020 commune au tribunal d'arrondissement de Luxembourg et au Barreau de Luxembourg.

Circulaire du 14 mars 2020 relative à l'adaptation de l'activité pénale et civile des juridictions aux mesures de prévention et de lutte contre la pandémie COVID-19, disponible sur : https://www.legifrance.gouv.fr/download/pdf/circ?id=44946.

Circulaire du 17 mars 2020, Juge de paix directeur, Accessible sur le site du Barreau de Luxembourg.

CoE, *Guide on Article 15 of the Convention – Derogation in time of emergency* (31 August 2020) ("Guide on Article 15"), available at: https://www.echr.coe.int/Documents/Guide_Art_15_ENG.pdf.

Commission consultative des Droits de l'Homme du Grand-Duché de Luxembourg, Avis sur le projet de loi n°7606 portant introduction d'une série de mesures concernant les personnes physiques dans le cadre de la lutte contre le virus SARS-CoV-2 (COVID-19), Avis 05/2020, 9 juin 2020.

Commission consultative des Droits de l'Homme du Grand-Duché de Luxembourg, Avis sur le projet de loi n°7683, Avis 11/2020, 27 octobre 2020.

Committee of Ministers, Resolution DH (81) 2, 3 E.H.R.R. 615 (1981).

Conseil d'État (Luxembourg), opinion of 15.7. 2016, doc. parl. n° 6938(4).

Conseil d'État of Luxembourg: Conseil d'État, *Avis du 15 juillet 2016 sur la proposition de revision de l'article 32 (4) de la Constitution*, doc. parl. No. 6938 (4).

Coronavirus: Local Coronavirus Regulations Tier 3 | The Crown Prosecution Service', 2020.

Council of Europe, Notifications Under Article 15 of the Convention in the Context of the COVID-19 Pandemic.

Cour supérieure de Justice, Déclaration adoptée à l'assemblée générale de la Cour du 16 mars 2020. Accessible sur le site du Barreau de Luxembourg.

COVID-19 : deuxième rapport d'étape sur la mise en œuvre de l'état d'urgence sanitaire, 29 avril 2020.

COVID-19 De-escalation Plan adopted by the Council of Ministers on 28 April 2020.

Déclaration du CCBE sur la réactivation de la justice en Europe, https://www.ccbe.eu/fileadmin/speciality_distribution/public/documents/Statements/2020/FR_AtJ_20200515_CCBE-Statement-for-the-reactivation-of-Justice-in-Europe.pdf.

Défenseur des droits, Lettre adressée ce jour aux Présidents du Sénat et de l'Assemblée nationale ainsi qu'aux présidents des commissions des lois des deux assemblées, Paris, le 2 mai 2020.

Der Bundesminister für Gesundheit,"Bundesministerium für Gesundheit Verordnung zur Testpflicht von Einreisenden aus Risikogebieten", November 2020

EU Fundamental Rights Agency, *Coronavirus Pandemic in the EU – Fundamental Rights Implications: Focus on Social Rights,* (November 2020), available at: https://fra.europa.eu/sites/default/files/fra_uploads/fra-2020-coronavirus-pandemic-eu-bulletin-november_en.pdf.

European Data Journalism Network, 'COVID-19 Has Served as the Pretext for Widespread Surveillance' (European Data Journalism Network), December 2020

European Union Agency for Fundamental Rights, Coronavirus pandemic in the EU – fundamental rights implications, 2020.

Exposé des motifs du projet de loi n°7587.

France, Conseil d'Etat, La lettre de la justice administrative, Edition spéciale « la justice administrative pendant la crise sanitaire », n°60, juillet 2020, accessible sur le site internet du Conseil d'Etat.

Glob. Comm'n on HIV and the Law: Risks, Rights & Health, https://hivlawcommission.org/report/.

Global Access to Justice, « Impacts of COVID-19 on Justice Systems », http://globalaccesstojustice.com/impacts-of-covid-19/.

HRC, Statement on derogations from the Covenant in connection with the COVID-19 pandemic (24 April 2020), CCPR/C/128/2.

HRW, *Human Rights Dimensions of COVID-19 Response* (19 March 2020), available at; https://www.hrw.org/news/2020/03/19/human-rights-dimensions-covid-19-response.

Human Rights Committee, General Comment 29, States of Emergency (article 4), U.N. Doc. CCPR/C/21/Rev.1/Add.11 (2001).

Interim Report On The Measures Taken In The EU Member States As A Result Of The COVID-19 Crisis And Their Impact On Democracy, The Rule Of Law And Fundamental Rights Adopted by the Venice Commission at its 124th online Plenary Session (8–9 October 2020), n°78.

International Commission of Jurists, Siracusa, Principles on the Limitation and Derogation Provisions in the International Covenant on Civil and Political Rights (1985), available at: https://www.icj.org/wp-content/uploads/1984/07/Siracusa-principles-ICCPR-legal-submission-1985-eng.pdf.

International Commission of Jurists, *States Of Emergency: Their Impact On Human Rights*, Geneva 1983, 466 p.

John Atkinson, Open Letter to Prime Minister Lee, 12 December 2021

Joint Committee on Human Rights (n 194) para 6.

Joint Committee on Human Rights (n 195) s 157.

Joint Committee on Human Rights (n 195) s 167.

Joint Committee on Human Rights, 'Human Rights and the Government's Response to COVID-19: Digital Contact Tracing', December 2020.

Kießling, "Infektionsschutzgesetz: IfSG, Kommentar", 2020.

Lettre de la justice de paix d'Esch-sur-Alzette adressée au Bâtonnier, 19 mars 2020. Accessible sur le site du Barreau de Luxembourg.

Lettre du juge aux affaires familiales adressée au Bâtonnier le 12 mars 2020. Accessible sur sur le site du Barreau de Luxembourg.

Lettre ouverte du président de la CCDH au Premier Ministre en date du 27 mars 2020, https://ccdh.public.lu/fr/actualites/2020/20200327_COVID-19_Droits_Humains.html.

List of Lead Government Departments' Responsibilities for Planning, Response, and Recovery from Emergencies' (GOV.UK).

Ministry of Health Singapore, 'End of Circuit le site du Barreau de Luxembourg.

Lettre du juge aux affaires familiales adressée au Bâtonnier le 16 mars 2020. Accessible sur le site du Barreau de Luxembourg.

Lettre du tribunal d'arrondissement de Diekirch adressée au Bâtonnier le 16 mars 2020. Accessible

Breaker, Phased Approach to Resuming Activities Safely' May 2020.

Ministry of Health Singapore(MOH), 'Circuit Breaker to Minimise Further Spread of COVID-19', April 2020.

Ministry of Manpower (MOM), 'Advisory on salary payment to foreign workers residing in dormitories', April 2020.

MOH of Singapore 'Antigen Rapid Test Kits Venting Machines Deployed Islandwide and Updates to Home Recovery and Travel Classifications', Sept 2021.

MOH of Singapore, "Multi-Ministry Taskforce on Wuhan Coronavffirus:Terms of Reference and Composition", January 2020).

MOH, 'Bringing COVID-19 Vaccination to the Heartlands for Seniors', July 2021.

MOH, 'No Prior Appointment needed at Moderna Vaccination Centres' 2 Aug 2021.

MOH, 'Vaccination incentive', Sept 2021.

OSCE, « The Functioning of Courts in the COVID-19 Pandemic », https://www.osce.org/files/f/documents/5/5/469170.pdf.

OSCE, « The Functioning of Courts in the COVID-19 Pandemic », https://www.osce.org/files/f/documents/5/5/469170.pdf.

Rechtsprechung, " OVG Münster, Beschl. v. 30.4.2020 – 13 B 539/20".

Rechtsprechung,"OVG Lüneburg, Beschl. v. 6.7.2020 – 13 MN 238/20".

Robert Koch Institut,'Täglicher Lagebericht des RKI zur Coronavirus Krankheit 2019', March 2020

Sénat, COVID-19 : deuxième rapport d'étape sur la mise en œuvre de l'état d'urgence sanitaire, rapport d'information n° 608, 8 juillet 2020.

Sénat, Mission de suivi de la loi d'urgence pour faire face à l'épidémie de COVID-19-Rapport d'information au nom de la commission des lois constitutionnelles, de législation, du suffrage universel, du Règlement et d'administration générale sur les 10 premiers jours d'état d'urgence sanitaire : premiers constats – Analyse des décrets et ordonnances (justice, intérieur, collectivités territoriales, fonction publique, 8 juillet 2020.

The BSE Inquiry. Vol. 1: Findings & Conclusions' (Stationery Office 2000) s 1277.

The European Commission for Democracy through Law (Venice Commission), *Respect for Democracy, Human Rights and the Rule of Law During States of Emergency – Reflections* (Venice Commission, May 2020) (26 May 2020).

Tribunal d'arrondissement de Luxembourg, Information de service COVID-19 pour garantir la continuité du service du tribunal d'arrondissement de Luxembourg, 13 mars 2020. Accessible sur le site du Barreau de Luxembourg.

UN HRC, CCPR/C/128/2 (30 April 2020).

UN Human Rights Committee (HRC), CCPR General Comment No. 29: Article 4: Derogations during a State of Emergency, UN Doc. CCPR/C/21/Rev.1/Add.11 (Aug. 31, 2001) (GC29), para. 3.

UNAIDS, 'Ending overly broad criminalization of HIV non-disclosure, exposure and transmission: Critical scientific, medical and legal considerations' (Guidance note, 2013) 2 <https://www.unaids.org/sites/default/files/media_asset/20130530_Guidance_Ending_Criminalisation_0.pdf> accessed 4 March 2021.

Venice Commission, 'Opinions and Reports on State of Emergency' (16 April 2020), CDL-PI(2020)003

Venice Commission, *Respect for Democracy, Human Rights and the Rule of Law During States of Emergency – Reflections* (Venice Commission May 2020) (26 May 2020).

Zeit Online, „Wie das Coronavirus nach Deutschland kam", 2020.

Annexes

Annex I : Législation liée à la pandémie de COVID-19

Loi organique d'urgence pour faire face à l'épidémie de COVID-19.

Gesetz zur Verhütung und Bekämpfung von Infektionskrankheiten beim Menschen (Infektionsschutzgesetz – IfSG), 20 July 2000, BGBl. I S. 1045 ('IPA 2000').

Loi n° 55–385 du 3 avril 1955 relative à l'état d'urgence, JORF n° 0085 du 7 avril 1955.

Loi n° 2004–806 du 9 août 2004 relative à la politique de santé publique, JORF n° 185 du 11 août 2004.

Italian Decree No. 19 of 25th March 2020.

Arrêté du 14 mars 2020 portant diverses mesures relatives à la lutte contre la propagation du virus COVID-19, JORF n° 0064 du 15 mars 2020.

Décret n° 2020–260 du 16 mars 2020 portant réglementation des déplacements dans le cadre de la lutte contre la propagation du virus COVID-19, JORF n° 0066 du 17 mars 2020.

Belgique, Arrêté ministériel du 18 mars 2020 portant des mesures d'urgence pour limiter la propagation du coronavirus COVID-19, Annexe à l'arrêté ministériel du 18 mars 2020.

Loi n° 2020–290 du 23 mars 2020 d'urgence pour faire face à l'épidémie de COVID-19, JORF n°72 du 24 mars 2020, texte n° 2.

Règlement grand-ducal du 25 mars 2020 portant suspension des délais en matière juridictionnelle et adaptation temporaire de certaines autres modalités procédurales, http://data.legilux.public.lu/eli/etat/leg/rgd/2020/03/25/a185/jo.

Ordonnance n° 2020–303 du 25 mars 2020 portant adaptation de règles de procédure pénale sur le fondement de la loi n° 2020–290 du 23 mars 2020 d'urgence pour faire face à l'épidémie de COVID-19, JORF n°0074 du 26 mars 2020.

Loi organique n° 2020–365 du 30 mars 2020 d'urgence pour faire face à l'épidémie de COVID-19, JORF n° 0078 du 31 mars 2020, texte n° 2.

Règlement grand-ducal du 3 avril 2020 portant modification du règlement grand-ducal du 1er avril 2020 portant dérogation aux articles L. 322–2 et L. 326–1 à L. 326–12 du Code du travail.

Règlement grand-ducal du 17 avril 2020 portant modification du règlement grand-ducal modifié du 18 mars 2020 portant introduction d'une série de mesures dans le cadre de la lutte contre le COVID-19.

grand-ducal du 29 avril 2020 portant adaptation temporaire de certaines modalités procédurales en matière pénale, http://data.legilux.public.lu/eli/etat/leg/rgd/2020/04/29/a341/jo.

Règlement grand-ducal du 29 avril 2020 portant adaptation temporaire de certaines modalités procédurales en matière pénale, http://data.legilux.public.lu/eli/etat/leg/rgd/2020/04/29/a341/jo.

Décret n° 2020–572 du 15 mai 2020 relatif au Comité de contrôle et de liaison COVID-19, JORF n°0120 du 16 mai 2020.

Règlement grand-ducal du 29 mai 2020 portant modification du règlement grand-ducal modifié du 18 mars 2020 portant introduction d'une série de mesures dans le cadre de la lutte contre le COVID-19.

Règlement grand-ducal du 12 juin 2020 portant dérogation aux dispositions des articles 3, 6, 7 et 9 de la loi du 1er août 2019 concernant les mutuelles.

Loi du 20 juin 2020 portant prorogation de mesures concernant la tenue d'audiences publiques pendant l'état de crise devant les juridictions dans les affaires soumises à la procédure écrite, certaines adaptations de la procédure de référé exceptionnel devant le juge aux affaires familiales, la suspension des délais en matière juridictionnelle, et d'autres modalités procédurales, http://data.legilux.public.lu/eli/etat/leg/loi/2020/06/20/a523/jo.

Loi du 20 juin 2020 portant adaptation temporaire de certaines modalités procédurales en matière pénale, http://data.legilux.public.lu/eli/etat/leg/loi/2020/06/20/a542/jo.

Loi du 20 juin 2020 portant prorogation de mesures concernant la tenue d'audiences publiques pendant l'état de crise devant les juridictions dans les affaires soumises à la procédure écrite, certaines adaptations de la procédure de référé exceptionnel devant le juge aux affaires familiales, la suspension des délais en matière juridictionnelle, et d'autres modalités procédurales.

Loi du 20 juin 2020 portant adaptation temporaire de certaines modalités procédurales en matière pénale.

Loi du 24 juin 2020 portant introduction d'une série de mesures concernant les activités sportives, les activités culturelles ainsi que les établissements recevant du public, dans le cadre de la lutte contre la pandémie COVID-19 et

Loi du 24 juin 2020 portant introduction d'une série de mesures concernant les activités sportives, les activités culturelles ainsi que les établissements recevant du public, dans le cadre de la lutte contre la pandémie COVID-19.

Loi modifiée du 17 juillet 2020 portant sur les mesures de lutte contre la pandémie COVID-19.

Règlement grand-ducal du 29 juillet 2020 modifiant le règlement grand-ducal modifié du 18 septembre 1995 concernant l'assistance judiciaire.

Ordonnance n° 2020–1401 du 18 novembre 2020 portant adaptation des règles applicables aux juridictions de l'ordre judiciaire statuant en matière pénale, JORF 280 du 19 novembre 2020.

Loi du 25 novembre 2020, http://legilux.public.lu/eli/etat/leg/loi/2020/11/25/a932/consolide/20201223.

Loi du 25 novembre 2020 modifiant :
1° la loi modifiée du 17 juillet 2020 sur les mesures de lutte contre la pandémie COVID-19;
2° la loi modifiée du 10 décembre 2009 relative à l'hospitalisation sans leur consentement de personnes atteintes de troubles mentaux, http://data.legilux.public.lu/eli/etat/leg/loi/2020/11/25/a933/jo.

Loi du 19 décembre 2020 portant adaptation temporaire de certaines modalités procédurales en matière civile et commerciale, http://data.legilux.public.lu/eli/etat/leg/loi/2020/12/19/a1056/jo.

Loi du 19 décembre 2020 portant modification de la loi modifiée du 20 juin 2020 portant adaptation temporaire de certaines modalités procédurales en matière pénale, http://data.legilux.public.lu/eli/etat/leg/loi/2020/12/19/a1046/jo.

Loi du 19 décembre 2020 portant adaptation temporaire de certaines modalités procédurales en matière civile et commerciale, http://data.legilux.public.lu/eli/etat/leg/loi/2020/12/19/a1056/jo.

Loi du 19 décembre 2020 portant modification de la loi modifiée du 20 juin 2020 portant adaptation temporaire de certaines modalités procédurales en matière pénale, http://data.legilux.public.lu/eli/etat/leg/loi/2020/12/19/a1046/jo.

Loi du 30 juin 2021 portant modification : 1° de la loi modifiée du 23 septembre 2020 portant des mesures concernant la tenue de réunions dans les sociétés et dans les autres personnes morales; 2° de la loi du 19 décembre 2020 portant adaptation temporaire de certaines modalités procédurales en matière civile et commerciale, https://legilux.public.lu/eli/etat/leg/loi/2021/06/30/a485/jo.

Loi du 30 juillet 2021 portant modification : 1° de la loi du 19 décembre 2020 portant adaptation temporaire de certaines modalités procédurales en matière civile et commerciale; 2° de la loi modifiée du 8 mars 2017 sur la nationalité luxembourgeoise, https://legilux.public.lu/eli/etat/leg/loi/2021/07/30/a626/jo.

Loi n° 2021–1465 du 10 novembre 2021 portant diverses dispositions de vigilance sanitaire, JORF n°263 du 11 novembre 202.

UK Legislation, Civil Defence Act 1948 s 9(2), https://www.legislation.gov.uk/ukpga/Geo6/12-13-14/5/section/9/enacted.

'The Civil Defence (General Local Authority Functions) Regulations' (Home Office 1974)S.I.1974/70s4 <https://www.legislation.gov.uk/uksi/1974/70/contents/made>.

The Health Protection (Coronavirus, Restrictions) (England) Regulations 2020 [SI 2020/350] s 12.

'UK Coronavirus Legislation' <https://www.legislation.gov.uk/coronavirus> accessed 14 November 2020.

Spanish Law, Ley 17/2015 del Sistema Nacional de Protección Civil;

Spanish Law Ley 36/2015 de Seguridad Nacional

Order SND/297/2020, https://www.boe.es/buscar/doc.php?id=BOE-A-2020-4162

Singapore Immigration Act Section 8(3)b
Section 34, COVID-19 (Temporary Measures) Act 2020
Singapore Interpretation Act (Cap 1) Section 23

Annexe II related to 'Evaluation des mesures juridiques de gestion de la pandémie de COVID-19 en France'

Annex 1) La chronologie rapide

Instauré pour deux mois par **la loi du 23 mars 2020**, l'état d'urgence sanitaire avait été prolongé jusqu'au 10 juillet inclus. Un délit de violation du confinement est créé.

Suite au début du déconfinement à partir du 11 mai 2020, **la loi du 9 juillet 2020** organisant la sortie de l'état d'urgence sanitaire avait mis en place un régime transitoire à partir du 11 juillet autorisant le gouvernement à prendre des mesures exceptionnelles jusqu'au 31 octobre 2020 pour faire face à l'épidémie de COVID-19.

L'état d'urgence sanitaire sur l'ensemble du territoire national a été à nouveau déclaré par décret à compter du 17 octobre 2020. Cet état d'urgence sanitaire a permis la mise en place d'un couvre-feu entre 21h et 6h dans les départements les plus touchés par l'épidémie de COVID-19 que sont les métropoles de Paris, Grenoble, Lille, Lyon, Aix-Marseille, Saint-Etienne, Rouen, Montpellier et Toulouse. Puis le couvre-feu a été étendu à tout le territoire de 18h, puis 19h à 6h. Le second confinement général de la population est instauré par décret du 29 octobre 2020.

La **loi du 14 novembre 2020** a prolongé, une première fois, l'état d'urgence sanitaire jusqu'au 16 février 2021. **La loi du 15 février 2021** prolonge l'état d'urgence sanitaire jusqu'au 1er juin 2021. Le texte reporte, par ailleurs, au 31 décembre 2021 la caducité des dispositions du code de la santé publique organisant le régime général d'état d'urgence sanitaire.

La **loi n° 2021–689 du 31 mai 2021** organise la sortie de l'état d'urgence sanitaire à compter du 2 juin et jusqu'au 31 octobre 2021. Ce régime a repris la loi du 9 juillet 2020 et permet au pouvoir réglementaire de garder la possibilité de limiter les déplacements et l'utilisation des moyens de transport, de restreindre les conditions d'ouverture de certains établissements recevant du public et de limiter les réunions et rassemblements sur la voie publique et dans les lieux ouverts au public. Dans ce cadre, le Premier ministre peut imposer aux personnes souhaitant se déplacer à destination ou en provenance du territoire hexagonal, de la Corse ou d'une collectivité d'outre-mer de présenter un test de dépistage négatif, un certificat de vaccination ou un document attestant de leur rétablissement à la suite d'une contamination par la COVID-19. Le « pass sanitaire » est créé et doit être présenté dans le cadre de grands évènements de loisir.

La **loi n° 2021–1040 du 5 août 2021** relative à la gestion de la crise sanitaire prévoit principalement qu'à compter du 30 août 2021, les salariés travaillant dans les secteurs où le pass sanitaire est obligatoire (*activités de loisirs, restauration commerciale (hors vente à emporter et restauration collective), débits de boissons, services, établissements de santé, sociaux et médico-sociaux, certains grands magasins et certains centres commerciaux...*), devront eux aussi en justifier. Elle prolonge le régime de sortie de l'état d'urgence sanitaire jusqu'au 15 septembre 2021. Que la **loi n°2021–1465 du 10 novembre 2021** portant diverses dispositions de vigilance sanitaire étend au **31 juillet 2022.**

Annexe 2) : Les sanctions pénales

La loi du 23 mars 2020, a fixé les sanctions encourues en cas de violation des mesures prescrites par les autorités publiques dans le cadre de l'état d'urgence sanitaire (art. L 3136–1 du code de la Santé publique). Elles ont été plusieurs fois modifiées, la dernière fois par le décret n° 2021–490 du 22 avril 2021 intégrant la violation des mesures de mises en quarantaine et des mesures de mises à l'isolement.

Une application graduée de ces sanctions est prévue pour les déplacements non justifiés.

Ainsi, la première violation est punie d'une contravention de la 4ème classe et la réitération, dans un délai inférieur de 15 jours, d'une contravention de la 5ème classe.

Le fait de commettre au moins quatre violations en moins de 30 jours est constitutif d'un délit, puni d'une peine de 6 mois d'emprisonnement et de 3 750 euros d'amende ainsi qu'une peine complémentaire de travail d'intérêt général et la suspension du permis de conduire lorsque l'infraction a été commise à l'aide d'un véhicule.

Enfin, le fait de ne pas respecter les réquisitions est puni de 6 mois d'emprisonnement et de 10 000 euros d'amende.

Le non-respect du port du masque est sanctionné par une contravention de 4ème classe de 135 euros d'amende. En cas de récidive dans les 15 jours, l'amende passe à 1 500 €.

En application de l'article 131–38 du Code pénal, les personnes morales peuvent se voir infliger cinq fois le montant de l'amende prévue pour les personnes physiques par la loi qui réprime l'infraction.

Annexe 3) : Le cadre juridique de l'état d'urgence sanitaire

L'état d'urgence sanitaire est déclaré par décret en conseil des ministres sur la base du rapport, rendu public, du ministre chargé de la santé, pour une durée maximale d'un mois. Le décret détermine la ou les circonscriptions territoriales dans lesquelles il s'applique.

Au-delà d'un mois, sa prorogation est autorisée par la loi. Celle-ci fixe la durée de l'état d'urgence sanitaire.

Un décret pris en Conseil des ministres peut mettre fin à l'application du régime avant l'expiration du délai fixé par la loi.

À défaut, les mesures adoptées dans le cadre de l'état d'urgence sanitaire prennent fin à l'issue de la période fixée.

Durant toute la période d'application de l'état d'urgence sanitaire, le Premier ministre est autorisé à adopter des mesures portant atteinte à la liberté d'aller et de venir, à la liberté d'entreprendre et la liberté de réunion, tandis que le ministre de la santé a vocation à prendre les autres mesures, en particulier sanitaires, réclamées par les circonstances.

Selon ce qui paraît le plus approprié dans chaque cas de figure, ces mesures peuvent être décidées au niveau national ou laissées pour partie à l'appréciation du représentant de l'État dans le département.

The Authors

Silvia Allegrezza, Professor of Criminal Law at the University of Luxembourg.

Géraldine Bachoué, Ph.D., Senior Lecturer, Director « Centre de documentation et de recherches européennes (CDRE) », Université de Pau et des Pays de l'Adour.

Basak Baglayan, Ph.D., Luxembourg Ministry of Economy, Expert on Responsible Business Conduct and Secretary General of the OECD National Contact Point for Luxembourg.

Stefan Braum, Professor of Criminal Law at the University of Luxembourg.

Fatima Chaouche, Ph.D., Referent to the Administrative Court, Lecturer University of Luxembourg.

Jörg Gerkrath, Professor of European and Constitutional Law at the University of Luxembourg.

Katrin Kappler, Ph.D., Post-Doc in Public Law at Max-Planck-Institute for Crime, Security and Law.

Séverine Menétrey, Professor of Judicial Constitutional Law and Comparative Law at the University of Luxembourg.

Adan Nieto Martin, Professor of Criminal Law, University of Castilla-La Mancha.

Valsamis Mitsilegas, Professor of European Criminal Law and Global Security, Deputy Dean for Global Engagement (Europe), Queen Mary University London.

Sandra M.B. Picicuto, PhD student in Law, University of Catania.

Maitena Poelemans, Ph.D., « Ingénieur de Recherches », « Centre de documentation et de recherches européennes (CDRE) », Université de Pau et des Pays de l'Adour.

Ralf Poscher, Professor in Public Law, Director Max-Planck-Institute for Crime, Security and Law.

Rosaria Sicurella, Professor in Criminal Law, University of Catania.

Li-ann Thio, Provost Chair Professor (Human Rights Law, Public International Law), Faculty of Law, National University of Singapore.

Santiago Wortman Jofre, Policy Analyst at OECD, Queen Mary University London.